COLOR STRUCK

Essays on Race and Ethnicity in Global Perspective

Julius O. Adekunle and Hettie V. Williams

University Press of America,® Inc.
Lanham · Boulder · New York · Toronto · Plymouth, UK

Copyright © 2010 by
University Press of America,® Inc.
4501 Forbes Boulevard
Suite 200
Lanham, Maryland 20706
UPA Acquisitions Department (301) 459-3366

Estover Road
Plymouth PL6 7PY
United Kingdom

Library of Congress Control Number: 2009943009
ISBN: 978-0-7618-5064-9 (paperback : alk. paper)

Contents

Preface

Color Struck: Essays on Race and Ethnicity in Global Perspective is a compilation of expositions on race and ethnicity written from multiple disciplinary approaches including history, sociology, women's studies, and anthropology. This volume is organized around a topical chronological framework and divided into three sections that begin with earliest times to the contemporary world. Part I is titled "The First Complex Societies to Modern Times," Part II "Race and Mixed Race in the Americas," and Part III is titled "Race, Ethnicity, and Conflict in Contemporary Societies." Scholars have contemplated the subjects of race and ethnicity for decades in a variety of textbooks or in a plethora of edited volumes. The great majority of this "plethora" has come largely from singular disciplinary approaches often with a distinct regional focus such as North America, Latin America, Asia, or Africa. Some of the more recognizable works with a distinct regional concentration include Paul Spickard, *Mixed Blood: Intermarriage and Ethnic Identity in Twentieth Century America* (1989); Frank Dikkster, ed., *The Construction of Racial Identity in China and Japan* (1997); and Peter S. Li, *Race and Ethnic Relations in Canada* (1999). Several studies on Africa, Latin America, and the Caribbean include Peter G. Forster, Michael Hitchcock, and Francis F. Lyimo, eds., *Race and Ethnicity in East Africa* (2000); Ralph Premdas, ed. *The Enigma of Ethnicity: An Analysis of Race in the Caribbean World;* and Arlene Torres and N.E. Whitten, ed., *Blackness in Latin America and the Caribbean: Social Dynamics and Cultural Transformation.* In this book, we have brought together contributors writing across time, discipline, and region.

The term race has nearly become synonymous with the word ethnicity, given the most recent findings in the study of human genetics that have led to the mapping of the human DNA. These findings indicate that "race" as applied to distinct categories of human communities is virtually obsolete. With the human genetic code having been revealed by scientists in 2001, studies of race and ethnicity have taken a new turn. The most recent volumes on the subject of race and ethnicity have indeed taken a combined approach and become more expansive in terms of geographic coverage. The first book to compare the racial *and* ethnic systems that have emerged around the world, including essays on China, the West Indies, Africa, Brazil, and the Americas, is Paul Spickard's edited volume, *Race and Nation: Ethnic Systems in the Modern World* (2004). This text includes chapters on the subject of race and ethnicity written by historians, sociologists, anthropologists and political scientists. The Spickard text involves contributors writing about race and ethnicity across multiple disciplines, time periods, and geography. Rodney D. Coates, author of *Race and Ethnicity: Across Time, Space and Discipline* (2006), adopts a similar methodology as Spickard, in terms of space and disciplines, but his work is not as comprehensive as the Spickard book in terms of geographic regions covered.

In the Coates work, the concentration is primarily on the African American experience in North America. The edited volume by Charles Gallagher *Rethinking the Color Line: Readings in Race and Ethnicity* (2008) although embraces a comprehensive format seems to also emphasize the experience of a particular group in a distinct region (primarily ethnic communities in North America). *Color Struck* is therefore an attempt to reconcile the time-space considerations along with a more comprehensive interdisciplinary overview while at the same time allowing for a complete section on the emergent field of Mixed Race Studies.

Mixed Race Studies is a fast growing field, and a highly controversial area within the context of American ethnic studies. Part II of this volume is directly devoted to the rising sub-discipline of Mixed Race Studies. Mixed Race Studies has engaged scholars in multiple disciplines and the issues of mixed race identity and community have been examined in various books and edited volumes since the early 1990s. The clinical psychologist Maria P. P. Root has played an important role in the development of important literature on mixed race subjects. Her edited volumes *Racially Mixed People in America* (1992) and *The Multiracial Experience: Racial Borders as the New Frontier* (1996) are considered standard works in the Mixed Race Studies debate. Paul Spickard's *Mixed Blood*, is also considered a key text in the emergent discipline. The sociological study by G. Reginald Daniel's *More than Black: Multiracial Identity and the New Racial Order* (2001) can be classified, along with the works of Root and Spickard, as foundational texts in the study of mixed race identity and community in America. Philosopher Naomi Zack has also made significant contributions to the study of mixed race communities with her books *Race and Mixed Race* (1993) and *American Mixed Race: The Culture of "Microdiversity"* (1995). Controversy abounds in this "new" field due to the fact that scholars, such as Rainier Spencer, have challenged the very foundation upon which mixed race identity studies rests.

It is our hope that this volume will answer some questions and provide scholarly insight into issues related to race and ethnicity. Realizing that these are complex issues with unending arguments and criticisms, this volume is intended to generate further discussion and research in global racial and ethnic relations. Given the constaints of clarity and brevity, we have deliberately placed an emphasis, in terms of coverage, on the major world societies in Africa, Asia, and North America while also recognizing the complexity of issues related to race/ethnicity in places such as Suriname.

Julius O. Adekunle and Hettie V. Williams
Monmouth University
August 2009

Acknowledgements

The idea to publish an interdisciplinary book on race and ethnicity began two years ago. The growing discussions and increasing demand for books on race and ethnicity motivated us to develop a collection of scholarly works on the race and ethnicity. We also decided to give the volume a global perspective. This grand plan involved tremendous contributions and assistance from many people and for this we would like to acknowledge those who have made the publication of this volume possible.

We acknowledge our family members and friends for bearing with us during the hectic time. We also recognize the encouragement we received from our colleagues at Monmouth University, especially in the Department of History and Anthropology. They have been instrumental in helping us to see this project through to completion. We appreciate the contributions of the members of the Interlibrary Loan department of the Guggenheim Library, Monmouth University for their cooperation in finding books and articles that we used to write and edit the chapters in this volume.

We would like to specially thank our contributors without whom this volume would not have been possible. They have worked tirelessly to write analytical papers on various world societies to understand race and ethnicity. We thank them for their time, patience, and dedication to the subject of this book.

Hettie V. Williams would like to particularly thank Reg Daniel for his kind support in this endeavor as well as for his phenomenal contributions to the field of critical Mixed Race Studies. Hettie and Julius would both like to acknowledge our colleagues, Kathy Shapiro and Bob Grasso, for their editorial assistance. We are greatly indebted to Ruth Jamnik, Assistant Computer Trainer at Monmouth University, for her efforts and patience in formatting the manuscript. Her hours of work are profoundly appreciated.

It has been an enjoyable experience working on this volume. As editors, we have benefited tremendously from the different perspectives of the contributors and it is our hope that readers of this volume would find it both interesting and informative.

Introduction

Race and Ethnicity in Global Societies

Hettie V. Williams

The blackness is visible and yet it is invisible, for I see that I cannot see it...

-Jamaica Kinkaid, "Blackness"

Race in history as word and idea is a fluid, ephemeral, and ambiguous concept in societies around the world. It is a phenomenon largely produced by culture and often misunderstood as physical appearance or color. Race is indeed a socio-cultural construction across time and space in human affairs. Humans have been struck by color as a moniker of human difference from the earliest complex societies to modern times. The Indo-Aryans who settled in the Indus Valley c. 1500 B.C.E. classified themselves as "wheat colored" noble people while the dark skinned Dravidians they encountered were identified as *dasas* or subject people. The ancient Egyptians considered notions of color in their ancient text *The Book of Gates*. Race, construed as color, evolved with the rise of the transcontinental enslavement of black Africans during the Islamic and Atlantic slave trades in the modern world. Muslim merchants in North Africa began to draw distinctions between slaves with a light complexion that they termed *mamluks* and slaves with a noticeably darker complexion that they called *'abids* centuries before the Europeans embarked on their Age of Discovery. In this volume, we argue that neither color nor geography is enough to classify the human community into fixed biological units called races. Given the ever fluctuating status of race as "idea" in human affairs across time, space, and place, the multidisciplinary approach is the most conducive approach to the study of race in human societies. The chapters in this volume therefore collectively represent multidisciplinary understandings of race in history and contemporary societies.

The phrase race is problematical. The 2000 U.S census survey illustrated the term race as associated with place of national origin or as a self-ascribed data item in which those surveyed felt they could most identify with. Respondents were also allowed to "write in" their race of choice. It was neither scientifically nor anthropologically based. The five categories of race that appeared on the survey were aligned with country of origin. Essentially, the U.S. Census portrayed the concept of race as a socio-political construction. The editors of this volume believe and argue that race as a biological moniker lacks taxonomic integrity. The pioneering mixed race studies philosopher Naomi Zack has argued that race is "conceptually driven" while the American Anthropological Association has literally come to accept that race is largely a social construction. Yale historian David Brion Davis, who cautioned that historians must begin to trace vociferously the idea of race in world history, has echoed these sentiments. The *Encyclopedia Britannica* also defined race as "idea" or "construction." Concepts of race have expanded along with the worldwide population explosion of persons with mixed-race identities as also reflected in the U.S. Census report of 2000. The findings of the Human Genome Project released in 2001 revealed that difference between human groups is at best miniscule (less than 1%) and is in fact, slightly more varied within supposed "racial" groups. Race, when applied as a socio-political concept, is nearly comparable with ethnicity, which is a sociological concept defined by human behaviors, beliefs, customs and "ways."

The process of globalization has profoundly shaped the social geography of world societies. As migrants from countries all over the world have entered into American society, the ethnic composition of America has shifted dramatically as has been the case in nearly every major western society between 1950 and 2005. Why then does race and ethnicity matter if America has always been a nation of immigrants? Despite these dramatic changes in the contemporary ethnic base of American society, the binary system of racial classification remains yet is shattering. The chapters in this collection are [in part] about challenging concepts of race and ethnicity beyond national boundaries.

Historically, human migration from place to place has ensured the dispersion of diverse cultural traditions and ethnicities around the world. Human migration has increased dramatically in modern times particularly with the upsurge of the Industrial Revolution in the 1700s. An estimated 1 billion people since the industrial revolution have settled in countries beyond their place of birth. This has greatly modified global social geography. The UN sponsored Global Commission on International Migration study published in 2005 indicated that 150 million people or an estimated 3% of the world's population reside outside of their country of birth. This Commission has also determined that transnational migrations doubled between the years 1980 to 2000 and that migrants "depart from and arrive in" every country of the world as of 2005. In fact, most of the world's developed countries have become diverse multi-ethnic societies since the 1950s. Many of these migrants have left Africa for Europe, Canada, and the United States. Thus, it is pertinent to examine thoroughly race and ethnicity in global perspectives from earliest times to the present as these concepts have been continuously reconfigured over time. This volume is divided into three parts exploring race and ethnicity from earliest times to contemporary world societies.

Part I

This segment consists of seven chapters that focus on race, ethnicity, and culture from human beginnings through the seventeenth century covering world societies in Africa, India, the Middle East, colonial America, Suriname, and the Middle Ages in Europe. The first chapter considers race, science, and human origins in Africa. Using the scientific and archaeological evidence of human origins in Africa, the chapter shows that race was not an issue, but migrations occurred from time to time and from place to place. Human development, from the era of Hominids to the emergence of Homo sapiens, sapiens, has been marked by transcontinental population flows. Homo sapiens having evolved, learned to walk upright, manipulate tools, and become wise first migrated out of Africa c.150, 000 years ago. Hunting and gathering communities of the Paleolithic age (2 million years ago to c. 12,000 B.C.E.) populated the world through a series of successive migratory waves out of Africa into the Near East and Asia. These migrations ultimately led to the establishment of societies and cultural traditions throughout the world with the emergence of civilized life from Neolithic villages in c. 5,000 B.C.E. Archeological evidence from the oldest known human ancestors has been found in such places as Olduvai Gorge in Tanzania and Hadar in Ethiopia. The science of DNA mapping has allowed evolutionary biologists and geneticists to compare mutations in the DNA of people around the globe. These scientists have found that African DNA is the most diverse and trace elements of ancient African DNA can be found in all modern humans. The history of the world is a history of an African Diaspora. Chapter two, which examines the rise of Swahili culture in Africa, is a follow up to the concept of migration and human interactions, which produced the emergence of a unique society, called Swahili.

The third chapter examines caste and gender in ancient Hindu society. India historically contains one of the oldest civilizations in the world and this chapter speaks to the ancient text that defined society in the ancient Indus valley. The remaining chapters in this section consider race and ethnicity in the Middle East, Europe, and the Americas.

Part II

Part II begins with a passionate plea from Andrew Jolivette related to the subject of mixed race identity, scholarship, and social justice. The nine chapters in this section focus on mixed race identity and communities in the Americas including chapters on black biracial identity, the limitations of binary thinking, Creole and American Indian identity, and the politics of mixed race identity in Brazil. The contentious dialogue between traditionalists and revionists scholars engaged in the study of mixed race identity and communities is well evidenced in this section of the book. The "passionate plea" by Jolivette is not echoed in the work of Rainier Spencer nor is this plea echoed in that of some of the other contributors in this section. We thought it necessary to highlight the subject of

Mixed Race Studies in this section given that it is the fastest growing field within the context of American ethnic studies while avoiding a one-dimensional presentation of the subject. This section includes writings from some of the leading scholars working in the field of Mixed Race Studies today.

Part III

Part III begins with chapter seventeen, which examines the new race science and the potential impact it may have on the lives of African Americans. The chapter argues that the use of color to determine race is not appropriate. Hence, black, used to refer to African Americans is the color of discrimination. By using the findings of the Human Genome project (HGP) and DNA evidence, it is proven that whiteness or blackness is not biological, but social determinants for convenience of identification. Chapter eighteen also contests the use of color as a mark of identity. This chapter uses the interviews of African female immigrants in Canada to support the argument that color is not an adequate marker of race. Chapter nineteen focuses on the unique burdens Black women in the United States have endured as a consequence of living experiences of the intersection of race, gender, class, and sexuality. The remaining chapters in this section provide analytical views on ethnic conflicts in the Middle East, China, Russia, and Chechnya.

Part I

The First Complex Societies to Modern Times

Chapter 1

Race, Science, and Human Origins in Africa

Julius O. Adekunle

Scientific evidence, which began with the study of fossils, shows that Africa was the cradle of human beings. Fossils, found in various parts of Africa, dated more than four million years ago. The early human species spread throughout the world and developed a culture upon which modern humans have built. The scientific interpretation of the fossils did not indicate the race to which the early humans belonged. However, the issue of race has become one of the centers of historical and anthropological discourse as science has routinely classified Africans as "Negroid." To address the question of race, science, and human origins in Africa, this chapter will consider the pivotal role of archaeology. Understandably, the prehistoric period of Africa reveals not only the origins of humans, but also the movement of early people from one place to the other, adapting to different climatic and environmental conditions. The pertinent question to be answered is what scientific evidence do we have to support the existence of different races in Africa?

Introduction[1]

The role of archaeology cannot be overlooked in the prehistory of Africa. Archaeology and its interpretations present the scientific part of the history of Africa. Where oral traditions fail to provide some needed information for the reconstruction of African past, archaeology fills the gap. The recovery and interpretation of artifacts produce vital information on the early history and culture of the peoples of Africa. In his *Descent of Man* (1871), Charles Darwin suggested that Africa was the cradle of humankind and subsequent scientific researches and archaeological discoveries proved him right. The shift in focus of the cradle of humans moved from Asia to Africa. Africans themselves had only oral traditions and culture to show, but not scientific evidence to prove their long existence. Paleoanthropologists, archaeologists, and anthropologists then began to carry out researches into the origins of human beings. Excavations have been carried out in Africa with new finds producing new information and new interpretations. The discovery of fossilized bones places Africa as the cradle of modern humankind. Although human fossils are rare because it takes a long time and certain conditions for humans to form into fossilized bones, nevertheless, some have been found in Kenya, Tanzania, Ethiopia, and South Africa. Thus, Louis Leakey asserts that the first contribution of Africa to human progress is "the evolution of man himself."[2]

The history and culture of the peoples of Africa, however, shows that their interpretation of the origins of humans is different and non-scientific. Their cultural beliefs and practices as well as their interpretation of human origins are entrenched in religion. Accordingly, they explain human origins in terms of creation stories. In their traditions, they refer to the creator of all living things. For one thing, traditions are cultural and not empirical. Therefore, they do not provide universally acceptable explanations to the origins of humans. For another, traditions are sacred and constitute the history, culture, and indeed the totality of African people's existence. In that respect, they cannot be entirely ignored. However, because of the abundance of scientific and universally accepted evidence, emphasis will be placed on scientific and archaeological interpretations of human origins in Africa.

Archaeological Discoveries and Interpretations

Paleoanthropologists believe that the earliest humans (hominids) had close relationship with the great apes, the chimpanzee, and gorilla (pongids) most of which were found in central Africa. Charles Darwin pointed out that "it is probable that Africa was formerly inhabited by extinct apes closely allied to the gorilla and chimpanzee."[3] The split between hominids and pongids took place during the late Miocene (about 10-5 million years ago).[4] Clifford Jolly states that, 'from rocks of this age [Miocene] have been found the earliest fossils representing the primates of sub-Saharan Africa, the home of many living monkeys and apes and the probable place of the origin of the human family."[5] In search of the "missing link," archaeologists have excavated many sites in East and South Africa with amazing results. Fossils have been found, analyzed, and dated thereby enlightening the understanding of the history and culture of the early people of Africa.

The search for the origins of humans is carried out through the study and interpretation of fossils. In the 1850s, scientists found only two fossils; one was that of an ape and the other was a near-human bone called the Neanderthal man.[6] The Neanderthal man was classified as later archaic *Homo sapiens* with the striking features of a large brain, stone tools and weapons, hunting, artwork, and burying of the dead. Eugene Dubois (1858-1940) in 1891 found the first remains of *Homo erectus* from the fossiliferous gravels in Java, Asia. Dubois believed that his discovery provided the "missing link" between humans and apes.[7]

In 1924 some fossilized bones of australopithecines were discovered, studied, and interpreted by Raymond Dart, a paleontologist and professor of anatomy at the University of the Witwatersrand in Johannesburg, South Africa. A skull, which represented early humankind, was discovered at Taung. The skull was different from either the Neanderthal or *H. erectus.* Dart named it *Australopithecus africanus* ("The South African Ape" or "Southern Ape from Africa"). *Australopithecus africanus,* with a larger brain than that of a modern ape, was dated about 2-3 million years ago.[8] Australopithecines have been found also in Tanzania, Kenya, and southern Ethiopia. Later discoveries show that *Australopithecus afarensis* fossils found at Hadar in Ethiopia lived between 3 and 4 million years ago.[9] A later species of the genus Authralopithecus was *A. aethiopicus.* In the 1930s, Robert Broom found adult samples of *A. robustus.* Both *A. robustus* and *A. africanus* belonged to the hominid family.[10]

Excavations and Results after the Second World War

Archaeological excavations increased after the Second World War and new hominid remains were unearthed. The Olduvai Gorge in northern Tanzania was the center of excavations for Louis and Mary Leakey, who uncovered a series of fossils of Pleistocene age and discovered a new form of robust *Australopithecus* in 1959. Because the Leakeys believed that the fossil was different from the australopithecines, they termed it a new genus and therefore named it *Zinjanthropus boisei* ("East African Man"), after Charles Boisei who funded the excavations.[11] *Z. boisei* had larger molars and heavier skull than either *A. aethiopicus* or *A. robustus.* Although Louis Leakey reported that he had discovered *Homo habilis*, paleoanthropologists consider it to be a new species of the genus *Australopithecus.*

In the1960s the Leakeys made another discovery in the Olduvai Gorge. The new find was closer to humankind than *A. boisei.* It was bipedal, had a brain that was getting larger, dental proportions that were humanlike, and legs that were longer. Bipedalism was considered to be one of the hallmarks of human beings. Because of these distinct features, the new find was classified in the genus *Homo* and the species *habilis.* Found about 1-2 million years ago, *H. habilis* had a brain size of about 600 to 750 cubic centimeters.[12] *H. habilis* made tools such as choppers, scrapers, and hammer stones. Of all the finds, *H. habilis* had the most pronounced features. That is why it has been described as the true human ancestor.[13] Bernard Campbell and Joseph Vogel point out that *A. boisei* coexisted with *H. habilis* and with *H. erectus* that was found by Richard Leakey at Koobi Fora, Kenya in 1971.[14] F. C. Clark, Yves Coppens, and Camille Arambourg, in different excavations, have also found earliest hominids in Omo Valley and East Turkana.

An international group led by Donald Johanson made a scientifically informative discovery at the Afar Triangle in Ethiopia in 1974. The fossil was identified as *A. afarensis* and nicknamed "*Lucy.*" Dated between 3 and 4 million years ago, Lucy was bipedal with the morphology of its bones functionally identical to that of more recent humans. Aside from Lucy, Johanson found a group of hominid bones, which has been called the "first family."[15]

The genus *Homo* split into another species called *erectus* about 1.9 million years ago. *H. erectus* had a large body, a thick skull, and prominent jaws. It had a brain capacity of 725 cubic centimeters, which makes it larger than the brain of *H. habilis*.[16] As *Homo erectus* replaced *H. habilis*, there is an improvement in mobility and toolkits. *H. erectus* migrated from Africa to Europe and Asia with the knowledge of tool-making. The spread suggests why similar stone tools have been found in most of the archaeological sites all over the world. However, the Acheulean tools of Africa and Europe are not found in India and eastward but the Java fossil discovered in Asia was *H. erectus*. Based on the differences between the *H. erectus* found in Africa and those in Asia, Bernard Wood suggests that African *H. erectus* should be identified as *H. ergaster*.[17] Some archaeologists argue that there were two species of early *Homo* (*habilis* and *rudolfensis*) while others contend that there was only one species. Some researchers also argue that *H. rudolfensis* was contemporary with *habilis*, while others say that *H. ergaster* rather than *erectus* was the successor.[18]

A new species is designated as archaic *H. sapiens* ("the wise or thinking human"). The term archaic *H. sapiens* is used to distinguish them because they exhibited a mosaic of *H. erectus* and *H. sapiens* characteristics.[19] They may be distinguishable as early as 400,000 years ago and modern *Homo sapiens* emerged between 100,000 and 200,000 years ago in Africa.[20] Archaic *Homo sapiens*, also labeled *H. rhodesiensis* ("Rhodesian Man"), corresponded to the *Homo neanderthalensis* in Europe. Both of them possessed heavier bones, larger nose, bigger brain, and superior tools than *H. erectus*. Furthermore, there were changes in their teeth toward modern humans. The *Neanderthal* people lived in cold areas thus their location mostly in Europe and the Middle East. Archaic *Homo sapiens* were found at Kabwe in Zambia and some parts of South Africa and the dominant invention was the Levallois method of forging specialized tools such as flaked-stone tools.

The Bodo skull was found in Ethiopia in 1971 with a span of 200,000 to 700,000 years ago. That was the same period Richard Leakey and his team discovered a complete skeleton of *Homo erectus* at Koobi Fora in Kenya. The Bodo skull was more advanced than *H. erectus* in spite of their similar features. It had nasal opening, substantially large brain, and humanlike face. Another specimen appeared about 35,000 to 40,000 years ago. It was the Ndutu skull from Tanzania. Its face was smaller than that of the Bodo skull and its brain was larger than that of *H. erectus*.[21]

Anatomically modern human beings, known as *Homo sapiens sapiens*, appeared in Africa about 200,000 years ago. Sally McBrearty suggests that, "African archaic *Homo sapiens* populations probably gave rise to the first modern humans, *Homo sapiens sapiens*."[22] Archaeologists have found fossilized remains of *Homo sapiens sapiens* from the Klasies River Mouth in Ethiopia and South Africa. They survived during the Middle Pleistocene period. Paleoanthropologists, however, debate the origins of the *Homo sapiens sapiens*. There are three hypotheses. The first proposes that *H. sapiens sapiens* originated from Africa, migrated to, and completely replaced the populations in Europe and Asia. The second believes in partial replacement, and the third proposes multiregional evolution.[23] *Homo sapiens sapiens* manufactured complicated tools and weapons of wood, stone, and metal. They made handles for tools, ornaments for their bodies, and lived in larger and complex communities. Adaptation to ecological and climatic dictates also led to differences and improvement in toolkits.

In 1978, Mary Leakey discovered the fossilized footprints of hominids at Laetoli. The three sets of hominid footprints formed a trail more than 75-80 feet long. They were found in a layer of volcanic tuff in sediments dated between 3.59 and 3.77 million years ago.[24] Mary Leakey was convinced that the footprints existed about half a million years before the fossils that Johanson had unearthed in the Afar region of Ethiopia in 1973.[25] Archaeologists have found more footprints to prove that bipedal locomotion was an important characteristic of early hominids. Aside from the footprints, Louis and Mary Leakey discovered thousands of stone tools made, used, and left behind by the early people at the Olduvai Gorge in Tanzania.

Archaeology has facilitated the study of the early human beings not only in Africa but also in other parts of the world. As Richard Leakey put it, "Archaeologists have assembled a wealth of data on early human technology in Africa that tells us a great deal about the appearance of man."[26] With all the archaeological evidence at our disposal, it is possible to trace the technology of the early humans.

The Stone Age and the Oldowan Culture

Tool-making activities dominated the early stages of human history. It was one of the hallmarks of human development in technology, especially in Africa. Foraging for food by human beings as well as animals such as chimpanzees led to the manufacturing of tools. Stone tools were associated with *Homo habilis*. The Stone Age is used to designate the period when stones were important in the development of human technology. The Stone Age has been divided into three: *Paleolithic* (Old Stone), *Mesolithic* (Middle Stone), and *Neolithic* (New Stone). In studying these periods, some problems have emerged. First, there is the difficulty in presenting the events of the ancient times in a neat chronological sequence. Second, there is no uniform development of technology and civilizations of the world.

The emergence of tool technology took place during the *Paleolithic* (Old Stone) Age. The Paleolithic period diffused over much of the world, beginning from Africa. The period has been sub-divided into three—the Upper, Middle, and Lower Paleolithic. The three have been defined by the invention of new techniques of stone tools. During the Upper Paleolithic, the technique for manufacturing was stone blades, although flakes too were produced. These new tools increased efficiency in hunting and gathering. The Upper Paleolithic people discovered which plant to eat and which animal to kill for meat. They, however, did not develop the concept of planting or domesticating animals.

Archaeologists and anthropologists suggest that the people of this Age lived in small nomadic bands.

In 1959, the Leakeys recovered some tools from the Olduvai Gorge. They were believed to be the oldest tools made by either *H. habilis* or *H. rudolfensis*. They called the finds the Oldowan Culture. According to Louis Leakey, the Oldowan culture is the oldest well-authenticated stone-age culture that has yet been discovered in the world. He emphasized the making of tools because "it was this step which lifted 'near-man' from the purely animal level to that of human status."[27] The period was characterized by bifacial flaking technology. Some of the Oldowan stone tools such as the choppers, scrapers, chisels, cleavers, hammer stones, and flakes were simple and did not perform specialized functions. All of them showed the variety of tool manufacturing as well as the different purposes for which they were used. Oldowan tools date to between 2.4 and 2.6 million years ago. Other Oldowan sites include Ethiopia, Kenya, Angola, and Sterkfontein and Swartkrans in South Africa.[28]

The Acheulian Culture

The Acheulian technology succeeded the Oldowan industry in Africa. Remarkable transformations in manufacturing standardized tools such as hand axes and cleavers characterized the period. Chipping was finer, handles were improved upon, and smaller and handy tools were produced through the use of the Levallois technique. First identified in France, the Levallois method was used to detach flakes to produce blades.

The Acheulian culture belonged to the Lower Paleolithic Age and extended to the Middle Paleolithic. The most prominent tool of the Acheulian technology were the bifacial cutting tools known as *hand-axes*, which were first identified in France at the site of St. Acheul but as indicated by Louis Leakey, the earliest ones came from the Olduvai Gorge.[29] Hand-axe was a multi-purpose implement because it was used for piercing, cutting, and scraping. Its invention was indeed a revolution in technology. While the Oldowan was found only in Africa, the Acheulian culture was not limited to any particular group of people. It was found in Africa, Western Europe, and the Middle East but very rare in eastern Asia.

The sites of the Acheulian culture in Africa were more widely distributed than the Oldowan. Clifford Jolly and Randall White contend that, "the Acheulians were the first humans to expand out of Africa, having done so about a million years ago."[30] This accounts for the widespread distribution of *Homo erectus* and their technology all over the world. Archaic *Homo sapiens* had emerged by the time the Acheulian culture came to an end and replaced by more sophisticated industrial equipment such as core-axes, choppers, and core-scrapers.[31]

The Middle Stone Age

The Middle Stone Age replaced the Acheulian, although the nature of transition is not clear. In North Africa and the Sahara, this period is known as the Middle Paleolithic and it began between 100,000 and 200,000 years ago and lasted until 40,000 and 20,000 years ago.[32] There was considerable improvement in the manufacturing of flake tools such as knives, spears, and daggers. Flint became a very useful material for tool making. Because of the complexity of tool making during this time, Augustin Holl suggests that the Middle Stone Age should be regarded as a *techno-complex* period.[33] Sites of the Middle Stone Age such as the Nok were found in West Africa. Others were Kromdraai, Swartkrans, Hopefield, and Langebaanweg in southern Africa. The Nok culture in the Jos plateau of Nigeria was classified as belonging to the Middle Stone Age. The Middle Stone Age culture is called *Sangoan* in Equatorial and West Africa. Unlike the Acheulian population, the Middle Stone Age people scattered into the interior, rather than clustering around water areas. The Middle Stone Age people in Africa were contemporaries with the Neanderthal population in Europe.

The Late Stone Age

The Late Stone Age is characterized by the making of small stone tools called "microliths," which were used as composite implements. They were neatly trimmed and slotted into arrow shafts to form points and barbs. The use of the new stone technology was widespread. It improved the hunting technology and the economy, especially in hunting and fishing.[34] Microliths were made about 35,000 years ago at various sites such as the Olduvai Gorge, Mumba-Hohle in northern Tanzania, and Matupi Cave in Zaire.[35]

In West Africa, microlithic centers have been found at Iwo Eleru, Mejiro Cave, and the rock-shelters at Rop in Nigeria, the Bosumpra Cave in Ghana, the Shum Laka in Cameroon, and Kourounkorokalé in Mali.[36] Other stone tools of the Late Stone Age included knives, scrapers, anvils, grinding stones, hammer stones, and saws. The bone tools discovered in the Katanda region of Zaire, compare with the European Upper Paleolithic technology.[37]

Iron Age

The development of food-production in contrast to foraging called for the use of metal-based implements. Metals such as copper, bronze, and iron were used. Africa did not experience the Copper or Bronze Age. However, there was a large deposit of copper at Akjoujt in Mauritania, central Mali, Niger, Angola, and Central African Copperbelt in South Africa. Copper was used mainly for decorative objects such as bracelets and it was later associated with political power. It also became an important article of trade in the indigenous commercial networks.[38] Bronze was used in northern Africa, especially along the

Mediterranean.[39] Thurstan Shaw suggests that Africa jumped from the Stone to the Iron Age because the desiccation of the Sahara broke the connection between Egypt and sub-Saharan Africa and "the link was not re-established until...some three thousand years later."[40]

During the Iron Age, which spread between 500 B. C. and A. D. 500, iron-based equipment such as axes, hoes, knives, arrows, spears, and razors were produced thereby transforming the economic system and culture of the early people. As agricultural communities increased, it became necessary to produce powerful, durable, and handy implements, which were used to clear rough and rugged lands.

Indigenous iron working in Africa involved two activities: smelting and smithing. The procedure for iron smelting is complexity. There is an argument that the smelting of iron was introduced to Africa from Anatolia (modern Turkey) from about 1500 B. C.[41] A contrary argument is that iron smelting was an independent development in Africa because iron ore was plenty and various types of ore were exploited. The Nok civilization, which flourished in 500 B. C. in central Nigeria, diffused to other parts of West Africa where there was no contact with the outside world in the early part of the Iron Age. Iron smelting industries were established at Taruga (central Nigeria) in the fifth to the third centuries B. C.[42] Archaeological excavations recovered terracotta figurines in the Nok region, which suggests that the makers were iron smelters. Other early Iron Age sites in West Africa were Jenne in the Niger Delta, Agadez, and Do Dimi in the Sahel region.[43] The continuity of the culture of the Neolithic peoples and the early Iron Age populations made the rapid spread of iron technology possible in West Africa.[44]

Another site of independent development of iron smelting was the kingdom of Kush. Meroe was both the political headquarter and the industrial center of Kush. Meroe played an important role in the diffusion of iron working in Africa.[45] Archaeological excavations indicate that metallurgical technology developed in Axum where iron and bronze artifacts have been recovered. In Egypt, the role of iron in agriculture and commerce became important during the period of the Saite kings (663-525 B. C.)[46] Iron was mined and smelted in Ethiopia and there were communities that used iron in the region around the Great Lakes. A recent survey by Pierre de Maret and G. Thiry indicates that the first appearance of iron in Central Africa was among villagers and it diffused slowly among other groups. They also indicate that agricultural populations in modern Rwanda, Burundi, and the Kivu region of Zaire (Democratic Republic of Congo) emerged as productive iron-smelters. It is, however, difficult to arrive at a specific date of the spread of iron technology in Africa because a spectrum of dates has been suggested.[47]

In East Africa, Roland Oliver used pottery types and patterns to trace the spread of iron by the Bantu-speaking people. Their farming and pottery occupations required the use of iron thus; the technology was spread in the course of their migration. Oliver associated the growth and diffusion of pottery in Rwanda, Burundi, Kivu, Uganda, and western Kenya with the Early Iron Age.[48]

A recent linguistic study of loan words in Bantu reveals that the early Bantu people borrowed iron working from Central Sudanic speakers.[49] Archaeological excavations by Peter Schmidt on the western shore of Lake Victoria have recovered some furnace pits. He argued that the Buhaya, a Bantu-speaking agricultural people inhabiting the Kagera region of Lake Victoria, are one of the groups of people with a living iron working tradition in Africa. They practiced iron smelting in 200-600 B. C., the same period when iron technology flourished in the Nok culture.[50]

The use of iron brought about significant changes in technology and the economic system of African peoples, whether it was introduced or it developed independently. It strengthened and facilitated the practice of agriculture and commerce. Iron smelters and blacksmiths produced hoes, knives, and diggers, which were used for farming, arrowheads, spears, and swords, which were weapons used especially against wild animals. Thus, iron was used for tools and weapons. The possession of iron materials was a status symbol, particularly among blacksmiths and rulers. Broadly, iron performed socio-political and economic functions.

Agriculture and Pastoralism

Towards the end of the Late Stone Age, there was a gradual transition from hunting and gathering to a production economy with the practice of agriculture and pastoralism. Improved metallurgy with the adoption of iron implements and microlithic technologies played a major role in the transition. Along with farming arose permanent settlements and large communities. Settlements were located around fertile areas and rivers such as the Nile, Niger, Gambia, Senegal, Congo, and Zambezi. Lake Chad in West Africa and the Great Lakes in Central Africa accommodated agricultural communities. Societies began to adapt to varied environments that permitted food production and diversification of the economy. As a result of increase in population, more food was produced.

Egypt, West Africa, and the Ethiopian highlands were cores of agricultural development. In these places, most of the food crops were cereals and vegetables such as wheat, sorghum, barley, millet, melons, beans, African rice (*Oryza glaberrima*), *Tef,* and *fonio*. Root crops such as African yams were also cultivated. In West Africa, cowpeas and black beniseed were grown and vegetable oils were obtained from oil-palm and shea butter trees. Graham Connah suggests that agricultural system began in West Africa in the first millennium A. D. when rotational bush-fallow cultivation was adopted. [51] Some of these crops were also found in the Nile valley, especially in Khartoum where microlithic tools and polished axes were used.

While the domestication of plants was an indigenous development in Africa, animal domestication, especially sheep and goats, was a result of influences from South-West Asia.[52] J. E. G. Sutton contends that the raising of sheep, followed by goats and cattle developed among East African peoples between the third and the second millennium.[53] The Tuareg of the Sahara, the Fulani of West Africa, and the Masai of East Africa are nomadic people with great skills in domesticating animals such as sheep, horses, donkeys, goats, and cattle. Some Bantu groups, according to A. L. Mabogunje, combined animal husbandry with plant cultivation to the mutual advantage of both, and in Rwanda there was a symbiotic economic relationship where the Tutsi kept cattle and the Hutu practiced agriculture.[54]

Archaeological evidence suggests that irrigation system was adopted in pharaonic Egypt and the middle Nile to support agriculture and to protect people's shelter. Dike-building, canal-digging, and artificial dams were some of the techniques employed to check the annual inundation of the land. It is to be noted that "floods may be either too great—destroying everything in their passage—or too slight—failing to provide adequate irrigation."[55] In Upper Nubia, particularly on the Kerma plateau, vestiges of irrigation works have been found. The mechanisms used were the *shaduf*, which were later replaced by the *saqiya*. A. A. Hakem states that the introduction of *saqiya* had a significant impact on agriculture, especially in Dongola because it saved more time and labor than the *shaduf*.[56] In most of the areas that experienced annual flooding, grains and cereals such as barley, wheat, peas, maize, and beans were cultivated. Cucumbers, lentils, and melons were also planted. Soil conservation was practiced through intercropping and crop rotation. Irrigation system was also practiced in southern Ethiopia, northern Tanzania, and Kenya.

Crafts such as pottery and woodcarving supplemented agriculture and animal husbandry. Archaeological excavations along the coast of West Africa suggest that a complex structure of ironworking, woodcarving, and pottery was developed during the first millennium B. C. when foragers began to interact with farmers. The emergence of pottery was another innovation in technology among the ancient societies of Africa. Two pottery industries at Punpun and Kintampo in Ghana had developed by 1400 B. C.[57] Both sites show evidence of intermixture of material culture between the Saharan and forest people. Apart from pottery and rich deposits of iron ore that facilitated iron smelting and food production, there is evidence of domestication of animals at Kitampo by the Akan people.[58] However, the Bantu-speaking people were said to be responsible for the spread or ironworking and pottery in sub-Saharan Africa during their migrations. The Eastern stream of the Bantu spread the Urewe and Kwale styles of pottery designs.[59]

In tracing the origins of humans and the development of technology, archaeology has provided tremendous information. Prehistoric societies of Africa interacted, borrowed ideas, and evolved agricultural, economic, and social patterns, which became significant aspects of human transition to historic times. Through archaeological studies, it is possible to identify similarities in agricultural tools and crops that existed from one region to another.

Race and Human Development

Because human species have developed some characteristics, they have been classified as belonging to different races. For example, skin color, stature and other physical features have become identification tools for race classification.

In modern classification, there are four races: Australoid, Caucasoid, Mongoloid, and Negroid. The Australoids, known as the Australian Aboriginal Group, are often regarded as a subgroup of the Caucasoids because of their similar features. However, the Australoids have dark skin color. Going by the scientific evidence that there is only one human species—*Homo sapiens*, it is possible to argue that there is also only one human race.

The use of color to indicate the race an individual belongs may be misleading. This is because within a group, there may be slight variations in skin color. For example, people in northern Africa are lighter in skin color than their counterparts in sub-Saharan Africa, and all of them are classified as Negroid. Although biologists have their scientific methods of explaining skin color and determining race, historically, the movement of the early human species due to climatic conditions and subsequent intermarriages were among possible factors for the differences in the skin color. According to Boyce Rensberger, "Race mixing has not only been a fact of human history but is, in this day of unprecedented global mobility, taking place at a more rapid rate than ever."[60] Kevin Young points out that:

> The term *race* is used in various contexts to denote human political, social, ethnic, biological, or cultural traits, or a combination of them. Sociologists, anthropologists, and politicians offer widely divergent definitions. Regardless of context, however, race is a classification tool to distinguish among categories of people where there is perceived need to establish a *difference*, or otherness. It is a label by which a group (or groups) of people strives to affirm or validate its difference for a purpose.[61]

Since *race* is used to denote varieties of things, it is plausible to conclude that in modern times, the term is merely a social construct rather than biological or historical fact.

Conclusion

Science, through paleoanthropological and archaeological studies, has played a major role in determining the early people who inhabited Africa and their culture material. It has been possible to trace human development and to identify the demographic movement, which took place as a result of climatic conditions. The recovered and studied fossils have yielded significant anthropological, historical, and paleoanthropological results, but they have not clearly explained or answered the pertinent and intricate question of race. This chapter has indicated that the evidence about the genesis of humans from archaeology is overwhelming. Its scientific approach and universal acceptability is not in doubt. Numerous artifacts that have been recovered indicate how early people developed and advanced in technology, agriculture, and social relations. While it is true that early human species lived in certain geographical environment and established political territories, it has been difficult identifying specific races due to intermixture of the people.

The application of race to distinguish people, especially in Africa did not exist in the early times; it was a later development in African history. As African historiography shows, the attempt through the heavily criticized, but now jettisoned Hamitic hypothesis was intended to emphasize color differentiation in Africa and to arrogate racial superiority to light-skinned people who civilized Africans. Race has become a convenient instrument for exploitation and for gaining political, economic, and cultural dominance. This only indicates that race is a social and not biological term for distinguishing human beings.

Notes

1. This chapter has been modified to include race and science, but the original version was published as "Early History: Traditions of Origins and Archaeological Interpretations," in *Africa: African History Before 1885*, vol.1, ed. Toyin Falola (Durham, NC: Carolina Academic Press, 2000), 55-72. The author acknowledges Dr. Toyin Falola, the editor and the publisher for the permission to use the chapter. The discussion on race and science replaces the section on traditions of origins.
2. L. S. B. Leakey. *The Progress of Man in Africa* (London: Oxford University Press, 1961), 3.
3. Charles Darwin. *The Origin of Species and Descent of Man* (New York: Random House, 1936), 520.
4. Robert Jurmain, et al. *Introduction to Physical Anthropology* (Belmont, CA: West/Wadsworth, seventh edition, 1997), 316-321.
5. Clifford Jolly. "Prehistoric Humans," *Academic American Encyclopedia*, Vol. 15 (Connecticut: Danbury), 1994, 516.
6. Neanderthal is named after the Neander Valley in Germany where the fossils were first found in 1856. Robert Jurmain, et al. *Essentials of Physical Anthropology* (Belmont, CA: West/Wadsworth, third edition, 1998), 306-309; Bernard G. Campbell. *Humankind Emerging* (New York: Harper Collins Publishers, sixth edition, 1992), 24.
7. Jurmain, *Essentials of Physical Anthropology*, 281-282.
8. Campbell, 187.
9. Mary Leakey also found *A. afarensis* at Laetoli. Kenneth L. Feder, *The Past in Perspective: An Introduction to Human Prehistory* (Mountainview: Mayfield Publishing Company, 1996), 89.
10. Joseph O. Vogel. "Search for Human Origins in Africa: A Historical Note," in *Encyclopedia of Precolonial Africa*, ed., Joseph O. Vogel (Walnut Creek: AltaMira Press, 1997), 84-90.
11. Ibid. 88.
12. Karthy D. Schick, "Prehistoric Africa," in *Africa*, ed., Phyllis M. Martin and Patrick O'Meara (Bloomington: Indiana University Press, third edition, 1995), 52.
13. Robert W. July. *A History of the African People* (Prospect Heights, IL: Waveland Press, Inc., fifth edition, 1998, 10).
14. Richard Leakey and his team were very successful because they were able to recover about 150 fossil hominids from Lake Turkana. Campbell, 201; Vogel, "Search for Human Origins," 89.
15. Fred Smith, "Hominid Origins," in Vogel, 247-256.
16. Ibid., 255.
17. Bernard Wood. *Koobi Fora Research Project IV: Hominid Cranial Remains from Koobi Fora* (Oxford: Clarendon Press), 1991, cited in Jurmain, et al., 289.

18. Jurmain, et al., 265.

19. Ibid. 321.

20. Fred Smith. "Modern Human Origins," in Vogel, 262-263.

21. Ibid. 261.

22. Sally McBrearty. "Early African Hominids: Behavior and Environments," in Vogel, 273.

23. Jurmain, et al., 324-328.

24. Mary D. Leakey and R. H. Hay. "Pliocene Footprints in Lateolil Beds at Lateoli, Northern Tanzania," *Nature*, 278, 1979, 317-323; Mary D. Leakey. "Footprints in the Ashes of Time," *National Geographic*, April 1979; Roland Oliver, *The African Experience* (New York: Harper Collins Publishers, 1991), 8.

25. Mary D. Leakey. "Footprints in the Ashes of Time," *National Geographic*, April 1979, 446-457.

26. Leakey, "African Fossil Man," 440.

27. Leakey, *The Progress and Evolution*, 3.

28.. Lawrence S. Barham, "Stoneworking Technology: Its Evolution," in Vogel, 109-115.

29. Leakey, *The Progress*, 7.

30. Clifford J. Jolly and Randall White. *Physical Anthropology and Archaeology* (New York: McGraw-Hill, Inc., 1995), 340.

31. J. D. Clark. "Prehistory in Southern Africa," in *Methodology and African Prehistory*, General History of Africa, Vol. 1, ed., J. Ki-Zerbo (Berkeley, CA: University of California Press, 1981), 505-506.

32. Schick, 59.

33. Augustin F. C. Holl. "Western Africa: The Prehistoric Sequence," in Vogel, 305-312.

34. Shaw, "The Prehistory," 622.

35. Lawrence H. Robbins. "Eastern African Advanced Foragers," in Vogel, 341.

36. The Late Stone Age is divided into three periods-the Upper, Middle, and Lower Stone Age. Several sites of the three periods are mentioned by Holl, "Western Africa," 305-312 and Shaw, "The Prehistory," 624.

37. Jurmain, 343-344.

38. Michael S. Bisson. "Copper Metallurgy," in Vogel, 125-132.

39. Kevin Shillington, *History of Africa* (New York, St. Martin's Press, 1995), 37.

40. Thurstan Shaw. "The Prehistory of West Africa," in *History of West Africa*, vol. 1, ed., J. F. Ade. Ajayi and Michael Crowder (London: Longman, 1976), 61.

41. Shillington, 39.

42. C. T. Shaw. "The Prehistory of West Africa," in Ki-Zerbo, 628-629.

43. Graham Connah. *African Civilizations: Precolonial Cities and States in Tropical Africa: An Archaeological Perspective* (Cambridge: Cambridge University Press, 1993), 113-114.

44. Scott MacEachern. "Western African Iron Age," in Vogel, 426-429.

45. Bruce Williams. "Egypt and sub-Saharan Africa: Their Interaction," in Vogel, 465-472.

46. Elizabeth Isichei. *A History of African Societies to 1870* (Cambridge: Cambridge University Press, 1997), 70-71.

47. Pierre de Maret and G. Thiry. "How Old is the Iron Age in Central Africa?" in *The Culture and Technology of African Iron Production*, ed., Peter R. Schmidt (Gainesville, University Press of Florida, 1996),29-30.

48. Roland Oliver. "The Emergence of Bantu Africa," in *The Cambridge History*, ed., Fage, 366-87.

49. Peter R. Schmidt. *Iron Technology in East Africa: Symbolism, Science, and Archaeology* (Bloomington: Indiana University Press, 1997), 15, cited in David

Schoenbrun. "Early History of Eastern Africa's Great Lakes Region: Linguistic, Ecological, and Archaeological Approaches ca. 500 B. C. to ca. A. D. 1000," Ph. D. Dissertation, University of California, Los Angeles, 268.

50. Peter R. Schmidt and S. Terry Childs. "Ancient African Iron Production," *American Scientist*, November-December 1995, 524-33.

51. Connah, 140-141.

52. Ibid.

53. J. E. G. Sutton. "The Prehistory of East Africa," in Ki-Zerbo, *Methodology and African Prehistory*, 481.

54. A. L. Mabogunje. "Historical Geography: Economic Aspects," in Ki-Zerbo, *Methodology and African Prehistory*, 342.

55. G. Mokhtar. "Introduction," in *Ancient Civilizations of Africa: General History of Africa*, Vol II, ed., G. Mokhtar (Berkeley, University of California Press, 1981), 12-13.

56. A. A. Hakem. "The Civilization of Napata and Meroe," in Mokhtar, 308-310.

57. Francis Musonda. "Foragers and Farmers: Their Interaction," in Vogel, 398-403 .

58. Connah, 130, 140.

59. For the process of how pottery was manufactured, see Richard A. Krause. "Pottery Manufacture," and the spread of pottery, Joseph O. Vogel, "Bantu Expansion," in Vogel, 115-124.

60. Boyce Rensberger. "Racial Odyssey," *Science Digest*, 89[1], January 1981, 50-57.

61. Kevin C. Young. "Race as an Instrument of control and Exploitation in the Caribbean Region, From the Colonial to the Modern Era," *The Sojourn*, Spring 2009, 125-154.

References

Connah, Graham. *African Civilizations: Precolonial Cities and States inTropical Africa: An Archaeological Perspective*. Cambridge: Cambridge University Press, 1993.

Leakey, Mary D. "Footprints in the Ashes of Time." *National Geographic* (April 1979): 446-457.

Schmidt, Peter R. *Iron Technology in East Africa: Symbolism, Science, and Archaeology*. Bloomington: Indiana University Press, 1997.

Schmidt, Peter R. ed. *The Culture and Technology of African Iron Production* Gainesville, FL: University Press of Florida, 1996.

Shaw, Thurstan. "The Prehistory of West Africa," in *History of West Africa*, vol. 1. ed. J. F. Ade. Ajayi and Michael Crowder. London: Longman, 1976.

Joseph O. Vogel, ed. *Encyclopedia of Precolonial Africa*. Walnut Creek: AltaMira Press, 1997.

Chapter 2

Race and the Rise of the Swahili Culture

Julius O. Adekunle

This chapter examines the interplay of race, religion, and trade in the evolution of the Swahili culture along the coast of East Africa. The rise of the Swahili society and culture dates back to c. 800 A.D. when traders from the Arabian peninsular, Persia, China, and India penetrated the East African coast. Three primary factors were responsible for the rise of the Swahili culture: trade, religion, and racial intermarriage. Over centuries of economic interaction, the indigenous Africans and Arabs along the coast of East Africa intermarried and produced a new and distinct society known as the Swahili. And, as a complex inter-regional network of trade evolved and expanded, there occurred a proliferation of inter-racial marriages, which led to the emergence of a new culture. The founding of Islam and its spread to Africa in the seventh century also changed the history of East Africa where the coastal people came into direct contact with the religion, its concomitant civilization, and oriental trade. Over centuries of relations particularly with the Arabs, a new culture evolved and gradually expanded into the interior.

Introduction

The historiography of East Africa and archaeological evidence suggest that since the first century, the history of the Swahili society has not been static, but dynamic. There were economic activities in the region in the pre-Arab period, but commercial changes occurred with the arrival of the Arabs, and by the late fifteenth century, the Portuguese penetrated and a new dimension was introduced to the economic and political relations of the Swahili states. Swahili, derived from the Arabic word "sawahil" meaning "coast," was the Arabic word for the culture that evolved. Swahili culture has endured and bequeathed lasting legacies not only on the people on the coast, but also on a large part of East Africa. This chapter will provide a historical background to the economic development in East Africa before the arrival of the Arabs, examine racial relations that led to the emergence of the Swahili culture, and discuss the collapse of the Swahili states.

The Geography and People of East Africa

East Africa enjoyed varied geographical and climatic conditions. For example, the interlacustrine region (the Great Lakes area) and the narrow coastal strip have humid atmospheres and adequate rainfall thus providing good soil for the cultivation of food crops such as rice, bananas, sorghum, and vegetables. The arid desert and semi-desert regions from northern Kenya to southeast Tanzania have little rainfall and therefore do not support extensive farming but are suitable for keeping livestock. While some areas were "dominated by the tsetse fly and the malaria-carrying mosquito," others were mountainous highland and steep escarpments.[1] For many centuries, movement to the interior from the coast was restricted due to natural barriers. Sonia Cole sums up the varied geographical conditions of East Africa as follows:

> The warm waters of the Indian Ocean lap against coral reefs and mangrove swamps. The narrow coastal plain has a climate tolerable to Europeans since it is tempered by sea breezes; here sisal and pineapple plantations are interspersed with coconut palms and gnarled baobab trees. Beyond this belt is hot bush country, much of it uninhabited because of lack of water and the presence of the tsetse fly, which makes cattle-keeping impossible. Further west again, the equator cuts through the climatically favorable volcanic highlands above 5,000 feet, which support a flourishing population, both black and white. Here stock can be grazed on the plains and agriculture practiced on the rich soils of hillsides.[2]

It is apparent that the strategic location along the coast allowed the Swahili states to thrive in agriculture and commerce, and to establish cultural and racial relations between indigenous Africans and foreigners who percolated the coast. The Indian Ocean played a major role in the economic development and racial population of the East African coast.

The numerous islands or city-states such as Lamu, Mafia, Manda, Pate, Pemba, and Zanzibar not only developed as urban centers, but also benefited from the proliferation of Arab, Indian, Indonesian, and Persian immigrants. Trade with the immigrants was facilitated by the monsoon winds. Monsoons are strong, often violent winds that change direction with the change of season. Monsoon winds blow from cold to warm regions and they blow from the northeast between November and April and from the southwest between May and October. Although there was usually "a period of calm or rain in between,"[3] Arab and Indian sailing vessels (the dhows) came to East Africa to purchase locally made goods and to sell their oriental or exotic products. The Indonesians, reputed for building large ocean-going vessels, used the monsoons to penetrate the East African coast in pursuit of their economic interests. Neville Chittick and Robert Rotberg pointed out that as immigrants arrived in the city-states, what they brought and what they contributed eventually resulted in cultural synthesis.[4] The Arabs enjoyed staying on the coast because they found a better climatic environment as well as trade, political, and religious opportunities.[5]

The Historiography of the Swahili Coast

The historical developments in the Swahili states can be gleaned through archaeology and numerous written records of the Arab and European geographers, scholars, merchants, and missionaries who visited or wrote on the coast between the second and nineteenth centuries. Paleoanthropologists have indicated that the earliest human beings came from Africa and archaeologists have excavated many sites in eastern and southern Africa to support the emergence of culture in this part of the world. Australopithecines, the earliest humanlike primates known to have come from fossil remains in Africa, were found in southern Ethiopia, Kenya, and Tanzania, and the discoveries of Louis and Mary Leakey at the Olduvai Gorge in Tanzania were testaments to the peopling and development of early civilization in East Africa.[6] While the interlacustrine region benefited from the development of agriculture, the coast gained from the growth of trade. Through a slow process, immigration to the coast took place within Africa, especially by the Bantu-speaking people, and the population soared because of the thriving economy. The Bantu-speaking people migrated from southern Cameroons, their cradle, by 1000 B.C., forging through the Congo forest to populate several parts of central, eastern, and southern Africa. They split into two major language families: the Eastern and the Western Bantu. Upon arrival in their different locations, they first interacted with the indigenous people before coming in contact with either the Arabs or Europeans. With time, their language intermixed with Arabic to produce Swahili. Bantu is neither a race nor a culture, but a member of the Niger-Kongo family of African languages.[7] Speaking over four hundred related languages and practicing a common culture, the Bantu developed as an agricultural and technologically advanced people with a complex political system. Aside from speaking related languages, the Bantu also had similar socio-economic characteristics.

Arab, Chinese, and European writers of early documents about the East African coast had different interests and therefore their information was varied and diverse, though mainly related to commerce and religion. Emphasis was on commerce because of the presence of essential articles of trade in East Africa and the Indian Ocean provided a convenient connecting factor. Religion, specifically Islam, was used to cement socio-cultural relations. Many of the documents, however, failed to discuss in any significant detail the issue of race relations. This was presumably because race did not create a problem in socio-economic relations in the Swahili states. The foreign merchants interacted peacefully with the indigenous people with whom they traded.

The earliest written record was the *Periplus of the Erythrean Sea*, a single-authored Greek record, written in the second century.[8] Focusing on the thriving commerce along the coast and supplying detailed information on the scattered urban and market centers that served as ports, the record also mentioned that custom duties were paid in several emporia. This suggests that a well-structured commercial arrangement evolved between indigenous Africans and foreign merchants. Among the essential articles of trade were gold, frankincense, and ivory. The closest information about race in the *Periplus* was that the Arab merchants "intermarried with East Africans—probably pre-Bantu—learned their languages, and exported the exotic products of the coast – notably ivory and . . . slaves."[9] In his analysis of the *Periplus of the Erythrean Sea*, Gervase Mathew believed that the document was "the account of an eyewitness . . . who traveled on the trade routes of the Indian Ocean."[10]

Another early document was the *Geography* of Ptolemy written in the fifth century. The author, Claudius Ptolemaeus (commonly known as Ptolemy), was a Roman scholar who lived in Egypt during the second century. Among his scholarly works, the *Geography* was the most important. Ptolemy referred to the people in East Africa as "man-eating Ethiopians," suggesting that the people were cannibals. Like the *Periplus*, the main theme of the *Geography* was the thriving commerce along the coast, and again like the author of the *Periplus*, Ptolemy described the inhabitants as boat makers and seafarers, and mentioned some places such as Opone as an important emporium.[11]

The early inhabitants of the coast have been described in various ways. For example, the *Periplus* described them as very tall people while the Arabs called them Zanj or Bilad az-Zanj (the land of the Black people).[12] The *Periplus* did not identify the different racial groups along the coast and did not specifically refer to the presence of the Bantu-speaking people, but it is certain that the Nilotic and Bantu-speaking peoples had populated East Africa for many centuries before the advent of foreigners. Among them were the Dinker and Nuer in the Sudan and Luo in western Kenya and Uganda. The dominant group of people were the Bantu who were advanced in agriculture, technology, pottery, and political organization.

The Christian Topography of Cosmas Indicopleutes, written in the mid-sixth century also used the Arabic term, Zanj to identify the people of East Africa. Cosmas Indicopleutes was a Greek seafaring merchant and Christian who travelled to Adulis, which he described as an important port. He did not travel to the southern part of the East African coast, but provided an indication that the Arab merchants controlled trade, intermarried, and spoke local languages.[13]

Numerous written sources in Arabic such as *Kitab al Zanj* were more concerned about the expansion of Islam and the growth of trade than about race relations. *Kitab al Zanj* mentioned Arab influence through two Omani brothers. The Omani Arabs became politically influential, especially in Zanzibar until the arrival of the Portuguese. João de Barros, a Portuguese and the writer of *Decada da Asia* in the early sixteenth century, provided information on the immigration of different groups of Arabs to the coast. Because the Arabs were unwilling to compromise their religion by living among infidels, they forced the inhabitants to move to the interior. In reference to race and language, Duarte Barbosa, a Portuguese mariner, identified the people of the coastal city-states as "black men, and men of colour—some speak Arabic, and the rest make use of the language of the Gentiles [Bantu language] of the country."[14] It also mentioned the intermarriage that took place among the Arabs thus leading to the establishment of dynasties, especially the Persian Shirazi dynasty of Kilwa.[15]

João de Barros must have derived his information from the *Chronicle of Kilwa*, which credited the founding of Kilwa's dynasty to seven Persian brothers (the Shirazi dynasty). The relations between the Persian immigrants and the indigenous inhabitants were cordial in spite of their religious differences. The *Chronicle of Kilwa*, like those of Pate and Lamu, made little reference to race, but mentioned some Swahili-sounding names.

The Arabs and East African Economy

As discussed earlier, before the penetration of the Arabs, the Swahili city-states thrived economically through the production of agricultural goods and the sale of mineral resources. Although there was no strong political connection other than the powerful Zimbabwe kingdom in the interior, there seemed to be some evidence of economic relations through the exchange of agricultural goods. The specialization in the production of goods and the growth of urbanized societies combined to improve the economy. Chapurukha Kusimba asserts that:

> The Swahili Coast has played a prominent role in world history from the beginnings of recorded time – Solomon and Tyrean allies were reputed to have dispatched trading fleets to the coasts of eastern Africa. The Romans trafficked there and Egyptian goods penetrated its interior. In historic times, the north, the Somali coast, offered entrepôts to the caravan routes leading to the Nile valley through such foreboding towns as the legendary city of Harar - a prominent slaving center with a thriving business in cotton and coffee. Its central reaches in Kenya and Tanzania connected the people and produce of the flourishing kingdoms of the Great Lakes region – Karagwe, Bunyoro, and Buganda – on the Highlands to the Coastal towns, the markets on Zanzibar and the island archipelagos. In the south, ports along the Mozambique Strait trafficked inland to the plateaus of Zambezia and the mineral riches controlled by maShona kingdoms, ruled from marvelous places like Great Zimbabwe.[16]

The city-states also developed their architectural ability by constructing houses and palaces with stone. They were fortified. Duarte Barbosa described Kilwa as a town with "many fair houses of stone and mortar, with many windows after our fashion, very well arranged in streets, with many flat roofs."[17] Murphy shows that, "ruins of palaces indicate that a few homes were designed for the most luxurious kind of living. Small but exquisitely built mosques were scattered about the coasts. Mosques of wood and mud were found in most small towns and villages."[18]

Trading became an important and integral part of the economy when the Arabs arrived. The city-states became trading ports for foreign merchants. The Arabs established trade routes through the Indian Ocean, not only to India, but also to the East African coast and to the interior for the lucrative gold trade found in Zimbabwe and Sofala. With the advantage of by the Indian Ocean on their side, Swahili men developed as seafarers, traveling to India, China, and

Europe for commercial purposes. The city-states established strong trading connections with India and China through the Indian Ocean.

Mogadishu, the northernmost Swahili state, controlled the commerce of the region until the twelfth century when Kilwa supplanted it by dominating the major trade routes, especially the one from the Sofala gold mines and Katanga copper region. Kilwa also established commercial outposts at Tete and Sena, both located on the River Zambezi. Numismatic studies reveal that although Kilwa minted its own coins, there was evidence of Arab, Chinese, Greek, Indian, and Roman coins in the Swahili states.[19] There was also evidence of Indian cotton as well as Chinese porcelain, glassware, and silk. Swahili merchants from Kilwa, Sofala, Tete, and Sena traveled to the interior to purchase machilla cotton cloth woven in the Maravi Empire in exchange for ivory and gold in Zimbabwe. The decline of Kilwa in the thirteenth century was due to the rise of Pate and the beginning of the dominance of Islam. Since a Swahili kingdom was not established, the civilization was built around city-states and no city-state was able to exercise complete dominance or hegemony over the others.

The Emergence of the Swahili Culture

Swahili applied to the people, culture, and language that evolved along the coast of East Africa. The earliest form of Swahili civilization emerged in the Lamu Archipelago where a sizeable number of Arab merchants and missionaries had settled and built a mosque by 800 A.D. A plausible argument can be made that since the Bantu were widely spread along the coast and related with their Arab trading partners, they laid the foundations for the Swahili civilization.[20]

By the thirteenth century, the racial, cultural, and linguistic interactions between the indigenous Bantu-speaking Africans and foreign merchants, especially the Arabs and Persians, had become prominent, and extensive intermarriage had taken place that enabled a new society to emerge. Over time, "a mixed culture developed as alien settlers arrived on the coast, were absorbed into East African life, and intermarried locally. Their children were the local hosts to later generations of immigrants."[21] Alongside the emergence of a new culture, Swahili cities such as Kilwa, Lamu, Mombasa, and Pate became urbanized, thriving economically (controlling much of the gold trade from Zimbabwe). Through the influence of the Arabs, the cities became Islamized. Jefferson Murphy points out that "the cities had an appearance and quality of urban life that was different from the traditional Bantu settlements along the coastal region. Forms of architecture and building techniques were non-Bantu; they were imported by the Arabs and they became essential parts of the emerging Swahili culture."[22] As argued elsewhere, "Swahili indicates the fusion in an urban melting pot of Bantu and other peoples from around the Indian Ocean in its culture, rituals, ceremonies, beliefs, and dances. Possibly its most well-known symbol was the elaborate carved wooden doors common to all the city-states."[23]

Trade and religion played major roles in the rise of the Swahili culture. The relations between the trading Arab communities and the indigenous Africans of East Africa brought about the birth of the Swahili society. Thomas Wilson emphatically stated that Swahili was "a result of the centuries of trade that occurred between the coastal peoples of East Africa and the Arab world."[24] Their favorable geographical location along the coast with access to natural harbors strategically placed them in the position to control both inland and overseas long-distance trade. Islam penetrated as early as the seventh century when the Arabs embarked on the conquest of many parts of North and East Africa. Islam had grown to the extent that Muhammad ibn Battuta, an Arab scholar who visited East Africa in the fourteenth century, was able to report that many of the people practiced Islam. Battuta referred to Mogadishu as "a very large town," and to Kilwa as "one of the most beautiful and well constructed towns in the world."[25] The Great Mosque in Kilwa, one of the finest mosques in medieval Africa, provided a forum for inter-racial worship and for socio-cultural relations. John Hansin contended that, "The Swahili eventually adopted their [Islamic] commercial values and religious beliefs and extended them throughout the coastal settlements . . . [and] by the thirteenth century Swahili merchants had moved down the coast and monopolized the international trade."[26]

As Africans accepted Islam and adopted Islamic customs and practices, the distinction between Africans and Arabs gradually diminished. Africans read the Qur'an in Arabic and spoke the language for commercial purposes. Thus they mixed indigenous African languages with Arabic, which remained a language of commerce and religion. Heavily influenced by African Bantu words, the Swahili became a popular language spoken in Zanzibar, Mombasa, Malindi, Kilwa and other city-states, although Arabic remained the official language. Swahili became a written language between the sixteenth and eighteenth centuries. It is generally believed that Swahili (KiSwahili) had its origin in Zanzibar through the influence of the Omani Arabs and Persians. The overall consequence of economic, religious, and linguistic relations was the emergence of a unique group of people known as the Swahili society.

The Swahili Language

Ki-Swahili, the language of the coastal people, is a mixture of Bantu and Arabic languages: a result of commercial, racial, religious, and social relations. The language has taken centuries to evolve because the process of meshing the different languages spoken on the coast was a slow one. Derek Nurse and Thomas Spear emphasize the fact that:

> Swahili is clearly an African language in its basic sound system and grammar and is closely related to Bantu languages of Kenya, northeast Tanzania, and the Comoro Islands, with which it shared a common development long prior to the widespread adoption of Arabic vocabulary. Though some Arabic words were assimilated into Swahili before A.D. 1500, most are attributable to the post-

Portuguese period. The Arabic material is a recent graft onto an old old-bantu tree.[27]

Although the Swahili language was formed largely with Bantu and Arab words, it also contains loanwords from both the Persian and Indian languages as well.[28]

Like other African languages, the Swahili was largely oral, but it became a written language using the Arabic and Roman alphabet in the seventeenth century when a few manuscripts emerged. As a language of commerce, Swahili spread rapidly from Lamu in the north to Kilwa in the south. It not only became a dominant language throughout the region, but also served to strengthened racial relations. The language, however, had a cluster of dialects: the northern, central, and southern clusters. Accordingly, Derek Nurse and Thomas Spear state, "all Swahili dialects were greatly influenced by the assimilation of considerable numbers of speakers of other languages."[29]

The Swahili language is rich in oral traditions, poetry, proverbs, and riddles. Elders blithely narrated stories that dealt with regional history, politics, and economics. Some oral traditions were about their ruler's genealogy or their people's migration from Arabia or Persia. There were family traditions or town traditions, which also revealed the racial background of the people. Since traditions are part of history and culture, they became a source of reconstructing the racial, economic, and political history of the Swahili states. Early writers of the Swahili states based part of their information on oral literature, especially oral traditions, which became the main sources for chronicles on the city-states, such as the *Chronicle of Kilwa* written in 1530, the *Chronicle of Pate* (claimed that the Omani Arabs established the dynasty of Pate), and the *Chronicle of Lamu* (which revealed that Lamu was inhabited by immigrants from Syria).

A large corpus of poetry exists, especially among the northern cluster of dialects. As Lyndon Harries indicates, the Swahili-speaking people express themselves in literary form and that "poems are still written in the traditional manner," and Swahili poetry continues to hold an entrenched position in the popular press, especially in Tanganyika [Tanzania]."[30] Some poems are recited and sung while others are read aloud.[31] Different forms of poem include the *tendi,* which are long narrative poems that contain oral traditions and historical events. The s*hairi* (chanted during traditional *gungu* dances); the *mavugo* (performed during weddings; and the *shairiare* (sung for national dances).

Hayawi, hayawi huwa, ("Time and tide wait for no man") is a Swahili proverb that expresses the importance of time and why it is necessary to make use of every opportunity when it avails itself. Another proverb, which is common in Africa, is *Tembo wawili wakipigana ziumiazo ni nyasi* ("When two elephants fight it is the grass that gets hurt").[32] This proverb relates how innocent people suffer when there is conflict between two powerful groups. In addition riddles were part of the entertainment component of the Swahili language. There were riddles such as *Nyumba yangu ndogo ina madirisha mengi* ("My house is small, but it has many windows"). This riddle refers to a fishing trap, which has several holes, which enable the catch of a large number of fish. The riddle can also express how people of diverse backgrounds can co-exist.

The other side of the riddle is *Nyumba yang kuu ina mlango mdogo* ("My house is large, but its door is small"). This riddle refers to a bottle, which does not have a wide opening. This riddle can apply to close-door political and economic relations, which may hamper growth and development in a society.

The spread of the Swahili language can be attributed to various factors such as the long period of trade, the diversity of the population, the coming of the European missionaries who needed the language to spread the Gospel, and colonialism. The colonial authorities used Swahili as the language of communication and gradually, Portuguese, German, and English words penetrated into the Swahili language as well. The Swahili language is now taught in schools and used in mass media. Aside from East Africa, Swahili is also spoken in Oman, where, according to Marc Valeri, the Swahili-speaking Omani returnees from Zanzibar "faced prejudices from the population who stayed at home and were forced to give guarantees to others of their full belonging to the nation."[33]

Swahili Cultural Features

Although the Swahili culture is often identified by its racial intermixture and language, there are other cultural features. Poems and proverbs are expressed through the Swahili language, but there are other features such as music and dance, which are closely related phenomena. Songs are composed for different occasions. For example, there are warrior, dream, and love songs. There are varieties of musical instruments such as drums, tambourines, along with bells and rattles, as well as wind instruments. In Lamu the *gungu* is a special dance, but in Zanzibar it is regarded as a wedding dance.

Another cultural feature was pottery, which the Bantu people had developed. Archaeologists have identified pottery as one of the most distinctive aspects of culture in eastern Africa generally, and in the Swahili states in particular. That was due to the influence of the Bantu-speaking people. Pottery was created in different shapes, techniques, and designs, which can be identified through their origins. Although pottery had a long historical development along the coast, evidence suggests that there were also imported ceramics such as tin glazed ware, Chinese sue ware, Indian purple ware, and Egyptian glass. Also, kilns were imported from China and Persia. The various forms of pottery found in the Swahili states was as a result of the immigration of the Arabs, Chinese, Indians, and Persians.[34]

Islamic civilization, trade, and the influence of the Persians, Arabs, and Omanis played a major role in the growth of Swahili architecture. Islam, which was initially the religion of the foreigners on the coast, had become widely accepted by the twelve century. One of the distinctive features of Islamic architecture was the construction of mosques, the most notable one being the Great Mosque of Kilwa. The use of coral for building was first noticed on this mosque. Expressing the interrelationship between religion and trade, Nurse and Spear argued that:

Trade boomed, and during the prosperity that followed merchants from Hadhramaut in southern Arabia became prominent community leaders, immigrant *sharifs* reformed and revitalized coastal Islam along contemporary Arabian lines, and people build elegant houses copying current Arabian and Indian features.[35]

As more people converted to Islam, many more mosques were built with coral and domes. While the mainland population lived in houses built of mud and thatched roofs, the urbanized people of the coast constructed houses and palaces with squared coral blocks. The difference in house pattern and size was a reflection of elitism and economic prosperity on the coast.

The Collapse of the Swahili States

The thriving culture and economy of the Swahili states witnessed a gradual decline with the arrival of the Portuguese under the leadership of Vasco da Gama in the late fifteenth century. In their attempt to find a sea route to India to participate in the lucrative spice trade, the Portuguese sailed to East Africa to trade in gold, ivory, and slaves. Vasco da Gama was attracted by the prosperity of Malindi and Mombasa, both controlling the gold trade from Sofala. To divert the trade in gold from the Arabs to themselves, the Portuguese adopted aggressive and destructive strategies. Their activities led to the destruction of the erstwhile booming trade and disrupted the network of trade routes among the Swahili states. With technological advantage over Africans, the Portuguese bombarded and destroyed leading commercial cities such as Kilwa, Mombasa, and Mogadishu. The Portuguese not only weakened the military and economic effectiveness of the Swahili states because of their greed, but they also slowed down the growth of the Swahili civilization.

After destroying most of the Swahili states along the coast, the Portuguese moved into the interior where they came into direct contact with the powerful Mwenemutapa Empire.[36] The economic greed of the Portuguese and their stiff opposition to Islam (which was an agent of the Swahili culture) initiated the collapse of the relationship between the Swahili rulers and Islamic foreigners both along the coast and in the interior. Ultimately, the Portuguese were attacked and defeated by the Omani Arabs and the Zimba (a fierce and militarily powerful group of people from Mozambique).

Conclusion

The East African coast, like the rest of the continent, was not a homogenous society and the emergence of the Swahili culture was a result of racial relations between Africans and foreigners, especially Arabs along the eastern coast of Africa. Although the Swahili states were initially diverse in culture and language, they were meshed together thus giving them a mosaic nature. However, through extensive socio-economic interactions and intermarriages, a cultural and linguistic identity was forged. Swahili was not the creation of a new race, but a synthesis of African and Arab cultures and languages. It was simply a distinct hybrid civilization, which was neither a political unit nor a militarized society. The Swahili-speaking peoples did not describe themselves as a race, but as Mombasans (Swahili waMvita), Pateans (waPate), Kilwans (waKilwa), and Arabs (waArabu) who shared a common culture and language.[37]

The historiography of East African states does not reveal any racial problem until the collapse of the Swahili states. Initially, people of different cultural and linguistic backgrounds were more interested in commerce and religion than in racial differences. When Islam first arrived, it served as a means of segregation because Muslims lived in separate quarters from the indigenous Africans who worshipped traditional religions. However, as Africans adopted Islam and its cultural practices, the line of separation became less apparent. Intermarriage also helped to close the racial gap. Hence, the new society focused on strengthening cultural and linguistic relations rather than emphasizing racial differences.

Trade was the first tool that cemented racial relations. Religion followed. These two factors led to intermarriage through which the Swahili culture evolved. As early Arab and European writers identified the inhabitants of the coast without any special reference to racial problems, even by the time the Swahili states collapsed, there was no evidence of racial tension. This long term and complex relationship eventually led to an amalgam of cultures and languages, which is known as Swahili culture.

In modern times, Swahili is no longer a racial phenomenon and is not a distinctive civilization. It remains a language that has endured for centuries without affiliation to any specific race. The Swahili language is widely spoken in countries such as Burundi, Comoro Islands, Democratic Republic of Congo, Kenya, Mozambique, Rwanda, Somalia, Uganda, and Tanzania, and it is taught in universities within and outside Africa. It is used as the national language and primary language of instruction in Tanzania. Although the Swahili states have collapsed and the Swahili culture has disappeared, the Swahili language still exists in several countries of East Africa. The collapse of the Swahili states terminated the continued distinctiveness of the Swahili culture, which is now recognized only by the language.

Notes

1. G. S. Were and D. A. Wilson. *East Africa through a Thousand Years: A.D. 1000 to the Present Day* (London: Evans Brothers Limited, 1968), 4-5.

2. Sonia Cole. *The Prehistory of East Africa* (New York: Mentor Books, 1963), 31-32.

3. H. Neville Chittick and Robert I. Rotberg. "Introduction," in *East Africa and the Orient: Cultural Synthesis in Pre-colonial Times*, eds., H. Neville Chittick and Robert I. Rotberg (New York: Africana Publishing Company, 1975), 1.

4. Ibid., 4.

5. B. G. Martin. "Arab Migration to East Africa in Medieval Times," *The International Journal of African Historical Studies*, vol. 7, no. 3, 1974, 367-390.

6. For example, see L. S. B. Leakey. *The Progress of Man in Africa* (London: Oxford University Press, 1961); Mary D. Leakey and R. H. Hay. "Pliocene Footprints in Lateolil Beds at Lateolil, Northern Tanzania," *Nature*, 278, 1979, 317-323.

7. J. B. Webster. "The Mystery of Bantu Expansion," in *Fundamentals of African History*, eds. Apollos Nwauwa and Bertin Webster (Unpublished manuscript, Dalhousie University, 1993), 69-75.

8. Gervase Mathew. "The East African Coast Until the Coming of the Portuguese," in Roland Oliver and Gervase Mathew, eds. *History of East Africa* (London: Oxford University Press, 1963), 95-96.

9. Chittick and Rotberg, 8.

10. Gervase Mathew. "The Dating and the Significance of the *Periplus of the Erythrean Sea*," in *East Africa and the Orient: Cultural Synthesis in Pre-colonial Times*, eds., H. Neville Chittick and Robert I. Rotberg, 153.

11. Neville Chittick. "The Peopling of the East African Coast," in *East Africa and the Orient: Cultural Synthesis in Pre-colonial Times*, eds., H. Neville Chittick and Robert I. Rotberg, 20; 161-162.

12. "Zanj" or "Zenj" vaguely referred to the Black people along the coast. They were most likely the Bantu who had settled in the region following their migration. J. E. G. Sutton. "The East African Coast: An Historical and Archaeological Review," *Historical Association of Tanzania*, Paper no. 1, 1966, 6-7.

13. L. P. Kirwan. "The Christian Topography and the Kingdom of Axum," *The Geographical Journal*, vol. 138, vo. 2 (Jun., 1972), 166-177.

14. Robert O. Collins. *Eastern African History, Vol. II of African History: Text and Reading* (Princeton, NJ: Markus Wiener Publishers, 1997), 66-67, reproduced from Duarte Barbosa. *A Description of the Coasts of East Africa and Malabar in the Beginning of the Sixteenth Century*, translated by Henry E. J. Stanley (London: Hakluyt Society, 1266, 4-15, 19-21.

15. G. S. P. Freeman-Grenville. *The Medieval History of the Coast of Tanganyika, with Special Reference to Recent Archaeological Discoveries* (London: Oxford University Press, 1962), 75-78.

16. Chapurukha M. Kusimba. *The Rise and Fall of Swahili States* (Walnut Creek, CA: Altamira Press, 1999), 19-20.

17. As quoted in E. Jefferson Murphy. *History of African Civilization* (New York: Thomas Y. Crowell Company, 1972), 234.

18. Ibid., 233.

19. Gervase Matthew. "The East African Coast Until the Coming of the Portuguese," in *History of East Africa*, eds., Roland Oliver and Gervase Matthew (London: Oxford university Press, 1963), 31.

20. Murphy, 225.

21. Philip Curtin, Steven Feierman, Leonard Thompson, and Jan Vansina. *African History* (Boston, MA: Little, Brown and Company, 1978), 144.
22. Murphy, 230.
23. Julius O. Adekunle. "The East African Coast and Its Diaspora," in *Fundamentals of African History*, 63.
24. Thomas H. Wilson. *City-states of the Swahili Coast* (New York: Franklin Watts, 1998), 7.
25. As quoted in Murphy, 231 and 232.
26. John Hansin. "Islam and African Societies," in *Africa*, ed., Phyliss Martin 1995, 103.
27. Derek Nurse and Thomas Spear. *The Swahili: Reconstructing the History and Language of an African Society, 800-1500* (Philadelphia, PA: University of Pennsylvania Press, 1985), 6.
28. Philip Curtin, et al. 144.
29. Ibid., 6-15.
30. Lyndon Harries. *Swahili Poetry* (London: Oxford University Press, 1962), 1-3.
31. A. H. J. Prins. *The Swahili-speaking Peoples of Zanzibar and the East African Coast (Arabs, Shirazi and Swahili)* (London: International African Institute, 1967), 110-111.
32. For these and more Swahili proverbs, see Bernard K. Muganda. *Speaking Kiswahili: A Grammar and Reader* (Washington, D.C.: Drum and Spear Press, 1970), 52-54.
33. Marc Valeri. "Nation-building and Communities in Oman since 1970: The Swahili-speaking Omani in Search for Identity," *African Affairs*, 106 (424): 2007, 479-496.
34. Chapurukha M. Kusimba. "Swahili and the Coastal City-states," in *Encyclopedia of Precolonial Africa: Archaeology, History, Languages, Cultures, and Environments* (ed., Joseph O. Vogel (London: Altamira Press, 1997), 507-513.
35. Nurse and Spear, 4.
36. Mwenemutapa means "Master Pillage" in the Shona language (a branch of the Bantu languages).
37. James de Vere Allen. *Swahili Origins: Swahili Culture & the Shungwaya Phenomenon* (London: James Currey, 1993), 1.

References

Allen, James de Vere. *Swahili Origins: Swahili Culture & the Shungwaya Phenomenon.* London: James Currey, 1993.
Chittick, H. Neville and Robert I. Rotberg, eds. *East Africa and the Orient: Cultural Synthesis in Pre-colonial Times.* New York: Africana Publishing Company, 1975.
Freeman-Grenville, G. S. P. *The Medieval History of the Coast of Tanganyika, with Special Reference to Recent Archaeological Discoveries.* London: Oxford University Press, 1962.
Harries, Lyndon. *Swahili Poetry.* London: Oxford University Press, 1962.
Muganda, Bernard K. *Speaking Kiswahili: A Grammar and Reader.* Washington, D.C.: Drum and Spear Press, 1970.
Prins, A. H. J. *The Swahili-speaking Peoples of Zanzibar and the East African Coast (Arabs, Shirazi and Swahili).* London: International African Institute, 1967.
Kusimba, Chapurukha M. *The Rise and Fall of Swahili States.* Walnut Creek, CA: Altamira Press, 1999.

Chapter 3

'Caste'- [ing] Gender:
Caste and Patriarchy in Ancient Hindu Jurisprudence

Indira Jalli

This chapter attempts to look at how caste and gender together were handled in Hindu jurisprudence in ancient times. This chapter is not premised on a time-based analysis because there has been a plethora of confusion over the time period of different Hindu legal codes and injunctions. Thus, the present study primarily seeks to understand the evolutionary process of ancient Hindu jurisprudence. The focal point of this chapter is the manifestation of caste [ist] patriarchy in the religious legal codes of Hinduism during ancient times and its implications to dalit women. This chapter does not look at the chronology of these texts neither the development nor the "ups" or "downs" in the status of dalit women in India as indicated. In other words, since the periodization of these texts are not clear, this author does not try to focus on whither dalits and women's conditions progressed or deteriorated with the commencement of each legal text.

Introduction

The Dravidians (aboriginal inhabitants of India) built the earliest urban society in south Asia in the Indus river valley region. This Indus Valley civilization, reaching its height roughly between c. 3,000 B.C.E.-1900 B.C.E., emerged near the cities of Harappa and Mohenjo-daro located in present day Pakistan. These darker skinned Dravidians were subsequently conquered by invading "wheat colored" Indo-Aryans from central Asia who brought with them their horse drawn chariots, ancient language Sanskrit, beliefs, and social customs. The term *varna* used by the Aryans to refer to social distinctions is the Sanskrit word for "color." The Dravidians and the Aryans managed to forge one of the oldest civilizations in history. Thus, humans have been struck by color since earliest times. The Aryans left an indelible imprint on the development of the [now] recognizable socio-cultural traditions of India. Aryan civilization flourished during the Vedic Age roughly between c. 1500 and 500 B.C.E. Four distinct *varnas* came to be increasingly recognized by the Aryans after about 1000 B.C.E including priests (*brahmins*), warriors and aristocrats (*kshatriyas*), cultivators, artisans, and merchants (*viashyas*), along with landless peasants and serfs (*sudras*). The people of "no caste" referred to as untouchables constituted a separate category subsequently added perhaps by the end of the Vedic Age or shortly thereafter. People who became polluted from their work such as with the butchering of animals and the handling of dead bodies were eventually considered "untouchable." Thus, an elaborate system of caste and subcastes eventually evolved that expressed the blending of both Dravidian and Aryan traditions.

The Vedic Age is named as such due to the fact that ancient Hindu religious texts called *The Vedas* (collection of rituals, prayers, and songs) were promulgated during this period first orally then as transcribed by Aryan priests c. 600 B.C.E. There are a total of four texts that constitute *The Vedas* the oldest of which is entitled the *Rig Veda* (compilation of more than 1,000 hymns addressed to Aryan gods). These texts help to provide insight into Aryan life and culture in ancient India as well as religious beliefs and practices. The classical writings of ancient India also include the *Upanishads* (c. 800 to 400 B.C.E.) and the *Law Book of Manu* (c. first century B.C.E.).The *Upanishads* as expressed in a series of dialogues concern an examination of the *Vedas* while the *Law Book of Manu* or *Manu Smriti* contains instructions and guidance on social relations in early Indian civilization. The primary goal of this chapter is an analysis of the *Manu Smriti* and its role in caste -[ing] gender in ancient Hindu society.

It is to be noted that most of these ancient texts do not have specific comments or laws on the untouchable castes. There are, however, many injunctions against the *sudras*. Most of the legal codes treat and imply the same rules for *sudras* and untouchables although the untouchable castes typically were more discriminated against than the *sudra* castes. The major differences between the *sudra* and untouchable castes are that the former fall within the four fold theory of caste and the later do not. In other words, *sudras* are considered to be at the bottom of the caste system whereas the untouchables were treated as unfit to be a part of the caste structure *at all*.

This does not mean that caste rules never addressed the "lower" castes directly. Demographically and culturally speaking, the untouchable communities were segregated from the physical proximity of the "upper" castes. They were seen as inferior subjects in the presence of the "upper" castes only within the particular contexts of manual labor related to agriculture, death, and scavenging. So, the untouchable castes were not seen as potential threats to the property, privileges, and women of the "upper" castes as much as the *sudras*.[1] That is why we do not come across these legal codes directly addressing the untouchables but repeatedly dealing with *sudras* on every occasion. In the majority of contexts such as related to property, women, progeny, rituals (for example penances), and *sraddhas*, one can see these texts addressing the *sudras* immediately after addressing the *brahmins*. This author could only see the untouchable subject lurking at the fringes and shadows of these texts but not as a main part of them. Since all of these texts were extremely rigid towards *sudras* it should be noted that they must have been more brutal to the untouchable men, in general, and their women in particular, as they were considered the most despicable species by caste laws.

Another predicament that one faces while studying these codes, is that the categories of *sudras* were also repeatedly addressed as "lower castes." Thus, we have the untouchable "lower" castes and also *sudra* "lower" castes and it is difficult on several occasions to differentiate which specific lower caste the codes were addressing. But, it is not a very difficult task as these codes seems to consider all "lower" castes as generally inferior or polluted. This filthiness, or pollution, however is again graded according to the occupations they (lower castes) were allotted. It can be inferred that a *panchama* (literally means fifth people/those who do not belong to the four fold caste system) who carried and buried the corpses of men and animals were more looked down than a *sudra* who pressed the feet of a *brahman* or shampooed his genitals. For untouchable communities terms such as *nishadas, panchamas, parasavas, pukkasas,* and *avarnas,* (people with no color, color- less people or people with dark or tan complexion) were used. Thus, it becomes inevitable for this study to consider the clauses that address the *sudras* and also those which address lower castes and the untouchables. When it comes to the question of "lower" caste women, we do not see many codes, which are specific to them. This author could only make inferences about the implications of these laws in the general clauses, which address the Hindu women, and the "lower castes." Before attempting to deconstruct these legal codes, it would be important to understand the basic elements of Hindu law.

Law is often regarded as *dharma* in Hindu legal colloquial. This concept of *dharma* actually denotes two opposite meanings. In a literal sense, it means a righteous act or justice. But in the sense of Hindu religion, it means "following one's duty according to one's birth." In a biological sense, caste and gender were the parameters according to which one's *dharma* is determined. Age was not included as a basic biological parameter in determining one's status as examined in this discourse. This notion of justice is not premised on the principle of "rule of law." People are not viewed as the natural subjects of rule of law. Thus, the Hindu notion of *dharma* is quite contrary to the modern notion of justice. The liberal democratic concept of "justice" does not correlate with this concept at all.

This notion of *dharma* ruled both the personal and public life of Hindus. There was not much difference between Hindu religion and the socio-political life of the people. The personal and political were not separate spheres, but rather always appear to be merged. The other point to be noted is that the caste system is the backbone of Hindu religion. Therefore, the basic perception and conscience of the common "upper" caste Hindu is structured with caste [ism].

Before attempting to deconstruct these texts, it would be first appropriate to understand further what the caste system is all about. The theory of caste is very much based on a strict demarcation of people clustered into castes, which one inherits from birth. It is essentially based on the notions of purity and pollution. One is pure or polluted depending on the caste in which he/she is born. This status is neither achievable nor alterable. According to the grand caste tale/myth a brahmana is born from mouth, a *kshatriya* (warrior caste) from chest, *vaishya* (traders) from thighs, and *sudra* from the feet of the god *brahma*. The other lower communities are the "untouchables." Technically, they are a non-caste because they do not fall under the ladder of the caste system and thus perceived as more despicable than the *sudra* castes. The present article mentions more references from the *Manu Smriti* (from hereafter MS) because it was the first and oldest systematic legal code utilized in ancient India.

Brahmans are declared *Bhudevas* (Gods on earth)

According to Manu, "By his origin alone a Brahmana is a deity even for the gods, and (his teaching is) authoritative for men, because the Veda is the foundation for that."[2] There are several justifications made for the origin of caste theory. There is a theory of creation where all supreme qualities such as light and virtues are attributed to the *brahmanas* where as darkness, sin, and indulgences are attributed to the lower castes. In the last chapter of the MS, Manu sounds hesitant about the stability of the caste system. Thus, he hastily reminds the Hindus about the origin of castes:

> Immovable (beings), insects, both small and great, fishes, snakes, and tortoises, cattle and wild animals, are the lowest conditions to which (the quality of) Darkness leads. Elephants, horses, Sudras, despicable barbarians, lions, tigers, and boars (are) the middling states,caused by (the quality of) Darkness. Karanas, Suparnas and hypocrites, Rakshasas and Pisakas (belong to) the highest (rank of) conditions among those produced by Darkness. Ghallas, Mallas, Natas, men who subsist by despicable occupations and those addicted to gambling and drinking (form) the lowest (order of) conditions caused by Activity.

Thus, lower caste people are equal to all the non-human creatures of the earth.[3] Manu also reminds all castes to follow their caste norms and threatens them of severe punishments in the present and next several births. Prime goal of Hindu dharma is to see that caste privileges of 'upper' castes and oppression against lower castes was properly maintained. Legal and political powers are vested in the hands of brahmans because they are the "pure" caste:

> The very birth of a Brahmana is an eternal incarnation of the sacred law; for he is born to (fulfill) the sacred law, and becomes one with Brahman. A Brahmana,

coming into existence, is born as the highest on earth, the lord of all created beings, for the protection of the treasury of the law.[4]

Brhamans have rights over all creatures and things of the world. "Whatever exists in the world is, the property of the Brahmana; on account of the excellence of his origin the Brahmana is, indeed, entitled to all."[5] In no case was a lower caste man entitled to these powers.[6] The following clauses explain this, "The kingdom of that monarch, who who looks on while a Sudra settles the law, will sink (low), like a cow in a morass."[7] Brahmans were entitled to make new laws also. Powers of execution and interpretation were also vested in the hands of Brahman community:

> If it be asked how it should be with respect to (points of) the law which have not been (specially) mentioned, (the answer is), 'that which Brahmanas (who are) Sishtas propound, shall doubtlessly have legal (force).[8]

The process of legal execution was also conducted according to the castes:

> Let him examine a Brahmana (beginning with) 'Speak,' a Kshatriya (beginning with) 'Speak the truth,' a Vaisya (admonishing him) by (mentioning) his kine, grain, and gold, a Sudra (threatening him) with (the guilt of) every crime that causes loss of caste.[9]

> Let the (judge) cause a Brahmana to swear by his veracity, a Kshatriya by his chariot or the animal he rides on and by his weapons, a Vaisya by his kine, grain, and gold, and a Sudra by (imprecating on his own head the guilt) of all grievous offences (pataka).[10]

Thus, "lower" castes are always guilty by default. Manu has mentioned ten places where punishments can take place against the three lower castes, but a *brahman* will not undergo corporal punishment.[11] In most of the cases, *brahmans* emerge immune to any kind of punishment. In most of the instances only a small amount of fine is fixed which, again, is payable to the *brahmans* themselves not even to the king. Whatever be the judgment and how much injustice and harm done to the lower castes they are not expected to raise their voice: "If he ['lower' caste person] arrogantly teaches Brahmanas their duty, the king shall cause hot oil to be poured into his mouth and into his ears."[12]

It is also to be noted that there are very few injunctions directly referring to lower caste women. Keeping these basic features of ancient Hindu jurisprudence in mind, this author tries to look at how caste and gender (together) were tackled to sustain and promulgate caste-[ist] patriarchy. The lack of frequent and direct references to lower caste women implies that they never existed as subjects for the authors and executors of these texts. It does not mean that they overlooked lower caste women. It only means that they took every care to see that a lower caste woman never treads in the boundaries of the upper castes whether this boundary is a caste, community, religion, marriage, progeny, inheritance or any other "respectable" relationship. The present paper tries to touch upon these boundaries and explain what must have happened to lower caste women during ancient times in the Indian subcontinent. Several themes of these texts are categorically separated for methodological convenience. They are notions of purity and pollution, education and occupation, marriage, progeny& inheritance, property and gifts, crime and punishments, body/sexuality and so on.

Purity and Pollution

In the very first chapter of the Manu Smriti, the author attaches principles of purity and pollution to caste. Vasista describes lower castes to be burial grounds.[13] A human being becomes pure or remains polluted completely based on his/her caste, which comes with one's birth. It cannot be changed. "Man is stated to be purer above the navel (than below); hence the Self-existent (Svayambhu) has declared the purest (part) of him (to be) his mouth."[14] "As the Brahmana sprang from (Brahman's) mouth, as he was the first-born, and as he possesses the Veda, he is by right the lord of this whole creation."[15] Caste[ism] revolves around the principles of purity and pollution. There are endless rituals involved in purifying process in the daily activities of common people. "A Brahmana is purified by water that reaches his heart, a Kshatriya by water reaching his throat, a Vaisya by water taken into his mouth, (and) a Sudra by water touched with the extremity (of his lips)."[16] Thus water is purer than a sudra. Also these rituals are set in humiliating and relative terms for the 'lower' castes. "Let him [a brahmana man] gently place on the ground (some food) for dogs, outcasts, Kandalas (Svapak), those afflicted with diseases that are punishments of former sins, crows, and insects. That Brahmana who thus daily honours all beings, goes, endowed with a resplendent body, by a straight road to the highest dwelling-place (i.e. Brahman)."[17] Thus, for Manu, 'lower' castes are equal to dogs, crows, insects, cursed people, those severely afflicted with diseases inherited due to sins committed in their former births. In the following sentence he equates 'lower' castes with the category of thieves, eunuchs, and atheists.[18]

Active oppression is justice for them. Manu gives a long list of people who should be avoided at the time of performing a *sraddha*. This list includes: an actor or singer, one who has broken the vow of studentship, one whose (only or first) wife is a *Sudra* female, the son of a remarried woman, a one-eyed man, and he in whose house a paramour of his wife (resides). It also includes he who teaches for a stipulated fee and he who is taught under this condition. He who instructs *Sudra* pupils and he whose teacher is a *Sudra*, he who speaks rudely, the son of an adulteress, and the son of a widow, he who forsakes his mother, his father, or a teacher without a (sufficient) reason, he who has contracted an alliance with outcasts either through the Veda or through a marriage, an incendiary, a prisoner, he who eats the food given by the son of an adulteress, a seller of Soma, he who undertakes voyages by sea, a bard, an oil-man, a suborner to perjury, he who wrangles or goes to law with his father, the keeper of a gambling-house, a drunkard, he who is afflicted with a disease (in punishment of former) crimes, he who is accused of a mortal sin, a hypocrite, a seller of substances used for flavoring food, a maker of bows and of arrows, he who lasciviously dallies with a brother's widow, the betrayer of a friend, one who subsists by gambling, he who learns (the Veda) from his son, an epileptic man, who suffers from scrofulous swellings of the glands, one afflicted with white leprosy, an informer, a madman, a blind man, and he who cavils at the veda.[19] Manu has mixed the lower castes with all the possible criminal, crippled, and incapable categories here.

In the following injunctions he equated lower castes with the species, which are considered impure and inauspicious by the Hindus and with the handicapped people:

> A boar makes (the rite) useless by inhaling the smell (of the offerings), a cock by the air of his wings, a dog by throwing his eye (on them), a low-caste man by touching (them).

If a lame man, a one-eyed man, one deficient in a limb, or one with a redundant limb, be even the servant of the performer (of the Sraddha), he must be removed from that place (where the Sraddha is held)."[20] There is also a long list of foods to be offered to the dead that include all possible meats and drinks on the earth. Interestingly the list also includes that ancestors of men are satisfied for six months with flesh of children.[21] It indicates that human sacrifice was prescribed by Manu and now the question whose kids' flesh used to be sacrificed as part of satisfying the ghosts of 'upper' castes men? Definitely not the 'upper' castes kids were sacrificed. More importantly 'lower' caste women were put aloof from the rituals that take place in her 'upper' caste husband's house:

> Many wives of the same caste and of the other castes existing, the rite of churning, for producing the fire, should be done by the chaste wives of the same caste, on account of the superiority of birth...[in it] one should not employ a sudhra wife, or one who tries to injure her husband or is jealous of him, or one who does not perform religious observances, or one who lives with another men.[22]

Thus, again the equation is drawn between the lower caste woman, one who is jealous and tries to cause injury or death to her husband, one who is not religious and one who sleeps with another man. All these ill qualities are attributed to her due to her caste.

There is much stigma attached to the biology and notions of purity and pollution dominate these scriptures. From menstruation to childbirth, these legal codes covered almost everything that deals with female body. The other important feature is that the 'upper' caste woman is always posed against the lower caste woman. To not to oblige caste rule means a fall in the status of upper caste woman. She becomes 'equal' to the 'lower' caste woman.

By increasing degrees, the condition of caste brands people as pure and impure. It is a fixed expression of status differentiation. The division of the female population into chaste and unchaste categories is given important consideration in Hindu society because castes are produced through women. This has led to a more rigorous control of the bodies and selves of women of all categories. Any code relating to the female body has thus become a closely guarded matter and stringent punishments have been met out to those who transgress prescribed codes of behavior. Two areas were to be protected:

1. False blood should not contaminate pure blood.
2. Upper caste women were to be saved from the 'lower' caste men and simultaneously *dalit* women should be available to the 'upper' caste men. Thus an extremely clashing set of rules and standards were needed. The higher the caste the less 'bad' she becomes.

Menstruation in women is associated with the murder of a Brahmin male. An upper caste woman becomes pure again after her menstruation period is over. But this is not so with the lower caste women. Upper caste women and dalit women were not only placed differently but also as "opposite and stratified others." The following sanctions endorse to such differentiated treatments. The upper caste woman undergoes three levels of purification each time she gets her period.

> On the first day [of the menses], she is a chandala woman, on the second, she is the murderess of a brahmana; on the third, she is called a washer woman; and on the fourth day, she becomes purified [resumes to her original caste].[23]

> A barren woman should be known as a vrishali; a woman who gives birth to a dead child is a vrishali, a sudra ['lower' caste] woman is a vrishali, and similarly a maiden in her menses.[24]

Education

An untouchable is depicted as a burial ground. Thus, reciting *Vedas* in his presence amounts to sacrilege. The untouchables were also barred from education and they were expected to stick to their caste based hereditary occupations and not dream of going higher than that status. Hope for a better caste place in the next life could only happen by birth if the member of the lower caste devoutly served the "upper" castes. Education, political, and cultural power were considered privileges of the *brahmans*.

> In order to clearly settle his duties those of the other (castes) according to their order, wise Manu sprung from the Self-existent, composed these Institutes (of the sacred Law). A learned Brahmana must carefully study them, and he must duly instruct his pupils in them, but nobody else (shall do it).[25]

De facto power of running the kingdom and civil society was in their hands. Merit is attributed to their caste and automatically to the *brahmans*. The MS is pregnant with references, which chant supremacy of upper castes especially the relating to the brahmans. For instance: "The offering made through the mouth of a Brahmana, which is neither spilt, nor falls (on the ground), nor ever perishes, is far more excellent than Agnihotras."[26] Not only are upper castes advised how to protect their privileges, but they are also reprimanded to not to share their privileges to the lower castes. A *brahmana* is advised to not explain the sacred law (to a Sudra) or dictates to him a penance. He will sink together with that (man) into the hell (called) *Asamvrita*. He should not recite Vedas in a village where a corpse lies, in the presence of a (man who lives as unrighteously as a) Sudra, while (the sound of) weeping (is heard), and in a crowd of men. He shall not recite the Veda during three days, when he has accepted an invitation to a (funeral rite) in honour of one ancestor (ekoddishta), or when the king has become impure through a birth or death in his family (sutaka), or when Rahu by an eclipse makes the moon impure. He should not study it near a burial-ground, nor near a village, nor in a cow-pen, nor dressed in a garment that he wore during conjugal intercourse, nor after receiving a present at a funeral sacrifice. He also should not recite the Veda after accepting gift of a sraddha (for the hand of a Brahmana is his mouth), when the village has been beset by robbers, and when an alarm has been raised by fire.[27] Thus, lower caste-ness is associated with impurities and misery of death, sex, unrighteousness, burial ground, bestiality, human waste, danger and loss. The lower castes should not be educated as education should be the exclusive privilege of the upper castes.

Occupation

Severe punishments were imposed on lower castes who tried to deviate from traditional occupations.[28]

> But let a (Sudra) serve Brahmanas, either for the sake of heaven, or with a view to both (this life and the next); for he who is called the servant of a Brahmana thereby gains all his ends. The service of *brahmans* alone is declared (to be) an excellent occupation for a *Sudra*; for whatever else besides this he may perform will bear him no fruit. The remnants of their food must be given to him, as well as their old clothes, the refuse of their grain, and their old household furniture."[29]

Along with 'lower' caste men, their women are also barred from entering into the realms of education and respectable occupations. It should also be remembered that the upper caste women were not completely banned from education. The lower castes are not meant for any training, which can make them eligible for better things in life. Their duty is to serve the upper castes. Within the boundaries of their caste, they are free to do whatever they want:

> If a woman or a man of low caste perform anything (leading to) happiness, let him diligently practice it, as well as (any other permitted act) in which his heart finds pleasure.[30]

Property and Gifts

The lower castes are banned from holding any property and *brahmans* are entitled to all the property on the earth. They are also exempted from many kinds of taxes. "No collection of wealth must be made by a Sudra, even though he be able (to do it); for a Sudra who has acquired wealth, gives pain to Brahmanas."[31] Several gifts are listed to be given to the brahmans on several occasions and such practices are said to yield rewards to the giver "without end".[32] Salvation is assured to the giver who offers to a brahmana.[33] Women were listed among the war spoils and their conquerors can possess them.[34] War in ancient India is unimaginable without a *brahaman* designing it. A Brahman can claim and own all treasure if he happens to treasure, as he was, the "master of all things." But the other castes have to pay shares to the king and brahmans.[35] It is not an exaggeration to say that lower caste women were considered as part of the war spoils by the upper castes as they were always at war with the lower castes in the initial phases of the establishment of caste supremacy.[36]

Segregation

Indian geography is also imagined and shared according to caste norms. Physical proximity between castes was strictly regulated and guarded:

"Let twice-born men seek to dwell in those (above-mentioned countries) [fertile places]; but a Sudra, distressed for subsistence, may reside anywhere."[37] "Let him [a Brahman ascetic] not dwell in a country where the rulers are Sudras, nor in one which is surrounded by unrighteous men, nor in one which has become subject to heretics, nor in one swarming with men of the lowest castes. Let him not stay together with outcasts, nor with Kandalas, nor with Pukkasas, nor with fools, nor with overbearing men, nor with low-caste men, nor with Antyavasayins."[38] Thus, all possible physical proximity between upper and lower castes was controlled. Thus, chances of physical relations except though labor were severely limited.

Marriages

Upper caste female sexuality and lower caste male sexuality were the two live threats that were sensed. Fear of this commingling was manifested by all or most all law makers. From childhood, the upper caste girl is brought up with strict care and pre-menstrual marriages were recommended. If a girl got her menstruation before she was wedded, each embryo she releases is considered wasted and therefore her father is considered accountable for those murders and will inevitably go to hell in his next birth. Thus, she is married before she becomes aware of her sexuality and sexually subdued while still she is a child.

Women have historically been considered as a kind of property. Moreover, a male sees his lineage is secured and his property is secured to sons of his 'seed'. The parable of 'seed' (male semen) and earth (female womb) is repeated in many of the legal scriptures. This explains the proprietorship of Hindu male over female. There is also a clause on women's names: "The names of women should be easy to pronounce, not imply anything dreadful, possess a plain meaning, be pleasing and auspicious, end in long vowels, and contain a word of benediction."[39]

Of course this does not include *dalit* women. A lower caste woman's name should denote, service and should sound contemptible according to these rules.

> [a Brahman man should not marry] one named after a constellation, a tree, or a river, nor one bearing the name of a low caste, or of a mountain, nor one named after a bird, a snake, or a slave, nor one whose name inspires terror.[40]

Thus a lower caste woman is outlawed at the level of nomenclature itself.

In the 3rd chapter of MS we come across rules regarding marriage. Men should marry according to the caste order. *Anuloma* marriages were both looked down and not strictly restricted if not encouraged whereas the *pratiloma* marriages were completely outlawed and posed as greatest threats like invasion of enemies into one's own nation:

> For the first marriage of twice-born men (wives) of equal caste are recommended; but for those who through desire proceed (to marry again) the following females, (chosen) according to the (direct) order (of the castes), are most approved. It is declared that a Sudra woman alone (can be) the wife of a Sudra, she and one of his own caste (the wives) of a Vaisya, those two and one of his own caste (the wives) of a Kshatriya, those three and one of his own caste (the wives) of a Brahmana.[41]

There were marriages between upper caste men and lower caste women despite restrictions. But the untouchable women never seem to have become wives of upper caste men. The limit was closed with the sudra women, the *atisudra* (untouchable) women were never allowed. *Samhitas* deal with such contexts also. They are as follows: "A woman who forsakes her poor or diseased husband, is repeatedly born either as a bitch, a vulture, or a shark."[42] This implies that all the existing 'lower' caste women were born so due to their disloyal attitude to their husbands in their previous lives. Thus, the lower caste refers to a woman as somebody who is unfaithful to her husband. Some *samhitas* attribute severe curses on upper caste men who marry lower caste women, "By cohabiting with a chandala woman one is born without testes."[43]

> For cohabiting with women, who should not be known, originates the disease of dharuvamandala (a kind of leprosy). Having made images of cow... one should duly present it unto a vipra, and recite the mantra "May the mother of a surabhi, daughter of a Vishnu, destroy my sin."[44]

Though sexual relations were encouraged with the lower caste women, the upper caste men are strictly forbidden to have any strong familial relation with their lower caste wives:

> Sudra woman is not mentioned even in any (ancient) story as the (first) wife of a Brahmana or of a Kshatriya, though they lived in the (greatest) distress. Twice-born men who, in their folly, wed wives of the low (Sudra) caste, soon degrade their families and their children to the state of Sudras. According to Atri and to (Gautama) the son of Utathya, he who weds a Sudra woman becomes an outcast, according to Saunaka on the birth of a son, and according to Bhrigu he who has (male) offspring from a (Sudra female, alone). A Brahmana who takes a Sudra wife to his bed, will (after death) sink into hell; if he begets a child by her, he will lose the rank of a Brahmana. The manes and the gods will not eat the (offerings) of that man who performs the rites in honour of the gods, of the manes, and of guests chiefly with a (Sudra wife's) assistance, and such (a man) will not go to heaven. For him who drinks the moisture of a Sudra's lips, who is tainted by her breath, and who begets a son on her, no expiation is prescribed.[45]

Manu has also prescribed eight marriage rites. They are the rite of Brahman (Brahma), that of the gods (Daiva), that of the Rishis (Arsha), that of Pragapati (Pragapatya), that of the Asuras (Asura), that of the Gandharvas (Gandharva), that of the Rhashasas (Rakshasa), and that of the Pisakas (Paisaka). Good and evil results with respect to the offspring are attached with these rites: One may know that the first six according to the order (followed above) are lawful for a Brahmana, the four last for a Kshatriya, and the same four, excepting the Rakshasa rite, for a Vaisya and a Sudra."[46]

Throughout the text, 'Manu' warns upper caste man against approaching a lower caste woman.[47] By examining the above injunctions, the researcher can decipher that the untouchable women were not allowed to marry the 'upper' men but at the same time they were sexually put at the disposal of these men. However, *sudra* women entering into wedlock with upper caste men was not a rare phenomenon though she was not equally respected on par with the other upper castes wives of the man. Other points to be remembered are that a *sudra* can neither be a first wife or only wife to an 'upper' caste man. Manu comes up heavily against any marriage between the 'untouchable' caste women and 'upper' caste men. He threatens such men with acquiring dreadful diseases and curses. The marital status of a dalit woman is also not respected. As she is addressed as a vrishali, she cannot hold any legitimate right to have any decent personal life. In Sanka Smahita there are various rituals to be followed byt brides of different castes. According to these instructions a Brahmin girl, at the time of marriage should hold a mendicant's cup, a Kshatriya girl an arrow and Vaishya girl a stick.[48] There is no mention of any rite that a lower caste girl should follow.

Since mixture of blood was the main concern of the law makers they took every care to criminalize the lower caste women:

If one cohabits with a woman [of same caste] in [her] manses or with lower caste woman, he is known as being obliged to perform a panacea; he should [take his] bath before that.[49]

Having gone to a she-animal, prostitute, she buffalo, she –camel...one should practice prajapatya panacea."[50]

This, sodomy is equal cohabitation with a lower caste woman. She is a mere animal. She, who renouncing her husband, desires for the company of another man, is to be known as a vrishali.[51]

Lower caste women are also named as *vrishali.* Even in distress a twice born one should not wed a sudra girl, in as much as a son begotten by him on her person will never find his salvation."[52] "A house holder should marry a wife of his own caste...[53] Ostracizing is another effective way of punishing. "[One should not feed] a hurtful person, a deceitful person...one who is a servant, one who is a twan-coloured, a deaf...and one who has married a vrishali."[54] List of Vrishali women includes a lower caste woman also as mentioned above. At the same time dreadful threats are given by the same samhitas against any possible intrusions of lower caste man against Hindu women.[55] They are as follows:

A sudhra detected in the act of sexually knowing a brahamana woman, or guilty of that offence should be punished by cutting of his genitals.[56]

A woman, of a superior caste, having been found guilty of illicit intercourse with a man of an inferior caste, the king of the country shall caste her to be torn alive by dogs at a public space, or the guilty man should be dealt with in the same manner.[57]

Progeny

"The son whom a Brahmana begets through lust on a Sudra female is, (though) alive (parayan), a corpse (sava), and hence called a Parasava (a living corpse)."[58] The following implications/results are applicable according to the castes of people involved in the marriage. Here Manu deals with the rights of progeny born according to the castes of a couple. "In all castes (varna) those (children) only which are begotten in the direct order on wedded wives, equal (in caste and married as) virgins, are to be considered as belonging to the same caste (as their fathers). Sons, begotten by twice-born man on wives of the next lower castes, they declare to be similar (to their fathers, but) blamed on account of the fault (inherent) in their mothers."[59] Also, "The son of a wife wedded according to the Brahma rite [she ought to be a brahmana], if he performs meritorious acts, liberates from sin ten ancestors, ten descendants and himself as the twenty-first."[60] Children born out of these marriages are outlawed before birth."But from the remaining (four) blamable marriages spring sons who are cruel and speakers of untruth, who hate the Veda and the sacred law. In the blameless marriages blameless children are born to men, in blamable (marriages) blamable (offspring); one should therefore avoid the blamable (forms of marriage)."[61]

Also marriages are symbolically performed. If the bride and the groom belong to the same caste, their hands can be joined at the time of wedding.[62] But if the women happen to marry a man of upper caste they should:

> On marrying a man of a higher caste a Kshatriya bride must take hold of an arrow, a Vaisya bride of a goad, and a Sudra female of the hem of the (bridegroom's) garment.[63]

It implies that women of the three above castes retain their caste relations and also allowed to uphold them, but a lower caste woman will not have relations with her nuptial home nor can her people frequent her home. After acknowledging the possibility of inter-caste marriages, Manu immediately threatens the upper castes against such weddings:

> By low marriages, by omitting (the performance of) sacred rites, by neglecting the study of the Veda, and by irreverence towards Brahmanas, (great) families sink low.[64]

Pratiloma marriages were severely looked down upon more so than the anuloma ones.[65] Inter-caste marriages within the lower castes were also diligently dealt with.[66] By the end of the book, Manu articulates his awareness of the danger of intermixture of castes. So, he indicated that caste status of an individual can always be found by his/her occupation.[67] New "untouchable" caste names also appear in this section such as *pukkasa, ayogava, sairandhra, margava/dasa, kaivarta, karavara, vaideha, andhra, meda, kandala, sopaka, antyavasayin.*

By chapter ten, it seems Manu becomes more concerned about the lurking dangers of the admixture of castes and thus repeatedly and elaborately refers to the particular occupations, residences, and caste marks of lower castes.[68] "Those three base-born ones are severally begot on Ayogava women, who wear the clothes of the dead, are wicked, and eat reprehensible food."[69] Sinfulness, burial ground, death, dirt, manual labor, are always attributed in the description of the newly invented lower castes. "Even, he, who is foremost of all virtuous men . . . is degraded to the status of a sudhra by having the thirteen sraddas done unto him by a sudhra son."[70] "A son of an idiotic father shall take a share like a son begotten on sudhra mother."[71] While any child is addressed and identified after the father, in the case of a child born to a lower caste woman, and an upper caste man, this rule does not pertain. Property rules are very carefully laid down keeping the danger of inter-caste marriage in view. Chapter 9, 150-157 elaborately deals with this. "The son of a Brahmana, a Kshatriya, and a Vaisya by a Sudra (wife) receives no share of the inheritance; whatever his father may give to him that shall be his property."[72]

There is almost no area that is left untouched by the caste rules. The MS also elaborately deals with progeny, out of inter-caste marriages, and separate nomenclature was invented to address them.[73] For instance nomenclature is also ruled by these norms:

Let (the first part of) a Brahmana's name (denote something) auspicious, a Kshatriya's be connected with power, and a Vaisya's with wealth, but a Sudra's (express something) contemptible. (The second part of) a Brahmana's (name) shall be (a word) implying happiness, of a Kshatriya's (a word) implying protection, of a Vaisya's (a term) expressive of thriving, and of a Sudra's (an expression) denoting service.[74]

Children born out of anuloma relations are expected to be named after degradable titles, "The name of a Brahmin child should be a term of a blissful significance...while that of a sudra child should be of a lowly import."[75] There are also injunctions to see that the lower castes do not outnumber the upper castes. "That kingdom where Sudras are very numerous, which is infested by atheists and destitute of twice-born (inhabitants), soon entirely perishes, afflicted by famine and disease."[76]

Punishments

Brahmans are immune from punishments. They can get rid of any guilt just by reciting some part of the Veda.[77] But, even a minute hurt like waving a blade of grass in front of a brahmana is a sin for other castes.[78] Transgressing caste rules is a sin. "With whatever limb a man of a low caste does hurt to (a man of the three) highest (castes), even that limb shall be cut off; that is the teaching of Manu. He who raises his hand or a stick, shall have his hand cut off; he who in anger kicks with his foot, shall have his foot cut off. A low-caste man who tries to place himself on the same seat with a man of a high caste, shall be branded on his hip and be banished, or (the king) shall cause his buttock to be gashed. "[79] "A man of low caste who through covetousness lives by the occupations of a higher one, the king shall deprive of his property and banish."[80] Caste rules are unbreakable for the "lower" castes but always flexible for the upper castes. Manu sooths hearts of upper caste men by giving various instances in history where great Hindu sages stooped down to eating flesh of cows, their own children, and dogs,[81] when they were hungry.

In chapter eleven, Manu deals with punishments for killing a brahamana man. That killer should live in a forest alone for twelve years,[82] or make himself a willful target of archers in a battle, or should throw himself into a blazing fire for three times,[83] or offer a horse-sacrifice[84] (this must be fore the rest of the upper castes who can escape corporal punishments. A lower caste killer does not have this concession), or must surrender all his property to learned brahmanas,[85] or may walk against the whole course of the river Saraswati.[86] A killer of a brahamana also becomes pure from that sin by renouncing everything, shaving his head, and by serving the cows and brahmanas or by helping the brahmanas for gathering property.[87] After the offence of murdering a brahmana, it was the murder of cow, which occupied a prime position in the MS.[88] The killer of a Sudra, can perform a prescribed penance for six months, present ten cows and bull to a Brahman to be releseed from that sin.[89] "Having killed a cat, an ichneumon, a blue jay, a frog, a dog, an iguana, an owl, or a crow, he shall perform the penance for the murder of a Sudra."[90] Thus life of a lower caste man is equal to all these creatures. There are numerous solutions offered to purify upper caste men for having slept with lower caste women.[91]

"The slayer of a Brahmana enters the womb of a dog, a pig, an ass, a camel, a cow, a goat, a sheep, a deer, a bird, a Kandala, and a Pukkasa."[92] According to these codes, a lower caste woman's womb and reproductive capacity are equal to all these creatures. Thus, a lower caste person is equal to all these creatures and being born in such a community is the severest punishment. It also implies that all those who are untouchables are so due to the murders they committed in their earlier births. "Men who delight in doing hurt (become) carnivorous (animals); those who eat forbidden food, worms; thieves, creatures consuming their own kind; those who have intercourse with women of the lowest castes, Pretas (ghosts)."[93] This means those upper caste men who have intercourse with lower caste women become ghosts. Manu states this in the last chapter of the MS. In the whole text one does not see such severe injunctions against intercourse with lower caste women though he was always against any intimate communication with the lower castes. By the end of the book he becomes very focused on the breaking of caste hierarchy. The other punishments that are mentioned were to those who fail to follow caste rules. For example:

> A Brahmana who has fallen off from his duty (becomes) an Ulkamukha Preta, who feeds on what has been vomited; and a Kshatriya, a Kataputana (Preta), who eats impure substances and corpses.

A Vaisya who has fallen off from his duty becomes a Maitrakshagyotika Preta, who feeds on pus; and a Sudra, a Kailasaka (Preta, who feeds on moths)."[94] There are methods and ways to beat the women, slaves and lower castes.[95] Stealing of the cows of brahmans is more severe a sin than cruelty against lower castes.[96] There are almost no punishments imposed on upper caste men's assaults against lower caste women.[97]

Conclusion

Ancient Hindu laws[98] laid down strict rules against women in general. But they were surely more liberal towards the upper caste women than to the lower castes. For instance, Hindu women were allowed to remarry according to caste rules. *Punarbhu* was the word used by many of the writers to indicate a woman married more than once. The Manu Smriti, depicts re-marriage of women as beastly custom but still finds no fault with women who reject a husband who is an eunuch, out-caste, who lacks manly features. He also does not prescribe any punishment or fine for such women.[99] Widowed, or disserted women, or a remarried woman, were an acknowledged fact of those times.[100] Most of the ancient legal codes[101] mention remarriage of women as a common phenomenon.[102] All these explain that a Hindu woman can re-marry at her own will in cases where her husband is an outcaste, lunatic, impotent, out of station for a long period or dead. There is also mentioning of pre-marital and extra-marital relations. Thus, it can be said that the ancient Hindu legal codes were not as severe to women as many modern intellectuals have assumed. It is indicated either directly or indirectly by the authors of these codes that these practices were very much social realities of the times. The legal practices became severe only when caste rules are transgressed by the lower castes.

Upper caste women were very much seen as sinners and dangerous in the MS. Especially in its ninth chapter one witnesses many clauses which replicate Manu's fearful hatred of women. That, however, is only half the story. As many including Ambedkar have assumed, the ancient Hindu codes were not equally brutal to the upper caste women as they were to the *dalit* women. They were brutal to upper caste women only when they transgressed caste rules and made relations with the lower caste men. Since a woman's body was considered as a possession of the community and its pride was based on them, they were guarded very keenly. More importantly, the fear of admixture of castes made them pass rigid rules, which would ban any interaction between the 'upper' caste women and sudra men. For instance:

> Men who commit adultery with the wives of others, the king shall cause to be marked by punishments which cause terror, and afterwards banish. For by (adultery) is caused a mixture of the castes (varna) among men; thence (follows) sin, which cuts up even the roots and causes the destruction of everything..A man who is not a Brahmana ought to suffer death for adultery (samgrahana); for the wives of all the four castes even must always be carefully guarded.[103] A (man of) low (caste) who makes love to a maiden (of) the highest (caste) shall suffer corporal punishment; he who addresses a maiden (on) equal (caste) shall pay the nuptial fee, if her father desires it.[104]

But, such corporal punishments were absent in case where an upper caste woman emerges as a potential culprit of having un-approved sexual relations either knowingly or un-knowingly. Interestingly, there were societal arrangements to accommodate progeny born from such pre or extra-marital relations. "A son whom a damsel secretly bears in the house of her father, one shall name the son of an unmarried damsel (Kanina, and declare) such offspring of an unmarried girl (to belong) to him who weds her (afterwards). If one marries, either knowingly or unknowingly, a pregnant (bride), the child in her womb belongs to him who weds her, and is called (a son) received with the bride (Sahodha)."[105] Along with *anuloma* marriages, Manu also mentions all other kinds of extra-marital sexual contacts between upper caste women and men:

> The son of an unmarried damsel, the son received with the wife, the son bought, the son begotten on a re-married woman, the son self-given, and the son of a Sudra female, (are) the six (who are) not heirs, (but) kinsmen.[106]

This clause explains that re-marriages, pre-and extra marital relations, or a system of *niyoga* were not rare in those days if not common. This *Kanina* or *Sahodha* was placed in a better place than the son born of a lower caste female as described in under the "progeny'" section.

In the following clauses one can see how clearly they set feminine norms according to castes of women. Wives of actors and singers, female slaves kept by one man are freely accessible to upper caste men to make conversion, which costs only a small amount of fine.[107] Thus, one can observe that there were severe punishments imposed on cases of adultery between upper caste women and lower caste men. Marriages (if they managed to go to that extent) were not approved or respected. Pre-marital, extra-marital relations, re-marriages between approved caste equations were not faced as much severe punishments as the in the case of *pratiloma* sexual relations during ancient times.

This explains that adulterous relations between upper castes were kept very much in the negotiable terms by the ancient Hindu jurisprudence. Only a 'lower' can man faces severe corporal punishments like making him lie down on a hot iron bed, make him hug hot iron image of a woman etc. Sexual offences like adultery, rape, molestation between the above three castes were not to be necessarily met with death. Here all the law makers were clearly pragmatic, caste-[ist] and patriarchal. For instance in the eightht chapter, 375 and 375 of MS, Manu clearly sets rules on these parameters. Also, clauses from 378 to 381 and 385 deal with various amounts of fines for the 'upper' castes in cases of crimes related to sexuality.

Hindu legal codes also assumed severity as history passed. In ancient times the system of widow burning (Sati) was not there. Even Manu, a chief architect of caste-[ist] patriarchy never mentioned it nor the dowry system. It means that these cruel practices were later developments. Manu also acknowledged ths system of niyoga (levirate).[108] The point is that ancient Hindu jurisprudence was more caste-[ist] than patriarchal. It is more caste-[ist] patriarchal than mere patriarchal. It is wrong to assume that it was equally severe on both women and the lower castes in India. It was more severe to lower caste men and women than to any of the upper castes [including men or women]. To put it more clearly, in the ancient times (as in the contemporary India) jurisprudence was more anti-lower caste than anti-women. So, we can consider "caste" more than gender in these texts.[109]

The other area that may be used to prove this hypothesis is that the ancient Hindu jurisprudence was more caste-[ist] than patriarchal is related to laws of inheritance. All Hindu legal codes recognize only sons as legitimate heirs of property. In the absence of a son, each *dharmasutra* came up with a different solution. However, all of them state that property of a sonless Brahman male should go to a learned brahmana. In other cases each of these codes gave a list of potent heirs, which include widow of the diseased, daughters, or son of daughter, kith and kin. None of them mention a "lower" caste wife or son of the dead as heirs.[110] The progeny of slave women were considered as items of interest in cases of debts.[111]

At the same time, "lower" caste women were at the disposal of all upper castes. However, as the above text explains, these women of *sudra* communities were not treated equally or their progeny were included in their fathers' caste. Still, another question is about the untouchable women's status in marital and sexual matters vis-à-vis the upper caste both men and women. Rape, concubinage, and spiritual prostitution were the methods and systems that the upper caste men applied in case of the untouchable women. Of course, we do not get direct evidence of them in ancient Hindu jurisprudence, but the present status of *dalit* women in contemporary India does prove this hypothesis to be true.

Ancient Hindu jurisprudence is basically harsh. Indian law, though often assumed to have been thoroughly re 'caste'd, carries several of its features; much more so surely in the process of adjudication and interpretation. This often alters and often invalidates the democratic essence generally illustrated in the original laws.

Notes

1. The historically called sudras are now the powerful ruling classes. Now, what we have as sudras are the BC (backward communities like barbers, washermen etc. The untouchable castes are now called dalits.
2 .Manu, "Manu Smriti-The Law Codes of Manu," *Bharatadesam:* Everything About India, http://www. bharatadesam.com/spiritual/manu, 85.
3 Taitreya Samhita, Vii, 1.1.6.; Satapata Brahmana, 14.1.1.31; Aitreya Brahmana, 35.3.
4. Manu, 98-99
5. Manu, 100.
6. Manu, 9-11; 20
7 .Manu, 8; 21
8. Manu, 108; 8; 56.
9. Manu, 8; 88
10. Manu, 113.
11. Manu, 124; 267-269
12 Manu, 270-272
13. Manmath Nath Dutt, trans., *Vasista Dharmasutra.* (Delhi: Cosmo Publications, 1979), 13-14.
14. Manu, 92.
15. Manu, 93
16. Manu, 62.
17. Manu, 92-93..
18. Manu, 150.
19. Manu, 155-161.
20. Manu, 241-242.
21 Manu, 267-271..
22. Manmath Nath Dutt, trans., *Katyana Samhita* (Delhi: Cosmo Publications, 1979), 372.
23. Manmath Nath Dutt, trans., *Angirasa Samhita* (Delhit: Cosmo Publications, 1979), 272; see also *Parasara Samhita.*
24. Yama Samhita, 279.

25. Manu, 102-103.
26. Manu, 82-84..
27. Manu, 80-81; 108-110; 116-118.
28. Kautilya, Arthasastra, iv. 85-10-4.
29. Manu, 122-123; 125
30. Manu, 223.
31. Manu, 129; 416-417.
32. Manu, 85.
33. Manu, 86.
34. Manu, 96.
35. Manu, 37-38.
36. There is an argument in the discipline of history and dalit studies that caste system was established by alien rulers and that there were several battles took place between the original inhabitants of the land, the 'lower' castes and those who came from outside/the three 'upper' castes. During this phase it is possible to hypothesize that the 'lower' caste women who were caught during such battles were subjugated under casteist patriarchy.
37. Manu, 24.
38. Manu, 61; 79
39. Manu, 33.
40. Manu, 9.
41. Manu, 12-13.
42. Manmath Nath Dutt, trans., Daksha Samhita (Delhi: Cosmo Publications, 1979), 447.
43. Manmath Nath Dutt, trans., Satapata Samhita (Delhi: Cosmo Publications, 1979), 475.
44. Manmath Nath Dutt, trans., Satapata Samhita (Delhi: Cosmo Publications, 1979), 477.
45 Manu, 14-19.
46. Manu, 23.
47. Manu, 176.
48. Manmath Nath Dutt, trans., Sanka Samhita (Delhi: Cosmo Publications, 1979), 617.
49. Aris Samhita, Vol.ll (270), p. 338; Samvartha Samhita, p. 348-350; Parasara Samhita, Chp. 10, 5,8.
50 Parasara Samhita, Chp. X (15), 59.
51. Samkya Samhita , Chp. 2 (3), 612.
52. Manmath Nath Dutt, trans., Sanka Samhita (Delhi: Cosmo Publications, 1979), 617.
53. Gautama Samhita,, 663.
54. Atri Smahita, 326; also see Parasara Samhita, Chp. 7 (9), 569. This samhita says that a Brahmin marrying a girl who achieved puberty, should be ill treated as the husband of a sudhra wife (vrishalipati). He should not be addresses, not accepted to sit at the same row with other brahmanas at a dinner.
55. Manmath Nath Dutt, trans., Yajnavalkaya Samhita (Delhi: Cosmo Publications, 1979), 286.
56. Gautama Samhita, Chp. 12, 683.
57. Ibid, Chp. 24, 710.
58. Manu, 178.
59. Manu, 5-6.
60. Manu, 37.
61. Manu, 41-42.
62. Manu, 43.
63. Manu, 44.
64. Manu, 63.

65. Manu, 12; 31.
66. Manu, 18; 32-38..
67. Manu, 40.
68. Manu, 45; 50-59; 61; 68.
69. Manu, 35.
70. Sanka Samhita, 10
71. Gauthama Samhita, 720.
72. Manu, 155.
73. Manu, 7-9.
74. Manu, 31-32.
75. Sankya Samhita, .612.
76. Manu, 22.
77. Manu, 264.
78. Manu, 206-207.
79. Manu, 274; 280-283.
80. Manu, 96.
81. Manu, 104-108.
82. Manu, 73.
83. Manu, 74.
84. Manu, 75.
85. Manu,77.
86. Manu, 78.
87. Manu, 79-82.
88. Manu, 109-116.
89. Manu, 131.
90. Manu, 132..
91. Manu, 180-185.
92. Manu, 55.
93. Manu, 59.
94. Manu, 71-72.
95. Manu, 299.
96. Manu, 325.
97. Yajnavalkya Samhita, 287.
98. Manu, 147-149
99. Manu, 78.
100. Manu, 175.
101. Baudhayana Dharmasutra, ii, 3. 27; Vasista Dharmasutra Xvii. 20 & 74; Yajnavalkyasmhita, i. 67; Visnusmriti, XV. 9; Naradasmriti, Xii. 46-48.
102. The concept of women's remarriage seems to exist from the times of Atharvana Veda. The word punarbhu appears in the Atharva Veda, ix. 5. 27-28
103. Manu, 352-352; 359.
104. Manu, 366.
105. Manu, 172-173.
106. Manu, 160..
107. Manu, 362-363.
108. Manu, 147..
109 .This hypothesis of 'gendering the caste' was done by Uma Chakravarty in her book "Gendering Caste: Through Feminist Lens", Stree, Culcutta, 2003.
110. Gautama Dharmasutra, XXViii. 21 & 41; Apasthabha Dharmasutra, ii. 6. 14. 2-5; Vasista Dharmasutra, Xvii. 81-85; Yajnavalkya Smriti, ii. 135;Bruhaspati Smriti, XXVi. 87& 90, 107&108, 134-136.
111. Yajnavalkya Smriti, 39.

References

Manu, "Manu Smriti-The Law Codes of Manu," Bharatadesam: Everything About India, http://www.bharatadesam.com/spiritual/manu_smriti/mau_smriti.php

Nath Dutt, Manmath, trans. *Aitreya Brahmana.* Delhi: Cosmo Publications, 1979.

Nath Dutt, Manmath, trans. *Angirasa Samhita.* Delhi: Cosmo Publications, 1979.

Nath Dutt, Manmath, trans. *Baudhayana Dharmasutra.* Delhi: Cosmo Publications, 1979.

Nath Dutt, Manmath, trans. *Daksha Samhita.* Delhi: Cosmo Publications, 1979.

Nath Dutt, Manmath, trans. *Gautama Samhita.* Delhi: Cosmo Publications, 1979.

Nath Dutt, Manmath, trans. *Katyana Samhita.* Delhi: Cosmo Publications, 1979.

Nath Dutt, Manmath, trans. *Satapata Brahmana.* Delhi: Cosmo Publications, 1979.

Nath Dutt, Manmath, trans. *Satapta Samhita.* Delhi: Cosmo Publications, 1979.

Nath Dutt, Manmath, trans. *Sanka Samhita.* Delhi: Cosmo Publications, 1979.

Nath Dutt, Manmath, trans. *Taitreya Samhita.* Delhi: Cosmo Publications, 1979.

Nath Dutt, Manmath, trans. *Vasista Dharmasutra.* Delhi: Cosmo Publications, 1979.

Nath Dutt, Manmath, trans. *Yajnavalkaya Samhita.* Delhi: Cosmo Publications, 1979.

Shamasastry, R. "Kautilya's Arthashastra," Bharatadesam: Everything About India, http://www.bharatadesam.com/literature/Kautilya_arthashastra/arthashastra.php

Chapter 4

Comparative Race and Slavery in Islam, Judaism, and Christianity: Texts, Practices and Current Implications

Magid Shihade

T his chapter seeks to provide a general overview and discussion of the questions of race and slavery in a comparative context between the three monolithic religions of Islam, Christianity and Judaism. It does so, first, by looking at how religious texts in the three religions view these questions, and secondly through a brief discussion of the history and politics of race and slavery in the civilizations of Judaism, Christianity, and Islam. The chapter shows that Islam, as a religion, did not justify slavery, but encouraged its abolition and opposed racism, while Judaism and Christianity condoned it. Furthermore, in practice, all cultures and people all over the world traded in slaves and practiced slavery. As the chapter will show, the racializing of slavery took hold only since the Inquisition and the colonization of the New World by European settlers and colonialists, a development that was unprecedented in history. Finally, the chapter will discuss the current implications of the issue of race and slavery in the context of the discourse of the "war on terror," the "Save Darfur" campaign, and the anti-Arab, anti-Islamic sentiments manifested in many forms and on different fronts, including propaganda against Arabs and Muslims regarding race and slavery, and the manipulation of history to present the Arab and the Muslim as the ultimate other; and finally, the chapter discusses a proposal on the changing terrains of slavery and race in modern times.

Introduction

Writing on race and slavery in Christianity, Islam, and Judaism, in a comparative context, and on the history of practice and development of race and slavery over hundreds of years, is a task that is fraught with the pitfalls of generalizations, and possible oversimplifications. Despite these possible pitfalls, the chapter takes this task seriously and attempts to provide a fair and general introductory discussion on this topic.[1]

This chapter will provide a general comparison of how each religion relates to the question of race and slavery, first theoretically through religious texts, and then how in practice this issue transpired. The chapter will also outline the historical development of the question race and how slavery became racialized, and in the final part, it will discuss the implications of the topic in the current period and especially in the context of the creeping discourse of "war on terror" that has been used to obscure western racism through the deflection of public opinion from Western racism, misrepresentation of conflicts such as that in the Darfur region, and how such campaigns have been used to vilify Arabs and Muslims by exploiting tragedies such as that in the Darfur-Sudan region and elsewhere, in which the Arab/Muslim is being represented as the oppressive, backward, and or violent vis-à-vis Africans, and Europeans at the same time. In the final part, the chapter pays particular attention to the emerging new forms of slavery and racism, that are not framed through the traditional European race theories and Darwinism, but rather through cultural tropes, which reflect a nascent non hereditary, non racialized, new form of slavery, that has been taking hold around the world through the Western dominant neoliberal hegemony and neoconservative aggressions.

Religious Texts and the Question of Slavery

Examining the religious texts, most importantly the Qur'an, in Islam, there is no evidence to any article that condones slavery and racism. On the contrary, when Islam took hold in the Arab world, the Prophet Muhammad made different statements as stated in the Qur'an and Hadith as to the effect that there is no difference in race or origin between people, and that the only difference lies in faith. That is, the devotion of the person to the faith is the most important condition as to the status of the person in the worldly and second life as well. Also the Prophet expressed displeasure for the practice of slavery, and in fact the freeing of a slave became an act that guaranteed reward for the Muslim who does that. In other words, Muslims were encouraged to stop practicing slavery that was present in the region, and those who were able to free slaves were supposedly to be rewarded in the second life.

In both Christianity and Judaism, there are explicit statements that justify slavery and even mandate it as a God-given order. For example, in the Old Testament, in Genesis 9:18-27, Ham's son Canaan was cursed with enslavement. Specifically stated in Genesis 19:25, "Cursed be Canaan; a slave of slaves shall he be to his brothers." Presumably, this verse refers to the conquest of and settlement in Canaan by the Israelites and the holding of Canaanites as slaves for the Jews. Later on, the word Canaanite became associated with slaves owned by Jews. Over time such statements and other passages from the New Testament led to perceptions that are very much linked to the ideology of racism and the practice of slavery in the history of Western civilization, and in Western colonial adventures in Africa, America, and Asia.

Later interpretations of the Old Testament constructed Ham and his descendants, the inhabitants of Africa, as black skinned. Hence, from the fifteenth century, the curse was transferred from Canaan to his father Ham, which configured the attitude towards the black man as inferior and primitive, thus becoming an accepted theological justification, and became a source and cause for the slave trade and slavery, in which black man's slavery became part of the divine order. In addition to the Old Testament and other Jewish religious sources, Christian Europeans also relied on verses in the New Testament such as those found in the books of Paul's letters, Mathew, and Luke to support racism and slavery against darker skinned and black Africans. This is especially the case since the Middle Ages. In this context, Judaism and Christianity accepted slavery as a self-evident institution, and instituted black slavery existed since then. Since medieval times European racism took several biblical verses as justification for institutionalized black slavery, and the biblical verses were often pointed to as divinely sanctioned punishment against blacks by pro-slavery advocates up to the nineteenth century America, and the racist reasoning of Jim Crow segregation.

Texts and Practice: Slavery and Skin Color

While in theory, only Christianity and Judaism condoned racism and slavery, in practice, people from all religious backgrounds traded in slaves and practiced slavery. And slavery and slave trade took place in Africa, Asia, Europe and the Americas, in which even Africans themselves took part, and in which not only blacks were enslaved but also whites, especially prior to the fifteenth century. The skin color, at least until the Inquisition period was not a defining issue in slavery. Although there is an agreement on the fact that skin color did not play part in racism and slavery early on, the difference among scholars is in the tracing of the origin of the conflation of blackness with race and slavery.

According to David Goldberg, even though the color black was mentioned in the Old Testament (Numbers 12:1, Isaiah 18:1-2, 7, Jeremiah 13:23), and that black became associated with sin, this should not be taken in term of racism. In his view, antipathy towards blacks is not of itself a negative evaluation. In fact, he shows that the darker color was seen positively in early Christianity, Islam, and Judaism. In all ancient civilizations, Goldberg argues, slaves were both black and white skinned and he believes that it was then the Arab period blackness and slaves became identical.[2] Thus, to Goldberg and Bernard Lewis before him, racism was not factor in slavery before the Arab period.[3] This is not only an erroneous point, it even contradicts statements he makes in the book and cited in this paragraph, which is also the case with Lewis, in which he aggress with Goldberg that there were black and white slaves in the Islamic period.

Goldberg and Lewis are scholars whose political motivation trumps their 'scholarly' work and their works are rendered hallow when examined with many other works that show the opposite of that with much evidence from texts, historical locations, contexts, and practices. That is, Islam neither condoned nor initiated racialized slavery, but quiet the opposite is the case, and this is evident from the different sources that I be discussed, in which the question of race and slavery is situated.

The questions of race and slavery did not exist only in texts, but they were also part of discussion in Islam, Christianity, and Judaism, as well as in Roman and Greek periods. They also existed in public debates among intellectuals. For example, as stated earlier, the question of race and slavery were not condoned, and were even opposed in Islam in texts and in public discussions. Ibn Khaldoun, the fourteenth century Arab Muslim philosopher, was astonished by the obsession of some with their ethnic origin. He argued that the most obsessed with this issue were the Israelites who continue to claim lineage to a certain head of a tribe.[4] In Ibn Khaldoun's view the question of origin is not only inaccurate but also a fallacy. In no way, Ibn Khaldoun argued, through living and mixing with different people there is any room for purity of blood, since people intermarry and have intercourses with all kind of people, especially in cities, which makes it impossible to maintain and claim purity of one's blood and certainty of origin or race.

Ibn Khaldoun further stated that the question of race is not a positivist or empiricist category. He argued that skin color is not an indication of race, but rather a reflection of environment, climate, nutrition, and labor. To illustrate his point, he took an example of a group of people that were known in a certain region in Africa for being dark skinned. Then he proved that when this group moved north to areas that are less hot, arid, sunny, and changed their working environment, life style, and nutrition, the skin color of their children changed over generations and became much lighter with time. Hence, he argued, skin color is not permanent when environment, and climate change, and thus it cannot be an indication of race.

Rather than blaming the Arabs and Muslims for racism and slavery as Goldberg, Lewis, and other scholars did, in an attempt to promote Islamophobia, and to help promote a wedge between Arabs/Muslims and Africans and African Americans, it would be more accurate to state that the answer of the beginning point of conflating skin/race/ and slavery lies in other religious traditions and took hold at a different time and place.[5]

Contrary to what Goldberg, Lewis, Zionists, and politically motivated scholars suggest, the reverse is true, which is that if racism against blacks or darker skinned attracted some in the Arab or Muslim societies, than it was as a result of influence of Christianity and Judaism on Islam as they interacted in the region—the Middle East as Baki Tezcan shows.[6] As Fawzi Abdulrazak argues in his review of Bernard Lewis's *Race and Slavery in the Middle East: An Historical Enquiry*, such scholarship is not only inaccurate, but also politically motivated, and selective. It is also part of a campaign to create a wedge between Muslims and Africans, as many Africans were attracted to Islam for its racial tolerance.[7]

While slavery and racism were present in all world cultures and societies prior to European hegemony, slavery was not particularly linked to race, since white slaves were abundant in the Arab and Muslim societies. It is only with the beginning of European colonialism and hegemony that race and slavery became conflated, and that slavery became synonymous with blackness. Prior to that slavery was not hereditary. Racialized and hereditary slavery came about with the rise of fundamentalist Christianity, especially since the Inquisition and later on was supported by secular Darwinism and European science, which rendered race "scientific" more than a matter of faith as the case with Jewish and Christian religious texts and interpretations. The seemingly contradiction between secular and religious worldviews can be explained through the reading of Talal Asad who argues, that while Europe and the West in general have perceived and presented themselves as being secular since the Enlightenment, in reality such separation of secular and religious is not only hard to establish but also misleading.[8] It is possible to argue that even racist scientific Darwinist and other European theories of race are not to be understood as a detachment from religion and faith and their influence on European societies.

Not only in science and practices, and not only in Europe but also in their colonial adventures, Europeans have always mixed religion and politics. As Michael Prior argues, despite the fact that many Europeans settlers, colonialists, and leaders were secular or not overly religious, they drew heavily on race and race theories in their colonial enterprise in Africa, Asia, and the Americas, and often times used biblical narratives to justify conquest, slavery and racism.[9] In a comparative work between European settlers in America as well as in Palestine, Steven Salaita argues that the narratives of biblical mandate, manifest destiny, and race were deployed by European settlers in Palestine as well as America, and were used as means to justify the colonization of the land and subjugation and displacement of the natives in both places.[10]

Prior also argues that European colonialists in Palestine as everywhere else drew on biblical claims for exclusive ownership of the land, justified expulsion and ethnic cleansing as well as in various colonial enterprises. Different Biblical narratives of "the chosen people" and the supposedly special mandate bestowed on them by God were deployed in direct colonization of Africa, Asia, America, and Australia, and in the enslavements of natives and Africans. He states further that similar to other European nationalisms, Zionism "used the biblical legend of Joshua with its racist, ethnicist, xenophobic, and militaristic tendencies, and justified the conquest of the land and the maltreatment of native population."[11] In Prior's view, all colonizing practices and racisms rested on the authority of the Bible:

> Since the conquest of the earth is not a pretty thing, colonizers sought after some ideological principle to justify their actions, and when these involved

significant exploitation, the search was all the more intense as European colonialism and imperialism stretch from Asia, Africa, to America, and in which the Biblical narratives and mandates served to redeem the violent racist colonial enterprise by the taking away from those with different complexion or slightly flatter noses than the Europeans.[12]

In other words, only European colonialism deployed religious mandates in the colonial conquest, slavery, and racism. Furthermore, as Keith Muhammad argues, slaves, before European hegemony, could buy themselves out if they were able to collect the sum amount of money that their owner had paid when purchased them.[13] In addition, slaves' children did not automatically become slaves. Thus slavery became hereditary only during European period of slavery in the Americas. Slaves were considered eternal slaves no matter how long they worked and their children inherited that slave status. In this context, slavery coincided definitely with skin color and no white slaves existed as the case during Islamic and other pre modern European global hegemony.

According to Keith Muhammad, not only that Europeans owned and named their slaves, they also did that with countries and continents due to their hegemonic power. Muhammad referred to that fact that continents and countries were named by Europeans, and were not chosen by their indigenous peoples. Even further, he argues, with slaves in America, slave masters chose names for their slaves. Muhammad noted further about an aspect of the slavery in America, that through the naming of slaves by their owners, separating them from their original lands, languages, and cultures, slaves' minds were also enslaved because they were made to become ignorant of their origins. While the argument of racialized, hereditary enslavement including ones' knowledge is definitely a European one, it did not start in the Americas as Muhammad suggest, as other scholars differ on the original date or period when this happened.

The origin and conflation of race and slavery, according to Roger Boase, began with racism against the darker skinned people, which predates the European colonization of the New World.[14] Rather than there and then, Boase suggests that the answer lies with the Inquisition, in which European Christians fought to end Muslim rule in Spain. At that time, Muslims who remained in Spain were forced to be either deported or convert to Christianity. Many did convert, but they were suspected in their loyalty to the Spanish state. In Boase's view, the fall of Grenada in 1492 marked a new phase in Muslim-Christian relations, and the Christian world -European relations with the rest of the world. In this period a theory of the purity of blood started to take hold in Spain and Europe in general, in which Christian faith became identified not only with the state, but also with the purity of blood. Many issues of concern to us today, as Boase argues, have their root in that period as well. Issues such as second class citizens, atrocities against a whole religious group, expulsion, land confiscation through legislation, ethnic-communal genocide through different forms including the thought of burning, demographic thought and calculation, expulsion, ethnic cleansing, transfer, Orientalism, European ethno-religious centrism, and finally racism and slavery have their strong origin in the

Inquisition period, and have influenced European thought and practices thereafter.

As to the colonization of the minds of slaves, Boase contends that the phenomenon also had its roots in Spain during the Inquisition. At that time, Muslim children of less than seven years of age were taken away from their parents, and were educated in order to forget their heritage and adopt a Christian worldview. Slaves who were mostly Muslim converts to Christianity were educated to a level less than Christian White Spanish children, and were only taught subjects that lead to only manual labor. Not only children were enslaved, but older ones were also made to work without wages or any other form of compensation. In Boase details, Muslims since the Inquisition were seen as darker, or at least so represented by Christians. In that period, in which religious ethnic racism was developed and practiced by White Christians against darker Muslims, and in which the "Chosen People" biblical myth was deployed against Muslims and Jews. Boase wonders how Jews themselves later on since the nineteenth century have deployed the same rhetoric and framework to colonize Palestine and displace its Arab inhabitants. Puritans in the Americas used the same biblical passages that justified genocide and ethnic cleansing in Spain.

Fairchild Ruggles also explored the linkage of the Inquisition to institutionalized slavery, racism, and skin color.[15] According to him, Muslims, Africans, and Arabs and dark skinned people were represented as an identical category by the supposedly Christian, European, and white. Ruggles further shows that in Islamic society white skin was not rather praised as much as darker skin, and especially darker hair and eyes. Although slavery was practiced in Islamic slaves, slavery was not hereditary and slaves were more Europeans than Africans. Not only slavery was not yet racialized under Islamic rule nor was it hereditary, but also many cases proved that slave women married men from royalty class, and their children became part of the royal class and some even became rulers at that time.[16]

As Ruggles further shows, under Islamic rule, slave women who bore children were granted certain rights including a permanent residence in her owner's house and were legible to inheritance when the owner died. Additionally, slave women's children were granted equal rights as others regardless of the status of their mothers. This was part of the larger picture in which women in Islam in that period enjoyed a prominent role in the society, and were free to practice their religion regardless of their husband's faith.[17]

In Muslim Spain, people achieved high status, high government offices, and even became rulers/kings regardless of where they came from, and the lineage of their family. This is even rare today not only in the Arab or Islamic world, especially since the ascension of the nation state, but even in the supposedly liberal nation states in the West, especially in the most supposedly "multicultural" society of the West - the United States, in which those are not born in the US cannot according to the law become presidents. The hybridity, openness, and tolerance of Muslim Spain is something that the modern world with its patriarchal and racist structures cannot comprehend.

Felicity Nussbaum is of the opinion that only with modern Western institution of slavery, especially in the colonial expansion and Atlantic trade, that slavery became a racialized and associated with Africa and blackness. Thus, as emerges for the discussion here is that while the scholars debate the time period and place of the origin of racialized hereditary slavery, the difference is whether it started during the Inquisition or during European colonial expansion, especially in the Americas, and there is broad agreement that racialized and hereditary slavery was only the making of Europeans.[18]

This is an important point to keep in mind considering the molestation of history and scholarship, evident in works such as that of Bernard Lewis and David Goldberg, as it is related to the current discourse deployed by politicized scholarship against Arabs and Muslims, which attempts to hide Western racism then and now against non-Westerners all around. This is the context of the next part of this chapter, which will discuss some misunderstandings and misrepresentation of the question of race in the West about conflicts in Africa.

Current Implication of Race and Slavery

The history and context of race, racism, and slavery can serve as a lesson to learn from. While one must not remain hostage to history, one cannot be either selective in the process or be in complete denial, state of amnesia or selective omission. This is especially useful in the current debates regarding slavery and racism in Africa, in which the Arab/Muslim is represented as the oppressor of the African/Black, which is rather a politicized discourse that aims at further dehumanizing Arabs/Muslims and create further wedge between Arabs and Arab Americans and Africans and African Americans. The proponents of such discourse are in part Zionists, as the case with Bernard Lewis among others, and in part Christian conservatives who both seek to obscure the racism against Palestinians and the colonization of Palestine, and want to deflect attention from what is taking place in Afghanistan, Iraq, and Palestine, by selectively focusing on Africa.

Similar to the history of Europeans in Africa, Asia, and America, in its different forms and ideologies, and how the Bible has served it and continue to do so, Zionism and racism are very much interlinked as Israel Shahak shows in his work.[19] Shahak claims that history and religion matter very much in understanding the treatment of Palestinians by Jews, which is part of Jews' racism against goyim (non-Jews), which is beyond the color skin, and aimed at any one who is not a Jews. While other factors played and continue to play in the shaping of treatment of Jews and Israelis of Palestinians, religious doctrines and biblical interpretations are often deployed in the process, as Shahak, Prior, and Salaita maintain, as discussed earlier in the chapter. Salaita again contends that racism against Arabs and Muslims in the US and elsewhere has its roots in the religious foundations, settler colonial nature and imperialist historical development, and racist foundations of the U.S.[20]

While one might find such arguments of such scholars to be too essentialist, others have complete denial of their own history of racism and how the Bible played a role in it. Rather than taking some effort to reflect on racism in their own backyards in the past as well as the present, other have chosen to displace their crimes by campaigning to highlight some distant crimes, and often misrepresent these crimes as being driven by race, slavery, and religion, obscuring other factors and oblivious to the role they have played and continue to play in its making and shaping. A good example of such is the "Save Darfur" campaign in the U.S. that is highly present on and off college campuses.

In an article in the *American Quarterly*, Jodi Eichler-Levine and Rosemary Hicks discuss the campaign to highlight the crisis in Darfur as being led by many liberals, religious Christian zealots, and Zionists, who want to bring attention to plight of people in Darfur.[21] While making efforts to bring attention to the plight of miserable lives of people is highly commended, what is interesting is how such groups ignore the role their governments play in the plight and racism against Arabs, Muslims, Latinos, Asians, and African Americans in the U.S. before and after September 11, 2001 While Zionists with their Israeli flags fill the crowds of these events, as the article show, they seem to be oblivious and in denial to what is taking place by Jews against Palestinians.

While such involvement could be reasoned by the good well of some, the ill intentions of others is not hard to recognize as an attempt to one hand deflect attention of what is taking place in the U.S., Afghanistan, Iraq, and Palestine, and on the other hand promote further grounds for racism against Arabs and Muslims in the US, and further turn away African and African Americans from Muslims and Arabs.

Mahmood Mamdani provides a similar opinion regarding the politics behind the Darfur campaign in the U.S. In his article, "The Politics of Naming," Mamdani examines the politics of naming of certain events, their misrepresentation, and political activism on American campuses.[22] Mamdani was astonished by the campaigns on US campuses that highlight the Darfur question, and wondered why Americans are not interested in their own genocide in Afghanistan or Iraq as well as other genocides in Somalia and the Congo. Mamdani reflects on the misrepresentation of the Darfur conflict as it is often presented as one between Arabs and dark Africans. He argues that the conflict is political and economic, and it is not by Arabs versus dark Africans as those who want to present the conflict as such. As many other sources show, the Right wing Christians and Zionists used the conflict in Darfur in the campaign to dehumanize Arabs, and by downplaying the role of U.S. and Israel in Africa and its implications.

Taking Mamdani's argument further, Bruce Dixon is of the opinion that the "Save Darfur" campaign is part of "the regular manufacture and the constant maintenance of false realities in the service of the American empire," which is, "a core function of the public relations profession and the corporate new media . . . Among the latest false realities being pushed on the American people are the simplistic pictures of Black vs. Arab genocide in Darfur . . ."[23] In his view, this public relation campaign is intended to justify U.S intervention, similar to other cases in the past in which "genocide" was pushed as a humanitarian intervention, covering for U.S. economic, strategic, and imperialistic interests.

Dixon further states why is it that not the Congo, but rather Sudan is the target of this PR campaign, when in the Congo five million people have died due to the conflict there, compared to the 200,000 in the Sudan? Not to minimize human suffering according to numbers, but why focus on smaller genocide and ignore another? Upon scrutiny, one finds that the Congo is a site were U.S. interests for natural resources are secured, while in the Sudan there are not, rather they are being exploited by China instead, as Dixon shows. Thus the Sudan is targeted in this PR campaign not for the human suffering there, but for its natural resources such as oil, uranium, and gum Arabic, and for its strategic location across from the Persian Gulf, and its strong position that controls the flow of the Nile River on which Egypt is dependent, Dixon argues.

The campaign, according to Dixon, is part of dehumanizing Arabs and Muslims, which seems an open game at the moment, and he also reveals in his article that the sources deployed for the PR campaign are in millions of dollars and joined by Hollywood and media celebrities such as Angelina Jolie, George Clooney, and Oprah Winfrey as participants celebrities who are supposedly concerned with humanitarian causes, yet who dared not to do the same regarding the killing in the Congo, or Somalia in which the U.S. is directly or indirectly complicit.

Dixon believes that "Save Darfur" campaign was launched by the American Jewish World Service, and the U.S. Holocaust Memorial Museum, and were joined by right wing Christian evangelists, who want to push an agenda against Muslims and Arabs, and in my view also to deflect from American and Israeli crimes in Afghanistan, Iraq, and Palestine, as well as other countries in Asia and Africa, and at the same time help further create a wedge between Arabs and Arab Americans and Africans and African Americans.

At this point of history, in which Western countries, chief among them the U.S., are interfering in every corner of the world, causing death and suffering, and their policies in their own countries are not less than racists when it comes to "minorities" who happen often to be Africans, Asians, and Natives, as well as their policies in Africa, Asia, and Latin American is nothing short of racism and greed, it is highly suspicious to believe their claim to be the champions of human rights and fighters against racism.

The Changing Terrains of Racism

In the current context of these internal and external racist policies in the West, the theorizing of racism must go beyond the color lines. Western racism has been transformed from racial and genetic tropes to a Neo-Darwinism, using cultural tropes instead genes and science, and this has been taking hold as the West is a dominant force within the global discourse in the current context of the so called war on terror. In his *Orientalism,* Edward W. Said pointed out that racism, myth making, and fantasy of Westerners against non-Westerners (Asians, Africans, Natives) were clothed in many scholarly garbage that continues to provide legitimacy to Western policies of domination, hegemony, and exploitation of non-Westerners around the world.[24]

In his work, Derek Gregory examines the recent wave of racism and brutality by Westerners in Afghanistan, Iraq, and Palestine.[25] In this new context the color of racism is changing to include those who are not dark or Africans only. Racism in contemporary times has gone beyond the color line. Similarly, in the contemporary period of neoliberalism and globalization slavery has also gone beyond the standard European exclusively racialized and hereditary framework. The poor in the West continue to be exploited as also the case with the poor in the rest of the World. In the current circumstances of exploitation, where old style racism and slavery are hard to practice openly, a neoracism and neoslavery are taking place with devastating effects on people in Latin America, Africa, and Asia, and the poor or marginalized groups in the West. Both groups continue to suffer under oppressive and harsh circumstances. Globalization, that is, Western (led by the U.S.) economic, political, cultural, and military global hegemony has been causing suffering to the poor in the West, and many in the rest of the world, as for example the case with framer suicide high rates in India, and the dispossession and dislocation of many around the world.

This is very much should be predicted as Ibn Khaldoun (discussed earlier) has noted. In his theory, states that expand beyond their borders, and states that wish to live beyond their means, end up oppressing and exploiting people at home and people abroad. Thus, according to this theory, foreign policies are often mirrored in domestic ones.

Angela Davis asserts that things, which seem separate and disconnected, have much in common than one might think.[26] For example, the prison in the U.S. where victims are disproportionately 'minorities' and heavily populated by Latinos and African Americans is a new form of slavery where non-White bodies serve and provide cheap labor in the different prisons in the U.S. In her views, the link between practices of racism and torture in U.S. prisons, as well as U.S. prisons and camps in Guantanamo, Iraq, and Afghanistan, are very much linked to the same rational—that the lives and bodies of those who are deemed unworthy and unequal can go through suffering and exploitation without much public attention through their stigmatization as criminals, while in fact those who hold them in these prisons are the real criminals. Davis' view of the prison industry as a new form of slavery adds to my argument, that the news forms of slavery and racism practiced in the West and by the West suggest a call to a new theorizing that needs to take into account the legacy of old racism and slavery, racialized and hereditary, and its new forms and colors that no politicized scholarship such as that of Goldberg or Lewis, neither politicized "humanitarian" campaigns such as that of "Safe Darfur" campaign can go unexamined for their attempt to deflect from Western and Western sponsored racism and slavery, and divide those who are the victims of such policies in the U.S. and elsewhere.

Conclusion

The topic of this chapter is vast and difficult to give it a sufficient treatment. For a general discussion of the subject of race and slavery in a comparative religious and historical perspective and its current implications and manifestation, the chapter has served to offer and establish a basic understanding of these questions. This, by taking into account the context of race and slavery in theory as well as in practice as it is reflected in the three religions and civilizations of Islam, Judaism, and Christianity, and the implications of such debates around such topics in contemporary context as well.

What emerged from the discussion in the chapter about the three religions and their implication in race and slavery, except for Islam, who, in texts, opposed slavery and racism, is that the other monolithic religions in question— Judaism and Christianity — have explicitly condoned racism and slavery. While in practice peoples from all religions and civilizations participated in slave trade and slavery, including Africans, racialized and hereditary slavery and racism did not take place before the Inquisition and modern European colonial expansion. Thus, it was a Western invention and practice that was never experienced in history before.

As the chapter aimed at dealing with current implications with the subject of slavery and race, and the points made include: First, the tendency is to manipulate the subject and rewrite history as to serve the political agenda of many groups involved in conflict and attacks on Arabs and Muslims, who aim to dehumanize and set Africans against Arabs specifically and Muslims in general, a discourse in which Westerners and Israelis present themselves as defenders of human rights, in contradiction to past and current policies of these countries in Africa, and Asia, as well as all the rest of the world.

Second, while such dominant discourses are also an attempt to also justify U.S., Western imperialism, and Israeli colonialism, they are also an attempt to veil the role of the West in these and other conflicts. They are also an attempt to veil the many new forms of slavery and racism that are taking place. New forms of racism using cultural tropes have replaced the old genes and science rhetoric. Now, like before, the West hold itself to be the bastion of progress and civility, thus erasing histories of past and present genocides, new forms of enslavements as seen in the prison industrial complex, or the economic sphere, in which poor people around the world are paying the price for the greed of Western states, chief among them the U.S.

Third, the future of a possible more humane, egalitarian, tolerant, and peaceful world depends on two things. One, on the resistance of conscious people, who are the true seekers of freedom, liberty, justice, and human rights, and the true seekers for a world without racism and any form of slavery. Second, this is also depends on the powerful Western states and those who serve them, who continue to hold global power beyond their numerical size of population, and who must first reckon wit their past and present racisms and crimes, whose victims continue to be the poor, and the non-Westerners, and then these states must make it possible for coexistence and tolerance of difference if they are true to their slogans—of liberty, equality and freedom. It meant liberty, equality, and freedom for some, and enslavement, oppression, and injustice for others. Putting much hope in Western governments and societies is not only a naïve proposal, but also ignored historical lessons. History has shown that the powerful and greedy never cedes power voluntarily, and that the struggle against racism and all forms of injustices must be taken as a continuous journey that never ends as humanity continue to exist.

Notes

1. I acknowledge Shahid Alam and Baki Tezcan for their helpful suggestions on sources for the chapter.
2. David M. Goldberg, *The Curse of Ham: Race and Slavery in Early Judaism, Christianity, and Islam.* (Princeton: Princeton University Press, 2003), 47-49.
3. Bernard Lewis, *Race and Slavery in the Middle East: An Historical Inquiry* (New York: Oxford University Press, 1990).
4. Ibn Khaldoun, *The Muqaddimah: An Introduction to History*, translated and introduced by Franz Rosenthal, abridged and ed., N.J. Dawood, with a new introduction by Bruce B. Lawrence, Bollingen Series, (New York and Oxford: Princeton University Press, 2005).
5. Matt Carr, "You are Entering Eurabia," *Race and Class*, Vol. 48. No. 1, 2006.
6. Baki Tezcan, "Dispelling the Darkness: The Politics of Race in Early Seventeenth Century Ottoman Empire in the Life and Work of Mullah Ali," in *International Journal of Turkish Studies*, Vol. 13, Nos. 1 & 2, 2007.
7. Fawzi Abdulrazak, review of "Race and Slavery in the Middle East, An Historical Enquiry by Bernard Lewis," in *The International Journal of African Historical Studies*, Vol. 24, No. 3, 1991, 682-685.
See also Ali A. Mazrui, "Zionism and Race in Afro-Semitic Relations," in *The Transformation of Palestine: Essays on the Origin and Development of the Arab-Israeli Conflict,* ed., Ibrahim Abu-Lughud (Evanston: Northwestern University Press, 1971). Also, Muddathir Abdel-Rahim El-Tayyeb, " African Perceptions of the Arab-Israeli Conflict," in *The Arabs and Africa,* ed., Khair El-Din Haseeb (London: CroomHelm, 1985), 344-66.
8. Talal Asad, *The Formation of the Secular: Christianity, Islam, and Modernity* (Sanford, CA: Stanford University Press, 2003).
9. Michael Prior, "Ethnic Cleansing and the Bible: A Moral Critique," *Holy Land Studies*, Volume 1, Number 1, September 2002, 37-59.
10. Salaita, Steven, *The Holy Land in Transit: Colonialism and the Quest for Canaan*, (Syracuse, NY, Syracuse University Press, 2006).
11 Prior, 37.
12. Ibid., 42-43.
13. Keith Muhammad, "Africans and the Diaspora," A talk at College of Alameda, 2/14/2008.
14. Roger Boase, "Muslim Expulsion from Spain." *History Today* 52. 4 (April 2002), 21(7).
15. Fairhild Ruggles, "Mothers of a Hybrid Dynasty: Race, Genealogy, and Acculturation in al-Andalus," *Journal of Medieval and Early Modern Studies* 34.1 (2004), 65-74.
16. Ruggles, 65.
17. Ibid., 72-76.

18. Felicity A. Nussbaum, "Slaver, blackness, and Islam: the Arabian nights in the eighteenth century," *Essays and Studies* (2007),150 (23).

19. Israel Shahak, *Jewish History, Jewish Religion: The Weight of Three Thousand Year* (London: Pluto Press, 1994).

20. Steven Salaita, *Anti-Arab Racism in the US: Where it Comes from and What it Means for Politics Today* (New York: Pluto Press, 2006).

21. Jodi Eichler-Levine and Rosemary R. Hicks. "As Americans Against Genocide: The Crisis in Darfur and Interreligious Political Activism," *American Quarterly*, Vol. 59, No. 3, September 2007, 711-736.

22. Mahmood Mamdani, "The Politics of Naming: Genocide, Civil War, and Insurgency," *London Review of Book*, Vol. 29, No. 5, March 8, 2007.

23. Bruce Dixon, "Ten Reasons to Suspect 'Save Darfur' is a PR Scam," *Black Agenda Report* posted on November 29, 2007, Printed on March 14, 2008. http://www.alternet.org/story/69170.

24. Edward W. Said, *Orientalism* (Vintage Books, 1979).

25. Derek Gregory, *The Colonial Present: Afghanistan, Iraq, and Palestine* (New York: Blackwell Publishing, 2004).

26. Angela Y. Davis. *Abolition Democracy: Beyond Empire, Prisons, and Torture*, Interviews with Angela Davis. (New York: Seven Stories Press, 2005).

References

Boase, Roger. "Muslim expulsion from Spain." History Today 52.4 (April 2002).

Fairhild Ruggles. "Mothers of a Hybrid Dynasty: Race, Genealogy, and Acculturation in al-Andalus." Journal of Medieval and Early Modern Studies, 34.1 (2004): 65-74.

Clearance-Smith, William. Islam and the Abolition of Slavery. London: Hurst & Company, 2006.

Davis, David Brion. "Slavery—White, Black, Muslim, Christian." New York Review of Books (5 July 2001).

Diamond, James S. Homeland or Holy Land? The 'Canaanite' Critique of Israel. Bloomington: Indiana University Press, 1986.

El-Tayyeb, Muddathir Abdel-Rahim. "African Perceptions of the Arab-Israeli Conflict," 344-366. In The Arabs and Africa, ed., Khair El-Din Haseeb. London: CroomHelm, 1985.

Gilroy, Paul. The Black Atlantic: Modernity and Double Consciousness. Cambridge, MA: Harvard University Press, 1993 reissued 2005.

Jayyusi, Kh. Salma, ed. The Legacy of Muslim Spain. E. J. Brill, 1992.

Mazrui, A. Ali. "Zionism and Race in Afro-Semitic Relations," in The Transformation of Palestine: Essays on the Origin and Development of the Arab-Israeli Conflict, ed. Ibrahim Abu-Lughud. Evanston: Northwestern University Press, 1971.

Miano, Peter J. The Word of God and the World of the Bible: An Introduction to the Cultural Background of the New Testament. London: Melisende, 2001.

Prior, Michael. "Ethnic Cleansing and the Bible: A Moral Critique." Holy Land Studies, vol. 1, no. 1, 2002, 37-59.

Sugirtharajah, R.S. The Bible and the Third World: Precolonial, Colonial, and Postcolonial Encounters. Cambridge: Cambridge University Press, 2001.

Chapter 5

The Dark Craven Jew:
Race and Religion in Medieval Europe

James M. Thomas[1]

This chapter is an attempt to engage with problems of periodicity in global histories on race and racism. While historians, literary scholars, and those within cultural studies have critically examined questions of periodicity and historical fluidity, sociology by and large has come to locate itself within a modernist framework where contemporary social issues and concepts only have relevance within a dialectic framework, which privileges post-Enlightenment thought as the thesis to the pre-modern antithesis. This chapter will examine the ways in which Jewish experiences in medieval Europe challenges the dualism of modern/premodern in how we look at the formation of modern racial/racist classificatory systems and practices. The experiences of Jews in medieval Christendom not only calls into question critical race scholarship which has located the birth of modern racism with the birth of modern capitalism, but also demands that new scholarship be attentive to the ways in which histories express a fluid interconnectivity, rather than a periodic breakage of epistemologies and ontologies.

Introduction

Sociological discourse on race and racism has often limited itself through processes of periodization and temporal constructions of racial differences. Many scholars in the field have often stood by a reductive epistemology, which seeks to understand race and racism only in conjunction with post-Enlightenment capitalist expansion and subsequent exploitation. One only has to look at some of the titles within our canon to see this phenomenon. For instance, Omi and Winant's classic work on racial formation in the United States concerns itself with racial formation from the period of the 1960s onwards, and in relation to U.S. social policy.[2] Racial projects in Omi and Winant are inherently temporal in that they occur as distinct, periodic episodes which reformulate notions of race and racism at the "instant" they occur.

Charles Mills' Racial Contract, while thorough in its argument that modern notions of race and racism are founded on a contract which privileges the ontology of modern Europe, still posits modern racism as distinctly different from whatever type of racism implicitly existed in a pre-modern epoch.[3] In fact, Mills canonical work does not acknowledge a discourse on racism prior to Enlightenment.[4]

Even W.E.B. DuBois succumbs to the seduction of periodization in his scholarly work on race and racism, writing that the history of race and racism "may be epitomized in one word—Empire; the domination of White Europe over black Africa and yellow Asia, *through political power built upon the economic control of labor, income, and ideas,*" (emphasis added).[5] For DuBois, as well as Mills, the genesis of modern racism can be found in the birth of capital, or rather the birth of the global production processes behind capital.[6]

What is needed is a reformation of critical race scholarship within sociology. Scholars in literary studies have already critically engaged themselves with issues of periodization through the ways in which they study race and racism,[7] and the challenge is to be up to date to avoid being outdated and without critical insight. Furthermore, for those who view sociology as a liberating method, must strive to reconceptualize the histories of difference making to make any worthwhile attempt to move past those legacies and begin to fashion and shape new legacies of kinship.

To provide grounds for moving forward (or backward?), an argument is constructed upon the Jewish experience in medieval Europe. In positioning this argument this chapter will articulate race and racism as concepts stemming out of the disidentification practices of Christendom. In positioning modern notions of race and racism as having their roots in the policies and practices of an anti-semitic medieval culture, it allows for critical race scholarship to see the emergence of modern racism not from a perversion of Contractarian logic,[8] nor from economic concentration and then expansion by European colonial powers[9], but from the more general construction of the European self and the generalized Other.[10] The objective is to indicate that the emergence of race as an element of intellectual discourse post-Enlightenment was a result of an elongated crisis within medieval Europe of how to differentiate the internal Other from the internal Christian self.[11]

In taking a position for a Meadian understanding of the development of the self and the social as the foundation of modern discourse on race and racism, this chapter will not engage in an argument of reduction, for it would not only be naïve, but essentially wrong.[12] The enslavement of people of color, the exploitation by the colonial powers of those they colonized, the European Holocaust, and the African Diaspora cannot be reduced to a simple logic of the

Me and the I without reducing the consequences and legacies of those practices as well. Rather, by seeing modern notions of racism through the breaking up of pre-modern/Modern dichotomies, we can fully engage ourselves with a history which acknowledges continuity rather than sharp breaks and points of distinctions.

Structure

This chapter structures the argument in three parts.[13] First, the conjectural history of critical race theory as it stands in relation to modernity. That will highlight many of the canonical works within critical race theory, and show how they have dealt with notions of Genesis in race and racism. These notions are limited by a lack of continuity in how history is studied, which has served to be just as hegemonic for discourses on race and racism as the racial ideologies that they attempt to address.

Second, there will be a brief survey of Jewish experiences within medieval Europe as a means of articulating the position that race and racism are not products of modernity, or capitalist logic.[14] The Jewish experience will not be totalized and there will be no attempt to convince the reader that the experiences that are articulated reflect all of medieval Jewish life. Rather, it will show that by and large the experiences of Jews in medieval Europe cannot be understood outside the context of Christianity and the effect that Christian thought and self-conception had upon both Jews and non-Jews at that time. The experiences of Jews in medieval Europe reflect what a post-Meadian conception of the self arising out of the construction of the generalized Other, but in a dualistic sense. The social "I" of Christendom arose not only out of the construction of the Christian generalized Other from which to reference towards, but also developed out of the construction of the Jewish Other as a group which held an essentialized identity inherently different from that of Christians. Thus, Christians came to know themselves by what, de facto, they were not.

Expanding upon Mead's work on the development of the social self, I wish to step out of the existential matters of epistemology, which Meadian pragmatism tends to dwell upon. The process of differentiation between the Christian self and the Jewish Other was much more than just a cognitive one, and contains distinct ontological experiences for the Jewish Other. Church officials in various parts of medieval Europe instituted Church policies meant to keep a mandated physical distance between Christians and Jews.[15] As well, laws of certain European kingdoms at the time also put into place edicts, which sought to further physically identify the Jewish body as profane and 'dark', in comparison to the Christian body, which signified wholeness and purity.[16] These policies and practices provide empirical data from which to extrapolate on Meadian concepts of the self, which are individual in Mead's body of work, and allow us to construct a pragmatist conception of racial discourse through which we can come to understand the construction of the social self as requiring, de facto, an Other from which to locate the self against.

The third section moves into a more in-depth discussion of Mead's (1932) concepts of the Me and the I in relation to historical continuities of racial discourses.[17] Mead's theory on the self and the social is useful because it articulates a process of difference making, which predates capitalist expansion or conjectural histories of contracts and pre-modern/modern periodizations. The self and society represent a way of understanding how the Other comes to be understood through the eyes of the self, a concept not unfamiliar to critical race scholarship.[18] In the case of medieval Europe, the self was understood through the development and expansion of Christendom, and the somatic Christian body was indeed a White body, as articulated through the writings of various medieval European thinkers. Thus, the Jew as the generalized Other represented not only non-Christian, but also non-White.[19]

Overall, the contribution from this work rests on two positions, interdependent and unique to sociological inquiry. The first position is the challenge to rid our work of the dualistic take on history, where we create artificial boundaries between modern and pre-modern, privileging the former over the latter in how we conceptualize and frame our research. Sociology as a whole has operated out of a modernist discourse, all the while problematizing other dualisms such as the universal and the particular. However, sociological discourse on race and racism has largely focused on race as only having relevance in modernity, and questions of pre-modernity are ignored.

The second position is that the location of race and racism as products of modernity has articulated race as a secularized concept with a particular type of rationality, which Weberian logic has only located within a post-Enlightenment discourse.[20] The distinction often made between pre-modernity and modernity has often been the secularization of thought and action, and race as a concept has been placed within a secularized framework of modernity. The problem with this framework (as will be shown later) is that Medieval Christendom did indeed operate off of a rationality in how the racialized Jewish Other was constructed, and this rationality was by and large guided by a theological epistemology.

Critical Race Scholarship, Periodization, and the Need to Disengage

Race and racism, as we have come to know it through both classical and contemporary sociological inquiry, is a product of the political entity known as the nation-state. Hobbes, Locke, Rousseau, and other contractarians have convinced many political and social scientists that the history of society begins with the history of the nation. This history, according to the Hobbesian logic, did not start until the epochal rising up out of our state of nature, and submitting ourselves to the rule of a few over the many for the sake of collective good will and security. Interestingly enough, one of the most poignant criticisms of such an idealistic narrative of society is found in the work of Georg Mead. In *Mind, Self, and Society*, Mead's posthumous collection of lectures and notes, he writes:

> . . . the contract theory of society assumes that the individuals are first all there as intelligent individuals, as selves, and that these individuals get together and form society. On this view societies have arisen like business corporations, by the deliberate coming-together of a group of investors, who elect their officers

and constitute themselves a society. The individuals come first and the societies arise out of the mastery of certain individuals...If, however, the position to which I have been referring is a correct one, *if the individual reaches his self only through the communication with others, only through the elaboration of social processes by means of significant communication*, then the self could not antedate the social organism. The latter would have to be there first (emphasis mine).[21]

Mead's theory on the development of the self as a precursor to the development of the social provides us with a different narrative, and one that recognizes historical development *by and through* social interaction, rather than the tautological narrative of development through social formation, which is itself a form of development.

Criticism of Contractarian logic, or the meta-narrative of modernity, was no deterrence for later generations of social theorists, however. Critical race scholarship has often found itself standing on the head of conflict theory, proclaiming to have the answer to the question of race, which Marx and the Marxian analysis that followed seemed to either ignore completely or push to the backburner as simply a product of the larger institution of capitalism. The problem with the emergence of critical race theories out of the weaknesses of conflict theory was that Marxist analysis engaged in a periodization of history that was reflective of the rise of economic classes from a capitalist system. Critical race theorists rightfully saw the neglect paid towards other social classification schemas, such as race, and later with feminist theory, gender, but they too engaged with the very same periodization of history that Marxist analysis did, without recognizing that perhaps their struggles had much earlier beginnings, and were simply old monsters rearing their ugly head again, rather than new monsters arising from the material relations of an unjust economic system.

To date, most theories on race have been unavoidably tied up in meta-narratives of history, plotting the growth of racial ideologies alongside the growth of modernity, colonialism, and science.[22] However, traditional periodization impedes our understanding of early crucial constructions of race and racism, and has resulted in the emergence of what we now temporally mark off as modern notions of race and racism.[23] As well, traditional periodization may contribute to the static, negative schematics of cultural interaction, which can have disastrous consequences at both the local and the global levels.[24] Furthermore, positing the ancient world as an era which predates prejudice amounts to imagining this 'ancient' world as a world without history.[25] It begins to be imagined as a kind of Age of Innocence that recognized multicultural identities as entities without contested, or even relational, status.[26]

While scholars within the fields of literature, medieval history, and cultural studies have acknowledged the problems with conceptualizing history in such a manner as that critiqued above, sociology appears too caught up in its own conventions to alter its mentality. Ever since DuBois' proclamation that the problem of the twentieth century is the problem of the color line,[27] critical race theorists have constructed a conjectural Genesis located within a discourse on

Modernity. DuBois himself wrote that the economic foundation of the modern world was built upon racial distinctions,[28] and while this is not necessarily an incorrect statement, the positioning of a modern world versus a pre-modern world presupposes a false sense of history. One can argue, as some historians have, that racial distinctions were the foundation upon which the 'pre-modern' world was founded as well,[29] and to do so would completely alter the common critique of capitalism as producing the dominant racial ideology of our global system.

One can point out of course that DuBois was writing at a time when most social theorists did not recognize this, and thus this critique of DuBois should not be taken very seriously. Undoubtedly, DuBois, writing in a Weberian vein, cannot be faulted for this oversight. Furthermore, none of his contemporaries argued any differently. The publications of that era reflect that many of the social scientists of DuBois' era saw racism as a product of modernity and economic exploitation by colonial powers.[30] Just how much were critical race scholars caught up in theorizing about race only in terms of European imperialism? According to an article in *The American Journal of Sociology* from 1935, there was "a period of some twelve or thirteen centuries in European history in which practically no literature dealing systematically with the subject of race was produced. [31] According to the prevailing ideology among social scientists in the middle of the twentieth century, race and racism were not even thought about for over twelve hundred years.

While recognizing the dated ideologies of our predecessors in the study of the nature of race and racism, there is the need to deal with the fact that even contemporary scholars of race and racism explore issues of race in the Western world,[32] whites and whiteness in a colorblind era,[33] the somatic construction of the Other,[34] and the history of racial construction[35] through the lens of a post-Enlightenment periodization of modern race versus pre-modern "distinctions." One problem from this approach is that it reifies post-Enlightenment biological models of racial classificatory systems by privileging modernist 'discoveries' of race as the starting point of social inquiry. Most theorists of racial differences still conceive of race as a post-Enlightenment ideology "forged on the twin anvils of colonialism and Atlantic slavery, which hinges on the pseudobiological notions of human differentiation, especially color, and is thus absent in premodern societies whose ideologies of difference were more 'cultural.'"[36] By using nineteenth and twentieth century biological models, derived from post-Enlightenment thought, as the golden standard for determining whether one can make connections between ideological formations in regards to race and racism hinders investigations into how medieval concepts on race may have shaped modern concepts on race in ways about which we are still unaware.[37]

It is for these reasons that the study of race and racism is positioned in the empirical inquiry into the social position of Jews in medieval Europe. Studying race in the medieval period demands that modernists follow through on the belief that race, as an indicator of difference, is always historically constructed and activated.[38] Furthermore, the historical construction of race does not begin with a construct such as modernity, but is rooted in a dynamic historical continuity of emergence. To succumb to the colonization of the Middle Ages by modernists is to create a pseudo-historical break in the study of human history, where the Middle Ages become a "dark" period, a precursor to the "real" history of human civilization.[39] This real history of civilization can only be found in the history of Europe, more specifically, the history of Europe post-Enlightenment. This Age of Reason corresponds to an Age of Expansion through the use of violence and force, both of which were common to the "dark" period of Europe that Occidental thought would like to throw away as incongruent to notions of Western progress.

The dynamics of medieval racial discourses may therefore fundamentally modify how work is done in the field because inquiries into medieval constructions of race, society, and other sociological analytics allows for us to deconstruct the dominant narrative of Western progress through forced political and social domination.[40] Studying the dominant ideology of race and racism from the medieval period allows for us to see that the mental habits and institutions of European racism and colonialism were byproducts of medieval European construction of the self and the social, thus finally shedding an illumination onto what has for too long been taken for granted as being dark and devoid of thought and significance.[41]

The Medieval Other

Medieval Social Policy and the Other

As stated earlier, Jews in medieval Europe reflected a larger construction of a generalized Other from which the European, Christian self would come to define its boundaries. In almost every facet of social life, the Jew remained separate from Christians, both de facto and de jure. Medieval constructions of race were predicated upon notions of a divine hierarchy, and these notions of manifest destiny for Christendom were largely being promoted through the official Church positions of that time.[42]

The philosophy of the Church in regard to the Jews had been formulated in the fourth century by St. Augustine, who compared the Jewish people to Cain.[43] Cain's punishment, if you recall, was to be a wanderer upon the earth all his life.[44] Augustine in "Against Faustus the Manichean" writes, "No emperor or monarch who finds under his government the people with this mark [of Cain] kills them, that is makes them cease to be Jews, and as Jews to be separate in their observance, and unlike the rest of the world."[45] Augustine argued that the Jew had to survive in Christendom if only to revealed the truth of Christian prophecy.[46] The Jews were always to be seen as the self without a place, but also, as will be discussed further, to be the generalized Other, which Christendom would come to locate its own self against. It is in this sense that the analysis becomes post-Median in how the Christian self develops. The generalized Other is more than just a point of reference for the development of the individual self. The generalized Other serves as a point of reference for the development of the Christian social self in both the ways in which the Christian self locates its social identity within the context of a larger Christendom, as well as in how the Christian self locates itself against the prismatic Jewish Other.[47]

Jewish ways of life were seen as threatening to the emerging Christian kingdoms arising after the fall of Rome. Various Church councils in France and Spain, for instance, headed a systematic struggle against what they deemed to be the dangerous influence of Judaism on the masses of newly converted Christians from the fourth to the eighth century.[48] As well, Church officials in various parts of Europe instituted Sunday Sabbath as a means of combating the influence of the Jewish Sabbath on both Jews and Christians, which fell a day earlier. The instituting of a different Sabbath was an indicator of separation between what would be considered sacred in Christendom and what was deemed profane.[49] This separation of the profane and the sacred is in the Durkhemian tradition, where the sacred and profane serve as sites around which social consciousness came to be constructed.

Up until the eleventh century, Jews were excluded from the existing Christian feudal class in four ways: Jews were denied the right to hold public office; by the thirteenth century Jews in England were denied the ownership of land; Jews could not own Christian slaves;[50] and Jews were often forbidden to participate in social interactions with Christians, or to intermarry.[51] Simmel writes that in Frankfort during the medieval period there existed a special tax upon the Jew dependent completely on the essentialist position of the Jew in relation to Christendom.[52] Whereas this same tax paid by Christians differed with the changes of the fortunes of the Christian, it was fixed for all times for every single Jew, no matter their economic position. This fixedness, according to Simmel, rested on the fact that the Jew's social position was that of a Jew first, not as the individual bearer of certain objective contents. The Jew was a Jew in the first place, not a taxpayer in the first place, so his tax situation had an invariable element, much like the identity given to him by the Christian self. The Jew could only be defined as a Jew because the interaction of the Christian self with both the generalized Christian Other and the generalized Jewish Other resulted in the invariable yet prismatic characteristic of Jewish social identity. Jewish identity at that point became a marker of indication for difference in relation to Christian identity. This marker of difference resulted not just in the denial of property, but also in the appropriation of wealth earned by the Jew.

This occurrence is similar to the Nuremburg laws of Nazi Germany, which sought to, among other things, appropriate the wealth and property of Jewish shopkeepers and landowners residing under the rule of the Third Reich. Jews in Nazi Germany also found their identities constructed through the interaction of the non-Jewish self with the generalized non-Jewish Other, and while this construction may not have been grounded in explicit theological rationality, it was the theological epistemology of Medieval Christendom which both precedes and to some extent predicted the apparent 'secularized' racism of the Third Reich.

The Somatic Other

Jews, as well as Muslims, stood both in proximity to and socially distant from Western European Christians during the medieval period, which guaranteed them a certain ideological and emotional significance within the processes of Christian self-definition.[53] For Jews, this nearness/farness dichotomy of existence represented a pariah status.[54] This pariah identity of the Jews has been traced back to Augustine's aforementioned declaration against the Jews.[55] This declaration reflects the differentiation of the Jews from Christians. Rather than exterminate the Jews completely, then, there comes to be a social utility involved in keeping them around, if only to serve the purpose to mark the boundary between the sacred and the profane.[56] Often, this marking of the sacred and the profane would occur through the body as a carrier of identification.

In many parts of medieval Europe, both Jews and Christians appear to have agreed that it was easy to know who was or was not a Jew, on grounds, which were biological, social, and religious.[57] Medieval Christian writers often grouped Muslims and Jews together in terms of physical characteristics, both in fiction and non-fiction.[58] While societal notions of Black and White were less stable in the twelfth century than they were through the twentieth century and up to the present, they were nonetheless demarcated in the Middle Ages by artists and the literati.[59] Medieval plays in England and France would often cast Muslims and Jews as physically black, or with other identifiable physical characteristics, to offer a reassurance that Christians could easily identify their difference.[60] De facto, the physicality of Christians remained unmarked, and in turn their physicality was seen in a somatic construction of Whiteness as Christian.

The practice of grouping together Muslims and Jews in medieval writings and works of art often resulted in the construction of a somatic body for both, opposed to a distinct Christian 'whiteness.'[61] Muslims and Jews were both described by Medieval Christians in terms of blackness and servitude, as the two would often go hand in hand in the justification of such servitude in the Kingdom of Christ.[62] In fact, in medieval as well as early modern romances, religious difference is persistently manifested in terms of color as a means of establishing a boundary between moral (read: Christian) bodies and immoral (read: non-Christian) bodies.[63]

To illustrate the importance of the somatic norm in the construction of Christian normative bodies, one can look at the last four decrees from the Fourth Lateran Council of 1215. These decrees dealt strictly with the Jews as a physical threat to Christendom. The Church accepted its drastic measures for the purpose of degrading the Jews and separating them from Christians, but not exterminating them.[64] As mentioned before, there was a social utility in keeping the enemy close, so to speak.

One of the decrees of the Lateran Council, for instance, was that the Jews should wear different clothing at all times, to further differentiate their bodies from those belonging to Christians. In fact, the Church even declared that no

Jew should depart from the strict tenets and practices of Orthodox Judaism.[65] In other words, even Jews who did not completely adhere to the laws of Mitzvot in the manner of the Orthodoxy were made to do so in order to further create a cognitive and social distinction between Christians and non-Christians. This shows that the boundaries around Christendom had to be clearly marked in order for the Christian self to recognize its own, and the Other, as a way to formulate a positive identification with a completely ordered Christian society.

The Lateran Council reflected a turn in polemic attitudes of Christians towards Jews and other non-Christians, as the polemic assumed a much more direct and aggressive character in the thirteenth century. The Church aimed to undermine the presence and security of the Jew in a properly ordered Christian society.[66] The most telling evidence of these developments was the assault by the Church on the Talmud. Nicholas Donin, described as an embittered Jewish apostate, indicted the Talmud before Pope Gregory IX in 1236, just three years after the initiation of the Inquisition by Gregory IX in 1233.[67] Consequently, the Talmud was denounced in a series of papal bulls in 1239 and 1244, burned in Paris under direction from the pope in 1242, and openly condemned by a commission of prelates and university masters in 1248.[68]

Along with the legal edicts issued under the papal authority, as well as the public condemnation of Jewish texts and Jewish rabbinical scholars, the somatic Other experienced an even more explicitly racist construction by Christian polemicists in the twelfth and thirteenth centuries. The overall consensus of the constructions depicted Jewish men as suffering from afflictions that only Christian blood can cure, because at the time Jews were seen as the possessors of diseased and debased bodies.[69] Popular forms of anti-semitism in medieval Europe often drew upon images of defective bodies and inferior bloodlines.[70] The accounts of these twelfth and thirteenth century polemics depicted Jewish men as being born mis-shapen, and even being afflicted with menstruations.[71] From this depiction, one can see how the somatic Other's identification came to be everything that at the time was viewed as unclean and incomplete. The overall racial ideology of the time equated a healthy body with a Christian body and soul. Wrapped up in this notion of health was an element of 'whiteness as pure', and wrapped up in the purity of whiteness was an essentialized notion of masculinity, which could only be allocated to a pure, White, Christian male.[72] Jewish men, then, became constructed not just as non-Christian and non-White, but also non-male.

Memory Practices in Race and Religion

In order to understand the continuity between medieval discourses on race and racism and the modern dominant racial ideology, I wish to implore the clustering process of historical epochs suggested by Mignolo.[73] Rather than a lineal succession of periods, beginning with the Dark Ages, moving to the Age of Reason, and now modernity, Mignolo conceives of a coexistence of clusters with quite a bit of overlap in between each cluster.[74] For instance, medieval texts were often translated and published in English in the sixteenth and seventeenth centuries.[75] The redistribution of the works medieval scholars and literati were not consumed as histories of a past, however, but rather as contemporary documents.[76] Thus, repeating and reformulating medieval as well as non-European ideologies of difference formulated the core values of early modern European slavery.[77] It was mentioned already the parallels between the appropriation by feudal governments of Jewish property and wealth and the appropriation of Jewish property and wealth by Nazi Germany. Using Nazi Germany as an analytical analogy of racist ideologies in practice, the marking off of the physical body of Jews under the Third Reich was parallel to that of Jews under the feudal systems of the medieval period. In twelfth and thirteenth century England, as well as twentieth century Nazi Germany, we find the assignment of badges or stars for Jews to wear as a means of marking the profane body.[78] As well, for over three hundred years after Edward I expelled the Jews were in 1290, they were more available as concepts than as persons to the English.[79] They became etched into the minds of English Christendom as sites of speculation, rather than active agents within the English kingdom.[80] Not surprisingly, Nazi Germany implored many of the caricatures from medieval England and elsewhere in their representation of the Jew as a social vagabond responsible for the economic condition of post-World War I Germany. The image of the Jew as a blood-sucker, to be feared by parents of pure Aryan children was not pulled out of thin air by the Third Reich, but reflected an already well-known historical memory of the Jew created by medieval Church officials and writers who wished to distance their imagined Christian sacredness from the imagined profanity of the Jewish people.[81]

Towards a History of the Self: A New Approach to Understanding Race and Racism

Having provided a background of evidence for which Christian Europe came to locate the Jewish Other, I now wish to turn to an in-depth look at the works of Georg Herbert Mead, and his writings on the development of the self and the social. For Mead, the human individual is a self only in so far as he takes the attitude of another toward himself.[82] The self, then, is a social development, arising out of the recognition of an I as a subject being in relation to other selves.[83] We are in possession of selves just in so far as we can and do take the attitudes of others toward ourselves and respond to those attitudes.[84] The others for whom we reference Mead refers to as the generalized other, and I wish to now make a very clear distinction between Mead's generalized other and my use of the generalized Other.

For Mead, the generalized other refers to all other members of the community for whose actions and reactions organize and control the actions of the self.[85] In this understanding of the concept, the Christian self of medieval Europe would be organized around the actions and reactions of other Christian selves towards the individual, and how the individual constitutes their own self in response. The use of the term here, however, denotes the Other, which has been so eloquently described by writers from the line of critical race studies, such as Edward Said and W.E.B. DuBois.[86] The Other, as used here, serves to locate the self through what the self is distinctly not. The actions of the self and the rest of the community, or the Meadian generalized Other, come to define not only their social location but also the position of the non-generalizable Other in relation to the rest of the community within which they reside.

To make this clear, the recognition of a self amongst a collection of other selves, which constitute a community, is to imply that we have played the role of those other selves.[87] As well, inner consciousness is socially organized by the importation of the social organization of the outer world.[88] The inner consciousness of the Christian self, which led to the development and maintenance of Christendom, required that the social organization of Christendom be imported into the Christian consciousness. This social organization was not just positioned around the teachings of Christ, but on the teachings of the Church in how to deal with the non-Christian presence in a Christian society. This non-Christian presence, as articulated in this paper, was perceived to be a threat to the constitution of the Christian self, and thus Christian society as a whole. The unity created by the Church rested upon the recognition of the Jew as the non-generalizable Other for which the Christian self could come to identify itself against. To join together against a common foe, whether it is internal or external to the society creates a sense of oneness amongst a community.[89]

In his work on the birth of the Jewish pariah, David Nirenberg asks the question: to what extent are the analytic concepts by which the modern social sciences approach the study of the Other themselves recapitulations of early Christian thinking about the Jews?[90] In other words, to what extent has the sociological inquiry of the Other become a secularized manifestation of the theological? Both a society's self-constitution and an individual 'self' depend upon the casting out of 'others.'[91]

One of the advantages to casting out distinctions between modern/pre-modern is that it allows us as scholars to see the continuity of networks from both periods. One of Bruno Latour's principles is that we can study all networks in the same way because there is no modern world.[92] Those who study the modern world have invented terms to distinguish it from the constructed pre-modern world. Modernists talk of modernity in terms of secularization, rationalization, mercantilism, scientization, one-dimensionalism, progress, etc.[93] This dividing up of time prevents us from seeing that the modern practice of periodizing history has been essential in creating the discourse of modernity as being inherently about progress. As Latour writes, "They are not interested in things in themselves, in following them along their paths; they are concerned only with man and the modifications to which he can be forced to submit."[94]

The identification of Jews as different through clothing and the branding of their bodies through badges on their clothing served the purpose of articulating the Self through the negation of the Other.[95] As well, their isolation in ghettos across European lands and the economy of expulsions from and readmittances to Christian lands also express a strong desire by the Church and its polemics to negate physical proximity to the Christian Self, either by segregating the Jewish community and thus neutralizing its 'power', or by literally expelling it from the body of Christianity.[96] Not surprisingly, the "modern" practices of the Third Reich shows the identification of the Jewish Other through the mandated branding of their clothing, the encircling of Jewish communities through the formation of ghettos, and the actual expulsion from the Christian body through concentration camps, which largely served as sites for extermination.[97] Furthermore, the figure of the Jew, both somatic and metaphorical, has functioned both as a way to further the sense of Christian cultural, social, and political unity as well as to project a vision of the Christian individual over against the religious Other. In other words, the Christian is whole, rational, and moral, while the Other is fragmented, irrational, and immoral.[98]

While Mead has by and large written of the self as developing out of the recognition of a generalized Other which it works in negotiation with, Mead also correctly points out that the whole history of conflict, both between and within societies, points to how much more readily the self finds its location in opposition to common enemies than in collaboration with them.[99] While the development of the introspective self requires that we enter into relations with other selves,[100] the formation of the Jewish Other by the Christian self required the Christian I to recognize in the Jewish Other that which it would not locate within itself.[101] Mead writes that the inner consciousness of the self is socially organized by the importation of the organization of the external social world.[102] It follows then that the inner consciousness of the Christian self, which led to the development and maintenance of Christendom, required that the social organization of Christendom be imported into the Christian consciousness. This social organization was not just positioned around the teachings of Christ, but on the teachings of the Church in how to deal with the non-Christian presence in a Christian society.

Through the development of an Other from which to position the self against, a 'hostile impulse' developed against the Jewish Other.[103] This hostile impulse then served as a point of unity for Christendom against what was seen as a common enemy. The formation of a hostile impulse allows for the social 'We' to bond in the common assault upon a common 'Them.' In bonding, the 'We' has become more than allies; it has formed a clan with a sense of oneness within the Christian community.[104]

Conclusion

Although the arguments in this chapter have been organized into three parts, there are two distinct points, which have been made separately, but should be moved into one formal position. First, the argument has been made for a new epistemology in the study of global race and racism. Current critical discourse on race and racism has by and large posited the origins of race as manifesting out of a larger colonial capitalist logic of expansion through exploitation. By consulting the works within history,[105] literature,[106] and cultural studies,[107] it has been shown how the periodization of history itself is a construct built into the discourse on modernity, and how development and discourse of the modern world through Western though cannot be seen as separate from the epistemological and ontological happenings of earlier European history, especially as it has related to the experiences of Jews in medieval Europe. The true wanderer of Europe was the medieval Jewish Other.[108] The medieval Jewish Other existed between the boundaries of Christianity and Judaism, forever moving between the two and a more general universalism.[109] The medieval Jewish Other, then, has served as the precursor of modernity in its struggle to obtain a stable identity configuration.[110]

In acknowledging a critique perhaps unfamiliar to sociology, but well-known to some of the other disciplines in humanities and the social sciences, this chapter has also sought to push forward a theoretical shift in sociology's approach to studying race and racism. Not only has it been argued that sociology must reposition itself *against* a modernist epistemology, but what many feel is an out-dated position on the development of society and the self, as well as the Other has been revisited. Mead's body of work was illuminating for its time, certainly, and has served as the beginnings for many works within the field of social psychology, inquiries into the development of consciousness, as well as works which have sought to incorporate larger calls for social justice. Yet by and large the study of race and racism seeks to understand the development and maintenance of racial classificatory systems through a Marxian model of economic expansion and development, rather than seeing it as a complex process of the Self, manifesting through the interaction with other Selves, as well as the Other.[111]

The Marxian model not only comes up short in its historical development of modern discourses on race and racism, but also collapses into a form of Oppression Olympics when discussing racial classificatory systems. The Marxian model has often privileged[112] colonization as the epitome of racism as praxis, with the trans-Atlantic slave trade positioned as the precursor to modern global imperialism and exploitation.[113] Some scholars have argued that slavery as it was practiced by the colonists was a fate worse than death, and that Africans stood as models of slaves specifically because they were not European, or *even* European Others.[114] This argument rests largely on the claim that enslaving Africans to work in European colonies outside of Africa was not economically efficient, but was at the same time morally and politically necessary.[115] The position of Jews in medieval Christendom and later colonial Europe was largely that of a non-human, and even *anti-human*. The widely held beliefs that Jews were diseased, deficient, and potentially cannibalistic would de facto construct them as unable and undesirable to work in the Master's house, as they would pose a direct threat to the Master's life.[116]

This chapter has sought to synthesize two arguments. The idea that Mead can serve as the unitary epistemological location for the liberation of sociological discourse on race and racism may be naïve at best, and counter-productive at worst. Criticism itself is a way of pushing dialogue forward, and it is hoped that this paper will inspire the type of criticism that is willing to acknowledge not only the shortcomings of my own theoretical orientation, but also the short-comings of those who came before me. Only by recognizing the global history behind our socially located inequalities may we liberate ourselves from an anti-humanist present and future.

Notes

1. I wish to thank David Brunsma and Amit Prasad for their insightful comments on previous drafts.
2. See Omi, M. and H. Winant, *Racial Formation in the United States* (New York: Routledge, 1994).
3. See Mills, C., *The Racial Contract* (Ithaca, NY: Cornell University Press, 1997).
4. For a survey of the field impacted by Mills' work, see Thomas, J,. "Re-Upping the Contract with Sociology: Charles Mills' *The Racial Contract* revisited a decade later," *Sociology Compass, 1(1)*, 2007a, 255-264. The reader should not walk away from this critique of Mills as if the Racial Contract is not a significant contribution to the field of sociological research on race and racism.
5. Du Bois, W.E.B., *Dusk of Dawn: An Essay Toward an Autobiography of a Race Concept* (Piscataway, New Jersey: Transaction Publishers, 1940, 2005), 96.
6. See Wallerstein, I., "The Rise and Future Demise of the World Capitalist System: Concepts for Comparative Analysis," *Comparative Studies in History and Society, 16(4)*, 1974, 387-415.
7. Lambert, L., "Race, Periodicity and the (Neo-) Middle Ages," *Modern Language Quarterly, 65 (3)*, 2004, 391-421. Also see Hahn, T., "The Difference the Middle Ages Makes: Color and Race before the Modern World," *Journal of Medieval and Early Modern Studies, 31(1)*, 2001, 1-37.
8. See Mills, C., 1997.
9. Du Bois, W.E.B., 1940.
10. With "generalized Other," I adopt the Meadian concept (see Mead, 1932) and expand upon it, creating a post-Median analysis which acknowledges the construction of a social self through processes of reference to a social Other which has a dualistic meaning. The social Other in one sense is much like the Meadian generalized Other (Mead, 1932) from which the I comes to locate itself in reference to. At the same time, there exists another Other from which the I comes to locate itself *against*.
11. Smaje, C. *Natural Hierarchies: The Historical Sociology of Race and Caste* (Oxford, UK: Blackwell Publishers, 2000), 8.
12. See Latour, B., *The Pasteurization of France*, trans. by Alan Sheridan and John Law (Cambridge, MA: Harvard University Press, 1988).
13. How hegemonic is the logic of distinction? So hegemonic that the argument itself is structured in a periodic method.
14. The use of "Jews experiences" rather than "the Jewish experience" is intentional, and reflects the author's position in a previous work that the term "Jew" or "Jewish experience" for that matter cannot and should not be seen in an essentializing manner, given that the criteria for determining what is authentically Jewish lacks consistency, even within the Jewish community at large. See Thomas, J., "The Other Within: Prismatic Identities and Authentic selves within the Marginalized," Masters Thesis, University of Missouri at Columbia, 2007b.
15. Deutsch, K. W., "Anti-Semitic Ideas in the Middle Ages: International Civilizations in Expansion and Conflict," *Journal of the History of Ideas, 6 (2)*, 1945, 239-251.
16. See Hahn, 2001.

17. Mead, G. H., *Mind, Self, and Society from the Standpoint of a Social Behaviorist* (Chicago, IL: University of Chicago Press, 1932).
18. See DuBois, W.E.B., *The Souls of Black Folk* (New York: Penguin Books, 1903 and 1996. Also see Said, E. *Orientalism* (New York, NY: Random House, 1978).
19. See Hahn, 2001; Lampert, 2004.
20. By and large, critical race studies in sociology have attributed modern notions of race and racism to what Weber would refer to as formal rationalization (see Weber, 1978), with a structural emphasis on the types of bureaucracies, which reproduce racial hegemony. One could even make the case that theoretical rationality in the sciences contributed to 'scientific' findings about the physical and mental abilities of different racial classifications. The fact remains that there was a rationality involved in the formation of the Christian self over and against the Jewish Other, which operated upon a rationality of difference. The Christian self needed the Jewish Other in order to come to a complete understanding of its own social world
21. Mead, 1932, 233.
22. Loomba, A., "Periodization, Race, and Global Contact," *Journal of Medieval and Early Modern Studies,* 37 (3), 2007), 597.
23. See Lampert, 2004.
24. Lampert, 420.
25. Hahn, 2001.
26. Hahn, 5.
27. Du Bois, 1903.
28. DuBois, 1940, 103.
29. See Hahn, 2001. Also see Heng, G., "Jews, Saracens, 'Black Men', Tartars: England in a world of racial difference," in *A Companion to Medieval English Literature and Culture, c.1350 – c.1500,* ed., Peter Brown (Malden, MA: Blackwell Publishing, 2006), 247-272.
30. Park, R., "The Basis of Race Prejudice," *The American Negro,* 140, 1,1928, 1-20; Cox, O., "The Nature of Race Relations: A Critique," *The Journal of Negro Education,* 16 (4), 1947, 506-510; also see Park, R., "The Nature of Race Relations," in *Race Relations and the Race Problem,* ed., Edgar T. Thompson (Durham, N.C.: 1939).
31. House, F., "Viewpoints and Methods in the Study of Race Relations," *The American Journal of Sociology,* 40 (4), 1935, 441.
32. Bonilla-Silva, E., "This is a White Country: The Racial Ideology of the Western Nations of the World-system," *Sociological Inquiry,* 70 (2), 2000, 188-214.
33. Lewis, A., "What Group?: Studying Whites and Whiteness in the Era of 'Colorblindness,'" *Sociological Theory,* 22 (4), 2004, 623-646.
34. Puwar, N., "The Racialized Somatic Norm and the Senior Civil Service," *Sociology,* 35 (3), 2001, 651-670; Puwar, N., "Multicultural Fashion...stirrings of another sense of aesthetics and memory," *Feminist Review,* 71, 2002, 63-87.
35. Roediger, D. *Colored White: Transcending the Racial Past* (University of California Press, 2002).
36. Loomba, 2007, 597.
37. Lampert, 2004, 396) makes it clear that theological concepts from the medieval period may play a central role in the determination of race and racism in the modern era.
38. See Hahn, 2001.
39. See Dagenais, J and M Greer, "Decolonizing the Middle Ages: Introduction," *Journal of Medieval and Early Modern Studies,* 30(3), 2000, 431-448. There is a paradox here, however, in that modern constructions of race have often rested upon biological categories. These biological categories give race a primordial characteristic that goes against the very logic of modernity.
40. Hahn, 2001, 4.

41. Bartlett, R., *The Making of Europe: Conquest, Colonialism, and Cultural Change, 950-1350.* (Princeton, N.J.: Princeton University Press, 1993, 313; also see Mead, 1932.

42. See Smaje, 2000, 8.

43. Rosenthal, J., "The Talmud on Trial: The Disputation at Paris in the year 1240," *The Jewish Quarterly Review,* 47 (1), 1956,.59.

44. Bauman (1996) writes of identity in a post-modern era: "Wherever the vagabond goes, he is a stranger, he can never be the 'native', the 'settled one', one with 'roots in the soil' (too fresh is the memory of his arrival – that is, of his being elsewhere before)," (1996, 28). Furthermore, in *Modernity and the Holocaust* (1989), Bauman rightfully mentions that in the context of European history, the Jew has almost always stood apart as the antithesis of every location which non-Jews occupy, thereby serving as the reference point for what identity one is not (1989: 41). This prismatic characteristic of Jewish identity (see Thomas, 2007b) allows for non-Jews to locate themselves in relation to whatever generalized Other (read: Jew) that they wish to compare themselves against: the non-Jewish working class versus the Jewish villain who gleams a pound of flesh off of those who cannot pay their debt in full; the wealthy non-Jew who must deal with the Jewish leach of society, always begging for a handout. No matter what position one takes in society, the Jew stands as the Oppressor both beneath and above them in social standing. Because of this prismatic characteristic, then, the Jew can never belong to their land of origin (Bauman, 1989, 54). They are never English, but simply a Jew in England. For to be English is to explicitly be non-Jewish.

45. From Nirenberg, D (. "The Birth of the Pariah: Jews, Christian dualism, and social science." *Social Research,* 70 (1), 2003, 201-238.

46. Cohen, J., "Scholarship and Intolerance in the Medieval Academy: The Study and Evaluation of Judaism in European Christendom," *The American Historical Review,* 91 (3), 1986, 594.

47. See Thomas (2007b). See also Bauman, Z., *Modernity and the Holocaust* (Ithaca, NY: Cornell University Press, 1989).

48. Deutsche, 1945, 240.

49. Deutsche, 1945, 242.

50. Ironically, Christians did not see it problematic to enslave other Christians along with non-Christians. The 'weight' of Christian identity, then, could be seen in the power of ownership, rather than the giving up of status in the name of servitude.

51. Deutsche, 1945, 245. Intermarriage was strictly forbidden at this time in terms of a Jewish male taking a Christian female for a wife. Christian men could, however, take action towards Jewish women as their wife. This reflects a larger male privilege that was tied into Christian identity at the time, and similar practices can be seen in the acceptance of White men in the antebellum South taking black women as their mistresses (quite often forcibly), while Black men were systematically beaten and lynched for even having the thought of a White female partner cross their minds.

52. Simmel, G., *The Sociology of Georg Simmel,* trans. by Kurt Wolff (New York: New York Free Press, 1950, 408.

53. Kruger, S., "Medieval Christian (Dis)identifications: Muslims and Jews in Guibert of Nogent," *New Literary History,* 28 (2), 1997, 186.

54. Nirenberg, 2003.

55. Nirenberg, 2003.

56. Nirenberg, D., *Communities of Violence: Persecution of Minorities in the Middle Ages* (Princeton, N.J.: Princeton University Press, 1996).

57. Berek, P., "The Jew as Renaissance Man," *Renaissance Quarterly,* 51 (1), 1998,129.

58. Lampert, 399.

59. Hahn, 24.

60. Loomba, 613.

61. See Lampert, 2004.

62. Loomba, 603.

63. Loomba, 611.

64. Rosenthal, 61.

65. Rosenthal, 1956.

66. Cohen, 1986.

67. See Cohen, 606; also see Rosenthal, 58.

68. Cohen, 606.

69. Kruger, S., "The Bodies of Jews in the Late Middle Ages," in *The Idea of Medieval Literature: New Essays on Chauncer and Medieval Culture in Honor of Donald R. Howard*, ed. by James M. Dean and Christian Zacher (Newark, DE: 1992),.303.

70. Smaje, 2000, 145; see also Poliakov, L., *The Aryan Myth: A History of Racist and Nationalist Ideas in Europe* (New York: New York Library, 1974); Burke, P., *Popular Culture in Early Modern Europe* (London, UK: Temple Smith, 1978); Lynch, J., *The Medieval Church: A Brief History*. (Harlow: Longman, 1992).

71. Resnick, I., "Medieval Roots of the Myth of Jewish Male Menses," *The Harvard Theological Review*, 93 (3), 2000), 244.

72 Resnick, 2000.

73. Mignolo, W., *The Darker Side of the Renaissance: Literacy, Territoriality, and Colonization* (Ann Arbor, MI: The University of Michigan Press, 1995.

74. Mignolo, 1995, vii

75. Loomba, 2007.

76. Loomba, 2007.

77. Loomba, 2007, 604.

78. Hahn, 2001, 7.

79. Berek, 1998.

80. Berek, 128.

81. See Resnick, 2000.

821 Mead, G. H., "The Genesis of the Self and Social Control," *International Journal of Ethics*, 35 (3), 1925, 274.

83. See Mead, 1932.

84. Mead, , 272.

85. Mead, 269.

86. See Said, 1978; DuBois, 1940.

87. Mead, G. H., "The Social Self," *The Journal of Philosophy, Psychology, and Scientific Methods*, 10 (14), 1913, 377.

88. Mead, G. H. (1912). "The Mechanism of Social Consciousness." *The Journal of Philosophy, Psychology, and Scientific Methods*, 9 (15), 1912, 406.

89. Mead, G. H., "National-Mindedness and International-Mindedness," *International Journal of Ethics*, 39 (4), 1929, 394.

90. Nirenberg, 201.

91. Kruger, 185; also see Mead, 1932.

92. Latour, 206.

93. Latour, 207.

94. Latour, 230. Latour has been used to make a point about race and racism in medieval Europe because of his reputation largely in the field of science and technology studies, and while he makes some distinctly sociological arguments, the above passages have been taken from his philosophical position outlined in his work on the construction of scientific knowledge (see Latour, 1988). But one has to recognize that even the dividing up of the sciences as natural/social, or the line drawn between epistemological/ontological, is a constructed boundary. Latour's position and mine are connected in the sense that we both seek to understand knowledge, and the social,

through a process of continuity. Latour's focus has been on the networking of actors and actants, and how they come to define a science in action that is very different from the science as progress narrative often described by other STS scholars. My focus, however, is on how history itself is a network of narratives, which cannot be partitioned off into sudden epistemological breaks, but must be understood as a continuum of experiences, which come to shape the present.

95. Kruger, 186.

96. Kruger, 186.

97. It should be noted that Bauman (1989) acknowledged the problematic of locating the Jewish Holocaust as an isolated event of modernity, a throwback to an earlier, barbaric period. Bauman rightfully acknowledges that it was modernity itself, which is to blame for the quantitative severity of Hitler's master plan. These thoughts and ideals were not unique to modernity, and yet they were unable to be carried through to their (il)logical end without the technology and political development that post-Enlightenment science and technology had born.

98. Kruger, 188.

99. Mead, 277.

100. Mead, 375.

101. Mead, 406.

102. Mead, 1912.

103. Mead, 1929.

104. Mead, 394.

105. Berek, 1998; Hahn, 2001.

106. Mignolo, 1995; Lampert, 2004; Loomba, 2007.

107. Nirenberg, 2003; Nirenberg, 1996.

108. Yovel, Y., *Spinoza and Other Heretics: The Marrano of Reason* (Princeton, N.J.: Princeton University Press, 1989).

109. Yovel, 49.

110. Yovel, 49; also see Bauman, 18.

111. This statement should not be interpreted to be a reduction of Marxian thought. The position that modern racism is a product of a capitalist world-system (see Wallerstein, 1976; Wallerstein, 1974) is not a simple position. Yet, it is inherently shortsighted, in that it periodizes global development as a whole. Why is it that we can acknowledge a philosophy on civilization as that beginning with the Greeks (or Egyptians, as Bernal (1987; 1991; 2006) has rightfully pointed out), yet we struggle to see how racism may have also been grounded in those same philosophical developments?

112. Obviously, the use of 'privilege' here is ironic, and is not meant to suggest that ancient or modern slavery was at all a privilege enjoyed by its victims and survivors.

113. For an example of this occurrence, see Patterson, 1982.

114. Patterson, O., *Slavery and Social Death* (Cambridge, MA: Harvard University Press, 1982); Eltis, D., "Europeans and the Rise and Fall of African Slavery in the Americas: An interpretation." *American Historical Review*, 98, 1993, 1399-1423.

115. See Smaje, 2000.

116. While not meaning to engage in the Oppression Olympics I have just criticized, it is important to acknowledge just how rampant ant-semitism in Europe was at a time when Africa was still largely unknown to many Europeans. Jews, even when expelled from European lands in the medieval period, still maintained a presence in art and literature, which further increased their status as a Somatic Other, as discussed in the chapter.

References

Bartlett, Robert. *The Making of Europe: Conquest, Colonialism, and Cultural Change, 950-1350*. Princeton, N.J.: Princeton University Press, 1993.

Bauman, Z. "From Pilgrim to Tourist – Or A Short History of Identity," in *Questions of Culture and Identity*, ed. Stuart Hall and Paul du Gay. Sage Publications, 1996.

_____ *Modernity and the Holocaust*. Ithaca, NY: Cornell University Press, 1989.

Berek, Peter. "The Jew as Renaissance Man." *Renaissance Quarterly*, 51(1), 1998, 128-162.

Bernal, M. *Black Athena: Afroasiatic Roots of Classical Civilization*. Vol. 1, *The Fabrication of Ancient Greece, 1785-1985*. Piscataway, NJ: Rutgers University Press, 1987.

_____. *Black Athena: Afroasiatic Roots of Classical Civilization*. Vol. 2, *The Archaeological and Documentary Evidence*. Piscataway, NJ: Rutgers University Press, 1991.

_____. *Black Athena: Afroasiatic Roots of Classical Civilization: The Linguistic Evidence*. Vol. 3, Piscataway, NJ: Rutgers University Press, 2006.

Bonilla-Silva, E. "'This is a White Country': The Racial Ideology of the Western Nations of the World-system," *Sociological Inquiry*, 70(2), 2000, 188-214.

Burke, P. *Popular Culture in Early Modern Europe*. London, UK: Temple Smith, 1978.

Cohen, J. "Scholarship and Intolerance in the Medieval Academy: The Study and Evaluation of Judaism in European Christendom," *The American Historical Review*, 91(3), 1986, 592-613.

Cox, O. "The Nature of Race Relations: A Critique." *The Journal of Negro Education*, 16(4), 1947, 506-510.

Dagenais, J and M Greer. "Decolonizing the Middle Ages: Introduction." *Journal of Medieval and Early Modern Studies*, 30(3), 2000, 431-448.

Deutsch, K.W. "Anti-Semitic Ideas in the Middle Ages: International Civilizations in Expansion and Conflict," *Journal of the History of Ideas*, 6(2), 1945, 239-251.

Dubois, W.E.B., *The Souls of Black Folk* (New York: Penguin Books, 1903 and 1996).

_____. *Dusk of Dawn: An Essay Toward An Autobiography of a Race Concept* (New Jersey: Transaction Publishers, (1940and 2005).

Eltis, D. "Europeans and the Rise and Fall of African Slavery in the Americas: An Interpretation," *American Historical Review*, 98, 1993, 1399-1423.

Hahn, T. "The Difference the Middle Ages Makes: Color and Race before the Modern World," *Journal of Medieval and Early Modern Studies, 31(1)*, 2001, 1-37.

Haraway, D. *Simians, Cyborgs, and Women: The Reinvention of Nature* (New York: Routledge, 1991).

Heng, G. "Jews, Saracens, 'Black Men,' Tartars: England in a World of Racial Difference," in *A Companion to Medieval English Literature and Culture, C.1350-c.1500*, ed. Peter Brown (Malden, MA: Blackwell Publishing, 2006). 247-272.

House, F. "Viewpoints and Methods in the Study of Race Relations." *The American Journal of Sociology*, 40(4), 1935, 440-452.

Kruger, S. "Medieval Christian (Dis)identifications: Muslims and Jews in Guibert of Nogent." *New Literary History*, 28(2), 1997, 185-203.

_____. "The Bodies of Jews in the Late Middle Ages." In *The Idea of Medieval Literature: New Essays on Chaucer and Medieval Culture in Honor of Donald R. Howard*, ed. James M. Dean and Christian Zacher. Newark, DE: University of Delaware Press, 1992.

Lampert, L. "Race, Periodicity, and the (Neo-) Middle Ages." *Modern Language Quarterly*, 65(3), 2004, 391-421.

Latour, B. *The Pasteurization of France*, trans. by Alan Sheridan and John Law. Cambridge, MA: Harvard University Press, 1988.

Lewis, A. "'What Group?': Studying whites and whiteness in the era of 'colorblindness.'" *Sociological Theory,* 22(4), 2004, 623-646.

Loomba, A. "Periodization, Race, and Global Contact," *Journal of Medieval and Early Modern Studies,* 37(3), 2007, 595-620.

Lynch, J. *The Medieval Church: A Brief History.* Harlow: Longman, 1992.

Marx, K. *Capital.* Volume 1. New York: Penguin Books, 1867and 1990.

Mead, G.H. *Mind, Self, and Society from the Standpoint of a Social Behaviorist.* Chicago, IL: University of Chicago Press, 1932.

_____. "National-Mindedness and International-Mindedness." *International Journal of Ethics,* 39(4), 1929, 385-407.

_____. "The Genesis of the Self and Social Control." *International Journal of Ethics,* 35(3), 1925, 251-277.

_____ "The Social Self." *The Journal of Philosophy, Psychology and Scientific Methods, 10(14), 1913,* 374-380.

_____. "The Mechanism of Social Consciousness." *The Journal of Philosophy, Psychology and Scientific Methods,* 9(15), 1912, 401-406.

Mignolo, W. *The Darker Side of the Renaissance: Literacy, Territoriality, and Colonization.* Ann Arbor, MI: The University of Michigan Press, 1995.

Mills, C. *The Racial Contract.* Ithaca, NY: Cornell University Press, 1997.

Nirenberg, D. "The Birth of the Pariah: Jews, Christian Dualism, and Social Science." *Social Research,* 70(1), 2003, 201-238.

_____. *Communities of Violence: Persecution of Minorities in the Middle Ages.* Princeton, NJ: Princeton University Press, 1996.

Omi, M. and H. Winant. *Racial Formation in the United States.* New York: Routledge, 1994.

Park, R. "The Basis of Race Prejudice," *The American Negro,* 140, 1928, 11-20.

_____, "The Nature of Race Relations." *From Race Relations and the Race Problem,* ed., Edgar T. Thompson (Durham, NC: Duke University Press, 1939).

Poliakov, L. *The Aryan Myth: A History of Racist and Nationalist Ideas in Europe.* New York: New York Library, 1974.

Puwar, N. "The racialized somatic norm and the senior civil service." *Sociology,* 35(3), 2001, 651-670.

_____. "Multicultural fashion...stirrings of another sense of aesthetics and memory," *Feminist Review* 71 (2002): 63-87.

Patterson, O. *Slavery and Social Death.* Cambridge, MA: Harvard University Press, 1982.

Resnick, I. "Medieval Roots of the Myth of Jewish Male Menses." *The Harvard Theological Review,* 93(3), 2000, 241-263.

Roediger, D. *Colored White: Transcending the Racial Past.* Berkeley, CA: University of California Press, 2002.

Rosenthal, J. "The Talmud on Trial: The Disputation at Paris in the year 1240." *The Jewish Quarterly Review, 47(1), 1956,* 58-76.

Said, E. *Orientalism.* New York: Random House, Inc., 1978.

Simmel, G., *The Sociology of Georg Simmel,* trans. by Kurt Wolff (New York: New York Free Press, 1950).

Smaje, C., *Natural Hierarchies: The Historical Sociology of Race and Caste.* Oxford, UK: Blackwell Publishers, 2000).

Thomas, J., "Re-upping the Contract with Sociology: Charles Mills' *The Racial Contract* revisited a decade later." *Sociology Compass,* 1(1), 2007a, 255-264. DOI: 10.1111/j.1751-9020.2007.00013.x

_____,"The Other Within: Prismatic Identities and Authentic Selves Within the Marginalized." Masters Thesis: University of Missouri at Columbia, 2007b.

Wallerstein, I., "The End of What Modernity?" *Theory and Society*, 24(4), 1995,471-488.

_____, "A World-System Perspective on the Social Sciences." *British Journal of Sociology, 27(3),* 1976.

_____, "The Rise and Future Demise of the World Capitalist System: Concepts for Comparative Analysis." *Comparative Studies in Society and History,* 16(4), 1974, 387-415.

Weber, M., *Economy and Society: An Outline of Interpretive Sociology* (Los Angeles, CA: University of California Press, 1978).

Yovel, Y., *Spinoza and Other Heretics: The Marrano of Reason* (Princeton, NJ: Princeton University Press, 1989).

Chapter 6

Growth of the Atlantic Slave Trade: Racial Slavery in the New World

Kwaku Osei-Tutu

The two essential issues to be addressed in this chapter are the growth of the Atlantic slave trade and the selling of black Africans. The central themes of this chapter include a discussion of the beginnings of the trade, motives, and reasons black Africans were used exclusively. The discourse also includes the key players in the trade. The chapter focuses on the growth of racial slavery, concerning itself with some varying aspects, culminating in a brief examination of the role of economics. The chronological parameter of this chapter is the beginning of the trans-Atlantic slave trade in the early 1400s through the mid 1600s with a particular emphasis on early North America, specifically on Virginia, as the data is plentiful on this subject.

Introduction

Financially secure, and well traveled, due to his "trade," Richard Drake, an Irish American, spoke about his lucrative, yet morally agonizing profit in such a way:

> I am growing sicker every day of this business of buying and selling human beings for beasts of burden...On the eight day [out at sea] I took my round of the half deck, holding a camphor bag in my teeth; for the stench was hideous. The sick and dying were chained together. I saw pregnant women give birth to babies whilst chained to corpses, which our drunken overseers had not removed. The blacks were literally jammed between decks as if in a coffin; and a coffin that dreadful hold became to nearly one half of our cargo before we reached Bahia.[1]

Thus, the reality for Drake and thousands of other slavers throughout the history of the trans-Atlantic slave trade was one of needed financial security attained through brutal, inhumane, and vicious treatment of their fellow beings. The conditions and the mortality rate on the ship of which Drake spoke was not unlike the thousands that crossed the Atlantic during the slave trade and the moral predicament he found himself grappling with was equally not unlike that of thousands of other slavers, traders, bankers, planters, politicians and the like throughout the trans-Atlantic slave trading world. This study seeks primarily to chart the early growth of the trade and how it gradually transformed into a trade in black African human beings.

This topic remains pertinent. The contentious racial issues currently taking place in Brazil and the United States today, and other world societies, are deeply related to how we remember and examine the emergence of global white supremacy; an event intrinsically bound to discussions of race and the rise of the Atlantic slave trade. The biological differences between races are so minute as to render them inconsequential yet the oppressive reality of overt and institutionalized racism is so blunt as to render it possibly the biggest impediment to world cooperation and progress, particularly in the western hemisphere. Striking imbalances continue to exist in the United States and Latin America, with regard to the employment and salaries of black vs. white workers, and economic development is cruelly disproportionate with regard to former slaving regions (US and Europe) and those regions from which slaves were drawn and sent (Africa, the Caribbean and Latin America) there are those who would argue most vehemently and passionately that the trans-Atlantic slave trade has no relation to these harsh realities whatsoever. In fact, as the world community often grapples over apologizing for slavery the economic imbalance between the "haves and have nots" persists.

The trans-Atlantic slave trade is a topic that has been abundantly studied; but there are questions that need to be asked and answered regarding this most gruesome period in human history. In fact, the question to begin with is: "Why Africans?" This chapter is in part an attempt to address more directly the issue of racial slavery, "why Africans," and how the trans-Atlantic slave trade was *the* most significant accelerant for this on going, unremitting, horrible thing we call racism.

Several recent studies have been done on the history of the slave trade and racial slavery. For example, Hugh Thomas's *The Slave Trade: The Story of the Atlantic Slave Trade: 1440-1870* (1997) is probably the most acclaimed of the more recent scholarship. Thomas of Boston University gives a well-researched balanced historical account of the slave trade. *The Invention of the White Race: The Origins of Racial Oppression in Anglo-America,* published in 1997, is a socioeconomic assessment of the relationship between economics and race. The author, Theodore Allen, argues quite passionately for the position that race was a tool used to maintain a stranglehold on the control of production (in the form of slaves) and more specifically, in breaking any semblance of unity between the poor white, indentured white and enslaved black against the establishment. Toyin Falola, a historian and professor at the University of Texas-Austin edited a significant five volume series on Africa. Falola assembled a well-rounded scholarly team to produce most urgently needed volumes centered on the study of Africa, its people, its culture, and its history. In the first volume of the series, *Africa Volume One: African History before 1885* (2003), one of the contributors, Joseph Inikori, gives an account of the trans-Atlantic slave trade and answers many significant questions with concise and succinct erudition and delivery.

Slave Nation: How Slavery United the Colonies and Sparked the American Revolution (2005), by Alfred and Ruth Blumrosen, two Rutgers University Law professors advanced the thesis that finances necessitated the continual enslavement of Africans and while the British were legally dismantling slavery, rich southern slaveholders in America saw their livelihood threatened and thus gained an incentive to join the already growing revolutionary movement in the northern colonies. The argument espoused by the Blumrosen's is original and consequently subject to great debate yet the research is primary source based and therefore very solid.

Robert Collins, a professor of history at the University of California, has produced a book of primary source documents on Africa spanning from the first century to the twenty first century. Frustrated with the difficulty in finding such a text, Collins compiled one the *Documents from the African Past* (2001). The need for these sorts of resources is invaluable to any historian particularly in the study of Africa, which has often been the victim of intentional and blatant historical miss-truths and outright lies.

The Birth of Black America: The First African Americans and the Pursuit of Freedom at Jamestown (2007) was written by an investigative reporter Tim Hashaw, and chronicles the first Africans brought to North America and the immediate aftermath. Hashaw claims to be descended from one of these Africans and provides an easy to read, entertaining, and adequately documented study that may appeal to even the most casual readers of history and should certainly be studied by historians. Thus, the body of literature related to this subject is varied although there are questions related to this historical period that we may continue to explore

The Beginnings of the Trade

According to Pope-Hennessy, "historians have generally agreed upon the year 1441 as that in which the slave trade was, so to speak, officially declared open. In that year ten Africans from the Northern Guinea coast were shipped to Portugal as a gift to Prince Henry the Navigator."[2] Thomas, reporting on the same event, states that there were, "some black Africans, twelve in number taken to Portugal."[3] Whether ten or twelve the matter is that Portugal ushered in open the most terrifying and brutal episode of the last millennium-the trans-Atlantic slave trade. Slavery was not a new enterprise. Particularly, among Europeans who had, even up to the voyage of Columbus continued the practice that was so deeply embedded into its feudal traditions.[4] While European slavery would eventually decline, the enslavement of Africans, involving Europeans and their African captives, was expanding. These Africans, who were seized by sailors under the command of Antao Goncalves from what today would be the Northern portion of Mauritania, were not the first to be shipped to Portugal. Indeed, in 1425, fifty-three or so Africans were brought to Portugal after being seized off of a Moroccan slave ship and, "profitably disposed of in Portugal."[5] Each year thereafter, Goncalves and Nuno Tristao would set out to the West African region to procure resources (including slaves). By 1444, a Portuguese trading company was formed and another shipment of about two hundred and thirty five Africans landed in Portugal.[6] The importance of this event is that the scope and principle of the trade had changed. On the one hand, the formation of the trading company gives a clear indication that continued trade with Africa was a Portuguese necessity and on the other hand, the sheer size of the African cargo suggests that slaving would most likely be a formidable, if not dominant part of that trade. Contrast this to the earlier voyages of 1441-1443 where enslavement seemed only a secondary objective or not an objective at all. Whether or not slaving was a primary or secondary motivating factor, the year 1444 is a critical turning point in the trans-Atlantic slave trade.

Early Motives

Prince Henry the Navigator was clearly interested in slaving as evidenced after 1425.[7] Motives and intents change, though depending on circumstance and opportunity. In regards to the slave trade it seems initially that:

> In the later decades of the fifteenth century the emphasis seems to have been upon the saving of black souls by their conversion to Christianity. Their enslavement was, moreover justified by tags from the Bible, most notably the curse Noah laid upon Canaan after the flood; that his descendants should be eternally subject to all races of the world.[8]

The evidence indicates that Europeans also sought profit and conquest early on.[9] For example, David Brion Davis argues that Portugal's intentions were initially driven by a desire to trade with the Africans, particularly the Mali Empire and to "outflank" the trade across the Sahara and land, dominated by the Arabs.[10] In addition, the Portuguese (who had achieved much of its maritime advantages by copying Moorish ship designs and utilizing Genoese captains on their ships) sought to increase their military advantages thereby improving its chances of maintaining hegemony over the new burgeoning trade with Africa and in Africans.

A great myth perpetrated by some scholars is that the Europeans were so overwhelmingly dominant militarily that Africans, in a most docile fashion, accepted their fates as slaves. Thornton presents strong contrary evidence:

> The West Africans had a well developed specialized maritime culture that was fully capable of protecting its own waters.[11]

Continuing, Thornton discussed the aforementioned excursions into Africa then makes the point that, "it was not long before African naval forces were alerted to the new dangers and the Portuguese ships began to meet strong and effective resistance."[12] When Nuno Tristao, in 1446 attempted to land armed forces near the Senegambia region, he and his force were soundly defeated. The following year, the same fate befell another Portuguese force, intent upon enslaving near Goree Island. Davis also points out that Portugal in 1415 while attempting to invade lands south of the Senegal River were soundly defeated.[13]

The motives of the Portuguese were particularly religious and economic. In addition, there were those misguided by arrogance and ignorance who felt that they were going to save Africans from their so-called barbaric lifestyle by enslaving them and bringing them Portuguese culture and religion. Even though Africans had some success in engaging and repelling early Portuguese excursions, the sheer numbers of future European visits and incursions coupled with the fragmented political entities that existed in the western region of Africa (exacerbated by the growing weakness of the Mali empire) as well as the growing military prowess of Europe, made fighting enslavement particularly challenging in the future. The various political entities and rulers within Africa also found trade with Portugal and later, other European nations beneficial.

Why Black Africans?

The growth of the trans-Atlantic slave trade was preceded by failed efforts to enslave other ethno-racial groups before black Africans. Indeed, these failures coupled with the unfeasibility to enslave other groups are a fact of history. For the trans-Atlantic slave trade to grow there needed to be two things in place. There needed to be a viable economic need and a viable labor source.

The Portuguese, as aforementioned, primarily brought their captured African slaves to Portugal and on occasion, islands in the Atlantic near Africa. Due to the absence of a viable economic need, there was no necessity in trading in huge numbers of Africans. This situation changed once the Americas became economically viable. According to Klein in *The Atlantic Slave Trade*, the need for labor in the New World, "most influenced" the growth of the trade.[14] When one looks at the entire history of the trade, it seems painfully evident that, "the entire New World enterprise depended on the enormous and expandable flow of slave labor from Africa."[15] The enterprise spoken of here is the profitable plantation system that developed in the Americas from the sixteenth century onward. To reiterate the point, David Eltis, who in *The Rise of African Slavery in the Americas* stated that European colonization of the New World was pursued for economic purposes.[16] Clearly, those purposes ultimately created a desire for a viable and effective labor force to cultivate the economic opportunities. Widely available data suggests that the cultivation of the New World caused a demand for labor that had to be fulfilled. Europeans, in constant and competition among themselves as well as with the Ottomans and Chinese, needed new sources of economic growth. Once the Americas proved to be *the* source, they entered it with the utmost zeal and fervor. Despite this reality, it is often asked why Africans?

Within the region of the Americas, there were millions of indigenous inhabitants who could seemingly be utilized with much less financial investment. Europe had a long tradition of enslavement and there was, at the time of Columbus' 1492 voyage, still slavery in Europe.[17] It would seem quite practical and more sensible, from an economic standpoint, to either use existing numbers from Europe or indigenous inhabitants from the Americas. Either method would eliminate the time and arduous nature of the trade in slaves from Africa. However, like all things, what seems apparent at first glance and on face value is not always accurate. The process by which Africans became the primary and almost exclusive source of slaves during the trans-Atlantic slave trade must now be explored.

Spain, since the late 1400s had procured slaves through various Portuguese slavers and through political alliances with Portugal thus making it the second European nation to enslave blacks. These slaves were not exclusively black African but were sometimes Moors (who could have been North African in origin, light skinned Arabs or dark skinned Africans or Arabs), or in rare instances other Europeans. Claud Anderson in *Black Labor, White Wealth* notes a "gift" of Moorish slaves from King Ferdinand to the Pope in 1488.[18] In terms of the Atlantic trade, it would be the indigenous inhabitants of the Americas to serve as the first slaves in the Americas and not black Africans. To that end, Christopher Columbus, in 1493, can be attributed with another "discovery" and that is the discovery of trans-Atlantic slaving:

> Determined to show some reason for his explorations, and with gold in short supply in the Caribbean, Columbus sent back from Santo Domingo to his Florentine friend in Seville, Juanotto Berardi, associate of Marchionni, the first known cargo of slaves to cross the Atlantic: Taino Indians, and in a west-east direction.[19]

In 1496, Columbus himself brought thirty indigenous slaves to Spain and hoped to annually send back upwards of four thousand. Spanish immigrants to Hispaniola returned to Spain in 1499 with a slave each and the enslavement of the indigenous people continued as Vespucci and other Spanish explorers brought back Native slaves.[20] The conversion from indigenous slaves to black African slaves was incremental and primarily motivated by the aforementioned economic factors. Initially, the Spanish authorities were reluctant to send any black slaves from Spain to the Americas for fear of insurrection. This fear was realized when in 1502 black Africans from Spain being utilized in the Caribbean were escaping and encouraging the Natives to rebel.[21] Another reason for preventing black Africans from being taken to the Americas was their apparent need in Spain. Whatever the reasons, the justifications for *not* using black Africans began to break down slowly during the first decade of the sixteenth century. There had always been a few exceptions to the ban on "slaves born in the power of Christians" (those born in Spain or Portugal) but when a report to Ferdinand in 1511 stated that the work of one black was four times that of an indigenous worker, the die was cast.[22]

As the mines of the Caribbean, particularly Hispaniola, became more economically productive, so did the need for labor. The Spanish used brutal methods ranging from kidnapping, maiming, and murder to get the Natives to work harder. However, death, due to disease and maltreatment, caused rampant labor shortages. Ultimately, these and other political and religious interests caused Spain to abandon, "the possibility of Indian slavery."[23] For example, Bartolome de Las Casas argued for the enslavement of blacks to alleviate the suffering of the natives.[24] De Las Casas and another religious figure, the Jesuit Manuel da Nobrega, urged for and ultimately received the importation of more black Africans to spare the lives of the Natives. While these religious figures questioned the moral and legal right of enslaving the indigenous peoples, they saw no conflict in enslaving black Africans. Nobrega even went on to claim that, "the legality of black slavery had been carefully weighed in the consciences of the people."[25] By 1510, Ferdinand, after being pressured by economic interests, ordered that fifty slaves be sent to the Caribbean to alleviate the labor problems. This was augmented by a further two-hundred sent weeks later. The instructions did not specify that they be black Africans but simply that they should be the best. Yet the make-up of the slaves would no longer be in question after the 1511 report. Included in Ferdinand's 1510 orders was the regulation of the trade with those wishing to participate being required to apply for a permit. As Thomas puts it, "This was the beginning of slave traffic to the Americas. Gold in Hispaniola was the lure."[26]

As the number of Africans transported to the Americas increased, the reliance on the indigenous populations of the Americas decreased. The reasons are clear: 1) the labor of one black African was equal to that of four Native workers, 2) the Native worker was more prone to successful escape being in his own homeland, yet the opposite was true for the black African 3) the Native worker was more susceptible to disease and had a poor life span. Anderson made the point that a critical drawback in utilizing the Native against black Africans was their ability to run off and "blend into the wilderness."[27] It is painfully clear that the enslavement of the indigenous American was not viable by any stretch of the imagination given the amount of labor needed.

Joseph Inikori in his text *Africa* makes the argument that after concluding that the indigenous populations of the Americas was not a legitimate labor source, only Europeans, sub-Saharan Africans, and East Asians were left to choose from.[28] He also discusses how sub-Saharan Africans became the most viable source of captives. First, the taking of captives from Europe had become exceedingly costly, both in manpower and money. Europe had, from at least the fourteenth century onward, slowly become politically and militarily organized and the weak disorganized political systems that had characterized it in earlier centuries no longer existed. Many peoples of Europe now belonged to strong empires that had a reason to curtail the slaving of its population and protect the integrity of its borders. Once the Americas became in need of labor, many European nations, hoped that its citizenry would populate and cultivate the Americas. Instituting various incentives and engaging in such practices as indentured servitude, the states of Europe hoped that labor from Europe itself could sufficiently develop the land. Unfortunately, not enough labor came from Europe and those that came, either escaped or worked out their indentured terms and went into business for themselves. During the last decades of the eighteenth century to the first two decades of the nineteenth century, there were shipped almost six black Africans for every one European who voluntarily came to the Americas. As we look at more numbers, it seems that by the second decade of the 1800s over 8.5 million black African slaves had been shipped from Africa to the Americas as opposed to a mere 2.6 million Europeans who had left Europe for the same destination (mostly convicts and indentured servants).[29] Even the labor of Europeans itself was haphazard as many were ignorant of the skills and tools it took to cultivate the land and crops of this new region. These realities left the Americas in dire need of a consistent, knowledgeable, labor force. The use of black Africans seemed to be the most efficient and economically correct choice:

> Unlike Native Americans, most West Africans were familiar with large-scale agriculture, labor discipline, and making iron or even steel tools. They also shared with Europeans some resistance to Old World diseases.[30]

While some Europeans had practiced enslavement of East Asians following the arrival of Portugal to that region in 1498, the sheer distance between that region and the Americas and the infant capabilities of the trans oceanic fleets of the time made the mass enslavement of East Asians in the western hemisphere quite impractical.[31] In addition, the continuing albeit declining power of China made this sort of intrusion into the Chinese sphere of influence unwise. By a process of elimination, sub-Saharan Africans, particularly West Africans, became the most viable source of labor for the Americas.

Other Actors and Reasons

Economics has long been identified as the primary reason for the growth of the trans-Atlantic slave trade, primarily for the cultivation of New World lands. From that end, Europeans were the catalyst. However, there were reasons Africans continued to trade as the trade itself most likely could not have continued without the agreement, tacit or not, with African leaders. It is widely accepted that Europeans could not have intruded into the African interior or even ventured anywhere much past their fortresses on the coast had they made a significant military push. Therefore, Europeans, beginning first with the Portuguese, chose to cooperate on equal scale with the Africans.[32] From the standpoint of the Africans, many scholars contend that military hardware was the key commodity desired and an urge that produced a significant catalyst for continual trade with the Europeans. For example, Thomas quoting primary sources states, "gunpowder was also popular," and notes the desire for guns as well as alcohol.[33] Thornton disagrees saying that at least prior to 1680 European military hardware was of no real essential use to Africans.[34] Thornton makes the argument that, within reason, the wars in Africa were not economically motivated, that is for the expressed purpose of procuring slaves, but were the mechanism of natural political endeavors engineered to procure land and power. The capture of prisoners of war was just an economic by-product.[35] Historians often view Africa as a homogenous entity with common political and economic objectives. This is quite incorrect as the various states and entities had their own foreign policy objectives and did not at all view themselves as, "African." This allowed them to sell others who may have been black also but foreign in their eyes.[36] The fact that they were similar in bodily traits and color did not appeal to any sort of racial camaraderie as it did amongst Europeans. Europeans quickly took advantage of this.[37]The point being made here is that the reasons and motivations of African leaders cannot be accurately discerned due to the varying nature of African political entities. Some leaders sought military advantages over their political rivals while others wanted economic advantages. Some leaders simply carried on trade as any political entity interested in development would. The major dilemma for most of these various yet small political bodies was that very soon the Europeans would view this fragmentation as a weakness and sought to exploit it.

The Dutch soon supplanted the Portuguese as the dominant power in the trade with West Africa having begun slaving on a small scale in the 1590s.[38] After the formation of the Dutch West India Company and a variety of economic and political occurrences, the Dutch eased the Portuguese from their dominant position in the Atlantic trade system.[39] In 1637 the Dutch had attacked and captured the Portuguese fortress of Elmina and thus ended the era of Portuguese dominance of slave trading along the African coast.[40]Although the Dutch had become the significant power players in the trade, other nations of Europe had by then entered the lucrative business. In 1618, England officially entered slave trading.[41] In 1626, a French company had been formed to conduct African trade.[42] In 1649 a Swedish company, modeled after the Dutch West India Company was formed for the same and in 1651 a Danish company had been created. [43] The purpose in the formation of these companies was to establish trade relationships with Africa to attain gold, ivory, and slaves. The end objective was to stimulate and develop the economies of the New World.

By the mid-seventeenth century all of the major players in the trans-Atlantic slave trade had begun their various enterprises. Also, by the mid-seventeenth century all of them had a foothold in the New World with Spain, Portugal, France, and Britain having significant areas of influence. Over 200 years later the last reported slave ship would land in Cuba in 1867, thus ending the trans-Atlantic Slave trade, although black African slavery in the Americas would continue for another two decades in Cuba and Brazil respectively.[44]

The Numbers

Of continuing controversy in the study of the Atlantic trade is the actual numbers of Africans taken from Africa. Note that this does not include those who were captured and died while still on African soil awaiting transport but those who were actually transported. While figures vary widely, the common figure is nine to fourteen million. Walter Rodney addresses the numbers by stating:

> The truth is that any figure of Africans imported into the Americas which is narrowly based on the surviving records is bound to be low, because there were so many people who had a vested interest in smuggling slaves (and withholding data).[45]

Additionally, given the nature of the trade and that a good proportion of it was contracted and sub-contracted work across nations and languages, the possibility of fraud, mistake and out right thievery was highly probable and most likely a not so uncommon occurrence. It is widely accepted that the Spanish and in particular, Portuguese were very lax in maintaining proper records and this reality undoubtedly allowed for the crossing and/or deaths of numerous Africans whose records have been lost to history.

During the last half of the twentieth century, scholars debated the numbers and engaged in a most extraordinary discourse on exactly how many Africans had been taken from Africa's shores during the trans-Atlantic slave trade. The prevailing problem was that no exact number could possibly be attained. Joseph Inikori notes that the era of slave trading dominated by the Spanish and Portuguese is devoid of proper data and numbers. He argues that the era has been very little studied and consequently archival data much less plentiful.[46] The British whom officially entered the trade well over 100 years after both Portugal and Spain have been accepted as the most accurate record-keepers, relatively speaking, even though most of their archival data deals primarily with the eighteenth century. As such, Inikori, in various studies conducted in the 1970s and 1980s supports a figure of around 15 million. Phillip Curtin, on the other hand, had previously introduced an empirical study in 1969 based on the aforementioned British data in which he surmised the numbers to be around 11 million (given a 15% mortality rate).[47] Recent scholarship has taken into account the absence of data from the first 250 years of the trade and Curtin's numbers have been generally and almost universally adjusted upward. At the time, Curtin's figures were widely accepted in what Walter Rodney viewed as an effort by intellectual collaborators and "apologists for the capitalist system" to minimize the numbers of Africans traded in an attempt to "whitewash the European slave trade."[48] David Brion Davis, completing his study in 2006, suggests that just from the period of 1700-1880, there were approximately 9.4 million black Africans transported from Africa.[49] Again, this estimate is devoid of any effort to address the first 250 years or the obvious smuggling and such that occurred but in and of itself intrudes upon the total figure given by Curtin. Klein argues for 9.5 million exported from Africa for the period spanning 1662-1867, a figure closer to Curtin but again not inclusive of about 150 years of slaving and not taking into account the dastardly aspects spoken of earlier.[50] In a paper submitted to Yale University, James H. Sweet suggests that recent scholarship places the figure of exported slaves from Africa approximately 500,000 between 1441 and 1619.[51]Thomas, arguing for a figure of around 11 million plus or minus 500,000 gives a brief accounting and critique of the figures presented by Inikori and Curtin as well as others. Thomas presents the arguments of various scholars and makes a brief case that an exact number is not possible or even necessary.[52]

The point here is that exact figures are not possible. Since the trade was a trade in millions a margin of error of a few percentage points result in the addition or loss of hundreds of thousands. That fact alone is a testimony to how significant the trade was. For an enterprise begun in the 1400s and at its peak in the 1780s, delivering an estimated 80,000 slaves per year from Africa indicates a worldwide significant affair of mind-boggling proportions.[53] Also, as this study discusses, the function of race in the history of the world, it is interesting to note the various positions of scholars often align by race. Primarily, scholars of African descent seem to support higher figures in this regard and European descended scholars just the opposite. Additionally, race must have played a part as the most obvious aspect of the trade was that the perpetrators by far were white and the victims were black. To imagine that race is not an issue in the production, conclusion, and analysis of the data is naïve.

Growth of Slavery and the Origins of European Racism

Europeans were conscious of race as early as the fifteenth century. For example, the Portuguese often referred to blacks as "dogs" and seemed to certainly believe they were superior to blacks and that blacks may have even been a different, perhaps evil species.[54] Sweet argues that ideas of the racial inferiority of blacks had been passed from the Arabs to those of Iberia who then infused them with already developing European thoughts of racial superiority. Although Sweet concedes that there were many (and in fact vicious) religious and cultural wars among Europeans, they all, viewed themselves racially the same. Since those that they were set to encounter (the indigenous inhabitants of the Americas and Africans) were neither Christian nor European, this made them "barbaric."[55] According to Sweet, Portuguese and Spanish royal authorities commented on blacks using such terminologies as "bestial, barbaric and savage." In addition, Sweet notes that the use of "negro" in the Portuguese language of the 1500s literally meant a race of people.[56] This lends credence to the fact that the Portuguese were certainly aware of race and categorized blacks as a separate race from themselves. Given the numbers of black Africans transported to Portugal, however, the Portuguese became accustomed to and even tolerant of the "coexistence of a range of skin colors from black to white." This provides further evidence of the consciousness of race. Davis argues that this Portuguese acceptance led to a more racially mixed and most likely more racially harmonious New World colonies.[57]

Portugal was not the only European nation to have negative viewpoints regarding blacks. Certain Spanish priests, specifically one Bartolome de Las Casas believed that black Africans were "natural" slaves.[58] He must have thought that blacks were inherently inferior human beings. In England during the sixteenth century, racial and racist ideas permeated the society. Although slavery had not yet penetrated England proper, the English clearly viewed black Africans as inferior noting them to be, "beastly," and "heathen," and generally uncivilized.[59] In other areas of Europe, including Scandinavia, peasants and serfs were often depicted as subhuman and black.[60]

.   The corruption of Christian teachings, specifically the so-called, "curse of Ham" where the descendents of Ham (taught to be blacks) were to be eternal slaves, shaped racial feelings of superiority among the white Christians of Europe. Also, the fact that the Catholic Church early on sanctioned the enslavement of blacks, further fueled the belief that blacks were inferior sub-humans who needed to be saved. What is clear from these examples is that by the time the early Europeans began to conquer and enslave, slavery itself already had racial connotations.[61] Sweet notes:

> Portuguese, Spaniards and other Europeans contested the African trade, but these were little more than internecine economic and political squabbles. From a social, cultural, and philosophical perspective, all were Europeans, and all underscored their rights to enslave Africans on the grounds that theirs were "civilizing" missions.[62]

The need to civilize one would suggest that you believe them to be beneath you in every aspect. Scientists, farmers and such often seek to "civilize" animals and beasts.

The evidence suggests that Europeans, prior to and during their enslavement of Africans viewed Africans as beasts and barbarians. Later, many Europeans continued to use this "civilizing" mission as a rationale for continuing slavery often going so far as to suggest that Africans were not capable of civilization except the one the Europeans brought to them.[63]

Some scholars also contend that the decline of the Mali Empire, which coincided with the first European contacts with West Africa, undermined Portuguese respect for black Africans as equals. Felipe Fernandez-Armesto termed this a "tragedy for the history of the world" as he concluded that the Portuguese began to ponder if blacks were capable of political sophistication.[64] Fernandez-Armesto notes that shortly after this contact, depictions of the Mali Mansa (ruler) would be caricatured as an inferior and that from that point forward whites could, "nourish convictions of superiority."[65]

Further, it is equally important to consider what Davis terms the "negative connotations and symbolism of the word black in medieval Europe."[66] Black was likened to evil, demonic, satanic including other negative connotations. Depictions of dark-skinned evildoers, torturers, and servants of Satan filled western literature. This made it easier for Europeans to view blacks with suspicion at the least with the more likely perception to be one of racial dislike or hatred. The culmination of such religious teachings is the moral comfort in believing that blacks were inferior and that perhaps, even God sanctioned such belief. The negative imagery of black as evil persists in contemporary western societies. It would be pure psychological madness to conclude that Church sanctioned religious intolerance would have no bearing on the behavior of the people. Indeed, by the early 1600s most Protestant denominations taught that in this life blacks were inferior beings and simply needed to accept their fates in order to achieve salvation.[67]

Clearly, the data has demonstrated that knowledge of race, and more specifically, the differences in race became commonly accepted in Europe. Europeans were color struck early into the era of slave trading. In addition, the data supports the thesis that racism was firmly entrenched in Portugal, Spain, England and the teachings of the Catholic and Protestant Church. While these ideas seem to have been more prevalent in the Iberian and Mediterranean region, there existed racist ideas in the northern and western portions of Europe as well. The idea of race preceded black African racial slavery and therefore counters the thesis that slavery created racism. The primary factors leading to these ideas of racial superiority were the absence of Christianity among the Africans, absence of what Europeans considered "civilization," their skin color having an already existing negative connotation and misguided religious teachings. The collapse of the Mali and later Songhai empires created a political vacuum that allowed for small rudimentary polities to thrive thereby preempting any semblance of a powerful kingdom or empire to check or even impress upon the Europeans that Africans had the capability to produce large stable empires.

Colonial Virginia

Regarding racial slavery, of particular interest is the fact that the trans-Atlantic slave trade became the only exclusively race based trade in slaves in history. Prior to the enslavements of blacks, one of the largest concentrations of slaves was the Mamelukes of North Africa. The *Mamluks* were primarily white and had been enslaved by Arabs and Moors. Ultimately, however the *Mamluks* overthrew their masters and established their own Sultanate. The overthrow was so brutal and vicious as to shock the world in a manner that caused the enslavement of whites to end forever.[68] Indeed, one of the primary reasons blacks became easy prey (so to speak) was their absence of a common nationalistic identity. As discussed earlier Africans identified themselves with their local political entity and were therefore not vigilant in ending enslavement of others whom Europeans viewed as black. Therefore, black racial slavery was able to rise and thrive absent of an African conceptualization of a "black" slavery.

Racial slavery in colonial America most likely has its roots in the aforementioned religious, social, and cultural racism that existed in Europe since medieval times. Further, some of the west's most revered Enlightenment thinkers were vicious racists. Both David Hume and Voltaire viewed blacks as intellectually inferior and questioned their humanity.[69] To a follower of Enlightenment thought these ideas would most assuredly seem attractive. Thomas Jefferson, for example, wrote that blacks were both physically and intellectually inferior to whites.[70] Jefferson's attitude was not unique to his eighteenth century contemporaries who had all grown up in a society in which the black African was viewed as inherently inferior is mind, body, and even spirit. Interestingly and hypocritically thought, Jefferson took great pleasure, as did many, of his other racist contemporaries, in sexual escapades with black African women. How on the one hand can you view a person as sub-human then in the next hand lay down with them to perform the very function of procreation?

As the colony of Virginia began to develop in the early 1600s, it has been argued that black and white laborers existed on equal footing. The first Africans, arriving on a pirated ship in 1619, were deposited to a struggling colony of half starved, unproductive English. It has been widely studied and reported that both black and white servants were not initially slaves but indentured servants and after fulfilling their contracts could leave.[71] This would no doubt be indicative of a system of servitude that was not based on race. Indeed, it was not uncommon to view English, Irish, and black African servants laboring and toiling side by side indistinguishable except by shade and color.[72] Anthony Johnson, probably the most discussed black African of colonial Virginia began as a servant, became free and eventually owned his own land and black and white servants![73] He also enjoyed such privileges as suing whites in court and other blacks and whites of the era routinely intermarried and lived among each other (quite interesting considering as recent as fifty years ago blacks in the southern US generally could not even testify in court against whites). By 1640, however, it became clear that racism and racial slavery was set to begin. In that year, three runaway servants were sentenced for their crime. Two were given extended service sentences, the third, a black man named John Punch was sentenced to serve, "for the time of his natural life."[74] The only difference between Punch and the others was skin color. There was no other compelling reason as to why Punch should have been made to serve for life. Some scholars contend that his sentence was imposed because he presumably was not Christian but the court cited Punch's race in the justification of his sentence thereby making it quite clear that race played a significant part of his sentence of lifelong servitude.[75] Later, in 1665 that same Anthony Johnson had his land stripped from him because he was black and that fact, the Virginia jury decided, made him, "an alien."[76] By the late 1600s, it became clear that blacks were on the road to permanent enslavement based on skin color.[77] The degradation of the black African was solidified when the Virginia General Assembly essentially declared in 1705 that blacks were the legal property (real estate) of whites and could be dealt with as such.[78] The era of black and white "equal" servitude was over.

But was there ever an era of equality in British North America? The 1628 will of Jamestown Governor Yeardley prominently distinguishes his "negars" from servants. The dates indicate that his "negars" had been held at least two years longer than the usual three to seven year period an indentured servant would serve. Later, in 1653 two young African girls aged ten and twelve were sold. This is three and five years respectively past the service years for an indentured servant.[79] This gives further evidence that some of the early Jamestown colonists may have viewed black Africans as chattel slaves rather than servants. From this evidence we can conclude that while some English in colonial America may have used the labor system as an economic system and chose their laborers regardless of race, there seems to be those that from the outset viewed Africans as natural slaves and therefore subscribed to the theory of racial slavery.

Growth of Racial Slavery: Economic Considerations

The prevailing theme in the study of racism and the slave trade has been to lay the blame for racism on the need for labor and hence racism on economics. Yet the evidence presented here and the volume of evidence out there begs for continued study and perhaps an acceptance that it was neither exclusively racism before slavery or slavery before racism but a combination of both. Eric Williams, the Trinidadian scholar who later became Prime Minister of the island, said in his landmark study, *Capitalism and Slavery*, "slavery was not born of racism: rather racism was the consequence of slavery."[80] This argument is old. Brinkley catalogues the debate from the 1950's in which the Handlin article concedes the uniqueness of black African racial slavery but concludes that it was done in an effort to increase the labor force. Citing the unavailability of the numbers of voluntary workers from Europe, Africans were viewed as an exploitable group that had no voice to speak for them. Later, scholars agreed arguing that the arduous nature of rice and tobacco cultivation and the fact that west and central Africans were accustomed to the climate and certain crops, made them ideal laborers. Yet despite the economic need in the Americas, it was hard for some scholars to ignore the blatant racism that Europeans came to America with.[81]

Given the vast numbers of laborers in the Chesapeake region in the seventeenth century, both black and white, the possibility of class rebellion struck fear in the hearts of the newly rich landowners of Virginia and Maryland. By 1676 there was an estimated 1,500 bond-laborers from Europe arriving annually to Virginia and there was great worry that they would join in a class struggle with black Africans.[82] These fears were realized that same year when thousands of black, white, and indigenous laborers united in what history would call Bacon's rebellion. In the aftermath of the rebellion, concerned politicians and landowners sought to prevent another one of these unified uprisings by passing laws to enforce racial segregation. Many of these laws were designed to create a sense of unity among whites that even the most menial laborer would feel more camaraderie with a rich white landowner than his fellow black laborer in the field. In fact, the laws created a feeling of privilege among the whites; that they belonged to a race higher and more sophisticated than the blacks. The concurrent racial slave system that was developing began to create a feeling of race consciousness and racism the depths of which had not been seen thus far in this region. Theodore Allen in *The Invention of the White Race* says this:

> The prospects for stability of a system of capitalist agriculture based on lifetime hereditary bond-servitude depended on the ability of the ruling elite to induce the non-"yeoman" European-Americans to settle for this counterfeit of social mobility. The solution was to establish a new birthright not only for Anglos

but for every Euro-American, the "white" identity that "set them at a distance",...from the laboring class African-Americans, and enlisted them as active, or at least passive, supporters of lifetime bondage of African-Americans.[83]

Allen continues this discourse arguing that in order to prevent a replica of Bacon's rebellion, (that is the unification of poor classes of blacks and whites), that racism was injected. This racism would, "separate dangerous free whites from dangerous slave blacks by a screen of racial contempt."[84] It is no fantasy that the unification of the laborers shook the ruling elites to the core and that unification represented a dangerous and significant threat to the economic situation, not only in colonial Virginia but also England. Allen's argument, as well as Eric Williams' and Robin Blackburn's are that economics played a powerful role in the development of racial slavery.

Conclusion

The evidence demonstrates that anti-black racism existed prior to Europeans' enslavement of black Africans. The evidence also allows for one to deduce that slavery helped to exacerbate racism. Once the power/powerless, master/slave relationship was established, the maintenance of power took precedent over all other considerations and the easiest most exploitable way to maintain power was to create an illusion of division between the poor classes that would persist uninterrupted for almost half a millennium. The way in which this was done was to create a system of institutionalized racism. This system of institutionalized racism continues today all over the world but particularly in the western hemisphere-seeks to perpetuate the old power/powerless, master/slave system. The contemporary version of this system serves corporate CEO's rather than landowners, and multi-national corporations rather than slave trading companies. The contemporary system of servitude and the face of oppression and enslavement are masked behind deficient education and labor systems and a sophisticated prison industrial complex.

Slavery in the western hemisphere did not end through a moral awakening on part of whites. It was likely that if not for economic, political and foreign policy differences among the major nations of Europe and the clashes that ensued, that slavery may have indeed continued into the 1900s.[85] Certainly, this fact suggests that the economic benefits of the system were still potent but also-racism and white supremacy remained. The fact that in the United States of America blacks are still disproportionately incarcerated, mis-educated, unemployed, and under employed, can almost certainly be traced to the ramifications of slavery and the brute reality of racism and its institutional components. The legacies of slavery continue to pounce upon the descendants of slaves like the whip of old. Conservative pundits, will in subtle and not so subtle fashion, suggest that there is an innate lack of work ethic, perhaps intelligence or even that there is a superior white work ethic and intellect that is the reason for these disproportionate realities.

Anderson argues that slavery was economic exploitation that specifically targeted blacks and created horrible disparities between blacks and whites.[86] Indeed America is, "indebted to the appalling sacrifices of millions of individual blacks who cleared the forests and tilled the soil."[87] That America owes the descendants of those free laborers a deep debt of gratitude is an understatement yet all they get and have gotten is a level of scorn, maltreatment and contempt not fit for the most un-American enemy. The bottom line is that blacks in America need to develop the unified identity that has so eluded them for eternity. People of African descent in America need unified, cooperative, economic programs in order to develop, build and maintain institutional systems of nation building. Systems that would include proper education, social programs and economic ventures are of a great necessity to this community. Such institutions would work toward destroying the walls of economic, social, and educational oppression. Racism and self hatred (an affliction found in many people of African descent) is a psychological disorder embedded in the minds of people that is multigenerational. This disorder took hundreds of years to produce and may take even more time to eliminate. Only patience, revolutionary action, and plain truth will do that.

Notes

1. James Pope Hennessy, *Sins of the Fathers: The Atlantic Slave Traders 1441-1807* (Edison, NJ; Castle Books, 2004), 4.
2. Ibid, 8.
3. Hugh Thomas, *The Slave Trade The Story of the Atlantic Slave Trade: 1440-1870* (New York: Touchstone, 1997), 54.
4. Herbert S. Klein, *The Atlantic Slave Trade* (Cambridge, MA; Cambridge University Press, 1999), 1
5. Thomas, 55.
6. Hennessy, 8.
7. Thomas, 55.
8. Hennessy, 9.
9. John Thornton, *Africa and Africans in the Making of the Atlantic World, 1400-1800* (Cambridge, MA; Cambridge University Press, 1998), 36.
10. David Brion Davis, *Inhuman Bondage: The Rise and Fall of Slavery in the New World* (New York, NY: Oxford University Press, 2006), 84
11. Thornton,, 37.
12. Ibid.
13. Davis,, 88
14. Klein, 18.
15. Davis,, 80.
16. David Eltis, *The Rise of African Slavery in the Americas* (Cambridge, MA; Cambridge University Press, 2000), 58.
17. Klein,, 1.
18. Claud Anderson, *Black Labor White Wealth: The Search for Power and Economic Justice* (Bethesda, MD; PowerNomics Corporation of America, 1994), 71.
19. Thomas,, 89.

201. Ibid, 89-90.
21. Ibid, 91.
22. Ibid, 92.
23. Klein,, 18.
24. Anderson,, 71
25. Davis,, 98.
26. Thomas,, 92-93.
27. Anderson,, 79.
28. Joseph Inikori, "Africa and the Trans-Atlantic Slave Trade," in *Africa Volume 1: African History Before 1885* ed. Toyin Falola (Durham, NC; Carolina Academic Press, 2003), 390.
29. Davis,, 80.
30. Ibid, 99.
31. Inikori,, 390.
32. Davis,, 88.
33. Thomas,, 326-327.
34. Thornton,, 99.
35. Ibid, 100.
36. Inikori,, 391.
37. Davis,, 88.
38. Thomas,, 160.
39 Adebayo Oyebade, "Euro-African Relations to 1885," *in Africa Volume 1: African History Before 1885* ed. Toyin Falola, (Durham, NC; Carolina Academic Press, 2003), 421.
40 . Thomas,, 171.
41 . Anderson,, 73
42. Thomas,, 172-173.
43. Ibid, 222-223.
44. Klein,, 192.
45. Inikori, 399-400.
46. Ibid, 406.
47. Ibid, 405.
48. Ibid, 399.
49. Davis,, 93.
50. Klein,, 208-209.
51. James H. Sweet, "Spanish and Portuguese Influences on Racial Slavery in British North America, 1492-1619" (paper presented at the proceedings of the fifth Annual Gilder, Lehrman Center International Conference at Yale University, New Haven, Connecticut, November 7-8, 2003).
52. Thomas,, 861-862.
53. Klein,, 193.
54. Davis,, 94.
55. Sweet, 2003).
56. Ibid.
57. Davis,, 79.
58. Eltis,, 15.
59. Sweet, 2003).
60. Davis,, 50-51.
61. Ibid, 73.
62. Sweet, 2003.

63. Mercator Honestus, *A Defense of the African Slave Trade. 1740,* ed. Robert O. Collins (Princeton: Markus Wiener Publishers, 2001), 135-136.
64. Felipe Fernandez-Armesto, *The World: A History* (Upper Saddle River, NJ: Pearson/Prentice Hall, 2007), 486.
65. Ibid.
66. Davis,, 79.
67. Anderson, 73.
68. Chancellor Williams, *The Destruction of Black Civilization: Great Issues of A Race From 4500 BC to 2000 AD* (Chicago: Third World Press, 1976), 162.
69. Davis,, 75.
70. Ibid, 74.
71. Public Broadcast System, "From Indentured Servitude to Racial Slavery" http//www.pbs.org/wgbh/aia/part1/1narr3_txt.html.
72. Ira Berlin, *Many Thousands Gone: The First Two Centuries of Slavery in North America* (Cambridge: Belknap Press of Harvard University Press, 1998), 29.
73. Tim Hashaw, *The Birth of Black America: The First African Americans and the Pursuit of Freedom at Jamestown* (New York: Carroll & Graf Publishers, 2007), 214.
74. Ibid.
75. Theodore W. Allen, *The Invention of the White Race Volume Two: The Origin of Racial Oppression in Anglo-America* (London: Verso, 1997), 178-179.
76. Public Broadcast System, "From Indentured Servitude to Racial Slavery" http//www.pbs.org/wgbh/aia/part1/1narr3_txt.html.
77. Alan Brinkley, *The Unfinished Nation: A Concise History of the American People* (New York: McGraw-Hill, 2004), 65.
78. Public Broadcast System, "From Indentured Servitude to Racial Slavery" http//www.pbs.org/wgbh/aia/part1/1narr3_txt.html.
79. Hashaw, 104-105.
80. Matt Wrack, "Slavery and the Rise of Capitalism," review of *The Making of New World Slavery: From Baroque to the Modern, 1492-1800* by Robin Blackburn.
81. Brinkley,, 66.
82. Allen,, 119.
83. Ibid, 248.
84. Ibid, 249.
85. Klein,, 202.
86. Anderson,, 73
87. Davis, 102.

References

Allen, Theodore W. *The Invention of the White Race Volume Two: The Origin of Racial Oppression in Anglo-America.* London: Verso, 1997.

Anderson, Claud. *Black Labor White Wealth: The Search for Power and Economic Justice.* Bethesda: Power Nomics Corporation of America, 1994.

Berlin, Ira. *Many Thousands Gone: The First Two Centuries of Slavery in North America.* Cambridge: Belknap Press of Harvard University Press, 1998.

Brinkley, Alan. *The Unfinished Nation: A Concise History of the American People.* New York: McGraw-Hill, 2004.

Davis, David Brion. *Inhuman Bondage: The Rise and Fall of Slavery in the New World.* New York: Oxford University Press, 2006.

Eltis, David. *The Rise of African Slavery in the Americas.* Cambridge: Cambridge University Press, 2000.

Fernandez-Armesto, Felipe. *The World: A History.* Upper Saddle River: Prentice Hall, 2007.

Hashaw, Tim. *The Birth of Black America: The First African Americans and the Pursuit of Freedom at Jamestown.* New York: Carroll & Graf Publishers, 2007.

Hennessy, James Pope. *Sins of the Fathers: The Atlantic Slave Traders 1441-1807.* Edison, NJ: Castle Books, 2004.

Honestus, Mercator. "A Defense of the African Slave Trade. 1740." In *Documents From the African Past,* ed. Robert O. Collins. Princeton: Markus Wiener Publishers, 2001.

Inikori, Joseph. "Africa and the Trans-Atlantic Slave Trade." In *Africa Volume 1: African History Before 1885,* ed., Toyin Falola. Durham: Carolina Academic Press, 2003.

Klein, Herbert S. *The Atlantic Slave Trade.* Cambridge: Cambridge University Press, 1999.

Oyebade, Adebayo. "Euro-African Relations to 1885." In *Africa Volume I: African History Before 188,* ed., Toyin Falola. Durham: Carolina Academic Press, 2003.

Public Broadcast System, "From Indentured Servitude to Racial Slavery" http://www.pbs.org/wgbh/aia/part1/1narr3_txt.html (accessed October 5, 2007).Sweet, James. "Spanish and Portuguese Influences on Racial Slavery in British North America, 1492-1619." Paper presented at the proceedings of the Fifth Annual Gilder, Lehrman Center International Conference at Yale University, New Haven Connecticut, November 7-8, 2003.

Thomas, Hugh. *The Slave Trade The Story of the Atlantic Slave Trade: 1440-1870.* New York: Touchstone, 1997.

Thornton, John. *African and Africans in the Making of the Atlantic World, 1400-1800.* Cambridge: Cambridge University Press, 1998.

Williams, Chancellor. *The Destruction of Black Civilization: Great Issues of a Race 4500 BC to 2000 AD.* Chicago: Third World Press, 1976.

Wrack, Matt. "Slavery and the Rise of Capitalism." Review of Robin Blackburn, *The Making of New World Slavery: From Baroque to the Modern, 1492-1800.*London: Verso, 1998.

Chapter 7

The Yellow Lady: Mulatto Women in the Suriname Plantocracy

Hilde Neus

Suriname, a former Dutch colony on the northern coast of South America, as one of the three Guianas, belongs to the Caribbean circumference within the context of the Atlantic World. Established as a British property in 1651 by Lord Francis Willoughby, count of Parham and Governor to Barbados, it was conquered by the Dutch in 1667. In that same year, the signing of the Peace Treaty of Breda took place and Suriname was considered a Dutch colony. From the time of colonization, European planters brought African enslaved people to the Caribbean to replace the Amerindians who, susceptible to imported infectious diseases, were unsuitable to work the plantations. In the Antebellum America's, the divide between black and white people was enormous. In most of the Caribbean however (and thus Suriname as well), the situation was totally different due to demographic figures. Creolization resulted in a new, typical Suriname society with its own specific cultural spaces.

The mulattoes born out of unions between black women and white men were able to develop their own room in society and sustain their own cultural routines. During the entire period of the formation of Plantation society in America slaves, especially mulattoes, were manumitted and set free. Two thirds of these were women. In former research, certainly in the case of Suriname, women were hardly acknowledged as a group of importance and very little special attention was paid to them. It is argued in this chapter that, by rereading old texts and placing colored (or 'yellow') women within the center of this research, it is possible to show that they were able to determine their own life quality to a great extent and construct their dignity by their own means, even in pre abolition times. This makes Suriname a good exemplary case of a three class society. In introducing and rereading contemporary literature, discussing the marriage laws and the day to day situation of reality –and a myth- this article will show that Suriname's society was much more mingled than previously accepted. Although the colonizers were certainly color struck, a strict color line was certainly not a rigid fundamental in this Dutch colony.

Introduction

The Yellow lady

A woman who minds virtues and watches her plights
Out of sheer joy might sing a song now and then
Plays the clavichord and some times dances gracefully
To replenish the tired brain of her man

Who is decisive in household and clean kitchen laws
Despises squanderers and saves her fees
But gives freely to those in need who ask
And to all matters with scrutiny sees

Who is nevertheless despised, envied and talked about
By malicious gossip hurt in honor out loud
By ill will called non virtuous or mellow

Because ... my tongue halts, abhorrence is my part
I have to speak out, so all know from the start
This good woman, instead of being white, was yellow

Hendrik Schouten, a famed member of the white elite in Suriname, wrote this poem in 1785.[1] He primarily wrote poetry that reflected on society with a tongue in cheek sarcasm, published in the collections of the Poets Society *'Surinaamsche lettervrinden'* (1783-1785). Hendrik married the beautiful mulatto Suzanna Johanna Hanssen in 1772.[2] She was a well-educated girl and niece of Elisabeth Samson. It was not uncommon for white men to marry mulatto women. Elisabeth's colored half sister Maria wedded the Swiss, Pierre Mivela in 1714. For black women, it was an altogether different case. And Elisabeth was black, born free in 1715. After a lot of opposition from the planter government in Suriname and letter writing to the societal authorities in the Netherlands, she was the first black woman allowed to marry a white man in Paramaribo in 1776. This marriage caused a lot of upheaval. The council in Suriname feared precedence to this case leading to marriages between black men and white women.[3] It was quite customary for planters to form liaisons with mulatto women and sometimes even marry them.[4] Even these marriages were not fully accepted socially, as shown in the above poem. And this is the imagery most people have of Suriname's society, although by rereading old texts and placing them into context, we will be able to conclude that the reality was much more nuanced.

Marriage Laws

In Suriname, the first marriage act, drawn by Governor C. Van Aerssen van Sommelsdijck in 1686, stipulates clearly that any sexual contact between whites and non-whites was forbidden.[5] White men were not to commit 'fleshly conversation' with black or free Amerindian women on punishment of two pounds of sugar. This placard was repeatedly published (in 1725, 1749 and 1761) but it remained a dead letter. As Goslinga states:

> The institution of concubinage nicely filled the gap in the absence of a sufficient number of white women and satisfied the sexual urges of the promiscuous white male to a large extent.[6]

The number of mulatto children born also proves this point. In this respect, the relations were always consummated between a white male and (initially) a black female. Already in 1738, when the first census was taken, there were 598 colored frees in Suriname, against 2037 whites. The colored children born in slavery were not even counted back then.[7] A later figure of 1830 presents 3941 colored free persons against 1206 colored slaves, on a total population of 56.463.[8] Only in 1784 a law was passed in which interracial relations were accepted officially, unless they caused upheaval at the plantations. By 1817 this article was completely stricken from the judicial records.[9] Official marriages, by law or church, were restricted to free people. Slaves were forbidden to marry; nor was marriage allowed if one of the partners was a free person.[10] In fact, the governor had to grant permission for a marriage and all the conditions, dictated by law, had to be fulfilled. Foreigners had to hand over sufficient proof that there were no objections to be expected from their countries of origin.[11]

Sexual contact between black men and white women was strictly forbidden. Early on in the stature of the colony, Governor De Gooijer wrote a special law on January 28, 1711 because, "To our large regret we have experienced that some female persons have not abstained from fleshly conversation with the Negroes whilst these are cases of the utmost shame to the entire colony." This law was based on two incidents. First, Judith de Castre had gotten pregnant by a black male. Second, Barend Roelofs requested divorce from his wife Maria Keijser because she bore a little mulatto girl after having lain with a Negro. To prevent these unnatural "whorings and adulteries" in the future it was stipulated that an unmarried white woman, caught in the act was to be flogged and banned from the colony for life. In case she was married, she would receive an additional branding. The black man involved, would be killed without any consideration, in any case. To make sure that everybody was informed about this law, it was published widely and read at all plantations.[12] Just one other case (1730) has been quoted, but it is not quite clear if a black or Amerindian man was involved, since he was called Jantje the Indian. This slave of Jacob Aron Polack was caught in having an affair with the daughter of Levy Hartogh, Ganna. Jantje was hanged by the gallows and Ganna was banned from the colony after being flogged.[13] One of the reasons why many officials rejected the marriage between the black free Elisabeth Samson and a white man was, so they argued in court, "to prevent this union to lead to being an example for black men to marry white women. And this, the Council considered to be "naturally incestuous."[14]

Some people in Suriname did protest against these strict miscegenation laws. For instance, Reverend Kals, who arrived in the colony in 1731, was known for his difficult behavior. He proposed a harmonious and equal partnership between whites and coloreds. He agitated against unlawful cohabitation and adultery. Kals suggested, in order to end this sinful behavior, "equally to give her daughters in marriage and their sons as brothers in-law, so you too, will be able to share the land lawfully amongst each other."[15] He approved of legal ties, disregarding the ethnicity of either the female or male partner. The government did not take Kals' advice seriously. On the contrary, they got so tired of his ranting, that they removed him from office and banned him from the colony two years later. Interestingly enough, when compared to the marriage situation in Barbados or the Antebellum American states these laws were not so much drawn upon racial grounds but on ratio. In the English territories, a marriage between a black man and a white woman was initially allowed, but later the law restricted these alliances.[16] The reason for this was the fact that children born from free white women were automatically free. This meant that patriarchy did not have instant control anymore over the births of free colored children.[17]

The first census in Suriname indicates separate figures for men and women was held in 1830. There were 766 men living in Paramaribo, the main town, against 545 women. For the districts the balance was even more uneven. On the plantations were 500 men against 37 women. In total, the entire country had a surplus of 684 white males.[18] One could say there was one woman to every five men. Previously, these figures were probably even more dramatic. The amount of 11% of white plantation mistresses in 1729 declined to 6% in 1752. These figures were drawn from tax lists since, for every person at the plantation, the owner had to pay a yearly tax (hoofdgeld).[19] At least half of the European planters probably arrived without a wife. Soldiers and poor adventurers always came without relatives. Suriname was not a colony to attract females from Europe, especially single ones. The Netherlands did not have a policy to send indentured laborers to Suriname, like Britain did to Barbados.

The Dutch East India (now Indonesia) was however initially a somewhat different case. The VOC (United East India Company) challenged women to migrate in however small numbers. Already in 1622, six impoverished young girls were shipped to East India and signed to stay for at least five years. This undertaking did not have an active follow up: the costs of transport were too high; the women were too much attached to Holland and would eventually just keep the men from staying on their posts. The final argument was that white children were not suited to the climate.[20] In Suriname active import of white women never materialized.

Manumission Laws

From the beginning of the settlement of the colony, there has been manumission: the freeing of individual people who lived in slavery.[21] The first mentioning of freed slaves was in a notification, published on March 12, 1670. Act Three of this law states that all Negroes who received freedom from their patrons should hire themselves out. Otherwise, flooging would be their punishment. In regard to manumission, however, the first law was published in July 1733, repeated in 1741, and again with slight changes in 1761.[22] Several state legislatures passed restrictions on free Negroes and coloreds over the entire period of slavery. During the initial period of colonization, any white owner could free any slave he chose to manumit. With the passing of the 1733 law on this subject, the rule became much stricter. It stipulated that owners were only allowed to free a slave after receiving permission from the colonial authorities, under the guarantee that the freed man should be able to earn his own keep for the rest of his life, and the government was never to carry any responsibility to provide for them if they were not able to do so themselves. Master and slave were obliged to support each other in the future, in case of need. Free people of color were not eligible for poor relief. They would lose their freedom and become slaves again, thus taken care of by their owner. Some people gained their freedom but returned to their master or mistress to bid them to keep them as slaves again, because they could not fend for themselves properly. These rules and regulations clearly mark the ambivalent position of the slaves: they were objects (property) and subjects (individuals) at the same time.[23]

The practice of manumission in Suriname was different from the one in Curaçao.[24] In Curaçao, planters were not required to receive permission and pay the government a manumission fee. As a result, the rate superseded that of Suriname by far. In Suriname, freed people had to be in possession of their manumission letter at all times and were not allowed to walk the streets after nine o'clock at night. Creditors were not allowed to free slaves who belonged to someone else, to make up for financial losses. The notification of 1743 pointed out that in regular cases free mulattoes were equal to whites by law. They had gained the rights to testify against and inherit from whites.

Freed people enjoyed the same rights as free born: full legal equality. In practice, this turned out to be a far cry from reality. Governor Mauritius issued a notification stating that manumitted persons were forbidden to commit insolences against the whites. They would be considered as slaves if not paying enough respect to any white person or not keeping negroes from acting so. They were instructed especially not to disrespect their previous owners. The governor wrote in his journal on July 9, 1743 that it had come to his notice that this stipulation was misinterpreted and misused. He claimed the free colored were insulted and badly mistreated while naming the concrete example of a certain Wilfort, who hit a mulatto clerk because he did not raise his hat quickly enough. As a result, in the same year the governor was obliged to warn the white population not to tread upon the rights of free colored people, not to hit them and mistreat them, especially not in public places.

Because of the large number of manumitted people, at a certain point the planters in the Political Council (the highest ruling board in the Suriname government) decided that freed people were not allowed to run for Council. This position was restricted only to free born and baptized people. By 1788, the amount of taxes the owner was obliged to pay was one hundred guilders for manumitting men older than fourteen years of age. For women, it was fifty guilders. By the end of the eighteenth century, the number of manumitted people had risen enormously and the government decided to obstruct this in 1804 by increasing the figures to 500 guilders fee for men and women and 250 for children under the age of fourteen. It was also decided that the previous owner needed to pay a guarantee of 2000 guilders if any freed person wanted to leave the country. It happened once. So, often they (ex-slaves) accompanied their former masters as traveling companion.

Previous to 1832, there are no exact figures on the number of people manumitted. Research on this subject was quite hampered by the scattered information.[25] In that same year however, a law was passed which stated that all free people had to adopt a Christian name, and since the implementation all were officially registered. As soon as the free population became a threat to the whites we see efforts to a debasement of their legal status by creating restrictive new laws. The free colored had their own social hierarchies and specific nomenclature to account for their varied racial origins. Once they became free they were expected to assimilate the forms of behavior directed to them. But as we know, thinking is free, and probably by abiding by the etiquette many wore a mask to hide what they truly felt. According to Doyle, on manumission a slave acquired a fixed legal status. But the definition of his social status, both by himself and by others, remained a problem.[26] Some researchers claim that the government was constantly trying to regulate the freedom of slaves, but this seems contrary to the numbers of manumittees.[27] When concluded that in Suriname not many slaves were freed, this figure is in comparison to the number of slaves, not to the number of whites. Already in 1738, free colored and their offspring made 22% of the total free population.[28] By 1800, their numbers had surpassed those of the whites living in the colony.

A Three-Caste Society

As we have seen, there was a large imbalance between the amount of white men and white women during slavery times in Suriname. The process of amalgamation happens more rapidly where society is most accessible and mobile, as Fitchett states.[29] He also thinks that slaves who are most able to make a claim upon the white master have the best chance of escaping the most negative effects of the system. Most importantly, Fitchett thinks that children born from a mix of high and low class parents tend to occupy an intermediate position. Similar types tend to develop relationships that encourage the growth of a new ethnic type. Even though the amount of women among the slave population never succeeded 40 %, two-thirds of the freed slaves were women. At the beginning of colonial times these were mostly black women; in later years there were more mulattoes.[30] Slave women learned early the value of sexual ties with European men and sometimes aggressively sought them.[31] The reason for this was that they had a much larger chance to be manumitted than black women, simply because they had more opportunities to form relationships with white males and, as a result, bear them children. Household and domestic service tended to be areas of life bound up most closely with kinship and family affairs. Mulattoes were chosen to perform household duties because, according to a number of whites, they were more susceptible to improvement and could handle tasks requiring higher capabilities. From plantation inventories it is also obvious they were priced at a higher rate. Some of the slaves held an irrevocable claim upon their masters either because of close kinship relations or on account of sentimental attachment or due to meritorious services, which warranted recognition.[32]

All these criteria are applicable to the demographics of Suriname population. Paramaribo, as an urban port context, provided most opportunities for colored women to meet white men. Cities contain a far greater proportion of mulatto slaves and freedmen than most plantation districts.[33] In Curaçao, a free port and also a Dutch territory, any man who married on the island was considered a full citizen. So it was not at all uncommon for white males in Curaçao to marry a mulatto woman.[34] This was not the case for Suriname where only a few couples were officially married. These belonged to the upper class. For instance, plantation directors were forbidden to marry. If they did anyhow, this resulted in their discharge.[35] These policies led to the fact that most white men lived together with a housekeeper (huishoudster), a woman of color as opposed to a housewife (huisvrouw), mostly a white woman to whom the man was officially married. Concubinage of a white male and a colored female acquired the semi-official term of 'Suriname marriage' (Surinaams huwelijk).[36] These colored concubines were called "Missies." An alliance with a white male, represented upward mobility in both economic and racial status for free women of color.

Some people were avertedly against the institution of the "Suriname marriage" and its natural consequences: amalgamation and the development of a mixed-blood group. A few contemporary authors were passers by; a few of them stayed a long term. Their opinions vary, but not so much according to the duration of the time they spent in Suriname. Teenstra (1842) called the colored "arrogant, haughty, conceited, lazy and insolent."[37] Fermin was much more positive; he praised their strength and vigor and claimed they were "industrious, alert and hard working. They learn quickly and apply their knowledge skillfully. They have a tenacity bordering on temerity."[38] Von Sack, a Prussian baron who visited Suriname in 1821, states, "One often prefers a woman of color; and though these seem to be of happy character, her company can just be favorable to her gentleman." Von Sack paints a favorable picture of these women, "The persons of color, who were born here, almost have the same constitution as those who descend from European parents, and are good looking. The women distinguish themselves by a beautiful figure and teeth; but the dark color of their skin robs them of the rosy hue on their cheeks, their hair is curly. The 'mestiezen,' born from a European father and a mulatto woman are a grade further from the Negroes and often so white, they cannot be distinguished from the Europeans. The 'quarteroons' are one grade closer to the Europeans and are their equals, the laws provided them with the same rights. They are by nature very lively and witty and, as one says, they are very generous in showing their affection."[39]

The military lieutenant JHN published a book on his stay in Suriname in 1840. In this text, he complained about the cruel practice of some directors or 'blankofficiers' (drivers) who are seldom married. They choose a housekeeper from among the slave women at the plantation. Sometimes they have children with black women and depart for Holland, leaving their colored offspring behind as slaves. He himself seems choosey, "Refusing to follow the example of most of the officers to take a house keeper, I hired a young negro fellow, who was offered to me, and seemed very suitable."[40] These descriptions were prone to be favored by abolitionists and adopted by them, referring to the supposed physical attractiveness and high intelligence of the mulattoes, making the acceptance of black people as equals a step closer.

In America, society was divided in black and white. It seems that under the influence of black movies and literature the burden of proof amongst Suriname internalization of facts has tended to apply American racial situations to our society.[41] Apparently the miscegenation taboo made interracial marriage a rare phenomenon in the United States in the twentieth century, whilst the attitudes and values toward mixed racial families, ranging from the racial openness that was an essential element of the Afro-Creole and Creole cultures that for instance developed in eighteenth century Louisiana.[42] As a counter example we can look at Montserrat. The white population halved between 1805 and 1822 while the free colored population grew by 274% to outnumber it. Similar changes occurred in Jamaica and Barbados, but white oligarchy in Montserrat stubbornly excluded free persons of color and did not recruit them as allies against the slave majority. At the same time, adult women outnumbered white men in Montserrat during the entire period, but few white children were born.[43]

Ten Hove and Dragtenstein state in their study on Suriname manumission that the color line was fundamental for Suriname society, "On this, all social, economic and political structures were based." Of course color was important. It was for instance stated by law (1732) that free Negroes and mulattoe's were only allowed to marry a free person of equal color. [44] This law could however not be upheld because the majority of mulatto women chose a white partner. As a result, most colored men had black partners. The law in which a manumitted person was forbidden to wed a non-free person could not be practiced and was banned in 1763. The importance of skin color was evident, but not an all deciding fact of life. We will see that Suriname society was more of a continuum, from lily white to black. Slaves were brought straight from Africa (being called "zoutwaternegers": salt water Negroes) until the time the slave trade was abolished in Suriname in 1807.[45] In between the extremities there was a whole range of people of different color, class, and position in the daily life of

Suriname. Or, as Hoogbergen and Ten Hove stated, a lot of white people lived in Suriname, who in other parts of America would be classified as black.[46]

Daily Life in Paramaribo

From the early days of colonization, white men mingled with black and colored women. Even though some research points out that these relationships only established towards the end of the eighteenth century, they started much earlier.[47] Already in 1750, Governor Mauricius wrote in his journals about the union between a plantation director, Willem Ouwater, and a widow, Anna Julien, an older mulatto woman. Anna had two daughters from a previous marriage with Hendrik Buys. She must have been very rich, owning several houses in the town of Paramaribo and at least four plantations. Elisabeth, Anna's daughter, married Isaac Stolkert. Widowed in 1766, Elisabeth remarried Jan Nepveu, soon to hold the highest position in the colony. He became governor in 1770.[48] Elisabeth's son, Frederic Cornelis Stolkert, became, as a 'light' colored person, a member of the Political Council. He was married to the infamous plantation mistress Susanna du Plessis, of whom we will speak later.

Governor Wichers, who as Governor ruled the colony from 1784 until 1790, played an important role in the acceptance of the rising societal position of the mulatto population. He wrote in 1784, "The females [. . .] because of their association with whites, imbibe the latter's prejudices; they consider whites as infinitely superior and coloreds as being of somewhat lower order, preferring to live a life of wantonness with the former to confining themselves to the letter in the narrow circle of conjugal love."[49] Van Lier concluded, "It seems that the free people of class considered it demeaning to marry beneath their own stature."[50] Wichers consciously pursued a social policy trying to solve population and economic problems. He feared that within a period of twelve years, all but a few white planters would leave Suriname, following the monetary crisis in Amsterdam (1773) and foreigners might come and drain the colony of the remaining funds. As a result of the crisis, many planters took loans on their properties and spent too much of their income on luxuries. Wichers proposed to raise a mulatto middle class of experts who could take over the positions abandoned by the plantation owners. These Creole coloreds were born within the colony and were more likely to stay. He even planned to encourage white plantation masters to father children by black slave mothers and declare the children free, adding an indemnification of one-hundred guilders for the master.[51] Eventually, many of the planters did not leave, but the result of the "political system," partially implemented by Governor Wichers, was at least that a number of talented mulattoes were able to get a good education and learn a trade.[52] He sent his own colored son, Wicheridus, to Holland to study. He got married to a Dutch girl, but died at the early age of twenty-five.

Sometimes the colored children had traveled and were quite well educated. G. van Lennep Coster, who stayed in the West Indies and in Suriname, for three years (1837-1840), mentions meeting a girl:

The company was manyfold, existing of directors from the neighborhood as well as girls, or housekeepers, being mulattoes; amongst them was one who distinguished herself very favorably from the others. She possessed the additional civility and knowledge achieved by traveling to America and England, which added much charm to her conversation.[53]

He enjoyed spending the day with her and they danced all night long. Van Lennep Coster observed that the people in Paramaribo tended to live a more quiet life and paid more attention to etiquette, by having more regard for the ceremonial.[54] He made the following remark, "The encounters between the Whites and important people of color I found to have become more common, and now one meets women of color in the company of European ladies, a thing which occurred very seldom in previous years." According to Von Sack, Negroes disliked mulattoes and expressed their feelings in songs, of which one says, "the whites have their fatherland, the blacks also have their fatherland but the mulattoes have nothing."[55]

Baptism and Schooling

Initially, the church did not have much contact with the largest part of the Suriname population, the slaves. Slowly, white European fathers began to request that their mulatto children born of black mothers be baptized. Only one parent was present at this occasion. The fact that the parents were not married caused a large problem for the church. The number of free colored people rose enormously during the eighteenth century, causing the church population, especially in Paramaribo, to grow, as well. This is not surprising, since the notification of 1733 stated that owners were obliged to educate their ex-slaves in the basics of Christian religion. As a result, most manumitted colored chose the denomination of their former owners. Many of the baptized turned out to be very pious people. By the end of the eighteenth century approximately 1400 souls were Dutch Reformed and some 600 Lutheran. The Roman Catholic Church did not find much support in Suriname. Mostly, Moravian Brethren were active in baptizing among the plantation slaves and the Maroon population and Amerindians within the interior of Suriname. Slaves attended their masters and mistresses going to church. Public funerals would include a gathering of both black and white.

After a long period of discussion among the *Conventus Deputatorum* of the Reformed Church, in 1760, the Political Council decided to open a school for mulatto, black and Amerindian children. The schoolmaster was to choose which children would profit from education, along with religious tutoring. Even at night, he held classes, especially for youths who already worked a job during the day. The people, who had manumitted the children, were obliged to contribute to the school funding. This automatically resulted in a census: all freed persons should be registered.[56] Often freed concubines of plantation managers moved to Paramaribo with their children so they would be able to attend school.[57]

"The children, born from these cohabitations, stay in the keeps of the mother, even though an honest father will not withdraw from his responsibilities," wrote an anonymous visitor to Suriname in 1825. He made a suggestion to place the colored children who did not benefit from their fathers "philanthropy" in a schooling institution, the girls to learn female handicrafts so they all would become prudent citizens.[58] Some fathers really wanted the best for their children. According to Fermin (1770), most of the mulatto children were freed, as long as the mother was also property of the begetter. These children were raised well and learned a trade. White fathers sometimes felt great responsibility for the upbringing of their illegal children. In 1730, two preachers investigated the position of these children in the colony. The clergy questioned one father on a mulatto girl, who he acknowledged as his own child. He told them the girl was able to say her prayers quite reasonably and was able to answer some questions from the catechism in Dutch and French. He was married now and had other children by his lawful (white) wife. She apparently mistreated the girl and oppressed her cruelly. This had caused discord between him and his wife and was the reason why he asked the clergy to house the girl some place else. He was willing to pay 100 to 140 guilders yearly for her upkeep. The church board discussed this predicament and the clergy unfortunately decided they were not able to respond in a positive way, on grounds the girl had not been manumitted yet.[59]

Sometimes white men frankly acknowledged their unions with colored women and named these housekeepers as the guardians of their natural children, appointing to them the enjoyments of [his] goods in usufructs for the duration of their lives. At times, cohabitants were not mentioned in wills, but the fact that natural children of color were appointed as heirs, clarifies the racial background of the mother. At times, the housekeeper is mentioned in the will as major beneficiary of 'a debt,' to avoid white kin to get precedence from the law. These wills suggest stable interracial unions.[60] These cases come to light because more and more people show interest in researching their family history.[61] Mulattoes were important both in terms of numbers as well as social privileges. Even though most of them were born out of wedlock, they were often mentioned in wills.

From Property to Owner

The supposition does not hold ground that mostly women were manumitted because of their ongoing dependency on men once they were free. In recent studies, it has been demonstrated that in Barbados, for instance, many freed women were able to build a future for by working hard.[62] Free persons of color were able to gather property, by receiving an inheritance or owning their own keep. This was also the case in Suriname. For tax purposes a list was drawn up in 1772 containing all the renting values of Paramaribo town houses. In all, the list contains a number of 667 houses. The rental costs of these houses varied from 120 to 3,720 Dutch guilders, probably per annum. In the Graavestaat, on the left hand side, we see mentioned Angelica V. de Lelie, the free Philida and Affiba van de Loge, all three living in houses estimated at 300 guilders. Judging by the names in the inventory, a number of properties belonged to manumitted men or women. Some 56 of these belonged to free women of color. The records do not state if these women were mulatto or black. Just in one case it says "Mulattin Geertruijd."[63] This entire list might contain more names of freed women, but just the ones of which one can be certain were counted. Some women owned more properties, like Betje van Pardo, who is registered in the "Maagde straat" and in the "Keijserstraat." Nanette (Nanoe) Samson had two houses in the "Waage wegstraat," valued at 720 and 1,560 guilders.[64] She used to be the housekeeper of Wijnand van Herpen, the white director of a plantation. Nanette was the last of the Samson sisters to die in 1793. She executed all the wills of her siblings. Her black half sister Elisabeth married Nanette's neighbor, Hermanus Daniel Zobre. Remarkably enough, people of all shades are found scattered among the diverse streets, living as neighbors next to whites and blacks.

Slaves did not have Christian names. Often their African names were changed into European ones. Before 1828 freed persons often received the name of the owner on manumission, indicated by "van." As an example, the mulatto slave Caro, belonging to Mozes Meyer de Hart was manumitted on February 25, 1827. From that day on she carried the name Carolina Petronella van het Hart. Apparently she married her previous owner. In his final will her name had changed into Carolina Petronella de Hart and she was mentioned as his widow. She and her thirteen children received a large inheritance. Among this portion were 87 slaves, most of them working at Plantation Sardam. Unfortunately, there was also a substantial amount of debts.[65] Some female mulattoes, being the concubines of white men, possessed a number of slaves. Masters in the city often owned more slaves than they could profitably employ daily within household tasks. They were often allowed to hire themselves to people who either needed more help or to persons who, unable to purchase their own slaves, nevertheless sought out the status of slave owners.

Pieter Constantijn Groen visited the West Indies in 1792 and kept a diary of his journey for a year. In his manuscript, he writes that the daily habits of women in Suriname differ greatly from other countries. They received him very well, once introduced. He finds the mulatto women more reserved and more difficult than in other places. They think, while lurking around, they will catch a rich administrator or even a planter. And this often even happened.[66] There was no open discussion on prostitution in Suriname, although some remarks of visitors point into that direction. We can all understand that there was only a thin line between getting into a benefiting relationship with a white male and selling your body for a 'sweet'. The number of venereal diseases was high in Suriname, or, as Von Sack pointed out, "The climate here is especially beneficiary to women; they reach high ages, being married and widowed for maybe four or five times. No doubt their long lasting life lies in the way they live their life. There is no need for strict abstinence, but it is better to enjoy life in a moderate way."[67] As a profession women practiced sewing, knitting or washing clothes. "Even, (what is not advisable and amongst us free Christians is not too much of a practice) often serves as girls of pleasure, and usually earn a sweet; although this is not openly allowed, but has to happen in silence," wrote Von Sack in 1821.[68] Brereton is quoted saying that the woman as prostitute reversed the canons of respectability, the norms of the superstructure with her bravery, her wit, her talent in song and dance, her deference to the law, her sexual prowess. This during the nineteenth century when the Victorian "Angel of the house ideal was riding the waves of popularity at home and abroad."[69] In Suriname there was no open discussion about prostitution, just some cryptic remarks. This was unlike the remarks made on mulatta's and their sexual prowess in Charleston, South Carolina or Barbados. In 1811, a census was held under British rule, to obtain an accurate statement of the returns of the population. All free citizens listed their profession, among them 57.8 % mulatta's of a total of 1,330 freed women.

When freed persons of color secured enough money, it was not an uncommon act for them to buy slaves. This might seem surprising, considering the fact that slavery was such a despicable institution that they themselves had experienced. It turns out, however, that family members were often bought and manumitted afterwards. This "chain manumission" resulted sometimes in entire families being set free.

The Du

Dancing was very important to the slaves. At certain times of the year they were allowed to have their balls. Sometimes these were strictly religious and more or less hidden from observers ("winti-prey") sometimes they were profane ("banja" or "du"). [70] In Suriname, there never were any large uprisings because the slaves were able to run away from the plantations and establish their own Maroon communities within the jungle, behind the waterfalls ("sula's") in the river where it was very difficult for government soldiers to capture them. But when a slave owner refused to allow the slaves to have their yearly balls, it was cause for them to protest fiercely, thus, most of the time they were allowed to dance. A number of notifications warned against drunkenness and loud noise within the vicinity of the main town. Over time this habit of dancing got a special connotation and became a display of wealth and beauty, thus the names: golden or diamond "du." Eventually, these events turned into plays that were staged with set figures and a story line of love and jealousy. These gatherings have been described as such, "When the Missies feel insulted, they call each other to some sorts of court of women and set a date and place, often a nice garden with a large tent that is beautifully lit by night."[71] The Missies would sit in the middle of this tent and watch as their slaves enacted the story, through song and dance.

Benoit, a painter from Brussels, visited Suriname around 1830. He made a number of beautiful drawings of slaves and free people. Two wonderful drawings to illustrate this discourse are by his hand.

They love to dress up and give up everything to be able to participate in the Du, (beautiful, shiny gathering) in which they try to compete. Dress was a way to visualize the class distinctions and was used as an intentional symbolization. These Missies are not very shy, but do not like to venture outside during the day. The fact that they used to be slaves does not keep them from owning some themselves. They very much like to show off.[72]

In the painting we see "A Missie bringing her child to be christened, preceded and followed by a slave-girl." This Missie was probably a free woman. She wears a very long dress, it is not possible to tell if she was wearing any shoes or not. Benoit has drawn a number of women, mostly without shoes on their feet. This was of importance, because in Suriname slaves were not allowed to wear shoes. We gather this from Notification, August 15, 1777 Act 1:

> No slaves, be it Mulatto's, Indians or negro's without distinction, may wear stockings, shoes, decorated hats or any gold or jewelry unless permission granted for small golden earrings, necklaces or armbands with little golden lockets.[73]

These notifications were printed and spread throughout the colony and read aloud on every plantation, since slaves were forbidden to read and write. It was important to the dominant class that the slaves were made aware of the contents of the law.

Judge A.F. Lammens lived in Suriname from 1816 to1835. He kept an elaborate diary and assembled a number of contemporary documents such as newspapers and pamphlets. In his collection he described a wonderful, detailed picture of Suriname life during his times. He did make some remarks concerning mulatto women. He stated that white people only look down on coloreds and feel nothing but contempt. But, on the other hand, he criticized the entire range of Suriname inhabitants. His view was probably not entirely without prejudice. He married the much younger mulatto woman, Carolina Maria Schouten in 1827. She was the granddaughter of poet Hendrik Schouten, who wrote the poem "The Yellow Lady."[74] Lammens despised "the distinction that a colored woman makes towards her black mother, and the fact that she sees her lighter child as higher in rank than herself, because these ideas might lead to tension within the society. And this will happen everywhere, if people award any value or addition, not based on common sense or virtue." He observed that most colored women did not accompany their partner when going out visiting; she gathered with friends and family. Since the women were used to this, they seemed not to mind. Sometimes the children joined their fathers on journeys to Europe while she stayed at home and practiced the utmost virtue while he was away.

Lammens described the *du* as a favorite past time for the Missies. He claimed that sometimes people even stooped to stealing in order to be able to contribute to the festivities and be dressed as nicely as possible. The opulence reminds us of the Quadroon balls organized in New Orleans that were uncommonly popular. A Spanish law of 1786 ordered free women of color to dress plainly and wear a special turban so as not to be mistaken for whites. This example is used to argue that French and Spanish laws were just as prohibitive as American ones.[75] It seems the *"du"* was an exclusive organization, based on color and economic status, mostly displayed in clothing and jewelry. The Missies wore as many pieces of cloth as possible, and of the finest quality. This was material of the most exquisite designs, embroidered waistcoats, patent leather shoes, silk hats, kid gloves, and chintzes. The Missies draped the slave girls with chains of beads (with special names for certain kinds) and golden jewelry; so much so, that, as we have seen, at a certain point it was forbidden by the government, because the slaves would not feel any distinction anymore between themselves and the white population.

This dress turned over time into the "koto," a heavy dress worn, to this day, as a Creole national costume during festivities. The woman wearing this costume is called a "Koto Missie."[76] At a certain point it was propagated that this dress was invented by cruel and jealous plantation mistresses, to hide the beautiful forms of the colored girls. This appears in contradiction to the paintings of Benoit, where he shows girls with elaborate skirts but bear breasted, not wearing a top. The koto became a much-favored dress, the scarves were folded in all kinds of shapes, conveying messages, and during the *du* all kinds of proverbs were exclaimed (*"odo"*). These proverbs are still very popular. Many of them stem from the old days of slavery and had a hidden meaning, so the plantation master could not grasp what the slaves were communicating (like the undercurrent content of a number of Negro-spirituals). One quite in tune with the subject of this article is *"Si bun nanga fri a no wan"* which translates as "Seeing good and free is not the same," meaning you should be satisfied with what you have got. [77] The lingua franca in Suriname is Sranan Tongo, a Creole language made up from West African idiom and words from an English, Dutch, French or Portuguese origin. And these *odo's* are theatrically exclaimed with a lot of fervor in Sranan.

A True Story: The Beautiful Mulatto Joanna

The most widely researched book on Suriname is *Narrative of a Five Years Expedition against the Revolted Negroes of Suriname* by John Gabriel Stedman. His view on slavery differed in tone from most other contemporary authors, probably because he fell in love with Joanna, a beautiful mulatto girl. His father was a Scotsman. Stedman wrote a journal in English while he lived in Suriname (1772-1777) and J. Johnson in London first published the book in 1796. It was translated into a number of languages and reprinted in numerous editions, especially due to the some 80 engravings. Stedman drew Suriname flora and fauna, the journeys undertaken by the military to chase the "revolted" Negroes, the Maroons, and the way the planters lived. Besides the descriptions of daily Suriname life in the years from his arrival by vessel in Paramaribo in February 1773 until his departure in April 1777, he visualized this life with illustrations. The drawings on slavery are well known and played an important role during the discussions on the ending of the slave trade and slavery in general by the abolitionists in the British parliament.

Within the context of this article I would like to focus on the love life of Stedman. He met the young mulatto girl Joanna and lived with her during the times he was not chasing Maroons. She was his "house-keeper." Already on March 1, not even a month after his arrival in Suriname, Stedman met a fine young mulatto woman. His meeting with Joanna is described as follows, "I first saw at the house of M. Demelly [. . .] and of whose Lady, Joanna aged then but 15 years was a very remarkable favorite." He describes her frame and beauty: The easy way she moved her body gave her an uncommon elegance. Modesty and gentleness were expressed in her face. He asks Mrs. Demelly about the girl's history. It turns out her father was a respectable gentleman named Kruithoff and her mother the slave woman, Cery, from Plantation Faukenburgh. The owner refused manumission of the five children, upon which the father died of shear misery. The fact that the owners of Cery, and her children, had to flee the country, because of creditors chasing them, turned out to be Joanna's good fortune. This was why she stayed in Paramaribo with an aunt and met Stedman, whom she would spend some happy years with. She took care of him during several illnesses and they were always together when he was not chasing Maroons (runaway slaves). Theirs was a case of true love: he even sowed some grains in the shape of the names of Joanna and Johnny, their son on his little piece of land. Many from the white elite complimented him on his choice of this fine colored lady.

Stedman and Joanna were never married, even though the young soldier was able to convince his friend, the Scottish plantation mistress Elisabeth Danford, to pay for her freedom. Danford was the widow of the French Huguenot Charles Godefroy and owned Plantation Alkmaar on the Commewijne River. This upper class lady also bought the manumission letter for Johnny, Joanna's son born in 1774. Stedman tried to convince Joanna to travel with him to Holland, after his soldier's contract had expired. She refused putting up the argument that she was fully convinced that, once in Europe, she would not be treated with the same respect as she was in Suriname.[78] She did not want to be a cause for contempt, or a burden to him. When Stedman left in 1777, she stayed behind as a companion to Mrs. Danford. Some years later she died, probably due to poisoning because of jealousy. Other slaves envied her privileged position. Johnny was sent to Holland, where he was raised in Stedman's new family. He died a sailor's death near the coast of Jamaica, at only seventeen years old.

Curiously enough, the original 1790 manuscript written by Stedman was found in the James Ford Bell Library at the University of Minnesota. Richard and Sally Price have researched the differences between this manuscript and the heavily edited first published edition of 1796.[79] Stedman wrote about being approached by mothers who offered young women for sexual intimacy in exchange for money or gifts. Economic motives and dealings might be rewarded by a slave woman's freedom or by food, clothing, and luxuries for herself and her kin. The men preferred young and light-complexioned women. Free women were in the position to seek out the company of white males, by joining dances, balls and other social rituals where European men came for entertainment. The women dressed up for these occasions. Prospects of manumission were enhanced by intimate contact with Europeans. Light skinned women occasionally attained considerable wealth and status as the mistresses of prominent white males. Many prominent Suriname officials were known to have free colored mistresses. The jealousy of the white Creole ladies was, according to Stedman, intense. The easy availability of other women reduced their status. The white women were intended to breed legitimate heirs and little else. Some were indifferent towards or condoned the relationships between their husbands and colored concubines, according to Stedman.

A Myth: The Beautiful Mulatto Alida

A large majority of white men, as compared to the smaller number of white women, made up part of Suriname plantation society. These men often had children with black or colored women. More than once their affairs were cause for discord. An anonymous visitor to Paramaribo stated in 1844:

> Because of this misbehavior, proper entertaining suffers a lot. One can understand that nice European ladies do not visit the houses of these men; as a result of this they also do not pay return visits often. This ends in a general lack of social interaction.[80]

Often these Suriname marriages caused white mistresses to be jealous. The free, libertine mores the white men practiced did not restrict them (in some cases) from having extra-marital relations with colored women.[81] When asked about slavery in Suriname, most people do not mention a male planter, but refer to the cruel plantation mistress Susanna du Plessis.[82] Rumor has it she was extremely jealous.

A long time ago in Suriname, there lived a beautiful slave girl whose name was Alida. She worked as a domestic servant for her mistress, Susanna du Plessis. Her husband liked the slave girl a lot, and ogled the slender figure of Alida all the time. One day, one bad day, Susanna caught her husband looking lovingly and longingly at the breasts of the beautiful Alida, who served them at their dinner table. This turned the plantation mistress into a monster green with jealousy. She ordered to have the breasts of the girl cut of and with the cruelest of words she said: 'You liked these breasts so much, well, here they are, nicely prepared for you.' and served them as a delicacy at dinner. Another dark day Susanna planned to visit her plantation "In spite of envy." On her tent boat across the river Commewijne she also took a slave with her child to go to the plantation. This child was crying its eyes out. Susanna asked the mother several times to hush the baby, each time more crossly. The woman tried to silence the child, but to no avail. Susanna then commended: "Hand me the child, I will make sure it stays quiet." She then kept the child under water until it drowned. The desperate mother threw herself into the river, to die a drowning death.

This case is used to argue how in recent history the figure of the mulatto woman in Suriname has been mystified. The stories on Du Plessis are very well known and the most quoted ones on slavery in Suriname. Is the current story on both women just a malicious rumor, or a true drama that unfolded between a cruel slave mistress and her beautiful slave girl? In many studies on the rise and fall of plantation societies women play a marginal role. This is the case for slaves, free colored women as well as white mistresses. In the archives we find limited information on the lives of individual slaves. We do, however, find scattered data on a number of white women. Based on the research involving the plantation mistress Susanna du Plessis, a number of aspects regarding the lives of women in eighteenth century Suriname could be reconstructed.[83] The historiography of the beautiful slave girl and her jealous mistress goes back to John Gabriel Stedman. In his *Narrative of a five years Expedition*, he wrote on several occasions about the cruel nature of one "Mrs. S." Mind though, it was all hearsay. He mentioned the events concerning the drowned baby. He also tells about a murdered mulatto girl at the corner of the Waterfront and the Town Square, just in front of the house where Susanna was living. The last story seems to have been the base on which the myth about the cut off breast of Alida was build.

During the reconstruction of the life of Susanna du Plessis a number of facts were uncovered. Her father, a Huguenot, came to the colonies as an advocate of the Dutch West India Company and married a rich widow. Because of his tribulations with Governor Mauricius, he was banned from the colony. His wife and four children stayed behind. Susanna was born in Paramaribo in the year 1739. Just before she turned fifteen, she married her neighbor Frans Willem Grand. He died in 1762 and Susanna remarried in 1767 under strict prenuptial conditions with Frederic Cornelis Stolkert, who was her junior by seven years and the stepson of the governor to be. The notary deeds were mainly in the interest of the bride. At all times she was to decide on the management of her plantation "In Spite of Envy" and current income was to be shared. In 1783, they separated because, according to the wife, he turned her life into a living hell. She died a rich, childless, woman in 1795. Her tombstone in the reformed church bears the inscription, "Finally, I found my peace." Susanna stated in her last will that Stolkert was never to partake in any financial involvement regarding her possessions. Most of her inheritance ended up in the Netherlands at the will of the descendants of her eldest half brother, Pichot-du Plessis. Looking at the inventories, we see colored babies born at Susanna's plantation. She freed slaves, women and men, and a little mulatto boy named Frederik. These actions seem not quite in accordance with her reputation.

De- and Re-construction

No facts regarding Susanna's cruelty can be deduced from deconstructing the written sources. They all seem hearsay. Through recurrent changes, the story became mystified. This happened in written non-fiction as well as oral sources. Even though the reconstruction of Susanna's life was published in 2002, modern day non-fiction authors still portray her as the most inhumane slave mistress in Suriname. This picture was mainly painted within Afro-Creole oral history. During the 1950s, within the Suriname nationalistic era, we detect a tendency to rewrite Suriname history.[84] Paasman, professor of colonial and post colonial cultural history and literatures at the University of Amsterdam, poses an intriguing question, "Would we still get the same version of the story in a poly perspective colonial or post colonial historiography with different authors, texts and interpretations?" His answer is, "Of course, every literature or cultural history only states one of many versions of the possible stories, and there still is a discrepancy between the black and the white story."[85] The reason why the story is so diverse depends on the differences in written and oral history. De Groot explains that written societies base their histories on written texts from archives, primary and secondary sources. In societies without writing, men and women hand over their (his) story to their children: oral history.[86] Chamberlaine investigated these differences according to gender and remembrance. She concluded that oral sources vary from conventional ones because they are laden with interpretations and subjectivity. Oral sources go back to individual remembrance with imagination providing a large contribution. Also, storytellers may cater to the needs of the listening public to facilitate a greater impact by the story. The value of oral history lays not so much in the conveyance of information, but in the impact of such. The story has become a product of a social process, as a collective remembrance.[87]

In the case of the story about Alida and Susanna du Plessis, oral history and conventional written sources go side by side, through means of a theatre play that was staged a number of times during the 1960s. The reason for the mystification is clearly stated in a valid question posed within many a post-colonial society, "How do you cope, as someone from Suriname, with a past that seems to offer so little to be proud of and so much to be ashamed of. How do you find yourself, your feelings of self esteem, in a history overshadowed by white supremacy?"[88] Eersel, a Suriname linguist who contributed to the Suriname nationalistic consciousness movement in the fifties ("Wie eegi sanie"; "Our Own Thing") tells us about an existence full of myths and stories, "They (the Dutch) have Piet Hein, we have our own heroes, Boni and Alida." Since 1991, the Miss Alida Society has organized a Miss Alida pageant every year, on the eve of Suriname Slavery abolition day, which occurred on July 1, 1863. The Creole girl, who was able to present her cultural heritage in the best possible way, was chosen.[89] This event was even celebrated among the Suriname community in the the Netherlands. The pageant consists of elements distilled from Afro-Surinamese cultural history. We see dancing, parading in "Bigi Koto" and exclaiming a relevant *"odo."* These are all elements we know from the *du*, and are considered as important female traditions. This fits within the societal and political goals as seen by women to claim their own rightful space.[90] In Suriname, internal organizational and financial problems have unfortunately caused this particular pageant to end. In 2006, former winners and contestants proclaimed a new organization (Fu den Alida) and chose an actual historical figure, the black run away slave Sery, to act as a role model.[91]

In the process of rewriting one's own history, slaves turned from anonymous shadows or vague personalities with sometimes just their first name known, into national heroes. Alida, the beautiful mulatto girl, paradoxically became an icon of bravery from slavery times and Susanna du Plessis was mystified into the cruelest of plantation mistresses.[92] It is obvious that people who suffered from slavery have a need to preserve their history within their own context and create their own heroic figures, like Alida. Curiously enough, the yellow girl who was murdered in front of Susanna's town house became black within this framework of mystification. Mulatto women form a minority within the present day population of Suriname. It seems rather predictable that the majority of black women deconstructed the story and reconstructed a new creation to their liking. This reconstruction was repeated when it became obvious through research that Alida was not an actual historical truth, but rather a figment of imagination. A new role model was chosen, Misi Sery, for black Afro-Suriname women to finally, rightfully and fully, reclaimed their own ethnic identity.

Conclusion

In early colonial Suriname, from 1651 on, white men outnumbered white women by far. As a result of this, the majority of these men formed relationships with black women. Their children were colored. The mulatto girls were favored in due course of the eighteenth century and beyond. In Suriname plantocracy, it was strictly forbidden for black males to marry white women. The first marriage between a black woman and a white male took place in 1776. Even though the law prohibited sexual liaisons between whites and blacks, ratio dictated otherwise. It turns out that over and over again the law was not in accordance with the facts of real life practice. White men did marry mulatto girls and had children by them. Female slave partners and their offspring were often freed, to the extent that by 1800 the colored free population had outnumbered the white. Two thirds of the manumitted were women. Because of their children they often inherited capital or slaves when their partner passed away. By 1840, the majority of slave owners were colored. The mulatto women were thus able to gather property and obtain a high social status, even though they were sometimes not fully accepted socially by part of the white elite. This did not keep some members of the privileged group from marrying colored women, even governors who held the highest position in the country. To show off their wealth, colored Missies organized dance plays, the *du's*. Some of the cultural aspects of these *du's* are still visible in Suriname society today even though the number of mulatto women has diminished. We see that in the Caribbean, each societal space had its own development of mulatto class, according to the process of creolization, demographics and government instilled processes of law creating and applying. For Suriname, it resulted in a continuum of people varying in color, from very dark to very light. Within this framework, people, especially women whose skin was lightly toned, were able to rise on the social ladder by gaining freedom, property and wealth.

In Suriname, within the nationalistic movement, a number of cultural expressions involving the *du* were adopted as favorite elements of black Afro-Suriname female heritage, tangible and intangible. The plantation time story of the cruel mistress Du Plessis and her unfortunate mulatto slave girl, Alida, was made into a drama and performed a number of times during the nationalistic period (1960s) and adopted by the Afro-Suriname population as part of their factual history. The story of Alida and the cultural heritage of the du's together culminated in the Miss Alida pageant on the evening before the yearly celebration of Emancipation, not surprisingly expressing the qualities of afro-Suriname young women. Even though the story was based on a mulatto girl, the pageant was about Afro-Suriname black identity. The Miss Alida event was renamed as the Miss Sery pageant, representing the strong, self-confident young Afro-Suriname women and not so much more the mystified mulatto victim of slavery. In general, mulatto women in Suriname plantocracy were not victims of slavery, but had opportunities to take the position of connecting dots between the master and the slave, between white and black.

Notes

I hereby express my gratitude to Drs. Laddy van Putten, director of the Suriname Museum Foundation, and Drs. Jerome Egger, chair of the History Department at the Teachers Training Institute (IOL), for constructive criticism and additional remarks to improve this text.

1. The original contemporary texts were written in Dutch. They were translated by the author of this article, with some unfortunate loss of nuance and flavor.
2. U.M. Lichtveld and J. Voorhoeve, *Suriname: Spiegel der vaderlandse kooplieden. Een historisch leesboek* (Den Haag: Martinus Nijhoff, 1980), 199-200.
3. Rudolf van Lier, *Samenleving in een grensgebied, een sociaal-historische studie van Suriname* (Amsterdam: Emmering, 1977, reprint from 1949). This is the most important mid-twentieth century over all study on Suriname, and is much quoted. Recent research however puts many of Van Lier's conclusions to doubt. Chapter 5 (70-85) deals with the free colored and black population.
4. Already in 1714, Elisabeth's mulatto half sister Maria had married a white man from Switzerland, Pierre Mivela. As a widow, she married the German F. C. Bossé in 1727. The marriage of Elisabeth Samson and her family was researched and documented by Cynthia McLeod, *Elisabeth Samson, een vrije zwarte vrouw in het achtiende-eeuwse Suriname* (Paramaribo: Vaco, 1994).
5. The colony was actually established in 1651 by the British under Francis Lord Willoughby who resided in Barbados. Slavery in British territories was abolished in 1834, but in Suriname Emancipation only took place on July 1st 1863.
6. For a good overview of Suriname histories in English see C. Ch. Goslinga, *The Dutch in the Caribbean and in the Guyana's* [Volume I and II] (Assen: Van Gorcum, 1985). For this quote: Vol. I, 358.
7. For 1791 the number of mulatto's (and free blacks) had already reached 1760, against 2030 white people in total. These figures were collected by Teenstra, *De landbouw in Suriname* (Groningen, H. Eekhof H.Z., 1842) and quoted by Lammens.
8. A.F. Lammens, *Bijdragen tot de kennis van de kolonie Suriname, tijdvak 1816-1822,* ed. G. A. de Bruijne
(Amsterdam: Vrije Universiteit, 1982).

9. All notifications and laws (plakaten en ordonantiën) executed in Suriname between 1667 and 1816 were collected, transcribed and edited by J. Schiltkamp and J. de Smidt, *West-Indisch plakaatboek: Plakaten, Ordonnantiën en andere wetten, uitgevaardigd in Suriname 1667-1816* (Amsterdam: Emmering, 1973).
All the laws mentioned in this article can be traced back on date in this publication.
10. W. Hoogbergen and Marjo de Theye, "Surinaamse vrouwen in de slavernij" in *Vrouwen in de Nederlandse Koloniën* (Nijmegen: SUN, 1986), 126.
11. E. Beier, *Suriname in deszelfs tegenwoordigen toestand door eenen inwoner aldaar* (Amsterdam: C. G. Sulpke, 1823), 55.
12. See Schiltkamp and Smidt.
13. Maria Lenders wrote on the Moravian church in Suriname in *Strijders voor het Lam* (Leiden: KITLV, 1996), 66.
14. Van Lier, 49.
15. Lichtveld and Voorhoeve, 138-142.
16. For Barbados see Hilary Beckles, "Sex and gender in the historiography of Caribbean Slavery" in *Engendering History. Caribbean women in Historical Perspective* ed. by Sheperd, Brereton and Baily (Kingston: Ian Randle Publishers 1995) and Beckles, *Centering Women. Gender discourse in Caribbean Slave Society* (Jamaica: Ian Randle Publishers, 1999).
Martha Hodes has done research on black men marrying white women in Ante Bellum America in Hodes, *White women, black men. Illicit Sex in the 19th-century South* (New Haven: Yale University Press, 1997).
17. See Hilde Neus "Ras of ratio? Verbod op het huwelijk tussen zwarte mannen en blanke vrouwen" in *OSO*, jrg. 26, nr. 2, okt. 2007, 306-322.
18. Van Lier, 54.
19. Between 1730 and 1750 the amount of white people in Suriname varied between 1000 and 1700. They were all registered to pay taxes. Since the tax amount for children under 14 years old was less, this division was clear from the list. In his study *Om werk van jullie te hebben. Plantageslaven in Suriname,1730-1750*, the author Ruud Beeldsnijder claims that amongst 2.062 slaves at the plantations only 31 (1,5 %) were mulatto. It is quite probable that the majority was send to Paramaribo to work as domestic house slaves. (Utrecht: Vakgroep Culturele Antropologie, 1994), 125.
20. Ann Stoler, *Carnal Knowledge and Imperial Power* (Berkeley: University of California Press, 2002) on métissage in Dutch East-India.
21. The term manumission comes from Latin 'manumittere' (manus is hand, mittere is to send away: let go from their hands).
22. See Schiltkamp and Smidt.
23. As also stated by Paul Koulen in "Schets van de historische ontwikkeling van de Manumissie in Suriname (1733-1863)" in: *Mededelingen van de Stichting Surinaams Museum*, no. 12, dec. 1973, 8-36.
24. Wim Klooster, "Subordinate but proud: Curacao's free blacks and mulattoes in the eighteenth century" in *New West Indian Guide* vol. 68, no 3&4, 1994, 283-300.
25. On manumission see Okko ten Hove & Frank Dragtenstein, *Manumissie in Suriname 1832-1863*, (Utrecht: Universiteit van Utrecht, Clacs & IBS, 1997).
26. Bertram B. Doyle talks about the government of ceremonial observances in "The etiquette of Race Relations – Past, Present and Future" in *The Journal of Negro Education*, vol. 5, no.2, 1936, 191-208, 202.
27. See Koulen, 13.
28. This according to Van Lier, 71.
29. E. Horace Fitchett identified six propositions for the formation of a free colored class in "The Origin and Growth of the free Negro Population of Charleston, South Carolina" in *The Journal of Negro History*, vol. 26, no. 4, 1941, 421-437.

30. Ten Hove & Dragtenstein, 28.

31. Marietta Morissey wrote a chapter on Sex, Punishment, and Protest in *Slave women in the New World. Gender Stratification in the Caribbean* (Lawrence: University Press of Kansas), 144-157.

32. See Fitchett, 425.

33. Paul F. Lachance elaborated on several types of wills as a source for the study of interracial unions in "The formation of a three cast society: Evidence from wills in Antebellum New Orleans" in *Social Science History* vol. 18, nr.2, 1994, 211-242.

34. Wim Klooster, 284.

35. M.D. Teenstra wrote in 1842 that many people in Suriname live within a corrupted society without morals and ethics that was forced upon them. Not just slaves were prohibited to marry, also plantation directors. See *De negerslaven in de kolonie Suriname en de uitbreiding van het christendom onder de heidensche bevolking* (Dordrecht: Lagerweij, 1842).

36. Angela van Leeuwen, "Het Surinaamse huwelijk" in *OSO*, jrg. 3 nr. 2, dec. 1984: 205-211.

37. See Teenstra, 87.

38. See Philip M.D. Fermin, *Nieuwe algemeene beschryving van de colonie van Suriname* (Harlingen: V. van der Plaats, 1770).

39. Albert von Sack, *Reize naar Surinamen, verblijf aldaar...* (Haarlem: De erven François Bohn, 1821), 148.

40. J.H.N., luitenant bij het 27ste Batt. Jagers wrote *Suriname in losse taferelen en schetsen* (Rotterdam: Wed. Locke & Zoon, 1840), 23, 60.

41. Oostindie writes for instance about the separation of families (mothers and children) at the auction block, this was not common practice in Suriname, and strictly forbidden by law in 1826. See Gert Oostindie, *Slavernij, canon en trauma.* (Oratie, University of Leiden, 2007). Movies like 'Mandingo' (1975) and 'Roots (1977) were played repeatedly in Suriname cinemas and turned out very popular. For instance the concept of selling mothers separately from their children was adopted by afro-Suriname people. This concept however was forbidden by law and not very practicable in Suriname since the distance between plantations was not that large.

42. This resulting from the transfer of sovereignty over Louisiana to the United States in 1803 – known as the Louisiana Purchase. See Lachance, 1994.

43. Tables quoted from Riva Berleant – Schiller, "The White Minority and the Emancipation process in Montserrat, 1807-32" in: *New West Indian Guide* vol. 70, no 3-4, 1996, 255-281.

44. Ten Hove and Dragtenstein, 14.

45. Suriname was ruled by a British interim government between 1799 and 1816. This coincided with the abolition of the slave trade throughout British territories. Suriname's emancipation however, took place only in 1863.

46. Wim Hoogbergen and Okko ten Hove wrote on the free colored and black inhabitants of Paramaribo in "De vrije gekleurde en zwarte bevolking van Paramaribo, 1762-1863" in *Oso*, 2001: nr.2, p. 306-320.

47. Rosemarijn Hoefte and Jean-Jaques Vrij, "Free Black and Colored Women in Early-Nineteenth-Century Paramaribo, Suriname" in *Beyond Bondage. Free Women of Color in the Americas* ed. David Barry Gaspar and Darlene Clark Hine (Urbane: University of Chicago Press, 2004), 143-168.

48. Cynthia Mcleod, 22.

49. Jean Jaques Vrij, "Jan Elias van Onna en het 'politiek systema' van de Surinaamse slaventijd, circa 1770-1820" in *OSO*, 1998: nr. 2, p.130-147.

50. Van Lier, 81.

51 Goslinga, Vol. I, 366.

52. Vrij, 136.

53. G. Van Lennep Coster, *Herinneringen mijner reizen naar onderscheidene werelddeelen* (Amsterdam: J.F. Schleyer, 1836), 96.

54. G. Van Lennep Coster, *Aantekeningen gehouden gedurende mijn verblijf in de West-Indien in de jaren 1837-1840* (Amsterdam: J.F. Schleyer, 1842), 40.

55. Von Sack, 179.

56. On the history of the reformed church in Suriname see J.W.C. Ort, *Vestiging van de hervormde kerk in Suriname. 1667-1800* (Amsterdam: Sticusa, 1963).

57. Hoefte and Vrij, 150.

58. Anonymous, *Aantekeningen, betrekkelijk de kolonie Suriname* (Arnhem: C.A. Thieme, 1825), 103.

59. This case is mentioned in Ruud Beeldsnijder, *Om werk van jullie te hebben. Plantageslaven in Suriname, 1730-1750* (Utrecht: Universiteit van Utrecht, 1994), 126.

60. Lachance, 235.

61. See the publications on Suriname genealogical research in the bi-monthly "Wi Rutu", first published in 2000.

62. See especially research done by Hilary Beckles (note 15) and Pedro Welch, *"Red" & Black over White: free Coloured Women in Pre-emancipation Barbados* (Bridgetown: Carib Research & Publications Inc.).

63. This list, drawn up in 1772, is published in C.L. Temminck Groll (et al), *De Architektuur van Suriname 1667-1930* (Zutphen: De Walburg Pers, 1973).

64. From this list, I was able to count 55 widows and 39 free colored or black men.

65. Ten Hove & Dragtenstein, 31.

66. This journal by Groen is mentioned in Michiel van Kempen, *Een geschiedenis van de Surinaamse literatuur* (Breda: Uitgeverij De Geus, 2003), 234.

67. Von Sack, 1821, 177.

68. A. Barrau, "De Waare staat van den slaaven-handel in onze Nederlandse colonien" in *Bijdragen tot het menselijk geluk 3* (1790): p. 341-388.

69. Bridget Brereton is quoted in "European Stereotypes and the position of Women in the Caribbean: An Historical Overview" by Kathleen Phillips-Lewis in *Crossroads of Empire; the Europe-Caribbean connection 1492-1992* ed. Alan Cobley (Bridgetown: University of the West Indies, 1994), 64-77.

70. An elaborate study on the 'du' was published by Trudi Martinus-Guda, *Drie eeuwen banya. De geschiedenis van een Surinaamse slavendans* (Paramaribo: Minov-Directoraat Cultuur, 2005).

71 Von Sack, 151.

73. J.P. Benoit: *Journey through Suriname, adapted from Voyage à Suriname (1839)* (Zutphen: De Walburg Pers, 1980).

73. See Schiltkamp and De Smidt.

74. Clazien Medendorp, *Gerrit Schouten (1779-1839)* (Amsterdam/Paramaribo: KIT/SSM, 1999), 31.

75. According to Lachance this law was implemented by Governor Miro's Bando de Buen Gobierno.

76. On koto and headdress see L. van Putten and J. Zantinge, "Let them talk", as *Mededelingen van het Surinaams Museum*, okt. 1988, nr. 43. They describe how only in 1879 was it obliged by law to wear clothing on the upper bodey when entering the town of Paramaribo.

77. A number of proverbs are assembled by Julian H.A. Nijhorst in *Bigisma Taki* (Paramaribo, 2002).

78. Gloria Wekker made an effort to write from the perspective of Joanna herself in "De mooie Joanna en haar huurling" in *OSO* jrg. 3, nr. 2 dec. 1984, 192-203.

79. The original by John Gabriel Stedman, *Journey through Suriname* ... was published in 1796. In Suriname the best known version is *Reize naar Surinamen*, reprint of the revised 1796 edition (Zutphen: De Walburg Pers, 1987). Transcribed from the original 1790 manuscript by Richard and Sally Price is *Narrative of a Five Years Expedition against the Revolted Negroes of Surinam* (Baltimore: John Hopkins University Press, 1988).

80. Anonymus, *Bijdragen de Nederlandsche en vreemde kolonien bijzonder betrekkelijk de vrijlating der slaven* (Utrecht, C. van der Post, 1844), 198.

81. On the role of the 'Mulâtresse' see *The Libertine colony. Creolization in the early French Caribbean* by Doris Garraway (Durham: Duke University Press, 2005), esp. Ch. 4.

Angela van Leeuwen claims that jealousy was caused mostly because the white married man had a colored mistress, 209.

82. A likewise story exists in Jamaica. The cruel Annee Palmer lived at Rose Hall Plantation in Montego Bay. H. de Lisser wrote a novel telling her story (*The white Witch of Rose Hall*, London: McMillan 1995, repr. from 1929), but carefull research by G.S. Yates has not proven any facts (C. Black, *Tales of Old Jamaica*, Kingston: Longman Caribbean, 1993), 9.

83. Hilde Neus researched the life and myths surrounding this plantation mistress and published *Susanna du Plessis. Portret van een slavenmeesteres* (Amsterdam: KIT, 2003).

84. This is not exclusive to Suriname, but occurred in most post-colonial societies. See for instance Bridget Brereton 'Contesting the past: narratives of Trinidad & Tobago History' in *New West Indian Guide* vol. 81 no 3 & 4, 2007, p. 169-196.

85. Bert Paasman, *Wandelen onder de palmen. De morele actualiteit van het koloniale verleden* (Amsterdam: Vossius Pers, 2002), 16.

86. On oral history see Sylvia de Groot "Boni's hoofd en Boni's dood" in *De Gids* 143, 1980, 3-15.

87. Mary Chamberlaine, "Gender and Memory: Oral History and Women's History" in *Engendering History: Caribbean Women in Historical Perspective* ed. Verene Shepherd (Kingston: Ian Randle Press, 1995), 95.

88. In the newspaper article "De lange schaduw van de slavernij" by M. Oomes and J. Palm (*Vrij Nederland*, July 30th, 2001).

89. Creole in Suriname means black or colored town people (as opposite to runaway slaves; the maroons) and has a different meaning from the one in other Caribbean countries, where it also stands for born within the country, either black or white.

90. On pageants and the articulation of ethnic identity see Yvon van der Pijl, "Missverkiezingen en de articulatie van etnische identiteit" in *OSO* nr. 1, jrg. 24, 2005, 115-135.

91. The organisation was advised on this historical role model by Cynthia McLeod, who researched Elisabeth Samson and wrote a number of historical novels (see note 3).

92. Hilde Neus, "Een quaad gerucht? Het verhaal van Alida en Susanna du Plessis" in *OSO* nr. 2, jrg. 21, 2002, 305-317.

References

Anonymus. *Aantekeningen, betrekkelijk de kolonie Suriname*. Arnhem: C.A. Thieme, 1825.

Anonymus. *Bijdragen de Nederlandsche en vreemde kolonien bijzonder betrekkelijk de vrijlating der slaven*. Utrecht: C. van der Post, 1844.

Barrau, A. "De Waare staat van den slaaven-handel in onze Nederlandse colonien." In *Bijdragen tot het menselijk geluk 3* (1790): 341-388.

Beckles, Hilary. "Sex and gender in the historiography of Caribbean Slavery." In *Engendering History: Caribbean Women in Historical Perspective,* ed. Shepherd, Brereton and Baily. Kingston Jamaica: Ian Randle Publishers, 1995.

_____. *Centering Women. Gender discourse in Caribbean Slave Society* (Jamaica: Ian Randle Publishers, 1999).

Beeldsnijder, Ruud. *Om werk van jullie te hebben. Plantageslaven in Suriname, 1730-1750.* Utrecht: Vakgroep Culturele Antropologie, 1994.

Beier, E. *Suriname in deszelfs tegenwoordigen toestand door eenen inwoner aldaar.* Amsterdam: C. G. Sulpke, 1823.

Benoit, J.P. *Journey through Suriname, adapted from Voyage à Suriname, 1839.* Zutphen: De Walburg Pers, 1980.

Berleant – Schiller, Riva. "The White Minority and the Emancipation process in Montserrat, 1807-32." *New West Indian Guide* vol. 70, no 3-4 (1996): 255-281.

Black, C. *Tales of Old Jamaica..* Kingston: Longman Caribbean, 1993.

Brereton, Bridget. "Contesting the Past: Narratives of Trinidad & Tobago History." *New West Indian Guide* vol. 81 no 3 & 4 (2007): 169-196.

Chamberlaine, Mary. "Gender and Memory: Oral History and Women's History." In *Engendering History: Caribbean Women in Historical Perspective*, ed. Sheperd, Brereton and Baily (Kingston Jamaica: Ian Randle Publishers, 1995).

Doyle, Bertram B. "The Etiquette of Race Relations – Past, Present and Future." *The Journal of Negro Education*, vol. 5, no. 2 (1936): 191-208.

Fermin, Philip M.D. *Nieuwe algemeene beschryving van de colonie van Suriname.* Harlingen: V. van der Plaats, 1770.

Fitchett, E. Horace. "The Origin and Growth of the free Negro Population of Charleston, South Carolina." *The Journal of Negro History*, vol. 26, no. 4 (1941): 421-437.

Garraway, Doris. *The Libertine Colony: Creolization in the Early French Caribbean.* Durham: Duke University Press, 2005.

Goslinga, C. Ch. *The Dutch in the Caribbean and in the Guyana's* [Volume I and II]. Assen: Van Gorcum, 1985.

Groot, Sylvia de. "Boni's hoofd en Boni's dood." *De Gids* 143 (1980): 3-15.

Hodes, Martha. *White Women, Black Men. Illicit Sex in the 19th-century* South. New Haven: Yale University Press, 1997.

Hoefte, Rosemarijn and Jean-Jaques Vrij. "Free Black and Colored Women in Early-Nineteenth-Century Paramaribo, Suriname," 143-168. In *Beyond Bondage. Free Women of Color in the Americas,* ed. David Barry Gaspar and Darlene Clark Hine. Urbane: University of Chicago Press, 2004.

Hoogbergen, W. and Marjo de Theye. "Surinaamse vrouwen in de slavernij." In *Vrouwen in de Nederlandse* Koloniën. Nijmegen: SUN, 1986.

Hoogbergen, Wim and Okko ten Hove. "De vrije gekleurde en zwarte bevolking van Paramaribo, 1762-1863." *Oso* jrg. 20, nr. 2 (2001): 306-320.

Hove, Okko ten and Frank Dragtenstein. *Manumissie in Suriname 1832-1863.* Utrecht: Universiteit van Utrecht, Clacs & IBS, 1997.

Klooster, Wim. "Subordinate but proud: Curacao's free blacks and mulattoes in the eighteenth century." *New West Indian Guide*, vol. 68, no 3&4 (1994): 283-300.

Koulen, Paul. "Schets van de historische ontwikkeling van de Manumissie in Suriname (1733-1863)." In *Mededelingen van de Stichting Surinaams Museum*, no. 12 (1973): 8-36.

Lachance, Paul F. "The formation of a three cast society: Evidence from wills in Antebellum New Orleans." *Social Science History* vol. 18, nr. 2 (1994): 211-242.

Lammens, A.F. *Bijdragen tot de kennis van de kolonie Suriname, tijdvak 1816-1822,* ed.

G. A. de Bruijne. Amsterdam: Vrije Universiteit, 1982.

Leeuwen, Angela van. "Het Surinaamse huwelijk." *OSO* jrg. 3, nr. 2 (1984): 205-211.

Lenders, Maria. *Strijders voor het Lam.* Leiden: KITLV, 1996.

Lennep Coster, G. Van. *Herinneringen mijner reizen naar onderscheidene werelddeelen.* Amsterdam: J.F. Schleyer, 1836.

_____. *Aantekeningen gehouden gedurende mijn verblijf in de West-Indien in de jaren 1837-1840.* Amsterdam: J.F. Schleyer, 1842.

Lichtveld, U.M. and J. Voorhoeve. *Suriname: Spiegel der vaderlandse kooplieden. Een historisch leesboek.* Den Haag:Martinus Nijhoff, 1980.

Lier, Rudolf van. *Samenleving in een grensgebied, een sociaal-historische studie van Suriname.* Amsterdam: Emmering, 1977 [repr. from 1949].

Lisser, H. De. *The White Witch of Rose Hall.* London: McMillan 1995 [repr. from 1929].

Martinus-Guda, Trudi. *Drie eeuwen banya. De geschiedenis van een Surinaamse Slavendans.* Paramaribo: Minov-Directoraat Cultuur, 2005.

McLeod, Cynthia, *Elisabeth Samson, een vrije zwarte vrouw in het achtiende-eeuwse Suriname.* Paramaribo: Vaco, 1994.

Medendorp, Clazien, *Gerrit Schouten (1779-1839).* Amsterdam/Paramaribo: KIT/SSM, 1999.

Morissey, Marietta. *Slave women in the New World. Gender Stratification in the Caribbean.* Lawrence: University Press of Kansas, 1989.

N., J.H. *Suriname in losse taferelen en schetsen.* Rotterdam: Wed. Locke & Zoon, 1840.

Neus, Hilde. "Een quaad gerucht? Het verhaal van Alida en Susanna du Plessis." *OSO* jrg. 21, nr. 2 (2002): 305-317.

_____. *Susanna du Plessis. Portret van een slavenmeesteres.* Amsterdam: KIT, 2003.

_____. "Ras of ratio? Verbod op het huwelijk tussen zwarte mannen en blanke vrouwen." *OSO* jrg. 26, nr. 2 (2007): 306-322.

Nijhorst, Julian H.A. *Bigisma Taki.* Paramaribo, 2002.

Oostindie, Gert. *Slavernij, canon en trauma.* Oratie, University of Leiden, 2007.

Ort, J.W.C. *Vestiging van de hervormde kerk in Suriname. 1667-1800.* Amsterdam: Sticusa, 1963.

Paasman, Bert. *Wandelen onder de palmen. De morele actualiteit van het koloniale Verleden.* Amsterdam: Vossius Pers, 2002.

Pijl, Yvon van der. "Missverkiezingen en de articulatie van etnische identiteit." *OSO* jrg. 24, nr. 1 (2005):115-135.

Phillips-Lewis, Kathleen. "European Stereotypes and the position of Women in the Caribbean: An Historical Overview." In *Crossroads of Empire: The Europe-Caribbean Connection 1492-1992,* ed. Alan Cobley. Bridgetown: University of the West Indies, 1994.

Putten, L. van and J. Zantinge. "Let them talk." As *Mededelingen van het Surinaams Museum,* nr. 43, Oct. 1988.

Sack, Albert von. *Reize naar Surinamen, verblijf aldaar...* Haarlem: De erven François Bohn, 1821.

Schiltkamp, J. and J. de Smidt. *West-Indisch plakaatboek: Plakaten, Ordonnantiën en andere wetten, uitgevaardigd in Suriname 1667-1816.* Amsterdam: Emmering, 1973.

Stedman, John Gabriel. *Reize naar Surinamen* [reprint of the revised 1796 edition]. Zutphen: De Walburg Pers, 1987.

_____, *Narrative of a Five Years Expedition against the Revolted Negroes of Surinam,* ed. by Richard and Sally Price. Baltimore: John Hopkins University Press, 1988.

Stoler, Ann. *Carnal Knowledge and Imperial Power.* Berkeley: University of California Press, 2002.

Teenstra, M.D. *De landbouw in Suriname.* Groningen: H. Eekhof H.Z., 1835.

_____, *De negerslaven in de kolonie Suriname en de uitbreiding van het christendom onder de heidensche bevolking.* Dordrecht: Lagerweij, 1842.

Temminck Groll, C.L. (et al). *De Architektuur van Suriname 1667-1930.* Zutphen: De Walburg Pers, 1973.

Vrij, Jean Jaques. "Jan Elias van Onna en het 'politiek systema' van de Surinaamse slaventijd, circa 1770-1820." *OSO* jrg. 17, nr. 2 (1998): 130-147.

Wekker, Gloria. "De mooie Joanna en haar huurling." *OSO* jrg. 3, nr. 2 (1984): 192-203.

Welch, Pedro. *"Red" & Black over White: free Coloured Women in Pre-emancipation Barbados.* Bridgetown Barbados: Carib Research & Publications Inc., 2000.

Part II

Race and Mixed Race in the Americas

Chapter 8

Critical Mixed Race Studies: New Approaches to Resistance and Social Justice

Andrew Jolivétte

The following address was delivered at the University of Washington, Seattle on May 16, 2007 as a part of the Ethnic and Cultural Center's annual Social Justice event. The theme for the evening was, "Mixed Race Ethnicity: New Demographics & Communities". The objective of the event was to present a cohesive plan for addressing issues impacting multiracial communities within the context of social justice and overarching issues in communities of color. What is offered below is a new framework for thinking about mixed-race studies as a critical intervention into discussion of race, power, culture and civil rights. In particular I argue for a critical re-assessment of whiteness as a viable ideological construct and cultural formation's potential for re-thinking ethnicities and identities as they change over time without losing a sense of connection to communities of origin and struggles for justice and equity.

Introduction

Good evening and thank you for the invitation to speak to you here today. I'd like to begin by acknowledging and thanking my ancestors, the French Creole people of Southwest, Louisiana---a multiracial, Afro-Latin community made-up of American-Indian, French, African, and Spanish people who give me the life blood that is necessary to live in today's world with all of its challenges.

In the early 1970s when my grandfather told my grandmother he didn't want "those niggas" (referring to my older half brothers whose biological father is African American) sitting next to "my grandchildren" (referring to my first cousins who are Creole and Puerto Rican). His actions were but the latest reflection of societal conflict played out on the familial stage. Fifteen years earlier, my father -- along with my aunts, uncle, and paternal grandparents -- had moved from southwest Louisiana to California. In the process, my grandparents informed him and the rest of the family that they were "becoming" a family of French Canadians, leaving their Creole identities behind. Why "French Canadians" as opposed to something else? This question, along with the rejection of blackness expressed in my grandfather's statement about "those niggas" continued to puzzle me across the years. It was not the privileging of whiteness that surprised me, as much as the complexities of a racialization process that so thoroughly neglected the regionally and culturally specific identity of Creoles as a multi-generational mixed race population. Our family situation speaks to the complex historical situation and socio-cultural context in this country through which white is privileged over not only black, but over mixed race populations.[1]

It was not until 2000, that individuals and communities like the Creoles of Louisiana even had the opportunity to identify themselves as full human beings when the census was forever changed in the United States. In the year 2000, the Office of Management and Budget for the first time in our nation's history allowed individuals and families, with multiracial backgrounds, to check two or more races on the federal census. Public debate and discourse was highly contested leading up to this historic change. On the one hand you had multiracial organizations such as the Association for Multiethnic Americans and Project Race debating whether or not we should have an actual multiracial category or the option to check two or more races. On the other hand, civil rights groups and organizations, particularly in the African American community were opposed to this change.

The fear has been a long and historic one, embedded in the very history of this nation's anti-miscegenation laws. Communities of color saw this as a "color-blind" race policy that would lead to the loss of monoracial population demographics and a retreat from race. While I can agree that there has been a long history of privileging white-of color mixtures, there has also been a long history of denying the role that multiracial people have played in historic civil rights legislation. Homer Plessy, a French Creole man helped to expose the segregation of the Jim Crow south's railroad cars, a case that eventually led to another key decision by the Supreme Court in 1954---*Brown v. the Board of Education*---argued by the multiracial attorney who would become the first African American Supreme Court Justice: Thurgood Marshall.

These are but two examples of a long list of multiracial social justice workers, leaders and advocates who acknowledged their multiracial identities while also working for social justice and against inequality in communities of color. But let me return here briefly to the contestation and debate over mixed-race identity and the census. Because this nation was founded by imperialists and terrorists, we are still reeling from the devastating impact of the American Indian genocide and holocaust that stripped lands away from so many indigenous and First Nations groups, not just in the United States, but throughout Latin America, Canada, and the Caribbean as well.

Because of the brutal, inhumane middle passage and the use of African slaves in this country, we know that the first mixed-race relationships in this nation were not consensual; they were the most vile, harsh forms of state sanctioned terror, violence, and sexual conquest perpetrated against the bodies of women of color, in particular against the bodies of African and Indigenous women. This history makes it very difficult and painful for some to acknowledge that relationships of true love came to exist even during the use of the Black Slaves Codes, the Antebellum Period, the Reconstruction period, all the way up through the Civil Rights Movement.

A contemporary example of the way in which mixed-race women's bodies have served as controllable by the state was the role played by biracial actress Halle Berry in *Monster's Ball*, for which she won an Oscar Award for Best Actress. Why does a woman of color, of mixed-descent have to be sexually exploited in a film to win an award in the twenty-first century? Part of the explanation for this is the on-going colonial gaze placed on the bodies of women of color and most often mixed-race women's bodies.

As we look to the future of our nation we can see that California's fastest growing youth demographic age 18 and under is multiracial. This is a trend to be found across the United States. What does all of this racial mixing and these new demographics indicate? That we have "overcome"? Surely a Critical Mixed Race Studies does not find this to be the answer. People have increasing access to each other cross-culturally and ethnically and the children of interracial marriages like their multiracial predecessors must continue to struggle against contemporary colonialism and globalization.

I must assert that it is by creating a Critical Mixed Race Studies Movement that we can move beyond simple racial formation theories to explain individual and group identity. We must move toward a collective consciousness that embraces our full humanity and this is only possible through and examination of cultural formation. Today, we as people of color, as mixed-race people, we share a common goal of dismantling hierarchies, but not our group specific cultural identities and practices.

I hear so often that, "we're all mixed-race anyway" but if we continue down this road that we're all just mixed then eventually we will become a nation without a culturally specific connection to our ancestors. We must ask will we lose valuable histories and potential coalitions in the fight for social justice and liberation? There is a soul wound in this country, which has come to exist because in intergenerational trauma that has never been addressed since the process of colonization began. This soul wound though is ironically most pronounced among white Americans who often say, "I don't have a culture or identity." I'm just human. When I hear people say I'm just human or everyone is mixed anyway…what I'm really hearing is that I do not know who I truly am and what my ancestors, all of my ancestors did to make this country what it is today. Good, bad, and indifferent.

What we need most to heal the soul wound is a deep return to community based healing and collective responsibility. This means un-doing the category white for ethnic specific categories so that in the same way whiteness was created to separate people its un-doing must attempt to bring people back together. This is a long process that will take many years to accomplish. But by acknowledging European ethnicity and returning to an identity beyond one's simple humanity or personhood, there is hope for something different.[2]

A Critical Mixed-Race Studies Movement will allow us to interrogate racial discourse in new ways. Not toward color-blindness, but toward critical cultural consciousness and new ideologies of equity. As we, the United States of America, become a more multiracial society and there is no more "white majority" or a "monoracial majority", how will be keep our culturally specific heritages intact if we do not acknowledge our full humanity?

This means we cannot and must not look back to a history of one-drop rules, hypodescent, blood quantum or mutually exclusive definitions that say we cannot be both or all-in-all. In other words, can we be both Mexican and Black, Chinese and German, Choctaw and French? I would say not only can we, but we must be all of the things that we are or we will run the risk of becoming the color-blind society we fear. To not recognize this new ethnic demographic is to ignore the future of our country and our world.

The power elite of this country already recognize this trend and as such we see key public figures making a number of racial comments that harbor the worst type of fear and soul wound. From Kramer the Seinfeld sitcom actor (during a comedy show made lynching comments to African Americans in the crowd because he felt he was "heckled" to Newt Gingrich (who said Spanish was the language of the "ghetto") and most recently Don Imus (called the Rutger's University women's basketball team a bunch of "nappy headed hos") people think it is okay to publicly lash out at people of color because they fear who we are and that they might continue to exist in the same ways as they have in the past. If we are to prevent a South African stile model where a minority population controls a majority of people of color including mixed-bloods, hen we must ask the question, Who is White?

Sitting around my grandmother's living room on Sunday afternoons as a child always left me feeling curious about my identity. One incident in particular reminds me of the problem of race and ethnicity when it comes to people of mixed descent. My aunts were talking with my grandma about work and some of her co-workers. I can still hear the words coming from her mouth when she re-told the story of a man who asked her what her race was, "Well I said I was White." I suddenly looked up and around the room to catch the eyes of my brothers and sister for a reaction. But there was none until we got home to debrief in private. Questioning who is white is something that I grew-up doing with my immediate family. Perhaps this is a common theme to be found in other multi-ethnic families throughout the United States. Growing up Creole meant that we knew that our dad's family was racially mixed despite the fact that two of our aunts, my grandmother and all of our cousins pretty much identified themselves as white throughout the 1980s and early 1990s (some have since changed the way that they self-identify).

Questioning who is white subverts the typical power dynamic in racial classification that usually marks as other those who are not white. Further, to question who is white is to challenge the structures of racial categorization and the arbitrary assignment of race and ethnicity by phenotype. In the twentieth century, sociologists argued that ethnicity and race would disappear because of changes in the modern world (Cornell & Hartmann, 1998: 4). Despite the predictions of important sociological scholars such as Robert Park, not only has race not disappeared, it has seemingly become an even more potent feature of contemporary society in the United States. Park argued that global forces such as trade, migration, new communication technologies, even the cinema-were bringing about a vast "interpenetration of peoples" (Cornell & Hartmann, 1998:4). Since the early twentieth century scholars have turned their attention to reasons for the prevalence of race among individuals and groups.

Thus, to question whiteness-as I questioned my own grandmother's whiteness-is to question the fixed and primordial nature of race and ethnicity for not only White Americans, but for mixed race Americans as well. Equally important is to challenge "whiteness" as a simple racial category as opposed to an ethnic one. Therefore, to question the "purity of white" is to understand how historical circumstances have worked to create, produce, transform, and reproduce European ethnics into American whites.[3]

In other words, to question whiteness is to change the racial model that we have used in this country for our entire history: a model that leaves us always speaking back to whiteness, rather than forcing whiteness to be something altogether new. I do believe that the 2000 census was an example of grassroots organizing led by multiracial people and their families and I would argue that mixed-race students on college campuses and in communities across this nation must commit themselves without reservation or hesitation to being who they are by not allowing others to tell them they cannot be in social justice movements because they are mixed.

People are often privileged by having at least one white parent or ancestor, but in fact many mixed-bloods have two parents of color or come from multigenerational mixed blood families. An example of how important this new work is to both local and national movements can be witnessed in two recent studies. One conducted in Seattle, Washington in 2006 that found that multiracial adolescents were more likely than their monoracial counterparts to engage in violence and substance abuse. Another study conducted in 2000 found that mixed-race gay men 15-22 have the second highest prevalence rate for HIV infection.[4]

These are real social problems. People of mixed descent are also facing extreme economic, social, and health disparities. We must work to understand these at both local and national levels. Two examples of the possibility for social change can be seen in the work of organizations like iPride (http://ipride.org) that work on a local and national level to do both anti-racism work, while also empowering young mixed-race race youth through the Multiethnic Education Program and the recent film, *My People Are* as well as the FUSION Program for mixed-heritage and transracially adopted youth.

One area where we can and must be most active is in organizing around youth empowerment, educational access, and multicultural education. Organizations like iPride are seeing tremendous success because they engage communities of color with an inclusive model for people of color from mixed backgrounds. To give young people of mixed descent the tools and language for self-definition and to combat racism will go along way in developing the future leaders of our country and world.

Starting at the elementary and middle school level is fundamental to ensuring that more people understand the experiences of mixed-race population demographics and the complexities that they often face, especially as double minorities—who are often marginalized as people of color and as mixed-race individuals. When you add other identity variables such as gender and sexual orientation, the experiences of marginalization can be even more extreme. This double minority status is central to the disparities faced by multiracial people today. By working to provide more access to education and critical multicultural curriculum we can do a lot to foster greater knowledge and understanding about racial justice.

Currently, in California, we see more young men of African and Latino descent incarcerated in prisons than attending the California State University and University of California systems combined. The only way we can create more access is by working directly with communities to understand how ideologies and structural inequalities go hand in hand in devastating entire communities. We must attack the rhetoric that diversity is the goal of multicultural education. Multiculturalism has been co-opted by neo-liberals and conservatives across this nation to mean diversity—which simply stated is a quantitative measure. True multiculturalism is about democratic education, equity, and access to a balanced curriculum and a non-Eurocentric paradigm for educating young people in this country.

Multiculturalism is about qualitative difference in the systems of support, access, retention, and successful matriculation of our students, not just as graduates, but as activists and community leaders. When universities, high schools, and employers use diversity only models they assume as long as people of color are present, then there is no problem. This is why some fifty-three years after the desegregation of public schools that we see a deliberate re-segregation of our nation's schools. Because just having people of color present without a voice/power and without cross-cultural dialogue there can never truly be change.

I would ask all of you: What are you willing to do to make sure that more people in your communities have access to education? Are you willing to initiate leadership and information campaigns in communities that do not experience the same privileges we do by our very presence in college campuses? Are you willing to partner your college club with local high school and middle school programs to actively engage in these issues…not just on your campus but out in our communities as well?

Another very serious issue facing our nation right now is immigrant rights. I find it very ironic that this, like so many other "ethnic specific" issues, is seen as something only immigrants should be concerned about or marching for. The media has cast the immigration movement as a Latino movement as if Latinos number one are the only people to emigrate to the U.S. when there are countless European, African, and Asian immigrants coming to this country every year. This issue impacts all of us. The other irony is that many of the immigrants being represented as coming from Latin America, especially Mexico are not immigrants. Their ancestors have lived on this continent for centuries and as mixed-race people, we must stand with our mixed-blood relatives who are not just Latino, but First Nations, Indigenous peoples who have a right to be here in the land of their ancestors.

This is a movement we should all be in engaged in and it is an example of how structural racism and inequality function to separate and divide people of color so we cannot mobilize together for the liberation of us all. A very wonderful example of how much coalitions can work is when people came together from the community to demand human rights as they did in San Francisco in October of 2006. I served as a member of the Native American Task Force to look at the status of American Indians in the city of San Francisco during the summer of 2006.

It was an amazing hearing before the city's Human Rights Commission and one of the best things about it is that there was so much diversity in terms of the indigenous peoples represented. Many of us were mixed-bloods. Some from Latin America, some Black-Indians, White-Indians, others were from Canada, but we were all united in our struggle for basic human dignity, cultural recovery and a right to our self-determination. Mixed-race people must be a part of every people of color movement in this country because we are a part of so many of these communities. We should not buy into the white supremacist model of divide and conquer that pits mixed-race people of color against those who identify as monoracial.

In 1967 we saw the historic Supreme Court decision in *Loving v. Virginia* strike down the last anti-miscegenation laws in seventeen states throughout this country. This past June, the 40th anniversary of the Loving decision was marked by a national conference held in Chicago, Illinois. Let us use this historic moment to invite ourselves into yet another fight for marriage equality and freedom. The Loving decision was possible because the court interpreted and applied the 14th amendment of equal protection and equal rights under the law to interracial couples. In the same way, the courts must see same-sex marriage as a struggle for equal protection under the 14th amendment.

We have seen for far too long in this country that difference equals the periphery. So, mixed-bloods, queers, people of color, women, people with different physical abilities have all been marginalized and disenfranchised from the "imagined American dream". We can recover that dream if we turn our attention to local and national level change. The American dream should be one that we narrate. You and I, all of us, we have the power if we dare to be brave and bold enough to take it. To turn the American dream into the American people's dream. We the everyday citizens did not craft the American dream, we inherited it and we must give it back because it is no proper inheritance. We must learn how to build community and then a dream for prosperity for everyone will begin to at least be possible.

This community building should focus on five areas: Health, Education, Employment, the Arts and what I would call The Streets. Health disparities in communities of color are on the risk in all areas. The five steps necessary to build a movement, a critical Mixed-Race Movement include:

1. Community involvement at local and regional levels.
2. A proactive commitment to addressing structural inequalities across racial and ethnic boundaries that have historically kept us from building inclusive coalitions.
3. The development of mixed race studies academic departments across the United States of America and on every university campus.
4. The development of social justice and anti-racist mixed race community based organizations at the grassroots level.
5. And finally, national and international mixed race conference and forums to set a movement agenda that includes an active deconstruction of global capitalism, on-going colonialism, and terrorists acts against the civil and human right of people of color.

One area of social justice that has been personally and professionally significant in my own life is HIV/AIDS among gay men of color and in particular among mixed-race gay men. There is little to no data on HIV and other health related problems for people of mixed descent. We have little knowledge about the experiences of this new emerging ethnic demographic in terms of schooling, prison incarceration, employment or other important social and economic areas. In order to make a difference we cannot wait to build movements and coalitions for social justice on local and national levels until they directly impact us. In my new research on mixed-race gay men I will be working closely with established ethnic specific HIV organizations such as the Black Coalition on AIDS, Hermanos de Luna y Sol, the Asian Pacific Islander Wellness Center, and the National Native American Prevention Center to understand how the needs of mixed-race clients are either met or unmet by these monoracial organizations. I use myself as an example of someone who has for all of my life focused on social problems, but who has also waited to respond to certain pressing issues until they impacted me directly. If there is one thing I would encourage you all to do today, it is to decide how you want to be involved and to join others even of the issues they face may not be the same issues that you are dealing with.

In the fall of 2002, HIV was something that I was aware of as a gay man of color, but I was more focused on more general issues of racial inequality. It wasn't until I was unexpectedly hospitalized and diagnosed with AIDS five years ago that I began to see, really see how race and sexuality were so closely linked to oppression in the United States. At 27, I was diagnosed with AIDS. I had 34 T-Cells (normal range is 500-1800) and over 500,000 copies of HIV per milliliter of blood in my body (the closer the viral load is to 1 million, the closer you are to death). Today I have over 600 T-Cells and my viral load is undetectable. I made a choice after this to do all I could to understand not only how this happened to me, but how it happens to so many other men like me. I disclosed my HIV/AIDS status at San Francisco State University where I have been a professor for the past five years during World AIDS Day in December of 2005.

> I wasn't sure if I should've disclosed my status in this way. I spoke with a colleague about it and he said, How will disclosing impact you? Will it benefit you? Are you giving anything up? I thought to myself, as a gay man of color, I have a responsibility to disclose. This is a very personal decision, but in communities of color we lack faces to make this pandemic real. If you've never known someone living with AIDS, now you do. You know my story and in sharing it I hope that others will know that they can live with this. They can have a career, a family, they too can find love again. Over the last five years I have learned AIDS is not me. I am me. AIDS is only one other part of my life.

This is a quote from the talk that I delivered two years ago at SF State. It is one way that I found to contribute and we all have to find our own ways to connect with our communities to make true change possible. Transformation can only happen in stages. The first stage of transformation in the current multiracial movement is full acknowledgement of our very existence. This means providing a means of documenting the number of mixed-race students attending schools at the elementary, middle, secondary and post-secondary levels...it means creating mixed-race studies departments across the country and mixed-heritage organizations in the community that will not work against, but along side and in struggle with other people of color organizations and academic departments. We should be working to create more small schools to keep our young people out of prisons, we should be soldiers on the streets making our voices, our experiences and our realities visible.

The representation of multiracial people in this country continues to focus on the exotic other, assumed to be always already tragic, privileged, a traitor, confused, or sexually available. We need to use current resources that we have like the MAVIN foundation, iPride, SWIRL, and other multiethnic organizations as a starting point to reach out to other multiracial demographics, people who are mixed within African American, Latino, and American Indian....these are populations that need more specific programs that address the unique forms of racial inequality that these communities face on a daily basis.

Let me conclude by returning to the census:

According to the 2000 census, less than 3% of the overall population (6.8 million) reported more than one race. "Of the 6.8 million respondents who reported two or more races, 93 percent reported exactly two. The most common combination was "White and Some Other race," representing 32 percent of the two or more races population. This was followed by White and American Indian and Alaska Native," representing 16%, "White and Asian," representing 13%, and "White and Black or African American," representing 11% (U.S. Census Bureau, 2000). There are, however, several questions that are left unanswered after analyzing the 2000 census and the additional options available since the 1990 census. First, it is unclear what the racial and ethnic backgrounds are of the people who checked Some Other Race as their ethnic background. This group represents 5.5% of the population or 15.3 million Americans.

> The most profound change to the question on race for Census 2000 is that respondents are allowed to identify one or more races to indicate their racial identity. There are 15 check box response categories and 3 write-in areas on the census 2000 questionnaire, compared with 16 check box response categories and 2 write-in areas in 1990. . . Finally, the category Some Other Race, which is intended to capture responses such as Mulatto, Creole, and Mestizo, also has a write-in area. All of the responses collected in Census 2000 can be collapsed into the minimum race categories identified in the 1997 revisions to the standards on race and ethnicity issued by the Office of Management and Budget, plus the category Some Other Race.[5]

One has to ask, how many multiracial people checked this box because none of the other categories accurately reflect their ethic and cultural background? How many Creoles and Mestizos for example chose to check two or more races? How many knew clearly that Some Other Race was intended for Creoles, Mestizos and Mulattos? The two or more races group also represents a large number 2.4% of the population or 6.8 million Americans. Combining these two figures, you get 22.1 million Americans (because Mestizos, Creoles and Mulattos are all multiracial). This number is larger than the Asian, American Indian, and Hawaiian categories respectively. One has to ask why there is a certain inclination on the part of Americans to check the other or two races or more categories? One obvious answer is that none of the other existing categories accurately reflect the identities of these 22.1 million people.

Over the last fifteen years the field of mixed-race studies has emerged in various disciplines: psychology, sociology, literature, and ethnic studies. Despite the forecasting of many scholars the field has failed to fully live up to its potential in part because defining such a community is such an enormous task with contested meanings on multiple levels. There has been little research focusing on the specific social problems faced by multiracial people in the United States.

Most of the early writing in this area has tended to focus on social and psychological development without going to the next stage of translating what this developmental process means in terms of real, applicable outcomes in the daily lives of this population. For mixed-race Americans, dealing with the "authenticity test" means answering the question: "Who do you belong to?" Where is the mixed-race person's allegiance? This binary of either/or right/wrong has inhibited the ability of multiracial Americans to get to a place where they can successfully negotiate what it means to be who they are, to form community, and to see themselves as legitimate members of any ethnic community. As definitions of relationships between different communities change, especially two marginal communities or one marginal and one dominant community, it means re-inventing or understanding one's place in the racial order of society.

Critical Mixed-Race Studies can recuperate itself by building bridges between communities, by partnering with youth, local civic leaders, and experienced civil rights activists to impact changes in public policy. The key to social justice today in the twenty-first century should be centered on constructing new paradigms for understanding social justice as more than an ideology. Social justice is an everyday practice that involves constant reflection, the ability to give something up, so that others might have access to the things we so freely enjoy. Our very existence, our very humanity depends upon recognizing and understanding the full complexities of racialized discourse in the face of global and imperialist capitalism. If we can begin to see beyond our own immediate needs and disagreements we can build a bridge to deconstruct the last five hundred years of colonial rule.

> Look into to my eyes...
> Recognize my humanity
> Look into my soul...
> I am a human being
> Look into my body...
> I am dark skinned
> You are light skinned
> Look into my blood...
> My ancestry contains the same blood as yours
> Look into my heart, see my experience....
> I am your brother, your sister, your mother, your father
> I am your child, be responsible for my future
> Look into yourself and tell me if you don't see that we are linked together in this struggle.
>
> Tell me, are we not most powerful when we stand together?
> When we look to the sun ON THE HORIZON OF A NEW DAY, of different paths we have crossed...
>
> We can see a future
> a soft whispering wind
> rushing forward
> to carry us closer
> to our own liberation and self-actualization.

Notes

1. This passage also appears in my book, *Louisiana Creoles: Cultural Recovery and Mixed-Race Native American Identity*. Lanham: Lexington Books, 2007.
2. The concept of soul wound that I use here is based on the work of Native American psychologists Eduardo and Bonnie Duran in their book, *Native American Post-Colonial*

Psychology. New York: SUNY, 1995. I discuss this concept in further detail in the essay, "Crash: An Centered Approach to Healing the Soul Wound" in *Crash Course: Reflections on the Film Crash for Critical Dialogues About Race, Power and Privilege* edited by Michael Benitez, Jr. and Felicia Gustin. Published by the Institute for Democratic Education and Culture. Available at http://www.speakoutnow.org

3. This section on whiteness is also discussed in Louisiana Creoles: Cultural Recovery and Mixed-Race Native American Identity. Lanham: Lexington Books, 2007. The passage also cites the book, Ethnicity and Race: Making Identities in a Changing World by Stephen Cornell and Douglas Hartmann. Thousand Oaks: Pine Forge Press, 1997.

4. The two studies referred to, "Are Multiracial Adolescents at Greater Risk? Comparisons of Rates, Patterns, and Correlates of Substance Use and Violence Between Monoracial and Multiracial Adolescents", Choi, Y. 2006American Journal of *Orthopsychiatry*, 76(1) 2006 and "HIV Prevalence and Associated Risks in Young Men Who Have Sex with Men" Valleroy, L. *Journal of the American Medical Vol. 284, No. 2, P. 198*

5. This is a quote from my text on Louisiana Creoles.

References

Choi, Y. "Are Multiracial Adolescents at Greater Risk? Comparisons of Rates, Patterns, And Correlates of Substance Abuse and Violence between Monoracial and Multiracial Adolescents." *American Journal of Orthopsychiatry* 76 (Winter 2006).

Cornell, Stephen, and Douglas Hartmann. *Ethnicity and Race: Making Identities in a Changing World*. Thousand Oaks, California: Pine Forge Press, 1997.

Duran, Eduardo, and Bonnie Duran. *Native American Post-Colonial Psychology*. Albany: SUNY University Press, 1995.

Jolivette, Andrew. *Louisiana Creoles: Cultural Recovery and Mixed Race Native American Identity*. Lanham, Maryland: Lexington Books, 2007.

Jolivette, Andrew. "Crash: A Centered Approach to Healing the Soul Wound." *Crash Course: Reflections on the Film Crash for Critical Dialogues about Race, Power, and Privilege,* ed. Michael Benitez, Jr., and Felicia Gustin. *The Institute for Democratic Education and Culture.* http://www.speakoutnow.org

Valleroy, Linda, and Duncan A. MacKellar. "HIV Prevalence and Associated Risks in Young Men Who Have Sex with Men." *Journal of the American Medical Association* 284 (July 2000): 198-2004

Chapter 9

Militant Multiraciality:
Rejecting Race and Rejecting the Conveniences of Complicity

Rainier Spencer

"Multiracial Solidarity!" "Multiracial Power!"[1]

What would a truly militant American politics of multiraciality look like? By this I mean a politics of multiraciality that did not merely declare its militancy, but one that actually was militant. Precisely what would it be militating against? Exactly what would it be protesting for? As might already be evident by the preceding few sentences, I do not consider multiracial activism in the United States to be a militant project. In fact, I do not think the American multiracial identity movement possesses a single militant bone in its entire ideological body. To be sure, current versions of multiracial identity politics are at times scrappy, bellicose, and belligerent; however—and this is a most critical point— those versions of multiracial identity politics are at no time scrappy, bellicose, or belligerent in opposition to the idea of race or to the American racial paradigm.[2] As I shall argue in this chapter, multiracial ideology is far more complicit with than it is subversive of current deployments of race in the United States. This, to my thinking, renders it a decidedly non-militant enterprise.

Introduction

Current popular wisdom asserts that we are in the midst of a paradigm shift concerning the way race is constructed in the United States. According to this view, individuals of mixed-race—most specifically, so-called first-generation multiracial persons—are confounding the American racial paradigm by virtue of their ambiguous phenotypes and their supposedly more cosmopolitan cultural outlooks.[3] This perspective is reflected in television and magazine advertising, in popular newsmagazine coverage, and in books both academic and non-academic. Kathleen Korgen provides a typical rendition of this standpoint with her announcement that "today mixed-race Americans challenge the very foundation of our racial structure."[4] *Newsweek* writer Lynette Clemetson concurs with Korgen, reporting that demographic changes in the United States "give many teens a chance to challenge old notions of race," and quoting in an affirmative light one high-school student's startling declaration that race "doesn't even really exist anymore."[5]

An Insurgent Multiracial Identity?

We hear that today's multiracial young adults accept a multiracial identity in far greater proportion than did their predecessors, but precisely what are they assenting to and what does it mean, if anything, beyond the pronouncement of a parentally indoctrinated fad? Advocates of multiracial identity have long argued that their position is destructive of race, that acceptance of multiracial identity will bring about the demise of the American racial paradigm. The arguments of scholars who favor multiracial identity, as well as the sentiments expressed via popular culture outlets by members of the multiracial movement, suggest that multiracial identity possesses an insurgent character, that advocacy of multiracial identity is therefore a militant stance for one to assume vis-à-vis the idea of race in the United States.

I as well as others have argued in turn that such a claim is without merit; that indeed it is quite self-contradictory since the very assertion of multiracial identity requires prior belief in biological race. If it is true that multiracial identity is a real and valid identity, then such an identity is sensible only *as* a biological racial identity. If words are to mean anything, and I very seriously believe they should, it quite obviously simply cannot be that a multiracial identity is somehow *not* a biological racial identity. If the issue were ethnicity, we would be debating the idea of multiethnic identity. If the issue were nationality, we would be debating the idea of multinational identity. If the issue were cultural affinity we would be debating the idea of multicultural identity. But as we are debating the idea of multiracial identity, the nature of that identity is made clear by the very wording in which the debate is framed. Nor is there any escape from this contradiction through asserting that racial identities are socially designated and not biological, since it is the sexual (and thereby biological) union of ostensibly differently raced parents that supposedly produces multiracial children. They are what they are said to be due to biological mixing, not social designation.

Multiracial Activists and Scholars Proclaim a "Militant Project"

Multiracial identity activists and the scholars who provide intellectual support for them share a belief that multiraciality is a militant project. Maria Root opens her second anthology on multiracial identity, *The Multiracial Experience: Racial Borders as the New Frontier*, with a chapter titled "A Bill of Rights for Racially Mixed People."[6] The major sub-headings for this chapter are "Resistance," "Revolution," and "Change," with Root averring that the "affirmation of rights" in her Bill "reflects *resistance, revolution*, and ultimately *change* for the system that has weakened the social, moral, and spiritual fiber of this country.[7] Moreover, Root offers this set of "affirmations or 'rights' as reminders to break the spell of the delusion that creates race to the detriment of us all."[8] Based on the clear intent of its author's own words, Jill Olumide is certainly correct in describing Root's Bill as a "programme of resistance," as is Kimberly DaCosta in terming it "a manifesto of sorts."[9]

Philosophically, it seems to me that this manifesto stands on two primary presumptions: (1) that multiracial activism is a militant cause [resistance, revolution, and change], and (2) that this activist project is corrosive of ideologies of biological race [such ideologies being marked by the manifesto as constituting a delusional spell that ought to be broken]. These presumptions undergirding Root's manifesto are also the primary presumptions of the multiracial identity movement at large, as the latter has been constructed consciously and conspicuously upon the former.

Root's Bill of Rights is somewhat dated, but nevertheless nothing has since come along to displace it. Rather, it has solidified and achieved for itself a sort of cult status within the ideology of the multiracial identity movement, and therefore must be said to still be very much alive in a deeply pervasive sense. Indeed, G. Reginald Daniel reports that, "ritualistic practices within the multiracial community include the reading of Maria Root's 'Bill of Rights for Racially Mixed People' at support group meetings and conferences."[10] In addition, Marion Kilson and Loretta Winters close their respective book and anthology on multiracial identity by reprinting the complete text of Root's Bill of Rights in the Epilogue of each.[11]

Kim Williams further highlights the continuing significance of Root's Bill by noting that "perhaps the most extensively reproduced statement exemplifying the movement's broad goals can be found in Maria Root's 'Bill of Rights for Racially Mixed People,' which has become something of a charter statement within the activist multiracial community."[12] Because of the status of Root's Bill within multiracial activist circles and its continuing impact on the movement as a whole, I want to hold its two premises (that multiracial activism and advocacy is a militant project, and that multiracial activism works to undermine race) as central to my overall analysis in this chapter.

The thesis in this chapter is that the multiracial movement, which congratulates itself so continuously and so effusively for its success at being militant and at working against notions of biological race, is not at all successful in accomplishing these two goals. In fact, critical analysis reveals quite clearly that it is engaged in neither task in an active way. Indeed, due to the nature of its true goals the movement cannot undertake these tasks with anything approaching sincerity and integrity. Rather, the American multiracial identity movement is a self-indulgent social enterprise whose primary aim is to bend the bars of race just enough to move its adherents upward from lesser- to more-privileged positions within the structure of the American racial paradigm.

This might not seem evident if one's information about the multiracial movement comes from the voices of movement leaders and adherents via the generally unreflective pages of popular newsmagazines such as *Time* and *Newsweek*, or through academic works written by movement scholars such as Daniel, Kilson, Korgen, and Ursula Brown, for instance.[13] Significantly, discussing pro-movement academics whose work was utilized by multiracial organizers during the federal multiracial category debates of the mid-1990s, DaCosta makes the important point that "the messages in some of the writings by these academics, most of whom identify as mixed race or are themselves intermarried, are indistinguishable from those of activists," noting further that Root's Bill of Rights "illustrates the extent of this parity."[14]

The Logical Contradiction

The writings of these scholar-activists, alongside a consistent brand of popular media coverage that can only be described as overwhelmingly bathetic, are responsible for the remarkable success of the multiracial movement; however, the remarkable success to which I am here referring is not at all related to the stated goals of the movement (militancy and the undermining of race), which as I have noted have been neither achieved nor even attempted. Rather, the remarkable success—indeed, one might argue, the only success—of the multiracial movement has been in conflating in a highly effective way those stated goals with what are in reality the de facto goals of the movement (enhancement of personal self-esteem and a concerted movement away from blackness). In the most basic sense it is a case of stating one thing while actually doing the opposite, a logical flaw with which the multiracial movement has found itself ensnared from the very beginning of its existence. Its consistent response to that flaw has been to emphasize the stating of the one thing and to ignore or camouflage the doing of that "opposite."

When introducing her Bill of Rights, in a discussion of the multiracial person's not having to justify her or his existence in this world, Root, referring to invasive questions posed by people (by monoracial people, quite obviously) mentions a few of the "stereotypes that make up the schema by which the *other* attempts to make meaning out of the multiracial person's existence."[15] What is most interesting to me in reading this passage, however, are not the stereotypes Root mentions, but rather her instructive choice of language in situating monoracials as the "*other*" in the context of a discussion in which she also advises multiracial persons to refuse to "uncritically apply to others the very concepts that have made some of us casualties of race wars."[16]

This leads quite obviously to the question of what the multiracial person is to do. Does she heed Root by refusing to take part in categorical stereotypes that facilitate the construction of racial boundaries or does she heed Root by imagining the diverse collectivity of monoracial persons as a stereotypical and unitary category of *"other"* against which she then constitutes her own identity? Moreover, given that one of the true operative dynamics of the multiracial movement is the attempt to move its constituents upward within the racial hierarchy toward whiteness and, most especially, away from blackness, it is reasonable to assume that the monoracial *"other"* Root imagines here is a non-white *"other."* In any case, engaging in the former would seem to preclude the latter and vice versa, highlighting the logical contradiction inherent in saying one thing and doing the opposite.

This sort of logical contradiction has been and still is being reproduced continuously through the ideology of the multiracial movement that looks to Root's Bill of Rights for Racially Mixed People as a foundational document. As an example of this reproduction, Erica Childs, writing about major multiracial websites, reports that "despite fostering a sense of community and place of acceptance for multiracial individuals and families, a sense of 'us versus them' is created, pitting the multiracial community against the 'enemy,' who is readily identified as people of color who identify with traditional racial and ethnic communities."[17] Given that such websites are often a person's initial encounter with organized multiracial activism, their influence should not be underestimated in terms of how they shape perceptions of what authentic multiraciality entails and of how this identity should be constituted vis-à-vis outsider *"others."* The influence and the double nature of Root's Bill are clear in this example, where the natural consequence of the multiracial impulse can be seen to have played itself out.

In making the case for the movement's militant character, advocates of multiracial identity politics often pronounce themselves to be free of race, to be beyond race, to have transcended the American fixation on and paranoia with race. Certainly this would be a most worthy accomplishment, but as I and others have argued many times, multiracial identity is unintelligible without the foundation of biological race upon which it depends. Thus, the celebratory tones in which adherents of multiracial identity and "Generation Mixed"-ness trumpet their freedom from the chains of race are every bit as self-conflicting as they are self-congratulatory.[18] This is apparent on at least two fronts—in the proclamations of adherents themselves and in the glossy magazine advertisements and television spots that use these people, usually young people and especially young women, to sell merchandise through the exploitation of an image of racial mixedness.

In instances of the latter, the showcased mixedness is actually no more than a fad, while it masquerades as something much more powerful and significant than it actually is. In elevating a self-indulgent social fad to the status of a socially conscious, transgressive politics the advertisers succeed in prostituting the manufactured exoticness of Generation Mixed in order to sell a false image of progress against the racial superstructure while at the same time prevailing perversely in cementing that very superstructure ever more firmly into place. Readers might wonder why the assertion and proliferation of mixed-race identity and imagery do not weaken the American racial paradigm. As I intend to demonstrate through the remainder of this chapter, the answer to such a query has to do with the difference between real structural change at the foundational level of the paradigm and purely cosmetic adjustments on its surface.

Ambiguous Imagery

Something that has failed to generate adequate attention is the fact that it is a very specific type of mixed-race imagery that is proliferating lately—an imagery that is often part-Asian or thoroughly ambiguous (with an important caveat), and *if* partaking in blackness is usually of a very much lighter-skinned variety. The caveat referred to above has to do with my use of the term "ambiguous." This imagery is ambiguous in the sense that it is not easily categorizable as—for lack of better language—100 percent white, but is nonetheless not clearly black. As will be described below, despite the celebration of mixedness and the equality it might be presumed to imply, a motivation of increasing distance from blackness and increasing nearness to whiteness is very much at work here.

Sushi Das, writing in an Australian publication about marketing trends in global perspective and also making several specific references to the United States, notes that "ambiguity, it seems, is in vogue and the current fascination with racial hybrid is reflected in the myriad ethnic looks eagerly adopted by models and other trend setters."[19] She finds that "ad campaigns for top-end brands such as Louis Vuitton, YSL and Lancome all use models with racially indeterminate features, and the look is also being embraced in the music world."[20] Das conveys the words of a Melbourne modeling agency executive who "knows exactly what advertisers want" and who "reports a hike in demand for mixedrace models."[21] Speaking of a trend in regard to which Australia is attempting to catch-up with the rest of the world, this executive asserts that "over the last couple of years, there has been an increase in using Asian people in advertising, and also a lot of people like the mixed-race look as well: not too Asian, but with a bit of a Western feel. We handle a lot of Asian and Eurasian models."[22]

Specifically linking these kinds of advertisers with the rising general trendiness of multiracial identity, Das opens the door for a questioning of which is cause and which is effect here, and also for an assessment of how deeply rooted either in reality or in any sort of progressive politics this display of multiracial imagery is: "Cheekily referring to themselves as the 'remix generation,' this group of young people sees a future born out of a mixed-race heritage. While models, superstars and pop idols chase the latest 'look,' advertisers and marketing teams are frantically pumping out images that they say reflect a multicultural society."[23] If this frantic pumping out of multiracial imagery in search of the most recent popular "look" is nothing more than pure marketing, if it contains no element of political consciousness, then it is subject to the same critique Caroline Streeter makes in regard to a Levi-Strauss American billboard advertisement featuring a mulatto woman that in her view "relies on celebratory and ahistorical rhetoric that elides the vexed strategies that racially mixed subjects have deployed to negotiate hierarchies of race and color."[24]

In Streeter's view, "this kind of multicultural imagery makes racially mixed people symbolic embodiments of antidiscrimination while using their images to mask persistent inequalities."[25] It is a view that meshes nicely with that of Julie Matthews, who in analyzing the supposed transgressiveness of Eurasian mixed race identity politics through the lens of performativity discovers that:

> "Its vacant hollowness overflows with alluring impressions of cosmopolitan transnational/transcultural attributes and embodied visual aesthetics. Fear and antipathy to miscegenation is smoothed over, rather than effaced when the mixed-race other is recoded as 'cosmo chic—familiar, knowable, sophisticated and worldly."[26]

But while the imagery in these non-transgressive and non-politically conscious advertising campaigns tends for the most part to be either part-Asian or ambiguous, the narrative articulated by local and national multiracial identity organizations and support groups is—owing to the principal membership and leadership of those organizations, which tends to be white mothers of black/white children—overwhelmingly a message about black/white mixture and its supposed transformative effect on the structuring of race in the United States. In highlighting this divergence, I am arguing that there is a sense in which that black/white narrative is riding a wave of part-Asian/ambiguous multiracial imagery and part-Asian/ambiguous upward movement within the American racial paradigm, and taking advantage of the content of a particular conversation that it is actually not a party to.[27]

In other words, to use one particular and very relevant example, while an increase in so-called interracial marriages and multiracial births is tied to a marked surge in immigration from Asia and Central and South America stemming from the easing of United States immigration laws in 1965, and while black/white marriages and black/white multiracial births continue to represent the lowest percentages of all, the American multiracial identity movement nonetheless consistently deploys the erroneous message that the 1967 *Loving v. Commonwealth of Virginia* Supreme Court decision outlawing state anti-miscegenation statutes is directly responsible for these purely immigration-fed increases; and further, that black/white marriages and interracial births represent a significant portion of this so-called "boom." This erroneous narrative delivers a twin set of false impressions: (1) that *Loving*, although relevant in a technical sense to all intermarriages, had a significant practical impact beyond the black/white scenario, and (2) that *Loving* was itself a watershed moment in the history of American consensual black/white intimacy.

The fact, though, is that excepting black/white marriages, all of the other intermarriages since the loosening of immigration laws in 1965 would have taken place even if the *Loving* decision had not been rendered. This is because the good people of Alabama, Mississippi, and the remainder of the 1967 anti-miscegenation states who were concerned about intermarriage were concerned specifically about black/white intermarriage. They were not concerned about Native American/white, Hispanic/white, or Asian/white marriage. Only on the west coast was Asian/white intermarriage a major issue historically, and it had been placed well on the way toward resolution seventeen years earlier by the 1948 outlawing of anti-miscegenation laws in California.[28] Moreover, *Loving's* wrongly celebrated significance as an emblem of black/white intimacy is shown to be fallacious by very fact that black/white intermarriages remain statistically the lowest of all in the United States—despite the telling reality that blacks have been in this country far longer than the Asian and Hispanic immigrants now welcomed by many whites as marriage partners.

It is absolutely essential to see that any assertions that black/white intermarriage rates are booming or that black/white births are soaring through appeal to national intermarriage and multiracial birth rates is misinformation that depends on conflating a specifically immigration-driven phenomenon involving Asians and Hispanics with a relatively static situation obtaining between whites and blacks in the United States. That this kind of conflation is precisely what popular newsmagazines such as *Time* and *Newsweek* engage in on a consistent basis should come as no surprise.[29] And this is significant since most Americans surely obtain their information on the multiracial identity debate from popular sources such as these, accepting the misinformation with which they have been presented, and as a consequence believing, wrongly, that they have thereby been educated.

Is multiraciality initiating an upheaval in the construction of race in America? It is true that racially ambiguous looks are certainly more in vogue in the advertising world. It is also true that immigrants from Asia and Central and South America are intermixing with white Americans in far greater proportion than are American blacks. These are phenomena that have far, far much more to do with Asians and Hispanics than with blacks, yet white mothers of black/white children ride the wave of Asian/white and Hispanic/white mixing and the national consumption of racially ambiguous advertising models in an attempt to make the case that race in general is breaking down, when in fact their children are at the absolute farthest remove from any breakdown of the American racial paradigm.

The Continuous Evolution of Race

Regardless of one's standpoint, race in America is not breaking down or otherwise being deconstructed. It is evolving, as it has done for centuries, in response to new pressures. As whites become a numerically smaller proportion of the American populace, race is evolving so as to allow some persons of Asian and Hispanic descent to enter through the coveted door to whiteness. Although this surface modification occurs, others who are not as close to whiteness as these—including those with sub-Saharan African ancestry but who are nonetheless not perceived to be 100 percent black—are moving away from blackness toward an intermediate status. For activist white mothers of black/white children, this intermediate status is multiracial identity.

Recent research has captured the shift I am referring to here.[30] This research points out the relatively new freedom for some Asians to become "honorary whites," and for their part-white children and grandchildren to become accepted fully as white—even though their Asian ancestry is known. This phenomenon, relatively new for Asians, has long been operative for Native Americans; and since it is already the case that Hispanics may be either white or non-white, it quite obviously applies to them as well. However, this experience of "honorary whiteness" and of racially mixed children and grandchildren being accepted fully as white—despite their non-white ancestry being known—is simply not possible in the black context. Regardless of the newfound upward mobility within the American racial paradigm of some persons of Asian and Hispanic descent, acknowledged sub-Saharan African ancestry disqualifies black/white persons from participating in whiteness. If whiteness is truly desired in their cases, racial passing as white remains the only full solution. Short of passing as white, the best that may be hoped for is a movement away from blackness, a movement into the intermediate multiracial status mentioned above.

But it is critical to understand that none of these moves toward whiteness and away from blackness serve to disrupt the race concept. The American racial paradigm evolves continually but is in no sense ever deposed or even challenged, because at its most elemental level of structure lies a simple binary equation of white purity and black impurity. Everything else regarding race in America is erected upon this structure. Without a significant alteration of this most basic equation—an equation requiring the deployment of hypodescent—any other changes to the American racial paradigm are essentially cosmetic only.[31] In other words, until such time as it is no longer accepted that a white woman may give naturally conceived birth to a black child but a black woman may never give naturally conceived birth to a white child, white purity and race in America remain unchallenged and unchanged. This is the only truly relevant test of change.

That the continuing maintenance of whiteness requires that it now accept the occasional incorporation of some measure of Asian or Hispanic ancestry is no threat to white purity, for that purity—which has always been merely illusory anyway—has simply been rearticulated accordingly. We must remember, after all, that biological race is in the first place hardly a logical enterprise, and that such a rearticulation therefore incurs no penalty in the thought process of the American imaginary. As a simple confirmation of this, we might consider the certainty that many white Americans of decades and centuries past would have been incredulous at the proposition of Greeks, Italians, or the Irish being considered white; yet these groups are unproblematically white today.

The only development that actually could shake the foundation of race in the United States would be a clear and total rejection of hypodescent, but no such clear and total rejection has been demanded in the protests and militancy of multiracial activists, and no such clear and total rejection will be forthcoming. Despite their claim of despising hypodescent, multiracial activists cannot reject it for they require monoracial black parents in order to create the false consciousness of first-generation black/white mixed-race children, and those monoracial black parents are made possible expressly through the selective application of hypodescent. Multiracial activists will howl in complaint if a black/white child is made subject to hypodescent; yet these same activists demonstrate no concern whatsoever in making the same child's black parent subject to a selective hypodescent that effaces completely that person's substantial history of population mixture. Due in part to the work of these multiracial identity activists, hypodescent—the popularly understood illustration of the foundational black/white binary upon which the American racial paradigm is based—remains very much alive and well in the United States.

In emphasizing the centrality of the black/white binary to the construction of race in America, this in no way implies that Asians do not endure racism or that Native Americans and Hispanics lead unproblematic lives in a racist America. Rather, it is to point out quite specifically that the fundamental underpinning of the race concept in America goes back hundreds of years to the creation of whiteness in constitutional opposition to blackness. This binary relationship is the foundation of race as Americans know it. In the simplest sense, it is to say that although whiteness has expanded its previous limits and can now be a bit Asian, somewhat Hispanic, or partly Native American, it can in no sense be a little black and still remain white. That is the fundamental predicate, the defining characteristic, of the American racial paradigm. Multiraciality, regardless of its seemingly endless and self-congratulatory celebration, does nothing to contest or disrupt this deep structure.

A few elemental questions therefore follow from this reality. Do the solemn recitation of Root's Bill of Rights for Racially Mixed People, the self-conscious exhibitionism of Generation-Mixed hipness, and the politically vacant exoticization and eroticization of mixed-race advertising models rise to the level of militant activism? Does the constant pleading of white mothers of black/white children to free their children from blackness and move those children nearer to whiteness represent a motivation or intention to challenge the American racial paradigm and its primary operative dynamic of white purity and black impurity? How can the surface alteration of the paradigm so that some former non-whites may become "honorary whites," and so that their children and grandchildren may become full whites be taken seriously as anything related remotely to "resistance," "revolution," and "change"? Where is the militancy in begging to be part of a paradigm of biological race as opposed to working actively to destroy that paradigm? In what sense is a paradigm of biological race undermined, deconstructed, or even challenged if one's desperate goal is to become a recognized constituent of it via the formal advocacy of multiracial identity within the structure of that very paradigm?

There is no revolutionary suicide in the American multiracial identity movement, for it is instead a movement of reactionary accommodation and nothing more.[32] In Charles Gallagher's view, "rejecting the monoracial categories imposed on multiracial people is taken as an act of revolution and ultimately such insurgency can bring about positive social change by acknowledging how the idea of race as a socially constructed category reflects power, politics, and the maintenance of white privilege."[33] Yet according to Gallagher, this has not taken place. Instead, "what appears to be taking place is a reconfiguring of existing racial categories."[34] This reconfiguration is one in which proximity to whiteness and the consequent distance from blackness is what is valued. Assessing descriptions of multiracial people conceived as ushering in the deconstruction of race, Rebecca King-O'Riain finds that "key in all of these predictions is the importance of not visually sticking out and being able to blend in with whiteness as the basis of equality."[35]

In the view of Jennifer Lee and Frank Bean, "at this time, America's shift in color lines points to the emergence of a new split that replaces the old black/white divide and one that separates blacks from nonblacks, or what sociologists refer to as a black/nonblack divide. In a black/nonblack divide, Latinos and Asians fall into the nonblack category."[36] Eduardo Bonilla-Silva comes to a similar conclusion in what he terms the "Latin-Americanization of Whiteness in the United States."[37] One struggles in vain to discern evidence of any revolutionary character in this alarming development, one in which moving away from blackness is a principal motivation.

In the same vein, and specifically examining the black/white case, Minkah Makalani's work "raises serious doubts about the biracial project's claim to be a progressive social movement. Rather than seeking to overthrow the racialized social system, it is a reactionary political response to the racialization of people of African descent in the United States as Black. Specifically, it uses whiteness to distinguish PMP [people of mixed parentage] from African Americans as a new race that would be positioned between Blacks and whites in a reordered, racialized social system."[38] The fact that the multiracial movement operates from within the structural organization of the American racial paradigm necessitates, indeed guarantees, this reality.

The multiracial movement's accommodation to, as opposed to any opposition to, white purity and selective hypodescent is tied to the movement's unquenchable desire for distance from blackness and its absolutely comfortable positioning within America's racial and racist structure. As Jared Sexton describes, "it is because the position of the multiracial does not break from the assumptive logic of anti-miscegenation that it can be accommodated by white supremacy. It threatens the racial schema from within but does not seek to challenge the regime of meaning, reason, interpretive capture, and definition that white Anglo racism paints in such bold strokes. It merely seeks to refine or reconfigure the apparatus, to establish a space for the full play of a multiracial identity or a race-transcendent human identity. It is, in other words, a battle within the bounds of the strategic field, contained by the fear of being undone or losing itself in the struggle."[39]

Is it progressive and militant or is it retrograde and discriminatory for a movement to advocate the continued veneration of white purity via acceptance of biological race and selective hypodescent? There is a clear sense of superiority—and, one supposes, it would have be a racial superiority—in the transcendent celebrations of Generation Mixed. The idea seems to be that these young people are mixed and mixing with abandon, and that such mixing is in itself some sort of revolutionary act deserving of celebration.[40] But precisely what is being celebrated? If the mere fact of population mixture is being celebrated, it is already an old story that certainly does not begin with Generation Mixed. It has been done before, both coercively and consensually, and is at least centuries old.

Discussing the threat that may be posed by unstable identities, Martha Cutter notes that "a player who refuses to play by the rules calls those rules into question, suggesting that they are not permanent, fixed, and closed but changeable, unstable, and open."[41] In what way, we might ask, does the advocacy of multiracial identity accord with the latter as opposed to the former? To be sure, most Americans may take it as a commonplace that mixedness destabilizes and undermines the racial structure. This is, after all, the consistent message from scholars writing in favor of multiracial identity and from popular media sources. So our questions are these: Does Generation Mixed in fact refuse to play by the rules? Is it true that these youthful purveyors of multiracial identity call the system of racial categorization into question by confounding the possibilities for the assignation of racial identities?

Playing by the rules in regard to race consists in assenting to belief in biological race, in biological racial groups, and in the assignment of persons to particular biological racial groups.[42] This is the racial superstructure that Generation Mixed is supposedly bringing down to a crashing ruin. Yet in celebrating their mixedness, the members of Generation Mixed are celebrating precisely the fact—not that they are transcending biological race at all—but that they are engaged in a very active way in the race work of instituting a new biological racial identity in the United States. The celebration of Generation Mixed is nothing less than a celebration of the active construction of biological race. As Minelle Matani notes, "clearly, 'mixed race' people have been made intelligible in ways that maintain racial hierarchies."[43]

This reality marks it as a retrograde movement in the sense that it resurrects the long-buried mulatto category of times past. Of course, the members of Generation Mixed do not claim the mulatto mantle overtly; to do so would be too explicit an embrace of biological race. However, under the guise of rejecting and transcending biological race, Generation Mixed brings the mulatto back to life, but without tragedy. Indeed, far from tragedy, the Generation Mixed version of the mulatto is celebrated as a racially superior being insofar as belief in biologically multiracial people amongst biologically monoracial people is privileged over belief in biologically monoracial people only.

The New Millennium Mulatto

Moreover, this new millennium mulatto is not only black/white, but may encompass all varieties of biological racial mixture. In a sense, then, the mulatto concept is being resurrected even though people are not embracing a mulatto identity in an overt way. In other words, if one asked the members Generation Mixed if they were adopting a new mulatto identity, they would surely say that they are not. Yet, the structure they are erecting is precisely the resurrection of the mulatto—the mixed-race person who is distinct racially from either ostensibly pure parent. This resurrected mulatto is no more than a confirmation of the logical reality that mixed-race advocacy depends absolutely on acceptance of biological race. Regardless of how many empty manifestos one might recite, there is no separating biological race from the quest for multiracial identity, which once again highlights the logical contradiction inherent in saying one thing and doing the opposite.

Interrogating the American mixed race movement, including mention of Root's Bill of Rights, Stephen Small reaches a similar conclusion in his observation that "it is clear that 'race' remains central to their enterprise."[44] That race occupies this central position in the movement is made clear by Root herself. One of the affirmations listed in Root's Bill is the right "not to keep the races separate within me."[45] Given that in the same piece of writing she also refers to race as a delusion whose spell ought to be broken, it is difficult to see how that ostensibly revolutionary goal is to be accomplished in the context of an acknowledgement of biological races that are "within" people. The truly radical position would be to deny that any races—whether separate or mixed—are "within" anyone.

According to Root, "the multiracial person's existence challenges the rigidity of racial lines that are a prerequisite for maintaining the delusion that race is a scientific fact."[46] Root's statement turns out to have been rather superbly crafted, however, since her seemingly deconstructive and seemingly radical words actually only allow for a very specific and very limited reading of racial revolution. It is a faux militancy that is reflected in the movement itself, for the racial project of the multiracial movement and of Generation Mixed is very specifically to challenge the "rigidity" of racial lines only; it is not to challenge the racial lines themselves. In other words, what the members of Generation Mixed work to do is to bend those lines so as to blend themselves more comfortably into the American racial paradigm—either through the successful infiltration to whiteness or through the construction of multiracial identity as a discrete biological racial identity both distinct from and superior to blackness. The only militancy deployed in this effort by Generation Mixed is militancy directed against a connection to blackness, which hardly represents a revolutionary stance in the United States either yesterday or today.

If one is to truly engage in "resistance," "revolution," and "change" vis-à-vis the American racial paradigm, one must first undergo personal "racial death," which simply means that one must allow one's belief in and accommodation to biological race to die. One must actively put one's own biological racial identity to death oneself before one is qualified to be a racial revolutionary, before one can engage in militant multiraciality.[47] True militant multiraciality requires a suicidal stance, not an attitude of accommodation. True militant multiraciality requires the vigorous assassination of race; it is certainly not represented or enabled by Daniel's "kumbaya" image of mixed-race racial wannabes holding hands and reciting Root's Bill of Rights around the metaphorical campfire.

Actual militancy would involve a good bit more than celebrating one's mixedness and reciting a set of desired rights. It would involve active work against the notion of biological race, and it would be directed toward results that would actually be destructive of race. It would not, as are the efforts of Generation Mixed, be directed at accommodating oneself to the American racial paradigm by requesting the addition to that paradigm of a single new category somewhere above the black category. True militancy would aim at effecting real change to race, and as such would demand the elimination of hypodescent in all its deployments—including the selective hypodescent that makes possible the monoracial black parents of supposed black/white multiracial children. True resistance, true revolution, and true change cannot be achieved by the proponents of Generation Mixed celebrating themselves as a new biological race made possible by the imaginary and scientifically vacant racial differences of their parents. Real change can only be a consequence of real work undertaken by real militants.

Conclusion

The somewhat frustrating reality in all of this is that the absolute best agents of militant multiraciality would be multiracial individuals themselves, most especially black/white persons. Imagine if such persons truly were interested in racial militancy. Instead of celebrating the fallacious nonsense of there being "races within them," they would reject race, they would refuse the conveniences of being complicit with the American racial paradigm, and they would resist constructing yet another biological racial identity in the United States. Imagine if rather than strutting their alleged biological alterity, the members of Generation Mixed instead offered themselves as physical examples of the fact that biological race does not exist, that they cannot be placed scientifically or logically in any biological racial group (including a multiracial one), that subjecting them to hypodescent is no more than the perpetuation of a completely corrupt social caste system, and that they have no interest whatsoever in either being nearer to whiteness or in distancing themselves from blackness—such proximity and distance being illusory accommodations to a nonexistent biological racial schema.

Rather than claiming to be biologically multiracial, the members of Generation Mixed would instead refuse racial identity altogether, taking the revolutionary step of preferring racial suicide to racial accommodation. Rather than dodging blackness by pleading for a multiracial category, white mothers of black/white children would instead argue that hypodescent in all forms is corrupt and that their children are neither black, white, nor multiracial—that those children are in fact, living proof that race, and along with it hypodescent, is a false consciousness. Such uncomfortable positions would represent true radicalism in opposition to race in the United States. They would represent significant steps away from the hegemony and the hierarchy of race.

If the multiracial identity movement were actually concerned with real militancy in regard to race—if "resistance," "revolution," and "change" were truly sought, rather than accommodation to and complicity with the American racial paradigm—the movement could represent an insurgent impulse. But as long as it involves itself in the logical contradiction of declaring on the one hand that race is a delusion whose spell ought to be broken, while on the other lobbying actively for the construction of biological multiracial identity, the American multiracial identity movement will remain open to the charge of saying one thing and doing the opposite. That kind of philosophical stance, that sort of ideological orientation, whatever else it might be called, surely cannot in any meaningful way be described as militant.

Notes

1. From a flyer announcing the Multiracial Solidarity March of July 20, 1996.
2. Race terms in this chapter are always a reference to people's misguided belief in biological race and the American racial paradigm. Given that my topic concerns the notion of racially mixed people in the United States, my use of such terms is necessary as I endeavor to engage the debate using the linguistic tools currently at our disposal. Race terms in this chapter, therefore, should always be read as if preceded by the words *so-called*. The only alternatives would have been to utilize far too many italicizations or to deploy cumbersome phraseology such as "persons who are perceived as, or who consider themselves to be, black," (or "white," "black/white," or "multiracial," etc.) either of which would have distracted unacceptably from the text itself.
3. "First-generation" multiracial individuals are taken to be those whose parents are presumed to be unmixed members of two distinct racial groups (i.e., black/white, Asian/Native American, etc.). The fact that this is scientific nonsense appears to have no impact on the thinking of those who advocate this particular identity.
4. Kathleen O. Korgen, *From Black to Biracial: Transforming Identity Among Americans* (Westport, CT: Praeger, 1999), 7.
5. Lynette Clemetson, "Color My World: The Promise and Perils of Life in the New Multiracial Mainstream," *Newsweek*, May 8, 2000, 70.
6. Maria P. P. Root, "A Bill of Rights for Racially Mixed People," in *The Multiracial Experience: Racial Borders as the New Frontier*, ed. Maria P. P. Root (Thousand Oaks, CA: Sage, 1996), 3.
7. Ibid., 6, 9, 12. Italics in original.
8. Ibid., 6.
9. Jill Olumide, *Raiding the Gene Pool: The Social Construction of Mixed Race* (London: Pluto Press, 2002), 63; Kimberly M. DaCosta, *Making Multiracials: State, Family, and Market in the Redrawing of the Color Line* (Stanford: Stanford University Press, 2007), 219n10.
10. G. Reginald Daniel, *More Than Black? Multiracial Identity and the New Racial Order* (Philadelphia: Temple University Press, 2002), 116.
11. Marion Kilson, *Claiming Place: Biracial Young Adults of the Post-Civil Rights Era* (Westport: Bergin and Garvey, 2001), 172; Loretta I. Winters, "Epilogue: The Multiracial Movement: Harmony and Discord," in *New Faces in a Changing America: Multiracial*

Identity in the 21st Century, eds. Loretta I. Winters and Herman DeBose (Thousand Oaks, CA: Sage, 2003), 373.

12. Kim M. Williams, "Linking the Civil Rights and Multiracial Movements" in *The Politics of Multiracialism: Challenging Racial Thinking*, ed. Heather M. Dalmage (Albany: State University of New York Press, 2004), 88.

13. Ursula Brown, *The Interracial Experience: Growing Up Black/White Racially Mixed in the United States* (Westport, CT: Praeger, 2001).

14. DaCosta, *Making Multiracials*, 34–35.

15. Root, "A Bill of Rights," 7. Italics in original.

16. Ibid., 6.

17. Erica C. Childs. "Multirace.com: Multiracial Cyberspace," in *The Politics of Multiracialism: Challenging Racial Thinking*, ed. Heather M. Dalmage (Albany: State University of New York Press, 2004), 154.

18. "Generation Mixed" and "Generation Remix" are two terms sometimes used self-descriptively by young advocates of multiracial identity.

19. Sushi Das, "They've got the Look," *The Age*, April 20, 2004 <http://www.theage.com.au/articles/2004/04/19/1082357106748.html>.

20. Ibid.

21. Ibid.

22. Ibid.

23. Ibid.

24 .Caroline A. Streeter, "The Hazards of Visibility: 'Biracial' Women, Media Images, and Narratives of Identity," in *New Faces in a Changing America: Multiracial Identity in the 21st Century*, eds. Loretta I. Winters and Herman DeBose (Thousand Oaks, CA: Sage, 2003), 308–311.

25. Ibid., 311.

26. Julie Matthews, "Eurasian Persuasions: Mixed Race, Performativity and Cosmopolitanism," *Journal of Intercultural Studies* 28, no. 1 (February 2007): 43.

27. A less charitable assessment would be that it has hijacked that conversation.

28. King-O'Riain, Rebecca C., *Pure Beauty: Judging Race in Japanese American Beauty Pageants* (Minneapolis: University of Minnesota Press, 2006), 46, 202.

29. John Leland and Gregory Beals, "In Living Colors," *Newsweek*, May 5, 1997, 60; Connie Leslie, Regina Elam, Allison Samuels, and Danzy Senna, "The Loving Generation: Biracial Children Seek Their Own Place," *Newsweek*, February 13, 1995, 72; Jack E. White, "'I'm Just Who I Am,'" *Time*, May 5, 1997, 33. These several articles are typical. Even though the graphs in such pieces may indicate the fact that black/white intermarriages or birthrates are far lower than those of other groups, the overall message, nonetheless, is that interracial marriages multiracial and births are skyrocketing in a way that is shaking the foundation of race in America, and that the black/white component is significant.

30. See, for instance, Charles A. Gallagher, "Racial Redistricting: Expanding the Boundaries of Whiteness," in *The Politics of Multiracialism: Challenging Racial Thinking*, ed. Heather M. Dalmage (Albany: State University of New York Press, 2004); Jennifer Lee and Frank D. Bean, "America's Changing Color Lines: Immigration, Race/Ethnicity, and Multiracial identification," *Annual Review of Sociology* 30 (2004); and Eduardo Bonilla-Silva, "'New Racism', Color-Blind Racism, and the Future of Whiteness in America," in *White Out: The Continuing Significance of Racism*, ed. Ashley W. Doane and Eduardo Bonilla-Silva (New York: Routledge, 2003).

31. Hypodescent should now be a well recognized and understood term in scholarly writings about multiracial identity, so I have decided to no longer introduce it in the text with the words "or the one-drop rule."

32. I acknowledge appropriation of the language of Huey Newton here.

33. Gallagher, "Racial Redistricting," 72.
34. Ibid.
35. King-O'Riain, *Pure Beauty*, 27.
36. Lee and Bean, "America's Changing Color Lines," 237.
37 Bonilla-Silva, "'New Racism,'" 277–282.
38. Minkah Makalani, "Rejecting Blackness and Claiming Whiteness: Antiblack Whiteness in the Biracial Project," in *White Out: The Continuing Significance of Racism*, ed. Ashley W. Doane and Eduardo Bonilla-Silva (New York: Routledge, 2003), 81.
39. Jared Sexton, "The Consequence of Race Mixture: Racialised Barriers and the Politics of Desire, *Social Identities* 9, no. 2 (2003): 265.
40. I acknowledge having borrowed the phrase "mixed and mixing" from Olumide.
41. Martha J. Cutter, "Sliding Significations: Passing as a Narrative and Textual Strategy in Nella Larsen's Fiction," in *Passing & the Fictions of Identity*, ed. Elaine K. Ginsberg (Durham: Duke University Press, 1997), 90.
42. This would include, quite obviously, biological multiracial groups as well.
43. Minelle Mahtani, "What's in a Name? Exploring the Employment of 'Mixed Race' as an Identification," *Ethnicities* 2, no. 4 (2002): 471.
44. Stephen Small, "Colour, Culture and Class: Interrogating Interracial Marriage and People of Mixed Racial Descent in the USA," in *Rethinking 'Mixed Race,'* ed. David Parker and Miri Song (London, Pluto Press, 2001), 126–127.
45. Root, "A Bill of Rights," 7.
46. Ibid.
47. To eschew a biological racial identity does not imply the giving up of political consciousness or the giving up of commitments to anti-racism efforts

References

Bonilla-Silva, Eduardo. "'New Racism', Color-Blind Racism, and the Future of Whiteness in America, 271–284." In *White Out: The Continuing Significance of Racism*, ed. Ashley W. Doane and Eduardo Bonilla-Silva. New York: Routledge, 2003.

Brown, Ursula. *The Interracial Experience: Growing Up Black/White Racially Mixed in the United States*. Westport, CT: Praeger, 2001.

Childs, Erica C. "Multirace.com: Multiracial Cyberspace," 143–159. In *The Politics of Multiracialism: Challenging Racial Thinking*, ed. Heather M. Dalmage. Albany: State University of New York Press, 2004.

Clemetson, Lynette, "Color My World: The Promise and Perils of Life in the New Multiracial Mainstream." *Newsweek*, May 8, 2000, 70–74.

Cutter, Martha J. "Sliding Significations: Passing as a Narrative and Textual Strategy in Nella Larsen's Fiction," 75–100. In *Passing & the Fictions of Identity*, ed. Elaine K. Ginsberg. Durham: Duke University Press, 1997.

DaCosta, Kimberly M. *Making Multiracials: State, Family, and Market in the Redrawing of the Color Line*. Stanford: Stanford University Press, 2007.

Daniel, G. Reginald. *More Than Black? Multiracial Identity and the New Racial Order*. Philadelphia: Temple University Press, 2002.

Das, Sushi. "They've got the Look." *The Age*, April 20, 2004 <http://www.theage.com.au/articles/2004/04/19/1082357106748.html>.

Gallagher, Charles A. "Racial Redistricting: Expanding the Boundaries of Whiteness," 59–76. In *The Politics of Multiracialism: Challenging Racial Thinking*, ed. Heather M. Dalmage. Albany: State University of New York Press, 2004.

Kilson, Marion. *Claiming Place: Biracial Young Adults of the Post-Civil Rights Era* .Westport: Bergin and Garvey, 2001.

King-O'Riain, Rebecca C. *Pure Beauty: Judging Race in Japanese American Beauty Pageants*. Minneapolis, University of Minnesota Press, 2006.

Korgen, Kathleen O. *From Black to Biracial: Transforming Racial Identity Among Americans*. Westport, CT: Praeger, 1999.

Lee, Jennifer, and Frank D. Bean. "America's Changing Color Lines: Immigration, Race/Ethnicity, and Multiracial Identification." *Annual Review of Sociology* 30 (2004): 221–242.

Mahtani, Minelle. What's in a Name? Exploring the Employment of 'Mixed Race' as an Identification. *Ethnicities* 2, no. 4 (2002): 469–490.

Makalani, Minkah. "Rejecting Blackness and Claiming Whiteness: Antiblack Whiteness in the Biracial Project," 81–94. In *White Out: The Continuing Significance of Racism*, ed. Ashley W. Doane and Eduardo Bonilla-Silva. New York: Routledge, 2003.

Matthews, Julie. "Euarasian Persuasions: Mixed Race, Performativity and Cosmopolitanism." *Journal of Intercultural Studies* 28, no. 1 (February 2007): 41–54.

Olumide, Jill. *Raiding the Gene Pool: The Social Construction of Mixed Race*. London: Pluto Press, 2002.

Root, Maria P. P. "A Bill of Rights for Racially Mixed People," 3–14. In *The Multiracial Experience: Racial Borders as the New Frontier*, ed. Maria P. P. Root. (Thousand Oaks, CA: Sage, 1996.

Sexton, Jared. "The Consequence of Race Mixture: Racialised Barriers and the Politics of Desire." *Social Identities* 9, no. 2 (2003): 241–275.

Small, Stephen. "Colour, Culture and Class: Interrogating Interracial Marriage and People of Mixed Racial Descent in the USA," 117–133. In *Rethinking 'Mixed Race,'* ed. David Parker and Miri Song. London: Pluto Press, 2001.

Streeter, Caroline A. "The Hazards of Visibility: 'Biracial' Women, Media Images, and Narratives of Identity," 301–322. In *New Faces in a Changing America: Multiracial Identity in the 21st Century*, eds. Loretta I. Winters and Herman DeBose. Thousand Oaks, CA: Sage, 2003.

Williams, Kim M. "Linking the Civil Rights and Multiracial Movements," 77–97. In *The Politics of Multiracialism: Challenging Racial Thinking*, ed. Heather M. Dalmage. Albany: State University of New York Press, 2004.

Winters, Loretta I. "Epilogue: The Multiracial Movement: Harmony and Discord," 373–379. In *New Faces in a Changing America: Multiracial Identity in the 21st Century*, eds. Loretta I. Winters and Herman DeBose. Thousand Oaks, CA: Sage, 2003.

Chapter 10

Whiteness Reconstructed: Multiracial Identity as a Category of "New White"

Kerry Ann Rockquemore and David L. Brunsma

It is perennially true that U.S. society reconstructs and rearticulates the ways that race, racialization, racism and racial identity work to support white supremacy. Currently, this can be seen in the blurring of racial categories in cultural representations, bureaucratic forms, public discourse, and the ways that individuals understand their racial group membership(s). While racial groups are considered social constructions with no genetic grounding, they continue to influence everyday interactions and life chances. Some forty years after the passage of Civil Rights legislation, structurally rooted racial inequalities continue to exist in every domain of social and economic life. Despite these persistent inequalities, Americans increasingly believe that race is declining in significance and have adopted a "colorblind" ideology. This concurrent denial of racial inequalities and widespread desire to move "beyond race," has triggered a challenge to the use of racial categories in public policy, social science research, and college admissions suggesting that the very existence of such designations perpetuates the problems. Such shifts, where once clear and mutually exclusive racial categorizations are giving way to ambiguity, have been popularly portrayed as the "browning" of American culture, "the end of racism," and as the Gingrich's and Connerly's would argue, a progression towards one classification – "American."

Introduction

Scholars have been enmeshed in a debate regarding the various ways in which the American racial structure is rearticulating itself. F. James Davis, in *Who Is Black?* and subsequent writings has discussed seven possible directions the United States could go, especially with regards to the incorporation of multiracial individuals—stating that the Hawaiian model of egalitarian pluralism is the most likely. George Yancey, in Who Is White? and other writings has empirically developed a theory on a developing Black/NonBlack divide. In contrast to Yancey and Davis is the work of Eduardo Bonilla-Silva and the potential Latin-Americanization of the racial structure in the United States. Due to immigration-altered demographics, globalized of race relations, maintaining white supremacy via non-racial practices, and changing the way racial statistics, is experiencing a "Latin Americanization of race." For instance, Eduardo Bonilla-Silva argues that historical dichotomous (white/non-white) categorizations are mutating into a tri-racial system, mirroring the racial hierarchy of Latin American countries that emphasize national identity, deny racial difference, and understand social stratification in terms of class. This three-tiered hierarchy consists of: 1) "whites" (Euroamericans, "new whites" such as Russians and Albanians, assimilated white Latinos, some multiracials, recovered memory and assimilated urban Native Americans, and a few Asian-origin people), 2) "honorary whites" (white middle class Latinos, Japanese Americans, Korean Americans, Asian Indians, Chinese Americans and Arab Americans), and 3) the "collective black" (Filipinos, Vietnamese, Hmong, Laotians, dark-skinned and poor Latinos, blacks, New West Indian and African immigrants and reservation-bound Native Americans). Scholars writing about this emergent hierarchy argue that it simultaneously masks the persistence of racial inequalities while fundamentally changing the way individuals understand themselves and others in terms of racial categories: in many ways, multiracials and multiraciality, have been at the center of this debate—as the new white.

To explore whether or not this may be the case, we focus here on a study of racial identity choices made by multiracial people.[1] Narrowing our gaze to those who straddle extant racial divides provides critical cases to observe the micro-level effects of changes in race relations by providing an indicator of where the most rigid boundaries may be blurring at the edges. The racial identity choices made by multiracial people serve as a barometer of change because historically, the black-white dichotomy, grounded in the ideology of white supremacy and manifested in the one-drop rule, has determined that they understand themselves (as they are understood by others) as black. However, if fundamental structural changes in race relations are underway, then one would expect variation in racial identification among multiracial people that corresponds to the emerging system (e.g., Latin-Americanization, tri-racial) and its internal pigmentocracy. We would expect to find some multiracial people (i.e., those who "look white") defying the one-drop rule and identifying as white while others who phenotypically appear black are confined to the honorary white or collective black stratum.

Racial Identity, the Legacy of the One-Drop rule, and Multiracials

Racial identity refers mainly to one's subjective understanding as a racialized person – that one is both *similar to* and *different from* others. Racial identities are derived from recognizing a distinction between oneself and others. As an example, in the U.S., being black means that one is "not-white." Yet, whiteness is often seen as not-black, not-Asian, not-Latino, and not-Native American, etc.; "white" is rarely seen as a race at all—a signifier of the absence of race in everyday life. While difference is often celebrated in relation to cultural heterogeneity, the historical link between difference and inequality remains. For African Americans, racial identity often refers to an historical sense of self that has emerged from the struggle against white supremacy and oppression. Ultimately, racial identity is bound up in both the historically specific politics of representation and experience and the effects of repression that occur upon entry into the symbolic structures of language and culture, the social and political relations of everyday life, and active involvement with the racial projects of contemporary society.

As the racial terrain is constantly in flux (the ever-changing same under white supremacy), racial identity is derived from individuals' direct engagement with the process of racial formation in contemporary society including both the official "racial projects" advanced by the state and corporate capital and the rituals of everyday life that constitute hegemonic assumptions about race. To consciously engage with racial formations is to advance, sustain, or challenge a particular understanding of race and its implications for social life. It is here that we find individuals embedded within racialized social contexts that designate what categories of racial identification are legitimate, how racial group memberships are defined, and their relative importance. These designations are historically specific, exist to support the status quo, and change only in times of flux and transition in race relations.

To understand the link between structure and black identity, we must consider that the American system of racial stratification did not emerge spontaneously, but has deep roots in eighteenth century European classification schemes, the eugenics movement, and the racialized history of imperialism. Early colonists brought their hegemonic ideology of racial difference and white supremacy to North America, creating hierarchical social structures and setting the stage for the uniquely American form of slavery to emerge. Slavery exaggerated existing ideas of racial difference and the inferiority of people of color, serving as a rationalization of the exploitation of Africans in America. That same racist ideology continued, in mutated form, after the emancipation of slaves, guaranteeing their subordinate status for generations. Considering the history of the *idea* of racial categorization illustrates how the fallacy of race has been constructed by dominant groups, socially reproduced over generations, remains embedded within the institutions, culture, and social consciousness of

American society, and determines the parameters for individual self-identification.

Because the definition of black is historically unique from the rules of inclusion for other racial groups, and inseparable from the social and economic institution of slavery, it allows a clear illustration of the link between structure and identity. Specifically, black group membership has been defined by a strict application of the one-drop rule that deems individuals with any black ancestry whatsoever (regardless of their physical appearance) as members of the black race. The result is an inescapable pattern of hypodescent, where multiracial individuals – no matter how far removed from black ancestry—share the same position as the lower-status parent. From the outset of slavery, miscegenation was strictly prohibited so that black blood would not taint the purity of the white race. Despite this prohibition, black female slaves were routinely raped and because of the one-drop rule, their multiracial children were considered black. After the Civil War, Jim Crow segregation necessitated the legal codification of segregation and anti-miscegenation laws in most states producing a legal definition of whom, precisely, belonged in the category "black." While no longer a matter of legal definition, the one-drop rule has remained a firm traditional, cultural, and bureaucratic grasp on individual racial categorization.

The historical legacy of the one-drop rule demonstrates the longstanding existence of racial hierarchies in the U.S. and their firm grounding in white supremacist ideology. The definition of who is black has consistently supported existing racist systems of stratification. Despite the fact that the one-drop rule has no basis in biological reality, and has been continually used as an ideological weapon to support the continued exploitation of African Americans, it has enjoyed near universal social acceptance. Of course, in reality we are all multiracial, but what is analytically important is how structural factors determine the rules of racial group membership. For black/white multiracial people, slavery and segregation necessitated the one-drop rule, which persistently determined their racial categorization and racial self-identification as black. The existence of multiracial people is not a new social phenomenon. Instead, it is the emergence of open resistance to the one-drop rule that is worthy of sociological attention. Not because new ways of racial identification are the *cause* of changes in race relations, but because they are *reflective* of broader structural changes. If we are in the midst of a changing racial structure, we should expect to find new rules of definition for blackness and expansion of the parameters of individual identity construction in ways that are unprecedented.

Methodology

The cases used for this analysis are part of a sample (n = 259) of individuals with one self-identifying black and one self-identifying white biological parent collected between 1997 and 2002. The data were drawn from Michigan, Indiana, Connecticut, Massachusetts, and Alabama. Respondents were obtained by contacting all students at one of six educational institutions (a community college, two private universities, two state universities, and one historically black college) who had designated themselves on their admission form as: a) "black or African-American," b) "other," or c) left the race question blank. Of a total of 10,149 students contacted, 303 fit the selection criteria and received a survey consisting of 106 closed ended questions. The response rate among respondents was 85 percent, yielding a survey sample of 259 respondents. From the total survey sample, we selected a sub-sample of 16 respondents for in-depth interviews representing each of the geographic areas and educational institutions.

The measure used to determine racial identity was constructed based upon Rockquemore's typology. Respondents were asked which of the following seven statements best described their racial identity: (1) I consider myself exclusively black (or African American), (2) I sometimes consider myself black, sometimes my other race, and sometimes biracial depending on the circumstances, (3) I consider myself biracial, but I experience the world as a black person, (4) I consider myself exclusively as biracial (neither black nor white), (5) I consider myself exclusively as my other race (not black or biracial), (6) Race is meaningless, I do not believe in racial identities, or (7) Other (fill in the blank).[2]

The interviews were loosely structured and followed an open-ended instrument composed of general topic areas including descriptions of childhood experiences, schooling, friendships, significant others, interactions with strangers, and self-perceptions. The interviews lasted between one and three hours and were audio taped and transcribed. Additionally, interviewees completed a demographic questionnaire and created a "life map," together with the interviewer. The "life map" is a brief history of where the respondent has lived, and the racial composition of their households, neighborhoods, schools, and friendship networks at various points in time.

To understand the basic patterns of racial self-identification within our sample, we draw first upon the survey data. However, given that our primary interest is to explore how respondents understand their social location as multiracial people and the processes by which they construct and maintain their racial identities, the analysis presented draws heavily upon two semi-structured in-depth interviews as case studies.

Findings

Variation in Racial Identification

If the U.S. is experiencing a shift away from a white/non-white dichotomy, and moving towards a tri-partite model of race relations, we should expect to find that multiracial people will understand their racial identity in ways that defy the one-drop rule. In fact, recent research has documented the fact that multiracial people do vary in their racial identification.

We find similar variation within our sample. Some multiracial people see themselves as biracial, in a way that blends both of their racial backgrounds into a new and unique category of self-understanding. More than half of our respondents (61.3 percent) described themselves as biracial. However, this large group is composed of two separate responses: 1) "I consider myself exclusively biracial (neither black nor white)" and 2) "I consider myself biracial, but I experience the world as a black person." Both of these responses represent individuals who understand their own racial identity as biracial. They differ, however, because the first response indicates that others in the person's social network accept and *validate* "biracial" as a legitimate category of racial identity. The second response reveals a more complicated scenario in which the respondents understand themselves as biracial, but their self-understanding is rejected by others who do not consider "biracial" a meaningful racial identification.

In contrast to the integrated merging of racial background that produces the biracial self-identification, others choose a singular identity by selecting only one of their parents' races. Some identify exclusively as black while others identify exclusively as white. In our sample, 13.1 percent identified exclusively as black, while 3.6 percent described themselves as white.

Less frequently discussed in the empirical literature and among multiracial activists is that there are some multiracial people that have developed not one, but several ways of identifying. These individuals shift between black, white, and biracial identities, depending on the racial composition of the group they are interacting within. Only 4.8 percent of our respondents said that they had multiple, contextually specific racial identities (sometimes they were black, sometimes white, and sometimes biracial).

Finally, there are multiracial individuals who eschew any racial designation whatsoever and describe their racial identity in ways that transcend race. They frequently refuse to answer demographic questions about race and/or write in "human." Thirteen percent of our respondents indicated that the best way to describe their racial identity was: "Race is meaningless, I do not believe in racial identities." [3]

The variation that we find in our data points to an expanding range of racial self-understanding among multiracial individuals.[4] If, in fact, the one-drop rule remained the primary determinant of racial identity, then the vast majority (if not all) the individuals in our sample would identify as black. However, this is not the case. The fact that they choose so many different racial identities suggests a subtle shift in the application of the one-drop rule. More importantly, the mere existence of individuals with one black and one white parent that identify as white is both unexpected and unprecedented.[5] They are not *passing* for white, which implies that they really have a black identity but pretend to be white. Instead, they have constructed a white identity to the degree that they understand themselves and their social location as white. Because of the unusual nature of these cases, we explore two as in-depth case studies in order to understand the social context in which an individual with black ancestry can develop and maintain a validated white identity.

Case Studies: On Being White and Honorary White

Michelle and Samantha are two college students who have had remarkably similar lives.[6] The primary difference between the two lies in their physical appearance and its importance in their construction of a white identity. Both were raised by a black father and white mother in upper middle class nuclear families. Michelle grew up on the East Coast, while Samantha lived in the Midwest. All four parents have at least a bachelor's degree. Further, both Michelle's and Samantha's paternal (black) grandparents are deceased and did not play a major role in their childhood socialization. Both expressed discomfort in all black environments, neither have close friendships with African Americans, nor could they recall experiencing discrimination from whites. Finally, both identify primarily with white culture, yet describe enjoying their African American "heritage" as making them "unique" "interesting," and even "exotic."

Michelle is a nineteen year-old student beginning her second year at a private, Catholic university in the northeast who described her racial identity as white on her survey. After moving several times before she was 5, Michelle's parents settled in an affluent suburb of Boston, where they are now both practicing physicians. She grew up in an all white neighborhood and attended private elementary and then public high schools that were both primarily white. Though she did have a close relationship with one black girl, and her current best friend is "Asian," Michelle's friendship networks have been largely white, as have all of her boyfriends. She describes her few experiences in all black environments as "uncomfortable." By way of example, she shared with the interviewer her experience at a scholarship brunch for African American college applicants:

> ...there were probably about 40 or 50 people, high school seniors, and they were all black and a few of them, maybe three were mixed and I was just like, I was really quiet and I just like felt kind of uncomfortable...and I mean, no one was discriminating...no one was shunning me or whatever, but I didn't really have a good time. It was just very different. It was a lot different from the other weekends I visited at colleges where it was white, white students mostly.

Here Michelle consciously recognizes that her experience in black environments is "different" than the white environments to which she is accustomed. At the same time, her uneasiness can be attribute to her lack of identification with the other attendees.

Michelle describes her physical appearance as white, having olive colored skin and "good" curly hair. She said that people are often surprised to find out she is "part African American." For Michelle, being African American is a *symbolic identity* akin to the way other third and fourth generation whites often relate to being, perhaps German American or Italian American. She stated the following:

> Well, I think that because I've been raised mostly around white people, in a white neighborhood in white schools, I wouldn't say that I'm black. Maybe if I had been raised in an all black community, and I think... sometimes I see myself as just kind of white, like my culture and my ethnicity I guess. But I would put in the part that I'm part African-American part Native American because, I don't know, I kind of, I think it's interesting and unique, and I like people to know, I guess. Sometimes I'm also curious, like I never really know if people can tell, and sometimes people will ask, like what's your ethnic background?

It is clear from this statement that "African American" and "Native American" are aspects of her identity that she can choose to expose or to hide and that she understands both as features of her *ethnic* background. Interestingly, until Michelle made this particular statement in the interview, she had never indicated that she had any Native American ancestry. Yet here, she offers that she is "part African-American and part Native American" as things that distinguish her from bland whiteness. Bonilla-Silva includes in the "white" strata of his three-tiered hierarchy "some multiracials" and what he calls "recovered memory and assimilated urban Native Americans." Here, he is referring to white individuals who claim some vague Native American ancestry yet have no tribal affiliation, speak no other language, and have no socialization into any tribal culture whatsoever. When pressed in her interview Michelle related that she did not know from which side of her father's family the Native American heritage originated, nor did it have any impact on her everyday life. Clearly her physical appearance affords her the privileges of whiteness, her socioeconomic status and socialization have provided her with white middle class cultural capital, and she has the choice to acknowledge her black and/or Native American ancestry when interesting or convenient, yet it has no consequences for her life chances. When Michelle self-identifies as white, she has that identification readily accepted and validated by others.

Other comments Michelle made confirm her self-understanding as white and the fact that she experiences the world as a white person, despite occasionally telling others of her "ethnic" background. For example, Michelle described an experience in high school in which she forgot that she had a multiracial background:

> My junior year, I was reading a book for English class and it was about a multiracial family and a multiracial community on Martha's Vineyard and... umm it's called "The Wedding," and there's a young girl who is mixed and she is part black...And umm, but she had pretty fair skin and her hair was curly, but it was actually blond, especially when she was young and she asked one of her parents, or her grandmother maybe, "am I black or am I white or am I like you" or some questions like that, and the grandmother was like...she had to try and explain it and ... I remember that part and I was like "oh that'd be so weird not to know what you are" and then I was like, I completely forgot that I was multiracial, umm so it was kind of interesting.

Michelle's description of this experience illustrates the deep roots of her self-understanding as white. In her mind, having a black parent does not disqualify her from whiteness. She so thoroughly conceptualizes herself as a white person, that she is able to forget that she has parents of different races. It is in the taken for granted moments of everyday life that Michelle's white identity has been developed and is consistently maintained.

Honorary Whiteness

Samantha is a twenty four year old, third year graduate student in a professional program who was born and raised in a Midwest college town. On her survey, she described herself as transcending race ("Race is meaningless, I do not believe in racial identities"). The daughter of a black, male professor and white, female homemaker, Samantha grew up living primarily in university owned housing, surrounded by the children of other faculty and graduate students. Though the community was ethnically and racially diverse due to the large population of international graduate students and their children, Samantha had little contact with African Americans, and no experience living in an African American community. Her mother was her primary caregiver and while she describes being close to both of her parents, she developed an especially intimate relationship with her mother.

Like Michelle, Samantha described feeling "uncomfortable" and "different" in black social contexts, such as when visiting her black relatives. Samantha described having friendly relations with the black children that were in her school and neighborhood, but often felt "different" from them as well. Specifically, she described not living up to their expectations of blackness. She states:

> There's this perception that I like, try to be white. Well, I don't try; if I'm white that's just cause that's how I am. Like, if you perceive me to be different in a white way, like well, that's how I grew up, it's not like a choice that I made.

While having no serious altercations with black children, she often heard that they saw her as having an easier life because she was light skinned and had a white mother. Samantha's close friends were primarily white children, but also non-black children of color, a trend that continues in her current social networks. She often befriended exchange students and the children of graduate students from places such as China, India and the Sudan. While describing herself as dating men of "all races," every boyfriend she could recall specifically in the interview had been white.

Despite writing on her survey that she had "no racial identity", Samantha described herself as "biracial" in a straightforward and consistent manner throughout the interview. The story of how she developed that understanding grew more complex as the conversation progressed. In addition to having little experience interacting with black people, Samantha identified multiple factors that have shaped her identity as "biracial." First, she felt that having a white parent disqualified her from being black, because, according to her definition of "black", the majority of black people do not have the experience of having a white parent. Second, she has no memory of any negative experiences with whites: no name calling, no surveillance by security guards in stores, no discrimination of which she is aware. The only related incident she could recall was when her grandmother gave her brother a *Dukes of Hazzard* lunchbox on which was a confederate flag, and how that mildly upset her mother. She could not relate to feelings of racial oppression and viewed blacks as having misconceptions about, and an "overly pessimistic" view of, white people. Third, Samantha feels that black people have expectations that she should have experienced "black culture," while whites have no "preconceived notions" or expectations for her in that same regard. Fourth, she identifies herself culturally as white by saying that if "mainstream culture . . .can be said to be white," then so is she. Fifth, Samantha knows that when people look at her, they identify her as a person of color by her appearance. She is very light skinned, but has dark eyes and hair texture that signifies that she is of African descent. She enjoys appearing "exotic" or a "little bit different," and feels that this makes her unique and interesting.

To clarify, Samantha stated that she had "no racial identity" on her survey, that her racial identity was "biracial" in her interview, and that her cultural self-understanding was "white". It appears that Samantha's racial self-understanding can best be described as a white person who happens to look black. She repeatedly emphasized a distinction between race and culture in the way she conceptualized her identity. Samantha sees race as biological heritage, which may or may not be isomorphic to the practice and experience of the culture usually associated with that heritage. In her cognitive racial schema, the fact that she is of African descent does not mean that she knows anything about African American culture or experiences life as a black person.

It may be helpful to compare Samantha's understanding of her "biracial identity" to other participants in the wider sample. Other individuals claimed a biracial identity for a variety of reasons, including: (1) they did not want to deny either parent's influence on their lives, (2) they embraced both their white and black cultural heritage, (3) they *saw themselves* as both black *and* white, or (4) they understood that *biracial* described something entirely *other* than *either* black *or* white. In these instances "biracial" represents a particular *quality* or *meaning* in the individuals' lives that they are drawn *toward*. For Samantha, biracial is a default category, an *other*. It is what you become when you do not want to be black, and know that you will be rejected by anyone as white because of your physical appearance. The presence of physical cues that signify African heritage (hair that marks her as *black*) would so easily discredit a claim to white identity that it is highly unlikely that she would/could even try to pass as white, despite identifying with mainstream white culture.

In the Latin-Americanization framework, Samantha illustrates the ideology of colorblindness and, because of her physical appearance, falls into the "honorary white" strata. Though she culturally sees herself as white and has many of the social privileges that accompany her socioeconomic position, she is constrained from fully appropriating a white identity by her physicality and, therefore, experiences only conditional acceptance among whites.

It is important to emphasize that both Michelle and Samantha's cases are the exception, and not the rule, for racial identification among multiracial people. Most understand themselves as biracial or black. We chose to analyze these two cases in further depth because they represent the furthest deviation from the one-drop rule and raise important questions for the study of black identity. Is it possible for a multiracial person in post-Civil Rights America to have a validated identity as white? Is the white identity we observed a new form of passing or has passing become obsolete in a changing racial hierarchy? Is the demise of the one-drop rule paralleled by changing rules of inclusion for whiteness? It is to these questions that we now turn.

The Changing Nature of Race, Racial Identity, and Passing

The findings we present illustrate the changing nature of racial self-identification in the U.S. for those straddling long-standing racial group categories. As opposed to uniformly identifying as black (in accordance with the one-drop rule), the multiracial people in our sample identify in at least 5 different ways including: 1) black, 2) white, 3) biracial, 4) black, white, and biracial depending on the social setting, and 5) no racial identity. We believe the most compelling finding is that people of African descent are constructing white identities as an expression of their self-understanding and that their identity is validated in their social context.

The variation in racial identification among our respondents provides support for the Latin Americanization thesis, although we agree with his assertion that this process is in formation and may not be fully realized for several decades. More interesting is the prevalence of multiracial people in the "honorary white" tier. We consider those within our sample who identify as biracial, those who have multiple and shifting racial identities, and those who claim no racial identity as "honorary whites." We believe that it is in this middle tier that the vast majority of multiracial people will be located, forming the core of a buffer class of individuals who fulfill some criteria of a new "whiteness" (i.e., they are culturally white) but who are barred from full inclusion as white because of their phenotype. While occasionally sympathetic to the collective black, they will be most closely politically aligned with white middle-class interests.

The buffer status is best illustrated in our case study of Samantha who explicitly articulates the "we are all Americans" rhetoric while simultaneously reinforcing the existence of racial difference. She emphasizes the fact that when traveling outside of the United States, individuals saw her as an "American" rather than an "African American," and approves of what she interprets as whites' ability to interact with blacks without having expectations of them based on their race, at the same time as she sees blacks as unable to do so. For her, white people are those who can see that "we are all Americans," while blacks are different, meaning incapable, and "overly pessimistic." Samantha has adopted white attitudes about race and would be considered honorary white precisely because she is not completely accepted as white (by whites), because her social network is largely populated with other people of color who are not members of the "collective black," and because she has a palpable disdain for members of the "collective black."

We can begin to see the opening of a social space where new ways of racial identity development emerge. The process of identification, whereby the unconscious self recognizes and has an affinity to other, similar people, does not happen for either Samantha or Michelle in relation to African Americans. This can be attributed in part to the fact that both of their primary caregivers were white women. The primary caregiver is critical because she/he is the most influential individual in a child's life at the time the child develops his or her first self concept as a unitary, whole person. We hope to see more research that focuses specifically on children with black mothers and white fathers (or with black male primary caregivers) in the future in order to tease out the relationship between caregiver's race and racial socialization more fully.

While we observe white identification in both Michelle and Samantha, neither of trhem embraces it positively and without reservation. Michelle sees herself as white mainly because she does not see herself as black, did not grow up in a black community, and doesn't believe having a black parent bars her from whiteness. Samantha does not feel that she can legitimately claim a black identity because she does not pass the racial litmus test for being black. She understands that what counts as black is socially constructed, including specific behavior strategies and political attitudes. But instead of challenging those notions and trying to change what she perceives to count as blackness, Samantha has come to see herself as "not-black." Again, both Michelle and Samantha's racial identities are significantly constructed out of the experience of being different from black people. The fact that they reluctantly understand themselves as white speaks to the way whiteness is often not seen as a race in U.S. society. The ideology of whiteness as the unmarked is not new, but it does have an elective affinity with the recently emerging Latin Americanization of race relations which de-emphasizes racial difference. Samantha sees herself as "normal" or as a member of the mainstream. She only considers herself to be white if this mainstream can be said to be white as well.

Curiously, it is only in the interaction with the formal racial project in the U.S. known as Affirmative Action that both Michelle and Samantha were willing to designate themselves as black. Although Michelle's father ideologically opposes Affirmative Action, he encouraged her to identify as black when it would increase her opportunities, such as on her college admissions applications. Samantha too believed that checking "black" in response to the race question on her professional school application would give her an advantage, and that there was "no doubt" she received preferential admission at the graduate school she now attends because of that designation. In a black/white stratification system, "passing" occurs when an individual defined as black (via the one-drop rule), who physically appears white, presents a white identity for economic and social gain. However, in a tri-racial system, supported by an ideology of color-blindness, an inversion of passing seems to have emerged. Specifically, in the context of societal perceptions that Affirmative Action is equivalent to "reverse discrimination" and that it is *blacks* who are institutionally and structurally privileged, multiracial individuals, who understand themselves as white, *pass for black* in order to receive social, economic, and educational opportunities.

Finally, our data suggests a need for more complex and nuanced modeling of black identity. We believe this is necessary because existing theoretical models of black identity assume a black/white racial landscape in which racial identity is monolithic and entirely structurally imposed. Individuals are socially designated black and their racial identity is measured by such factors as their group evaluation, feelings of closeness to other blacks, and black autonomy. Other models highlight racial group identification or one's development across the life span from a non-Afrocentric to an Afrocentric black identity. All of these theoretical models of black identity take blackness as a given and measure the degree to which one adjusts to their racialized status. While this remains the case for the vast majority of black people in the U.S., these models fail to allow space for the newly emerging patterns of negotiation, fluidity, and choice that we have observed in our sample. We believe that the Latin Americanization framework challenges the assumptions underlying existing conceptualizations of race, racial categories, and racial identity and demands a fundamentally new way of understanding micro-level racial identity construction that balances both the social reality of blurring racial boundaries and the historical and structural reality of changes in racial stratification.

The growing multiracial population in the U.S. is racially identifying in historically new ways, including as white members of society. This demonstrates a break from historically rooted binary models of racial categorization, implying an erosion of the one-drop rule in determining who is black, and an expansion of the rules of whiteness that reduce the absolute need for "racial purity," and instead imply socioeconomic standards and cultural assimilation as the price of admission. While we observe new racial identifications among our multiracial respondents, we continue to see the lingering constraints of physical appearance that make the range of identity choices differentially available. It is among this group that we see both the first signifiers of broader change, and the psychological, political, and cultural complexities that accompany that change.

Notes

1. In this article the term multiracial refers specifically to individuals with one self-identifying black and one self-identifying white biological parent. While black/white biracial people are not the most prevalent sub-group within the multiracial population, they represent the most contested combination given the strict historical, legal, and cultural definition of blackness and prohibition of miscegenation. We also use the term

"self-identifying black" and "self-identifying white" to reflect the fact that most members of each population ("black" and "white") have some racial mixture and that their racial identities reflect socially constructed understandings of race more than any genetic reality.

2. See Rockquemore and Brunsma (2002) for the complete questionnaire and interview guide.

3. Approximately 4.2 percent of our sample felt that none of the existing survey responses represented their racial self-understanding (i.e., they chose "other").

4. Several factors influence the racial identity choices made by multiracial people 1) the racial composition of social networks, 2) experiences of acceptance or rejection within those networks and 3) physical appearance.

5. The white-identifying multiracial respondents were unexpected methodologically because we did not solicit participants from those who marked "white" on their admissions forms. We may have found more individuals in this category had we solicited all students instead of restricting the sample.

6. All respondents names are pseudonyms.

References

Bonilla-Silva, Eduardo. *Racism without Racists: Color-Blind Racism and the Persistence of Racial Inequality in the United States.* Lanham, Maryland: Rowman & Littlefield, 2006.

Davis, James F. *Who is Black? One Nations Definition.* University Park: Penn State University Press, 1991.

Rockquemore, Kerry Ann, and David L. Brunsma. *Beyond Black: Biracial Identity in America.* Thousand Oaks, California: Sage Publications, 2001.

Chapter 11

Conversations in Black and White: The Limitations of Binary Thinking about Race in America

Johanna E. Foster

$\mathbf{M}$uch has been written in contemporary academic discourse about the ways in which binary thinking has been, and continues to be, at the core of Western hegemonic cultural systems. One of the most fruitful and voluminous academic critiques of binary thinking that has emerged in the social sciences and humanities in recent decades is the challenge to the pervasive and politically problematic conceptualization of race in the United States as an essential dichotomy between "Black" and "White." Despite challenges and changes in thinking about racial classification there are still limitations to binary thinking about race that are not widely acknowledged inside and outside of the academy. This chapter clarifies key theoretical contributions of a social constructionist critique of Black/White binary thinking as it has emerged in the social sciences in the past few decades, and extends the theoretical analysis of the limits of dichotomous conceptualizations of race by calling attention to important but underemphasized themes. The chapter concludes with theoretical reflections on the ways in which existing critiques of dichotomous thinking have advanced struggles for racial justice, and how a more nuanced critique of dichotomous thinking might prove even more useful for confronting global White supremacy.

Introduction

Much has been written in contemporary academic discourse about the ways in which binary thinking persists in American cultural practices, institutions, and in academic scholarship itself, whether it is through the dichotomous categories including: "light/dark," "good/evil," "Christian/pagan," "West/East," "right/wrong," and "human/animal." Other terms such as "reason/emotion,"

"mind/body,"   "subject/object,"   "seaf/other,"   "masculine/feminine,"
"science/religion," or "free/slave," despite important critiques across scholarly
disciplines. One of the most fruitful and voluminous academic critiques of
binary thinking that has emerged in the social sciences and humanities in recent
decades is the challenge to the pervasive and politically problematic
conceptualization of race in the United States as an essential dichotomy between
"Black" and "White." Indeed, it is hard to deny that a Black/White[1] dichotomy
is central to organizing all our social institutions and our cultural arrangements
in America today- as it has been over centuries. Equally hard to deny is the
extensiveness and gravity of past and present White assaults against people of
African decent, assaults that are embedded in the very fabric of U.S. society and
societies around the world, forming a ubiquitous and enduring political dynamic
that fundamentally shapes everyday social interaction and larger cultural and
structural arrangements in our nation for the benefit of those classified as
"White." What is easier to deny, in both popular and academic conversations
alike, is that this binary Black/White classification system, like all classification
systems, is now, and has always been, a social fiction, a cultural logic used to
implement what amounts to centuries of crimes against humanity.

Having said this, White supremacy as a social and political system is more
complicated than the operations of a Black/White dichotomy, even as individual
White people, and White institutions, continue to make ready use of such a
binarism, and the relegation of "Blackness" as symbolic other, to decimate not
only Black communities but communities of color here in the United States and
around the world. Today, as a result of a generation of critical scholars who have
approached the study of race from a social constructionist perspective, there is
now a considerable body of interdisciplinary academic work that exposes the
limitations of binary thinking about race. Despite these challenges and changes
in thinking about racial classification in particular, and social identity
classification in general, it can be argued that there are still limitations to binary
thinking about race that are not widely acknowledged inside and outside of the
academy. As such, in this chapter, an attempt will be made to broadly clarify
some of the key theoretical contributions of a social constructionist critique of
Black/White binary thinking as it has emerged in the social sciences[2] in the past
few decades, and then extend the theoretical analysis of the limits of
dichotomous conceptualizations of race by calling attention to the important but
underemphasized themes. This approach will help to clarify how existing
critiques of dichotomous thinking have advanced struggles for racial justice, and
how a more nuanced critique of dichotomous thinking might prove even more
useful for confronting global white supremacy.

Social Constructionist Challenges to Binary Thinking about Race in America

In the social sciences, critical examinations of the contemporary limits of
binary thinking about race in the United States are indebted to tremendous shifts

in thinking about identity and inequalities, and the relationship that has occurred between the two over the last century in academic discourses, but accelerated in the last thirty years. A full intellectual history of these shifting ideas would no doubt take volumes. Suffice it to say here that as the twentieth century came to a close, critical theorists in the social sciences and humanities had widely called into question the limitations of binary thinking about social identity categories for both theory and progressive political practice. For sure, it is not too much of an overstatement to say that it has been, precisely, this analytical process of deconstructing identity categories that has been the hallmark of much contemporary theorizing in critical theories of not only race, but nation, gender and sexualities, such that there is now an enormous body of interdisciplinary research that confronts the political and conceptual problems of thinking about the meaning of all social identity categories as essential, universal, and fixed. There is also a tremendous body of interdisciplinary scholarship that critically examines the social and institutional processes and practices that create and maintain the very boundaries between these supposedly essential, universal, and fixed identity categories.

This move to deconstruct the meanings of, and boundaries between, the identity categories on which the major systems of social inequality rest in the United States can be traced as far back to Sojourner Truth[3] and Anna Julia Cooper[4] in their early critiques of White feminist conceptualizations of the category "woman," and carried into the contemporary period by feminists of color in the 1980s, such as Patricia Hill Collins, Paula Gunn Allen, Cherrie Moraga, and Gloria Anzaldua, who continued the call to hold White feminists accountable for racist notions of gender that rendered women of color invisible[5]. Feminist theorists Gayatri Chakravorty Spivak[6] and Diana Fuss[7] further laid the groundwork for a major theoretical turn toward the acceptance of not just social constructionist, but postmodernist, understandings of identity among critical scholars in the social sciences and humanities in their now classic analyses of identity. These theoretical contributions of what might Maxine Baca Zinn and Bonnie Thornton Dill termed "multiracial feminist theory"[8] are invaluable, and inarguably generated a paradigm shift in the theorizing of identity that has influenced all the "threads" of contemporary critical theory, from feminist theory, to cultural studies, postcolonialism, queer theory, and critical race theory—"threads" that are, themselves, intertwined. So profound has been the shift in thinking in the last decades of the twentieth century, we can now say with certainty that it is mainstream in sociology, and in many other schools of thought in the social sciences and humanities, to be enormously suspicious of, and to encourage thinking beyond, binary categories of identity.[9] It is argued in the following section that there have been several aspects of a social constructionist critique that have been more widely embraced than others in the contemporary social science discourses on race, including the critiques that binary thinking 1) erases the lived experiences of non-Black people of color; 2) reifies the shifting meanings and boundaries of racial identities; 2) obscures the institutional contexts in which racial identities are constructed; 3) and reifies the boundaries between race and ethnicity as systems of social identity.

Erases the Lived Experiences of Non-Black People of Color

The most obvious challenge that social constructionist perspectives have brought to a critique of conversations in "Black and White" are the ways in which the lived experiences of a substantial part of the United States population, as well as the world's population, who identify, or are classified by others, as neither White nor Black, are marginalized by scholars and laypeople alike, and in many cases completely ignored when race is understood to be essentially dichotomous. Such singular focus on a Black/White binary also marginalizes those who have White and/or Black ancestry but do not identify monoracially, or choose to identify as both Black and White. It is beyond the scope of this chapter to review the sociology of the lived experiences of non-Black communities of color in the United States, although scholars examining the lived experiences of people of Asian descent in America,[10] Native peoples,[11] and Latinas/os[12] have pushed the academic conversation in sociology toward an analysis of race that rightfully demonstrates the limits of a binary approach. Simply put, scholars have contended that in shining the light solely on the unequal power relations between Whites and Blacks, we not only fail to fully understand these dynamics accurately, but scholars then perpetuate the same kinds of racism against non-Black and/or multiracial people and communities as white scholars have perpetrated against African-American people. Moreover, as other contributors to this volume have examined, a significant scholarly and practical challenge to the binary system of race in the United States was extended in the early 1990s by such texts as Maria P.P. Root's, *Racially Mixed People in America*, and revised in 1995 as *The Multiracial Experience: Racial Borders as the New Frontier*,[13] anthologies which not only generated significant academic work,[14] but also helped to inspire the U.S. multiracial movement itself. To converse about race as if it were simply a Black/White binary clearly renders to the margins the lives of millions of people living in the United States, and minimizes our collective understanding of race and ethnicity as socially constructed ideas that nonetheless have been among the most consequential ones in our nation's history.

Reifies the Shifting Meanings and Boundaries of Racial Identities

Along with this most obvious and consequential critique of the limitations of binary thinking about race in the United States, a social constructionist approach to race has also informed more subtle, if still well-articulated, critiques that have become widely-accepted in contemporary sociology. One of the most important developments in the sociology of race in recent decades has been an increased attention and interest in the social construction of both the meanings of, and the boundaries between, identity categories, most particularly those identity categories that are used to distribute valuable social resources. While the study of identity itself as fundamentally a process of social interaction has been a centerpiece of sociological inquiry[15] for over a century, the amount of scrutiny that contemporary social theorists have employed in the deconstruction of racial and ethnic meanings and boundaries has been increasing and with much to teach us about the problems of reifying a Black/White dichotomy. For example, in terms of the larger hegemonic western cultural system, uncritically redeploying a Black/White dichotomy leads us, first of all, to recreate similar analytical binary traps that have their own problems for sure, but more importantly, contribute to the symbolic mapping of the meaning of Blackness on to that which the larger White culture deems undesirable. Too easily, a Black/White binary gets charted conveniently on to other dichotomies with which scholars in philosophy and cultural studies have interrogated at length. These include: "good/evil"; "free/slave"; "Christian/pagan"; "west/east"; "right/wrong"; "human/animal"; "reason/emotion"; "mind/body"; "subject/object"; "self/other." In each case, the second term in each pair is overtly or implicitly subjugated to the first term in ways that help rearticulate White supremacy.[16]

On top of this well-known critique of the problem of setting up Whiteness in relation to Blackness, and its impact on the maintenance of systemic White privilege, a wealth of empirical research, some of which is also included in this volume, now examines the shifting and fluid meanings of racial categories themselves, including the ways in which biological and cultural essentialism have been historically and culturally constructed and used precisely to maintain economic, political, social privilege.[17] Again, this literature is too much to review in this short essay here, but social constructionist critiques of racial binarisms have paved the way for, as an example, Neil Foley's[18] work on the history of middle-class Mexican-American identity and the ways in which contested claims to Whiteness were deployed in relation to a stigmatized Blackness, and for Min Zhou's[19] work on the contemporary meaning of "Asian-American" identity and the complicated ways in which racist notions of Asians as a "model minority" intersect with a historical legacy of ideologies that construct people of Asian descent as "forever foreigners." Social constructionist perspectives have also laid the groundwork for the analyses of shifting hegemonic notions of the meaning of "Native American" and the early colonist understandings of "Indians" as essentially racially White people capable of "civilized," unlike people of African descent whom Europeans defined as racially different and thus unredeemable.[20] Indebted, too, are the scholars who study the shifting and contested meanings of "mixed" and the politics of an emergent "multiracial" identity.[21]

Similarly, scholars that take issue with the shifting meanings of race over time and place have also look explicitly, although not always, at the ways in which the very lines, or boundaries, between racial categories themselves are drawn in social and political and historical contexts, and in ways that are always fraught with conflict and power. The scholarship on the social construction of racial classification schemas is also enormous, and includes, F. James Davis's[22] classic work on the history of the one-drop rule, Hanley-Lopez's work[23] on the legal construction of White racial identities, Wander, Martin and Nakaya's work[24] on the historical roots of racial classification, Noel Ignatiev's work[25] on the process by which Irish people in the U.S. were afforded the privileges of Whiteness, Karen Brodkin's[26] well-known work examining how Jews became classified as White people, Lee and Bean's work[27] on the shifting color line at the turn of the 21st century in the context of predictions that Hispanics will soon constitute the largest minority group in the United States. In addition, it also includes Eduardo Bonilla-Silva and David Embrick's work[28] that theorizes the process of "triracialization" emerging in America, a process whereby a privileged category of "Whites and New Whites" exercises power over an intermediate racial category of "honorary Whites" as well over a bottom-rung category of marginalized people defined as members of the "collective Black."

Obscures the Institutional Contexts in which Racial Identities are Constructed

While academics who have examined the shifting boundaries of racial categories do not always attend to the shifting meanings of these identities, in sociology it is safe to say that this contemporary scholarship, taken together, has called into question the essence of race as ranked biological differences, the notions that racial categories are inevitably binary and mutually exclusive, as well as the very universality of racial classification schemas. It is also safe to say that the intellectual impetus to challenge these taken-for-granted notions of race emerged out of a theoretical understanding of the ways in which the social construction of these categories is happens within a range of institutional contexts and is explicitly related to the creation and maintenance of structural inequalities. Without question, contemporary scholars engaged in this kind of intellectual work of deconstructing the meaning and boundaries within their institutional contexts are indebted to early critiques of the creation and protection of a Black/White color line, such as that found in the classic works of Dubois,[29] and the more contemporary, but foundational work of Davis.[30] Given the centrality of the exploitation of Black labor and the cultural use of "Blackness" in the American White imagination, this research on the creation and maintenance of a Black/White binary is necessary and rightfully voluminous.

Moreover, in the past decades, contemporary sociology has learned from critical scholarship across disciplines that a conceptual focus on a Black/White binarism also distorts the ways in which this particular color line has been drawn in relation to other racialized meanings and boundaries. The Black/White binarism in the United States, while pivotal, has always been situated in a larger context that has included more complicated meanings, and in institutional/structural contexts that include communities of people who have been defined as "White" or "of color" but have not been of European or African decent. Perhaps most fundamental, then, the focus on the social construction of

Black/White identities outside the context of other racialized meanings, obscures the reality of how all, not just some, racial identities are constructed in relation to one another in a cultural system, as well as in larger institutional contexts that are not simply organized by a Black/White binary system. In other words, such a dichotomous focus reifies, or makes invisible, the complex institutional arrangements that create racial meanings and categories in the first place. This analytical simplicity is also compounded by the lack of analysis of how the social construction of a racial binarism intersects with other cultural and institutional practices of inequality, such as class, gender, and sexuality, a point I address in detail below.

Reifies the Boundaries between Race and Ethnicity as Systems of Social Identity

In examining the social construction of racial and ethnic categories, recent social science literature has taken previous mainstream social scientific analysis of race and ethnicity to task for reifying "race" as system of essential biological difference, and "ethnicity" as a system of cultural difference. Current scholarship in critical social scientific studies of race and ethnicity, like that of contemporary feminist social science in their critique of liberal conceptions of sex and gender, calls into question the lack of analysis of power in traditional studies of race and ethnic "difference," and also calls into question the very meaning of the categories of race and ethnicity as fundamentally distinct social systems. Arguably, we have entered a time of conceptual debate in sociology over whether or not, and to what extent, race and ethnicity are distinct, interrelated, or fundamentally the same concepts. As such, to converse about race in "Black and White" terms makes it difficult to identify the complicated relationships between racial and ethnic systems, and the historical sliding of ethnic categories into racial categories, and vice versa. More specifically, as social constructionist perspectives have illuminated, racial and ethnic meanings are deployed in complex and varying ways across time and place, and the meanings and relationships between these categories are steeped in power relations such that our belief in the clear-cut boundaries between one's race and one's ethnicity distorts the operation of power.[31]

Ultimately, in focusing on a Black/White dichotomy, social scientists and lay people alike remain ill-informed about the ways in which cultural notions of ethnicity are, themselves, used not only against Black people, but are used to rearticulate racist practices that harm all people who are not classified as White. Yet, despite what has amounted to a paradigm shift in the social sciences around our thinking about racial classification, in particular, and social identity classification more generally, binary thinking about race still permeates popular and academic discourses, and there remain important critiques of such a cultural logic that emerge from social constructionist perspectives that are still minimized when we attend largely to racial justice matters "in Black and White."

Clarifying Additional Limits to Thinking in Black and White

It is no overstatement to say that the focus on the social construction of identity has taken center stage in contemporary analyses of race and ethnicity in the social sciences, and especially in sociology. While this area of research has been voluminous and necessary, there are elements of this influential critique that could stand to be clarified and more widely articulated. As this volume aims to demonstrate, the advantages of moving beyond essentialist and binary thinking about race (although essentialist and dichotomous are not synonymous problems) are tremendous both conceptually and politically insofar as this conceptual lens allows us to confront scientific and cultural racism.

Nonetheless, the focus on the cultural politics of boundary construction and meaning has, ironically, overshadowed what are equally important and major limits to binary thinking, namely 1) the erasure of the history and complexity of structural racism; 2) the minimization of the intersections of inequalities; 3) the erasure of the global context of White supremacy; 4) the distortion of the historical and contemporary context of racial justice movements; and 5) the overemphasis on "the politics of ambiguity"[32] at the expense of a focus on global White supremacy and global capitalism.

Erases the History and Complexity of Structural Racism

Unlike scholars in other disciplines, sociologists take as a central analytical task the job of articulating how cultural ideas about race are used to distribute wealth, power, and prestige at the social structural level. While one of the major contributions of sociology to the study of social inequalities is this analytical attention to institutional and structural processes in the creation, organization and maintenance of oppression, conversations about race that are primarily dichotomous facilitate a number of additional analytical and political problems by marginalizing a more complex analysis of structural inequality. More specifically, a binary analysis of race in the American context erases the manifestation of institutional and structural racism that impacts Latino, Asian-American, Native-American and other communities of color, obscures the complexity of the historical trajectory of White privilege, and obscures how White supremacy works in the present social context by giving primacy to certain regions in U.S.

The impact of institutional and structural racism against people of African decent is among the social phenomena, which sociologists have documented very well. Analyses of racism, albeit themselves often products of the very same racialized institutions and politics, have long-defined the field of sociology as distinct from other disciplines that pay little or no scholarly attention to White supremacy. And while these analyses have added much to both academic and popular understandings of racial injustice, and indeed have directly impacted social change agents, analyses of the impact of structural and institutional racism on non-Black communities have received much less recognition, despite the extent of the literature. If we use a "Black and White" analytical lens, even one that takes the social construction of these categories into account, we miss, for example, Alejandro Portes'[33] on the macro shifts in the global economy and the impact on immigrant experiences in the United States, or Barajas and Pierce's work[34] on the impact of race and gender structures on Latinos access to education, or Haunani Kay Trask's[35] work on global capitalism and the cultural imperialism and the impact on Native Hawaiians.

Not only does a focus on a Black/White binarism leave little room to attend to the lessons in these important works, it impedes a more nuanced understanding of the history of White supremacy, a history that is vast and torturous, and includes but is not limited to the unimaginable horrors of White racism against people of African decent. This collective amnesia to the complexity of structural racism in the past thus makes it that much more difficult to understand the very workings of racial inequality in the present and its impact all communities of color as the current power relations are borne from these past arrangements, as sociologists and historians like George Lipsitz[36] and Howard Zinn,[37] respectively, have demonstrated thoroughly elsewhere. Framing the problems of race and structural racism as fundamentally matters in "Black and White" creates the related dilemma of prioritizing particular regions in American geography and their structural realities, namely those in the eastern and southern parts of the United States where Black people have been more likely to live given the history of slavery and industrial migration. In doing so, the historical and contemporary manifestation of institutional and structural racism in the American West or Southwest, for example, which has very different racialized patterns is ignored, and the politics of the Northeast and American South are taken as universal. Bonnie Thornton Dill,[38] in her comparative work on the intersections of race, class, gender and nation on the unequal conditions of social reproductive labor for Black, Chicana, Chinese, and White women in U.S. history makes a clear case for the ways in which structural racism has played itself out differently depending on the social geography.

Minimizes the Intersections of Inequalities

Along with a sensitivity to the culturally-specific, historical, and cumulative dimensions of White structural advantage exemplified in empirical work such as Dill's, contemporary social science has been informed by feminist scholarship on inequalities that has called for examinations of racism that take into account the intersections of systems of privilege and oppression. First articulated widely by the critiques of black feminist scholars such as Deborah King,[39] in her establishment of the concept of "double jeopardy," Patricia Hill Collins,[40] in her development of the idea of a "matrix of domination," and Kimberle Crenshaw[41] in her explicit use of the term, "intersectionality,"[42] the notion that racism is always already "compounded," to use Nancy Hewitt's[43] analogy, by other systems of difference and inequality, such as gender, class, sexuality and nation, is now a staple idea in any basic critical analysis of racism in sociology. In fact, there is an entire subfield in sociology devoted to race, class and gender studies, and the analysis of intersectionalities is also the conceptual starting point in the field of women and gender studies. The empirical work in race, class and gender studies is substantial and interdisciplinary and includes, for instance, Ayana Byrd's[44] analysis of Black female subjectivity in hip hop, Ruth Atkin and Adrienne Rich's[45] analysis of the intersections of gender, race, ethnicity and class in the vicious scapegoating of young Jewish women on college campuses, Becky Thompson's[46] intersectional analysis women's eating problems and weight preoccupation, and Ruth Frankenburg's[47] now classic work on the intersection of race and gender on the construction of White women's racial identities. And, here, again, the lessons from research like this that comprises the flourishing bodies of work now becoming increasingly mainstream in sociological approaches to race are ignored when the conversation about race assumes an essential Black/White binarism. As long as a decade ago, Crenshaw[48] warned against this very marginalization of analyses that attend to the intersections of inequalities. As will be addressed shortly, the contemporary focus on maintaining and deconstructing a Black/White binary risks, giving primacy to a politics of intrasectionality, or identity contests over the workings of a singular identity system, rather than a more macro; it is politically promising, focused on the workings of multiple stratification systems as they operate simultaneously.

Renders Invisible the Global Context of White Supremacy

A social constructionist perspective also teaches us that thinking about race in the United States in "Black and White" terms obscures the current global context of White supremacy, as well as the changing demographics of race and ethnicity in the U.S. brought on by globalization. Surely, in many analyses of American social life in the twenty-first century, it would be woefully inadequate to disregard the enormous impact of globalization on even the smallest units of social interaction. In the same way in which it would have been a colossal mistake for social analysts to fail to situate, for example, Native American genocide, American slavery, the annexation of Mexico, or Japanese internment, in the larger contexts of European colonialism and the rise of U.S. imperialism, it is an equally serious error to decontextualize the centrality of globalization and the role of the U.S. as a global Empire in the social landscape of race in America today. As has been our history, race and racism in the United States has always been deeply and necessarily tied to larger global economic and political forces, even when our manifestations of racial classification systems have been more particular to our national institutional arrangements and legal and political institutions.

A narrow focus on Black and White, however, makes it difficult to understand these historical connections, and to see how U.S. racial structures have been built by, but are also changing as a result of, global capitalism. Moreover, in failing to look through a more macro analytical lens, we miss, for instance, how and why racialized tensions, both between Whites and Blacks, between Whites and people of color, and between communities of color themselves, have escalated and/or changed shape in the recent periods as a result of global economic restructuring. We miss the racialized impact of global corporate rule on the political and economic health of developing nations and the consequential mass migration across the globe of people who are often defined as "of color." When we focus on racism as a matter of Black and White only, we fail to fully articulate how anti-immigrant sentiment and policy in the U.S. is as much a matter of protecting White privilege as it is anything else. We fail to see how the global "war on terror" is deeply racialized and gendered, as Rosalind Petchesky[49] argued in her widely acclaimed "Phantom Towers" reflection on the attacks of September 11, 2001. A limited focus on a Black/White binarism misses the ways in which the "war on terror" and the subsequent threat to people of color in the United States, in the form of weakened civil rights protections and strengthened powers of the state to use surveillance and incarceration against its people, is connected to the rise of U.S. empire and the exportation of American penal policies around the world in the name of so-called democracy. To take it one step further, the narrow attention to matters of Black and White in the U.S., decontextualized from racialized global capitalism makes it difficult to fully understand the links between domestic attacks on people of color, the restriction of civil liberties, the rise of prisons, the expanding racialized wealth gap, the "war on terror," and the threat to democratic institutions here and around the world—an argument cogently argued by such preeminent scholars such as Angela Davis in her most recent work on the threat to democracy posed by the rise of a privatized international incarceration industry as a major engine of racialized global capitalism.[50]

Moreover, in the midst of a trend in migration from the "global South" to the "global North" unprecedented in world history, a binary focus on the politics of Black and White in the U.S. that does not attend to these most macro of racialized patterns also misses the ways in which the entire meaning systems and boundary drawing between racial categories is changing as we speak. Who counts as White now? Who is non-White? How are we to understand Eduardo Bonilla-Silva and David Embrick[51] when they suggest that we are approaching the "triracialization" of American society if we are not using a global lens? How would a lack of understanding of the past, present, and changing context of a global racial system impact racial justice activists' call for reparations for slavery for people of the African diaspora who span the world? How will a lack of understanding of the current intersections of race, class, and gender in the global context impact scholars' and activists' understanding of the emergence of new systems of slavery in the form of global sweatshops, nanny chains, sex work and sex trafficking-- all conditions of exploitation that are most likely to be endured by women of color in the global South? Paradoxically, in the absence of a critical analysis of race and racial categories in a global context, the relentless and enthnocentric focus on a U.S. Black/White binarism serves to recenter Whiteness over and over again, making it difficult to understand racialized interactions that are largely contests among communities that are not defined as White, even if the context of the interactions, and the meanings of the identities, are constructed within institutions shaped by systemic White privilege, and in relation to Whiteness as an identity category.

Distorts the History and Complexity of Racial Justice Movements in the U.S.

Not only do social constructionist perspectives allow us to more fully understand the history, complexity, and persistence of global White supremacy, such perspectives can afford us a more nuanced understanding of the history and complexity of social resistance to racial injustice. To be sure, the American Civil Rights Movement of the 1950s and 1960s not only altered the very fabric of U.S. race relations forever, but also inspired subsequent successful movements for human rights that have spanned the world.[52] In the same way that a narrow focus on a Black/White binary leads us to attend solely to the problems of White supremacy as if they only impact people of African decent in relation to those defined as White, such an analytical lens also discourages serious investigation of social movements among non-black communities, serious investigation of racial justice movements that cross racial-ethnic boundaries and are coalitional, serious investigation of the links between racial justice movements and other kinds of struggles for human rights, or serious investigation of strategic racial identity politics that are outside the bounds of monoracial identity practices.

Here, too, critical scholars have moved the conversation beyond a Black/White binary and have illuminated practical action against entrenched structures of racism that is not always considered in popular understandings of civil rights movements. For instance, Josephy, Nagel, and Johnson[53] have documented the rise of the American Indian Movement, while Fransisco Rosales and Guadalupe San Miguel have both examined the Chicano movement.[54] In another example, and taking to task the obstacles to social justice organizing posed by the emergence of a culture of identity politics in the 1980s and 1990s, John Anner[55] studied social justice movements that were explicitly dedicated to multiracial coalition work. As global capitalism spins out of control, and corporate plundering gets increased popular attention in the form of news reports on global warming and other "natural" disasters like Hurricane Katrina, scholarly analyses of anti-globalization movements have begun to look more closely at the connections between global White supremacy and eco-terrorism. In a study of the multiracial, intersex, and disability rights movements in the U.S. in the late 1990s, I examined the claims of social movement activists who were using social constructionist claims about race, sex, and ability to challenge binary systems of identity classification on behalf of those caught "betwixt and between" supposedly mutually exclusive identity categories. I was primarily interested in whether or not activists' critiques of these respective binary systems, and any related claims to the transgressive character of boundary-crossing identities, were linked by activists to claims about the maintenance of structural inequalities, and if so, with what impact on social movement efforts to confront such institutional—as opposed to cultural—arrangements. In all these cases, the analytical lens is one that takes into account the institutional, intersectional, and global dimensions of White privilege.

Encourages a Focus on Cultural Politics at the Expense of Structural Analyses

As a result of the vigilant policing of a Black/White color line, and the enormous cultural energy that goes into recreating the social fiction of an essential Black/White dichotomy, there has been an understandable and intense focus on identifying the shifting, multiple and fluid meanings of racial identity categories- as this very article itself has done. In the end, however, there should be a caution when putting our scholarly and activist attention to identity boundary crossing and disruption itself at the expense of an analysis that takes all of the conceptual limits noted above into consideration. Despite the enormous contributions of social constructionism to theoretical understandings of and practical solutions to the problems of White supremacy, the turn toward cultural politics in the last decades has been somewhat regrettable to the extent that the focus on structural analyses of race in their intersectional and global context have been de-emphasized as scholars and activists alike embrace a more individualistic "politics of hybridity," or a "politics of ambiguity."[56] In other words, in confronting the very limits of binary thinking about race, there is the risk of "over-rotating," as mentioned elsewhere,[57] such that the very critique of essentialist and binary notions of race has gotten used to assert supposedly new and distinct racial identities that are "beyond binarisms." Indeed, this is the critique of some of the more conservative dimensions of the U.S. multiracial movement other writers raised in this volume.[58] This move to emphasize "intrasectionality" in progressive politics has overshadowed the more complicated analyses of "intersectionality" that would prove more fruitful for understanding more clearly the manifestations of global White supremacy in the current period, and is a set of cultural moves that we see in not only in contests around racial classification and inequality, but around gender, sexuality and nation as well.

Conclusion

In the United States, the relegation of people of African decent to the bottom of the social, political and economic ladder has a long history and persists in inarguable ways today, from marginalization in employment, to the impact of resegregation in public schools, to the disproportionate and mass imprisonment of Black people. At the same time, and made possible by the intergenerational, structural, and cumulative disenfranchisement of people defined as Black, White Americans, many of whom remain largely unaware of, or resistant to, the notion of unearned White privilege, are afforded structural advantages in all areas of social life- even sixty years after the American Civil Rights Movement. However, structural inequalities are far from binary. Along with the refusal of Whites, bigoted and well-meaning alike, to fundamentally alter structural arrangements that accrue them such material advantage, the persistence of systemic White supremacy is also made possible because of our continued willingness as academics and laypeople to prioritize a "Black/White" racial dynamic in our collective thinking about racial inequalities and racial justice. For, indeed, as this essay has attempted to demonstrate, the meanings and boundaries of race, and the impact of White racism on all people of color in the United States rely on such a binary, but are not entirely constitutive of it. As such, this chapter has tried to bring into sharper focus the limits of a sole focus on a Black/White racial dichotomy as informed by a generation of social constructionist scholarship around race and racial identities. An attempt has also been made to extend an analysis of these limits to argue that twenty-first century racial justice efforts, and critical social scientific analyses of these efforts, must address in more depth the ways in which binary thinking obscures our understanding of how White racism operates in an increasingly global world. In doing so, social science may hold increased promise for in its attempts to illuminate the contours of White supremacy in the United States in the contemporary period, and to suggest fruitful avenues to confront its many manifestations.

Notes

The author wishes to thank Erin Stattel and Jamie Masco for their invaluable research assistance and Keumjae Park for her insightful comments on an earlier version of the manuscript.
1. In this chapter, I use the terms "Black" and "White" in the conventional sense to refer to demographic categories of people defined as those who are of African decent and European decent respectively.
2. Given space considerations, I have chosen to focus largely on the theoretical contributions to the social sciences, and sociology more particularly, as these are the discourses in which I am trained and am most familiar.
3. Sojourner Truth, "Ain't I a Woman?" in *The Norton Anthology of Literature by Women* (New York: Norton, 1985).
4 Anna Julia Cooper, *A Voice From the South: By a Black Woman of the South* (Xenia, OH: The Aldine Printing House, 1892).
5. Paula Gunn Allen, "Who is Your Mother? Red Roots of White Feminism," in *The Sacred Hoop: Recovering the Feminine in American Indian Traditions*, ed. Paula Gunn Allen, (Boston: Beacon Press, 1986), 209-221; Gloria Anzaldua, *Borderlands / La Frontera: The New Mestiza* (San Francisco: Aunt Lute Press, 1987); Patricia Hill Collins, "Learning From the Outsider Within: The Sociological Significance of Black Feminist Thought," *Social Problems* 33 (1986): 14-32; bell hooks, *Talking Back: Thinking Feminist, Thinking Black* (Boston: South End Press, 1989); Gloria T. Hull, Patricia Bell Scott, and Barbara Smith, *All the Women are White, All the Blacks are Men, but Some of us are Brave: Black Women's Studies* (Old Westbury, NY: Feminist Press, 1982); Cherrie Moraga and Gloria Anzaldua, eds., *This Bridge Called my Back: Writings by Radical Women of Color* (San Francisco: Aunt Lute Press, 1981).
6. Gayatri Chakravorty Spivak, *In Other Words: Essays in Cultural Politics* (New York: Routledge, 1987).
7. Diana Fuss, *Essentially Speaking: Feminisation, Nature, and Difference* (New York: Routledge, 1989).
8. Maxine Baca Zinn and Bonnie Thorton Dill, "Theorizing Difference From Multiracial Feminism," *Feminist Studies* 22 (1996): 321-333.
9. For examples, see Beth Hess, "Beyond Dichotomy: Drawing Distinctions and Embracing Differences," *Sociological Forum* 5 (1990).
10. For examples, see Yen Le. Espiritu, *Asian American Panethnicity: Bridging Institutions and Identities* (Philadelphia: Temple University Press, 1992); Keumjae Park, "Constructing

Transnational Identities without Leaving Home: Korean Immigrant Women's Cognitive Border-crossing," *Sociological Forum* 22.2 (June 2007): 70-88; Min Zhou, "Are Asian Americans Becoming 'White'?" *Contexts* 3.1 (2004): 29-37.

11. For examples, see Mary Crow Dog and Richard Erdoes, "Civilize Them With a Stick," in *Lakota Woman*, (New York: Grove Weidenfeld, 1990), 28-41; Diane-Michele Prindeville, "Identity and the Politics of American Indian and Hispanic Women Leaders," *Gender and Society* 17.4 (2003): 591-608; Andrea Smith, *Conquest: Sexual Violence and American Indian Genocide* (Cambridge, MA: South End Press, 2005); Haunani Kay Trask, "Lovely Hula Hands: Corporate Tourism and the Prostitution of Hawaiian Culture," in *Mapping the Social Landscape* (4th edition), ed. Susan J. Ferguson (New York: McGraw Hill, 2005), 111-118.

12. For examples, see Robert S. Lichter and Daniel R. Amundson, "Distorted Reality: Hispanic Characters in TV Entertainment," in *Latin Looks*, ed. Clara Rodriguez (Boulder, CO: Westview Press, 1997), 57-72; Pierette Hondagneu-Sotelo, *Gendered Transitions: Mexican Experiences of Immigration* (Berkley, CA: University of California Press, 1994); Elizabeth Martinez, "Seeing More Than Black and White: Latinos, Racism, and the Cultural Divides," in *The Social Construction of Difference and Inequality*, ed. Tracy E. Ore, (New York: McGraw-Hill, 2006), 692-699.

13. Maria P. P. Root, ed., *Racially Mixed People in America* (Newbury Park, CA: Sage Publications, 1992); Maria P. P. Root, ed., *The Multiracial Experience: Racial Borders as the New Frontier* (Thousand Oaks, CA: Sage Publications, 1995).

14 David L. Brunsma, "Mixed Messages: Doing Race in the Color-Blind Era," in *Mixed Messages: Multiracial Identities in the "Color-Blind Era,"* ed. David L. Brunsma, (Boulder, CO: Lynne Rienner Publishers, 2006), 1-11; Kim Williams, "Linking Theory and Action: Social Movements Frameworks and Multiracial Activism" (paper presented at Colorlines in the 21st Century: Multiracism in a Racially Divided World, Roosevelt University, Chicago, September, 26, 1998).

15. W. E. B. DuBois, *The Souls of Black Folk* (New York: Penguin Books, 1903[1898]); George Herbert Mead, *Mind, Self, and Society: From the Standpoint of a Social Behavioralist* (Chicago: University of Chicago Press, 1934); Charles Horton Cooley, *Human Nature and the Social Order* (New York: Charles Scribner's Sons, 1902[1922]); Erving Goffman, *The Presentation of Self in Everyday Life* (New York: Doubleday, 1959).

16. Richard Dyer, "The Matter of Whiteness," in *White Privilege*, ed. Paula S. Rothenberg (New York: Worth, 2002), 9-14; Robert B. Moore, *Racism in the English Language* (New York: Council on Interracial Books for Children, 1976).

17. Eduardo Bonilla-Silva, *Racism without Racists: Color-Blind Racism and the Persistence of Racial Inequality in the United States* (Lanham, MD: Rowman & Littlefield, 2003); Prince Brown Jr., "Biology and the Social Construction of the 'Race' Concept," in *The Social Construction of Race and Ethnicity in the United States*, ed. Joan Ferrante and Prince Brown Jr. (New York: Longman Press, 1998), 131-138; Prince Brown Jr., "Why 'Race' Makes no Scientific Sense: The Case of Africans and Native Americans," in *The Social Construction of Race and Ethnicity in the United States*, ed. Joan Ferrante and Prince Brown Jr. (New York: Longman Press, 1998), 320-325; Abby L. Feber, "White Supremacists in the Color-Blind Era: Redefining Multiracial and White Identities," in *Mixed Messages: Multiracial Identities in the "Color-Blind Era,"* ed. David L. Brunsma (Boulder, CO: Lynne Rienner Publishers, 2006), 147-159; Barbara J. Fields, "Slavery, Race, and Ideology in the United States of America," *The New Left Review* 181 (1990): 95-118; Henry Louis Gates Jr., ed., "Race as the Trope of the World," in *"Race," Writings, and Difference*, (Chicago: University of Chicago Press, 1986), 4-13; Michael Omi and Howard Winant, "Racial Formations," in *The Social Construction of Difference and Inequality*, ed. Tracy E. Ore (New York: McGraw-Hill, 2006), 19-29; Howard F. Taylor, "Defining Race," in *Race and Ethnicity in Society: The Changing Landscape*, ed. Elizabeth Higginbotham and Margaret L. Anderson (Belmont, CA: Thompson Wadsworth, 2006), 47-54.

18. Neil Foley, "Becoming Hispanic: Mexican Americans and Whiteness," in *White Privilege*, ed. Paula S. Rothenberg (New York: Worth, 2002), 55-65.

19. Zhou, 2004, 29-37.

20. *Race: The Power of an Illusion*. Broadcast 24 April, 1 May, and 8 May 2003 by PBS (Public Broadcasting Service). Produced by Larry Adelman. San Francisco: California Newsreel. (http://www.pbs.org/race/000_General/000_00-Home.htm)

21. Kimberly McClain DaCosta, "Selling Mixedness: Marketing with Multiracial Identities," in *Mixed Messages: Multiracial Identities in the "Color-Blind Era,"* ed. David L. Brunsma (Boulder, CO: Lynne Rienner Publishers, 2006), 183-199; Feber, 2006, 147-159; Johanna E. Foster, "Strategic

Ambiguity Meets Strategic Essentialism: Multiracial, Intersex, and Disability Rights Activism and the Paradoxes of Identity Politics," *Research in Political Sociology* 13 (2004): 139-178; Judy Scales-Trent, *Notes of a White Black Woman* (University Park, PA: Pennsylvania State University Press, 1995); Jon Michael Spencer, *The New Colored People: The Mixed-Race Movement in America* (New York: New York University Press, 1997); Rainier Spencer, "New Racial Identities, Old Arguments: Continuing Biological Reification," in *Mixed Messages: Multiracial Identities in the "Color-Blind Era,"* ed. by David L. Brunsma (Boulder, CO: Lynne Rienner Publishers, 2006), 83-102.

22. James F. Davis, *Who is Black?: One Nation's Definition* (University Park: The Pennsylvania State University Press, 1991).

23. Ian Haney-Lopez, *White by Law: The Legal Construction of Race* (New York: New York University Press, 1996)

24. Philip C. Wander, Judith N. Martin, and Thomas K. Nakayama, "The Roots of Racial Classification," in *White Privilege*, ed. Paula S. Rothenberg (New York: Worth, 2002, 29-33.

25. Noel Ignatiev, *How the Irish Became White* (New York: Routeledge, 1995).

26. Karen Brodkin, *How Jews Became White Folks and What That Says About Race in America* (New Brunswick, NJ: Rutgers University Press, 1998).

27. Jennifer Lee and Frank D. Bean, "Beyond Black and White: Remaking Race in America," *Contexts* 2.3 (2003): 26-33.

28. Eduardo Bonilla-Silva and David G. Embrick, "Black, Honorary White, White: The Future of Race in the United States?" in *Mixed Messages: Multiracial Identities in the "Color-Blind Era,"* ed. David L. Brunsma (Boulder, CO: Lynne Rienner Publishers, 2006), 33-48.

29. DuBois, 1903.

30. Davis, 1991.

31. James E. Barrett and David Roediger, "How White People Became White," in *White Privilege: Essential Readings on the Other Side of Racism*, ed. Paula S. Rothenberg (New York: Worth Publishers, 2002), 30-32; Joan Ferrante and Prince Brown Jr., "Classifying People by Race," in *The Social Construction of Race and Ethnicity in the United States*, ed. Joan Ferrante and Prince Brown Jr., (New York: Longman Press, 1998), 113-128; Mary C. Waters, "Optional Ethnicities: For Whites Only?" in *Origins and Destinies*, ed. Sylvia Pedraza and Ruben G. Rumbaut (Belmont, CA: Wadsworth Publishing Company, 1996), 444-454.

32. Foster, 2004, 139-178.

33. Alejandro Portes, "Immigration's Aftermath," *The American Prospect* 13.7 (8 April 2002): 35-37

34. Heidi L. Barajas and Jennifer L. Pierce, "The Significance of Race and Gender in School Success Among Latinas and Latinos in College," *Gender and Society* 15.6 (2005): 859-878.

35. Trask, 2005, 111-118.

36. George Lipsitz, "The Possessive Investment in Whiteness," in *White Privilege*, ed. Paula S. Rothenberg (New York: Worth, 2002), 67-90.

37. Howard Zinn, *A People's History of the United State: 1492-present:* (New York: HarperCollins, 2003).

38. Bonnie Thornton Dill, "Our Mothers' Grief: Racial-Ethnic Women and the Maintenance of Families," *Journal of Family History* 13 (1988): 415-431.

39. Deborah King, "Multiple Jeopardy, Multiple Consciousness: The Context of Black Feminist Ideology," *Signs: Journal of Women in Culture and Society* 14 (1988): 42-72.

40. Patricia Hill Collins, *Black Feminist Thought: Knowledge, Consciousness, and the Politics of Empowerment* (Boston: Unwin Hyman, 1990).

41. Kimberle W. Crenshaw, "Mapping the Margins: Intersectionality, Identity Politics, and Violence Against Women of Color," *Stanford Law Review* 43.6 (1991): 1241-1299.

42. Thanks to Brooke Campbell for pointing out Crenshaw's explicit coining of the term "intersectionality."

43. Nancy, Hewitt, "Compounding Differences," *Feminist Studies* 18 (1992): 313-326.

44. Ayana Byrd, "Claiming Jezebel: Black Female Subjectivity and Sexual Expressions in Hip Hop," in *The Fire This Time: Young Activists and the New Feminism*, ed. Vivien Labaton and Dawn Lundy Martine (New York: Anchor Books, 2004), 3-18.

45. Ruth Atkin and Rich Adrienne, "'J.A.P.'–Slapping: The Politics of Scapegoating," in *Reconstructing Gender: A Multicultural Anthology*, ed. Estelle Disch (New York: McGraw-Hill, 2006), 67-70.

46. Becky W. Thompson, *A Hunger So Wide and So Deep: A Multiracial View of Women's Eating Problems* (Minneapolis, MN: University of Minnesota Press, 1994).
47. Erica Frankenberg and Chungmei Lee, "Race in American Public Schools: Rapidly Resegregating," (Cambridge, MA: The Harvard Civil Rights Project, Aug 2002), http://www.civilrightsproject.ucla.edu/research/deseg/Race_in_American_Public_Schools1.pdf.
48. Kimberle W. Crenshaw, "Demarginalizing the Intersection of Race and Sex: A Black Feminist Critique of Antidiscrimination Doctrine, Feminist Theory, and Antiracist Politics," *Feminism and Politics* (1998): 314-343.
49. Rosalind Petchesky, "Phantom Towers: Feminist Reflections on the Battle Between Global Capitalism and Fundamentalist Terrorism," *Ms.* 12.1 (2002): 10.
50. Angela Y. Davis, *Abolition Democracy* (New York: Seven Stories Press, 2005).
51. Bonilla-Silva and Embrick, 2006, 33-48.
52. Aldon D. Morris, *The Origins of the Civil Rights Movement: Black Communities Organizing for Change* (New York: The Free Press, 1984).
53. Alvin M. Josephy, Joane Nagel, and Troy Johnson, eds., *Red Power: The American Indians' Fight for Freedom*, 2nd Edition (Lincoln: University of Nebraska Press, 1999).
54. Francisco A. Rosales, *Chicano: The History of the Mexican American Civil Rights Movement* (Houston, TX: Arte Publico Press, 1997); Guadalupe San Miguel Jr., Brown, *Not White: School Integration and the Chicano Movement in Houston* (College Station, TX: Texas A&M University Press, 2001).
55. John Anner, *Beyond Identity Politics: Emerging Social Movements in Communities of Color* (Boston, MA: South End Press, 1996).
56. Foster, 2004, 139-178.
57. Ibid
58. For examples, see Brunsma, 2006, 1-11.

References

Allen, Paula Gunn. "Who is Your Mother? Red Roots of White Feminism," 209-221. In *The Sacred Hoop: Recovering the Feminine in American Indian Traditions*, ed. Paula Gunn Allen. Boston: Beacon Press, 1986.

Anner, John. *Beyond Identity Politics: Emerging Social Movements in Communities of Color.* Boston, MA: South End Press, 1996.

Anzaldua, Gloria. *Borderlands / La Frontera: The New Mestiza.* San Francisco: Aunt Lute Press, 1987.

Atkin, Ruth, and Rich Adrienne. "'J.A.P.'–Slapping: The Politics of Scapegoating." In *Reconstructing Gender: A Multicultural Anthology*, ed. Estelle Disch, 67-70. New York: McGraw-Hill, 2006.

Baca Zinn, Maxine, and Bonnie Thorton Dill. "Theorizing Difference From Multiracial Feminism." *Feminist Studies* 22 (1996): 321-333.

Barajas, Heidi L., and Jennifer L. Pierce. "The Significance of Race and Gender in School Success Among Latinas and Latinos in College." *Gender and Society* 15.6 (2005): 859-878.

Barrett, James E., and David Roediger. "How White People Became White," 30-32. In *White Privilege: Essential Readings on the Other Side of Racism*, edited by Paula S. Rothenberg. New York: Worth Publishers, 2002.

Bonilla-Silva, Eduardo. *Racism without Racists: Color-Blind Racism and the Persistence of Racial Inequality in the United States.* Lanham, MD: Rowman & Littlefield, 2003.

Bonilla-Silva, Eduardo, and David G. Embrick. "Black, Honorary White, White: The Future of Race in the United States?" 33-48. In *Mixed Messages: Multiracial Identities in the "Color-Blind Era,"* ed. David L. Brunsma. Boulder, CO: Lynne Rienner Publishers, 2006.

Brodkin, Karen. *How Jews Became White Folks and What That Says About Race in America.* New Brunswick, NJ: Rutgers University Press, 1998.

Brown, Prince, Jr. "Biology and the Social Construction of the 'Race' Concept." In *The Social Construction of Race and Ethnicity in the United States*, edited by Joan Ferrante and Prince Brown Jr., 131-138. New York: Longman Press, 1998.

Brown, Prince, Jr. "Why 'Race' Makes no Scientific Sense: The Case of Africans and Native Americans," 320-325. In *The Social Construction of Race and Ethnicity in the United States*, edited by Joan Ferrante and Prince Brown Jr. New York: Longman Press, 1998.

Brunsma, David L. "Mixed Messages: Doing Race in the Color-Blind Era," 1-11. In *Mixed Messages: Multiracial Identities in the "Color-Blind Era*," ed. David L. Brunsma. Boulder, CO: Lynne Rienner Publishers, 2006.

Byrd, Ayana. "Claiming Jezebel: Black Female Subjectivity and Sexual Expressions in Hip Hop," 3-18. In *The Fire This Time: Young Activists and the New Feminism*, ed. Vivien Labaton and Dawn Lundy Martine. New York: Anchor Books, 2004.

Collins, Patricia Hill. "Learning From the Outsider Within: The Sociological Significance of Black Feminist Thought." *Social Problems* 33 (1986): 14-32.

Collins, Patricia Hill. *Black Feminist Thought: Knowledge, Consciousness, and the Politics of Empowerment*. Boston: Unwin Hyman, 1990.

Cooley, Charles Horton. *Human Nature and the Social Order*. New York: Charles Scribner's Sons, 1902[1922].

Cooper, Anna Julia. *A Voice From the South: By a Black Woman of the South*. Xenia, OH: The Aldine Printing House, 1892.

Crenshaw, Kimberle W. "Mapping the Margins: Intersectionality, Identity Politics, and Violence Against Women of Color." *Stanford Law Review* 43.6 (1991): 1241-1299.

Crenshaw, Kimberle W. "Demarginalizing the Intersection of Race and Sex: A Black Feminist Critique of Antidiscrimination Doctrine, Feminist Theory, and Antiracist Politics." *Feminism and Politics* (1998): 314-343.

Crow Dog, Mary, and Richard Erdoes. "Civilize Them With a Stick." In *Lakota Woman*, 28-41. New York: Grove Weidenfeld, 1990.

DaCosta, Kimberly McClain, "Selling Mixedness: Marketing with Multiracial Identities," 183-199. In *Mixed Messages: Multiracial Identities in the "Color-Blind Era*," ed. David L. Brunsma. Boulder, CO: Lynne Rienner Publishers, 2006.

Davis, Angela Y. *Abolition Democracy*. New York: Seven Stories Press, 2005.

Davis, James F. *Who is Black?: One Nation's Definition*. University Park: The Pennsylvania State University Press, 1991.

Dill, Bonnie Thornton. "Our Mothers' Grief: Racial-Ethnic Women and the Maintenance of Families." *Journal of Family History* 13 (1988): 415-431.

DuBois, W. E. B. *The Souls of Black Folk*. New York: Penguin Books, 1903[1898].

Dyer, Richard. "The Matter of Whiteness," 9-14. In *White Privilege*, edited by Paula S. Rothenberg. New York: Worth, 2002.

Espiritu, Yen Le. *Asian American Panethnicity: Bridging Institutions and Identities*. Philadelphia: Temple University Press, 1992.

Feber, Abby L. "White Supremacists in the Color-Blind Era: Redefining Multiracial and White Identities," 147-159. In *Mixed Messages: Multiracial Identities in the "Color-Blind Era*," ed. David L. Brunsma. Boulder, CO: Lynne Rienner Publishers, 2006.

Ferrante, Joan, and Prince Brown Jr. "Classifying People by Race," 113-128. In *The Social Construction of Race and Ethnicity in the United States*, ed. Joan Ferrante and Prince Brown Jr.. New York: Longman Press, 1998.

Fields, Barbara J. "Slavery, Race, and Ideology in the United States of America." *The New Left Review* 181 (1990): 95-118.

Foley, Neil. "Becoming Hispanic: Mexican Americans and Whiteness," 55-65. In *White Privilege*, edited by Paula S. Rothenberg. New York: Worth, 2002.

Foster, Johanna E. "An Invitation to Dialogue: Clarifying the Position of Feminist Gender Theory in Relation to Sexual Difference Theory." *Gender and Society* 13 (1999): 431-456.

Foster, Johanna E. "Strategic Ambiguity Meets Strategic Essentialism: Multiracial, Intersex, and Disability Rights Activism and the Paradoxes of Identity Politics." *Research in Political Sociology* 13 (2004): 139-178.

Foster, Johanna E. "Defining Racism to Achieve Goals: The Multiracial and Black Reparations Movement," 161-181. In *Mixed Messages: Multiracial Identities in the "Color-Blind Era,"* ed. David L. Brunsma. Boulder, CO: Lynne Rienner Publishers, 2006.

Frankenberg, Ruth. *White Women, Race Matters: The Social Construction of Whiteness.* Minneapolis, MN: University of Minnesota Press, 1993.

Fuss, Diana. *Essentially Speaking: Feminism, Nature, and Difference.* New York: Routledge, 1989.

Gates, Henry Louis, Jr., ed. "Race as the Trope of the World." In *"Race," Writings, and Difference*, 4-13. Chicago: University of Chicago Press, 1986.

Goffman, Erving. *The Presentation of Self in Everyday Life.* New York: Doubleday, 1959.

Haney-Lopez, Ian. *White by Law: The Legal Construction of Race.* New York: New York University Press, 1996.

Hess, Beth. "Beyond Dichotomy: Drawing Distinctions and Embracing Differences." *Sociological Forum* 5 (1990).

Hewitt, Nancy. "Compounding Differences." *Feminist Studies* 18 (1992): 313-326.

Hondagneu-Sotelo, Pierette. *Gendered Transitions: Mexican Experiences of Immigration.* Berkley, CA: University of California Press, 1994.

Hooks, Bell. *Talking Back: Thinking Feminist, Thinking Black.* Boston: South End Press, 1989.

Hull, Gloria T., Patricia Bell Scott, and Barbara Smith. *All the Women are White, All the Blacks are Men, but Some of us are Brave: Black Women's Studies.* Old Westbury, NY: Feminist Press, 1982.

Ignatiev, Noel. *How the Irish Became White.* New York: Routeledge, 1995.

Josephy, Alvin M., Joane Nagel, and Troy Johnson, eds. *Red Power: The American Indians' Fight for Freedom* (2nd Edition). Lincoln: University of Nebraska Press, 1999.

King, Deborah. "Multiple Jeopardy, Multiple Consciousness: The Context of Black Feminist Ideology." *Signs: Journal of Women in Culture and Society* 14 (1988): 42-72.

Lee, Jennifer, and Frank D. Bean. "Beyond Black and White: Remaking Race in America." *Contexts* 2.3 (2003): 26-33.

Lichter, Robert S., and Daniel R. Amundson. "Distorted Reality: Hispanic Characters in TV Entertainment," 57-72. In *Latin Looks*, edited by Clara Rodriguez. Boulder, CO: Westview Press, 1997.

Lipsitz, George. "The Possessive Investment in Whiteness," 67-90. In *White Privilege*, ed. Paula S. Rothenberg. New York: Worth, 2002.

Martinez, Elizabeth. "Seeing More Than Black and White: Latinos, Racism, and the Cultural Divides," 692-699. In *The Social Construction of Difference and Inequality*, ed. Tracy E. Ore. New York: McGraw-Hill, 2006.

Mead, George Herbert. *Mind, Self, and Society: From the Standpoint of a Social Behavioralist.* Chicago: University of Chicago Press, 1934.

Moore, Robert B. *Racism in the English Language.* New York: Council on Interracial Books for Children, 1976.

Moraga, Cherrie, and Gloria Anzaldua, eds. *This Bridge Called my Back: Writings by Radical Women of Color.* San Francisco: Aunt Lute Press, 1981.

Morris, Aldon D. *The Origins of the Civil Rights Movement: Black Communities Organizing for Change.* New York: The Free Press, 1984.

Oliver, Melvin L., and Thomas M. Shapiro. *Black Wealth/White Wealth: A New Perspective on Racial Inequality.* New York: Routledge, 1995.

Omi, Michael, and Howard Winant. "Racial Formations," 19-29. In *The Social Construction of Difference and Inequality*, ed. Tracy E. Ore. New York: McGraw-Hill, 2006.

Park, Keumjae. "Constructing Transnational Identities without Leaving Home: Korean Immigrant Women's Cognitive Border-crossing." *Sociological Forum* 22.2 (June 2007): 70-88.

Petchesky, Rosalind. "Phantom Towers: Feminist Reflections on the Battle Between Global Capitalism and Fundamentalist Terrorism." *Ms.* 12.1 (2002): 10.

Portes, Alejandro. "Immigration's Aftermath." *The American Prospect* 13.7 (8 April 2002): 35-37.

Prindeville, Diane-Michele. "Identity and the Politics of American Indian and Hispanic Women Leaders." *Gender and Society* 17.4 (2003): 591-608.

Race: The Power of an Illusion. Broadcast 24 April, 1 May, and 8 May 2003 by PBS (Public Broadcasting Service). Produced by Larry Adelman. San Francisco: California Newsreel. (http://www.pbs.org/race/000_General/000_00-Home.htm).

Root, Maria P. P., ed. *Racially Mixed People in America.* Newbury Park, CA: Sage Publications, 1992.

Root, Maria P. P., ed. *The Multiracial Experience: Racial Borders as the New Frontier.* Thousand Oaks, CA: Sage Publications, 1995.

Rosales, Francisco A. *Chicano: The History of the Mexican American Civil Rights Movement.* Houston, TX: Arte Publico Press, 1997.

San Miguel, Guadalupe, Jr. *Brown, Not White: School Integration and the Chicano Movement in Houston.* College Station, TX: Texas A&M University Press, 2001.

Scales-Trent, Judy. *Notes of a White Black Woman.* University Park, PA: Pennsylvania State University Press, 1995.

Smith, Andrea. *Conquest: Sexual Violence and American Indian Genocide.* Cambridge, MA: South End Press, 2005.

Spencer, Jon Michael. *The New Colored People: The Mixed-Race Movement in America.* New York: New York University Press, 1997.

Spencer, Rainier. "New Racial Identities, Old Arguments: Continuing Biological Reification," 83-102. In *Mixed Messages: Multiracial Identities in the "Color-Blind Era,"* ed. David L. Brunsma. Boulder, CO: Lynne Rienner Publishers, 2006.

Spivak, Gayatri Chakravorty. *In Other Words: Essays in Cultural Politics.* New York: Routledge, 1987.

Taylor, Howard F. "Defining Race," 47-54. In *Race and Ethnicity in Society: The Changing Landscape,* ed. Elizabeth Higginbotham and Margaret L. Anderson. Belmont, CA: Thompson Wadsworth, 2006.

Thompson, Becky W. *A Hunger So Wide and So Deep: A Multiracial View of Women's Eating Problems.* Minneapolis, MN: University of Minnesota Press, 1994.

Trask, Haunani Kay. "Lovely Hula Hands: Corporate Tourism and the Prostitution of Hawaiian Culture," 111-118. In *Mapping the Social Landscape* (4th edition), edited by Susan J. Ferguson. New York: McGraw Hill, 2005.

Truth, Sojourner. "Ain't I a Woman?" In *The Norton Anthology of Literature by Women.* New York: Norton, 1985.

Wander, Philip C., Judith N. Martin, and Thomas K. Nakayama. "The Roots of Racial Classification," 29-33. In *White Privilege,* ed. Paula S. Rothenberg. New York: Worth, 2002.

Waters, Mary C. "Optional Ethnicities: For Whites Only?" 444-454. In *Origins and Destinies,* ed. Sylvia Pedraza and Ruben G. Rumbaut. Belmont, CA: Wadsworth Publishing Company, 1996.

Williams, Kim. "Linking Theory and Action: Social Movements Frameworks and Multiracial Activism." Paper presented at *Colorlines in the 21st Century: Multiracism in a Racially Divided World,* Roosevelt University, Chicago, September 26, 1998.

Zhou, Min. "Are Asian Americans Becoming 'White'?" *Contexts* 3.1 (2004): 29-37.

Zinn, Howard. *A People's History of the United State: 1492-present.* New York: HarperCollins, 2003.

Chapter 12

The Necessity of a Multiracial Category in a Race-Conscious Society

Francis Wardle

This chapter addresses the need for multiracial and multiethnic children and adults in the United States to have a category to use for their own identity. The issue, however, is not just about a category on the US Census and all other federal forms—particularly those used in K-12 schools; it is also about the developmental needs of these children as they grow, develop, and interact with single-race children and adults in a variety of social settings. We need a commonly used term in our general language, so that children of mixed-heritage not only have a group to which they belong, but also so that others recognize them as being part of a distinct group.

Introduction

Developing a healthy racial/ethnic identity is a process that occurs over time as children interact with their social environment and construct their own reality.[1] A central component of this healthy identity development process is directly related to complex social and private use language.[2] Further, because scholarship is so driven by the US census categories—everything from research, critical theory analysis of public policy, curriculum development and training of teachers and human service professionals, a term for multiracial and multiethnic people is essential. The reality of both the expanding mixed-race population, and the overall deconstruction of race in America, requires a change.

There is no commonly accepted term for mixed race children and adults. The terms multiracial, multiethnic, mixed-race and mixed-heritage are utilized in this chapter to refer to individuals who self-identify with two or more of the current U.S. census categories.[3] These individuals may be first generation, or many, many generations removed from a single-race/ethnic identity. Inherent in the definition is the understanding that each of the five US racial/ethnic groups is, in fact, multiracial. Within the 2000 census categories, the Hispanic/Latino ethnic category is particularly confusing, being obviously multiracial, and thus highly problematic when looking at a "single-race" view of society.[4] Obviously, these definitions change from country to country, as do single-race definitions. For example, in Belize there are several government racial categories that, viewed from a U.S. perspective, would be considered mixed-race; the same, of course, is true of Brazil.[5]

Critics of the multiracial movement have often focused on our insistence of a separate category, arguing that this insistence actually perpetuates the racial categories that we wish to abolish.[6] The need for a category *is not* inconsistent with deconstructing race! Those who argue that a concrete mixed race category helps to perpetuate the old racial hierarchy are simply using the issue to cover up their own disagreement with the whole idea of identifying as multiracial.

This chapter argues for a common word or label to describe people and children who are multiethnic and multiracial. Arguments against this view are articulated in various essays in this volume and thus will not be examined within this discourse.

Assumptions

The study of multiracial and multiethnic communities lacks a coherent body of knowledge. This field is interdisciplinary in that it tends to borrow from sociology, history, ethnology, anthropology, psychology, women's studies, and U.S. single-race ethnic studies (African America, Latino, and Native American). However, sociologists dominate the field. There is a great deal of confusion and misinformation surrounding scholarship related to mixed race identity, and the extant body of knowledge, and there is a bias toward each of the disciplines described. Further, Wallace[7] suggests that this perspective also leads to a view of mixed-race people only in terms of a specific minority group (i.e. African American; Asians) as opposed to a general mixed-race/ethnic construct. To clarify the body of knowledge used for this chapter, an outline of assumptions, ambiguities, and misconceptions related to mixed race identity is necessary along with this author's stance on controversial issues:

- Anyone with any black heritage is black.[8] This, of course, applies to people with other than black/white combinations, and when the mixture is a combination of minorities, the one with the lowest status is the only one recognized—this is known as the rule of hypodescent or "one drop rule." The US is the only society in the world with a strict one-drop rule. In Brazil most mixed-race people are identified as either mulatta/o or morena/o;[9] in India people with some African or Caribbean heritage are not considered black,[10] and mixed-race people worldwide have various mixed labels.[11] In South American countries other than Brazil, a person's racial label is based on their phenotype (physical appearance), which means that some people with Black heritage are considered European or Asian or Indian. But even in the US this is not always the case. The American Latino category includes in it mestizos, who are people with Native American, European, and black backgrounds.[12] According to Fernandez, about 85-90% of today's Mexican population is mestizo (Native, Spanish, and African) and thus many who identify as Latino in the US are mestizo. Many Native American groups have members with considerable black heritage, particularly those from tribes that harbored slaves during the American Civil War. One of the bands (tribes) that comprise the Seminole Nation is considered a black group. And, of course, there are those with some African heritage who pass as white—knowingly or unknowingly. As Aves-Silva, Santos, Guimarás, Ferreira, Bandelt, Pena & Prado discovered in their DNA studies of Brazilian's racial background, many Brazilians who consider themselves white have some African heritage in their linage, and visa-versa with those who consider themselves Amerindian and Afro Brazilian

- Academics must frame the discussion of race and multiracial issues in this country and the world.[13] Academics have the peculiar arrogance to assume that they must be the architects of all social movements, and must be the framers of all social and political debates. Not only is this generally untrue, but it is particularly untrue of the multiracial movement, which is truly a grass-roots movement.[14] It is a movement that developed from the real, lived, experiences of multiracial families, multiracial children, and mixed-race people struggling to survive and prosper in a society dominated by a fixed-race view of humanity.[15] At best academics have come late into the struggle; at worst, some continue to be detractors and in opposition to the gains of the movement.[16]

- Academics are the experts on multiracial issues. Similar to the previous point, many academics have accused grass-roots leaders of the movement of being "self-appointed experts."[17] This, of course, belies the question, "and who made them experts?" Since there are no departments of multiracial studies in our universities and colleges, and no PhDs that specialize in multiracial and multiethnic studies, none of these academicians can truly claim to be experts, either. Because of the nature of the academic preparation required for advanced degrees, and because current faculty positions are situated within single-race/discipline departments, academics are embedded within the politics, group-think, and scholarship of a single-race/discipline context that controls their thinking, scholarship, academic advancement, and politics. Many of these "experts" have no real personal connection to the multiracial movement.

- Multiracial children look black (or the phenotype of their minority parent). This, of course, is one of the most popular myths about our children.[18] Thus if they look black they should be raised black, because society sees them as black, the argument then continues. The basis of the argument of white privilege and black—or minority—oppression is based on looks (phenotype). This myth is partly based on the concept that if you do not look black you are not recognized as mixed – but rather as belonging to another single-race-ethnicity group (thus a self-fulfilling perception). My children have been "seen" as Samoan, Brazilian, Latino, Vietnamese, Cambodian, Asian Indian, Native American, Fijian, North African and sometimes African American.

- Multiracial children are ashamed of their black heritage. There is a great amount of material suggesting that the only reason for insisting on identifying multiracial children as multiracial and not black is because they and/or their parents are ashamed of their black heritage.[19] Multiracial children come in all shapes and sizes: blond hair, blue and green eyes, white skin, freckles, along with whatever is the stereotypical look of a mixed-race child, and everything in between.

- In terms of phenotype, many are certainly not African. They have some African heritage, but also European, Native American, Latino and Asian, and others. Most multiracial-multiethnic people who want to identify as multiracial and or multiethnic do so because they believe it is genetically, culturally and socially a an accurate category to describe their true identity.[20] In a recent discussion I had with my 23-year-old daughter, she referred to the fact that she does not feel any particular affinity or allegiance to any of her single-race heritages (white, Black or Chickasaw) largely because each of them does not recognize or support a label that is inclusive of her mixed-race identity. It should be noted here that the US census has often claimed that they are not in the business of describing a person's race/ethnicity; that the system relies on "self-identification."[21]

- To withstand racism, multiracial children must be raised as black.[22] Multiracial and multiethnic children receive harassment from single-race children and adults, often including teachers, social workers and psychologists. This is not always deliberate, but its impact is still harassment. My own children have experienced more harassment from minorities than whites. The black or other minority parent in the marriage can and will certainly assist their children in understanding how to resist racism. Also, white partners in interracial relationships experience their own harassment and prejudice and can certainly identify with some of the issues their children must face. Many minority parents in white/minority relationships have themselves experienced racism from individuals in their own racial/ethnic group.

- Those who advocate for a multiracial category are colorblind. This is an extremely popular position.[23] Not only do multiracial children and people experience prejudice based on race, but they experience it from members of all single-race groups. White members of interracial unions have been fully indoctrinated into racism by our minority spouses, not to mention our own experiences! To argue against the one-drop rule does not automatically mean one is colorblind. One would have to certainly become much more sensitive to racism within an interracial relationship.

- Liberals are good, conservatives are bad, and advocates of multiracial identity are conservatives.[24] This discussion of a multiracial label goes way beyond the inclusion of a separate category on federal forms; however, many of the detractors of the multiracial movement have fixated on this specific area of debate as the only issue of importance to the multiracial movement. And, as one would expect, they frame the debate in a liberal versus conservative, enlightened versus ignorant, educated versus uninformed manner. In fact, Rainier Spencer calls these conservative representatives right wing demagogues who will do anything to thwart civil rights progress.[25] Thus, advocating of a multiracial category is viewed as preventing civil rights progress. Part of this argument comes as a result of the support of a multiracial category on the US Census by some republicans, including very conservative ones but this is much more a critical theory argument.[26] From this perspective, liberals—and their policies and approaches—are pro humanity and pro civil rights, while conservatives are viewed a pro big business and anti-human rights or racists.

- Multiracial identities in counties such as Brazil and S. Africa have prevented true racial equality in those countries.[27] To make these statements about Brazil shows that these writers have a limited understanding of the complex colonial history, politics, religion and cultures of Brazil. Inequality in Brazil is based much more on social class than it is on color; further, Brazil's society is based on Portuguese and French (Napoleon) laws and the mores of the Catholic Church, not on a Judeo-Christian history. Finally, Brazil's democracy is very new. It has only been about thirty years since Brazil was ruled by a dictator.

The Necessity of a Multiracial Category in a Race-Conscious Society: Need for an Accurate Label

Listed below are several arguments for the need of a multiracial/multiethnic word in both our academic and our general terminology. As aforementioned, this necessity goes beyond a category on federal employment, assessment, school, and college entry documents and other official forms. This category has to become a part of our academic knowledge base and common language; also, it must be internalized to become a part of the way individuals develop their identity and label themselves.

As the father of four multiracial children, I am still constantly amazed at how complete strangers will come up to my children and/or their parents, and ask, "well, what are you?" "Where do you live?" (i.e. are you from a European or an Africa nation?) "Are you black or are you white?" "How come your mother is black and your father is white?" As mentioned before, strangers label these children as Latino, Native American (several different tribes), Samoan, Brazilian, Asian/Indian, Filipino, Cambodian, N. African, Vietnamese, Moroccan, and others. This labeling has occurred when my children were in the US, Europe, Africa, and Brazil.

On one occasion, a complete stranger in a convenience store accosted my then college-age daughter. This stranger asked my daughter, "Do you speak Spanish?" When my daughter got over her initial confusion to answer, "No," the stranger launched into a diatribe about how bad my daughter's parents were for not teaching her Spanish! On my youngest daughter's study-aboard visit to Samoa, the native Samoans were very perplexed by her color and features. While their only experience with American students was with white students, they knew she was not Black. At first they believed she was from Fiji, and actually tried to convince themselves of this, but then realized she did not speak the Fijian language and exhibited very different behaviors from their Fijian friends.

For Sunday breakfast my wife, son and I shared a table with a stranger. She asked my college-age son if he was Indian (Asian). After he pointed out to her that we were his parents, she insisted on repeating the question. She obviously believed that he was adopted. Of course, on a more serious note, much of the questioning and downright harassment of multiracial and multiethnic children occurs at school and comes from peers of all races and ethnicities.[28] While some of this questioning is outright prejudice (addressed later in this chapter), some is simply a result of confusion on the part of the questioner, particularly children. Since we do not culturally and socially acknowledge multiracial people (they are always labeled with a single-race label), children and adults alike are very confused. Further, as we well know, when an accurate label does not exist, all sorts of derogatory and unacceptable terms are used, both by adults—that it marginal man—and certainly by children.[29] Thus a multiracial/ multiethnic word or label will essentially enable both our language and our society to "catch up with the times"; it will also provide an appropriate term and a defense against using inappropriate and unacceptable putdowns.[30]

Third Culture Children

Two of my children live and work in Paris. They can do so because they speak French (as well as English), and have British passports (as well as U.S. passports), which make them members of the European Union. One of my children is a member of the Chickasaw tribe (as well as being multiracial—black/white). Eventually, all my children will have US and British passports, view themselves as having a Black-white heritage, and be members of the Chickasaw tribe.

According to West, my children are third culture children.[31] Third culture children are children "whose lives span two cultures—children sometimes referred to as third culture, so-called for the third culture created within them," also, according to West, the number of these children is growing.[32]

The challenge for professionals is how to respond to these children's third culture—not each separate culture, but "the one created within them."[33] West indicates that, "responding authentically to children whose backgrounds include more than one cultural group exposes the fallacy of a single race approach to diversity."[34] Further, according to Bronfenbrenner, children exist within their own unique contexts, and integrate all the different ecological components that make up their unique context: race, culture, gender, disability/ability, family, community and SES, as opposed to having a context where they are forced to choose between opposing environmental factors such as black and white race/culture.[35] Thus, teachers must move from helping children connect to a single cultural or racial group to relating to each child's uniquely constructed, complex contexts.

This view presented by West and Bronfenbrenner is a constructivist view that honors each child's active exploration and development of their entire identity. Part of the constructivists approach is to explore the use of language that honors, affirms and helps scaffold the child's learning about his/her identity development.[36] When it comes to the third culture child, this means language that celebrates and constructs the child's unique, global, multiracial, and multicultural identity.

Self Identity Development

The concept of children constructing their own unique identity though a developmental progression must include a discussion on exactly how, in a society fixated on a single-race view and single-race language, words act as central components in this identity development.

It makes little sense for a society to finally allow a Tiger Woods to play golf at any country club he so chooses, but not allow him to proclaim a self-identity as multiracial, which of course he has done. America is a country that has historically focused on individual rights and individual freedoms. The right to self-identity must be one of our fundamental rights to life, liberty, and the pursuit of happiness.

As the number of multiethnic and multiracial people increases, the need for a label to self-identity increases.[37] This need for the use of supportive language is particularly important for children as they progress though each critical developmental stage.[38] During the preoperational stage (2-7 years of age), children notice physical differences and similarities.[39] At this age they also start using words to label objects, ideals and emotions, and the physical differences they observe.[40] Preoperational children can only handle one piece of information at a time; they lack what we call class inclusion. Thus it is critically important that children this age have a single term or label to describe their heritage. I recommend brown when they are young; as they get older they can use a multiracial or multiethnic.[41] But they cannot understand black and white, or Hispanic and Native American, or Japanese and Hispanic. And their same-age peers cannot understand a dual identity, either, (For example, this age child cannot conceive that a teacher is also a mother). This is the age when children will honesty ask, "well, what are you, anyway, your mother's black and your father's white?"[42] Children this age are also use labels to create categories for files in their minds. These become the files they use to sort and order their long-term memory. They clearly need a place to put information about one of the most important aspects of positive self-concept development—their ethnic/racial identity.

During the concrete operations stage (7-11 years old), children can think logically and handle multiple ideas simultaneously.[43] Thus, they have the mental capacity to handle multiple identities. But, given that other children, adults, teachers and professionals continually ask these children, in a variety of polite and not-so-polite ways, "well, what are you?" they need a simple, single label. Further, they need a single file in their long-term memory in which to place all the issues regarding the construction of a healthy identity, rather than many different files that they must continually refer to every time the issue of race comes up (within their own private speech, or within their social contexts). A child who is always sorting racial and ethnic categories and labels will soon begin to question which ones really apply; and what his/her identity really is.[44]

However, as most people involved with multiracial children (parents, educators, psychologists and researchers) know, adolescence is the critical timeframe—what Erikson calls the period of the identity crisis. This is the time of the in group-out group struggle. This in group-out group conflict occurs with a variety of group identities—athletes and geeks, country and popular music, punks and preppies, etc., and is a natural part of the struggle all adolescences (regardless of race) experience as they struggle to find their true, and not false, identities.[45] Regarding racial and cultural identity, the in-group is single-race identity, the out-group students with more than one identity, and single-race students who do not meet the very rigid stereotypical view of racial/ ethnic identity and behavior held by those who control the in-group.[46] This is the age of Tatum's *Why are all the black kids sitting together in the cafeteria?* It is when behavior, language, and clothes are used to define group membership, including racial and ethnic group belonging.[47]

I have worked with mixed-race adolescents, and my four children all have progressed through this stage. The harassment and put-downs from single-race students at this age are extreme and very destructive.[48] "I just try to hang out with whomever I want to. I'm in the band; I play basketball. That's like two opposites. All my black friends ask, 'Why are you playing music? Why aren't you playing football this season? Why are you being all weak, you're hanging out with all those weak people?' People want you to fit into one group. I don't fit into one group."[49] Further, teachers—including diversity experts—have no idea how to provide activities that include multiracial and multiethnic children in a positive and appropriate manner.[50]

Children in this developmental stage—Piaget's stage of formal operations, and in Erikson's stage of identity versus role confusion, need a commonly understood term both for their own self-concept development (personal identity) —"I am multiracial" —and for their reference group orientation—"I belong to the multiracial group."[51] This latter concept is particularly critical because, as I have already stated, on the one hand single-race students, teachers and psychologists continually point out to these children that the do not fit into single-race group, and on the other hand diversity experts insist that individual identity is a product of reference group (single-race) orientation.[52]

Multiracial and multiethnic children not only need a clear and district reference group to belong to, but they also need a commonly understood label or heading for that group.[53] It is clear that one of the main ways we categorize files in our minds is using words (initially young children use icons, which are then replaced by words).[54] Thus, multiethnic and multiracial children need a word to label their identity files, both for their own meta-cognitive development of a healthy identity, and to respond to a social world fixated on single-race labels – albeit inaccurate ones – to describe a one's race and culture.

To Move Beyond Black and White

There are many mixed-race people who are not black/white.[55] Further, while some cultures such as Brazil, fully accept people with a vast variety of mixed-race backgrounds, other cultures are emphatically single-race in their view of diversity. It is interesting to note that in the US there are multiracial support groups and virtual support groups for individuals to find a community in which to explore their identity and that of their children, while in Brazil there are similar groups for people who identify as Afro Brazilian).[56] It is well known that Amerasians in many Asian countries, such as Vietnam, are social outcasts subject to discrimination not experienced by any single-race group.[57] In cases and counties like this, the race/ethnic combination of the person of mixed-heritage does not matter; what mattes it that the person is obviously mixed. Japan is also known for its intolerance of people with mixed heritage, as is, of course, the U.S.[58] Thus, globally there are places where anyone with any racial or ethnic mixture, especially in racial homogenous societies, is placed at the bottom of the social order.

In the U.S., we tend to focus on mixed-race children and people whose background is Black-white.[59] This is probably due to two reasons, 1) many in the U.S. view b/w interracial marriages as the most extreme of choices (due to our history of slavery, Jim Crow laws), and, 2) because many detractors of the current move towards acceptance of multiracial and multiethnic label and acceptance tend to be associated with Afro-American university departments. As aforementioned, the creation of the Hispanic/Latino category, unique to the US, has prevented the US from truly exploring the mixed-heritage of most Latinos.[60]However, as stated earlier, both in the U.S. and globally there are as many ethnic and racial combinations of people of mixed heritage as there are single race-ethnicities (however defined). Further, race of course is defined differently from country to country.[61] One of the purposes of embracing a multiracial and/or multiethnic label is to move the debate beyond simply black-white, to all children and people who challenge the single-race view of humanity within their social and cultural contents.

Research

Recently, the British Department of Education conducted research on multiracial (white/Caribbean) students in British schools.[62] Results of the research showed that, while British public schools are making progress in assisting signal-race minority children, the unique needs of multiracial children are not being addressed.[63] However, in the United States we cannot conduct this kind of research because schools still do not collect demographic information on multiracial children.

Some years ago I received a question on my website (Center for the Study of Biracial Children). It was more of a statement than a question, "Why is it that so many mixed-race children are in special education?" Obviously, this question is a variation of the "mixed race children are confused" stereotype. And, of note, this question came from a teacher. We do not have the most basic body of knowledge about how mixed-race children perform in schools, the number of these children in special education, and whether mixed-race children are disproportionably disciplined and/or suspended. Thus, I was unable to provide a response based on actual statistics.

There is a small body of information that is suggesting that mixed-race children in the U.S. face unique problems growing up in a society fixated on single-race identity.[64] To more fully and comprehensively address this issue, we must begin to collect baseline data to create a scientific body of knowledge. Further, to explore many of the stereotypes and myths that surround this population, we must increase our research.[65]

One of the most popular arguments for not having a multiracial category on school forms is that this will make it too difficult to track the successes or failures of single-race, minority children in our schools. This very argument, of course, proves my point. It is interesting that such a controversial area—mixed-race children—accompanied by a plethora of both popular and academic myths and folk law lacks any true scientific body of knowledge.[66] In most academic areas when accurate information does not exist, scholars insist on creating methods and approaches to collect this information. Maybe detractors of the multiracial cause like the fact that our knowledge base is so small, because this allows for the perpetuation of false and negative myths and beliefs.[67]

Funding

The contemporary multiracial movement has achieved enormous progress with no government funding and almost no foundation funding.[68] Recently, I attended a multiracial conference in Chicago sponsored by AMEA (Association of Multiethnic Americans). There were five or six vendors, and conference presenters paid for their own travel and lodging. Contrast this to conference of the National Black Child Institute, which I have attended on several occasions. As all conference participants know, funding for conferences comes from participants and from vendors who exhibit in huge halls. For the National Black Child Institute conference there were many vendors. Of particular interest, over 75% of the vendors were U.S government agencies of one kind or another: CDC, U.S. Department of Education, HHS, Head Start, Early Start, Jump Start, Children's Bureau, and the USDA. It seems very clear that both the federal government and major charitable foundations target minority groups for outreach, services, access, and education. And this is as it should be, but why should multiracial and multiethnic children, families, and adults, be left out of these endeavors?

An interesting example illustrates a certain irony here. For the last several years, American foundations have sponsored visits of African American graduate experts to Brazil to spearhead a process of creating Affirmative Action programs based on the one-drop rule in Brazil.[69] This is happening at the very time US multiracial organizations are pushing for a move away from the one-drop rule, and who use Brazil's reality as a model to be followed in the US.

There are a variety of services, educational, and outreach organizations that attempt to meet the needs of the ever-growing multiracial population in the U.S. These organizations need and desire funds to serve children, families, and adults. But, if one does not have numbers it becomes difficult to make a case for funding. We do not have the numbers because multiracial and multiethnic children and adults are invariably not counted as a separate category. And because, we lack research about these children and their families - in our schools, early childhood programs, juvenile programs, jails, communities and colleges.

The Training of Professionals

There is a huge disconnect, between a growing number of multiracial and multiethnic children and families, and the education of professionals who come into direct contact with these children and families. These professionals are teachers, therapists, nurses, social workers, councilors, school psychologists, community workers, youth recreation leaders, Head Start staff, and others. While the teaching profession lacks minority teachers in the same proportion as students,[70] there is at least large body of knowledge used in classes, graduate programs, workshops and in-service training to help train white teachers to work with minority students.[71] I have taught diversity classes to teachers. All the texts and curricula I use do mention multiethnic and multiracial children. At some point in all of these classes a student always asks, "what about mixed-race children? Why are they not included here?" Others join in, declaring the number of mixed-race children they have in their classes and the challenges they pose. Then much of the class begins to share about all the friends and relatives they have who are involved in interracial relationships, and who have multiracial children. It seems that everyone know someone with a multiethnic or multiracial child!

We also provide little if any advice to helping professionals working with multiracial and multiethnic adults: therapists, social workers, nurses, and doctors. At a local community college, I teach child psychology classes. My students include future nurses, radiologists, and other healthcare professionals, clinical psychologists, child psychologists, and teachers. While the psychology books I use—and review continually do make needed changes—continually add information about traditional U.S. racial/ethnic groups, almost none of them in any way address multiracial and multiethnic children, adults and families.[72]

The new book *Classic Edition Sources: Multicural Education* by J. Noel contains 36 articles "to reflect the direction of the field of multicultural education today." Not one addresses education for multiethnic and multiracial children. And in the current *Handbook of Multicultural Education*, only one of the 49 articles addresses this topic at all.[73]

The major focus of all articles on multicultural education emphasize the importance of tailoring our educational efforts to match the unique learning styles and social/cultural context of each child, and to make sure that marginalized children of minority racial, ethnic, language, gender and other status have their needs addressed.[74] Gonzalez-Mena argues that all children need a sense of belonging. A growing number of books and articles for counselors, social workers, and therapists also provide this multicultural perspective to assist professionals in working effectively with children and adults from minority, single—race and ethnic backgrounds, what the field is now calling cultural competence. Not only do all of these books and articles continue to perpetuate the very non-diverse and inaccurate notion that the entire U.S. (and global) population fits neatly within the traditional five U.S. census categories, but these approaches provide no advice to assist teachers and other helping professionals in meeting the unique learning and mental health needs of children and adults whose parents crossed traditional and orthodox boundaries to marry and have children.[75] This lack of inclusion of multiethnic and multiethnic children and adults in diversity books and articles—from multicultural textbooks to position statements by psychological associations—is quite bewildering and astonishing, especially in texts that profess to "honor diversity!."

Harvard psychiatrist Alvin Poussaint changed his view of multiracial children, from confused and disoriented, to together and potentially very successful. He stated that his former view was based on what he had been taught in graduate school; the latter view was based on what he had discovered through his own research and clinical experience.[76]

How can professionals respond to the needs of multiracial and multiethnic children and adults if they are not trained to do so? Further, how do we change the biased and inaccurate views that many professionals bring to the field about this population, without specific instruction in college?

Providing a specific label for multiracial children will provide everyone in all academic fields with a single construct which will lead to an increase in research, scholarship, theory, diversity activities, books, curricula, and the training of professionals on issues related to multiethnic and multiracial people (teachers, counselors, social workers, and healthcare professionals). This will result in the academic community finally creating a solid body of knowledge about this unique population, encourage graduate students to study the unique needs of these students, in their various academic disciplines, and provide specific training to assist professionals in working with this every-increasing population.

Resisting Harassment

One of the ironies of our current racial climate is that in our attempts to affirm the belonging of minority children to their single-race minority group,[77] we have actually produced a very negative byproduct: asserting one's own ethnic and racial pride and self-esteem at the expense of others. This activity is practically strong during adolescence, when students are engaged in what Erikson calls determining in-group and out-group belonging. And more often than not, the students placed in the out-group are multiracial and multiethnic students, particularly those who proudly proclaim a multiracial or multiethnic heritage.[78] This group solidarity approach to racial pride and identity formation is partially powerful and destructive at this age. We've all heard the phrases, "you are not black enough, you think you are better than us, you are ashamed of your black blood." Replace black with other minority status for other children.[79] These attacks are often very vicious and very destructive to a child's self-esteem and healthy identify development. In bullying language, this harassment constitutes relational bullying (Berger 2006).

Some years ago a white mother called me and said that the children at her daughter's predominantly African American public school told her daughter that her mother was a whore. When this mother complained to the school's administration, they did nothing, suggesting she brought this upon herself for marrying a black man. There are many incidents, through my website and personal contacts, of harassment that are reported by multiracial people that are perpetuated by other minorities against multiracial children.[80]

The only way to address this issue of harassment of multiethnic and multiracial students is to fully embrace their full heritage, and to assert their right to being proudly multiracial. We have to make it totally unacceptable for anyone, including peers, to harass, put down, or question the identity of any child. While a multiracial label will not automatically do this, it will provide acknowledgment and legitimacy for each of these children.

Accept Reality

Demographic data is supposed to be an accurate statistical description of a specific population. Over 6.8 million Americans (2%) identified themselves as having more than one race in the 2000 U.S. Census. However, for political reasons, this change of the method to collect demographic data still has not found its way into our schools, even though it was adopted by OMB in 1997). When we enrolled one of our daughters into the International Baccalaureate Program at a local high school, the form used to collect demographic date asked the respondents to "check the most accurate category" for race/ethnicity. When we told the school official that we would have to check almost all of them, she responded, "Oh, no, you must only check one!" How is this accurate?

The school district in which I live (all my children have graduated) sent to all post office addresses in the district a *Shareholders' Report (fall 2007), Vision, Mission and Values*. In this document the district's twelve core values are covered. Number six is, "Cherry Creek Schools . . . value respecting and understanding the diversity of the students and families we serve."[81] Then, under the section that describes diversity in the district, the document lists African-American, American Indian, Asian-Pacific, Hispanic and Caucasian students.[82] Needless to say, according to this list, Cherry Creek School District *does not* understand or respect my family (which is mixed white, Chickasaw and African American).

DNA research in Brazil has shown that Europeans in Brazil have more African heritage than they believe, while Afro Brazilians have a greater white heritage than they acknowledge.[83] About 70% of African Americans have some heritage from other races, including white, Native American and Asian.[84] My African-American- Chickasaw wife has all these heritages, which explains why my children have been "seen" in so many different ways. Thus, the reality is that many people in this country can rightfully claim a multiracial or multiethnic heritage. With the vast amount of global immigration and the increased acceptance of interracial and interethnic (and intertribal) marriages, the entire world, from Brazil and the US to Belize and Australia, is becoming multiracial and multiethnic.

Why postpone the inevitable? Language is supposed to change as society changes. Why hang on to the past, when it is clear that we need words to accurately describe this new demographic reality. It should be noted here that the current single-race system used in the U.S. does not apply well to many other societies.[85]

Challenging Single-race Thinking

In a graduate curriculum development class, some of my students designed a curriculum unit for high schools students. In the narrative for the unit they described how, unlike European schools, U.S. schools face unique challenges because they very multicultural and multilingual. I had to point out to my students the great diversity of many contemporary European societies, such as Britain and France. They had assumed that, since the term European American means white or Caucasian, all Europeans and all European societies are all still homogenously white!

This, of course, is one of the many examples of the problems with our current system for categorizing race and ethnicity. Other problems with the US Census approach include the fallacy of placing bitter, historical enemies together in the same categories, such as Chinese and Japanese, Korean and Japanese; placing Maya Indians together with Latinos (in central America Latinos have violently oppressed Mayas and other indigenous people for hundreds of years), viewing Middle-Easterners as white, and considering all members of the Latino ethnic group as oppressed minorities.[86] Many Latinos in the U.S. today are racially white, and are descended directly from the wealthy ruling classes of Central and South American societies.[87] Brazilians speak Portuguese, and are as multiracial a society as we are—if not more: Asians, Middle-Easterners, European (including Spanish), Amerindian, Afro-Brazilians, and many who proudly claim a mixed heritage. [88]

Part of the problem, of course, is that we tend to view the US as multicural, and all other countries a racially homogeneous. This is not only untrue of much of Europe and all of Central and south Americas, but historically homogenous counties such as Australia are becoming very multicural. The other day I talked to a white Muslim woman from Morocco who said that her white Muslim son checks the African American category on his college forms. And, of course he was not lying! This one-race view of the population of all counties except the US is largely a result of our obsolete view of categorizing people by social-political characteristics that belie both genetics and current social trends.[89]

The Federal Forms

Much of the debate around a multiracial label has centered on the OMB federal categories. While the need for a universal multiracial and/or multiethnic label is much broader than a federal designation, the federal category is critically important. It should be noted here that, while the detractors of a multiracial label continue to ague that the only purpose of the single—race categories is to monitor civil rights compliance,[90] this, in fact, is not true. I recently re-applied for my Alien Registration Card and was required to identify my race on the application form. The only non-single-race option was, "race unknown." First, having accurate federal forms is important because U.S. academics seem to think that anything that the federal government creates is somehow the truth.

The fixation of the multicultural education movement on the OBM racial and ethnic categories is proof enough of this strange phenomenon. [91]But, of more importance is the fact that many of the issues addressed in this discourse are themselves dependent on the OMB categories. These issues include funding, the schools' acknowledgment of multiracial children's unique needs, research, and inclusion of multiracial and multiethnic children in developmental, educational and diversity texts.

It is my sincere belief that, eventually, race will not be a part of the data collected by the U.S. government. But until this day arrives, it is critical that the federal forms used to designate funds for research, determine equality and access in our schools, and provide the structure for diversity and multicural tests, research, and training, we must have a multiracial/multiethnic category. This category must enable us to collect data on children and people who view themselves as multiracial and multiethnic, not as someone who is part African American and part white, or part Native American and part Hispanic. We need real figures of the numbers of children who challenge the very powerful and inaccurate orthodoxy of viewing people as belonging only to an exclusive single-race minority group, and who acknowledge that racial/ethnic identity can be diverse, complex, inclusive and comprehensive.

Conclusion

In this chapter, the need for a common multiracial/multiethnic word in both our academic and general language has been addressed. Clearly, the need would not exist if we were not fixated—as a academic body and as a culture – on categorizing everything by U.S. government census categories, from daily newspaper articles on prisons, schools and neighborhoods, to scholarly books and articles in child development, education, juvenile crime, and employment. While detractors view this issue as purely one of civil rights compliance (and thus those of us who advocate a separate category as soft on civil rights), this discourse represents a broader argument on the subject of mixed race identity and categories. Eventually, of course, counting by government defined racial and ethnic categories will become obsolete, but until America becomes less color struck a growing number of multiracial and multiethnic children and adults in this society and throughout the world need and deserve their own label.

Notes

1. See Eric Erikson *Childhood and Society* 2nd edition (1963) and J. Piaget *The Origins of Intelligence in Young Children* (1936).
2. Here I draw upon the L. Vygotsky's *Mind in Society: The Development of Higher Mental Processes* (1978).
3. The U.S. Bureau of the Census officially mandated changes that allow for the selection of "one or more" categories in terms of individual racial classification in the 1990s.
4. C.A. Fernandez, "La Raza and the Melting Pot: A Comparative Look at Multiethnicity," ed. Maria P.P. Root *Racially Mixed People in America* (Newbury Park: Sage, 1992), 126.

5. J.M. Fish, "The Myth of Race," ed. J.M. Fish *Race and Intelligence: Separating Science from Myth* (Mahwah: Lawrence Elbaum Publishers, 2002), 133.

6. For an expanded discussion of this argument see A. Smedley "Science and the Idea of Race" in *Race and Intelligence: Separating Science from Myth* (2002), J.M. Spencer's *The New Colored People: the Mixed Race Movement in America* and Rainier Spencer's "Assessing Multiracial Identity and Politics" (2004).

7. See M.M. Wallace *Working with Multiracial Students: Critical Perspectives on Research and Practice* (2004).

8. See C.A. Banks and J.A. Banks *Handbook of Research on Multiracial Education* 2nd edition (2003); Heather Dalmage *Tripping on the Color Line: Black-White Multiracial Families in a Racially Divided World* (2000), A. Smedley "Science and the Idea of Race" in *Race and Intelligence: Separating Science from Myth* (2002), Rainier Spencer "Census 2000: Assessments and Significance" in *New Faces in a Changing America: Multiracial Identity in the 21st Century* (2003), M.T. Texeira "The New Multiracialism: An Affirmation of or an End to Race as We Know it?" and Kim Williams *Mark One or More: Civil Rights in Multiracial America* (2006).

9. Fernandez, 126-143. See also S. L. Ferreira "Interview of a Multiracial Woman" in *Trip Report* (2005) and J.M. Fish "The Myth of Race" in *Race and Intelligence: Separating Science from Myth* (2002).

10. Fish, 133-144.

11. Ibid.

12. Fernandez, 126-143; See also J.M. Fish "The Myth of Race," Paul Spickard "The Illogic of American Racial Categories" in *Racially Mixed People in America* and Francis Wardle and M.I. Cruz-Janzen *Meeting the Needs of Multiethnic and Multiracial Children in Schools* (2004).

13. Smedley, 145; See also J.M. Spencer *The New Colored People: the Mixed Race Movement in America* (1997), Rainier Spencer "Census 2000: Assessments and Significance" (2003) and "Assessing Multiracial Identity Theory and Politics" (2004); and Kim Williams *Mark One or More: Civil Rights in Multiracial America* (2006).

14. N.G. Brown and R.E. Douglass, "Making the Invisible Visible: The Growth of Community Network Organizations," in *The Multiracial Experience: Racial Borders as the New Frontier* ed. Maria P.P. Root (Thousand Oaks, Sage, 1996), 323-341; See also Fish "The Myth of Race," and Wardle "History of the Contemporary Multiracial Movement" (2005).

15. M.I. Cruz-Janzen, E.W. King, and Francis Wardle, "The Challenge of Declaring an Interethnic and/or Interracial Identity in Postmodern Societies," *Race Relations Abstracts* 28 (2003): 5-20.

16. Smedley, 145; See also the work of J.M. Spencer in *The New Colored People* and Rainier Spencer in "Census 2000: Assessment and Significance."

17. See the works of J.M. Spencer and Rainier Spencer for an expanded discussion of these arguments.

18. See C.A.M. Banks and J.A. Banks *Multicultural Education: Issues and Perception* 5th edition (2006); See also R. Kennedy *Interracial Intimacies* (2003), J.M. Spencer *The New Colored People* (1997), and Debose and Winters "The Dilemma of Biracial People of African American Descent" (2003).

19. See the work of J.M. Spencer, Rainier Spencer, M.T. Texeira, and Kim Williams for this argument.

20. M.I. Cruz-Janzen, E.W. King, and Francis Wardle, 5-20. See also the work of Naomi Zack.

21. See the U.S. Bureau of the Census 2000.

22. H.L. Debose and L.I Winters, 127-153. See also Kennedy *Interracial Intimacies* and R. McRoy and E. Freedman "Racial Identity Issues Among Mixed Race Children" in *Social Work in Education.*

23. Refer to the work of J.M. Spencer, Rainier Spencer, and Kim Williams for an expanded discussion of this argument.

24. See the work of Rainier Spencer and Kim Williams as related to the "conservative vs. liberal" argument.

25. Rainier Spencer, "Census 2000: Assessments and Significance," in *New Faces in a Changing America: Multiracial Identity in the 21st Century* ed. L.I. Winters and H.L. Dubose (Thousand Oaks: Sage, 2003), 99-110.

26. Ibid.

27. See J.M. Spencer, R. Spencer, and Heather Dalmage in their various works on this issue.

28. See my work with M.I. Cruz-Janzen in *Meeting the Needs of Multiethnic and Multiracial Children in Schools* (2004).

29. Ibid.

30. Morrison and Bordere, "Supporting Biracial Children's Identity Devolopment," *Childhoo Education 77* (2001), 134-141.

31. M. West, "Teaching the Third Culture Child," in *Readings on Teaching Young Children in a Diverse Society* ed. C. Copple (Washington, D.C.: NAEYC, 2005), 29-32.

32. Ibid.

33. Ibid.

34. West, 30.

35. Francis Wardle, "Proposal: An Antibias and Ecological Model for Multicultural Education," *Childhood Education 72* (1996), 152-156. See also my other writings such as with *Tomorrow's Children: Meeting the Needs of Multiracial and Multiethnic Children.*

36. See Vygotsky's *Mind in Society: the Development of Higher Mental Processes.*

37. Morrison and Bordere, 134.

38. See once again the works of Erikson and Piaget.

39. See my findings in *Introduction to Early Childhood: A Multidimensional Approach to Care Centered Care and Learning* (2003).

40. Ibid.

41. See again my writings on childhood development.

42. Morrison and Bordere, 134-141.

43. See my book *Introduction to Early Childhood Education: A Multidimensional Approach to Care Centered Care and Learning.*

44. Morrison and Bordere, 134-141.

45. See K. Berger *The Developing Person: Through Childhood and Adolescence* and Erik Eric Erikson's *Childhood and Society.*

46. See B. Tatum's *Why are all of the Black Kids Sitting Together in the Cafeteria?*

47. Ibid.

48. See my work with Cruz-Janzen *Meeting the Needs of Multiethnic and Multiracial Children in Schools.*

49. Francis Wardle and M.I. Cruz Janzen, *Meeting the Needs of Multiethnic and Multiracial Children in Schools* (Boston: Allyn and Bacon, 2004), 117.

50. See S. York *Roots and Wings: Affirming Culture in Early Childhood Programs* and Wardle and Cruz Janzen in *Meeting the Needs of Multiethnic and Multiracial Children in Schools.*

51. W.E. Cross, "A Two Factor Theory of Black Identity Development in Minority Children," in *Children's Ethnic Socialization* ed. J.S. Phinney and M.J. Rotherman (Newbury Park: Sage, 2003), 117-134.

52. L. Derman Sparks, and P.C. Ramsey, "A Framework for Culturally Relevant, Multicultural, and Anti-Bias Education in the 21st Century," in *Approaches to Early Childhood education* 3rd edition ed. J.L. Roopnarine and J.E. Johnson (Upper Saddle River: Merrill, 2002), 127-153. See also Gonzalez & Mena *Diversity in Early Care and Education: Honoring Differences* and Gollnick & Chin's *Multicultural Education in a Pluralistic Society.*

53. Morrison and Bordere, 134-141.

54. See my essay "Of Race and Racism in Brazil."

55. Maria Root, "The Bill of Rights for Mixed Race People, in *The Multiracial Experience: Racial Borders as the New Frontier,* ed. Maria P.P. Root (Thousand Oaks: Sage, 1996), 3-1. See also Wardle and Cruz Janzen *Meeting the Needs of Multiethnic and Multiracial Children in Schools.*

56. Brown and Douglass, "Making the Invisible Visible," 323-341. See also my essay "History of the Multiracial Movement."

57. K.C. Valverde, "From Dust to Gold: The Vietnamese Amerasian Experience," in *Racially Mixed People in America*, ed. Maria P.P. Root (Newbury Park: Sage, 1992), 144-161.

58. See the work of Paul Spickard in *Mixed Blood: Intermarriage and Ethnic Identity in Twentieth Century America*, and Wardle & Cruz-Janzen *Meeting the Needs of Multiethnic and Multiracial Children in Schools.*

59. K.R. Wallace, "Introduction," in *Working with Multiracial Students*, ed. K.R. Wallace (Greenwich: Information Age Publishing, 1987), x-xxiv.

60. C.A. Fenandez, "La Raza and the Melting Pot: A Comparative Look at Multiethnicity," in *Racially Mixed People in America* ed. Maria P.P. Root (Newbury Park: Sage, 1992), 126-143. See also Fish, "The Myth of Race," and Wardle and Cruz-Janzen *Meeting the Needs of Multiethnic and Multiracial Children in Schools.*

61. Fish, 133-144.

62. See L. Tikly, Caballero, and Haynes, *Understanding the Educational Needs of Mixed Heritage Pupils.*

65. Ibid.

64. D.D. Bowles, "Biracial Identity: Children born to African American and White Couples," *Clinical Social Work Journal* 21, No.4, 417-428. See also Cooney & Radina "Adjustment Problems in Adolescents: Are Multiracial Children at Risk," and Mcroy and Freeman "Racial Identity Issues Among Mixed Race Children."

65. See my text *Tomorrow's Children: Meeting the Needs of Multiracial and Multiethnic Children at Home.*

66. Fish, 133. See also *Tomorrow's Children.*

67. Ibid.

68. See my essay "History of the Multiracial Movement."

69. See the essay on Brazil by G. Reginald Daniel in this volume.

70. See S. Nieto *Affirming Diversity: the Sociopolitical Context of Multicultural Education.*

71. See J.A. Banks and C.A.M. Banks *Multicultural Education: Issues and Perception*, and J. Gonzalez-Mena *Diversity in Early Care and Education: Honoring Differences*, and S. Nieto *Affirming Diversity.*

72. See my essay "Multicultural Children in Childhood Development Textbooks."

73. This is in reference to the Banks & Banks text *Handbook of Research on Multicultural Education* edition two (2003).

74. See J.A. Banks and C.A.M. Banks *Multicultural Education: Issues and Perception*, and Gonzalez-Mena *Diversity in Early Care and Education: Honoring Differences.*

75. C.E. Cortes, "Mixed Race Children: Building Bridges to New Identities," *Reaching Today's Youth 3* (1999), 28-31.

76. Alvin Poussaint, "Study of Interracial Children Presents Positive Pictures," *Interracial Books for Children* 15, No.6, 9-10.

77. See Banks & Banks *Multicultural Education*, Gonzalez-Mena *Diversity in Early Care and Education,* and S. Nieto *Affirming Diversity.*

78. See Wardle and Cruz- Janzen, *Meeting the Needs of Multiethnic and Multicultural Children in Schools.*

79. Ibid.

80. Ibid.

81. See the 2007 Cherry Creek School fall *Shareholder's Report.*

82. Ibid.

83. J. Alves-Silva, M.S. Santos, and P.E. Guimaras, "The Ancestry of Brazilian mtDNA Lineages," *American Journal of Human Genetics* 76, 444-461.

84. See Kim Williams *Mark One or More: Civil Rights in Multiracial America.*

85. Fish, 133-144.

86. Fernandez, 126-143.

87. Ibid.

88. Fernandez, 126-143. See also Ferreira's "Interview with a Brazilian Woman," in *Trip Report* Fish "The Myth of Race," and my own work on this subject.
89. Cortes, 28-31.
90. See the work of R. Spencer, Smedley, and Texeira for this argument.
91. See G. Reginald Daniel "Black and White Identity in the New Millennium: Unsevering the Ties that Bind," and Kim Williams *Mark One or More: Civil Rights in Multiracial America.*

References

Alves-Silva, J. Santos, M. S., Guimaras, P. E. M., Ferreira, A. C. S., Bandelt, H. J., Pena, J. D., & Prado, V. M. "The Ancestry of Brazilian mtDNA lineages." *American Journal of Human Genetics* 76, (2000), 444-61.

Banks, J. A., & Banks, C. A. M. *Handbook of Research on Multicultural Education,* 2nd ed. Hoboken, NJ: Wiley: Jossey-Bass, 2003.

Banks, J. A., & Banks, C. A. M. *Multicultural education: Issues and Perception,* 5th ed. Hoboken, NJ: John Wiley and Sons, 2004.

Berger, K. *The Developing Person: Through Childhood and Adolescence,* 7th ed. New York: Worth, 2006.

Bowles, D. D. "Biracial identity: Children born to African American and White Couples." *Clinical Social Work Journal, 21* (4), (1993), 417-428.

Bronfenbrenner, U. *The Ecology of Human Development: Experiments by Design* Cambridge, MA: Harvard University Press, 1979.

Brown, N. G., & Douglass, R. E. "Making the Invisible Visible: The Growth of Community Network Organizations," 323-341. In *The Multiracial Experience: Racial Borders as the New Frontier,* ed., Maria P.P. Root. Thousand Oaks, CA: Sage, 1996.

Cherry Creek School District. *Shareholders' Report Fall 2007: Vision, Mission, Values.* Greenwood Village, CO: Cherry Creek Schools, 2007.

Cooney, T. M., and Radina, M. S. "Adjustment Problems in Adolescents: Are Multiracial Children at Risk? *American Journal of Orthopsychiatry, 70* (4), (2000): 433-444.

Cortes, C. E. Mixed-race Children: Building Bridges to New Identities. *Reaching Today's Youth, 3* (2), (1999): 28-31

Cortes, C. E. The Diversity Within: Intermarriage, Identity and Campus Community. *About Campus, 5* (1), (2000), 5-10.

Cross, W. E. "A two-factor Theory of Black Identity Development in Minority Children." In *Children's Ethnic Socialization,* edited by J.S. Phinney and M.J. Rotheram (Newbury Park, CA: Sage, 1987), 117-134.

Cruz-Janzen, M. I., King, E. W., & Wardle, F. "The Challenge of Declaring an interethnic and/or Interracial Identity in Postmodern Societies. *Sage Race Relations Abstracts. 28* (1), (2003): 5-20.

Daniel, G. Reginald ."Black and White Identify in the New Millennium: Unsevering the Ties that Bind," 121-139. In *The Multicultural Experience: Racial Borders as the New Frontier* ed., Maria P.P. Root. Thousand Oaks, CA: Sage, 1996.

Derman Sparks, L., & Ramsey, P. C. "A framework for Culturally Relevant, Multicultural and Anti-bias Education in the 21st Century," 379-404. In *Approaches to Early Childhood Education* 3rd ed. Ed., J.L. Roopnarine, and J.E. Johnson. Upper Saddle River, NJ: Merrill, 2002.

Dalmage, H. M. *Tripping on the Color Line: Black-white Multiracial Families in a Racially Divided World.* New Brunswick, NJ: Rutgers University Press, 2000.

Erikson, E. *Childhood and Society.* 2nd ed. New York: Norton, 1963.

Fernandez, C. A. "La Raza and the Melting Pot: A Comparative Look at Multiethnicity," 126-143. In *Racially Mixed People in America,* ed. Maria P.P. Root Newbury Park, CA: Sage, 1992.

Fish, J. M. "The Myth of Race," 133-144. *Race and Intelligence: Separating Science from Myth,* ed., J.M. Fish. Mahwah, NJ: Lawrence Erlbaum, Publishers, 2002.

Ferreira, S. L. "Interview of a Multiracial Brazilian Woman." In *Trip Report,* ed., Francis Wardle. Washington, DC: Partners of the Americas, 2005.

Gall, M. D., Borg, W. R., & Gall, J. P. *Educational Research: An Introduction* 6th ed. White Plains, NY: Longman, 1996.

Gollnick, D. M., and Chinn, P. C. *Multicultural Education in a Pluralistic Society.* 4th ed. Upper Saddle River, NJ: Merrill, 1994.

Gonzalez-Mena, J. *Diversity in Early Care and Education: Honoring Differences.* 5th ed. New York: McGraw-Hill Company, 2008.

Kendall, W. I. *Diversity in the Classroom: New Approaches to the Education of Young Children* 2nd ed. New York: Teachers College Press, 1996.

Kennedy, R. *Interracial Intimacies.* New York: Pantheon Books, 2003.

McRoy, R., & Freeman, E. "Racial Identity Issues among Mixed-race Children." *Social Work in Education, 8,* (1986), 164-174.

Mills, G. E. *Action Research: A Guide for the Teacher Researcher.* Upper Saddle River, NJ: Merrill, 2000.

Morrison, J. W., & Bordere, T. "Supporting Biracial Children's Identity Development. Childhood Education," *Association for Childhood Education International,* 77 (13), (2001), 134-141.

Nieto, S. *Affirming Diversity. The Sociopolitical Context of Multicultural Education,* 4th ed. Boston, MA: Allyn & Bacon, 2004.

Noel, J. ed. *Classical Edition Sources: Multicultural Education,* 2nd ed. New York: McGraw Hill Higher Education, 2008.

Page, J. A., *The Brazilians.* New York: Da Capo Press, 1995.

Piaget, J. *The Origins of Intelligence in Young Children.* New York; Norton, 1936; 1963.

Poussaint, A. P. "Study of Interracial Children Presents Positive Picture. *Interracial Books for Children Bulletin, 15,* No. 6, (1984), 9-10.

Ramsey, P. *Teaching and Learning in a Diverse World. Multicultural Education for Young Children* 3rd ed. New York: Teachers College Press, 2004.

Root, M. M. "The Bill of Rights for Mixed-race People," 3-14. In *The Multiracial Experience: Racial Borders as the New Frontier,* ed., Maria P.P. Root Thousand Oaks, CA: Sage, 1996.

Spradlin, L. K., & Parsons, R. D. *Diversity Matters: Understanding Diversity in Schools* (Belmont, CA: Thompson Higher Education, 2008).

Smedley. A. "Science and the idea of race: A Brief History," 145-176. In *Race and Intelligence: Separating Science from Myth,* ed. J.M. Fish. Mahwah, NJ: Lawrence Erlbaum Publishers, 2002.

Spencer, J. M. *The New Colored People: The Mixed–race Movement in America.* New York: New York University Press, 1997.

Spencer, R. "Assessing Multiracial Identity Theory and Politics." *Ethnicities* 4, No. 3, (2004), 357-379.

Spickard, P. *Mixed blood: Intermarriage and Ethnic Identity in Twentieth Century America.* Madison, WI: University of Wisconsin Press, 1989.

Spickard, P. "The Illogic of American Racial Categories," 12-23. In *Racially Mixed People in America,* ed., Maria P.P. Root. Newbury Park, CA: Sage, 1992.

Tatum, B. *Why are all the black kids sitting together in the cafeteria?* New York: Basic Books, 1999.

Tikly, L., Caballero, C., & Haynes, J. *Understanding the Educational Needs of Mixed Heritage Pupils.* Research Brief # RB549. London: UK Department of Education and Skills, 2004.

U. S. Bureau of the Census. *Office of Management and Budget Revision of the Standards for the Classification of Federal Data on Race and Ethnicity* (58782-58790; 58792). Washington, DC: U.S. Government, 1997. U. S. Bureau of the Census 2000. *USA Census 2000.* Washington, DC: U.S. Government, 2000.

Valverde, K. C. "From Dust to Gold: The Vietnamese Amerasian Experience," 144-161. In *Racially Mixed People in America,* ed., Maria P.P. Root. Newbury Park, CA: Sage, 1992.

Vygotsky, L. *Mind in Society: The Development of Higher Mental Processes,* eds. and trans, M. Cole, V. John-Steiner, S. Scribner, & E. Souberman. Cambridge, MA: Harvard University Press, 1978.

Wallace, K. R. "Introduction," x-xxiv. In *Working with Multiracial Students: Critical Perspectives on Research and Practice,* ed., K.R. Wallace. Greenwich, CT: Information Age Publishing, 2004.

Wardle, F. *Biracial Identity Model: An Ecological and Developmental Model.* Denver, CO: Center for the Study of Biracial Children, 1992.

Wardle, F. "Proposal: An anti-bias and Ecological Model for Multicultural Education." *Childhood Education 72,* (1996), 152-156.

Wardle, F. *Tomorrow's children: Meeting the needs of Multiracial and Multiethnic Children at Home, in Early Childhood Programs, and at School.* Denver, CO; CSBC, 1999.

Wardle, F. "Multiracial and Multiethnic Students: How they Must Belong." *Multicultural Perspectives 2,* No. 4, (2000), 11-16.

Wardle, F. "Of Race and Racism in Brazil." *Interracial Voice Magazine.* 2003, http://www.webcom.com/intvoice

Wardle, F. *Introduction to Early Childhood Education: A Multidimensional Approach to Care-centered Care and Learning.* Boston, MA: Allyn and Bacon, 2003.

Wardle, F. "History of the Contemporary Multiracial Movement Part I." *Interracial Voice Magazine,* 2005, http://www.webcom.com/intvoice

Wardle, F., & Cruz-Janzen, M. I. *Meeting the Needs of Multiethnic and Multiracial Children in Schools.* Boston, MA: Allyn and Bacon, 2004.

West, M. M. "Teaching the Third Culture Child," 29-32. In *A world of Difference: Readings on Teaching Young Children in a Diverse Society,* ed., C. Copple. Washington, DC: NAEYC, 2005.

Williams, K, *Mark One or More: Civil Rights in Multiracial America.* Ann Arbor, MI: University of Michigan Press, 2006.

Winters, L.I. and H.I. Debose, ed. *New Faces in a Changing America: Multiracial Identity in the 21st Century.* Thousand Oaks, CA: Sage, 2003.

York, S. *Roots and Wings. Affirming Culture in Early Childhood Programs.* St. Paul, MN: Redleaf Press, 2003.

Zack, Naomi. "American Mixed-race: The 2000 Census and Related Issues." Guest Editorial, *Interracial Voice Magazine,* 2002. http://www.webcom.com/intvoice.

Chapter 13

Mixed Race Terminologies in the Americas: Globalizing the Creole in the Twenty First Century

DeMond S. Miller, Jason D. Rivera, and Joel C. Yelin

T he concept of creolization can be found in many colonial settings throughout history. The word Creole itself has only been used in the Caribbean and Southern North America colonies, mostly owned by France and Spain. Creole, as a word, was first developed by the Portuguese and later used by the Spanish and French; as used to describe a person born to European parents in the New World colonies. Currently, the term typically refers to a person of mixed race and is most common in the southern states, such as Louisiana, as well as the Caribbean. Since its creation, the word has carried both negative and positive connotations, depending on the point of view of the person who uses it. In the British American colonies, the term has gone as far as being completely avoided by the colonists, who chose instead to consider themselves British until they realized that Britain would never consider them equal. At this point, the colonists reverted to calling themselves Americans rather than Creoles. This chapter seeks to discuss the evolution of the term Creole through the history of colonial society in the New World to the connotations the word has in today's society.

Introduction

The meaning of the word *Creole* has changed throughout history. Creole as a concept and as a category of people of mixed heritage has evolved through the ages depending on the people who use the term and the region in which the people live. In modern vernacular, Creole generally refers to a person of mixed heritage; however, Creole was originally used in reference to pure origins with no mention of hybridity. For example, once "Creole denoted the offspring of Old World progenitors born and raised in the New World"[1] The concept was met with negative connotations at first because "[e]migration to a distant environment was thought to transform Europeans into a different sort of people."[2] People born in the New World were seen as individuals lacking the refinement of Europeans. The environment of the New World was thought to adversely affect the people born and raised there; it was feared that children of the colonists were more like the natives than their European forefathers. The idea that the environment shaped character was common among Europeans and people took strides to avoid this change in character. Moreover, the notion that environment had such an influence on one's character helped to further shape the negative connotations that accompanied the concept of Creole. The children of the colonists were regarded as lesser than their Old World parents for merely being born in a different environment For example, among Spanish colonies:

> Even if he [or she] was born within one week of his father's migration, the accident of birth in the Americas cosigned him [or her] to subordination—even though in terms of language, religion, ancestry, or manners he [or she] was largely indistinguishable from the Spain-born Spaniard. There was nothing to be done about it: he was *irremediably* a [C]reole.[3]

Though regarded as inferior, Creoles enjoyed a social status higher in society than the indigenous people and African slaves because of their pure heritage.

The word Creole originated on the Iberian Penninsula, which ". . . first arose in Portuguese (*crioulo*) sometime in the sixteenth century, although it was first attested in Spanish in 1590 with the meaning of 'Spaniard born in the New World.'"[4] The word denoted different aspects of a racial or ethnic group; however, sixteenth century use of the concept made no mention of race mixing. When "applied to Europeans, 'creole' distinguished those locally born from those born in the Old World, who in Spanish were sometimes referred to as *peninsulares* (that is, hailing form Iberia), and in Portuguese as *renois* (from the Realm) or *marinheiros* (sailors) . . ."[5]

The term Creole shifts from negative to positive when independence movements began to build national identities among the colonists of the New World. Charles Stewart contends that, "The rise of independence movements in the Americas, often led by [C]reoles, required forging a unified national identity as 'local' as opposed to the European, colonial power."[6] At this time, many of the settlers intermarried with the Indian and black slaves, creating a mixed culture that was neither European nor Indian. When the descendants of the original colonists desired to govern themselves, they rallied behind the word Creole. Furthermore, when more colony-born people could no longer consider themselves pure Europeans, they began revolting against their European forefathers. Thus, the term Creole received a radical transformation from its negative roots. Joyce Chaplin in Creoles in British America asserted that, "Spanish settlers at first resented the term 'creole.' Their descendants began to accept, by the late eighteenth century, only when their desire to become independent of Spain supported a new sense of difference from the Spanish."[7] Later, the term became a rallying call to form political and social movements. However, many areas of the New World under European control did not share this meaning.

Throughout history, the word Creole has denoted different meanings in different places. For example, in Haiti, where shortly after independence the white population was expelled, "Creole could refer only to black people, whereas on Martinique, which remained within the French orbit, the same word referred to white people, as it did in Louisiana."[8] Creole is a flexible term that is attributed different meanings according to the people using it. It is interesting to see how a single term has both similar and completely different meanings throughout the New World colonies. In the following sections, Creole and creolization will be explored in their origin, meaning, and evolution within different societies throughout the New World.

Creoles in French America/Louisiana

Creole identity was essentially split into two groups in Louisiana, which was one of the colonies that maintained a significant French influence. According to Cecyle Trepanier, "The first group is the white Creoles. It includes descendants of the first French and French-Canadian colonists, early Gallicized Germans, and later French political refugees. Second are the black Creoles, some of whose ancestors come from African directly, others via the Caribbean."[9] This division occurred when America developed a significant presence in Louisiana after the Louisiana Purchase. Borrowing the term Creole from the Spanish, the French used it as a label for its citizens in the colony of Louisiana, making "any native of Louisiana was a Creole. After the Louisiana Purchase of 1803, the Creoles added to the definition a cultural dimension to exclude the American newcomers."[10] After the purchase of Louisiana from France, the term Creole served as a way to demarcate a group of people within a newly imposed social structure; ". . . the American system of ethnic classification had no place for a racially undifferentiated social society."[11]

In Louisiana, the traditional definition of a Creole had no mention of purity of racial ancestry as it did among the French, Spanish, and Portuguese colonies. To the Americans, people of white ancestry and people of color could be considered of equal status in society. Virginia Dominguez points out that "The reference to color marked them [colored Creoles] off as a special subclass of the group, but the use of Creole as noun signified their full inclusion in the category labeled Creole."[12] The American people initially viewed a Creole of a lighter skin tone as white, but inferior. Thus, they were unable to understand Creoles as a separate social class in Louisiana that could include both whites and colored people as equal citizens because, in the American classification system, the hint of African ancestry relegated a person to a lower social status. Dominguez further asserts that, "If the Creoles insisted on their inclusive categorization, they would be classified within the 'colored' sector of society. As a last resort, the white Creoles who were still in socially and politically respectable positions began systematically to exclude the 'colored Creole' from their group."[13]

The white Creoles sought to make Creole a category exclusive to whites, but "blacks with a French culture never recognized this new definition and members of both groups continue to refer to themselves as Creoles."[14] The division between white and colored Creoles was created out of necessity, for survival and acceptance in the American society. However, "when the Anglo-Americans began to stress that Creole indicated mixed-racial origins, a new racial order based on black–white duality was imposed on Louisiana . . ."[15]

In the case of Haiti, creolization developed as a definite social class system. The colony was originally a Spanish holding until it was ceded to France in 1697 and was renamed Saint-Domingue, which ". . . played a pivotal role in the French economy, accounting for almost two-thirds of French commercial interests abroad and about 40 percent of foreign trade."[16] Because slavery was a staple part of the agricultural economy of Haiti, as many as five hundred thousand slaves were brought from Africa to work in the colony.[17] The import of so many African slaves into Haiti resulted in the development of a separate caste of people. It has been argued that, "The mixture of races that eventually divided Haiti into a small, mainly mulatto elite and an impoverished black majority began with the slavemasters' concubinage of African women."[18] In Haiti, the term Creole can be seen as including a hybrid ancestry in its definition. Haitian Creoles maintained a place in society above that of the African slave majority and below that of the French white minority. In Saint-Domingue (Haiti), "a virtual one-drop rule differentiated free people of colour from whites by the time of the revolution of the 1790's."[19]

After a series of failed revolts in Saint-Domingue, a rebellion in 1791 led by the runaway slaves and Creoles (or *gens de couleur*)[20] succeeded in liberating the country from the white French minority. The August 1791 revolt "represented the culmination of a protracted conspiracy among black leaders."[21] Haiti became the first black republic in modern times due to the only successful slave revolt in world history.[22] However, racial implications from slavery carried over into the new republic and "the racial prejudice inherent in the colonial system survived under the black republic. A light-skinned elite assumed a disproportionate share of political and economic power."[23]

Creoles in British America

British American colonists avoided the term Creole altogether. The British American colonists can be considered Creoles by the nature of the concept, yet the colonists refused to consider themselves Creoles. In Chaplin's opinion, "It's a puzzle: the first surge of [C]reole patriotism that challenged European empires in the Americas was propelled by people who emphatically rejected the name '[C]reole.'"[24] They were opposed to the word itself because "it was an Iberian designation that described how Europeans (and Africans) became native to America, adapting to the physical environment and adopting selected parts of Native-American culture."[25] To label themselves as Creoles was to forfeit their titles as Englishmen, which would turn the colonists into a separate people from England. Following the belief that environment creates certain personality traits in people, the British colonists could never consider themselves similar to the Native Americans by adopting pieces of their culture.

They did not want to be like the original peoples of the Americas, the pagan Indians whose bodies were native to the Americas, those bizarre places where the gospel had never been heard. Nor did they want to be like the Spaniards and the Portuguese, those people originally called Creoles, whose catholic religion, Mediterranean culture, and warm climate represented what the English thought they should not be.[26]

It was unthinkable for the British settlers to call themselves Creoles because, to them, it meant that they had adopted a part of foreign culture that would have a detrimental effect on English culture.

The English settlers, like their English forefathers, preferred cultural continuity rather than cultural adaptation. The English way of life depended on custom and tradition, rather than innovation or importation, as the foundations of common law, public culture, and the Anglo-colonial experience and identity.[27] Any deviation from custom was viewed as degenerative, further alienating settlers from the English homeland and culture. If the settlers referred to themselves as Creoles, not only would it have meant a separation from England, but they would have also recognized that the culture had been tainted. Alteration of British culture by British citizens was viewed as extremely negative. The British tended to regard changes in custom, religion, and language as evidence of degeneration; cultural continuity was greatly preferred, whether in pedigree, text, ceremony, or law.[28] Settlers tried to maintain their legitimacy as pure English even against claims that the environment would change them into a lesser people, such as those native to the area. Those arriving from Britain claimed to experience the environmental effect but preferred to distance themselves from the natives. The colonists explained that America's effects on them were cultural rather than physical; however, people of the British Isles were not willing to accept them as equal.[29]

Similar to the Spanish colonies, revolution and self-government created the necessity for the differences associated with a Creole culture to be accepted by the colonials. However, unlike the Spanish colonies, the word Creole was never used in British colonies. During the rumblings of independence after 1773, colonists began to call themselves Americans—only making a clear distinction between themselves and their British forefathers once they believed that Britons would never accept them as equal citizens.[30] After the American Revolution, citizens of the new nation continued to refer to themselves as Americans but almost never as Creoles, which would never catch on as a term of art outside of the lower Mississippi Valley.[31] The development of a people of mixed heritage is evident throughout British American colonies even though the settlers and their children born in the Americas emphatically refused to refer to themselves as Creoles. Though the process was the same as it was in the Spanish colonies, the word itself was replaced with American because a similarity to the Indians was more acceptable to the settlers than a similarity to Spain. That is to say, "an American was the north American (and northern European) counterpart to the Spanish American (and Iberian) Creole, even as the choice of the name American was final rejection of any similarity between English and Iberian populations in the Americas."[32]

Creoles in Spanish America

Creoles in the Spanish American colonies began as the first generation of the Spanish-born in the New World. Similar to the British American colonies, the Creoles of the Spanish American colonies were regarded as inferior to the *peninsulares* yet continued to consider themselves as Spanish. However, like the American colonists, pride in the name Creole did not occur until the rush to independence occurred. "Creole patriotism originated in the late sixteenth and early seventeenth centuries as the American-born descendants of Spanish conquistadors complained that the crown was turning its back on its original commitment to foster a class of grandees in the New World."[33]

The image the Creoles had of themselves was different than that of the image Spain had of them and "all over Spanish America, [C]reoles articulated a somewhat misleading view of themselves as dispossessed nobles outcompeted by ravenous, transient, peninsular upstarts."[34] The peoples of mixed heritage in Spanish America viewed themselves as both Spanish and Indian, with the better qualities of both.

> Racism toward Amerindian commoners notwithstanding, [C]reoles lionized the accomplishments and grandeur of past Amerindian civilizations such as the Incas and the Aztecs. Spanish American Creoles excluded the great Amerindian rulers of the past, their own ancestors, from the generalization of the Amerindians as degenerate or lazy.[35]

In viewing their Amerindian ancestors as great figures of the past, the Creoles created a positive image of the side of their heritage typically viewed as degenerate and inferior. This led to the run for independence as the Creoles began to rally behind the term and their mixed heritage. As Jorge Canizare-Esquerra put it, "Creoles saw themselves as *naturals* of their own local kingdoms and cast *peninsulares* as foreigners incapable of loving and caring for the local communities."[36] This glorified view of past Amerindian rulers allowed the Creoles to rally behind a positive image of their ancestors while fighting for independence from Spain; Creoles included Amerindians, mestizos and blacks as *naturals* of creolized Spanish American kingdoms, part of a larger Spanish commonwealth.[37]

During the push for independence in the Spanish American colonies, the Creoles stepped forward to take the place their pure Spanish forefathers had previously held in society. In most of Latin America during the independence period, "a kind of Creole aristocracy stepped into the places of privilege formerly occupied by Spaniards and Portuguese."[38] In separating themselves from Spanish rule, Creoles became the overruling elite class of Spanish American society, and according to J. J. Arrom, "it is worth noting that in postcolonial Mexico the identity term *criollo* carried, and still does carry, overtones of eliteness in contrast to *mestizo*."[39]

Creoles in Brazil

In Brazil, the term Creole had a different meaning for the people than it did in the Spanish and French colonies. Creole in Brazil "carries the negative connotation of lower-class 'black' identification and does not have the Spanish-American meaning of either mestizo or that of people of European ancestry born in the Americas."[40] Every other colony in the New World held a distinction between the people born in the colony from those of Old World birth. In the other colonies, the people born in the colonies were called Creoles, yet the term extended only to the slave population in Brazil. For the slave population, "it came from diverse ethnic backgrounds in Africa, but the relevant distinction was established between those born and raised in Brazil and in the plantations (*crioulos*) and those recently arrived (*bocais*).[41] This distinction, however, could have worked in favor of the African Creoles, but "among the slaves, slave holders also created a hierarchy based on origin and color. Creole and especially mulatto slaves were given more opportunities to acquire skilled jobs or to work in the house as servants rather than in the fields or mines."[42]

Race mixing became increasingly significant because it began to shape the Portuguese society in Brazil where "each recognized distinctions between African-born 'salt water' slaves who were almost invariably black (by European standards) and their American-born descendants, the Creole slaves some of whom were mulattoes as a result of sexual exploitation slave women or the process of miscegenation."[43] This was significant because of the high percentage of colored people in Brazil due to the slave trade.

> Brazil also had large numbers of imported Africans, but its more diverse population and economy, as well as a tradition of manumitting slaves and high levels of miscegenation, meant that slaves made up only about 35 percent of the population. Free people of color, the descendants of former slaves, however, made up about another one-third, so that together slaves and free colored constituted two thirds of the total population.[44]

As the races began to mix, they received privileges in society that were previously unavailable to them due to their now higher standing. "These mixed bloods," according to Frazier Franklin, "became important in the history of Brazil as the once stable rural patriarchal organization began to disintegrate and urban communities began to dominate the life of the country during the first half of the nineteenth century."[45]

Race mingling became an almost necessity for the African slaves and the mixed bloods who where considered black. There were no legal discriminations against persons of Negro blood, but they were "isolated and discriminated against in subtle ways."[46] Mixing the other races created another group of people that, depending on the color of their parents, made them white. This social classification could award them opportunities that were previously denied to them and as Franklin argues, "As the Negro is pushed down in the economic scale, he is unable to acquire the education and skills which would enable him to compete successfully with other groups. The only escape for the Negro is to mingle his blood with that of the whites."[47] It was from here that the African Creoles of Brazil, mixed their blood over generations to become equivalent to the white minority.

Racial Classification in the Americas

The classification of race became increasingly significant as the races began to blend. There was a need for the law to distinguish whites from the "lesser" colored people in society. In America, as well as the French and Spanish colonies, different terms were created to ascertain lineage and pure ancestry. The ascribed status positions represented place and legal standing in society with all of the rights and privileges associated with one's station in life. Moreover, it is important to note how the legal system treated people of color when compared to those of white skin.

In Latin America, different terms were created as apart of a caste system designated to determine the rights of the mixed races as citizens and to clearly determine the rights to inheritance. Although it was possible for a male to have multiple children with multiple women, "the rights of these apparent heirs have to be defined, particularly when some of the mothers were not pure Europeans."[48] Creole was a general term used to denote offspring of the Spanish who were born in the New World. *Mestizo* and *Mulatto*[49] were legal terms created to specifically designate quantity the mixture of races present within an individual. These terms helped to determine a persons' standing in society by specifically designating the amount of European (in this case Spanish) ancestry. The more Spanish blood present in a person, the higher their place in society over the other mixed races. There are differing views throughout Latin America as to what constitutes a mestizo. For example, "In most countries, 'mestizo' apparently indicates a white-Indian cross; in El Salvador's last census, however, it was specifically defined as the type resulting from the mixture of white and Indian. In the latest Panamanian census, 'mestizo' was considered separately as 'persons of mixed race, of whatever class and proportion of blood.'"[50]

The French colonial system of race classification involved analyzing the purity of ancestry by devising a system of "parts." During the French colonial period in Haiti, "there were 9 categories of Africans and European mixture that was defined based on the assumption that people have 128 parts of inheritance."[51] This system has spawned terms such as Blanc (128 parts European), Negre (128 parts African), and Mulatre (64 parts European and 64 parts African),[52] as well as other categories meant to classify the differing number of parts of ancestry. These terms mainly included the mixture of whites and blacks, with little to no mention of Indian ancestry.

The Indians living in Louisiana were subject to many changes in how they were classified within the society. In "A Case of Identity," Dave Davis indicated that in 1810, "interpreting a state statute of 1808, the Louisiana Supreme Court (Adele v. Beauregard [1 Mart {O.S.} 184]) ruled that American Indians were people of color; by implication marriage between Indians and Negroes was legal, but marriage between Indians and whites was proscribed."[53] Indians and blacks were often given the same legal rights by the courts; for example, "any individual who possessed any degree of Indian or black ancestry was 'colored."[54] The legal standing of marriage between Indians and either whites or blacks changed several times. From 1870, with Louisiana repealing its anti-miscegenation laws, to 1920, where Indian marriages to people of color were not legally recognized,[55] Indians found their legal classification to be fluid in an ever "evolving legal context; Indians were both legally and socially viewed sometimes as people of color, sometimes as a class in their own right, and sometimes as the legal equals of whites."[56] The legal system for classifying race remained in flux; Indians found that what they could and could not do in society constantly changed.

The classification of race in the American colonies focused on the separation between white and black. Any minor shade in skin color amounted to black, whereas whites defined themselves by the absence of any other race. According to Davis, "The sum of what you were not—Indian, black, slave—made you what you were, in that you were white."[57] As mentioned earlier, the settlers would never consider themselves equal to the indigenous people and the same concept applies to the black slaves working for them. White blood was considered superior and should never be tainted by dark blood and "a little 'black blood' could make you black, but it took a great deal of 'white blood' to render a person white."[58] To preserve this idea of pure "white blood," American society used the power of the legal system to create laws such as the Jim Crow laws to prevent any mixture of the races. These laws included the dictation of segregated seating in railroad cars, buses, and restaurants; they also prohibited intermarrying, but the definition of what constitutes intermarriage differed from state to state. Arizona claimed any marriage between someone of Caucasian blood and a Negro would be considered null and void.[59] However, the state of Florida was much more specific in its definition of a Negro: "all marriages between a white person and a negro, or between a white person and a person of negro descent to the fourth generation inclusive, are hereby forever prohibited."[60] With the law dictating the rights of the "lesser" races, the white American people attempted to prevent any mixture of the races to avoid any dilution to their "purity". However, they ultimately failed because the realization came that race mixing is inevitable.

Creoles into the Twenty-first Century

Since the end of the late nineteenth century, many of the nations throughout the western hemisphere that were once under the colonial control of European states gained their independence. With the independence of these countries, new national identities had to be created that were distinguishably different from their prior colonizers,[61] prompting the creation of new Creole societies with varied perspectives. The mixing of races in prior centuries carried a negative connotation, especially in relation to the idea of degrading the "white race." However, with a need to recreate identities, nations in the western hemisphere that were once colonies, especially with slaves, began adopting more positive perspectives on a mixed national population.[62]

Creating national identities or cultures among fledgling nations was thought to aid in resolving differences and ideologies among a new country's racially varied population.[63] As discussed above, many of the nations in Central and South America and the Caribbean were dominated by large populations of blacks and mixed people, which raised the issue as to the true cultural or ethnic roots of these nations now separated from their white colonizers. Therefore, during the period after independence, terms such as Creole and *mestizaje* began to take on new meanings and possibilities.

> In many Latin American nation-states, the idea of *mestizaje* became the 'trope for the nation.' *Mestizaje* was seen as the source of all possibilities yet to come and a new image of the 'inferior races' eventually emerged. The racial and cultural mixing of 'inferior' with 'superior' races would provide Latin American nations with that would become their characteristic strength, superior event to the 'actual strength' of the white race.[64]

On a more micro level, the concept of *mestizaje* or Creole began to underscore the affirmation of cultural identity as constituted by "national characters" (i.e., Cuban, Mexican, or Brazilian). This new perspective was important because it recognized the plurality of cultural identities in a specific region and therefore aided in the construction of hybrid constitutions that recognized the identities of all ethnicities living within a bounded geographic area.[65]

Jose Marti illustrates an example of this phenomenon in the work *My Race*.[66] In his work, Marti discusses that being human is more than identification with a racial category such as white, mulatto, or black. Moreover, one's nationality is paramount to one's racial classification because the entire population is of that nationality. Marti's work promoted unity among all Cubans to create a national space in which, in principle, Cubans would accept the color-blind ideology whereby man equals citizen and citizen equals Cuban.[67] Nationalistic ideologies such as these were in no way devoid of racial undertones; acknowledgement of "less superior" races abounded. What was new in this line of thinking, however, was the notion in Latin America that continued mixing of the races would lead to a fifth race, the "cosmic race," which would be superior than or equal to the white race.[68]

As ambivalent and egalitarian as transculturation was notions of humanity or equality did not wholly motivate ideologies such as these, but rather by power. Martinez-Echazabal notes that true transculturation is not possible because relationships between racial groups, the rich and poor, and European and non-European are mediated by privilege and that there will always be an assigned value to one's level of transculturation.[69] In this way, there will always be a differentiation of hierarchy among either racial characteristics or social class. In an attempt to mediate this predicament, some ideologies emerged in reference to Creoles or other categories of mixed peoples that created a mythical type of people indicative to each national setting that epitomized the concept of what it meant to be from a specific place or nation.

These mythical creations exaggerate the positive virtues of a society in an attempt to promote people's pursuance of these virtues and become similar to the romanticized individuals depicted as Creoles. According to Francisco Scarano, the use of the term *jibaro* in Puerto Rico emerged during a period when the island was attempting to gain its independence from Spain. This term, created by the island's Creoles, was invented to distinguish the island's people from the other colonies of Spain and more importantly from Spain itself. Descriptions of *jibaros* in its early usage were racially inclusive and violated common ideas of Creole class privilege. Moreover, the term *jibaro* was meant to include all Puerto Ricans and not just a select few, which was hoped to unite the population behind the original privileged Creoles that created the term.[70]

> In the final decade of the twentieth century, Puerto Ricans of all classes and colors often show pride in, indeed, are prone to, defining their ethnicity in terms of a profound identification with the legendary *jibaro* (*jibaridad*). This phenomenon of identification with an ideologically constructed 'common man' has few parallels in the Caribbean or Latin America . . .[71]

By creating a category of people to which all could aspire to be regardless of race or social station strengthened the power of the local elite, which made it in their best interest to perpetuate notions of commonality among a population.

Although the twentieth century witnessed a more profound acceptance of different racial backgrounds, notions of the superiority of "whiteness" continue to exert itself in some places. As late as the 1980s, Brazil took aggressive political efforts to make immigration into the country more attractive to Europeans by boosting the economy; however, due to labor pool shortages, immigration into the country was needed to aid in stimulating the economy.[72] The question became who to bring into the country to work? The answer was made clear by the actions and positions of the government and interest groups, which believed that keeping the "purity" of the Brazilian people was more preferable than economic expansion.

> They preferred a 'civilized' future with a 'vigorous and conquering race' to easy profits and the possibility of weakening a Brazilian civilization still under construction through the supposed backwardness of the black and yellow races.[73]

For Brazil, notions of peace, security, progress, civilization, and order are dependent on race and are possible only through whitening. This perspective stimulated governmental Brazilian support for the immigration of more than two million people from Europe over the course of the twentieth century.[74] Progressive efforts to whiten the Brazilian population over the last century have contributed to the marginalization of not only Blacks and Asians, but also native peoples.

Conclusion

The idea of what it means to be Creole has changed over time. Initially, it described people with close family links to Europe in the New World. When more Europeans insisted they retain their legal rights in Europe, terms evolved to describe racial mixing within some New World colony inhabitants in addition to elite members of the colonial society. More recently, the notion of Creole has been given a more positive and inclusive meaning in some countries as a means to unite multiracial populations together in the formation of national identities; however, in some countries in the western hemisphere, the idea of Creole and other terms used to describe mixed races still carries negative connotations. These negative connotations contribute to the current disruption and marginalization of certain segments of society and perpetuate ideas of superiority, usually in reference to whites and more generally Europeans.

In the twentieth and twenty-first centuries, there seems to be a trend among nations to emphasize nationality as opposed to racial composition of its population. This trend has the ability to progressively break down barriers to race relations including ideas of racial superiority while encouraging transculturation. Progress toward transculturation is slow, especially in reference to countries that hold on to past prejudices on race such as Brazil because transculturation will mean the break down of social constructs that have benefited certain segments of society, which will resist change. True transculturation in the twenty-first century will mean that eventually everyone will be of mixed blood and that the term Creole, when used to describe race, will describe everyone and not a select few.

Notes

1. Charles Stewart, "Creolization: History, Ethnography, Theory," In *Creolization: History, Ethnography, Theory* ed. Charles Stewart (Walnut Creek, California: Left Coast Press, 2007), 1.
2. Ibid., 1.
3. Benedict Anderson, *Imagined Communities: Reflections on the Origin and Spread of Nationalism* (London, United Kingdom: Verso 1991), 57-58.
4. Stewart, 2007.
5. Ibid., 7.
6. Ibid., 8.
7. Joyce E. Chaplin, "Creoles in British America: From Denial to Acceptance," In *Creolization: History, Ethnography, Theory* ed. Charles Stewart (Walnut Creek, California: Left Coast Press, 2007), 47.
8. Stewart, 8.
9. Cecyle Trepanier, "The Cajunization of French Louisiana: Forging a Regional Identity," *The Geographic Journal*, Vol. 157, No. 2 (March, 1991): 161.
10. Ibid., 163.
11. Ibid., 164.

12. Virginia R.Dominguez, "Social classification in Creole Louisiana," *American Entomologist*, 4, No. 4 (Winter, 1977): 593.

13. Ibid., 594.

14. Trepanier, "The Cajunization of French Louisiana."

15. Ibid., 164.

16. Library of Congress Country Studies, "A Country Study: Haiti," 1989 from http://lcweb2.loc.gov/frd/cs/httoc.html (Accessed May 22, 2007).

17. Ibid.

18. Ibid.

19. George M. Fredrickson, *Mulattoes and Metis. Attitudes Toward Miscegenation in the United States and France Since the Seventeenth Century* (Boston, MA: UNESCO Blackwell Publishing, 2005), 106.

20. Fredrickson asserts that it was the *"gens de couleur"* that initially led the revolts in Haiti.

21. Library of Congress Country Studies,"A Country Study: Haiti."

22. Ibid.

23. Ibid.

24. Chaplin, "Creoles in British America," 46.

25. Ibid., 47.

26. Ibid., 47.

27. Ibid., 51.

28. Ibid., 51.

29. Joyce E. Chaplin, "Natural Philosophy and an Early Racial Idiom in North America: Comparing English and Indian Bodies," *The William and Mary Quarterly* 54, No. 1 (January, 1997): 244

30. Chaplin, "Creoles in British America," 58.

31. Ibid., 59.

32. Ibid., 60.

33. Jorge Canizares-Esguerra, "Creole Colonial Spanish America" In *Creolization: History, Ethnography, Theory* ed. Charles Stewart (Walnut Creek, California: Left Coast Press, 2007), 31.

34. Ibid., 31.

35. Ibid., 35.

36. Ibid., 42.

37. Ibid., 42.

38. Charles W. Arnade, Arthur P. Whitaker, Bailey W. Diffie, "Causes of Spanish-American Wars of Independence," *Journal of Inter-American Studies* 2, No. 2 (Summer, 1960): 137.

39. J. J. Arrom, "Criollo: Definicion y matices de un concepto," In *Creolization: History, Ethnography, Theory* ed. Charles Stewart (Walnut Creek, California: Left Coast Press, 2007), 34.

40. Miguel Vale de Almeida, "From Miscegenation to Creole Identity: Portuguese Coloniallism, Brazil, Cape Verde," In *Creolization: History, Ethnography, Theory* ed. Charles Stewart (Walnut Creek, California: Left Coast Press, 2007), 108.

41. Ibid., 110.

42. Peter N. Stearns, Michael Adas, Stuart B. Schwartz, "The African Diaspora," 1992 from http://history-world.org/African%20Diaspora.htm (Accessed June 21, 2007).

43. Ibid.

44. Ibid.

45. Frazier, E. Franklin, "Some Aspects of Race Relations in Brazil," *Phylon* 3, No. 3 (3rd Quarter, 1942: 1940-1956): 290.

46. Ibid., 294.

47. Ibid., 294.
48. Zona Latina, "Racial Classifications in Latin America," 2007 from www.zonalatina.com/zldata55.htm (Accessed June 6, 2007).
49. Mestizo is used to describe a person born of a Spanish father and Indian mother and Mulatto is used for a person born of a Spanish father and African mother. From these terms, as many as sixteen other terms were created to reflect additional mixtures.
50. Marylee Mason Vandiuer, "Racial Classifications in Latin American Censuses," *Social Forces* 28, No. 2 (December, 1949):139-140.
51. Dr. Dennis O'Neil, Behavioral Sciences Department, Palomar College, San Marcos, California,   "What   Are   You?"   2007,   from http://anthro.palomar.edu/ethnicity/ethnic_4.htm (Accessed June 12, 2007).
52. Ibid.
53. Dave D. Davis, "A Case of Identity: Ethnogenisis of the New Houma Indians," *Ethnohistory* 48, No. 3 (Summer 2001): 484.
54. Ibid., 484.
55. Ibid., 484.
56. Ibid., 485.
57. Scott L. Malcomson, "One Drop of Blood. The American Misadventure of Race," (New York: Farrar, Stratus, and Giroux, 2000), 291.
58. Ibid., 291.
59. Race, Racism, and the Law. "Examples of Jim Crow Laws." 2001, from http://academic.udayton.edu/race/02rights/jcrow02.htm (Accessed June 17, 2007).
60. Ibid.
61. Michael Gonzalez-Cruz. *Puerto Rican Revolutionary Nationalism (1956-2005): Immigration, Armed Struggle, Political Prisoners & Prisoners of War.* Doctoral dissertation for the Binghamton University, State University of New York. 2005.
621. Jean Muteba Rahier, "The Study of Latin American 'Racial Formations': Different Approaches and Different Contexts," *Latin American Research Review* 39, No. 3 (2004): 282-293.
63. Anderson, 1991.
64. Rahier, "The Study of Latin American," 284.
65. Lourdes Martinez-Echazabal, "*Mestizaje* and the Discourse of National/Cultural Identity in Latin America, 1845-1959," *Latin American Perspectives* 25, No. 3 (May, 1998): 21-42.
66. Jose Marti, "My Race," In *The America of Jose Marti*, trans. Juan de Onis (New York: Funk and Wagnalls. 1968).
67. Martinez-Echazabal, "*Mestizaje* and the Discourse," 31.
68. Rahier, "The Study of Latin American," 284.
69. Martinez-Echazabal, "*Mestizaje* and the Discourse," 37.
70. Francisco A. Scarano, "The Jibaro Masquerade and the Subaltern Political of Creole Identity Formation in Puerto Rico, 1745-1823," *The American Historical Review* 101, No. 5 (December, 1996): 1398-1431.
71. Ibid., 1404.
721. Sales Augusto dos Santos, "Historical Roots of the 'Whitening' of Brazil," *Latin American Perspectives* 29, no. 1 (January, 2002): 61-82.
73. Ibid., 65.
74. Ibid.

References

Anderson, Benedict. *Imagined Communities.* London: Verso, 2007.

Arnade, Charles, Arthur P. Whitaker, and Bailey W. Diffie. "Causes of the Spanish-American Wars of Independence." *Journal of Inter-American Studies* 2 (Summer 1960):137-157.

Arrom, J.J. "Criollo: Definicion y Matices de un Concepto."*Creolization: History, Ethnography, Theory.* Edited byCharles Stewart. Walnut Creek, California: Left Coast Press, 2007.

Augusto dos Santos, Sales. "Historical Roots of the Whitening of Brazil." *Latin American Perspectives* 29 (January 2002): 61-82.

Chaplin, Joyce E. "Natural Philosophy and an Early Racial Idiom in North America:

Comparing English and Indian Bodies."*The William and Mary Quarterly* 54 (January 1997):244-270.

Chaplin, Joyce E. "Creoles in British America from Denial to Acceptance." *Creolization: History, Ethnography, Theory.* Edited by Charles Stewart. Walnut Creek, California: Left Coast Press, 2007.

Davis, David D. "A Case of Identity: Ethnogenesis of the New Houma Indians." *Ethnohistory* 48 (Summer 2001): 484-504.

De Almeida, Miguel Vale. "From Miscegenation to Creole Identity: Portuguese Colonialism, Brazil, Cape Verde." *Creolization: History, Ethnography, Theory.* Edited byCharles Stewart. Walnut Creek, California: Left Coast Press, 2007.

Dominguez, Virginia R. "Social Classification in Creole Louisiana." *American Ethnologist* 4 (Winter 1977): 593.

Frazier, E. Franklin. "Some Aspects of Race Relations in Brazil." *Phylon* 3 (Fall 1942): 290-320.

Fredrickson, George M. *Mulattoes and Metis: Attitudes Toward Miscegenation in the United States and France Since the Seventeenth Century.* Boston, Massachusetts: Blackwell Publishing, 2005.

Library of Congress. "Country Studies: Haiti." May 22, 2007, http://lcweb2.loc.gov/frd/cs/httuc.html

Malcomson, Scott L. *One Drop of Blood: the American Misadventure of Race.* New York: Farrar, Strauss, and Giroux, 2000.

Marti, Jose. "My Race." *The America of Jose Marti.* Translated by Juan de Onis. New York: Funk and Wagnalls, 1968.

Martinez-Echazabel, Lourdes. "Mestizaje and the Discourse of National/Cultural Identity in Latin America, 1845-1959."*Latin American Perspectives* 25, No. 3 (May 1998): 21-42.

Muteba Rahier, Jean. "The Study of Latin American Racial Formations." *Latin American Research Review* 39(October 2004): 282-293.

O'Neil, Dennis. "What are You?" anthro.palomar.edu, June 12, 2007, http://anthro.palomar.edu/ethnicity/ethnic_4.htm

"Race, Racism, and the Law-Examples of Jim Crow Laws." udayton.edu, June 17, 2007, http://academic.udayton.edu/race/02rights/jcrow02.htm

"Racial Classification in Latin America." Zonalatina.com, June 6, 2007, www.zonalatina.com/zldata55.htm

Scarano, Francisco A. "The Jibaro Masquerade and the Subaltern Political of Creole Identity Formation in Puerto Rico, 1745-1813," *The American Historical Review* 101 (December 1996): 1398-1431.

Stearns, Peter N., and Michael Adas. "The African Diaspora." June 21, 2007, http://historyworld.org/African%20Diaspora.htm

Stewart, Charles. "Creolization: History, Ethnography, Theory." *Creolization: History, Ethnography, Theory.* Edited by Charles Stewart. Walnut Creek, California: Left Coast Press, 2007.

Vandiuer, Marylee Mason. "Racial Classifications in Latin American Censuses." *Social Forces* 28 (December 1949): 139-140.

Chapter 14

Examining the Regional and Multigenerational Context of Creole and American Indian Identity

Andrew Jolivétte

I came to the question of Creole identity relatively early in life, but the implications have taken decades to unravel. In the early 1970s when my grandfather told my grandmother he didn't want "those niggas" (referring to my older half brothers whose biological father is African American) sitting next to "my grandchildren" (referring to my first cousins who are Creole and Puerto Rican), his actions were but the latest reflection of societal conflict played out on the familial stage. Fifteen years earlier, my father—along with my aunts, uncle, and paternal grandparents—had moved from southwest Louisiana to California. In the process, my grandparents informed him and the rest of the family that they were "becoming" a family of French Canadians, leaving their Creole identities behind. Why "French Canadians" as opposed to something else? This question, along with the rejection of blackness expressed in my grandfather's statement about "those niggas," continued to puzzle me across the years. It was not the privileging of whiteness that surprised me as much as the complexities of a racialization process that so thoroughly neglected the regionally and culturally specific identity of Creoles as a multigenerational mixed-race population. Our family situation speaks to the complex historical situation and sociocultural context in this country through which white is privileged over not only black but over mixed-race populations. Through the years, my interest in understanding this complex process led me back to Louisiana to document the contemporary cultural experiences and practices of Creole people.

In the late 1990s, the author started to explore these issues from a different angle and began collecting data on Creole-Indian relations. In the process, discovering the Louisiana Creole Heritage Center (LCHC) at Northwestern State University in Natchitoches, Louisiana, and attending the conferences they sponsored in Los Angeles, California, in July 2001; in New Orleans, Louisiana, in October of 2003; and in Las Vegas, Nevada, in May 2004, in which national attention was focused upon Creole studies and important questions were raised about the place of Indian, African, French, and Spanish contributions in the history, culture, and preservation of this multiracial community. Following the publication of Gary Mills's landmark work, *The Forgotten People*, in 1977, several key texts examined the history of Creoles of Color in the state of Louisiana, focusing particularly on the city of New Orleans and on the social, legal, and racial classification of Creoles as black or white, or black and white, but never as Indian.[1]

In the United States and throughout the Americas, many communities of multiethnic, multicultural, and multiracial ancestry embody an aspect of American Indian identity that is seldom addressed publicly: the amalgamation of some indigenous tribes into new ethnic communities. The Creoles of southwest Louisiana are an example of one such community in which elements of the cultures of indigenous tribes have retained their vitality while intermingling with traditional Creole culture. By declaring many smaller Native communities in the Americas extinct due to disease, malnutrition, and European colonization, nineteenth- and twentieth-century scholars and researchers dismissed not just the contemporaneous contributions but also the continuing presence of indigenous groups such as the Atakapa and Opelousa descent Indians in southwest Louisiana, in effect erasing their existence by relegating it entirely to the past.

It is my contention, however, that groups such as the Opelousa and Atakapa not only still exist, but that they exist in new, complex, hybrid forms that thrive today within multiethnic and multicultural groups such as communities of Creoles of Color across the United States. In order to understand this phenomenon and to document the formation of ethnic and cultural identity among a complex multiethnic population, this author embarked, in 2001, upon an ethnographic study of Creoles of Color in North America, one of the few studies of Creole identity formation in the United States to explore contemporary Native identity among this population, and one of only a handful of studies which have drawn upon primary data collected from Creole people themselves. Those data, reported on in this article, contribute to our understanding of how racial identity and racial formation are articulated within a multigenerational, mixed-race Native population and provide a case study illustrating how other multiethnic populations throughout the Americas have blended with Indian groups to create a multiethnic American Indian diaspora.

Background

Despite a rich tradition of Creole studies in literature, media studies, and narratives of the antebellum South, little, if any work in these disciplines, has been devoted to examining the complex sociocultural relationship between Creole and American Indian identity. That is, few if any previous Creole studies link American Indian identity to the Creole American experience in the southern United States or to the growth of the Creole diaspora. Furthermore, most studies of Creole identity formation have been set in New Orleans, almost entirely overlooking the experience of Creoles in southwestern Louisiana. The three studies that examine the formation of a mixed-race French-Black Creole culture in New Orleans and thus offer a starting point for considering the social, political, and economic factors that have led to racializing Creoles in black and white terms—Mary Gehman's *The Free People of Color of New Orleans* (1994), Virginia Dominguez's *White By Definition: Social Classification in Creole Louisiana* (1997), and Gwendolyn Midlo Hall's *Africans in Colonial Louisiana: The Development of Afro-Creole Culture in the Eighteenth Century* (1992)—completely neglect to analyze the Indian experience within Creole culture during the eighteenth and nineteenth centuries.

No in-depth study to date of the U.S. policy of extermination through broken treaties, illegal land cession, and redefinition of Indian cultural and ethnic identity or community membership has looked specifically at mixed-race Indian identity in Louisiana. Similar lacunae characterize the research of scholars who have investigated the Creole experience of southwest and northwest Louisiana. Gary Mills's *The Forgotten People: Cane River's Creoles of Color* (1977) asserts that the Black Creole was originally accorded a third position (neither black nor white) within a three-tiered racial caste system but that this category has been collapsed over time to a black-only identity. Brasseaux, Fontenot, and Oubre's *Creoles of Color in the Bayou Country* (1996), focuses on areas of southwest Louisiana.

Although these authors go a step further than their counterparts by at least partially addressing the Indian experience, their analyses leave many questions about what became of the Indians in southwestern Louisiana, some of which are illustrated in the following passage:

> Because indigenous inhabitants of the lower prairies—The Atakapas Indians—were reputedly cannibalistic, the Atakapas and Opelousas districts were among the last areas of lower Louisiana to be developed by the colony's French government. Indeed, the French administration made no effort to establish formal relations with the Atakapas, the area's largest Indigenous group, and theOpelousas, a cultural and linguistic subgroup of the Atakapas, throughout the first four decades of Louisiana's existence, prompting the tribe to send a delegation to New Orleans in 1733 to forge commercial ties with the neighboring colony.[2]

Here, Brasseaux, Fontenot, and Oubre raise the issue of the Atakapa presence in the area but provide no further mention or analysis of what becomes of this the "area's largest Indigenous group." The authors never explain what becomes of the Atakapa or the Opelousa tribes, nor do they acknowledge or discuss intermarriage or interracial sex between Indians and the French. The undisputable historical fact that there were few French women in the early settlements, however, means in effect that the first Creoles had to be of color and had to have Indian and/or African ancestry. Also problematic is the effect attributed by the authors to the Louisiana Purchase on tribal self-determination, land, and treaty rights.[3] Since the Indians of the entire territory were uprooted, misplaced, and uncounted during this period, some scholars have inferred from the ensuing lack of records that all these Indians must have "died out," a position, which I assert is unwarranted and historically inaccurate.

As Terrel Delphin, a Creole scholar from Natchitoches, Louisiana, explains, "Creoles understand Anglo-American racism, especially their conception of 'Negro blood,' as a powerful tool for disenfranchisement, leaving them unprotected and at distinct legal and social disadvantages."[4] He goes on to say, Their Native American connections became confused in the Spanish period when, in the 1780s, Spain freed Indian slaves in Louisiana. Some were censused as Indians, others as freed slaves still others as mulattos or mixed and some as blacks. Whenever Creoles tried to explain who they were, who they felt they were, it ultimately was, and is, interpreted as an attempt to *passer pour blanc*, an effort to deny an African connection.[5] This assumption that Creoles *want* to pass for white continues to make identifying with their American Indian ancestry extremely difficult. The notion of "passing" is an important one in the face of ethnic resurgence theories, which contend, however inaccurately, that many mixed-race people identify as Indian today for primarily economic and/or political purposes. Our ability to trace Indian-Creole relations with any accuracy has been clouded by the misdesignation of Indians as "colored" for most of Louisiana's history.

Most interracial relationships in Louisiana were between European males and African or Indian females, who very often were the property of the men who seduced them. Research shows that most enslaved Indians were women, who, along with female Indian slaves were, "quickly absorbed into the Franco-African communities through concubinage and intermarriage."[6] Most of the slaves brought from Africa to Louisiana were male, whereas most Indian slaves were women who were sought primarily by French men to perform cooking, cleaning, farming, translating, and sexual duties. The large numbers of male African slaves and female Indian slaves inevitably meant that many slave families comprised African husbands and Indian wives. The slave communities on plantations and in cities like New Orleans developed as the respective Indian and African cultures evolved, melding into one common fabric. Children of African-Indian parentage were called "mulatto," while children of Indian females and French men were called "colored."

By the turn of the nineteenth century, the term "colored" was commonly used to describe people of either African or Indian heritage.[7] However, this aspect of Indian absorption into the Franco-African populations, yielding a hybrid and colonial Creole population, is mentioned only briefly if at all in most Creole studies, generally absent an analysis of how the Indian population, particularly the Native women, contributed to the continuity of the group's racial, ethnic, religious, and cultural identity. In fact, when Spanish governor Alejandro O'Reily outlawed Indian slavery in 1769, many slave owners simply reclassified the Indian slaves as black and thus kept them legally enslaved.[8]

The study reported upon here builds on the work of Creole scholars like Delphin, and Martin who have contributed to our understanding of historical aspects of the relations between Indians, Creoles, Africans, and Europeans, but places this history into a contemporary context. Additionally, I examine the failure of prominent anthropological and sociological theories in the twentieth century to document how American Indian individuals and groups, rather than falling into extinction as often claimed, were actually absorbed into multiethnic communities such as the Creole of Color communities in the state of Louisiana, where their living influence remains vibrant to this day.

Ethnic Identification and Self-Perceptions of Creoles in the United States

The present article examines ethnic self-identification of Creoles as well as factors associated with the misrepresentation of the group as biracial (black and white) rather than as multiracial (Indian, French, African, Spanish, etc.). This two-part ethnographic study deals first with quantitative data obtained through a national survey exploring Creole self-perceptions of identity as a multigenerational, mixed-race, Indian population. The second set of data reported upon here was gathered through a series of structured and semistructured individual and group interviews about the politics of identifying as both Creole and Indian.

Survey Design and Results

In order to explore the issue of how Creoles of Color have conceptualized, negotiated, and articulated their identities as members of a distinct multiracial community, the author conducted a survey in August 2001 of one hundred randomly sampled members of a Creole Heritage Center mailing list that was made available to me through Northwestern State University in Louisiana. The survey included thirty-five questions, some open-ended and others closed. In a deliberate attempt to move beyond the limitations of the binary paradigm of identity in all questions related to racial, ethnic, and cultural identity, participants were invited to check as many answers as applied or to provide as many details as they felt appropriate.

The survey was distributed nationally to one hundred individuals who were members or otherwise affiliated with St. Augustine's Historical Society and the Louisiana Creole Heritage Center. Included in the mailing was a cover letter briefly describing the proposed plan for my dissertation research at the University of California, Santa Cruz, and requesting the recipients' participation. Of these one hundred surveys, sixty were returned within a two-month period via the self-addressed, stamped envelopes that had been provided in order to protect participant anonymity, yielding an overall response rate of 60 percent. Participation in the study was strictly voluntary, with no remuneration or other financial incentives offered for participating.

The average age of the survey respondents was fifty-two years. More than 50 percent of the sample group worked as white-collar professionals. Fifty-three percent of the respondents were male, and 47 percent were female. Ten U.S. states: California, Illinois, Connecticut, Louisiana, Maryland, Mississippi, Missouri, New York, Tennessee, and Texas and more than forty cities are represented by the sample group. Despite the small size of the sample, the data collected clearly document a pervasive pattern of multiple self-identifications among Creoles that is inclusive of Indian, French, African, and Spanish ancestry. The pattern is illustrated graphically in figure 1 and described further below.

Among the sixty Creoles respondents, 87 percent identified themselves as Creole, 63 percent as French, 57 percent as African American, and 55 percent as Native American. These data in and of themselves challenge the notion of racial and cultural identities as unitary constructs and reveal the inadequacy of instruments and methodologies that are premised on these inherently limiting notions. The use of such instruments inevitably perpetuates disparities in the treatment of mixed-race peoples such as Creoles by limiting their recognition as distinct multiethnic populations and thus rendering them invisible.

Additional results of the survey speak to the complexity and pervasiveness of mixed-race identity within the Creole population and, in particular, the widespread inclusion of Native American identity within the Creole population, as demonstrated in figure 2. As illustrated below, 85 percent of the survey respondents endorsed the belief that one does *not* have to be 100 percent Native American to identify as Indian, and 40 percent endorsed the belief that Creoles should be considered Native Americans. Contributing further evidence of the complexity of the identification process, 75 percent thought that Creoles should be identified only as Creole, whereas 82 percent thought that individual Creoles with Native American ancestry should be able to identify as both Creole and Native American, and that the U.S. government should recognize individual Creoles with Native American ancestry. None of the respondents believed that Creoles should be identified as white or Native American only. Seven percent of respondents did not respond to the five questions just reported on respecting the interrelationship of Creole and Native American identities.

Figures 1 and 2 graphically depict the results of the survey and represent current trends in Creole thinking about the role and contributions of American Indian culture to Creole identity, addressing the controversial questions of whether Creoles should be legally recognized as an American Indian community and/or should be identified as a discrete category on the 2010 U.S. federal census. These findings suggest a complex pattern of ethnic identity among the contemporary generation of Creoles living within and outside of Louisiana. Internal group definitions of what it means to be Creole are overwhelmingly inclusive of Native American identity.

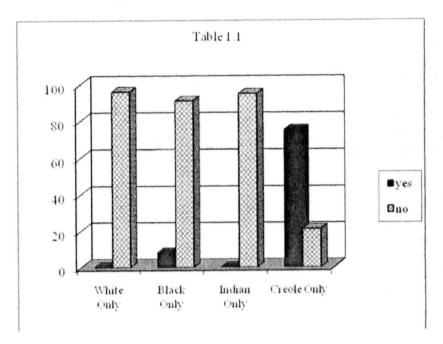

Figure 14.1 *Creole Identification Patterns.*
Source: One hundred surveys distributed nationally in the United States and collected by the author from August 2001 to October 2001. Margin of error: +/– 3. Response rate: 60 percent.

Furthermore, the findings reveal that, while Creoles are inclined to identify most heavily with their French roots, most also see themselves as equally Indian and African. The results demonstrate that the Creole connection to Indian identity is equal in strength to the Creole connection to African identity, though the former connection has been rendered invisible to the outside world and has been largely ignored in other studies of this community.

Individual and Group Interviews

The quantitative survey described above was supplemented by a series of individual and group interviews with Creoles across the continental United States. Data from the interviews further support and substantiate the reported survey findings and add important historical and contextual details about Creole life and identity from an intimate personal perspective.

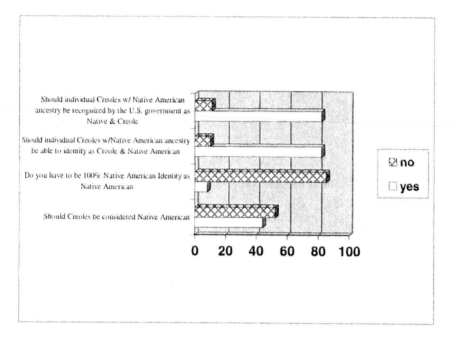

Figure 14.2 *Creole-Indian Identification Patterns.*
A. *Should individual Creoles with Native American ancestry be recognized by the U.S. government as Native and Creole?*
B. *Should individual Creoles with Native American ancestry be able to identify as*
Creole and Native American?
C. *Do you have to be 100 percent Native American to identify as Native American?*
D. *Should Creoles be considered Native American?*
Source: One hundred surveys distributed nationally in the United States and collected by the author from
August 2001 to October 2001. Margin of error: +/– 3. Response rate: 60 percent.

From July 2001 through May 2004, I conducted one-on-one and small group interviews with a total of thirty-five Creole individuals at conferences in New Orleans, Los Angeles, and Las Vegas. Participants were recruited by selective sampling through staff members at the LCHC, through random selection at conferences, and through snowball methods where individuals were either referred directly or were contacted by the investigator because a previous participant had referred them. All interviews were structured or semistructured and ranged in duration from thirty minutes to two hours. All participants signed informed consent forms that explained the study, its voluntary nature, and its use for my dissertation as well as my intentions for future publication. No compensation was offered for participation in the interviews.

The average age of the interview respondents was thirty-nine years. Of the thirty-five individuals who consented to and participated in interviews, sixteen were men and nineteen were women. Group interviews were mixed according to gender and age and were usually semistructured and more conversational in nature than were the individual interviews. Everyone was asked the same eighteen questions, with spontaneous follow-up questions posed to help clarify individual and group responses to these initial questions. Individual interviews followed the same format as group interviews but had a less open-ended flavor because they involved a two-way dialogue instead of a group discussion. Some group discussions and interviews actually took place during shared meals or after religious services or familial events such as family reunions.

All interviews were conducted with the principal investigator in the role of interviewer and were recorded using both audiotapes and handwritten notes. The tapes were then transcribed and analyzed to assess variables and patterns specific to the study's scope. The following comments of one interview participant summarize the frequent concerns expressed by respondents about the chronic invisibility of the Creole community, attributed in part by this participant to the conceptual and methodological biases of prior researchers:

> Part of it is the anthropologists' sort of colonialism that spawned anthropology in the first place. It's where you're always looking for the pristine people . . . people who have their culture. It's the old Boazian thing about finding a whole culture intact. See [John] Swanton wasn't interested in mixed families at all. He was looking for "real" Indians. Like there's a letter, you might run across it, he went below Azeel [sic] and he said, "I heard there were some Indians there and I went . . . but when I got there, there were just a bunch of Choctaws mixed with Black." There's a lot of races in those swamps there. I'm sure he was blind to it. But they were never interviewed. There was a linguist, who was married to Mary Haas. He was working on the Chitimacha and she was working on the Tunica and they found a Black man who spoke Chitimacha, what I hate is he probably also spoke Mobilian, but they didn't know that, but he did become one of their Chitimacha informants. But he's one of the few people who they talked to about Blacks and Indians. Nobody much talked to Mexican/mixed people.[9]

These comments speak directly to the issue of Indian-Creole relationships in the state of Louisiana. The reference to "anthropological colonialism" calls into question the tendency of early twentieth-century anthropologists to overemphasize "full blood" or "authentic" Indian culture while ignoring important aspects of Indian cultural participation and linguistic preservation in multigenerational mixed-race contexts. John Swanton, a Smithsonian anthropologist renowned for his studies of many Indian tribes in Mississippi and the lower South, failed to analyze or even document mixed Indian cultural and linguistic practices in his research in Louisiana. This glaring omission is a clear example of the ways in which methodological biases and limited understanding of the realities of identity among members of mixed racial and cultural groups drastically constrain the contents and utility of research data obtained in this area.

Rethinking Region and the Boundaries of White-Black Identity

Seeking a better life for themselves and their children, many Creole families moved out of Louisiana during the 1940s, 1950s, and early 1960s, with the intention of continuing to express and maintain their Creole culture in their new communities. The following comments by one Creole mother whose family participated in this emigration speak to the challenges faced by Creole migrant children who attended schools in the north during this period.

> I remember when we moved from Louisiana. My sons had a really hard time, especially my younger son who was darker than his brother, but still very light. In school kids didn't know what to think of him, or where he fit in. He always tried to go with the black kids, but to them he just wasn't "black enough" and there were days when he would get beat up just because he looked, in their words, "so white." To this day he still tries very hard to be acknowledged and accepted by the black community. He always asked me, "Mom . . . why do I have to look like this? Why do I have to be Creole?" And I told him that this was his culture and that yes, he was different, but that he should be proud of who he is and not try to change. [10]

As demonstrated in this first-person account, once settled in their new locations, Creole families found little external recognition of their cultural and racial identities. In fact, to their surprise, they found it was difficult for non-Creoles outside of Louisiana to understand what a Creole was, due largely to the social silence surrounding mixed-race identities and their total obfuscation under federal and state law and public policy, which essentially conceptualized race as a binary phenomenon. Many Creole parents were deeply influenced by these views, which were predominant throughout the segregated South and within the political climate of the 1950s and early 1960s. Some explicitly taught their children to relinquish deliberately their identity as Creoles, as recounted by the following respondent whose parents instructed him and his siblings to choose between black and white, the only options given during those days; what seemed to some to be a third option, "colored," included Indian but was ultimately interpreted to mean black.

> In the late 1950s my daddy went up to San Francisco. I think he drove his Cadillac. He went to meet my uncles who had already relocated to the Santa Rosa area. When my daddy came back he and my mama sat us kids down and explained that we were no longer Creoles. If anyone asked when we moved up North we should say that we were French Canadians. They then turned on the television and told us to watch the Imitation of Life. This was a movie about the tragic life of a mulatta girl who looked white and hated having a black mother. She had a terrible life and her mother died eventually leaving the young woman all alone. Then our parents told us to choose what we wanted to be. I always knew we were Indian and White, but I chose black. Of my five siblings I always said we had 2 1/2 blacks and 2 1/2 whites. We all identified differently and we didn't know much about our Indian people anymore, so we

all made our choices I guess, but it's a new generation for my kids who can make their own decisions now. [11]

Despite the difficulties they faced in the absence of external validation and with the pressure to conform to inaccurate and self-limiting concepts of racial identity, Creole families found various covert ways to preserve their identities and culture. One of the most significant of these areas involved the religious beliefs they passed along to Creole youth. In a 1989 study of the religious lives of Creoles in their twenties, Sr. Frances Jerome Woods reported that 64 percent of the Creole youth surveyed believed that their religion strengthened their family lives; while only 30 percent of other Catholic youth concurred with the statement. Sixty percent of the young Creoles attended Mass at least once weekly, compared to 23 percent of their non-Creole counterparts. Although young Creoles took exception to Church norms on abortion and non-marital status, they did so in equal measure with the other Catholic young people studied.

Eighty-two percent of the Creole youth endorsed a belief in life after death and in heaven as a paradise of pleasure and delights. These findings demonstrate the significant role played by Catholicism in the lives of many Creole youth and illustrate the extent to which older generations succeeded in conveying traditional values to them. The results are particularly noteworthy, Sr. Woods observes, because the respondents were "an age when establishing themselves as responsible adults might mean distancing themselves from the ways of their parents and older generations."[12] Sr. Woods' analysis obliquely raises the question of whether the processes of individual identity formation and psychological individuation differ qualitatively between youth of publicly unacknowledged mixed racial/cultural backgrounds and youth who grow up in publicly recognized, socially sanctioned, homogeneous cultural communities.

Woods's[13] study indicates that religion was an essential variable in the reconstruction and rearticulation of a Creole community that was less concerned with "authenticity" and "racial purity" and more frequently focused on the importance of culture and family traditions and rituals. Despite the problems surrounding white black identity construction, Creoles were able to maintain a sense of their culture outside of Louisiana through the many social clubs and activities they created and sponsored in urban areas such as Los Angeles, San Francisco, Oakland, Chicago, Detroit, and New York.[14] The broad sweep of these locations through all corners of the United States demonstrates that success of the Creole population in preserving its rich traditions and beliefs despite regional differences. For example, California-born Creole Janet Colson recounts that boucheries (butcheries) in urban and rural areas of California replicated exactly the experience of their Louisiana counterparts.[15] As the account in which Colson is quoted concludes, "Creoles carry their traditions with them."

These traditions reflect some of the subtle and not-so-subtle ways in which Creoles differ culturally from other ethnic groups with whom they have been associated, despite obvious similarities with the various groups that have contributed to their complex ethnic identity. Some Creole customs are American

Indian, while others directly resemble French, African, or Spanish traditions. Fontenot, also quoted in the *Creole Chronicles*,[16] remarks on the presence of social clubs in the Lake Charles area, where families and friends from small south Louisiana communities who had moved to Lake Charles for jobs and economic stability "came together for various events to keep the closeness of the Creole communities they left." Creoles outside of the rural country parish towns of the southwest and northwest have created a form of trans-state travel, much like immigrants from Europe, Asia, Africa, and Latin America who have formed transnational communities from which they leave and return to their places of origin, transplanting their cultures in new locations and regions of the world. When these trans-state travelers leave home to visit Creoles within the diaspora, they—much like their transnational counterparts—are inclined to bring things from "home." The reunion traditions of one Creole family are described vividly in the following passage:

> Family reunions in the LeDee family are not limited to Louisiana. Many of Elva's relatives moved to California. Her father, her mother's oldest brother, and a cousin moved to San Francisco. Her mother's sister lives in Anaheim, and many other relatives are spread through the San Francisco, Los Angeles County, and Orange County areas. When Elva visits, it becomes a reunion. Cousins arrive for special meals and spread out across the floor. Elva brings food items that are not found in California and prepares special dishes that remind the relatives of home. She brings Camelia brand red beans, sausage, boudin, tasso, and a particular favorite, gingerbread. The foods are handled with care. She freezes the meat items and packs them in a suitcase for the trip. The forty gingerbreads are layered between her clothes in another suitcase. Relatives encourage Elva to bring plenty of food with the admonition that they will furnish her with all of the clothes that she needs while visiting![17]

Family reunion events of this type are a regular feature of Creole life and were commented on repeatedly by the participants who were interviewed in this study as a primary means through which the community continued to assert itself as a distinct entity despite geographical separation. Many Creoles of Color have retained various aspects of their complex ethnic ancestries not only through religion and reunions, but through other cultural practices such as food, dance, music, and storytelling. Creoles have worked to move beyond the limited and limiting construction of blackness and whiteness that has plagued most of the mixed-race colonial and postcolonial population of the Americas. Creoles have not only been organizing locally, nationally, and internationally, but their everyday cultural rituals reflect an embedded sense of their indigenous ancestries. In one particular example, Creoles continue to preserve their American Indian heritage through the filé making process (a process and ingredient learned from the Choctaw), which involves the use of sassafras leaves to make filé for gumbos and other traditional Creole foods. Cane River Creole, historian, and preservationist, Michael Moran, better known as "Mickey," is very knowledgeable about filé making.

In 1982, Moran's uncle taught him how to process and gather the leaves to make the filé. Certain traditions as well as techniques are involved with making filé. Many people still hold to the older tradition of picking the leaves on August 15, a holy day in the Catholic religion and a day on which most people in past years did not have to work. However, another guideline is to pick after the first full moon in August. The leaves must be dried in a dark place, but only one who has learned the art can tell when the leaves are dry enough. The leaves are ground and sifted to produce a fine powder. The resulting filé is stored either in jars or in the freezer for use as a seasoning and thickener in gumbos and other Creole dishes. About four years ago, Moran taught the process to his boys, Michael and Matthew, then eleven and eight years old, respectively. Having handed this part of Creole culture and tradition down to his sons, filé making has become a family affair at the Moran household.[1]

Creole community activities and organizations across the country have grown to attract attention at the national level, bringing the general public to a greater recognition of the diversity of the Creole people's history and contemporary existence. Consider for example the following excerpt from a Creole Society publication:

> A special stamp hand cancellation was scheduled to be issued January 20–23 in honor of French Creole Migration according to Sherrell Bozeman, manager of Post Office Operations in Alexandria. A special presentation of the cancellation to the community is to be held at the St. Augustine Catholic Church in Melrose on Saturday, January 20. The Melrose Post Office is one of two postal stations honoring "Creole Heritage Day." The other postal location will be the Baldwin Hill's Crenshaw Plaza Station in Los Angeles California, where the Creole link happened in the mid '40s when the first wave of Creoles migrated from Louisiana to California. The Louisiana hand cancellation will feature maps of Louisiana and France in honor of the 230th anniversary of the French Creole Migration of Claude Thomas Pierre Metoyer from France to the new world (Louisiana) in 1766.[2]

Working to preserve their heritage and to connect with the larger Creole community has been an enormous task, but organizations like the LCHC, along with *Bayou Talk*, St. Augustine's Historical Society, and the Louisiana Folk Life Office have been instrumental in sustaining the current Creole Movement and articulating the ancestral and cultural connections among Creoles and Indians. In 2000, these organizations brought forth a very important presentation at Creole Heritage Day that focused precisely on the Native-Creole connection.

> Regional Folklorist Dr. Dayna Lee will present a paper "Native American Ancestry in the Cane River Community," and Professor of Anthropology, Dr.

H.F. "Pete" Gregory, curator of the Williamson Museum as NSU, will provide an exhibit on the Caddos and the Creoles.[3]

The growth of public attention and the specific inclusion of American Indian aspects of Creole culture reinforce the group's refusal to participate in its own reduction to the classifications of black and white. Rather, Creoles acknowledge and celebrate the vibrant components of a hybrid culture, instead of conforming to a monoracial identity. The community's struggle to move beyond the binary social construction of Creole identity as black-white is often exacerbated by the lack of clarity found in historic records. Lapses and omissions in the historical record more often than not represent the vision and preferences of the dominant culture and represent a challenge even for Creole-initiated genealogical research. For example, the Creole Family History Convention in Los Angeles, California, in 2002 gathered a series of important resources to help Creoles conducting genealogy research to identify their Spanish and American Indian ancestors, with two workshops focusing on the Indian and Spanish influences within Creole culture, a database of family surnames, and a newly established central location for Creole family research. Staff members note that, even in this inclusive context, the dimensions of Indian identity may be difficult to document because they have been unrecorded or obscured in the records from churches and other institutional sources.

> To the best of my knowledge, we have not been able to determine, like what tribe or anything, but I grew up, like I think a lot of people did, under the belief that there were Native Americans within our family. And one of my uncles, who married my father's sister, I knew that he was the descendant of Native Americans, just by the look. But I didn't know that his grandmother, yeah his grandmother, was a sister to my great-grandmother. I didn't know this. So we descended from that same people. I didn't know that until after I started doing research because I always figured that this was a name that married into our family, and come to find out, we were descendants to that family. . . . Oh definitely, because I cannot really say how, like a definite path that a person would take. Now one thing I can say, that I found last summer (myself personally) some of the church records and some of the census records that indicate a person as Native American in one census, may be labeled something else in the next census. So the other thing is that, in the church records, the baptismal records, they might keep a separate record of slaves or Indians (I found that a record of slaves, those people were actually Indian). So the only thing I could say is that when you're researching your heritage, is that you need to look at everything. If it says that this is a group of white people, do not rule out that your family may not [actually] be Indian. Or if it says slaves, do not rule out that they might not be within that group [Indian].[4]

Creole people, like members of other multiethnic populations with Indian ancestry, are often unsure of their exact tribal connection to indigenous groups of North America. Often, parents and grandparents pass down cultural traditions that they identify only as "Creole" because they themselves do not know for sure the identities of the individual tribes that contributed to these practices, or they know that society would not allow them to fully embrace these identities as "legitimate."

On the other hand, the current Creole ethnic resurgence movement continues to confront what has been characterized as an "overemphasis" on black aspects of Creole identity. Many Creoles I spoke with who identified closely with their African American roots spoke of simultaneously feeling pressured to deny the other aspects of their identities. One Creole woman from southeast Texas remarked, "I identify as Black because that's what they say I am, and I don't have a problem with that, but why should I *only* be Black when that's the smallest part of my ethnic background?" Another woman's comments suggest that many Creoles use the term "Creole" deliberately to reject such reductionism and embrace all of the many ethnicities that contribute to their overall identity.

> I think that that part of the culture [Indian] should be recognized. The thing that I always think about, because I've always been or whatever, is "Why don't you wanna recognize your Black heritage?" Its like we're purposefully not recognizing our Black heritage, which is [somewhat] true. How can you say, "Well, I'm gonna recognize the Black heritage today, but tomorrow we'll be Native American?" I think that part of what everyone should recognize is that all of the culture is captured by the center name, "Creole." It's just like, I had this one analogy that I always said I was gonna put on my website, talking about making a chocolate chip cookie. You end up with a chocolate chip cookie, but you don't just go and talk about the flour that went in there! It's a mixture. And what you're looking at is the end product, and there's no reason why I'm gonna just sit here and talk about the flour or the chocolate chips. So to me it's the same analogy; I'm gonna talk about that end product, and how it affects me and what made it—I'll give the ingredients but there's no reason why I'll just talk about one.[5]

The "chocolate chip cookie" metaphor expressed by this interviewee provides a rich analogy through which we can speak about the American Indian aspects of Creole culture. Over time, American Indians have been like the flour of that cookie. No one ever says, "Mmm, that flour sure made this a great cookie!" The flour is a hidden but necessary ingredient, without which the cookie itself would not exist. However, based on cultural conventions and social expectations, many people tend instead to focus on the chocolate chips or the sugar, just as many prefer to focus on the black or white elements of the Creole mixture. Unlike cookies, however, Creoles are complex human subjects, and the negotiation of their distinct, many-faceted identities during the last century has been a complex, multigenerational process.

Discussion

The data collected in this study clearly reveal a pattern of personal and community self-identification as both Creole and Native American among the majority of the research participants. Quantitative and qualitative analyses demonstrate that Creoles regard the cultural contributions from all aspects of their identity as being equal. As the rates of interracial mixing continue in Native American communities across the United States, the potential significance of the work presented here is enormous. Among other things, this research strongly supports the movement to ensure the rights of indigenous communities to self-identify, using culture and not biological determinism to define themselves over time. In order to fully understand these data, we need more research and in-depth theoretical analyses to address how cultural formation among multigenerational mixed-race populations can challenge binary racial classification and community authentication practices. These are just some of the many questions that can be raised only after we have done the work explicitly to recognize the social and cultural realities of racially and culturally mixed communities. With such outcomes in mind, the present study and others like it have the potential to lead to entirely new lines of inquiry within ethnic and Native American studies.

Creoles in the United States today are, for the first time, able to make visible their Native identities—in their own words and voices—as fluid, intact, and socially meaningful. As a multigenerational mixed-race Native community, Creoles are one of the last indigenous populations on the continent to be discussed in the scholarly literature because so much of the shared history between Creoles and Indians has been lost, hidden, destroyed, or unrecorded. To fully understand the operations of cultural formation, we need to cultivate a greater understanding of the politics and potential social effects of black-Indian relations, sociocultural disparities, identity perception, and community sustainability. And to fully interrogate the construction of discourse on "Black-Indians" as an overt form of racism when the converse category "White-Indians" does not exist and is never called into question. These racial distinctions are social constructions left over from colonization of tribal communities where these "White-Indians" who continue to deny the multiplicity of ethnic mixture among indigenous communities, especially when they include African ancestry often take up leadership.

There is also a need for further research into the possibilities of alliances between ethnic and cultural communities throughout the Americas who are similar to Creoles in their Latin (French and/or Spanish), Indian, European, and African ancestries, who have similarly melded Catholicism with Indian and African cultures and who have articulated post- and decolonial identities that can include Indian in the naming of their existence as Creole, Puerto Rican, Cuban, Dominican, Jamaican, Haitian . . . at once multiethnic and indigenous.

Throughout the Americas, indigenous communities are struggling to gain respect and acknowledgment of their sovereign political, social, economic, legal, and regional status as nations. Rearticulating a specific place for multiethnic indigenous communities that have historically been racialized along the lines of non-Native, biracial, European-African only communities can offer a new framework for understanding the importance of culture and cultural formation in shaping ethnicity and, perhaps more importantly, for linking ethnicity with individual and group identity: what people *do*, *feel*, and *articulate* as their own lived experience.

Creoles offer us an important lesson about the futility of reducing race and ethnicity to biology, law, and even history. Creoles of Color demonstrate that to understand the full complexity of identity as a sociological phenomenon, scholars must link all of these different variables and, in the process, withstand any temptation to simplify or reduce identity to a dichotomy of extremes. Creoles in the twenty-first century continue to fight to move outside of the extreme binary conceptualization of race and, in the process, to assert a clearly Creole identity that encompasses everything that we are—American Indian, French, Spanish, and African—as indigenous, multiethnic, Afro-Latin and diasporic peoples.

One of my concerns in designing and implementing this study was the notion that identities can become mutually exclusive when they apply to multiracial people. There are many examples of local Creole people who work to preserve their identities even as these change over time. It is important to note that no ethnic group goes without changing in terms of dress, language, appearance, and even in terms of culture. So then, at what point in history does one stop being Indian if this has been a part of one's identity? Does a multiracial identity necessarily negate or privilege one aspect of identity over others? I often comment to my students that if we used the same racial logic of Louisiana

Racial formation theory assumes that racial identities are socially constructed and therefore change over time as societal forces exert pressure on these constructs to become different or remain the same. The one-drop rule (the notion that one drop of black blood is all it takes to "qualify" a person as black) is one example of the way in which racial formation theory demonstrates the significance of race, while ignoring culture in influencing and even interrupting the notion that society completely controls individual ethnic identity options. The Creole case in fact provides evidence to the contrary. Despite the outside pressures and society's long history of racializing them as "black," Creoles have successfully maintained a coherent, albeit multifaceted, identity that they themselves experience and authenticate. The formation of Creole organizations throughout the twentieth century provides evidence of the ways in which groups organize themselves around community and culture rather than physical appearance alone. Cultural formation, in contradistinction to racial formation, provides for a deeper analysis of the ways in which cultural practice, cultural symbols, and signs of cultural identity contradict the static definitions of race against which they argue. More specifically, to understand fully how race and racism are products of ideology, one must understand the ways in which cultural formations disarticulate the "logics" of intact racial identities. To question the notions of race, racism, and the hegemony of racial projects, we must be able to produce an alternative framework for arguing against a racial agenda.

The Creoles provide us with an instructive case in point. Creoles distinguish themselves not so much by biology as by culture. In the interviews conducted in California, Texas, and Louisiana during the two-part study reported herein, most of the participants discussed the meaning of their Creole identities in the context of social gatherings, music, dances or La-La's, church ceremonies, and ethnic festivals. As their responses demonstrate, although racial identity or biology is the initial factor that gives a group its identity, it is not what maintains. Creoles have preserved their distinct identity not simply because of biology (which the research indicates has changed over time) but mostly through their vibrant, shared culture. Similarly, American Indians are defined today within most tribal communities not simply by biology, but also by community participation, geography, awareness of cultural traditions, and shared history. Thus, degree of blood—though still used in some parts of the country today as a determinant of race—is often far less significant to Indians and Creoles than cultural identification and participation.

Additionally, the interviews reported here argue against the historical view of Creoles as "performing" race. Instead, a constructionist or social interactionist model is of far greater utility in helping to clarify the many ways in which Creoles have been forced by their surroundings and by the hegemonic construction of racial identity to shift from a collective group identity as Creole to individual identification with specific points within the continuum of French, Indian, Spanish, and African ancestry. Larger structural state apparatuses have compelled Creole migrants to deny the complexity of their ethnic and cultural distinctiveness and have instead ensured the perpetuation of an inaccurate and overly simplified view of Creole people by not offering a "Creole" category on any census forms.

Conclusion

This chapter reports on the results of a two-part ethnographic study of ethnic self-identification and regional invisibility of Creoles in the United States, conducted from 2001 to 2004, which incorporated both a survey and a series of in-depth individual and group interviews with members of the contemporary Creole community across forty U.S. cities. The study adds to the handful of research reports that are based on data obtained primarily from Creole people themselves and represents the first research ever performed in the United States on Creole-Indian identity formation.

The survey reveals that Creoles from around the United States believe strongly that their group should first and foremost be identified legally and socially as Creole. Additionally, it is clear from the results of the survey that to the members of the Creole community themselves, the Native American aspects of the group's ancestry are equally as important a part of the group's heritage as are the African and European aspects.

Finally, data obtained from both the survey and from a parallel set of in-depth semi-structured interviews reveal that, despite various pressures to deny their multiracial ancestry, Creoles have maintained a continuous connection to the self-proclaimed identity as Creole and to their original homeland in Louisiana, expressing, celebrating, and perpetuating this identity through the practice of rituals related to religion and the Catholic Church, cooking and family social gatherings and celebrations throughout the Creole diaspora.

The implications of this work are profound and promising in their potential contribution to the body of literature on ethnic studies and American Indian identity, demonstrating, for example, the limitations of the black-white paradigm of racial identity in the United States. The reported findings also illustrate how the ethnic civil rights movements in the United States during the 1960s paradoxically led to particular constraints on the ability of Creoles to assert their own multiethnic identity as a community of French, American Indian, African, and Spanish descent. Despite the confluence of legal, political, and social factors that have denied its existence or sought to eradicate it, the identity of the Creole community continues to remain strong and vibrant—if largely unrecognized by outsiders—on the continent today and, therefore, has much to teach us about the ability of communities to, in the words of anthropologist James Clifford, "articulate themselves."

The survey and interview data reported here indicate that a clear majority of Creole respondents across the United States believe that Creoles should be able to identify as "multiracial," Creole and American Indian, French, African and Spanish all at the same time. As the elders in the community informed me over the course of my research, no individual identity within the larger Creole makeup is more valuable than any other. At the conferences I attended in Los Angeles, New Orleans, and Las Vegas, I participated in workshops on the Spanish, French, American Indian, Caribbean, and Haitian influence on the Louisiana Creole alongside a wide range of participants of clearly different phenotypes—ranging in appearance from European to American Indian, to Latino and African American. In this space, the unifying element was culture, a complex amalgamation of Louisiana ancestry, family names, and personal involvement in Creole cultural activities such as masses, dances, food, and historical celebrations. No matter what you looked liked, if you could participate, you were family: You were Creole.

Notes

I would like to acknowledge the support of my dissertation chair, John Brown Childs, at the University of California, Santa Cruz; Tomas Almaguer, my faculty mentor at San Francisco State University; Barbara Ustanko for her excellent editorial assistance; and the Ford Foundation Postdoctoral Fellowship Award Program, which allowed me to secure important release time from my teaching duties to complete this research project, which was in part based on research conducted for my dissertation at UC Santa Cruz. Versions of this article have appeared in, *Louisiana Creoles: Cultural Recovery and Mixed-Race Native American Identity* (Lanham: Lexington Books, 2007) and in *Cultural Representation in Native America* (Lanham: AltaMira Press, 2006), permission was obtained to reproduce the article in this anthology. Finally, my assertion in the conclusion that appearance doesn't matter is not to suggest that color hierarchies do not exist, but rather it is to assert that spaces where cultural practices can supersede color do exist and provide hope for dismantling race and color discrimination if we focus on experience as opposed to biology, but it will take many years to shift racial ideologies from race to critical cultural consciousness, as many years perhaps as it took to create white supremacist ideologies in the first place.

1. See Virginia Dominguez *White By Definition* (1997); Frances Jerome Woods *Value Retention Among Young Creoles* (1989); Carl A. Brasseaux, Keith P. Fontenot, and Claude F. Oubre *Color in the Bayou Country* (1996); Sybil Kein *Creole: The History and Legacy of Louisiana's Free People of Color* (2000) and G. Reginald Daniel *More Than Black* (2002).
2. Carl A. Brasseaux, Keith P. Fontenot, and Claude F. Oubre, *Creoles of Color in the Bayou Country* (Jackson: University of Mississippi Press, 1996), 6.
3. See Vine Deloria *Custer Died for Your Sins: An Indian Manifesto* (1988).
4. Terrel Delphin, *The Creole Struggle and Resurrection: Our Story as Told by Creoles* (Natchitoches: Northwestern State University Library, 1995), 14.
5. Ibid.
6. Joan Martin, "Placage and the Louisiana Gens De Couleur Libre: How Race and Sex Defined the Lifestyles of Free Women of Color," in *The History and*

Legacy of Louisiana's Free People of Color, ed. Sybil Kein (Baton Rouge: Louisiana State University Press, 2000), 59.

7. Jolene Adams, and Freida M. Fusilier, "He, La-Bas: A History of Louisiana Cajun and Zydea Music in California," cal.net, 2002, www.cal.net/louisianasue/ehlabas.htm

8. Martin, 59.

9. This statement was made by a French-Indian respondent in 2001 to the author.

10. Personal communication between author and attendee at Creole Family Convention Los Angeles, California 2002.

11. Statement made by Creole respondent in 2001.

12. Louis Metoyer, "Sr. Woods Update," *Bayou Talk Newspaper 5*, No. 11, 1991.

13. See Frances Jerome Woods, Sr. *Value Retention Among Creoles: Attitudes and Commitment of Contemporary Youth* (1989).

14. This notion is reinforced with statements by a Creole respondent at the Los Angeles Conference.

15. Michael Fontenot, "Boucheries and Other Celebrations," in *The Creole Chronicles* ed. NSU Creole Heritage Center (Natchitoches: Northwestern State University, 2002), 6.

16. Ibid.

17. Fontenot, 33.

18. Mickey Moran, "The File' Making Process," in *Creole Heritage Day Program Booklet* ed. NSU Creole Heritage Center (Natchitoches: Northwestern State University, 1998), 28.

19. Ibid.

20. See the *Creole Heritage Day Booklet* (2000) section authored by Janet Colson.

21. This statement was given by a Creole respondent in 2001.

22. Commentary by another Creole respondent in 2001.

References

Adams, Jolene M., and Fusilier, Freida M. "He, La-Bas!: A History of Louisiana Cajun and Zydeco Music in California." 2002. Available at www.cal.net/louisianasue/ehlabas.htm.

Brasseaux, Carl A., Keith P. Fontenot, and Calude F. Oubre. *Creoles of Color in the Bayou Country*. Jackson: University of Mississippi Press, 1996.

Clifford, James. "Indigenous Articulations." Address delivered at the conference "Native Pacific Cultural Studies at the Edge," Center for Cultural Studies, University of California, Santa Cruz, February 11–12, 2000.

Colson, Janet. *Creole Heritage Day Program Booklet*. Natchitoches, LA: Northwestern State University, 2000.

Daniel, Reginald G. *More Than Black?: Multiracial Identity and the New Racial Order*. Philadelphia: Temple University Press, 2002.

Deloria, Vine. *Custer Died for Your Sins: An Indian Manifesto*. Norman: University of Oklahoma Press, 1988.

Delphin, Terrel. *The Creole Struggle and Resurrection: Our Story as Told by Creoles*. Natchitoches, LA: Northwestern State University Library, 1995.

Dominguez, Virginia. *White By Definition: Social Classification in Creole Louisiana*. New Brunswick, NJ: Rutgers University Press, 1997 [1987].

Dormon, James H. "Ethnicity and Identity: Creoles of Color in Twentieth Century South Louisiana." In *Creoles of Color of the Gulf South*, edited by James H. Dormon. Knoxville: University of Tennessee Press, 1996.

Fontenot, Michael. "Boucheries and Other Celebrations: Lake Charles Louisiana." In *The Creole Chronicles*, Vol. 2. Natchitoches, LA: Northwestern State University, 2002.

Gehman, Mary. *The Free People of Color of New Orleans*. New Orleans: Margaret Media, 1994.

Hall, Gwendolyn Midlo. *Africans in Colonial Louisiana: The Development of Afro-Creole Culture in the Eighteenth Century*. Baton Rouge: Louisiana State University Press, 1992.

Kein, Sybil. *Creole: The History and Legacy of Louisiana's Free People of Color*. Baton Rouge: Louisiana State University, 2000.

Martin, Joan. "Placage and the Louisiana Gens De Couleur Libre: How Race and Sex Defined the Lifestyles of Free Women of Color." In *Creole: The History and Legacy of Louisiana's Free People of Color*, edited by SybilKein. Baton Rouge: Louisiana State University Press, 2000.

Metoyer, Louis. "Sr. Woods Update." In *Bayou Talk Newspaper*, Vol. 5, No. 11. Moreno Valley and West Covina: JO VAL, 1991.

Mills, Gary. *The Forgotten People: Cane River's Creoles of Color*. Baton Rouge: Louisiana State University, 1977.

Moran, Mickey. "The Filé Making Process." In *Creole Heritage Day Program Booklet*. Natchitoches, LA: Northwestern State University, 1998.

Ravare, Malinda. "Louisiana to California." In "The Natchitoches NSU Folk Festival." Natchitoches, LA: Northwestern State University.

Saint Augustine Historical Society. "Program Brochure." Natchitoches, LA: Author, 1998.

Saint Augustine Historical Society. "Creole Heritage Day Celebrations: The Past 7 Years, 1994-2000." Natchitoches, LA: Author, 2000.

Woods, Sr. Frances Jerome. *Value Retention Among Young Creoles: Attitudes and Commitment of Contemporary Youth.* Mellen Studies in Sociology, Vol. 5. Lewiston, NY: Edwin Mellen Press, 1989.

Chapter 15

Race, Class, and Power: The Politics of Multiraciality in Brazil[1]

G. Reginald Daniel and Gary L. Haddow

In Brazil, pervasive miscegenation and the lack of formal legal barriers to racial equality contributed to its image as a "racial democracy." Accordingly, the Brazilian racial order has historically been characterized by a ternary racial project that designates individuals as white, multiracial, and black and that supported the idea that social inequality is primarily attributable to differences in class and culture rather than race. Since the 1970s, the black movement has articulated a binary racial project that combines black and multiracial individuals into a single African Brazilian category distinct from whites to heighten awareness of and mobilize opposition to the real racial discrimination that exists in Brazil. Beginning in 2001, the multiracial movement began challenging this binary conceptualization of the Brazilian racial order. The goal has been to defend and reassert the historical process of racial blending that has characterized the Brazilian people as well as affirm the right of individuals and the nation by extension to identify as "multiracial." This chapter examines these competing narratives of Brazilian racial formation and national identity, particularly as they relate to ongoing formations of "blackness" and "whiteness." This is especially meaningful given the history of African slavery, and the unique attitudes, discourse, policy, and behavior that have crystallized around individuals of African descent in the formation of Brazil's national identity.[2]

Neither Black nor White: The Brazilian Racial Order

Brazil and the United States inherited European norms that accorded whites privileged status relative to all other racial groups. However, Brazil has traditionally been contrasted with the United States in terms of its long history of pervasive racial (phenotypical, ancestral) and cultural (beliefs, values, customs, artifacts) blending. Furthermore, Brazil has validated this process by implementing a ternary racial project that differentiates its population into European Brazilians (*brancos*), multiracial individuals (*pardos* in official texts, *mestiço* or *mulato* in everyday parlance), and blacks (*pretos*).[3] This has led to a notable fluidity in racial/cultural markers and has been accompanied by the absence of legalized barriers to equality in both the public and private spheres. Correspondingly, it has been argued that class and cultural, rather than racial, signifiers have come to determine one's identity and status in the social hierarchy, which has given rise to Brazil's ideology of racial democracy.[4]

Brazil's "racial democracy" stands out in stark contrast to the U.S. racial order. European Americans have sought to preserve their cultural and racial "purity," as well as their dominant status, by enforcing the one-drop rule of hypodescent that designates as black everyone of African descent. The resulting binary racial order has served as the underpinning for legal and informal exclusion of individuals of African descent from having contact with whites as equals in most aspects of social life—both public barriers (e.g. political, economic, educational) and private ones (e.g. residential, associational, interpersonal). At the turn of the twentieth century, these restrictions reached drastic proportions with the institutionalization of Jim Crow segregation.

Despite the absence of legalized barriers to racial equality in Brazil, as compared with the United States, data collected since the last half of the twentieth century indicate that physical appearance, if not ancestry (as in the United States), working in conjunction with class and cultural factors, significantly impact social stratification in Brazil.[5] The divide between haves and have-nots primarily coincides, respectively with the racial divide between whites (*brancos*) and the African Brazilian masses (*negros*), including both the black and multiracial populations, a finding that has challenged Brazil's racial democracy ideology.

The racial democracy ideology was popularized in the monumental studies by anthropologist Gilberto Freyre[6] who attributed Brazil's more fluid racial order to the exceptional openness to miscegenation, particularly with people of African descent, on the part of the Portuguese colonizers, and the altruism that underpinned their differentiation of mulattoes from blacks. Such arguments had more to do with racial romanticism than with reality. Throughout the Americas, and irrespective of the national and cultural origins of the colonizing Europeans, the quantity of miscegenation and the social distinctions made between individuals of varying degrees of African ancestry were motivated primarily by self-interest and closely related respectively to the ratio of European men to women and the ratio of whites to blacks.

In Brazil, and other areas of Latin America—including "Latin North America" such as the lower Mississippi Valley, the Gulf Coast, and South Carolina—the colonizing Europeans were a minority and mostly single males. Africans comprised a majority of the colonial population. Rape, fleeting extramarital relations, as well as extended concubinage and common-law unions between European men and women of African descent, therefore, were more or less approved, if not encouraged, by the prevailing unwritten moral code. There were, however, legal barriers to interracial marriages during most of the colonial period, and formidable social prejudice against these relationships that remained in place long afterwards.[7]

As slaves, the mulatto offspring of these unions were often assigned more exacting tasks that symbolized greater personal worth and that required greater skill (e.g. domestics and artisans). The pronounced scarcity of white women mitigated or prevented significant opposition from the legal wife and enhanced the likelihood that these offspring would be the recipients of socially tolerated demonstrations of affection, as well as economic and educational protection. Mulattoes were given preferential liberation over blacks, who overwhelmingly were slaves. This made it possible for them early in the colonial period to enter the free classes where they necessarily filled important interstitial roles in the economy—particularly in the artisanal and skilled trades—due to a shortage of European labor and for which the use of slave labor was considered to be impractical.[8]

Free Colored urban artisans, long before abolition, readily advanced from these favored interstitial positions into the arts, letters, and liberal professions (including medicine, engineering, law, and the civil service), although they were barred from holding public office, entering high status occupations in the clergy and governmental bureaucracy, experienced limitations on educational attainment, and were denied equal rights in a variety of categories. Free Coloreds did not achieve their vertical mobility through direct competition in the open market, but rather through the paternalistic support of patrons in the white elite who always controlled their advancement.[9] European Brazilians, by granting mulattoes a social location somewhat superior to that of blacks, but significantly inferior to that of whites, won their loyalty in efforts to exclude blacks from power without at the same time undermining white domination and control. As long as blacks were retained in the least remunerative sectors of the secondary labor force as agricultural, industrial, and service laborers, mulattoes willingly settled for token integration into the skilled trades, the petty bourgeoisie, intelligentsia, and primary labor force comprised of white-collar workers.[10]

The paradoxical nature of the Brazilian racial order has assured that African Brazilians collectively speaking are denied the privileges of whites, but mulattoes are at the same time rewarded in proportion to their cultural and phenotypical approximation to the European psychosomatic ideal.[11] This window of opportunity that Degler calls the "mulatto escape hatch" is an informal social mechanism by which a select few "visibly" multiracial individuals, for reasons of talent, culture, or education, have been allowed token vertical socioeconomic mobility into the middle class and with it the rank of situational "whiteness."[12] In its broadest sense, however, the escape hatch is a social device that has made it possible for other millions of individuals whose ancestry has included African forbearers, but who are phenotypically white, or near-white, to become socially designated and self-identified as white. This aspect of the escape hatch is indicative of a more inclusive definition of whiteness clearly setting apart the Brazilian racial order from that in the United

States where the one-drop rule can transform into black an individual who appears otherwise white.[13]

Brazil's long history of pervasive miscegenation, and its conspicuous absence of institutionalized White supremacy and legalized barriers to equality as compared to the United States, should not, however, not obscure the fact that "white" is synonymous with being superior, and inferiority is generally synonymous with being "black." As miscegenation became a central tenet in the twentieth-century evolution of Brazil's concept of racial democracy, racial and cultural blending was not posited on egalitarian (or horizontal) integration. There was not a random entropic integration of European, African, and by extension, Native American traits, seeking its own "natural" equilibrium, through a reciprocal *transracial/transcultural* process. It was rather, a process of inegalitarian (or hierarchical) integration, that is to say, *assimilation* in disguise, an unnatural contest between unequal participants artificially manipulated in order to purify the Brazilian pedigree and culture of its vast accumulation of "inferior" African (and Native American) traits with the goal of perpetuating only one: the European.[14]

Pervasive miscegenation and the escape hatch, by blurring and softening the line between whites and African Brazilians, indeed helped to diminish any collective problem in post-slavery Brazil stemming from race per se while simultaneously maintaining de facto white dominance and control. They have achieved this by creating the illusion that whatever prejudice and discrimination exists in Brazil, are not based on ascribed, and, thus, essentially immutable characteristics such as race. Rather, discrimination is supposedly based on acquired social, economic, and cultural characteristics that are subject to alteration by individual merit and achievement during ones' lifetime. However, the privilege of first-class citizenship is awarded selectively in accordance with ones' approximation to European phenotypical and cultural traits, working in combination with their economic standing.

For the most part, the socioeconomic polarization between haves and have-nots, respectively follows the racial divide between white and black. Multiracial individuals, more so than blacks, are the beneficiaries of this meritocracy. The escape hatch has retarded, if not prevented, political mobilization along racial lines, by guaranteeing that large numbers of those individuals most likely to possess the cultural, intellectual, and social skills to unmask the reality behind the racial democracy ideology, and serve as mouthpieces of the African Brazilian masses, are neutralized or coopted, if you will, into silence. Not being white, yet aspiring to be treated as first-class citizens, multiracial individuals at any time could be classified as racial inferiors by even the most socially and culturally "inferior" whites by simply being treated as second-class citizens racially, such that the escape hatch could easily become a "trap door."[15]

Either Black or White: The Black Movement

Brazil's image as a racial democracy began to erode under the weight of massive data compiled in the 1950s by both Brazilian and foreign social scientists revealing a complex web of correlations between phenotype, culture, and class in determining social stratification. Comprehensive data were lacking, and some important regional variations existed, and researchers' opinions varied on how physical appearance might affect future social mobility. There was a general consensus that Brazilians who were phenotypically more African—like their African American counterparts—were disproportionately found at the bottom of society in terms of education and occupation.[16]

Discrimination was more complex than in the United States binary racial project, and had never been codified since the colonial era. Nevertheless, the growing body of evidence not only made the Brazilian elite cautious about discussing their society's contemporary race relations, much less its racial future, but also made the racial democracy ideology even more crucial. It was systematically and staunchly defended by Brazil's ruling elite, and reinforced by the series of military dictatorships that dominated the Brazilian political scene between 1964 and 1985. The intense censorship of public discussion on the racial issues (despite the work of social scientists) was paralleled by the fact that no racial data were collected in the 1970 census. Government officials were seeking to promote the notion that racial criteria were insignificant in determining the distribution of societal wealth, power, privilege, and prestige— and thus meaningless statistical categories—by depriving researchers (and therefore the public and politicians) of nationwide figures which would make it possible to verify how poorly African Brazilians fared in terms of education, jobs, income, and health.[17]

Only since the last two decades of the twentieth century has there been the necessary political space and conceptual flexibility about race in Brazil to secure and reformulate racial meanings, forge an oppositional racial ideology, and constitute alternative racial institutions.[18] The long veil of silence on the discussion of racial inequality was not lifted until the 1970s during the gradual liberalization of the national sociopolitical ecology and the lifting of authoritarian rule (the "abertura democrática," or democratic opening). The growing, but covert, racial tension in Brazil in the early 1970s, as well as the Civil Rights movement in the United States all combined to set the stage for the formation of the Unified Black Movement (O Movimento Negro Unificado, MNU). African Brazilians, thus, made some progress in rekindling the previous militancy, which the MNU's predecessor, the Black Front (A Frente Negra), had exhibited during the 1930s before having reached its nadir during the repressive dictatorship of Getúlio Vargas (1937–1945).[19]

The MNU enjoyed a significant amount of publicity in the late 1970s and early 1980s, but gained greater attention from academics abroad than in Brazil. Class divisions within the MNU's ranks arose as a result of the primarily urban bourgeoisie leadership, which prevented it from garnering support from the urban and rural sectors of the African Brazilian community. Furthermore, the

MNU's goal of achieving a more equitable society by mobilizing an African Brazilian plurality to challenge the dominant assimilationist ideology was met with blatant hostility from sectors of the political and cultural establishment. At best, their tactics were termed as "un-Brazilian" and mindless imitations of the United States civil rights movement. At worst, the MNU's egalitarian (or horizontal) pluralist premises and goals (Figure 1.f) were described as racist in the manner of a reverse type of apartheid (Figure 1.e). The MNU is part of a larger black movement encompassing a wide variety of significant social, cultural, and political organizations and activities.

The black movement's efforts were also aided by a new generation of social scientists. These researchers (most of whom are white) assisted in getting the race question reinstated on the 1980 census by providing a rigorous analysis of official data contained in such sources as the 1940, 1950, and 1980 censuses, and the National Household Surveys of the 1970s and 1980s. As a result, they documented glaring disparities in the areas of health, income, and education between whites, who make up approximately 54 percent of the population, and African Brazilians, who make up approximately 46 percent.[20] Analysis of the 1980 census data indicate that in terms of overall socioeconomic stratification, the racial divide is primarily located between whites and African Brazilians including mulattoes and blacks.

It is true that rates of intermarriage and residential integration between multiracial individuals and whites are higher than between whites and blacks.[21] In addition, mulattoes have been able to enter the primary occupational tier as schoolteachers, journalists, artists, clerks, or low-level officials in municipal government and tax offices, and get promoted more easily. They also earn 42 percent more than their black counterparts. These wage differentials persist among *pretos*, *pardos*, and *brancos*, even when controlling for education and job experience. The multiracial population remains disproportionately concentrated in the secondary labor force (including agricultural, industrial workers, service employees, day laborers, and domestic servants), or in the ranks of the underemployed and unemployed. These factors hamper and erode their ability to pass on their achieved status from generation to generation. Racial inequalities in employment and earnings indicate that African Brazilians achieved lower financial returns than whites on their investments in education, particularly at higher educational levels. In addition, African Brazilians have a lesser chance of even entering and staying in a university and have higher rates of infant mortality and a greater risk of going to prison.[22]

These findings highlight the primacy of race apart from culture or class, in determining social inequality. The presence of African ancestry in one's genealogy and/or some phenotypically African traits does not preclude a self-identification or social designation as white. Consequently, the credentials distinguishing someone who is white from someone who is multiracial are ambiguous. If the achievements of individual African Brazilians can be pointed to as examples of meritocracy in action, they also help divert attention from the fact that black and multiracial individuals collectively speaking, not only have a more difficult time breaking out of the proletariat, but also suffer increasing disadvantages as their vertical class mobility increases. African Brazilians are handicapped by the cumulative disadvantages of previous, as well as persistent racial discrimination.

Accordingly, the 1988 Constitution, for the first time in Brazilian history, outlawed racism, declaring that "the practice of racism constitutes a crime that is unbailable and without statute of limitation and is subject to imprisonment according to the law."[23] However, the antiracist article in the Constitution, like the Affonso Arinos Law of 1951 (which outlawed racial discrimination in public accommodations), was more rhetoric than a societal commitment. Civil rights attorneys have frequently found it difficult to establish a legal basis for their criminal complaints even with the passage in 1989 of the necessary constitutional enabling statute—Law 7716—commonly referred to as the Caó Law (Lei Caó).[24]

Although African Brazilians mounted massive public demonstrations against racism during the centennial celebrations in the spring of 1988, a barrage of academic papers and civic ceremonies extolling Brazil's genius in having allegedly liquidated slavery without such upheavals as the Civil War in the United States, largely overshadowed their protests.[25] African Brazilian activists, however, regarded their battle as only in its preliminary stages. Beginning in 1978, one of their prime goals has been to awaken more individuals to the reality of Brazil's racial democracy ideology. Since they have successfully exposed this doctrine as a sinister myth that has translated into inegalitarian integration, or assimilation (Figure 1.b), for a privileged few multiracial individuals (and some rare blacks), who are, thus, coopted into an alliance as "insiders." Simultaneously, it has perpetuated gross inequalities in the areas of education, jobs, income, and health between whites and the African Brazilian masses through inegalitarian pluralism in the manner of de facto, if not de jure, apartheid (Figure 1.f).[26]

Black Identity and the Decennial Census

The black movement has sought to bring about social structural change by challenging institutions, policies, and conditions directly and indirectly based on the ternary racial project and the mulatto escape hatch. Activists have sought to forge a "new" African Brazilian identity by contracting the boundaries of racial whiteness and expanding those of racial blackness. Racial formation theory, which examines the ongoing sociohistorical construction and deconstruction of racial categories, makes it possible to analyze these changes and how a society determines racial meanings and assigns racial identities.

At any given spatiotemporal juncture many interpretations of race exist in the form of "racial projects." Every racial project is a discursive or cultural initiative. This involves an interpretation, representation, or explanation of racial dynamics by means of identity politics in order to rescue racial identities from their distortion and erasure by the dominant society. At the same time, each racial project is a political initiative. Its goal is to organize and redistribute resources, a process in which the state is often called upon to play a significant role.

The racial state and its institutions are the site of collective demands both for egalitarian reforms and for the enforcement of existing inegalitarian privileges. Yet rather than serve one coordinated racial objective, state institutions often work at cross-purposes, a condition of institutional competition and conflict within the state that is only exacerbated when the social changes set in motion by oppositional projects threaten to disrupt the racial equilibrium. The need to establish a new equilibrium thus becomes paramount and is achieved through a process of conflict and compromise between the racial state and racially based opposition.[27]

The black movement's cultural initiative is an explanation of racial dynamics by means of identity politics; its political initiative is most evident in appeals for changes in official racial classifications, as in the census, and the collection of racial data. As part of their strategy for achieving this goal, activists have called upon the state to implement a *negro* identifier in the federal standard for collecting and presenting data on race as in the census. By questioning the legitimacy of and demanding changes in extant racial categories, activists have forced recognition and discussion of the state's role in not only buttressing certain ideas about race and displacing others but also maintaining racial categories and the formation of identities.

In 1980, based on an analysis of the 1976 Household Survey (PNAD) and 1980 census, and responding to demands and recommendations by activists and social scientists, the Brazilian Institute of Geography and Statistics (IBGE), began documenting the social inequities between whites (*brancos*) and the African Brazilians masses (*negros*) when it began analyzing and publishing racial data in binary, rather than ternary, form.[28] This change in procedure was no doubt a response in part to demands made by African Brazilian activists and by the new generation of social scientists. It actually had broader implications. Previously, the IBGE had advanced policy decisions to serve the national project aimed at unifying Brazil's three parent racial groups—European, African, and Native American—to project a more integrated, albeit whiter, national image. Although the IBGE had not abandoned the traditional three-category concept of color (or four, if including *amarelos*, individuals of Asian ancestry) in the actual collecting of data, it had moved toward a conceptualization of Brazilian race relations similar to the United States binary racial project. Both the *preto* and *pardo* populations were combined as a single nonwhite racial group. Activists have placed a great deal of emphasis on these data, as it confirms their argument that the socioeconomic status of *pretos* and *pardos* is similar.[29]

Beginning in 1990, the black movement began concentrating on changing procedures for collecting official data on race-particularly on the decennial census. Activists argued that the tendency of individuals to identify themselves on previous surveys with a lighter color (racial) category than their "actual" phenotype might warrant has led to a "distortion" of racial demographics. Blacks numerically have lost much and gained nothing; multiracial individuals have gained more than they have lost, and whites have made substantial gains.[30]

The black movement has focused much attention on census and other survey data not only to emphasize that *pretos* and *pardos* have a similar socioeconomic status, but also to identify its constituency as a numerical majority. Individuals who identify themselves as *preto* on the census have never surpassed 10 percent of the population. If this 10 percent is combined with the roughly 42 percent who identify as *pardo*, the total surpasses 50 percent. Activists have very strong feelings about this fact, and in much of movement discourse and writing they employ an expanded definition of blackness that relies on African ancestry, claiming that the percentage of African Brazilians ranges from 50 to as high as 80 percent.[31]

The black movement was unsuccessful in getting IBGE to use *negro* as an official overarching term in collecting data on the 1990 census. Activists hoped that African Brazilians would identify with the concept *negro* to such an extent that census officials would be forced to make this change by the year 2000 census. The IBGE considered retaining the term *pardo* with a sub-option that would allow Brazilians to acknowledge African ancestry. *Branco, preto, amarelo*, and *Indígena* (Native American) would be retained. Traditionally, the Native American population was listed under the color category *pardo*, which essentially translates as "brown." However, beginning with 1990 census "Indigenous" appeared as a separate racial category.[32]

More important, Brazil's President Henrique Cardoso called upon the IBGE to continue its policy of grouping *pretos* and *pardos* together. This grouping would not appear in the actual tabulations but rather, would be used for the purposes of certain statistical work (e.g., some of the cross-tabulations on work income, education, etc).[33] In other words, the IBGE would continue to count by four separate categories, but for the purposes of public presentation and certain statistical work, the relevant categories would be "white," and "non-white," if not *negro* and *branco*. There was little likelihood that the IBGE would adopt *negro* as the all-encompassing term that black activists sought. The term carries a particular political connotation that the state was not willing to advance. The state's action reflected a policy of "insulation" that confined activists' concerns to an area that is, if not completely symbolic, at least not central to operating the racial order.[34]

Color data for the 1991 census (released in 1995) were consistent with previous censuses, which indicate a progressive decline in the percentage of individuals identifying as *preto* and *branco*. The percentage of Brazilians identified as white, however, still remained more than half of the population (52 percent), whereas those who identified as *preto* decreased slightly from 5.9 percent in 1980 to 5 percent. The percentage of individuals identifying as *pardo* increased from 38.8 percent in 1980 to 42 percent in 1991. These data are in keeping with previous trends. Neither the lack of significant change in 1991 census data nor the failure to persuade the Census Bureau to use *negro* as an official designator on the census weakened activists' resolve in pursuing their campaign goals for the 2000 census. As was the case in 1991, activists were unsuccessful in getting the term *negro* added to the 2000 census. The 2000 census figures indicate that 6.2 percent of the respondents identified as *preto*, which is a slight increase over the 5 percent on the 1991 census. At the same time, there was a decrease in the number of individuals who were identified as *pardo* (42.6 percent in 1991 to 39.1 percent in 2000). The census indicates that the majority of Brazilians (53.7 percent) still identified as *branco*, 39.1 percent identify as *pardo*, 6.2 percent as *preto*, 0.5 percent as *amarelo*, and 0.4 percent as *Indígena*.[35]

If the small increase in the numbers of *pretos* on the 2000 census can be attributed to the census campaign, the black movement nonetheless has a difficult task of consolidating its actual and potential constituents into a politically conscious collective subjectivity. Claims of representing an African Brazilian majority (or a large plurality) based on census data and actually mobilizing individuals into a collective subjectivity as *negros* are entirely separate, if related, tasks. The black movement will need to convince vast numbers of individuals who self-identify as *pardo* (or even as *brancos*) to view themselves as part of a larger African Brazilian (*negro*) constituency, or even as partners in a common cause with blacks. The movement's calculated African Brazilian (*negro*) majority of approximately 73 million people (half of Brazil's population), which it claims as its constituency, remain an abstraction that exists only on paper. The full social, economic, and political import of regarding Brazil as a nation with an African Brazilian majority or sizable plurality has not yet registered in the public consciousness.[36]

A "New" African Brazilian Identity: Closing the Escape Hatch

Given that racial formation in Brazil exists on a continuum, which has historically supported the racial democracy ideology, activists have faced the challenge of implementing cultural (or discursive) initiatives aimed at mobilizing blacks (*pretos*) and mulattoes (*pardos*) under a politicized identity as African Brazilian (*negro*). Since the 1970s, a major portion of the black movement's energy has thus been devoted to overcoming the secondary color divide between *pardos* and *pretos* associated with Brazil's colonial past. The goal has been to integrate them into a racial plurality as *negros* by reinforcing the primary racial divide between *negros* and *brancos*. Their tactic for achieving this goal has been to shift focus away from the color designations of *pardo* and *preto* and instead, sensitize individuals to the idea of ethno-racial origins (i.e. African ancestry) and assign positive value to the term *negro*.[37]

Accordingly, activists have rearticulated a "new" African Brazilian identity based on the dichotomization of whiteness and blackness as two distinct categories of experience (or more specifically, that expands the boundaries of blackness and contract those of whiteness) to dismantle the hierarchical relationship of whiteness over blackness. Many activists believe that the United States one-drop rule and binary racial project should be adopted in Brazil as a form of "strategic essentialism."[38] This tactic so the thinking goes would enable the mass mobilization of African Brazilians, just as it has mobilized African Americans. Activists believe that the absence in Brazil of the original negative factor of legal discrimination typified by the United States, which was buttressed by the one-drop rule, along with pervasive miscegenation, and the greater fluidity and ambiguity of racial identities and markers, have resulted in a less unified voice against the brutalities of racial discrimination and undermined the social progress of African Brazilians collectively.[39]

The gains of the 1970s and 1980s provided the diverse institutional and cultural terrain upon which more radical oppositional political projects could be built. Compared to previous strategies, group pluralism is considered more as a strategy for dismantling (rather than fulfilling) the national ideology of racial democracy as well as a means of recognizing and maintaining a distinct African Brazilian racial and cultural plurality. Pluralism is now considered an integral and legitimate aspect of the Brazilian racial order, compared with the traditional image of integration. Activists have sought to contract the boundaries of whiteness and break its association with both miscegenation and national identity. Activists do not consider Brazil to be a racially and culturally integrated (i.e., whiter) society, but rather composed of distinct pluralities of racial and ethnic groups. They envision a mosaic of mutually respectful and differentiated, if not mutually exclusive, African Brazilian and European Brazilian racial and cultural centers of reference. Contemporary strategies of resistance, much as previous ones, seek to achieve structural integration of African Brazilians as equals into the racial order in terms of occupation, income, education, political representation, etc. Both whites and blacks would have equal access to all aspects of the public sphere, with the option of integrating in the private sphere. In this case, the selective pattern would be voluntary, rather than mandated by whites, such that if and when African Brazilians choose to integrate, they do so as equals.[40]

Activists frequently complain that the African Brazilian masses are not receptive to their message of positive black identity and mobilization against racism, which is often attributed to the latter's ambiguous or vague awareness of racial identity and racial prejudice. Anthropologist John Burdick found in interviews conducted since the 1990s that most "lifelong black" informants had no difficulty identifying racial prejudice. Self-identified *negros* who express sympathy for fighting discrimination and valorizing an African Brazilian identity, but who view the objective of building a unified African Brazilian identity as personally less appealing may see little benefit in "assuming blackness," which they consider to be of greater concern for the identity ambiguities of elite (often lighter-skinned) African Brazilians. They often accuse the latter of being more concerned about reclaiming an identity that may have been lost in the journey through the escape hatch, than with addressing the everyday problems of racism faced by people without such identity ambiguities. Burdick acknowledges that this claim is deeply polemical. He suggests that there is a relatively large and untapped constituency of movement sympathizers; to politically reenroll these individuals may require overcoming ideological barriers *within* the black movement itself. At present it seems unlikely that large numbers of individuals will actually join African Brazilian political organizations, though many appear more willing to embrace the idea of a distinct African Brazilian culture and experience.[41]

From Racial Denial to Racial Affirmation

Beginning in the 1990s, there was increased discussion of compensatory measures like affirmative action. Since then, state agencies have announced affirmative action policies. Some entities, including several ministries and universities, have established percentages (or quotas) of positions that must be reserved for African Brazilians; the Foreign Ministry followed suit. This is a radical shift in policy, considering that Brazil's diplomatic corps has historically been overwhelmingly, if not totally, white. The Foreign Ministry's affirmative action program, which began in early 2003, makes annual scholarships available to twenty African Brazilian candidates to assist them in studying for the public service entrance exam. None of these changes were accompanied by the necessary federal legislation and implementation of public policy to achieve political, economic, and social redistribution.[42]

The implementation of affirmative action in Brazil is complicated by the fact that only a few agencies have historically tracked race or color. This situation is compounded by the absence of a clearly defined racial (or color) category, along with the uneven geographical distribution according to race within Brazil (itself giving rise to regional nuances in the way race is conceptualized). Critics also argue that racial "quotas" have no place in a multiracial society like Brazil. Opponents of race-based affirmative action argue that the most egregious racial inequalities could be reversed with class-based policies aimed at eradicating poverty. They argue that policies supporting mass education, basic sanitation, universal medical and dental care, affordable housing, basic infrastructure, increased employment, land distribution, and the civic participation of the poor would proportionally benefit more African Brazilians than whites given that most of the former are poor.[43]

In the wake of the U.N. World Conference on Racism, held in Durban, South Africa (August–September 2001), Brazilian state officials acknowledged that the primary source of persistent inequality in Brazil is racial discrimination. Following the Durban Conference, Rio de Janeiro State University (UERJ) and the Northern Fluminense State University (UENF), two of Brazil's largest and most prestigious centers of higher learning, became the first public institutions to comply with October 2, 2001 legislation in the state of Rio de Janeiro requiring universities to reserve a 40 percent quota for African Brazilians in its 2003 entering class.[44] This figure corresponded to the fact that approximately 45 percent of Brazil's 175 million people consider themselves African Brazilian (black and mulatto). The legislation mandated a 50 percent quota for graduates from public secondary schools (as well as 10 percent for students with physical disabilities or special needs). The average Brazilian attends public secondary schools, which are overcrowded, underfunded, and significantly inferior to the private schools, where middle class, wealthy (and overwhelmingly white) Brazilians send their children. Brazil's government-operated universities are among the most prestigious in Latin America and are the training ground for the corporate and political elite. They are also the bastion of the white and affluent: less than one student in five is African Brazilian.[45]

College admission is highly competitive, with many more applicants than places available, especially for the prominent public universities. The notorious *vestibular,* or college entrance exam, has become the arbiter for admission. According to some, this exam is a "democratic victory" that represents a noteworthy exception to the pervasive habit of gaining entry into the elite through one's social connections. Critics consider the *vestibular* to be a "game played with marked cards."[46] Students who attend private schools have an unfair advantage because they are better prepared to score well.[47] Of the 1.4 million students admitted to universities each year, only 3 percent have typically identified as African Brazilian and only 18 percent have come from public schools, where most African Brazilians are enrolled.[48] The implementation of affirmative action has effectively doubled (in some cases tripled) the enrollment of black and multiracial students in elite professional schools such as law, engineering, and medicine at UERJ.[49]

Although these policies have stimulated a national debate about racial inequality and encouraged more working-class students to apply, it has had ambiguous results and is proving to be an awkward solution to a complex problem. One caveat is that affluent African Brazilians and graduates of the few elite state high schools have been the primary beneficiaries of affirmative action. For example, only 243 (or 5 percent) of Rio de Janeiro State University's entering class of 4,970 black and multiracial students were admitted solely to meet racial quotas. The majority of African Brazilians had the test scores to be admitted anyway.[50] These individuals were able to pay for private high schools. In fact, one-third of the African Brazilians admitted had household incomes of about 2,000 *reais* (or approximately US $800) a month—at least ten times the minimum wage.[51] In order to rectify this problem and address the concerns of poor African Brazilians, state legislators are recommending that students who benefit from racial quotas also be required to prove their families earn no more than 300 *reais* a month—approximately US $100.[52]

The Ministry of Education, together with the Special Secretariat for the Promotion of Racial Equality, has been preparing guidelines on affirmative action for all public universities. Although the prospects for affirmative action in higher education appear promising, African Brazilian leaders acknowledge that other obstacles remain. In addition, some critics have expressed concerns about the noticeable change in student test scores since the implementation of affirmative action. The average score for individuals admitted into UERJ law school in 2002 was nearly 81 percent. According to university admissions officials, the average score was 64 percent under the quota system, which many interpret as a lowering of academic standards. Supporters of affirmative action counter that racial quotas are not the problem. Rather, the focus should be on improving the schools at every level and increasing employment opportunities.[53]

The quotas at UERJ were themselves controversial in that some critics argued that the 40 percent for African Brazilian students overlapped with the 50 percent for students from public secondary schools where African Brazilians are the majority. Many argue that the ceiling should be set at 20 percent, at least for the moment. Others contend that quotas should vary from state to state and be based on the percentage of the population that is black or multiracial.[54]

By 2003, Brazil's nascent affirmative action programs, much like those in the United States, had provoked a backlash from white students who worked hard and prepared themselves for college admissions, only to be rejected despite scoring higher on the entrance examination.[55] Indeed, the press reported that the administrations of these universities were already preparing to deal with possible lawsuits by white students who considered themselves jeopardized by the quota system, which in fact occurred on a broad scale during the subsequent months. As in the United States, they have challenged affirmative action in the courts. Brazil's racial quotas brought a flurry of lawsuits from some three hundred white students who won injunctions,[56] claiming they were being discriminated against and denied "equality of access to schooling guaranteed by Brazil's 1988 Constitution."[57] The controversy surrounding the quotas culminated in a constitutional challenge that reached Brazil's federal Supreme Court.[58]

Civil rights advocates predict that the debate will intensify and become more acrimonious if the sweeping Racial Equality Statute now before Congress is passed. This legislation, which is being met with resistance in the Senate,[59] recommends a 20 percent quota for African Brazilians in government jobs and public universities, enterprises with more than twenty employees, and actors in television programming, including soap operas and commercials. In addition, 30 percent of political party candidates must be African Brazilians.[60] Critics argue, however, that affirmative action is a solution imported from the United States—where racial definitions and relations are quite different—and therefore will exacerbate rather than ameliorate the situation in Brazil. Other opponents argue that conditions for African Brazilians will improve as poverty is gradually eliminated. Supporters respond that racial quotas are a legitimate means of expanding educational and other opportunities for African Brazilians, despite the imperfections.[61] Many observers believed the Brazilian Supreme Court, which began deliberating the constitutionality of racial quotas and a dispute by preparatory schools that the university quotas favor public schools, would determine the ultimate outcome of these developments.

Considering its reputation for caution and middle-of-the-road approaches, the high court was expected to give a moderate endorsement to racial preferences.[62] Some critics of racial quotas have evoked the U.S. Supreme Court's 1978 ruling in *Bakke* and 2003 verdicts in the University of Michigan cases, which permitted race to be considered as one factor in the admissions process but prohibited explicit quotas and point systems.[63] Afirmative action has been the most contested aspect of racial (and gender) politics because it has frequently been interpreted to mean quotas rather than target goals.[64] In Brazil, this interpretation can be attributed in part to the U.S. and global media, as well as public perceptions that often erroneously frame U.S. affirmative action policies as quotas. The history of the U.S. Supreme Court's affirmative rulings could provide Brazilians with a template for their own programs. Seeking to take advantage of U.S. expertise in affirmative action, the Ford Foundation in August 2003 arranged for a group of U.S. attorneys to visit Brazil. The visit by U.S. attorneys not only advanced the cause of Brazilian antidiscrimination groups but also resulted in the formation of the Affirmative Action Expert Group, which is an international network of attorneys, seeking to combat discrimination throughout Latin America.[65]

The university itself circumvented the possibility of a Supreme Court decision in the State University of Rio de Janeiro cases that would set a strong precedent supporting affirmative action. It proposed a new law to the Rio de Janeiro State Assembly that was approved in August 2003, in time to be implemented for the 2004 entrance exam. This statute halved the university's quotas to 20 percent for African Brazilians, 20 percent for public-school students, and 5 percent for students with physical disabilities as well as students of indigenous background. These changes in state law at least rendered the initial challenges null and void although the reduced quotas have also been challenged in the state court.[66]

Educators remain undaunted in their support of affirmative action. The Federal University of Brasília has adopted a 20 percent quota for African Brazilians.[67] The State University of Minas Gerais and Federal University of Bahia (UFBA) have also supported quotas. The University Council at UFBA, which is composed of administration, faculty, and students, voted to reserve 45 percent of the openings in various fields of study for students from Bahia's public schools, which are attended by the majority of the state's overwhelmingly African Brazilian population. According to the UFBA plan, 36 percent of slots would be reserved for African Brazilians, 2 percent for Native Americans, and the remaining 7 percent for other nonwhites who attend public schools.[68]

Affirmative action is not yet normative as social policy and support for these practices has grown considerably since Brazil's former president Cardoso introduced goals for the development and implementation of such policies. African Brazilian leaders now consider affirmative action an indispensable corrective to racial discrimination. These policies have gained considerable support in terms of university admissions, government employment, and public contracts, and perhaps eventually in private companies. Three federal ministries recently introduced quotas of 20 percent for African Brazilians in senior jobs. A few cities in the state of São Paulo have introduced racial quotas in the past several years. The city of São Paulo has recommended holding 30 percent of city jobs for *pretos* and *pardos*.[69]

As the idea of affirmative action has spread, many sympathetic whites have grown uneasy. Some propose a broader affirmative action program, including scholarships and subsidized pre-*vestibular* courses for African Brazilians and poor whites.[70] What is transpiring in Brazil, however, is not simply a dialogue about the merits of affirmative action. The current debate is reflective of a broader discourse on inequality, race, and what social debt, if any, the nation owes to African Brazilians. More important, it is indicative of a rearticulation of

African Brazilian collective identity (as well as Brazilian national identity) grounded in a positive valuation of blackness.[71] The ideology of whitening and the aesthetic bias attached to European physical appearance, although challenged and somewhat attenuated by the black movement, continues to permeate Brazilian mass culture and holds sway over the public imagination in determining an individual's perceived worth.[72]

Brazil is reexamining its image as a racial democracy. For many Brazilians, the nation's history of racial and cultural blending, which has sustained the racial democracy ideology, continues to be held in high esteem. Nevertheless, the affirmative action debate has forced the nation to acknowledge the existence of racial discrimination and exclusion. Many supporters of affirmative action believe that Brazil is a living refutation of any notion that racial intermarriage and multiracial offspring decreases or eliminates racism.[73] The question of formulating precise definitions of racial categories, which is pivotal to affirmative action, has been perplexing for Brazilian policymakers. Such a question challenges Brazilian racial thinking, considering that the overwhelming majority of Brazil's population of 175 million has some African ancestry— whether or not they acknowledge or identify with it.[74]

A "New" Multiracial Identity: The Multiracial Movement

The black movement defines as African Brazilian (or *negro*) anyone of African ancestry and requires de facto that active participants in political organizations identify themselves as such. This in turn has resulted in a strong ideological rejection of terminology referring to racially intermediate phenotypes and experiences. Burdick has noted that in political gatherings black movement participants have been chastised when they inadvertently use one of the intermediate terms (e.g., *mestiço*, *mulato*).[75] Given the programmatic effort to prevent the formation of a radical African Brazilian subjectivity, the strengths of the movement's identity politics are undeniable: the fostering of pride, group solidarity, and self-respect. There can be no denying that the one-drop rule was implemented to deny equality to African Americans, but also had the unintended consequence of forging group identity accordingly. This, in turn, enabled African Americans to organize and eventually culminated in the civil rights movement of the 1950s and 1960s, which dismantled Jim Crow segregation and achieved the passage of historic legislation that dissolved legal racial discrimination and inequality.[76]

An African Brazilian identifier such as *negro* that combines *pretos* and *pardos* into a single statistical category, whether for the purposes of collecting, analyzing, tabulating, or publishing data is a logical step in the pursuit of a genuine racial democracy. As long as public policy deems it necessary to collect racial data, particularly as a means of tracking Brazil's progress in achieving social equity; this has the potential to change social attitudes and alleviate the social oppression imbedded in traditional methods of data collection, which have supported Brazil's ternary racial project and the mulatto escape hatch.

Many individuals such as social anthropologists Peter Fry and Yvonne Maggie, along with some journalists such as Ali Kamel and Antonio Risério, have given stringent warnings about the real dangers of forcing binary racial thinking on Brazilian racial formation. They argue that the imposition of racial categories and definitions, particularly the effectiveness of any definition that relies on ancestry premised on the one-drop rule, poses serious logistical problems, and is inherently fraught with irreconcilable contradictions when applied to the Brazilian terrain.[77] African ancestry (not to mention African phenotypical traits) is widespread throughout the entire population, including among large numbers of self-identified and socially designated whites. French thinkers, Bourdieu and Wacquant, who considered the formulation of the "new" African Brazilian identity and related racial projects as the product of a "cultural imperialism," voiced similar criticism.[78] Accordingly, racial categories and strategies specific to a given context (i.e., the United States) are transformed into supposedly "natural, universal, and true" ones that are imposed on and made applicable to any and all situations, including that of Brazil, which perpetuates a situation of "symbolic violence."[79]

The black movement's opposition to the perpetuation of a multiracial identity, or rather, opposition to acknowledging the potentially legitimate differences between the experience, and therefore, identities of black and multiracial individuals, perpetuates a rather pernicious racial essentialism premised on the belief that these differences are inherently invidious distinctions. A multiracial identity is viewed as being not only antithetical but also inimical to the goal of forging African Brazilians into a cohesive political force. By focusing primarily on eradicating a multiracial identification, or absorbing it into a singular egalitarian African Brazilian identity, activists have overlooked, or outright rejected, the possibility of a multiracial identity formulated on egalitarian or antiracist premises.[80] This precludes the exploration of new possibilities for critiquing the pathologies of racism.

Ultimately, this may also keep at bay individuals who are sympathetic to the aims of the black movement, who genuinely wish to valorize their African slave ancestry, and unequivocally acknowledge they are the descendents of slaves, but who honestly cannot translate these sentiments into adopting *negro* as an appropriate means of self-identification. Some researchers suggest that disconnection from the term *negro* may originate in the awareness that their social experiences have been qualitatively different from those darker-skinned African-descent Brazilians. It is unclear as to whether the term *negro* can include individuals who generally would be considered "phenotypically white," but who have African ancestry and choose to identify as African Brazilian. It also remains to be seen whether individuals who previously self-identified and were designated as mulattoes or whites are fully welcomed as newly self-identified or "assumed blacks" (*negros assumidos*). Although self-definition is supposedly used to determine racial identification, some tension has arisen over who is "authentically" *negro* or African Brazilian.[81]

Part of the struggle for a radical black subjectivity should include finding ways of constructing self and identity that oppose reifying "the blackness that whiteness created."[82] This effort must be grounded in a decolonization process that challenges the perpetuation of racial essentialism and the reinscription of notions of authentic identity.This requires the recognition of the multiple experiences of African-descent identity rooted in the lived conditions that make diverse identities and cultural productions possible.[83] A "new" multiracial identity, rather than imploding African Brazilian identity, could potentially forge a more inclusive blackness and whiteness. This in turn would provide the basis for a "strategic antiessentialism"[84] that would accommodate the varieties of African Brazilian subjectivity without negating a larger African Brazilian group, or recreating that group as the complete antithesis of whiteness.[85]

As part of the goal of furthering this development, the multiracial movement (O Movimento Pardo-Mestiço), established in 2001 in Manaus, Amazonas, has begun to mobilize to challenge the imposition of a binary racial project in Brazil. According to multiracial movement president Jerson César Leão Alves, the goal is to support and rearticulate the historical process of racial blending (*mestiçagem*) that has characterized the Brazilian people and affirm the right of individuals and the nation by extension to identify as "multiracial" (*mestiço*).[86]

By 2007, the focus was on gaining official recognition of a Day of Multiraciality or Mixed-Race Day (Dia do Mestiço) in celebration of this racial blending. The Dia do Mestiço, which has been officially recognized at the municipal and state levels in several locales, occurs three days after the Day of the Caboclo (Dia do Caboclo), the *caboclo* (individuals of Native American and European descent) being the first multiracial individual to emerge in the colonial era.[87] The June 27 date, which was selected to commemorate this event, is a reference to the twenty-seven multiracial representatives elected during the 1st Conference for the Promotion of Racial Equality, which was held in the city of Manaus, Amazonas from April 7–9, 2005. It also refers to the month in which a multiracial woman, after systematic opposition from anti-multiracial organizations, was registered as the only multiracial representative at the 1st National Conference for the Promotion of Racial Equality, which occurred in Brasilia, from June 30–July 2, 2005.[88]

Many black movement activists and supporters have expressed vocal and sometimes aggressive antagonism toward this "new" expression of multiraciality in the form of "multiracialphobia" ("mestiçofobia") or "antimultiracial racism" ("racismo antimestiço"), which many multiracial activists argue is legitimated and abetted by the racial state. During a session of the General Committee convened by the Chamber of Deputies in Brasília on November 26, 2007 to discuss the Statute of Racial Equality, activist Alves responded to this enmity, and also criticized the legislation—particularly what he considered its erasure of or discrimination against multiracial individuals.[89] At the same hearing, Elda Castro de Sá, who represented the Association of Caboclos and River Peoples of the Amazon (Associação dos Caboclos e Ribeirinhos da Amazônia), voiced similar concerns, considering that a significant portion of the multiracial population in the Amazon region is predominantly of Native American and European descent.

Both Alves and Sá stressed the importance of addressing black racial inequality and the importance of respecting a black identity. They argued this should neither be achieved at the expense of multiracial-identified individuals nor does it justify disregarding their grievances in the pursuit of racial equality. Also, the multiracial movement has campaigned to get the IBGE to replace the color term *pardo* with the racial designator *mestiço* in the collection of official data as in the decennial census. The spirit of the campaign is captured in the slogan "Bring back MULTIRACIAL to the census of the IBGE" ("Coloque de volta MESTIÇO no censo do IBGE"). This is a reference to the fact that the 1890 census, unlike previous censuses, used the term *mestiço*. However, subsequent censuses replaced that term with *pardo* reflecting a return to previous terminology.[90]

"The Molecular Portrait of Brazil"

Despite this opposition, the "new" multiracial phenomenon has gained legitimacy from the current preeminence of research in the "new genetics," particularly the sequencing of parts of mitochondrial DNA, the Y chromosome, and nuclear DNA, which sheds light on the "genetic origins" of Brazilians.[91] The findings of the studies conducted in Brazil, known as "Retrato Molecular do Brazil" ("Molecular Portrait of Brazil),") were published in 2000. The study almost coincided with the 2003 publication in the United States and Europe (with further analysis still being published) of the initial conclusions of one of the largest and most international projects in modern science, the Human Genome Project (HGP) and the companion research of the Human Genome Diversity Project (HGDP). The original HGP project began in 1991 with the goal of not only determining more than 3 billion base pairs of nucleotides linked together in a specific order along the chromosomes in the human genome but also identifying all the genes in this vast amount of data. This latter part of the project is still ongoing, although a preliminary count indicates the human genome is composed of approximately 30,000 genes.[92]

At the molecular level, roughly 99.9 percent of genetic information is identical from individual to individual. However, approximately 0.1% of the 3 billion bases of human DNA (an estimated 10 million) are locations of common genetic variations called single nucleotide polymorphisms, or SNP's. SNP's are small gene variations that differ from individual to individual (and make individuals more prone to certain diseases, as well as determine how people react to drugs). Still, SNP's tend to occur in different patterns in different populations and are typically inherited in clusters called haplotype blocks. Like SNP's, varieties of haplotype blocks occur at different frequencies in different regions of the world, which has enabled population geneticists to reconstruct the history of human migration. Of all polymorphisms, only a small percentage is different as a function of ancestry and these are called AIM's (Ancestry

Informative Markers). AIM's are specific genetic polymorphisms that carry information about population structure, inter- and intra-individual diversity and the history of the human species. While SNP patterns do not reveal anything about the function of the genes, they can provide information about an individual's continent(s) of ancestry and, by extension, about pathways of migration throughout human history.[93]

Elucidating the significance and mapping the location of these phenomena has become a key focus of the "new" genetics. Mapping, among other things, can measure the blending of ancestral backgrounds within individuals, that is to say, Bio-Geographical Ancestry ("BGA"). This phenomenon was examined in a study entitled the "Molecular Portrait of Brazil" ("Retrato Molecular do Brasil"), which was coordinated by geneticist Sérgio Pena at the Universidade Federal de Minas Gerais (UFMG). By sequencing portions of mitochondrial DNA and the Y chromosome, geneticists sought to map the geographical distribution and patterns of the Brazilian population's respectively matrilineal and patrilineal ancestry, with a particular focus on the social and demographic reality of miscegenation. One of the objectives was to engage social scientists in a dialogue on genetics. Part of this strategy involved making references to some of the classical Brazilian anthropologist, sociologists, and historians (e.g., Gilberto Freyre, Darcy Ribeiro, and Sérgio Buarque de Holanda). And, this tactic did succeed in attracting considerable interest from social scientists, which is rather atypical for genetic and biological research.[94]

For logistical and theoretical reasons, Pena and his colleagues chose to examine a sample of 200 men who classified themselves as white.[95] The primary reason given for this exclusive focus on whites was based on IBGE data, which indicated that self-identified whites constitute more than half (51.6 percent) of Brazil's population. Furthermore, there are already several genetic studies on the proportion of European ancestry among African Brazilians but no comparable analyses of the presence of Native and African ancestry in the white population. The DNA sample was selected at random among university students and patients who submitted to paternity studies, primarily from the middle and upper-middle class. These participants, who had obtained education and higher socioeconomic, were encouraged to declare their color/race in contexts (paternity clinics and university laboratories) that are predominantly frequented by elite whites. The individuals were selected from four of Brazil's five sociopolitical and geographic regions (North, Northeast, Southeast, and South).[96] In addition to the main sample of 200 individuals, the study also included for purposes of comparison an analysis of DNA from a set of "white rural workers" from a poor region in the northern Minas Gerais state (the Jequitinhonha Valley). Parra and his colleagues studied this sample in greater detail. Alves-Silva and his team of researchers provided important additional information on the principal sample, which is to say that, "37 individuals were students or staff from our laboratory."[97]

In the investigation into Y chromosome DNA polymorphisms, the overwhelming majority of markers were of European origin. A very small percentage was of sub-Saharan African origin and none was of Native American origin.[98] Meanwhile, the results of the mitochondrial DNA analyses presented a more complex picture composed of 33% Native American and 28% African markers. This essentially indicates that the majority (approximately 60 percent) of matrilineal ancestry among the white Brazilian male participants is of Native American or African descent, which was higher than might have been expected.[99] These patterns corroborate the racial and sexual demographics of the colonization of Brazil beginning in the sixteenth century. The shortage of European women and the preponderance of single men meant that the latter necessarily formed sexual unions with Native American and later African women, in the form of rape, fleeting extramarital relations, as well as extended concubinage and common-law relationships.

The first article from the "Molecular Portrait of Brazil" was published in Portuguese in 2000 in the popular monthly science magazine *Ciência Hoje* (*Science Today*). Two related articles containing a detailed presentation of the findings for the scientific community were published in the *American Journal of Human Genetics* (AJHG).[100] Another article was published later in the *Proceedings of the National Academy of Sciences of the United States* (PNAS). In the two articles published in the AJHG the geneticists focused primarily on molecular genetics and phylogeographic aspects of their findings. In the *Ciência Hoje* article they made a bolder proposition. They were very careful to point out that Brazil is clearly not the racial democracy it has historically touted. However, they also argued that if the many whites who have Native American and African mitochondrial DNA became aware of this fact, they would perhaps be more inclined to value the genetic diversity of Brazilians and correspondingly become more engaged in the antiracist struggle.[101]

Not surprisingly, the "Molecular Portrait of Brazil" has sparked heated debate among biologists, social scientists, as well as social movement and other actors well beyond the academy. Many individuals have received the research with great enthusiasm. Some consider the report conclusive evidence of genetics' potential in reconstructing the biological history of the Brazilian people. Journalist Elio Gaspari wrote that "it provides scientific evidence of what Gilberto Freyre formulated in sociological terms," referring to the pervasiveness of miscegenation in Brazil.[102] Others, particularly African Brazilian activists, have greeted the research findings with great skepticism and caution and in extreme cases with alarm and blatant hostility.

Athayde Motta, for example, has been highly critical of the geneticists' work.[103] Motta's criticisms have focused on the similarities between the "Molecular Portrait of Brazil" and interpretations of Brazilian history, culture, and society—particularly the writings of Gilberto Freyre—that are regarded as erroneous, outdated, and conservative. Motta points out that the rather unlimited potential for manipulation of the research is the fault of neither the researchers nor the research itself.[104] He also acknowledges that the study combines the most sophisticated contemporary technology with good intentions to provide a genetic map of a sample of the population of white Brazilians.[105] Motta argues that the research has the liability of seeming to provide the racial democracy ideology with scientific support and indeed infuses it with new life.[106] Motta believes the "Molecular Portrait of Brazil" merely serves to maintain the racial *status quo* and ultimately mask existing racial inequality as well as assure its continued existence.

Motta[107] and others[108] argue that the antiessentialism stressed by the new genetics, as expressed in the "Molecular Portrait of Brazil" and similar research, does not simply challenge the feasibility of race as a concept. Rather, it also rearticulates a view of miscegenation that dilutes clearly defined racial identities. This in turn undermines the identity politics espoused by the black movement, which is the cornerstone of the collective identities organized to combat racism. Motta particularly expresses alarm about the implications these genetic data will have on affirmative action policies. Geneticist Sérgio Pena himself expressed similar concerns but from a somewhat different perspective. He argued that since there is no "objective basis for the introduction of racial quotas" in Brazil, "the only thing that can be used, and which is subject to many abuses, is self-classification. . . . We have no intention for this index [referring to genomic markers] to be used for individual evaluation. It would be a new form of racism."[109] On another occasion, Pena emphasized that "the definition of who is African Brazilian or African-descended in Brazil will necessarily be resolved in the political arena. From a biological perspective, the question makes no sense."[110]

Although self-classification is mentioned as the criterion to be adopted, in certain contexts the inclusion (or at least an indication) of biological and/or genetic criteria has been apparent. Then-Minister of Agrarian Development Raul Jungmann (2001) under the Cardoso administration spoke in defense of federal affirmative action programs. He stated that in case of doubt as to whether a given individual is African Brazilian or not, the person "can be submitted to tests."[111] The then State Secretary of Science and Technology Wanderley de Souza, a scientist from the field of biomedicine, stated that, "my main difficulty is determining who is black and brown in Brazil."[112] In order to address this concern, Souza announced he would set up a commission, including geneticists, anthropologists, and activists from the black movement, which would be charged with regulating the law.[113] On that occasion, Edna Roland, president of the African Brazilian women's NGO *Fala Preta!* (Speak Out Black Woman) in São Paulo, commented, "I think it is absurd to consult specialists in biology or genetics."[114] Attorney Hédio Silva Júnior, a specialist in race legislation, also voiced opposition to "genetic criterion."[115]

With the actual implementation of affirmative action quotas in Brazil, it is likely that arguments surrounding ancestry based on genetics will be brought into play, whether to strengthen or undermine given positions. On the occasion of the first *vestibular* in January 2003, a genetic argument along the lines of "Molecular Portrait of Brazil" was already making its presence felt (perhaps based on a direct reading of the article or through coverage of the article in the mainstream press). For example, a female applicant, who equivocated as to whether her physical appearance would make her eligible for the quota system, declared, "I have the typical Brazilian blend of DNA: Portuguese, African, and Native American. I was uncertain, but I opted to declare myself brown (*parda*)."[116] No less significant was a provocative statement by José Roberto Pinto de Góes, history professor at the State University of Rio de Janeiro (UERJ) and a vocal critic of the quota system. While he stressed the historical, cultural, and social aspects of the "Africanness" of all Brazilians, his framing of the discussion also transcended questions of national specificity and emphasized the genetic comity of the human species and its African origin: "If you are an applicant in the next admissions exams for UERJ, declare yourself black or brown. It is your right. You will not be lying. You may not know it, but you are also part-African. We're all offspring of Africa, whatever the color of our skin."[117]

Ultimately, the discussions sparked by the "Molecular Portrait of Brazil" challenge "common sense" views espoused by various currents in the social sciences that consider biology (and genetics) as inevitably supportive of deterministic and essentialist principles. Similar criticisms of the concept of race have been in existence for decades. The "Molecular Portrait of Brazil" is a direct descendent of a long influential tradition dating back at least to the first declarations on race drawn up by UNESCO in the 1950s. That pronouncement, which was concomitantly antiessentialist and antiracist, characterized much of the research on the human biology variation throughout the second half of the twentieth century. The findings of the "Molecular Portrait of Brazil" thus reiterate the limited relevance of the race concept in the biological sense and portray Brazilians as not so much immutable essences but rather, the products of extensive blending. This in turn underscores the fluidity, instability, and ill-defined nature of racial categories. In particular, these new bio-historical narratives reinforce a long-standing and deeply rooted social imagination that considers miscegenation a positive and defining element of Brazil's national identity.[118]

Armed with the tools of the new genetics, "Molecular Portrait of Brazil," is waging a pitched battle in defense of an antiessentialism that is at the same time considered deleterious to certain social and political agendas, as well as collective identities and their antiracist albeit essentialist premises, which have been formulated to organize resistance to racial oppression and injustice. Indeed, the discussions of genome research in Brazil are, at their core, debates about identity politics.[119] If the black movement has utilized strategic racial essentialism, which draws implicitly on biological or ancestral reductionism as the basis for cultural initiatives in the form of identity politics, as well as certain political initiatives, then the antiessentialism of the new genetics undermines some of the premises of those initiatives, while also serving to bolster those of the multiracial movement.

Conclusion

During the first half of the twentieth century the Brazilian racial order sustained a national ideology of racial democracy both implicitly and explicitly. By the 1970s and 1980s, the public and political debate increasingly included discussions about the importance of race, quiet apart from questions of class, in determining social stratification. Since the 1990s, there has been a gradual yet unmistakable decline in support of the racial democracy ideology in academic circles, official discourse, as well as national public opinion much of which can be attributed in large part to the efforts of the black movement.[120] State officials—including respectively the previous and present heads of state Henrique Cardoso and Luiz Inácio Lula da Silva—have publicly challenged the racial democracy ideology. Many Brazilians hold on tenaciously to the racial democracy ideology; some consider this ideology an unfilled potential that may be realized in the future; others have cast aside the ideology for a more critical focus on racial inequality. After taking office, President Lula took a number of steps, both practical and symbolic, to stress his commitment to racial equality. His cabinet included four African Brazilians, among them the minister of a newly created secretariat for the promotion of racial equality. Lula appointed the first African Brazilian justice to the Supreme Court.[121] A new statute makes the teaching of African Brazilian history and culture mandatory in the public schools.[122]

Also, attitudes, discourse, behavior, and policy surrounding race and national identity increasingly include references to Brazil's "racial diversity" and "multiculturalism" (egalitarian pluralism) as compared with the traditional reference to its "racial unity" (egalitarian integration), both of which are inextricably intertwined with census categories. The publication of color data in binary form and the debate over census categories, seek to alleviate the social oppression imbedded in traditional methods of data collection, which have supported the ternary racial project and the mulatto escape hatch. This new racial project challenges the ternary racial project and the mulatto escape hatch by contracting the boundaries of whiteness and expanding those of blackness as the basis for the formation of a new African Brazilian identity.

It is clear that this change is moving Brazilian racial discourse in a direction similar to the binary racial project, if not strictly enforcing the one-drop rule, traditionally associated with the United States. This "Anglo-Americanization" of Brazilian racial formation has been accompanied by recommendations for implementing affirmative action and other initiatives similar to those aimed at monitoring and eradicating patterns of racial discrimination in the United States. Whether and to what extent this "binary racial project" will actually lead to a new "binary racial order" in Brazil underpinned by the one-drop rule remains to be seen.

Just as the new African Brazilian identity cannot be equated with the articulation of black identity in the United States, the new multiracial identity in Brazil cannot be equated with previous manifestations of Brazilian multiraciality. The latter originated in a colonial system of exclusion that sought to control the threat of nonwhites to white dominance by allowing multiracial individuals to avoid the full brunt of discriminatory policies. A multiracial identity became a means by which individuals distanced themselves from the stigma of non-whiteness, even if this identity has not conferred upon them white racial privilege. In contrast, the new multiracial identity in Brazil is not a means by which individuals seek to avoid racial stigma or gain racial privilege. As a racial project, the new multiracial identity rearticulates Brazil's ternary racial project, but without the hierarchical valuation of whiteness over blackness that historically gave rise to that identity. This is indicative of an egalitarian dynamic that was at least the rhetoric and espoused premise of the racial democracy ideology if not its actual operationalization.

Part of the struggle for achieving a fully participatory racial democracy in Brazil involves deconstructing the very racial categories and identities that have served as the basis of racism and racial hierarchy in Brazil.[123] Ultimately, both the new African Brazilian identity and new multiracial identity as racial projects are therefore logical steps in the pursuit of this goal, with the potential to change social attitudes. They could initiate a long overdue and "honest" national conversation about the African ancestry shared by the majority of Brazilians, which has been obscured by the whitening ideal. This ideal is the very means by which racist ideology and racial privilege have been perpetuated in Brazil.[124]

These new articulations of racial identities are not inherently immune to larger social forces. Any effort to impose racial categories and definitions— particularly those premised on the one-drop rule—is intrinsically problematic in a racially blended and chromatic society such as Brazil despite the usefulness of an African Brazilian identifier, whether for the purpose of collecting, tabulating, analyzing, or publishing data. Furthermore, analyzing racial data in binary, rather than ternary, form is one thing. But erasing multiracial-identified individuals from the actual collection, tabulation, and publishing of data as well as the national consciousness is quite another matter. The current proposed formulation of a more inclusive blackness, whether in terms of statistics, public policy, or vernacular parlance impels individuals to distance themselves from acknowledging and/or identifying with their multiple backgrounds for the sake of African Brazilian unity in the struggle for racial equality. Conversely, the recent expressions of multiraciality may spawn simulacra that merely rearticulate the mulatto escape hatch in egalitarian guise. Individuals could elect to acknowledge and/or identify with multiple racial backgrounds as a means of distancing themselves from their blackness and from blacks. More important, this phenomenon would give renewed credence to the racial democracy ideology while masking continuing racial inequality, as well as undermine strategies aimed at eradicating its existence.

Discussion on this topic should not center on multiraciality as being inherently problematic. Multiraciality in a hierarchical system, whether pluralist or integrationist or both, can mean being a little less black, and thus a little less subordinate but does not assure equality with whites. Even the best-intentioned efforts to eradicate racial inequality will be continually thwarted as long as whites in Brazil refuse to confront and eradicate notions of white privilege, however subtle this phenomenon may be. If Brazil is to create a genuinely "new" racial order out of these "new" racial projects the critical challenge is to dismantle completely the Eurocentric underpinnings of the racial order by deconstructing the dichotomous and hierarchical relationship between blackness and whiteness. Such a development would hold promise for moving Brazilian race relations toward actualizing a new multiracial synthesis based on egalitarian premises.

The goal should be to affirm the equality of differences in the manner of egalitarian pluralism, while at the same time nurturing new kinds of inclusion based on equality in the manner of egalitarian integration. This in turn would not only acknowledge the complementary and simultaneous nature of pluralistic and integrative dynamics but also challenge the inegalitarian modalities of both pluralism and integration, which turn these differences into inequalities. This transformative consciousness would seek to achieve equality of similarity without advocating assimilation, to encourage unity without perpetuating uniformity, and to build new kinds of community without promoting conformity.[125] This integrative pluralism (or "pluralistic integration") is greater than the sum of its parts in that it exists at a deeper level of organization than either pluralism or integration alone. Differences become the basis upon which to forge a web of interdependent, yet flexibly integrated, racial and cultural pluralities that not only maintain relatively permanent centers of reference but also allow optimal autonomy for their individual constituents.[126] These dynamics acknowledge the reality of black-white differentiation but maintain porous boundaries that are easily crossed. Group pluralism functions in tandem with individual pluralism that is integrated under a larger national consciousness and identity.[127] Increased contact would result in a better understanding and appreciation of differences and commonalities and lead to a broader basis for cooperation and collaboration.

By now, the lessons of history should have taught Brazil that neither political reform nor appeals to conscience alone can solve issues of racial inequality. A new racial contract, as well as a new national consciousness and identity, based on integrative pluralism, would help coordinate political action and public policy. This in turn would facilitate building other issue-based coalitions, regardless of racial group differences, to work toward an inclusive politics that recognizes the complexity of various types of oppression and how each feeds on the others in order to thrive.[128] This kind of politics would create a constructive and beneficial relationship between the different groups, one marked by mutual respect, interdependence, a balance of power, and a shared commitment to community and nation (and ultimately to the larger human community).

Genuine integrative pluralism is unlikely to be achieved on a large scale until Brazil is willing to commit to the "social engineering, constant vigilance, government authority, official attention to racial behavior" and sacrifice necessary to achieve it.[129] It also requires a more honest assessment of the factors that keep individuals of African descent in a disadvantaged position, and those of European descent in an advantaged one, not to mention a more accurate rendering of the historical forces that put them there in the first place. It necessitates an open discussion of how systems of racial oppression not only deprive subordinate groups of basic human amenities but also deprive dominant groups of their own humanity by preventing them from embracing the humanity of racialized "Others."[130]

Forging this consciousness will require Brazil to disabuse its citizens of the illusions and falsehoods spawned by history. There must be a genuine commitment to undermining hierarchical and dichotomous thinking, particularly in the media and the classroom. The current trend toward multiculturalism, which many activists in Brazil proposed, tends to emphasize differences in the manner of group pluralism, but is not likely to nurture an integrative pluralism. Multiculturalism without a simultaneous commitment to transculturalism could easily harden into a pernicious isolationism, despite its egalitarian premises and goals.[131] Instead, comprehensive and nationally coordinated curricula that explore and validate are needed, not only racial and cultural diversity (egalitarian pluralism) but also shared racial and cultural commonalities (egalitarian integration). A comprehensive anti-bias curriculum and a program that teaches skills in conflict mediation must buttress this agenda.[132]

The acceptance of integrative pluralism should in time generate in the minds and hearts of larger numbers of whites greater sensitivity to the experience of people of color, or what sociologist Jon Cruz has called ethnosympathy.[133] Ultimately, white, black, and multiracial individuals would develop a greater level of identification with and appreciation of each other's experiences in the manner of ethnoempathy. This would enable all Brazilians to acknowledge the historical ramifications of these designations (without internalizing respectively any sense of "white guilt" and "victimization"), and take collective responsibility for their future socioeconomic and political implications.[134] Taken to its logical conclusion, this would ensure that wealth, power, privilege, and prestige are more equitably distributed among citizenry in Brazil in the political, socioeconomic, and educational spheres. Such a transformation in thought and behavior would move Brazil closer to its ideal of a genuine multiracial democracy.

Notes

1. This manuscript borrows on material in G. Reginald Daniel, *Race and Multiraciality in Brazil and the United States: Converging Paths?* (University Park, PA: Pennsylvania State University Press, 2006) and *More Than Black?: Multiracial Identity and the New Racial Order* (Philadelphia, PA.: Temple University Press, 2002).

2. The issues surrounding multiraciality in Brazil are by no means limited to the experience of individuals of African and European descent. Yet, unless otherwise indicated, the words "mulatto," "multiracial," and their Portuguese equivalents *mulato, mestiço*, etc. are used interchangeably in this book to refer to individuals of predominantly African and European descent, although other backgrounds—particularly Native American—may be included in their lineage. "Black" generally refers only to individuals who are considered to be completely (or at least predominantly) African, African American, or African Brazilian. However, the term is sometimes used as a synonym for "African Brazilian," "African American," "African-descent Brazilian," and "African-descent American," which encompass both "black" and "multiracial" individuals.

3. *Preto, branco*, and *mulato* (or *mestiço*) are used in everyday parlance to refer respectively to black, white, and multiracial individuals. *Pardo* (which literally means "brown") is more of an official term used to refer to multiracial individuals, particularly mulattoes. A vernacular term such as *moreno* (brunette), however, is a euphemism that can be used to describe a wide variety of "brunette" phenotypes, including those individuals who are designated as *preto, pardo*, or *branco* (if the latter have dark hair and eyes). Maria Palmira da Silva, "Identidade Racial Brasileira," in *Racismo no Brasil: Percepções da Discriminação e do Preconceito Racial no Século XXI*, ed. Gevanilda Santos and Maria Palmira da Silva, 37–44 (São Paulo: Editora Fundação Perseu Abramo, 2005), 41–2.

4. Some of the most important of these classic studies have included: Carl N. Degler, *Neither Black nor White: Slavery and Race Relations in Brazil and the United States.* (Madison, WI: University of Wisconsin Press, 1986); E. Franklin Frazier, "A Comparison of Negro-White Relations in Brazil and the United States," (Originally published 1944), in *African American Reflections on Brazil's Racial Paradise*, ed. David J. Helwig (Philadelphia, PA.: Temple University Press, 1992), 131–36; Gilberto Freyre, *The Masters and the Slaves: A Study in the Development of Brazilian Civilization*, trans. Harriet de Onís (New York: Alfred A. Knopf, 1933/1963); Gilberto Freyre, *The Mansions and the Shanties: The Making of Modern Brazil*, trans. Harriet de Onís (New York: Alfred A. Knopf, 1935/1963); Gilberto Freyre, *Order and Progress: Brazil from Monarchy to Republic*, trans. and ed. Rod W. Horton (New York: Alfred A. Knopf, 1959/1970); Marvin Harris, *Patterns of Race in the Americas* (New York: W. W. Norton: 1963); Donald Pierson, *Negroes in Brazil: A Study of Race Contact at Bahia* (Chicago, IL.: University of Chicago Press, 1942); Fernandes, Florestan. *A Integração do Negro na Sociedade de Classes.* São Paulo: Dominus Editora/Editora da USP, 1965; Thomas A. Skidmore, *Black into White: Race and Nationality in Brazilian Thought* (New York: Oxford University Press, 1974); Pierre van den Berghe, *Race and Racism: A Comparative Perspective.* (New York: Wiley, 1967); Thomas A. Skidmore, "Race Relations in Brazil," *Camões Center Quarterly*, 4 (Autumn and Winter 1992–1993), 49–57; Robert Brent Toplin, *Freedom and Prejudice: The Legacy of Slavery in The United States and Brazil* (Westport CT: Greenwood Press, 1981); Charles Wagley, *Race and Class in Rural Brazil* (Paris: UNESCO, 1963).

5. Oracy Nogueira, "Preconceito Racial de Marca e Preconceito Racial de Origem (Sugestão de um Quadro de Refêrencia para a Interpretação do Material sobre Relações Raciais no Brasil)" in *Tanto Preto Quanto Branco: Estudo de Relações Racias*, ed. Oracy Nogueira, 78–9 (São Paulo: T.A. Queiroz, 1985 [1954].

6. See endnote 4.

7. Degler, 226–38; Gerald Bender, *Angola Under the Portuguese: The Myth and the Reality* (Berkeley: University of California Press, 1978), 42–5; Degler, 213–16; Caio Prado, Junior, *The Colonial Background of Modern Brazil*, trans. Suzette Macedo (Berkeley: University of California Press, 1969), 117, 120; G. Reginald Daniel, "Passers and Pluralists: Subverting the Racial Divide," in *Racially Mixed People in America*, ed. Maria P. P. Root, 91–107 (Newbury Park, CA: Sage Publications, 1992).

8. Maria Luisa Marcílio, "The Population of Colonial Brazil," in *Colonial Latin America*, The Cambridge History of Latin America, vol. 2, ed. Leslie Bethell, 45–52 (Cambridge University Press, 1984). In fact, at the time of its colonization of Brazil in 1531, Portugal had a population of only about 1 million, and was able to send only 400 settlers despite having deliberately expanded its penal code to make some 200 crimes punishable by exile. Carlton S. Coon, *The Living Races of Man* (New York: Alfred A. Knopf, 1965), 293; David W. Cohen and Jack P. Greene, "Introduction," in *Neither Slave Nor Free: The Freemen of African Descent in the Slave Societies of the New World*, ed. David. W. Cohen and Jack P. Greene, 1–23 (Baltimore, MD: Johns Hopkins University Press, 1972); Herbert S. Klein, "Nineteenth-Century Brazil," in *Neither Slave Nor Free: The Freemen of African Descent in the Slave Societies of the New World*, ed. David. W. Cohen and Jack P. Greene, 309–34 (Baltimore, MD: Johns Hopkins University Press, 1972); A.J. R. Russell-Wood, "Colonial Brazil," in *Neither Slave Nor Free: The Freemen of African Descent in the Slave Societies of the New World*, ed. David. W. Cohen and Jack P. Greene, 84–133 (Baltimore, MD: Johns Hopkins University Press, 1972); Herbert S. Klein, *African Slavery in Latin America and the Caribbean* (New York: Oxford University Press, 1986), 227–228, 230; Hartimus Hoetink, *Slavery and Race Relations in the Americas: Comparative Notes on Their Nature and Nexus* (New York: Harper and Row, 1973), 108; John Burbick, "The Myth of Racial Democracy," *North American Congress on Latin America Report on the Americas*, 25, 4 (February 1992): 40–2. During the early colonial period, most multiracial individuals were *mamelucos*, or individuals of European and Native American descent. When the Native American population began to die by the thousands, colonists increasingly imported African slaves (although as late as the 1580s, Native Americans still made up two-thirds of the slave labor force). After 1600, when the transition to African labor was complete in most regions, there was a significant increase in the numbers of multiracial individuals of African

and European or African, European, and Native American descent (*mulatos*)—and to a lesser extent, individuals of African and Native American descent, or *cafusos*. *Cafusos* were less common because Africans and Native Americans had limited intimate and lasting contact after the early phase of colonization and slavery. Exceptions to this trend were the *quilombo* settlements of runaway slaves scattered throughout the interior, where unions (especially in the Northeast) between African men and Native American women were facilitated by the shortage of African women. Prado, 121–22; James Lockhart and Stuart B. Schwartz. *Early Latin America: A History of Colonial Spanish America and Brazil* (New York: Cambridge University Press, 1987), 197–200.

9. Emilia Viotti da Costa, *The Brazilian Empire: Myths and Histories* (Chicago, IL: University of Chicago Press, 1985), 239–43.

10. Cohen and Greene, 1–23; Klein, 309–34; Russell-Wood, 84–133; Hoetink, 108; Burdick 1992, 40–2.

11. The escape hatch allows vertical mobility primarily in terms of phenotypical, that is, somatic approximation to the dominant European norm image as defined by Hoetink. However, somatic (external) characteristics of a cultural and economic nature (e.g., speech, mannerisms, attire, occupation, income, etc.), and psychological (internal) factors, such as beliefs, values, and attitudes, are also taken into consideration. Consequently, a few exceptional blacks have gained vertical mobility in accordance with their socioeconomic and sociocultural, if not phenotypical, approximation to the dominant Whites. Hoetink 1973, 197–98, 200, 201; Hartimus Hoetink. *Caribbean Race Relations: A Study of Two Variants* (London: Oxford University Press, 1967), 88–9, 122.

12. Degler, 140, 196–199; Andrews, 249–54. This has historically been the dominant trend in the states from Rio de Janeiro northward—particularly the state of Bahia—where individuals of African descent have always been a majority. In that region, the line between black and white is far more elusive and has even given rise to the interesting designations *branco da terra* or *branco da Bahia*. These terms translate literally as "home grown white" and "Bahian white," and refer to individuals who clearly display some African phenotypical traits (or at least have known African ancestry), but who are regarded as whites in Bahia, and the Northeast by extension. This is a far more liberal attitude than in the states from São Paulo southward, where Europeans have been significantly more numerous, if not always a majority. The markers delineating blacks from whites, and more specifically multiracial individuals from whites is far more restrictive.

13. G. Reginald Daniel, *More Than Black? Multiracial Identity and the New Racial Order* (Philadelphia: Temple University Press, 2002), 49–63.

14. It should be pointed out, however, that Brazilian popular culture and the physiognomy of the Brazilian people remain strongly indebted to and influenced by the African component despite attempts by the elite to ignore and disguise, if not wipe out, its presence. Fernando Ortiz, *Cuban Counterpoint* (Original work published 1940), trans. Harriet de Onís (New York: Alfred A. Knopf, 1947), ix–xi; Anani Dzidzienyo, *The Position of Blacks in Brazilian Society,* Minority Group Rights Reports, No. 7 (London: Minority Rights Group, 1979), 2–11; Abdias do Nascimento, *Mixture or Massacre?: Essays on the Genocide of a Black People,* trans. Elisa Larkin Nascimento (State University of New York at Buffalo, Puerto Rican Studies and Research Center, 1979), 74–80; Skidmore, 64–77.

15. Degler, 182–3; Daniel, 33. The election of President Cardoso, who is considered white by Brazilian standards, is a clear indication of this process. Cardoso was one of the scholars who was purged from the University of São Paulo in the 1960s for his revisionist research on race relations. However, he remained silent on racism during his presidential campaign and for the most part has continued to do so during his administration. More important, he actually reinforced and perpetuated the myth of racial democracy in his inaugural address. hat is to say, in the tradition of so many socially designated and white-identified Brazilians, he offered himself up as proof of the genetic and ancestral democratization that has emerged in Brazil after centuries of miscegenation. He did this by publicly declaring himself to have some African ancestry, while at the same time remaining silent on both the whitening ideology implied in this racial and cultural blending and the existence of gross socioeconomic, educational, and political inequality based on

race. Rebecca Reichmann, "Brazil's Denial of Race," *North American Congress on Latin America Report on the Americas* 28, No. 6 (May/June 1995), 35–42.

16. Skidmore 1992–1993, 49–57; Charles H. Wood and José Alberto Magno de Carvalho, *The Demography of Inequality in Brazil* (New York: Cambridge University Press, 1988), 135–53.

17. Nascimento, 79–0; Peggy Lovell-Webster, "The Myth of Racial Equality: A Study of Race and Morality in Northeast Brazil," *Latinamericanist* (May 1987): 1–6; Thomas A. Skidmore, "Race and Class in Brazil: A Historical Perspective," in *Race, Class and Power in Brazil*, 24–41 (Center for Afro-American Studies, University of California, Los Angeles, 1985).

18. Omi and Winant, 77–91.

19. Andrews, 146–56; Michael George Hanchard, *Orpheus and Power: The Movimento Negro of Rio de Janeiro and São Paulo, Brazil, 1945–1988* (Princeton, New Jersey: Princeton University Press, 1994), 104–29; Michael Mitchell, "Blacks and the Abertura Democrática," in *Race, Class and Power in Brazil*, 95–119 (Center for Afro-American Studies, University of California, Los Angeles, 1985). There have been other collective and individual forms of resistance in the nineteenth and twentieth centuries that have sought to move against the wedge that has been driven between blacks and mulattoes. When abolition became a popular causes in the 1880s, many Free People of Color became very much involved in the mass-based movement inciting the wholesale flight of slaves from the plantations which dealt the final blow to the slave regime. Mulatto lawyer-journalist-poet, Luís Gama (1830-1882) and a handful of earlier voices in the Mulatto Press of the 1830s, openly discussed the more taboo subject of racism as an independent variable that kept the masses of Free People of Color in a position of second-class citizenship during slavery, and which guaranteed that African Brazilians collectively would remain in a position of second-class citizenship long after abolition in 1888. James Kennedy, "Luís Gama: Pioneer of Abolition in Brazil," *Journal of Negro History* LIX, No. 3 (July 1974): 255–67; Thomas Flory, "Race and Social Control in Independent Brazil," *Journal of Latin American Studies* 9, No. 2 (November 1977): 199–224. Considering the serious social, economic and political reprisals that Luís Gama suffered for his activities (he was fired from his job as clerk at the Police Department, imprisoned several times and the authorities closed down several of the radical newspapers in which he collaborated as a writer), it is not surprising that he had no predecessors in the frontal attack on racism. Few vertically mobile multiracial individuals in late-nineteenth-century and early twentieth-century Brazil followed Gama's lead. Exceptions to this trend included writers José do Patrocínio (1853–1905), who also was an abolitionist and ardent fighter for African-Brazilian rights, and Lima Barreto (1881–1922), who, we might add, found it difficult to get his works published, and suffered a fate similar to Gama's. Although the Black Front (A Frente Negra) had numerous successors in the 1940s and 1950s (Teatro Experimental do Negro, União dos Homens de Côr, Associação Cultural do Negro), none of these organizations achieved its level of prominence.

20. Ruth Simms Hamilton, "From the Editor," *Conexões: Africa Diaspora Research Project*, Michigan State University 4, no. 2 (November 1992), 2, 13; Mac Margolis, "The Invisible Issue: Race in Brazil," *Ford Foundation Report* 1, No. 2 (Summer, 1992), 3–7; Reichmann, 35–45; Regina Domingues, "The Color of a Majority Without Citizenship," *Conexões: Africa Diaspora Research Project*, Michigan State University 4, No. 2 (November 1993), 6–7; Carlos Hasenbalg, "Race and Socioeconomic Inequalities in Brazil," in *Race, Class and Power in Brazil*, ed. Pierre-Michel Fontaine, 25–41 (Center for Afro-American Studies, University of California, Los Angeles, 1985); Peggy Lovell-Webster, "The Myth of Racial Equality: A Study of Race and Mortality in Northeast Brazil," *Latinamericanist*, (May 1987): 1–6; Peggy Lovell-Webster and Jeffery Dwyer, "The Cost of Not Being White in Brazil," *Sociology and Social Research* 72, no. 2 (1988): 136–38; Anani Dzidzienho, "Brazil," in *International Handbook on Race and Race Relations*, ed. Jay A. Sigler, 23–42 (New York: Greenwood Press, 1987).

21. Edward E. Telles, "Residential Segregation by Skin Color in Brazil," *American Sociological Review* 57, No. 2 (April 1992): 186–98; Edward E. Telles, "Racial Distance and Region in Brazil: Intermarriage in Brazilian Urban Areas," *Latin American Research Review* 28, no. 2 (1993): 141–62.

22. Nelson do Valle Silva, "Updating the Cost of Not Being White in Brazil," in *Race, Class and Power in Brazil*, ed. Pierre-Michel Fontaine, 42–55 (Center for Afro-American Studies,

University of California, Los Angeles, 1985); Nelson do Valle Silva, "Racial Differences in Income in Brazil," in *Race Relations in Contemporary Brazil: From Indifference to Inequality,* ed. Rebecca Reichmann, 67–82 (University Park: Pennsylvania State University Press, 1999); Nelson do Valle and Carlos A. Hasenbalg, "Race and Educational Opportunity in Brazil," in *Race Relations in Contemporary Brazil: From Indifference to Equality,* ed. Rebecca Reichmann, 53–66 (University Park: Pennsylvania State University Press, 1999); Sérgio Adorno, "Racial Discrimination and Criminal Justice in São Paulo," in *Race Relations in Contemporary Brazil: From Indifference to Equality,* ed. Rebecca Reichmann, 123–38. (University Park, PA: Pennsylvania State University Press, 1999); Carlos Hasenbalg, "Perspectives on Race and Class in Brazil," in *Black Brazil: Culture, Identity, and Social Mobilization,* ed. Larry Crook and Randal Johnson, 61–84 (Los Angeles: UCLA Latin American Center); Lovell-Webster, 2–6; Peggy A. Lovell and Charles H. Wood, "Skin Color, Racial Inequality, and Life Chances in Brazil," in *Latin American Perspectives* 25, No. 3 (May 1998): 90–109; Margolis, 7; Wood and Carvalho, 139, 135–53.

23. Skidmore, 55.

24. Antonio Sérgio Alfredo Guimarães, "Measures to Combat Discrimination and Racial Inequality in Brazil," in *Race Relations in Contemporary Brazil: From Indifference to Equality,* ed. Rebecca Reichmann, 143–53 (University Park, PA: Pennsylvania State University Press, 1999); Melissa Nobles, *Shades of citizenship: Race and the Census in Modern Politics* (Stanford, CA.: Stanford University Press, 2000), 109; Skidmore 1992–1993, 49–57; Hasenbalg, "O Negro nas Vésperas do Centenário," *Estudos Afro-Asiáticos,* 13 (Março de 1987): 79–86.

25. Hasenbalg , 25–41; Andrews, 218–33; Skidmore, 49–57.

26. Skidmore, 49–57.

27. Michael Omi and Howard Winant, *Racial Formation in the United States: From the 1960s to the 1990s.* 2nd edition (New York: Routledge, 1994), 77–91.

28. Andrews, 250; Elvira Oliveira, "Dia Nacional da Consciencia Negra," *Nova Escola* (Novembro de 1993), 23–5; Lori S. Robinson, "The Two Faces of Brazil: A Black Movement Gives Voice to an Invisible Majority," *Emerge* (October 1994), 38–42.

29. Andrews, 250; Oliveira, 23–5; Robinson, 38–42; Skidmore 1992–1993, 49–57.

30. Mac Margolis 1992, 3–7; Nascimento, 74–80; Oliveira, 3–25; Robinson, 38–42; Wood and Carvalho, 135–53. In 1890, *pardos* composed 41.4 percent of the population. Their apparent decline from 41.4 percent to 21.2 percent between 1890 and 1940, and the growth of the white population from 43.97 to 63.5 percent during the same period is more related to the massive immigration of Europeans to Brazil than to increased miscegenation or racial self-recoding. Census figures make clear, however, that between 1940 and 1990, the *pardo* population was the country's s fastest growing racial group, rising from 21.2 percent to 38.8 percent (+/- 48 million) of the national population. During the same period Whites declined from 63.5 percent to 54.2 percent (+/- 86 million) and *pretos* from 14.6 percent to 5.9 percent (+/- 6 million). (Carlos A. Hasenbalg, Nelson do Valle Silva, and Luiz Claudio Barcelos, "Notas Sobre Miscegenação no Brasil," *Estudos Afro-Asiáticos* 16, 3 (1989): 189–97). This does indicate a progressive "lightening" of the population. It would be less appropriately described as a whitening, however, and more as a "browning." If upwardly mobile African Brazilians have been moving out of the *pardo* category into the *branco* category, it, therefore, has not been in numbers sufficient to reverse this trend (Andrews, 252).

31. John Burdick, *Blessed Anastácia: Women, Race and Popular Christianity in Brazil* (New York: Routledge, 1998a), 150.

32. Nobles, 123, 171–72.

33. Nobles, 123, 171–72; Rebecca Reichmann, "Introduction," in *Race Relations in Contemporary Brazil: From Indifference to Equality,* ed. Rebecca Reichmann, 13–14 (University Park, PA: Pennsylvania University Press, 1999).

34. Nobles, 123, 171-72, Daniel, 256.

35. Instituto Brasileiro de Geografía e Estadísticas (IBGE). *Censo Demográfico 2000. Características Gerais da População. Resultados da Amostra. Tabelas de Resultados.* Rio de Janeiro: Fundação IBGE, 2000; Francisco Neves, "Two Brazils." *Brazzil,* May 1, 2002.

http://www.brazzil.com/content/view/2562/68/; Marcelo Paixão, "Waiting for the Sun: Account of the (Precarious) Social Situation of the African Descendant Population in Contemporary Brazil," *Journal of Black Studies* 34, No. 6 (July): 747–48.

36. Nobles, 123–24, 127.

37. Daniel, 245.

38. "Strategic essentialism" is a term coined by the Indian literary critic and theorists Gayatri Chakravorty Spivak. It refers to a strategy that nationalities, ethnic groups, or minority groups can use to present themselves to achieve certain goals. While strong differences may exist between members of these groups, and amongst themselves as they engage in continuous debates, it is sometimes advantageous for them to temporarily "essentialize" themselves and bring forward their group identity in a simplified and reductionist manner that tends to focus on one axis of experience, identity, and ultimately oppression (Donna Landry and Gerald Maclean, *The Spivak Reader: Selected Works Gayatri Chakravorty Spivak* (New York: Routledge, 1995), 7, 54–71, 159, 204, 295.

39. Daniel, 244–46.

40. Daniel, 4, 245.

41. John Burdick, "The Lost Constituency of Brazil's Black Movement," *Latin American Perspectives* 25, No. 1 (January, 1998b): 150–52.

42. Daniel, 243.

43. Guimarães 1999, 147–48; Daniel 2006, 244; Sales Augusto dos Santos, "Ação Afirmativa e Mérito Individual," in *Ações Afirmativas:Políticas Contra as Desigualidades Raciais,* ed. Renato Emerson dos Santos and Fátima Lobato, 83–126 (Rio de Janeiro: DP&A Editora, 2003).

44. Antonio Sérgio Alfredo Guimarães, "Ações Afirmativas para a População Negra nas Universidades Brasileiras," in *Ações Afirmativas: Políticas Públicas Contra as Desigualdades Raciais,* ed. Renato Emerson dos Santos and Fátima Lobato, 75–82 (Rio de Janeiro: DP&A Editora, 2003); Daniela Galdino and Larissa Santos Pereira, "Acesso à Universidade: Condições de Produção de um Discurso Facioso," in *Levando a Raça a Sério: Ação Afirmativa e Universidade,* ed. Joaze Bernardino and Daniela Galdino, 157–72 (Rio de Janeiro: DP&A Editora, 2003); Delcele Mascarenhas Queiroz, "A Negro, Seu Acesso ao Ensino Superior e as Ações Afirmativas," in *Levando a Raça a Sério: Ação Afirmativa e Universidade,* ed. Joaze Bernardino and Daniela Galdino, 137–56 (Rio de Janeiro: DP&A Editora, 2003); Delcele Mascarenhas Queiroz, "A Negro, Seu Acesso ao Ensino Superior e as Ações Afirmativas, " in *Levando a Raça a Sério: Ação Afirmativa e Universidade,* ed. Joaze Bernardino and Daniela Galdino, 137–56 (Rio de Janeiro: DP&A Editora, 2003). The State University of Bahia instituted similar measures, followed in 2003 by the Federal University of Brasília, the Federal University of Alagoas, and the State University of Mato Grosso do Sul, which already had a quota for indigenous individuals (Martins, Medeiros, and Nascimento, 806–11).

45. Dias 2004; Jeter 2003; Margolis, 3, 46; Martins, Medeiros, and Nascimento, 806–11; "Race in Brazil, Out of Eden" 2003; Ricardo Rochetti, "Not As Easy as Black and White: The Implications of the University of Rio de Janeiro's Quota-Based Admissions Policy on Affirmative Action," *Vanderbilt Journal of Transnational Law* 37, no. 1432 (November 2004); Raquel Villardi, "Acesso à Universiadade pro Meio de Ações Afirmativas: Estudo da Situação dos Estudantes com Matrícula em 2003 e 2004 (Junho)." UERJ (Universidade do Estado do Rio de Janeiro) Report, 2004, 3.

46. "Race in Brazil, Out of Eden" 2003.

47. Margolis, 3, 46; Martins, Medeiros, and Nascimento, 806–11; "Race in Brazil, Out of Eden" 2003; Telles, 159

48. Jon Jeter, "Affirmative Action Debate Forces Brazil to Take Look in the Mirror," *Washington Post* Jun 16, 2003eter 2003; Larry Rohter, "Racial Quotas in Brazil Touch Off Fierce Debate," *New York Times*, April 5, 2003. http://www.nytimes.com/2003/04/05/international/Americas/05BRAZ.html/.

49. Jeter, 2003.

50. Michael Astor, "Brazil Tries Quotas to Get Racial Equality," *Los Angeles Times*, sec A3, February 29, 2004.

51. "Race in Brazil, Out of Eden" 2003.

52. Astor, 2004; Villardi, 3.

53. Jeter, 2003.

54. Rohter, 2003.

55. Astor, 2004; Jeter, 2003; Margolis, 3, 46.

56. Martins, Medeiros, and Nascimento, 806–11; Telles, 74.

57. Rohter ,2003.

58. "Brazil: Affirmative Action in Higher Education" 2003–2004, 3. However, some of these white students would still not have been admitted if the quota system were not in place (Martins, Medeiros, and Nascimento, 806–11).

59. Mario Osava, "Rights—Brazil: Blacks Demand Adoption of Promised Measures," Inter-Press Service News Agency, November 16, 2005. http://www.ipsnews.net/news.asp?idnews=31051/

60. Margolis 2003, 3, 46; "Race in Brazil, Out of Eden" 2003.

61. Dias 2004; Jeter 2003; Rochetti 2004; Rohter 2003; Pueng Vongs, J. Prakash, Marcelo Ballve, and Sandip Roy, "Around the World, Countries Grapple with Affirmative Action," *Pacific News Service*, July 11, 2003. http://news.pacificnews.org/news/view_article.html?article_id=3e26118fcdf4fba57da467da3ee b43d0/.

62. Margolis, 3, 46; Martins, Medeiros, and Nascimento, 806–11.

63. Vongs et al. 2003.

64. Reichmann, 21.

65. Ana Toni, "For Brazil, First Steps Toward Affirmative Action," Ford Foundation Report, winter 2004. http://www.fordfound.org/publications/ff_report/view_ff_report_detail.cfm?report_index=478.

66. "Brazil: Affirmative Action in Higher Education" 2003–2004, 3; Margolis, 3, 46; Martins, Medeiros, and Nascimento, 806–11; Telles, 74–5; Toni, 2004; Villardi, 3. Other important analyses on this topic include Teixeira's *Negros na Universidade: Identidade e Trajetórias de Ascenção Social no Rio de Janeiro* (Rio de Janeiro: Pallas, 2003), Carvalho's *Inclusão étnica e racial no Brasil: A Questão das Cotas no Ensino Superior* (São Paulo: Attar Editorial, 2006), and Gomes's and Martins's *Afirmando direitos: Acesso e Permanência de Jovens na Universidade* (Belo Horizonte: Autêntica, 2004).

67. Rodrigo Davies, "Brazil Takes Affirmative Action in HE," *Guardian,* August 4, 2003. http://education.guardian.co.uk/higher/worldwide/story/0%2C9959%2C1012157% 2C00.html/; "Race in Brazil, Out of Eden" 2003; Margolis, 3, 46; Martins, Medeiros, and Nascimento 2004, 806–11; Toni, 2004; Villardi 2004, 3.

68. Gregory Kane, "In Bahia, University Council Votes in Favor of Quotas," http://blackamericaweb.com/site.aspx/bawnews/diaspora/brazi/2004.

69. Margolis 2003, 3, 46; Martins, Medeiros, and Nascimento, 806–11.

70. Jeter 2003; "Race in Brazil, Out of Eden," 2003.

71. Joaze Bernardino, "Ação Afirmativa e a Rediscussão da Democracia Racial no Brazil," *Estudos Afro-Asiáticos* 24, no. 2 (2002): 247–73; Jeter 2003.

72. Telles 2004, 76–7.

73. Jeter 2003; Telles, 76–77.

74. Jeter, 2003; Margolis, 3, 46.

75. Burdick 1998b, 150–52.

76. Daniel, 245–6.

77. Daniel, 292–3; Peter Fry, "Politics, Nationality, and the Meaning of Race," *Daedalus* 129, No. 2 (2000): 83–118; Ali Kamel, *Não Somos Racistas: Uma Reação Aos Que Querem Nos Transformar Numa Nação Bicolor.* 2a impressão (Rio de Janeiro: Editora Nova Fronteira, 2006), 17–41, 49–57; Reichmann, 11–13; Peter Fry and Yvonne Maggie, "Política social de alto risco," in *Divisões Perogosas: Políticas Racias no Brasil Contemporâneo,* ed. Peter Fry and Yvonne Maggie, Marcos Chor Maio, Simone Monteiro, and Ricardo Ventura Santos, 277–81 (Rio de Janeiro: Civilização Brasileira, 2007); Antonio Risério, *A Utopia Brasileira e Os Movimentos Negros* (São Paulo: Editora 34 Ltda, 2007), 19, 24, 55, 67.

78. Pierre Bourdieu and Loïc Wacquant, "On the Cunning of Imperialist Reason," *Theory, Culture, and Society* 16, no. 1 (1999): 47–48.

79. Bourdieu and Wacquant, 47–48.

80. Fernando Conceição, "As Cotas Contra O Apocalipse," *Folha de Sao Paulo Caderno Mais*, 27 June 2004; Daniel, 72–179; Daniel, 293–4; Kamel, 17–41, 49–57; Hermano Vianna, "Mestiçagem Fora de Lugar," *Folha de Sao Paulo Caderno Mais*, 27 June 2004; Fry and Maggie, 277–81; Risério, 19, 24, 55, 67.

81. For example, journalist Nilza Iraci identifies as African Brazilian (*negro*) but could easily be seen as white. In a conference on racism in the early 1990s she heard an activist comment, "I didn't know our organization is already accepting whites." When defending the rights of African Brazilian women in another meeting. Ms. Iraci was questioned by a white colleague, who stated "But why are you saying all these things when you aren't even African Brazilian?" (Neves 2002).

82. Victor Anderson, *Beyond Ontological Blackness: An Essay on African American Religious Criticism* (New York: Continuum, 1995), 13; Daniel, 293–4.

83. bell hooks, *Yearning: Race, Gender, and Cultural Politics* (Boston: South End Press, 1995), 23–31; Daniel, 293–4.

84. "Strategic antiessentialism" refers to a tactic that nationalities, racial/ethnic groups, and other minorities can use to present themselves by emphasizing the strong differences that may exist between members of these groups, and amongst themselves as they engage in continuous debates in order achieve their goals. While strong similarities may exist between members of these groups, it considered advantageous for them to "antiessentialize" themselves and bring forward their group identity in a complex manner in order to address more than axis of experience, identity, and ultimately oppression, as well as the interlocking nature of these phenomena (George Lipsitz, "Noise in the Blood: Culture, Conflict, and Mixed Race Identities," in *Crossing Lines: Race and Mixed Race Across the Geohistorical Divide*, ed. Marc Coronado, Rudy P. Guevarra Jr., Jeffrey Moniz, and Laura Furlan Szanto, 32–35 (Santa Barbara, CA.: Multiethnic Student Outreach, in collaboration with the Center for Chicano Studies, University of California, Santa Barbara, 2003).

85. Fernando Conceição, "As Cotas Contra o Apocalipse." *Folha de São Paulo Caderno Mais*, June 27, 2004; Daniel 2002, 172–79; Daniel 2006, 219, 293–4; hooks, 23–31; HermanoVianna, "Mestiçagem Fora de Lugar," *Folha de São Paulo Caderno Mais*, June 27, 2004; Fry and Maggie, 277–81; Risério, 19, 24, 55, 67; Fry, 83–118.

86. Jerson César Leão Alves, e-mail correspondence with G. Reginald Daniel, October 9, 2007.

87. "Mestiçofobia É Racismo," http://www.nacaomestica.org/;"Diga Não Ao Racismo Antimestiço," http://www.nacaomestica.org/.

88. Jerson César Leão Alves, e-mail to G. Reginald Daniel, October 10, 2007; "Coloque de volta MESTIÇO no censo do IBGE," *Naçãomestiça* http://www.nacaomestica.org/.

89. "Brasília–DF. Comissão Geral para debater o Estatuto da Igualdade Racial," http://www.nacaomestica.org/.

90. Jerson César Leão Alves, e-mail to G. Reginald Daniel, October 10, 2007; "Coloque de volta MESTIÇO no censo do IBGE," http://www.nacaomestica.org/. By the nineteenth century the term *mameluco* had been replaced with *caboclo*, which generally signified ethnicity (or origin), encompassing the acculturated Native American or indigenous population and particularly their multiracial descendants (Nobles 2000, 89; Edith Piza and Fúlvia Rosemberg, "Color in the Brazilian Census," in *Race Relations in Contemporary Brazil: From Indifference to Equality*, ed. Rebecca Reichmann, 37–52 (University Park: Pennsylvania State University Press, 1999), 40–41.

91. See Part II, Chapter 10 and Part III, Chapter 1 in this book for a discussion of the limitations and dangers of the new genetics.

92. "An Overview of the Human Genome Project (HGP)," http://www.genome.gov/12011238; "Human Genome Project Goals", http://www.genome.gov/11006945; L. Luca Cavalli-Sforza, Paolo Menozzi, and Alberto Piazza, *The History and Geography of Human Genes* (Princeton, New Jersey: Princeton University Press, 1994), 377–78; Mark A. Jobling, Matthew Hurles,

and Chris Tyler-Smith, *Human Evolutionary Genetics: Origins, Peoples, and Disease* (New York: Garland Publishing, 2004), 274–75; Ricardo Ventura Santos and Marcos Chor Maio, "Race, Genomics, Identities and Politics in Contemporary Brazil," *Critique of Anthropology* 24, 4 (2004): 363–4; Ricardo Ventura Santos and Marcos Chor Maio, " Antropologia, Raça e os Dilemas das Identidades na Era da Genômica," *História, Ciências, Saúde—Manguinhos,* 12, no. 2 (May-August 2005): 447–68.

93. Robin Marantz Henig, "The Genome in Black and White (and Gray)," *New York Times Magazine,* October 10, 2004, http://www.nytimes.com/2004/10/10/magazine/10GENETIC .html/; Kristen Philipkoski, "Gene Map Presents Race Concerns," *Wired,* http://www.wired.com/science/discoveries/news/2001/02/41619; Santos and Maio 2004, 361–62; "Science," DNAPrint Genomics, http://www.dnaprint.com/welcome/science/; Lee Herring and Mercedes Rubio, "Scientists Warn of Conceptual Traps Concerning "Race" in New Genetic Map of Human Populations," *Footnotes,* April 2005 http://www2.asanet.org/footnotes/apr05/indextwo.html.

94. Santos and Maio 2004, 356–57; 2005, 3.

95. Sérgio D.J. Pena, Denise R. Carvalho-Silva, J. Alves-Silva, Vania Ferreira Prado, and Fabríco R. Santos, "Retrato Molecular do Brasil," *Ciência Hoje* 159 (2000): 16–25.

96. Pena, et. al., 16–25.

97. J. Alves-Silva, M.S. Santos, Pedro Edson Moreira Guimarães, A.C.S. Ferreira, Hans-Jürgen Bandelt, Sérgio D.J. Pena, and Vania Ferriera Prado, "The Ancestry of Brazilian mtDNA Lineages," *American Journal of Human Genetics* 67 (2000): 445.

98. Santos and Maio 2004, 361–2; Denise R. Carvalho-Silva, Fabrício R. Santos, Jorge Rocha, and Sérgio D. J. Pena, "The Phylogeography of Brazilian Y-Chromosome Lineages," *American Journal if Human Genetics* 68 (2001): 281–286.

99. Alves-Silva et. al., 454–55.

100. Santos and Maio 2004, 361–2; Alves-Silva et al. 2000, 444–61; Carvalho Silva et al. 2001, 281–286.

101. Pena et al., 25.

102. Elio Gaspari, "O branco tem a marca de Nana," *Folha de São Paulo,* Caderno A, 16 April 2000: 14; Santos and Maio 2004, 351; 2005, 3.

103. Athayde Motta, "Genética para as massas," 2000a, http://www.afirma.inf.br; Motta, "Genética para uma nova história," 2000b; "Contra a genética, o conhecimento," 2003 http://www. afirma.inf.br; Motta, "Com Raça, Sem Raça, Com Raça. . . " *Fala, Brasil!* 28 July 2005, http://www.brazil-brasil.com/content/view/528/78/; Motta, "Essencialismo Genético: Por que a genética do século 21 soa como a biologia do século 19?" 14 de Junho de 2007, *Mundo Negro. http://www.mundonegro.com.br/noticias2/?noticiaID=863.* Article was originally published on 1/6/2007 in Ibase: www.ibase.br.

104. Motta 2000a, 2000b; 2002; 2005; 2007.

105. Motta 2000a, 2000b; 2002; 2005; 2007.

106. Motta 2000a, 2000b; 2002; 2005; 2007.

107. Motta 2000a, 2000b; 2002; 2005; 2007.

108. Sueli Carneiro, "De novo a raça," *Revista Espaço Acadêmico,* ano II, no. 21 (2003), http://www.afirma.inf.br; E. L. Sales Júnior, "Genética e realidade," 2003. http://www.afirma.inf. br.

109. Marcelo Leite, "Raça é só conceito social, diz DNA brasileiro," *Folha de São Paulo,* sec A16, December 17, 2002.

110. Sérgio D. J Pena, "Há uma base objetiva para definir o conceito de raça?," *Folha de São Paulo,* sec A3, December 21, 2002.

111. Raul Jungmann, "Cotas para negros: dez questões," *O Globo,* December 15, 2001, 6.

112. Santos and Maio 2004, 369.

113. The racial roulette this entails was demonstrated in a recent case involving identical twins who applied for admission at the Federal University of Brasília (UnB). Like all students who self-identified as African Brazilian, the twins were required to pose for a photograph that would be evaluated by a secret certification committee to determine whether they were phenotypically "black" enough to qualify for admission under the quota system. Although the

twins have been mistaken for the each other throughout their lives, the panel designated one as African Brazilian, which made him eligible for admission through the racial quota system; the other was designated as white, which automatically disqualified him (Mike DeWitt and Adam Stepan, "Brazil in Black and White," http://www.pbs.org/wnet/wideangle/shows/brazil2/, 2007.

114. Santos and Maio 2004, 369.

115. Fernanda da Escóssia, "Determinar quem é negro vira polêmica na lei sobre cotas do Rio," *Folha de São Paulo*, sec D4, November 14, 2001.

116. Ronaldo França, "Não Deu Certo," *Veja* 1791 (February 26, 2003): 71.

117. José Roberto Pinto de Góes, "Sem vergonha de ser feliz," *O Globo*, Primeiro Caderno, February 19, 2003, 7.

118. Santos and Maio 2004, 362; Fry 83–118.

119. Santos and Maio 2005, 16.

120. Stanley R. Bailey, "The Race Construct and Public Opinion: Understanding Brazilian Beliefs About Racial Inequality and Their Determinants," *American Journal of Sociology* 108, no. 2 (September 2002): 406–39.

121. Rohter 2003.

122. Burdick 1998a, 3; Htun 2005, 24; Nobles, 123–24, 127; Reichmann, 23; Telles 2004, 76–77, 238, 261.

123. Paul R Spickard, Rowena Fong, and Patricia L. Ewalt. "Undermining the Very Basis of Racism—Its Categories," *Social Work* 40, no. 5 (1995): 581–84.

124. Conceição 2004; Vianna 2004.

125. John Higham. *Send These to Me: Jews and Other Immigrants in Urban America* (New York: Atheneum, 1975), 242–46.

126. Ervin Laszlo. *Evolution: The Grand Synthesis* (Boston: Shambhala, New Science Library, 1987), 133–49.

127. Mark A. Chesler. "Creating and Maintaining Interracial Coalitions," in *The Impacts of Racism on White Americans*, ed. Benjamin P. Bowser and Raymond G. Hunt, 217–43 (Thousand Oaks, CA.: Sage Publications, 1981); Higham, 242–46; Richard Merelman, *Representing Black Culture: Racial Conflict and Cultural Politics in the United States* (New York: Routledge, 1995), 284–99; Richard W. Thomas. *Understanding Interracial Unity: A Study of Race Relations* (Thousand Oaks, CA.: Sage Publications, 1996), 195–211.

128. Loriane Hutchins and Lani Kaahumanu, "Bicoastal Introduction," in *Bi Any Other Name: Bisexual People Speak Out*, xxii–xxiv, (Boston: Alyson Publications. 1991), xxii–xxiv.

129. Leonard Steinhorn and Barbara Diggs-Brown. *By the Color of Our Skin: The Illusion of Integration and the Reality of Race* (New York: Dutton, 1999), 222–23.

130. Thomas, 195–211.

131. Ahyas Siss, *Afro-Brasileiros, Cotas, e Ação Afirmativa: Razões Históricas* (Rio de Janeiro: Quartet Editora Siss, 2003), 86–109.

132. Louise Derman-Sparks. *Anti-Bias Curriculum: Tools for Empowering Young Children* (Washington, D.C.: National Association of the Education of Young Children, 1989), ix–10, 31–8; Arthur Schlesinger, Jr. *The Disuniting of America: Reflections on a Multicultural Society* (Knoxville, TN.: Whittle Direct Books, 1991), 1–3, 20–57.

133. Jon Cruz, *Culture on the Margins: The Black Spiritual and the Rise of American Cultural Interpretation* (Princeton, NJ: Princeton University Press, 1999), 3–4, 68.

134. Janet E. Helms, "An Overview of Black Racial Identity Theory," in *Black and White Identity: Theory, Research, and Practice*, ed. Janet E. Helms, 9–32 (Westport, CT.: Greenwood Press), 1990a; Janet E. Helms, "Toward a White Racial Identity Development," in *Black and White Identity: Theory, Research, and Practice*, ed. Janet E. Helms, 49–66 (Westport, Conn.: Greenwood Press, 1990b); Shelby Steele, *The Content of Our Character: A New Vision of Race in America*. (New York: St. Martin's Press, 1990), 48–49, 77–109.

References

Alves-Silva, J., M.S. Santos, Pedro Edson Moreira Guimarães, Antonio Carlos Santana Ferreira, Hans-Jürgen Bandelt, Sérgio D.J. Pena, and Vania Ferriera Prado, "The Ancestry of Brazilian mtDNA Lineages," *American Journal of Human Genetics* 67, 2000, 445.

"An Overview of the Human Genome Project (HGP)," http://www.genome.gov/12011238

Anderson, Victor. *Beyond Ontological Blackness: An Essay on African American Religious Criticism.* New York: Continuum, 1995.

Andrews, George Reid. *Blacks and White in São Paulo, Brazil, 1888–1988.* Madison, WI: University of Wisconsin Press, 1991.

Astor, Michael. "Brazil Tries Quotas to Get Racial Equality," *Los Angeles Times,* February 29, A3, 2004.

Bailey, Stanley R. "The Race Construct and Public Opinion: Understanding Brazilian Beliefs About Racial Inequality and Their Determinants," *American Journal of Sociology* 108, No. 2 (September 2002): 406–39.

Bender, Gerald. *Angola Under the Portuguese.* Berkeley and Los Angeles: University of California Press, 1978.

Bernardino, Joaze, "Ação Afirmativa e a Rediscussão da Democracia Racial no Brazil," *Estudos Afro-Asiáticos* 24, No. 2 (2002): 247–73.

Berghe, Pierre van den. *Race and Racism: A Comparative Perspective.* New York: Wiley, 1967.

Bourdieu, Pierre, and Loïc Wacquant. "On the Cunning of Imperialist Reason," *Theory, Culture, and Society* 16, No. 1 (1991): 41–58.

"Brasília– DF. Comissão Geral para Debater o Estatuto da Igualdade Racial" *Naçãomestiça* http://www.nacaomestica.org/

"Brazil: Affirmative Action in Higher Education," 2003–2004. Global Rights. http://www.globalrights.org/site/DocServer/LA_Fact_Sheets_AffirmActionBrazil.pdf?do cID=3623 "Brazil's Unfinished Battle for Racial Democracy." 2000. *Economist,* April 22, 31.

Burdick, John. "The Myth of Racial Democracy," *North American Congress on Latin America Report on the Americas* 25, No. 4 (February 1992): 40–42.

———. *Blessed Anastácia: Women, Race, and Popular Christianity in Brazil* (New York: Routledge, 1998a).

———. "The Lost Constituency of Brazil's Black Movement." *Latin American Perspectives* 25, No. 1 (January 1998b): 136–55.

Carneiro, Sueli, "De novo a raça," *Revista Espaço Acadêmico,* ano II, No. 21 (2003) (http://www.afirma.inf.br).

Carvalho, José Jorge de. *Inclusão Étnica e Racial no Brasil: A Questão das Cotas no Ensino Superior.* São Paulo: Attar Editorial, 2006.

Carvalho-Silva, Denise R., Fabrício R. Santos, Jorge Rocha, and Sérgio D. J. Pena, "The Phylogeography of Brazilian Y-Chromosome Lineages," *American Journal if Human Genetics* 68 (2001): 281–286.

Cavalli-Sforza, L. Luca, Paolo Menozzi, and Alberto Piazza, *The History and Geography of Human Genes* (Princeton, New Jersey: Princeton University Press, 1994).

Chesler, Mark A., "Creating and Maintaining Interracial Coalitions," in *The Impacts of Racism on White Americans,* ed. Benjamin P. Bowser and Raymond G. Hunt (Thousand Oaks, CA: Sage Publications, 1981), 217–43.

Cohen, David W. and Jack P. Greene, "Introduction," in *Neither Slave nor Free: The Freemen of African Descent in the Slave Societies of the New World,* ed. David. W. Cohen and Jack P. Greene (Baltimore, MD: Johns Hopkins University Press, 1972) 1–23.

"Coloque de volta MESTIÇO no censo do IBGE," *Naçãomestiça*

http://www.nacaomestica.org/.

Conceição, Fernando. "As cotas contra o apocalipse." *Folha de São Paulo, Caderno Mais,* June 27, 2004.

Coon, Carlton S., *The Living Races of Man.* New York: Alfred A. Knopf, 1965.

Costa, Emilia Viotti da., *The Brazilian Empire: Myths and Histories.* Chicago, IL: University of Chicago Press, 1985.

Cruz, Jon. *Culture on the Margins: The Black Spiritual and the Rise of American Cultural Interpretation.* Princeton, NJ: Princeton University Press, 1999.

Daniel, G. Reginald, *More Than Black? Multiracial Identity and the New Racial Order.* Philadelphia, PA: Temple University Press, 2002.

Davies, Rodrigo. 2003. "Brazil Takes Affirmative Action in HE." *Guardian,* August 4. http://education.guardian.co.uk/higher/worldwide/story/0%2C9959%2C1012157% 2C00.html/

Degler, Carl N. *Neither Black nor White: Slavery and Race Relations in Brazil and the United States.* Madison, WI: University of Wisconsin Press, 1971.

Derman-Sparks, Louise. *Anti-Bias Curriculum: Tools for Empowering Young Children.* Washington, D.C.: National Association of the Education of Young Children, 1989.

"Diga Não Ao Racismo Antimestiço" http://www.nacaomestica.org/

DeWitt, Mike and Adam Stepan, "Brazil in Black and White," http://www.pbs.org/wnet/wideangle/shows/brazil2/, 2007.

Domingues, Regina. "The Color of a Majority Without Citizenship." *Conexões: African Diaspora Research Project, Michigan State University* 4, no. 2 (November 1992): 6–7.

Dzidzienyo, Anani. *The Position of Blacks in Brazilian and Cuban Society.* Minority Group Rights Reports, no. 7. London: Minority Rights Group, 1979.

_____ "Brazil." In *International Handbook on Race and Race Relations,* ed. Jay A. Sigler. New York: Greenwood Press, 1987.

Escóssia, Fernanda da. "Determinar Qem é Negro Vira Polêmica na Lei Sobre Cotas do Rio." *Folha de São Paulo* (14 November 2001): D4.

Fernandes, Florestan. *A Integração do Negro na Sociedade de Classes.* São Paulo: Dominus Editora/Editora da USP, 1965.

Flory, Thomas. "Race and Social Control in Independent Brazil." *Latin American Studies* 9, no. 2 (November 1997): 199–224.

França, Ronaldo. "Não Deu Certo," *Veja* 1791 (26 February 2003): 71.

Freyre, Gilberto. *The Mansions and the Shanties.* Translated by Harriet de Onís. New York: Alfred A. Knopf, 1963a.

_____. *The Masters and the Slaves.* Translated by Harriet de Onís. New York: Alfred A. Knopf, 1963b.

_____. *Order and Progress.* Translated and edited by Rod W. Horton. New York: Alfred A. Knopf, 1970.

Frazier, E. Franklin. "A Comparison of Negro-White Relations in Brazil and the United States." (Originally published 1944). In *African American Reflections on Brazil's Racial Paradise,* ed. David J. Helwig. Philadelphia: Temple University Press, 1992.

Fry, Peter. "Politics, Nationality, and the Meaning of Race," *Daedalus* 129, no. 2 (2000): 83–118.

Fry, Peter and Yvonne Maggie. "Política Social de Alto Risco." In *Divisões Perigosas: Políticas Raciais no Brasil Contemporâneo,* ed. Peter Fry and Yvonne Maggie, Marcos Chor Maio, Simone Monteiro, and Ricardo Ventura Santos, 277–81. Rio de Janeiro: Civilização Brasileira, 2007.

Galdino, Daniela, and Larissa Santos Pereira. "Acesso à Universidade: Condições de Produção de um Discurso Facioso." In *Levando a Raça a Sério: Ação Afirmativa e Universidade,* ed. Joaze Bernardino and Daniela Galdino, 157–72. Rio de Janeiro: P&A Editora, 2003.

Gaspari, Elio. "O branco tem a marca de Nana," *Folha de São Paulo,* Caderno A, 16 April 2000: 14.

Góes, José Roberto Pinto de. "Sem vergonha de ser feliz," *O Globo,* Primeiro Caderno, 19 February 2003: 7.

Gomes, Nilma Lino and Aracy Alves Martins. *Afirmando Direitos: Acesso e Permanêcia de Jovens na Universidade.* Belo Horizonte: Autêntica, 2004.

Guimarães, Antonio Sérgio Alfredo. "Measures to Combat Discrimination and Racial Inequality in Brazil." In *Race Relations in Contemporary Brazil: From Indifference to Equality,* ed. Rebecca Reichmann, 143–53. University Park, PA: Pennsylvania State University Press, 1999.

———. "Ações Afirmativas para a População Negra nas Universidades Brasileiras." In *Ações Afirmativas: Políticas Públicas Contra as Desigualdades Raciais,* ed. Renato Emerson dos Santos and Fátima Lobato, 75–82. Rio de Janeiro: DP&A Editora, 2003.

Hamilton, Ruth Simms. "Conexões: Africa Diaspora Research Project," Michigan State University 4, no. 2 (November 1992), 2, 13.

Hanchard, Michael George. *Orpheus and Power: The Movimento Negro of Rio de Janeiro and São Paulo, Brazil, 1945–1988.* Princeton, NJ: Princeton University Press, 1994.

Harris, Marvin. *Patters of Race in the Americas.* New York: Walker, 1964.

Hasenbalg, Carlos. "O Negro nas Vésperas do Centenário." *Estudos Afro-Asiáticos* 13 (March 1987): 79–86.

———. "Perspectives on Race and Class in Brazil." In *Black Brazil: Culture, Identity, and Social Mobilization,* ed. Larry Crook and Randal Johnson, 61–84. Los Angeles: UCLA Latin American Center, 1999.

Hasenbalg, Carlos A., Nelson do Valle Silva, and Luiz Claudio Barcelos. "Notas Sobre Miscegenação no Brasil." *Estudos Afro-Asiáticos* 16, no. 3 (1989): 189–97.

Helms, Janet E. ed. *Black and White Identity: Theory, Research, and Practice.* Westport, CT: Greenwood Press, 1990.

Henig, Robin Maranyz. "The Genome in Black and White (and Gray)." *New York Times Magazine,* October 10 2004. http://www.nytimes.com/2004/10/10/magazine/10GENETIC.html/

Herring, Lee and Mercedes Rubio, "Scientists Warn of Conceptual Traps Concerning "Race" in New Genetic Map of Human Populations," Footnotes," April 2005 *American Sociological Association* http://www2.asanet.org/footnotes/apr05/indextwo.html

Higham, John. *Send These to Me: Jews and Other Immigrants in Urban America.* New York: Atheneum, 1975.

Hoetink, Hartimus. *Caribbean Race Relations: A Study of Two Variants.* London: Oxford University Press, 1967.

———. *Slavery and Race Relations in the Americas: Comparative Notes on Their Nature and Nexus.* New York: Harper and Row, 1973.

Hooks, Bell. *Yearning: Race, Gender, and Cultural Politics.* Boston: South End Press, 1995.

Htun, Mala. "Racial Quotas for a Racial Democracy." *NACLA Report on the Americas* 38, no. 4 (2005): 20–25.

"Human Genome Project Goals." http://www.genome.gov/11006945

Hutchins, Loriane, and Lani Kaahumanu. "Bicoastal Introduction." In *Bi Any Other Name: Bisexual People Speak Out,* xxii–xxiv. Boston: Alyson Publications, 1991.

IBGE. *See* Instituto Brasileiro de Geografía e Estadísticas.

Instituto Brasileiro de Geografía e Estadísticas (IBGE). *Censo Demográfico 2000. Características Gerais da População. Resultados da Amostra. Tabelas de Resultados.* Rio de Janeiro: Fundação IBGE, 2000.

Jeter, Jon. 2003. "Affirmative Action Debate Forces Brazil to Take Look in the Mirror." *Washington Post,* June 16.

Jobling, Mark A., Matthew Hurles, and Chris Tyler-Smith, *Human Evolutionary Genetics: Origins, Peoples, and Disease.* New York: Garland Publishing, 2004.

Jungmann, Raul. "Cotas para negros: dez questões," *O Globo,* December 15, 2001: 6.

Kamel, Ali. *Não Somos Racistas: Uma Reação Aos Que Querem Nos Transformar Numa Nação Bicolor.* 2a impressão. Rio de Janeiro: Editora Nova Fronteira, 2006.

Kane, Gregory. 2004. "In Bahia, University Council Votes in Favor of Quotas." Blackamericaweb.com. http://blackamericaweb.com/site.aspx/bawnews/diaspora/brazil3/.

Kennedy, James H. "Luiz Gama: Pioneer of Abolition in Brazil." *Journal of Negro History* 59, no. 3 (July 1974): 255–57.

Klein, Herbert S. "Nineteenth-Century Brazil," 309-334. In *Neither Slave nor Free: The Freemen of African Descent in the Slave Societies of the New World,* ed. David. W. Cohen and Jack P. Greene. Baltimore: Johns Hopkins University Press, 1972.

_____. *African Slavery in Latin America and the Caribbean.* New York: Oxford University Press, 1986.

Landry, Donna, and Gerald Maclean, ed. *The Spivak Reader: Selected Works of Gayatri Chakravorty Spivak.* New York: Routledge, 1995.

Laszlo, Ervin. *Evolution: The Grand Synthesis* (Boston: Shambhala, New Science Library, 1987).

Leite, Marcelo. "Raça é Só Conceito Social, Diz DNA Brasileiro," *Folha de São Paulo,* December 17, 2002: A16.

Lipsitz, George. "Noise in the Blood: Culture, Conflict, and Mixed Race Identities." In *Crossing Lines: Race and Mixed Race Across the Geohistorical Divide,* ed. Marc Coronado, Rudy P. Guevarra Jr., Jeffrey Moniz, and Laura Furlan Szanto, 32–35. Santa Barbara, Calif.: Multiethnic Student Outreach, in collaboration with the Center for Chicano Studies, University of California, Santa Barbara, 2003.

Lockhart, James, and Stuart B. Schwartz. *Early Latin America: A History of Colonial Spanish America and Brazil.* New York: Cambridge University Press, 1987.

Lovell-Webster, Peggy. "The Myth of Racial Equality: A Study of Race and Mortality in Northeast Brazil." *Latinamericanist,* (May 1987): 1–6.

Lovell-Webster, Peggy and Jeffery Dwyer. "The Cost of Not Being White in Brazil," *Sociology and Social Research* 72, no. 2 (1988): 136–38.

Lovell, Peggy A. and Charles H. Wood. "Skin Color, Racial Inequality, and Life Chances in Brazil." *Latin American Perspectives* 25, no. 3 (May 1998): 90–109.

Marcílio, Maria Luisa. "The Population of Colonial Brazil." In *Colonial Latin America,* vol. 2 of *The Cambridge History of Latin America,* ed. Leslie Bethell, 37–63. New York: Cambridge University Press, 1984.

Marger, Martin N. *Race and Ethnic Relations: American and Global Perspectives.* Belmont, Calif.: Wadsworth, 1991.

Margolis, Mac. "The Invisible Issue: Race in Brazil." *Ford Foundation Report* 23, no. 2 (Summer 1992): 3–7.

_____. 2003. "Brazil's Racial Revolution: Affirmative Action Has Finally Come of Age. And Latin America's Most Diverse Society May Change in Ways Few Had Ever Imagined." *Newsweek International,* November 3, 46.

Martins, Sérgio da Silva, Carlos Alberto Medeiros, and Elisa Larkin Nascimento. "Paving Paradise: The Road from 'Racial Democracy' to Affirmative Action in Brazil." *Journal of Black Studies* 34. no. 6 (July 2004): 787–816.

Merelman, Richard. *Representing Black Culture: Racial Conflict and Cultural Politics in the United States.* New York: Routledge, 1995.

"Mestiçofobia É Racismo." http://www.nacaomestica.org/

Motta, Athayde Motta (2000a) "Genética para as massas." http://www.afirma.inf.br; Motta, A. (2000b), "Genética para uma nova história." http://www. afirma.inf.br; Motta (2002) "Saem as raças, entram os genes." http://www.afirma. inf.br; Motta (2003) "Contra a genética, o conhecimento." "Com Raça, Sem Raça, Com Raça. . ." *Fala, Brasil!* 28 July 2005, http://www.brazil-brasil.com/content/view/528/78/; "Essencialismo Genético: por que a genética do século 21 soa como a biologia do século 19?" 14 de Junho de 2007 *http://www.mundonegro.com.br/noticias2/?noticiaID=863.*This article was originally published 1/6/2007 at IBASE: www.ibase.br).

Nascimento, Abdias do. *Mixture or Massacre? Essays on the Genocide of a Black People.* Translated by Elisa Larkin Nascimento. Buffalo: Puerto Rican Studies and Research Center, State University of New York at Buffalo, 1979.

Neves, Francisco, "Two Brazils." *Brazzil,* May 1, 2002. http://www.brazzil.com/content/view/2562/68/

Nobles, Melissa. *Shades of Citizenship: Race and the Census in Modern Politics.* Stanford: Stanford University Press, 2000.

Nogueira, Oracy. 1985 [1954]. "Preconceito Racial de Marca e Preconceito Racial de Origem (Sugestão de um Quadro de Referência para a Interpretação do Material sobre Relações Raciais no Brasil)," 78-79 In *Tanto Preto Quanto Branco: Estudo de Relações Racias,* ed. Oracy Nogueira. São Paulo: T.A. Queiroz.

Oliveira, Elvira. "Dia Nacional da Consciencia Negra." *Nova Escola,* (November 1993), 23–25.

Omi, Michael, and Howard Winant. *Racial Formation in the United States: From the 1960s to the 1990s,* 2nd edition. New York: Routledge, 1994.

Ortiz, Fernando. *Cuban Counterpoint.* Translated by Harriet de Onís. New York: Alfred A. Knopf, 1947.

Osava, Mario. "Rights—Brazil: Blacks Demand Adoption of Promised Measures." Inter-Press Service News Agency, November 16, 2005
http://www.ipsnews.net/news.asp?idnews=31051/

Paixão, Marcelo. "Waiting for the Sun: Account of the (Precarious) Social Situation of the African Descendant Population in Contemporary Brazil." *Journal of Black Studies* 34, no. 6 (July 2004): 743–65.

Pena, Sérgio D. J. "Há Uma Base Objetiva Para Definir o Conceito de Raça?," *Folha de São Paulo,* December 21, 2002: A3.

Pena, Sérgio D.J., Denise R. Carvalho-Silva, J. Alves-Silva, Vania Ferreira Prado, and Fabríco R. Santos, "Retrato Molecular do Brasil," *Ciência Hoje* 159 (2000): 16–25.

Philipkoski, Kristen. "Gene Map Presents Race Concerns,"
http://www.wired.com/science/discoveries/news/2001/02/41619

Pierre-Michel Fontaine, ed. *Race, Class, and Power in Brazil.* Los Angeles: UCLA Center for African American Studies, 1985.

Pierson, Donald. *Negroes in Brazil: A Study of Race Contact at Bahia.* Carbondale, IL: Southern Illinois University Press, 1967.

Prado, Caio, Jr. *The Colonial Background of Modern Brazil.* Translated by Suzette Macedo. Berkeley and Los Angeles: University of California Press, 1969.

Queiroz, Delcele Mascarenhas. "A Negro, Seu Acesso ao Ensino Superior e as Ações Afirmativas,"137-156. In *Levando a Raça a Sério: Ação Afirmativa e Universidade,* ed. Joaze Bernardino and Daniela Galdino. Rio de Janeiro: DP&A Editora, 2003.

"Race in Brazil, Out of Eden." *The Economist Print Edition,* July 3, 2003, http://www.economist .com/world/la/displayStory.cfm?story_id=1897546/

Reichmann, Rebecca. "Brazil's Denial of Race." *North American Congress on Latin America Report on the Americas* 28, no. 6 (1995): 35–42.

Reichmann, Rebecca. *Race Relations in Contemporary Brazil: From Indifference to Equality.* University Park, PA: Pennsylvania State University Press, 1999.

Risério, Antonio. *A Utopia Brasileira e Os Movimentos Negros.* São Paulo: Editora 34 Ltda, 2007.

Robinson, Lori S. "The Two Faces of Brazil; A Black Movement Gives Voice to an Invisible Majority." *Emerge,* (October 1994), 38–42.

Rochetti, Ricardo. "Not as Easy as Black and White: The Implications of the University of Rio de Janeiro's Quota-Based Admissions Policy on Affirmative Action." *Vanderbilt Journal of Transnational Law* 37, no. 1423 (November 2004). http://web .lexisnexis.com/universe/document?_m=5eb66ec1eb9aff3afe64e92c41a1df60_docnum=3 &wchp=dGLbVlb-zSkVb&_md5=0571753367a1a6b0fa45e7841eee1b9b/

Rohter, Larry. "Racial Quotas in Brazil Touch Off Fierce Debate." *New York Times,* April 5, 2003
http://www.nytimes.com/2003/04/05/international/Americas/05BRAZ.html/.

Russell-Wood, A.J.R. "Colonial Brazil,"84-133. In *Neither Slave nor Free: The Freemen of African Descent in the Slave Societies of the New World,* ed. David. W. Cohen and Jack P. Greene. Baltimore, MD: Johns Hopkins University Press, 1972.

Sales, E. L., Júnior. "Genética e realidade." http://www.afirma.inf.br.

Santos, Ricardo Ventura and Marcos Chor Maio. "Antropologia, Raça e os Dilemas das Identidades na Era da Genômica ," *História, Ciências, Saúde—Manguinhos,* 12, no. 2 (May-August 2005): 447–68.

Santos, Ricardo Ventura and Marcos Chor Maio, "Race, Genomics, Identities, and Politics in Contemporary Brazil," *Critique of Anthropology* 24, 4 (2004): 363–4.

Santos, Sales Augusto dos. "Ação Afirmativa e Mérito Individual." In *Ações Afirmativas: Políticas Contra as Desigualidades Raciais,* ed. Renato Emerson dos Santos and Fátima Lobato, Rio de Janeiro: DP&A Editora, 2003), 83–126.

Schlesinger, Arthur, Jr. *The Disuniting of America: Reflections on a Multicultural Society.* Knoxville, TN.: Whittle Direct Books, 1991.

Silva, Maria Palmira da. "Identidade Racial Brasileira." In *Racismo no Brasil: Percepções da Discriminação e do Preconceito Racial no Século XXI,* ed. Gevanilda Santos and Maria Palmira da Silva (São Paulo: Editora Fundação Perseu Abramo, 2005), 37–44.

Siss, Ahyas. *Afro-Brasileiros, Cotas, e Ação Afirmativa: Razões Históricas.* Rio de Janeiro: Quartet Editora, 2003.

Skidmore, Thomas A. "Bi-racial U.S.A. vs. Multi-racial Brazil: Is the Contrast Still Valid?" *Journal of Latin American Studies* 25, No. 2 (May 1993): 383–86.

———. *Black into White: Race and Nationality in Brazilian Thought.* New York: Oxford University Press, 1974.

———. "Race Relations in Brazil." *Camões Center Quarterly* 4, no. 3–4 (1992–1993): 49–57.

Spickard, Paul R., Rowena Fong, and Patricia L. Ewalt. "Undermining the Very Basis of Racism—Its Categories." *Social Work* 40, no. 5 (1995): 581–84.

Steele, Shelby. *The Content of Our Character: A New Vision of Race in America.* New York: St. Martin's Press, 1990.

Sundiata, I. K. "Late Twentieth-Century Patterns of Race Relations in Brazil and United States." *Phylon* 48, no. 1 (March 1987): 62–76.

Teixeira, Moema de Poli. "Negros em Ascensão Social: Trajectórias de Alunos e Professores Universitários no Rio de Janeiro. Rio de Janeiro: Pallas, 2003.

Telles, Edward. E. "Residential Segregation by Skin Color in Brazil." *American Sociological Review* 57, No. 2 (April 1991): 186–98.

———. "Racial Distance and Region in Brazil: Intermarriage in Brazilian Urban Areas." *Latin American Research Review* 28, no. 2 (1993):141–62.

———. *Race in Another America: The Significance of Skin Color in Brazil.* Princeton: Princeton University Press, 2004.

Thomas, Richard W. *Understanding Interracial Unity: A Study of Race Relations.* Thousand Oaks, CA.: Sage Publications, 1996.

Toni, Ana. 2004. "For Brazil, First Steps Toward Affirmative Action." *Ford Foundation Report,* Winter. http://www.fordfound.org/publications/ff_report/view_ff_report_detail.cfm?report_index=478/.

Toplin, Robert Brent, ed. In *Freedom and Prejudice: The Legacy of Slavery in the United States and Brazil.* Westport, CT.: Greenwood Press, 1981.

Vianna, Hermano. "Mestiçagem fora de lugar." *Folha de São Paulo Caderno Mais,* June 27, 2004.

Villardi, Raquel. "Acesso à Universiadade por Meio de Ações Afirmativas: Estudo da Situação dos Estudantes com Matrícula em 2003 e 2004 (Junho)." UERJ (Universidade do Estado do Rio de Janeiro) Report, 2004.

Vongs, Pueng, J. Prakash, Marcelo Ballve, and Sandip Roy. 2003. "Around the World, Countries Grapple with Affirmative Action." *Pacific News Service,* July 11, 2003. http://news.pacificnews.org/news/view_article.html?article_id=3e26118fcdf4fba57da467da3eeb43d0/.

Winant, Howard. *Racial Conditions: Politics, Theory, Comparisons.* Minneapolis: University of Minnesota Press, 1994.

Wood, Charles H., and José Alberto Magno de Carvalho. *The Demography of Inequality in Brazil.* New York: Cambridge University Press, 1988.

Chapter 16

All Mixed Up:
A New Racial Commonsense in Global Perspective[1]

G. Reginald Daniel and Gary L. Haddow

In this increasingly globalized world it is critical to deconstruct essentialized notions of racial (and cultural) difference that accompanied European colonialism as well as to demystify the notion of a self-contained Europe. Accordingly, the study of globalization and global human history should be grounded in the concept of postcolonial "critical hybridity." This also challenges the rigid strategic essentialism espoused by radical Afrocentrism and interrogates any globalization of the U.S. one-drop rule as an antiracist tactic. The goal should be to embrace a moderate Afrocentrism premised on strategic antiessentialism, which is not only compatible with postcolonial critical hybridity but also catalytic in the formation of a "postcolonial blackness." The 2003 publication of the initial conclusions of the Human Genome Project and Human Genome Diversity Project underscores the legitimacy of the concept of critical hybridity. This research indicates that although certain geno-phenotypical traits may mark off population aggregates as different from one another, in fact, a "multiracial" lineage is the norm rather than the exception. The implications of this "new genetics" have been a cause for both celebration and concern in terms of the connection between race, pharmacology, justice, genealogy, and intelligence. The "Molecular Portrait of Humanity" that emerges from these studies reiterates the limited relevance of race as a biological concept and portrays humans not as fixed "racial" essences but rather, the end result of extensive "racial" blending.

Eurocentrism and the Master Racial Project: European Colonialism and Expansion

Beginning in the late fifteenth and early sixteenth centuries, the colonial expansion of Western European nation-states—specifically Spain, Portugal, Italy, France, Germany, Holland, Denmark, and England—led to encounters between Europeans and populations that were very different culturally, and above all else, phenotypically from themselves. With the awareness among European nation-states of their power to dominate others they established empires throughout the New World, the Pacific, Asia, and Africa. The cultural and phenotypical differences between Europeans and their conquered populations laid the foundation for the concept of race.

It was not until the beginning of European colonial expansion that the necessary distinctions fundamental to the systematic, comprehensive, and reciprocal set of ideological beliefs capable of sustaining a racialized discourse and social structure emerged. All of the modern European philosophies, social theories, and literary traditions have been implicated in this process. Grounded in exploitive economic relations, racial divisions were used to justify a unique form of slavery involving primarily those of African descent. For millennia, expansion, conquest, exploitation, and enslavement had been an aspect of human history; however, these were not guided by ideologies or social systems based on race.[2] This does not dismiss the longer-standing ethnocentrism and prejudice based on color and other phenotypical attributes that had existed in some form since antiquity.[3] Even the antagonism that medieval Christian Europe displayed toward the two most significant non-Christian "Others"—the Muslim and Jewish populations—cannot be considered more than a "dress rehearsal" for racial formation.[4] Despite the chauvinism and atrocities of, for example, the Crusades, these hostilities were universally interpreted in religious terms even when they had racial metaphors.[5]

By the late eighteenth century racial formation gained legitimacy through supposed scientific investigation by naturalists and other learned individuals although it had no basis in natural science. It was the amalgamation of social beliefs and stereotypes that identified differences through the association of social groupings and physical appearances.[6] In this climate "race" increasingly came to designate a biologically defined group and rested on *genetic* arguments supporting ideas of inherent somatic as well as intellectual and cultural inferiority and superiority.[7] This was a direct result of Europe's rise to global domination as race became a way of classifying what were already considered naturally unequal populations. Racialized thinking reached maturity during the eighteenth and nineteenth centuries with the massive expansion of African slavery and when the rising imperial powers began to divide their "spoils" in Africa, as well as in Asia and the Pacific.[8]

A Eurocentric worldview was a consequence of the ascendance of European nation-states to global dominion. Europeans viewed themselves as an independent and self-contained entity relative to the rest of the world. This perspective designated Europe as a transcendental nexus of history due to its unprecedented accomplishments in the sensate sociocultural domain, which privileged materialist rationalism, science, and technology over other types of mentation and cultural expression.[9] Based on these achievements Eurocentrism is directly associated with the historical period referred to as modernity. In addition, Eurocentrism may be viewed as the master racial project that serves as a point of reference for all other racial projects. Becoming the unquestioned center of a global civilization, Europe radiated the idea of universalism through colonialism and imperialism forcing all non-Western "Others" to adapt European norms through systems of exploitation and domination. As a means of perpetuating essentialist notions of purity—racial and otherwise—Eurocentrism is specifically premised on an "either/or" mentation. Accordingly, it creates a dichotomous and hierarchical categorization of differences in terms of value, privilege, and experience, which attaches superior status and privileges to whiteness and inferior status and privileges to all racialized "Others."

Globalization and the New World Order

Colonialism was the process by which the European nation-states reached positions of economic, military, political, and cultural domination through conquest and direct settlement and control of "Others"—particularly in terms of occupation of their land—through both the distant control of resources, as well as of direct settlement. In an extended sense, the phenomenon was linked not only to the "First World" capitalist mode of production and mass culture, but also the concomitant destruction of pre-or non-capitalist forms of social organization.[10] The dismantling of European colonial empires in the twentieth century gave rise to awareness that West European civilization—and its outposts in Asia, the Pacific, Africa, and the Americas—was no longer "the unquestioned and dominant center of the world."[11] It also raised the hopes of the newly independent countries for the emergence of a truly postcolonial era.

Such optimism proved to be short-lived. It became apparent that the West had not in fact relinquished control although it had given up colonialism as its primary mechanism of control, which involved domination, exploitation, and exclusion of subordinate groups in their most explicit and abrasive form. Colonial structures based on domination and exclusion increasingly have been juxtaposed with or replaced by neocolonial structures. Characterized by what Italian political theorist and activist Antonio Gramsci describes as "hegemony," these structures allow dominant groups effectively to maintain control and hierarchy but create the illusion of equality by selectively including its subjects and incorporating its opposition.[12]

The persistence of neocolonial structures and practices is very obvious as compared to the less immediately perceptible emergence of capitalism as a truly global economy. The final demise of colonial regimes and subsequent collapse of the Soviet Union removed the barriers to the capitalist world market and opened the way for "an irresistible and seemingly irreversible globalization" of capitalist economic and cultural exchanges.[13] This has been accompanied by a transformation of the dominant productive process itself. There has been a reduction in the significance of industrial factory labor and an increase in the significance of "communicative, cooperative, and affective labor."[14] These forces in turn have transformed significantly the modern imperialist geography of the globe. The spatial divisions of what have been termed core, semi-peripheral, and peripheral regions—or more frequently, "First," "Second," and "Third" Worlds—seem to have become hopelessly commingled.[15]

Many lament the globalization of capitalist production and exchange as the closing of institutional channels through which workers and citizens can influence or contest the economic forces of exploitation; others celebrate globalization, along with the concomitant frequency and ease with which economic and cultural exchanges move across national boundaries, as the liberation of capitalist economic relations from the restrictions that political forces have imposed on them. The political sovereignty of the nation-state itself and its ability to regulate production and exchange, money, technology, people, and goods, while still powerful, has declined progressively. Even the most powerful nation-states can no longer be thought of as supreme and sovereign authorities associated with the imperialisms of the modern era. The decline in nation-state sovereignty, however, does not mean that sovereignty itself has declined. Along with the new global market and networks of production, sovereignty itself is taking a new globalized form. It is composed of a series of national and transnational entities united under a single logic of rule that progressively incorporates the spatial totality of the entire global realm within its open, expanding frontiers.[16]

Some individuals designate the United States as the ultimate authority that rules over the process of globalization. If imperialism in the strict meaning of the term was the domain of Europe, globalization is thus considered the province of the United States, which has become the center of a new global empire. According to this perspective the United States is at worse repeating the practices of old European imperialists; at best it is a more efficient and more benevolent world leader, rectifying the errors of the previous European dominated imperialist order originating in the modern era.[17] Both these views are based on the erroneous assumption, however, that the United States has simply donned the mantle of global power that was previously under the authority of European imperial nations. It is true that globalization in some sense originates in the United States and the underpinning of the global world order is in a sense Eurocentric. In addition, the United States does occupy a privileged position in the globalization process. In contrast to imperialism, which consisted of historical regimes originating in conquest, globalization is a social order that has no temporal boundaries and no territorial center of power or spatial limitations to its rule. In the emerging global order the United States cannot, and indeed no nation-state can maintain its position as a world leader in the dominative manner of modern European nation-states.[18]

This continuing global Western influence is rather, maintained through a flexible, yet, complex, interweaving of economic, political, military, ideological, and cultural dynamics and hegemonic power relations, including interventionist politics.[19] These power relations not only mask contemporary forms of control, subordination, and exploitation in the manner of neocolonialism but more important, indicate that globalization wields the potential to maintain hegemonic forms of cooptation and rule on an unprecedented scale.[20] On the one hand these forces are in combination binding humanity into a more global (or universal) network. These same forces also bring with them the real dangers of a bland uniformity and homogeneity and the dynamics have spawned reactionary forces seeking to resist the centripetal forces toward global convergence in the name of myriad types of fractious particularisms (racial, ethnic, cultural, religious, etc.) that fly in the face of every kind of larger social cooperation and civic mutuality.[21]

Globalization also offers new opportunities for the forces of resistance to develop political organization of global flows and exchanges reflective of structures and practices aimed toward more egalitarian ends. Those forces of resistance are themselves not limited to any geographical region. The political task is thus not to resist the forces of globalization per se. The goal should be to reorganize and redirect them as the basis for an alternative global society.[22] Clearly, the survival of a civilization that is increasingly global in dimensions and transnational in scope, and yet marked by many pluralities within pluralities, will depend on how successfully humans development new models of coexistence and cooperation. There is need to shift from dominator to partnership modes of interaction that nurture a sense of community (integration) without demanding uniformity.[23] Considering the current extremity of human history the continuing quest for domination be it racial or otherwise, has reached a point where such behavior is not only homicidal but also suicidal.[24]

From Colonial to Neocolonial and Postcolonial: Hybridity, Hierarchy, and Hegemony

Both "colonialism" and "neocolonialism" imply oppression and the possibility of resistance. However, "'postcolonialism" neither posits "clear domination nor conveys clear opposition."[25] The term "postcolonial" obscures the traces of colonialism that exist in the present.[26] By implying that colonialism has come to an end the term postcolonial lacks a political analysis of contemporary power relations.[27] "Postcolonial" implies going beyond not only colonialism but also anticolonial nationalist theory—which sought and led to the dismantling of formal political colonial domination—as well as a movement beyond a specific point in history. Postcolonial thought therefore stresses deterritorialization, the constructed nature of national borders and nationalism, as well as the obsolescence of anticolonialist discourse.[28]

Since the "post" in "postcolonial" suggests a stage "after" the demise of colonialism, it is imbued, quite apart from it users' intentions, with a spatial and temporal ambiguity. "Postcolonial" tends to be associated with Third World countries that gained independence after World War II. It can also refer to the Third World diasporic presence within First World metropolises. The "postcolonial" also collapses diverse chronologies such that the term potentially can be expanded exponentially. It can include processes of liberation originating in all societies "affected" by colonialism, including areas in North and South America that gained political independence during the late eighteenth and early nineteenth centuries. The majority of countries in Africa and Asia achieved independence during the twentieth century; "some in the 1930s (Iraq), others in the 1940s (India, Lebanon), and still others in the 1960s (Algeria, Senegal, the Congo) and the 1970s (Angola, Mozambique)," etc.[29]

These ambiguities and contradictions notwithstanding, the term "postcolonial" may be applied to a broader process that involves the dismantling of Eurocentric discourse in the emerging global order.[30] For example, the concept of "hybridity" in postcolonial discourse calls attention to the complex and multilayered identities generated by geographical displacements. Although racial and cultural hybridity have existed from time immemorial, European colonial expansion accelerated and actively shaped a new world of practices and ideologies of racial and cultural blending. This is particularly the case in the Americas, which have been the site of an unprecedented scale of blending in the form of "syncretism," "creolization," and "mestizaje" involving combinations of indigenous peoples, Africans, and Europeans, and later of diasporic immigrations from all over the world.[31]

On one level, the celebration of hybridity counters the colonialist obsession with racial "purity," which viewed different racial groups as different species created at different times that were therefore forbidden to "interbreed." The hostility to miscegenation—particularly in Anglo-North America—was encapsulated in such pejorative terms as "mongrelization" and "mulattoes" (seen as necessarily infertile).[32] While rejecting the colonialist obsession with purity, postcolonial hybridity also counterpoises itself against the rigid essentialism that often underpins Third World discourse, including radical Afrocentrism and much Black Nationalist thought. The concept of hybridity in postcolonial theory is admirably honed to deal with the complexities and contradictions "generated by the global circulation of peoples and cultural goods in a mediated and interconnected world."[33] The hybrid globalized human subject is confronted with the challenge of moving among the diverse modalities of sharply contrasting cultural and ideological worlds. Consequently, hybrid identities are not reducible to a fixed formula; rather, they form a changing repertory of cultural modalities.[34]

As part of the assault on Eurocentrism, postcolonial hybridity not only interrogates any notion of racial (and cultural) purity but also the concept of race itself. Indeed, given that science has been unable to produce empirical data that would confirm the existence of clearly delineated biophysical racial boundaries, many "deconstructive" postcolonial thinkers present race as a problem, a misconception, a legacy of the past that should be dispensed with altogether. They seek to "transcend race" in pursuit of a universal humanism as part of an emerging global consciousness.[35] Constructivist postcolonial thinkers argue that any notion of "transcending race" would be unthinkable until the struggle to achieve equality of racial difference has been won. These thinkers challenge the notion that race is something we can or should move beyond. Instead, they posit "racial transcendence" by acknowledging a more inclusive identity based on a multiplicity of ancestral backgrounds. Many of these "constructive" postcolonial thinkers agree that the concept of race invokes biologically based human characteristics in the form of "racial traits" but do not view racial categories and boundaries as being absolutely fixed in biological fact. Racial categories and identities are rather, considered unstable and decentered complexes of sociocultural meanings that are constantly being created, inhabited, contested, destroyed, and transformed by political struggle. Racial formation may be thought of not only as an element of social structure but also as a dimension of human cultural representation and signification—rather than an illusion.[36]

The impulses behind and implications of the celebration of hybridity are themselves "mixed," if you will.[37] The deconstruction of dichotomous notions of purity, along with the celebration of racial and cultural blending per se, is not sufficient. These dynamics must be articulated in the manner of "critical hybridity." Otherwise, they risk downplaying contemporary forms of neocolonialism that effectively maintain racial hierarchy.[38] Any discourse on hybridity must also take into consideration questions of hegemony and inclusion that create the illusion of equality without those in power actually giving up control. For example, national racial and cultural identities in Latin America have been officially articulated as hybrid, multiracial, and egalitarian (see Figure 7:1a of this book). They have been hypocritically integrationist, that is to say, assimilationist ideologies, seeking whitening through racial and cultural blending, which have deliberately obscured subtle hegemonies that reproduce racial hierarchies in a new guise (see Figure 7:1b).

Despite these caveats, the concept of postcolonial critical hybridity is part of a broader process instrumental to the study of globalization and global human history for deconstructing the essentialized, dichotomous, and hierarchical ranking of racial (and cultural) difference that accompanied European colonialism as well as demystifying the belief in a self-contained Europe. It is imperative to acknowledge the specificity of Europe's development by reading its history through multiple racial and cultural lenses. Indeed, what is referred to as European civilization is actually a global human heritage "that for historical, political, and geographical reasons" has been bestowed upon the modern world "in the guise of a European or Western synthesis."[39]

A closer analysis of the celebrated markers in the historical formation of Europe—Greece, Rome, Christianity, the Renaissance, the Enlightenment— indicates that each is a moment of hybridity and integration: Greece, strongly influenced by, if not an actual colony or outpost of Egyptian, Phoenician, and Asian civilization; Rome, "strongly indebted" to Greece, Egypt, and Carthage; Christianity, originally a religion of Asian origin, whose link with Byzantium, the Nestorians, and Gnostics at times "loomed larger" than it relationship with European, i.e., Latin, Christendom; the Renaissance, "a recovery of Hellenic civilization passed on thorough Arabic civilization and deeply engaged with non-European cultures"; the Enlightenment, "another period wide open to non-European influences, from China to Egypt."[40]

The impetus behind these revisions of Eurocentric history is not, however, necessarily to enhance the role of Africa and individuals of African descent, or the non-Western world, by linking them with the much-vaunted achievements of Western Europe. Their goal is to point out that many of the philosophies, political principles, forms of knowledge in physics, chemistry, technology, medicine, metallurgy, and art that have been attributed singularly to Western

Europe by virtue of its supposedly inherent superiority, have been to a considerable extent multicultural and multiracial, that is to say, plural in origin (see Figure 7:1d) and transcultural and transracial (or egalitarian integrative) in composition (Figure, 7:1a). It is significant that the synthesis of these elements is uniquely European. This should not obscure the fact that the sources are plural and intercontinental as well. European civilization becomes more transparent if we look at Europe as part of Eurasia, and Southern Europe as part of a larger Mediterranean continuity encompassing North Africa as well as influences that extend from West Africa. Indeed, the actual "borders" between the West and the larger non-Western world have been more blurred and porous "frontiers" than Eurocentric rhetoric and imagery have acknowledged.[41]

Afrocentrism and Strategic Essentialism

The Eurocentric paradigm, and its companion pieces white racism and white supremacy, have had a particularly oppressive impact on individuals of African descent across the globe. It served to justify African enslavement and became the basis for the U.S. one-drop rule of hypodescent, which is an extreme expression of Eurocentrism that designates as black everyone of African descent. The rule perpetuated a binary racial order that has necessitated individual identification as either black or white. And, by codifying the dichotomization and hierarchical valuation of whiteness over blackness in the manner of inegalitarian pluralism (figure 1.f) the rule not only served as part of the strategy for preserving European American cultural and racial "purity" but also as a means of maintaining white privilege.[42]

By drawing boundaries solidifying subordinated racial identity and excluding African Americans from interacting with European Americans as equals, the rule had the unintended consequence of legitimating and forging group identity. Originally a tool of oppression, the one-drop rule principle has become an important transnational element of what Gayatari Spivak calls "strategic essentialism." This concept refers to a tactic that nationalities, racial/ethnic, or "minority" groups can utilize to mobilize themselves in order to achieve certain goals. Strong differences may exist between members of these groups as they engage in continuous and indeed contentious debates. It may be considered strategic for them to project their group identity in an "essentialized" or reductionist manner that focuses on one axis of experience, identity, and ultimately, oppression (e.g., an emphasis on race as opposed to gender, class, etc.).[43]

Accordingly, the one-drop rule has served as an essentialist tactic that enabled African Americans to organize. This eventually culminated in the civil rights movement of the 1950s and 1960s that dismantled Jim Crow segregation and achieved the passage of historic legislation dissolving legal racial discrimination and inequality. Considering that globalization in some sense originates in the United States, it also follows that the one-drop rule principle would be appropriated or exported as a transnational antiracist and anticolonial tactic. This is most obvious, for example, in the formation of black movements in Brazil and other parts of Latin America as well as in South Africa since the 1960s and 1970s. In those societies, racial definitions and relations have historically been different from those in the United States, specifically their historical recognition of white, multiracial, and black individuals, despite their similarly inequitable treatment of all non-whites.

The implementation of essentialist formulations of blackness that draw on the U.S. one-drop rule principle as a tool for mobilizing the black and multiracial populations has led to irreconcilable conflicts, particularly in arriving at definitions of racial identity and composition. This in turn has helped undermine the mass mobilization the rule was supposedly intended to advance.[44] In addition, any globalized definitions of racial categories and identities premised on the rule mask its potential as a form of cooptation, control, subordination, and exploitation in the manner of neocolonialism. French thinkers such as Bourdieu and Wacquant voiced similar criticism.[45] They considered any globalized appropriation or imposition of the one-drop rule and related racial projects as the product of "cultural imperialism."[46] Racial categories and strategies specific to a given context, particularly the United States, are transformed into supposedly "natural, universal, and true" ones. These are made applicable to any and all situations, which perpetuates a situation of "symbolic violence."[47]

The legitimacy of the desire to give voice to the shared global oppression embedded in the African diasporic experience is not in question. Indeed, the strengths of this Afrocentric perspective are undeniable: the fostering of group pride, solidarity, and self-respect among African-descent individuals and an interrogation of the ideology of inegalitarian integration (assimilation) Figure 1.b and the perpetuation of differences in the manner of inegalitarian pluralism (apartheid, Figure 1.f).[48] But the effectiveness of any organizing principle as the basis for essentialized collectives (viewed as if they were "natural," static, and eternal units) is fraught with unavoidable contradictions.[49] Some of the discourses and practices of radical Afrocentrists are not merely pro-black but anti-white, if not actually "racist" in the current sociological meaning of the concept.[50] In extreme cases this has prompted many individuals to reject any association or alliances with, if not the demonization of whites, which has in turn led to accusations of a reverse type of apartheid (Figure 1.e).[51]

Exponents of radical Afrocentrism often criticize the validity of the biological concept of "race" on the one hand while reinscribing essentialist notions of black identity on the other.[52] They thus rearticulate the notion of "purity" that underpinned nineteenth-century scientific racism. The European and Anglo-North American theorists of the period argued that racial "purity" was a necessary prerequisite for a civilization to be creative. This made it increasingly unacceptable that Greece, as the designated birthplace of the modern West, and thus the source of Western rationalism, could have been the result of the blending of indigenous Europeans, African Egyptians, and Semitic Phoenicians, whether in the form of colonization or mere cultural (and racial) exchange resulting from contact through trade, war, etc. Once the forces of an emergent capitalism were propelled into full drive, Eurocentric theories served as the justification African enslavement. Africans were necessarily excluded from any discussion that focused on their contribution to the development of the West and global history by extension. It is therefore imperative to deconstruct the Eurocentric rendering of history.[53]

Many radical Afrocentrists, borrowing on the U.S. one-drop rule, apply the term "black" to anyone and anything of African origin no matter how remote in space or time.[54] They rarely explore, and sometimes openly dismiss, the profound dynamics of racial and cultural blending and multiple identities found throughout the African Diaspora. Furthermore, this perspective, when taken to Afrocentric extremes, ignores the complex global ancestral, genetic, and cultural diversity and blending that has taken place over the eons. This is a fact that radical Afrocentrists, much as Eurocentrists, generally have failed to acknowledge, or outright dismiss in their support of racial essentialism and search for racial "purity."[55] Radical Afrocentrists thus delineate the contours of blackness and the African diasporic experience from a photographic negative of whiteness.[56] Radical Afrocentric revisionism reaffirms the same oppressive mechanism inherent in the Eurocentric dichotomization of whiteness and blackness. At best, it perpetuates an oversimplification of prehistory and contemporary history, and at worst a new distortion. By incorporating to contemporary issues and value the notion of a transhistorical and transgeographical "black" essence radical Afrocentrists obscure the lived and empirical conditions that are the basis for diverse identities and cultural productions.They thus actually nurture even further the very collective historical amnesia they seek to cure.[57]

Toward a "Postcolonial Blackness:" Afrocentrism and Strategic Antiessentialism

If Afrocentrists wish to dismantle Eurocentrism they must also move beyond the "either/or" thinking that underpins both Eurocentric and radical Afrocentric thought. The goal should be to embrace a moderate Afrocentrism based on a "both/neither" way of thinking that is compatible with the postcolonial concept of "critical hybridity."[58] This moderate Afrocentrism is posited on an egalitarian blending of pluralism (Figure 7:1d) and integration (Figure 7:1a)—integrative pluralism (or pluralistic integration)—in which blackness and whiteness are seen as relative, rather than absolute, extremes on a continuum of grays. Many radical Afrocentrists view the concept of critical hybridity as tantamount to Eurocentrism in a new guise that would lead to the loss of black distinctiveness and political cohesiveness (Figure 7:1c).[59] Consequently, they have overlooked, or outright rejected, the possibility of a critical hybridity (or multiraciality) premised on egalitarian or antiracist terms, which emphasize a nondichotomous and nonhierarchial mentation. This criticism, nevertheless, obscures the potential that these concepts hold for challenging a myopic and constricting "ontological blackness."[60] This bias, in turn, precludes acknowledging and exploring new possibilities for the construction of self and community[61] but more important, for critiquing the pathologies of racism that originating in the Eurocentric master racial project.[62]

One factor that divides Afrocentrism—particularly moderate Afrocentrism—from the concept of critical hybridity is that "Afrocentrism" means different things to different people, and this has obscured its deeper significance. The most common perception is that Afrocentrism seeks to expose individuals—particularly through the education system—to the accomplishments and contributions of individuals of African descent in the manner of egalitarian pluralism (Figure 7:1c). Another view is that Afrocentrism is a new form of Black Nationalism that exposes white racism and promotes racial separatism (or inegalitarian pluralism). In extreme cases, the goal has been to replace white superiority with a new hierarchy premised on the superiority of blackness (Figure 7:1e). This is a response to the perceived failure of civil rights legislation and philosophy to ameliorate the economic, political, social, and psychological oppression that continues to plague African Americans.[63]

Although Afrocentrism is related to African history and originated in Black Nationalist thought, it is more appropriately described as a paradigm that places African-descent individuals at the center of their analyses. They become subjects rather simply objects of history. Afrocentrism is predicated on traditional African philosophical assumptions, which is particularly evident in its more moderate as compared to its more radical variants. It assumes that all elements of the universe have a metaphysical base, are created from a similar universal substance, and are functionally interconnected. In addition, this more moderate Afrocentric perspective makes no absolute demarcation between the metaphysical (or subjective) and the physical (or objective) domains. This rejection of clearly delineated boundaries extends to morality, temporality, and the very meaning of reality.[64] Afrocentrism values knowledge gained through intuition and feelings as much as that gained through the senses and the intellect. The Afrocentric paradigm fosters a human-centered orientation that values interpersonal connections more highly than material objects. This more moderate Afrocentrism rejects the dichotomization and hierarchical valuation of differences typified by Eurocentric (and radical Afrocentric) thinking, which divides things into mutually exclusive and unequal categories of value, privilege, and experience.[65]

Broadly speaking, moderate Afrocentrism is part of a generalized assault on the Eurocentric paradigm that polarizes things into black or white. It replaces the Eurocentric dichotomy with a paradigm that views these categories as relative rather than antithetical categories of experiences. This variant of Afrocentric though[t] rejects the hierarchical ranking of differences that characterize the Eurocentric (and modern) paradigm, which has placed Europe at the center of everything and dislocates African contributions. Moderate Afrocentrism recenters Africa, without ethnocentrism, to its rightful place in global human history, as the origins of humanity and civilization. More important, it originates in and is centered in an African worldview without privileging Africa and its contributions over other parts of the globe. Rather, it posits a cosmovision that happened to originate in Africa and is centered in an African worldview simply because Africa is the birthplace of humanity.

More moderate variants of Afrocentrism are basically engaged in a critique of the pathologies of modernity and the sensate-dominated worldview, which privileged materialist rationalist thinking and technology over other types of mentation and cultural expression. This moderate Afrocentric worldview is reflective of an even broader and more fundamental epistemological shift seeking to move civilization away from the dominant "either/or" paradigm that originated in modernity. This counter-paradigm argues that many things cannot be categorized by dichotomous thinking and emphasizes instead contexts, relationships, and wholes. Whereas the Eurocentric construction of identities in modern Western consciousness is thoroughly permeated by the erection of dichotomous oppositions that delineate things into mutually exclusive categories of experience, moderate Afrocentrism seeks to incorporate concepts of "partly," "mostly," or "both/neither."[66]

Moderate Afrocentrism, which is premised on the concept of critical hybridity, serves as a form of what George Lipsitz refers to as "strategic antiessentialism."[67] Jean-Paul Sartre (1905–1980) addresses similar concerns in "*Orphée Noir*" ("*Black Orpheus*"), which he wrote as an introduction to the *Anthologie de la Nouvelle Poésie Nègre et Malgache de Langue Francaise* (*Anthology of the New Black and Malagasy Poetry in the French Language*, 1948), edited by Leopold Sédar Sénghor (1906–2001), one of Negritude's most prominent exponents. It is perhaps the most famous and conceivably the most controversial essay on this topic. This essay sought to define the concept of Negritude for Western audiences, while at the same time seeking to encourage its writers to embrace Marxism in their search for a universal path beyond racial identity politics.[68]

On the one hand, Sartre understood Negritude and Afrocentricity by extension as an operative power of negation (or antithesis), a type of strategic essentialism formulated as an irreducible difference in the manner of egalitarian pluralism. It seeks to unify blacks in their struggle to constitute a unique history, reclaim their humanity, and shield themselves from outside contagion. Negritude (and Afrocentricity) is thus a rearticulation of blackness as an existentialist affirmation liberated from static and atavistic connotations (or thesis) in the French imaginary.[69] Sartre commended Negritude's racial essentialism in that he admired the African's closeness to the natural world and celebration of communal over individual concerns. He contrasted the synthetic African with the analytic European and black's capacity to display warmth and emotion against the whites's cold rationality. He praised the African's blameless role in modern history's litany of genocide, fascism, and racism.[70] On the other hand, Sartre was not content with defining Negritude simply as strategic essentialism (or "anti-racist racism")[71] and anticolonialism uniting people around race consciousness to combat French colonialism, paternalism, and imperialism. He also envisioned Negritude (and Afrocentricity broadly construed) as emblematic of a postcolonial and strategic antiessentialism. Blackness would be deployed as part of a larger project of abolishing all kinds of hierarchies, racial and otherwise, in the manner of egalitarian integration (or a new synthesis). Ultimately, this would serve as a vehicle for the transcendence of blackness in a future global and universal humanism.[72]

The concept of critical hybridity, which underpins moderate Afrocentricity as well as Sartre's concept of universal humanism, provides a means through which all individuals can liberate themselves from and move beyond the dichotomous, hierarchical, and myopic perspective bequeathed by Eurocentric discourse. It challenges essentialist notions of identity espoused by radical Afrocentrism and interrogates any global imposition or appropriation of the one-drop rule as a tactic in the antiracist struggle.[73] Instead, moderate Afrocentrism acknowledges the various types of African-derived subjectivity without negating a larger African-derived collectivity or maintaining that collectivity as a complete antithesis of whiteness. It challenges the limitations of Eurocentrism and radical Afrocentrism, question notions of authentic and essentialist identity,[74] and thus opposes any construction of self and community that reifies "the blackness that whiteness created."[75]

The reluctance of many individuals to critique the essentialist premises of radical Afrocentrism and subscribe to more moderate variants that posit critical hybridity is rooted in the legitimate fear that individuals will lose sight of the unique sensibilities and culture that have arisen from the African diasporic experience. Bell Hooks proposes that essentialism can be criticized while emphasizing the authority of experience. She argues there is a significant difference between repudiating the idea of an African-derived essence and recognizing that African-derived identity has been forged through the experience of exile and struggle.[76] This perspective would also make it possible to acknowledge the manner in which sex/gender, class, and a host of other categories of difference have altered the collective African diasporic experience.

The emphasis on strategic racial essentialism reflected in radical Afrocentric thought has typically required the erasure or leveling of concerns relating to other axes of experience and oppression (e.g., sexism/gendered racism, homophobia, etc.). It has in no small part helped perpetuate, rather than ameliorate inequities originating in these differences, which undercuts the very solidarity radical Afrocentrism seeks to achieve.[77] Essentialist tactics must be balanced with those premised on strategic antiessentialism. This would give voice to more than one axis of experience, identity, and ultimately oppression, which in turn would make it possible to recognize the interlocking and fluid nature of racial, class, gendered inequalities, etc., and how each feeds on each other. This would serve as the basis for greater inclusiveness by acknowledging a broader range of concerns, which would ultimately further the larger struggle for social justice.[78]

New Genetics or Scientific Racism in a New Guise: Race and Genetic Comity

The strategic antiessentialism embedded in the notion of critical hybridity, which is supported by moderate Afrocentric thought, would seem to have gained legitimacy from the current research in the "new genetics." This is particularly the case with sequencing of parts of mitochondrial DNA, the Y chromosome, and nuclear DNA, which sheds light on the "genetic origins" of humanity. The 2003 publication in the United States and Europe (with further analysis still being published) of the initial conclusions of the Human Genome Project (HGP) and the companion research of the Human Genome Diversity Project (HGDP) was the result of one of the largest and most international projects in modern science. The original HGP project began in 1991 with the goal of not only determining more than 3 billion base pairs of nucleotides strung together in a specific order along the chromosomes linked together in a specific order along the chromosomes in the human genome but also identifying all the genes in this vast amount of data. This latter part of the project is still ongoing, although a preliminary count indicates the human genome is composed of approximately 30,000 genes.[79]

At the molecular level, roughly 99.9 percent of genetic information is identical from individual to individual. That said, approximately 0.1% of the 3 billion bases of human DNA (an estimated 10 million) are locations of common genetic variations that differ from individual to individual, which are called single nucleotide polymorphisms (SNP's). Most SNP patterns have been preserved for thousands of years, despite the reshuffling of DNA that occurs with each new generation.[80] Still, SNP's tend to occur in different patterns in various populations and are typically inherited in clusters called haplotype blocks. Like SNP's, varieties of haplotype blocks occur at different frequencies in diverse regions of the world, which has enabled population geneticists to reconstruct the history of human migration. Of all polymorphisms, only a small percentage is different as a function of ancestry and these are called AIM's (Ancestry Informative Markers). AIM's are specific genetic polymorphisms that contain information about population structure, inter- and intra-individual diversity, and the history of the human species. Consequently, while SNP patterns do not reveal anything about the function of the genes, they can provide information about an individual's continent (s) of ancestry and, by extension, human paths of migration throughout history.[81]

Scientists have found that roughly 10 percent of SNP's are more common in certain continental groups and can be used to distinguish different geno-phenotypical differences that arose during the tens of thousands of years that humans populations evolved on separate continents after their ancestors dispersed from humanity's birthplace in Central Africa millennia ago.[82] Between 90,000 and 180,000 years ago, populations from Africa spread throughout Africa, Asia, Europe, and the Pacific; perhaps as early as 30,000 years ago but at least as recently as 15,000 years ago they migrated to the Americas. As they adapted to various environments they evolved into geographical aggregates of populations displaying differences in various bodily features. Some of the externally visible features—skin color, hair, and facial morphology—are commonly referred to as "racial traits." These physical differences (phenotypes) reflect some of the differences in genetic information (genotypes) that are transmitted through one's ancestors. There are human populations that, taken as aggregates, exhibit higher incidences of particular geno-phenotypical traits than do other human populations, taken as aggregates.[83]

If geno-phenotypical diversity of racial traits is a biological fact, the boundaries delineating geno-phenotypical subgroupings are not discrete or fixed entities. These boundaries have always been eroded by contact—through migration, trade, and war—that has inevitably set into motion a countertrend toward "racial entropy." Over time racial entropy levels out absolute differences by diffusing common genetic information—and ultimately common phenotypical traits—throughout the general population if no forces intervene to prevent this process. Consequently, the 0.1 percent of the genetic information that determines phenotypical traits associated with racial differentiation is itself the product of millennia of genetic "blending."[84] Although we recognize certain geno-phenotypical traits as marking off population aggregates as different from one another, in fact, humans are "all mixed up," such that a "multiracial" lineage is the norm rather than the exception. Indeed, if we trace a person's lineage back over the generations, the number of ancestors, as well as the myriad possibilities in terms of their "racial" composition, is staggering. Elucidating the significance and mapping the location of these phenomena has become a key focus of the "new" genetics. Mapping, among other things, can measure the ancestral backgrounds within individuals and populations.

Race and Genetic Pharmacology

While scientists were mapping the human genome in the early 1990s, the state for the first time mandated that all federally funded biomedical and behavioral research include members of historically excluded groups, particularly racial/ethnic "minorities" and women. After decades of research on mostly white, male subjects, this government-sponsored initiative was generally hailed as an advancement by politicians and scientists across the racial and gender spectrum.[85] However, as the Human Genome Project discredited the use of race in science, it had some rather unintended and paradoxical consequences in terms of biomedical and behavioral research. It prompted the pharmaceutical industry—particularly the Pharmacogenetics Research Network, a government funded follow-up to the Genome Project—to begin investigating possible genetic causes for racial disparities in disease and drug responses. Instead of focusing on the 99.9 percent of genes shared by all humans, they focused on the 0.01 percent that differs. The goal was to provide a detailed map of key genetic markers or SNP's considered to be potentially predictive of an individual's risk for particular diseases, and responsiveness to specific remedies. These data in turn would make it possible to design clinical trials and epidemiology studies that might aid in developing effective population-targeted pharmacological treatments.[86]

Documenting health disparities is imperative, given the significantly higher rates of disease and mortality from disease among racial/ethnic "minority" groups in the United States. A small group of African American scientists eventually voiced opposition to the fact that the federal mandate could foster, if only unwittingly, the very racism its originators hoped to undermine. They feared this development might endorse a gene basis for the social construct of race and nurture the belief that there are significant biological differences among perceived racial groups.[87] The small remaining percentage of genetic variations notwithstanding, gene-based explanations for differences in complex social outcomes have been endemic to scientific and vernacular discourse since the eighteenth century.

Opponents have been concerned that the new research could undermine principles of equitable treatment and opportunity that have relied on the presumption that all individuals are fundamentally equal. This is turn would lead to specific racial groups being invariably associated with specific diseases and physical conditions. This would infuse long-discredited racial prejudices with a new potency and lead to science-based racial discrimination.[88] The dye had been cast by the time critics voiced their concerns. The use of racial categories in applications for research funding and reporting of results has become normative. This in turn has resulted in a concentrated focus on and blind faith in genes as the basis of understanding and treating disease.[89] As federal funds continue to pour into research on the genetic sources for certain racial disparities in terms of disease (e.g., diabetes, asthma, alcoholism, etc.) race as a biological fact becomes more entrenched in the public consciousness.[90]

The dangers of the new genetic pharmacology were underscored by the nation's first designer "race-based drug" BiDil (isosorbide/hydralzaine hydrochloride), which was approved by the F.D.A. in June 2005. BiDil was marketed only after it was unsuccessful in wining regulatory approval because tests failed to demonstrate the drug's effectiveness for congestive heart failure in the general population. In the original test, there was the suggestion that the drug might benefit African Americans.[91] NitroMed of Lexington, Massachusetts, which manufactured the drug, did not develop a clinical trial to determine whether various racial/ethnic groups had different responses to the drug. The firm "reinvented" BiDil as an "ethnic drug,"[92] and went directly to the F.D.A. to request that it be tested specifically on 1,050 Africans.[93] The Association of Black Cardiologists co-sponsored the clinical trials and received $200,000 from NitroMed to organize them. In the study, which was composed of self-identified African Americans, BiDil reduced the death rate by 43% and the hospitalization rate by 39% as compared to the placebo. Those striking statistics secured FDA approval, which was enthusiastically applauded by the Association of Black Cardiologists.[94]

Troy Duster, a sociologist at the University of California, Berkeley, and a recent former president of the American Sociological Association, has been one of the most articulate and outspoken voices addressing not only the faulty reasoning of pharmacogenomics but also "genetic" profiling based on race that could conceivably be one of the nefarious, if unintended, uses of this technology.[95] Duster argues that cystic fibrosis, which is thought to be a European American disease, and indeed far greater among those individuals, also afflicts some African Americans.[96] Conversely, sickle cell anemia is generally considered an African American disease, and the likelihood of occurrence is in fact greater among individuals of West African descent, but it is also common among Greeks, individuals on the Arabian Peninsula, and in other regions of the Old World where the sickle-cell trait helps provide some immunity to malaria or lessens the symptoms in case of infection. These phenomena need not be race-based but rather, are markers from the regions where certain populations originated. Awareness of these variations is absolutely necessary.[97]

Duster also voiced concerns about the similarly flawed approach to the study of hypertension.[98] He points out it is true that African Americans ages 45 to 64 are more than 2.5 times likely than European Americans to die from heart failure, which suggests a biological basis. The disparity narrows after age 65. This is equally true for the higher rates of hypertension among African Americans than European Americans. The research indicates that the disease can be reduced when individuals are removed from stressful situations. And, it is undeniable that African Americans face daily situations that are inherently stressful and stem from the racial profiling that pervades their daily activities.[99] The disparity may be less attributable to biology and race than other documented quality of life factors in heart disease (e.g., diet, stress, lifestyle, etc.). Data outside of the United States further undermines the rationale for a race-based approach to hypertension. For example, Germany has the highest rate of the condition and Nigeria the lowest rate. Hypertension studies in the Caribbean indicate fewer racial disparities than in North America. If African Americans are presumed to be genetically similar to individuals of African descent in the Caribbean, then molecular genetics would indicate that that the cause of the disease is not endemic to that population.[100]

Similarly, African American males have twice the rate of prostate cancer as their European American counterparts. Scientists are not asking why men of African descent in the Caribbean and sub-Saharan Africa have much lower rates of prostate cancer than all American men. Instead, the National Cancer Institute is searching for cancer genes among African American males just as millions of dollars are being spent on trying to find a drug for black hypertension. This is not only significantly less costly than targeting poverty as a major contributing factor in much hypertension but also obscures the class or socioeconomic factors involved in the disease.[101] These data indicate an intricate relationship between genes and social environment. A necessarily interdisciplinary perspective would involve asking whether there is something in the United States environment that activates the high rates of these diseases.[102]

This is neither to suggest there is no correlation between diseases and race/ethnicity nor argue that scientists simply disregard the impact of environment and lifestyle on disease.[103] These issues are frequently framed in a simplistic manner that emphasizes what is transpiring inside to the body without taking into consideration the complex interaction between environment and disease and the impact of factors outside.[104] When biologists discuss genetic diseases, there is generally something in the environment that initiates their onset, which should be taken into consideration. Since the genomic revolution has gained momentum, many scientists appear to have increasingly disregarded these considerations. In other words, it is simpler to look inside the body because genes, proteins, and SNP patterns are far more measurable than the complexity of social dynamics.[105]

Duster is emphatic that the genomic revolution is moving considerably faster than humanity's ethical and practical abilities to handle it. He urges geneticists to slow down and examine their methods as they search for links between genes, disease, and race.[106] While cautionary in his approach, Duster does not actually oppose the research itself. Rather, he is critical of the manner in which some biologists interpret the data and privilege genetics as if it holds the answers to medical problems that afflict all individuals in a particular perceived racial/ethnic group. His concern is that the efforts by biotech firms or pharmaceutical companies can give these claims the official sanction of scientific authority. This would inadvertently fuel the public's propensity not only to perceive innate racial differences as responsible for one's health but also accept categories that all too easy led to the misconception that there are "racial" or "ethnic" diseases. This would foster the perception that treatment and therapy for these pathologies reside strictly in medicines tailored to specific racial groups. Neither a single gene nor even clusters of genes can be viewed as the root cause of most diseases that disproportionately affect African Americans and other racial groups (e.g., heart disease, cancer, diabetes, etc.). And there are no imminent miracle cures even in cases where illness is associated with specific genes (e.g., sickle cell anemia, Tay-Sachs disease, etc.).[107]

Considering that people of color have less access to health insurance and health care, social disparities may prevent them from having access to new treatments or the personalized medicine that remains the goal of many genetic scientists.[108] "Racial" pharmaceutical research sets a dangerous precedent by helping absolve social institutions, public and social policies, as well as social arrangements of any responsibility for the unequal distribution and treatment of diseases across groups. The new genetic technologies, like all technologies, develop within a political, economic, and social context. Responsible scientists clearly need to be vigilant in order to help educate the public about the fallacy of the biological concept of race and forestall nonscientists and scientists alike from "misreading" genomic maps as if they are "signposts of racial categories."[109]

Race and Genetic Justice

The significance of the new genetics is also evident in the area of criminal justice. This is most apparent in the FBI, which has been compiling SNP information into the Combined DNA Index System (CODIS) that contains DNA profiles from convicted offenders.[110] In spring 2007, the *New York Times* published an article entitled "The DNA 200," which spotlighted the implications of this new practice. The article was a short essay that included a collection of photographs of former inmates, most of them African American and Latino men, who had spent an average of 12 years in prison for crimes they had not committed. These men are among 213 cases (and counting) in which it has been proven, beyond a shadow of doubt, that genetic material uncovered at a crime scene did not match their own. Their convictions were overturned through the extensive efforts of the Innocence Project, a national litigation and public policy organization. Founded in 1992 by Barry C. Scheck and Peter J. Neufeld, the organization is dedicated to exonerating wrongly convicted individuals—particularly through DNA analysis—as well as reforming the criminal justice system to prevent future injustice.[111]

DNA tests led to the 2004 conviction of an African American suspected of a serial murders in Baton Rouge, Louisiana. Based on eyewitness testimony and the assumption that most serial killers are European American males, police initially were searching for a European American suspect. However, DNAPrint Genomics offered to examine a DNA sample taken from the crime scene. The company's conclusions were that the suspect was not European American but rather, a medium-to dark-skinned African American who was 85 percent sub-Saharan African and 15 percent Native American.[112] The DNA matched a sample given voluntarily to the police by Derrick Todd Lee, a man with an extensive criminal record. Lee was convicted and sentenced to death based in part on this DNA analysis. Critics, however, have argued that such tests are at best predictive of geographical ancestry, and even then not with 100 percent accuracy.[113]

The compiling of DNA samples from suspects and convicts has become normative in many states. Previously, DNA was collected only from individuals found guilty of the most heinous crimes. The new data bases helps to facilitate the incarceration of all criminals and the exoneration of the wrongly accused. The sampling is likely to have a disproportionately negative impact on communities of color considering the racially biased arrest and conviction rates in many locales across the United States.[114] While science can be instrumental in administering justice such racialized forensics presents numerous problems for individuals of color. DNA tests can definitively rule out suspects. They also give scientific legitimacy to the widespread but still controversial notion that certain genetic differences or markers correlate precisely with geographic regions and modern racial categories. Furthermore, they imbue the tracking of "ancestry informative markers"[115] with an aura of acceptability as a stand-in for and seemingly less offensive reference to racial identifiers in DNA. Even worse, they generate a market for an increasing array of genetic services that may, at best, provide reasonable speculations but not definitive answers.[116]

Critics fear that the use of such dubious science in criminal justice will result in the search for gene markers for criminal behavior. Given police practices that heavily target African Americans and Latinas/os, criminologists would inevitably begin with a database that is disproportionately composed of individuals from those communities, which would skew any computer-generated searches and findings.[117] With each DNA sample, the state takes possession of personal biographical information, depriving citizens of their right to privacy. Also, entire families are open to inspection considering that each sample provides information not only about individuals but also their relatives. In some cases, once a DNA sample is taken it is neither returned to the donor nor destroyed but rather, kept indefinitely, unless a particular state law instructs otherwise. There can be no doubt that science has often been used for positive ends, including those that benefit communities of color. As race is resurrected, redefined, and rearticulated by biologists, geneticists, and biotech firms, social justice advocates must also be actively engaged with these discussions.[118]

Race and Genetic Genealogy

The new genetics has also expanded opportunities for individuals interested in genealogical research. Curiosity about one's origins has motivated countless individuals across the racial and ethnic spectrum to have their DNA tested by numerous companies. These firms charge a fee for collecting samples by having individuals swab their cheeks and mail the sample for DNA analysis to determine their genealogy. One such test offered by DNAPrint seeks to pinpoint the geographical origins and estimated percentages of an individual's genes that are inherited from ancestors originating in populations in Asia, Europe, Africa, and in aboriginal America. DNAPrint maintains that it can use DNA to determine phenotypical traits such as skin and eye color, thus providing more detail to a particular individual's genetic portrait. Their web site makes claims of 100 percent accuracy in blind, company-administered tests.[119]

Another type of ancestral DNA analysis, which has been used in the Genographic Project of the National Geographic Society and IBM, typically traces

DNA along one of two lines—the paternal Y chromosome line or maternal mitochondrial line. Both males and females can take the mitochondrial test whereas only males can take the Y-chromosome test since that chromosome is found only in males. With $55 million dollars in funding and 10 centers across the globe, this ambitious project has sought to amass the largest DNA database of its kind with the goal of mapping ancient migration patterns and learning more about their geographical origins.[120]

Evolutionary biologists believe humans derive their Y chromosomes from an imagined "Y Adam" and their mtDNA from an imagined "mt Eve." Individuals' mitochondrial DNA is a copy of their mother's mother, their mother's mother's and so on, which reaches back to the dawn of humanity. The male's Y chromosome is essentially identical to that of his father, and can provide an individual accurate information about his father's father, his father's father's, and so on back indefinitely through all ancestral generations on the Y chromosome line. Humans derive most of their nuclear DNA from all the other reproductive females and males at that time in pre-history, and so on. Each individual's family lineage is much greater than one ancestral line. If you trace back twenty generations an individual has 1,048,576 grandparents.[121]

Y-DNA or mtDNA tests suffer from their own limitations and are no more precise than other ancestry testing services. Each utilizes proprietary computer programs to trace respectively only one of an individual's ancestors—either paternal (Y-DNA) or maternal (mtDNA) lines—as well as their descendants and siblings (same sexed siblings for Y-DNA or all siblings for mtDNA).[122] In other words, these mitochondrial DNA and Y chromosome analyses focus on one of the ancestors from whom individuals have inherited DNA, which leaves out a majority of their antecedents.[123] An individual can be someone's descendent without having inherited any of that ancestor's DNA at a specific location on the genome, or even without at all having inherited any of that ancestor's DNA. Generally speaking, the smaller the proportion of any given ancestry the more probable it is that the number of genes inherited from that ancestry is also proportionately smaller.

Genes are randomly distributed in individuals. Having one or more West African ancestors, for example, does not guarantee that an individual will inherit genetic information from those forebears or exhibit discernible West African phenotypical traits. Individuals may be of partial West African and West European ancestry and also inherit genetic material from those ancestors, yet appear completely European American.[124] This "illusion" of complete "whiteness" is attributable to the fact that the human visual system is unable to perceive information at the genetic level (except by technological means) where we could possibly see DNA inherited from both West African and West European ancestors. The U.S. one-drop rule, which uses ancestry as the criterion in arriving at racial designations, has designated as black all individuals of any traceable West African ancestry irrespective of one's geno-phenotype.[125]

Another caveat of the current DNA tests is that they tend to conflate geography with ancestry and culture. This can be easily interpreted by the lay public and even by some less conscientious scientists as a proxy for race at time when the same new genetics is arguing that race has no basis in science. The terms "ancestry" and "genetic diversity"[126] have emerged as alternative ways to refer to differences that have historically come to be known as racial ones. These terms may be no more accurate in conveying human genetic variation than are traditional racial categories.

Genetic markers, attributed to one group or region, are present in others. Whether scientists discuss the variations in terms of geography or ancestry, the end result is that race and racial differences are resurrected as concrete biological facts, encoded within human DNA.[127]

Race and Genetic Intelligence

As genetic information seeps out of the laboratory and into everyday life the false confidence many individuals draw from the results of ancestry testing inevitably conveys the notion that people of different perceived racial groups have different DNA. This could erroneously provide biological validation of sociocultural delineations of racial categories.[128] Laypersons are already beginning to formulate dangerous and highly speculative conclusions from the new genetics in terms of the historically incendiary debate about the relationship between race and intelligence.

While there are measurable, if not one hundred percent accurate, differences between people of different continental ancestries, the link between I.Q. and DNA is unsubstantiated.[129] Any relationship between genetics and intelligence is likely to be exceedingly difficult to pinpoint. Accordingly, geneticists and other scientists need to be prepared to provide more nuanced and refined perspectives on these socially charged discoveries in their eventuality. Otherwise, these developments hold the potential to ignite a new era of racist thought supporting the use of biological differences as a means of furthering racist practices. This could ultimately undermine the generally accepted conclusions drawn from research conducted beginning in the 1970s and confirmed by subsequent studies throughout the twentieth century, which support the premise that all racial groups are essentially equal.[130]

Popular conversation is already projecting into the future and asking questions about what would happen if genetically encoded racial differences in socially desirable—or undesirable—traits are identified and whether to support discriminatory practices against certain groups because they are less "intelligent."[131] This argument dangerously ignores the social forces that underpin inequalities of condition, which have significantly more impact on an individual's achievement than genes. These have been shown to have minimal influence, and this influence has proven difficult to measure. These discussions also beg the question as to whether society is prepared to handle the eventuality of scientifically revealed appreciable genetic differences between racial groups in terms of social traits.[132]

Some liberals believe the new genetic data could become the latest rallying point for conservatives seeking to dismantle social policies aimed at redress such as affirmative action. Even some liberal thinkers argue that accepting the possibility of some genetic differences between "racial groups" negligible is an important part of preparing to address them with politically. Public policy would need to take into consideration how to provide individuals with the educational and occupational opportunities most appropriate to their unique talents and limitations.[133] Others suggest that innate differences should be accepted but essentially ignored.[134] That said, social scientists have argued for decades that race is a social construct historically devised to justify discriminatory attitudes and practices. Preconceived and commonsense notions of race appear all the more authentic when quantified, reified, and indeed given the imprimatur of science and DNA.[135]

Conclusion

The notion of multiraciality embedded in the concept of critical hybridity and moderate Afrocentric discourse would seem to have gained legitimacy from the current preeminence of research in the new genetics. Given the authority the new genetics is currently wielding in Western civilization, the significance of racial differences, and their very essence and existence, are being reconstructed. This challenges current "common sense" views that have inevitably coupled racial formation with essentialist principles. The new "Molecular Portrait of Humanity" that emerges from this research is the most recent in a long influential tradition of antiessentialist and antiracist thought dating back at least to the first declarations on race drawn up by UNESCO in the 1950s. That statement characterized a significant portion of research on human biological variation throughout the second half of the twentieth century.[136] The findings of the new genetics thus reaffirm the limited significance of race as a biological concept and render humans not as immutable essences but rather, "all mixed up," that is, the product of extensive blending.[137]

Although the DNA-based genealogy tests offered by a growing number of companies may have the unintended consequence of reifying the link between ancestry, biology, and identity,[138] they also have the potential to raise awareness of the fluidity, instability, and imprecision of racial categories and call into question any lingering notions of racial purity. As larger numbers of individuals become more aware of the myriad ancestors in their lineage and DNA inherited from them, through genetic testing, as well as more traditional genealogical research, they may be prompted to display more fluid monoracial, if not actual multiracial identities. Positing the most optimistic scenario, this "Molecular Portrait of Humanity"[139] has implications that are similar yet broader and more global in its implications than the bold proposition by Brazilian geneticists who authored the "Molecular Portrait of Brazil."[140] It could induce more individuals across the globe to develop a new racial commonsense that values the genetic and ancestral diversity of humanity and become more engaged in working toward a more just and equitable world.[141]

Considering that genetic narratives interact with historical and social ones, we should not underestimate the repercussions of genetic knowledge as the basis for questioning and transforming notions of social cohesion and group identity. Furthermore, this knowledge has implications in terms of personal esteem and self-worth, access to resources, and redressing historical injustice. As this research achieves increased currency, historically recognized standards of identity may gain further legitimacy or be eclipsed as new formulations emerge.[142] The discussions of genomic research are in essence debates about identity politics. On the one hand, the identity politics of radical Afrocentrism and related ideologies have utilized strategic racial essentialism, which draws implicitly on biological or ancestral reductionism as the basis for cultural initiatives in the form of identity politics, as well as certain political initiatives. On the one hand, the antiessentialism of the new genetics embodied in the "Molecular Portrait of Humanity" serves to bolster those of critical hybridity and multiraciality. Correspondingly, individuals who choose to trace their ancestry through DNA research are not simply engaged in a laboratory analysis but also a political act.[143] This furthers an agenda that at the same time can be considered deleterious to some of the premises of Afrocentric social and political initiatives, as well as collective identities, which have been formulated to organize resistance to racial oppression and injustice.

It is critical to ask whether the new genetics and the accompanying technology will radically transform racial categorization or rearticulate and reinforce even more insidious, essentialist, and deterministic ways of perceiving racial differences. Racial formation is undergoing constant transformation as it interacts with emerging knowledge and technologies. Although the new genetic research has become a significantly influential component of contemporary identity politics, the outdated and discredited perspective of race and essentialized differences is far from being eclipsed.[144] One cannot assume that determinism, essentialism, and hierarchy will inevitably accompany this research, including its implications in the area of identity politics.[145] In the changing interaction between scientific knowledge, local and transnational contexts, and the agendas of various social actors and movements, the genome-based formulation of human differentiation is establishing itself as a tool that can alter the patterns of proximity and distance[146] between "beneficiaries of racial hierarchy" and "people who have been subordinated by race-thinking."[147] The research into human genetics can precipitate a deliberate and self-conscious repudiation of race as meaningful way of categorizing, dividing, and above all else, hierarchically ranking humanity.[148]

A similar perspective was expressed in *La Raza Cósmica* (*The Cosmic Race*, 1925), which is an essay written by José Vasconcelos (1882–1959), a Mexican philosopher, Secretary of Education (1921–1924), and 1929 presidential candidate. His central argument is best captured in the notion of a future "fifth race" in the Americas, which would be a blend of all the world's racial groups in the formation of a new global civilization: *Universópolis*.[149] According to Vasconcelos, armies of individuals would subsequently go across the globe and initiate the "universal era of humanity" and cosmic race.[150] Vasconcelos also argued that late nineteenth- and early twentieth century scientific theories of race were simply formulated to explain, validate, and justify the racial superiority of some groups, specifically Europeans, and the inferiority of others, who were people of color. He sought to refute these theories through his concept of the cosmic race, which embodies the notion that traditional, exclusive concepts of race and nation can be transcended in the name of humanity's common destiny.[151] Others have posited a similar outcome for humanity, one in which extensive racial and cultural blending will eventually result in a single tan or beige-hued species. A corollary to this process is the notion that racism would disappear by virtue of the accompanying fluidity and ambiguity of racial categories and designations.[152]

Still other observers are skeptical of the likelihood of a global racial blending. They argue that most racial intermarriage will take place either in regions where it has already recently occurred on a considerable scale since the modern era (Latin America and some remote islands), or in immigrant magnets (Western Europe, North America, and Australia). Barring a massive influx of new contributions from recent and future immigration, the racial composition of such societies is unlikely to change substantially in the near future. Critics question whether a thoroughly miscegenated global civilization would lead to genuinely multiracial democracies or hypocritically multiracial ones that have characterized Brazil and other parts of Latin America.[153] Vasconcelos espoused integration (or assimilation) as whitening, Europeanization, and homogenization through miscegenation rather than an equitable blend, despite his egalitarian and effusive rhetoric. The underlying premise of Vasconcelos's notion of the cosmic race thus follows along the lines of many other late nineteenth- and early twentieth-century Latin American thinkers. The goal of national unity and integration was the cultural and racial erasure of the Native American, African, and Asian elements of Mexican society. These views are particularly noteworthy in Vasconcelos's equivocation in terms of the role and significance of individuals of African descent in this racial and cultural blending.[154]

That said, in our contemporary world, which is increasingly marked by the forces of globalization, these issues can be addressed by examining the concept of critical hybridity or multiraciality, which is an excellent case study of recasting racial analyses of humanity's past, present, and future from a global perspective. While rejecting dichotomous notions of racial (and cultural) purity derivative of Eurocentric discourse, critical hybridity, as an expression of postcolonial discourse, also counters the rigid essentialism that is often the premise of anticolonial projects, including Third World discourse, as well as radical Afrocentrism and much Black Nationalist thought. The latter perspectives have the advantage of exposing white racism and supposedly espouse the equality of difference (or egalitarian pluralism). They have frequently promoted racial separatism that has been accused of rearticulating racial hierarchy in a reverse type of apartheid or inegalitarian pluralism.

Rather than reverse the dichotomy, however, the concept of critical hybridity questions fundamentally the very hierarchical and inegalitarian grounds on which the dichotomy is erected.[155] It helps guard against downplaying contemporary and future hegemonies that merely create the illusion of equity while obscuring subtle racial hierarchies that appear in a new guise.[156] It furthers this objective by opening up a long-overdue conversation about humanity's genetic comity, as well as shared ancestral and cultural connections, which have been ignored, obscured, and erased by several hundred years of Eurocentric thought.

Similarly, the concept of critical hybridity is catalytic in the formation of a postcolonial blackness that interrogates any reification, global imposition, or appropriation of the U.S. one-drop rule as an antiracist tactic. The struggle for black liberation must be grounded in a process of decolonization that continually challenges and goes beyond the perpetuation of racial essentialism and the reinscription of notions of authentic identity derived from the rule. This has led to one-dimensional and dichotomous formulations of blackness and whiteness that in many ways parallel those that have historically sought to reinforce and sustain white domination and black subordination.[157] Postcolonial blackness is quintessentially Afrocentric in the deepest meaning of the word. It not only has special meaning for people of the African Diaspora but also a universal significance for all humans as descendants of the first diaspora out of Africa.[158] Postcolonial blackness can be deployed as part of a larger project of abolishing all kinds of dichotomies and hierarchies, racial and otherwise, in which egalitarian pluralism becomes a prelude and counterpart to a new higher de-differentiation in the manner of egalitarian integration that serves as a vehicle for a future global and universal humanism.[159]

Notes

1. This chapter borrows on material in G. Reginald Daniel, *More Than Black?: Multiracial Identity and the New Racial Order* (Philadelphia, PA.: Temple University Press, 2002) and "Beyond Eurocentrism and Afrocentrism: Globalization, Critical Hybridity, and Postcolonial

Blackness," in *Critical Globalization Studies*, ed. Richard P. Appelbaum and William I. Robinson, 259–68 (New York: Routledge, 2005).

2. Audrey Smedley, *Race in North America: Origin and Evolution of a Worldview* (Boulder, Colorado: Westview Press, 1993), 14–16.

3. Carter A. Wilson, *Racism: From Slavery to Advanced Capitalism* (Thousand Oaks, CA: 1996), 37–47; Frank M. Snowden, Jr, *Before Color Prejudice: The Ancient View of Blacks* (Cambridge, Mass.: Harvard University Press, 1983), 78–80.

4. Michael Omi and Howard Winant, *Racial Formation in the 1980s and 1990s* (New York: Routledge, 1994), 61.

5. Ibid., 61.

6. Smedley, 14–16.

7. It may be meaningful to think of these ancient (or premodern) and modern attitudes as two formative periods in racial formation. Yet, to conflate these earlier attitudes with those that emerged in eighteenth-century Western Europe denies the singularity and historic specificity of the modern understanding of race as a biological concept. See Part I, Chapters 4, 5, 7 in this book for a detailed discussion of some of these phenomena. Smedley 14, 18; Omi and Winant, 61–62.

8. Smedley, 14, 18; Omi and Winant, 61–62.

9. Pitirim Sorokin, *Social and Cultural Dynamics: The Study of Change in Major Systems of Art, Truth, Ethics, Law and Social Relationships*. Revised and Abridged (Boston: Porter Sargent Books, 1957/1985), 623–628, 699–704.

10. Helen Tiffin, "Introduction," in *Past the Last Post: Theorizing Post-Colonialism and Post-modernism*, ed. Ian Adam and Helen Tiffin, vii–xvi (Calgary, Albert, Canada: University of Calgary Press, 1990); Ella Shohat and Robert Stam, *Unthinking Eurocentrism: Multiculturalism and the Media*. (New York: Routledge, 1994), 1–54; Patrick Williams and Laura Chrisman, "Colonial Discourse and Post-Colonial Theory: An Introduction," in *Colonial Discourse and Post-Colonial Theory: A Reader*, ed. Patrick Williams and Laura Chrisman (New York: Columbia University Press, 1994), 17.

11. David Slater, "Exploring Other Zones of the Postmodern: Problems of Ethnocentrism and Difference Across the North-South Divide," in *Racism, Modernity and Identity: On the Western Front*, ed. Ali Rattansi and Sallie Westwood (Cambridge: Polity Press, 1994), 88.

12. Omi and Winant, 55–61.

13. Michael Hardt and Antonio Negri, *Empire* (Cambridge, Massachusetts: Harvard University Press, 2000), xi.

14. Hardt and Negri, xiii.

15. Shohat and Stam, 1–54.

16. Hardt and Negri, xi–xvii.

17. Ibid.

18. Ibid.

19. Shohat & Stam, 1–54.

20. Shohat and Stam, 1–54; Hardt and Negri, xi–xvii.

21. Benjamin R. Barber, "Jihad Vs. McWorld," *The Atlantic Monthly* (March 1992), 53–65.

22. Riane Eisler, *The Chalice and the Blade: Our History, Our Future* (San Francisco: Harper and Row, 1988), 42–44, 66–69, 73–77; Johann P. Arnason, "Nationalism, Globalization, and Modernity," in *Global Culture: Nationalism, Globalization, and Modernity*, ed. Mike Featherstone (Thousand Oaks, CA.: Sage Publications, 1990) 207–36; Mike Featherstone, "Introduction," in *Global Culture: Nationalism, Globalization, Modernity*, ed. Mike Featherstone (Thousand Oaks, CA.: Sage Publications, 1990), 1–13; Václav Havel, "The Need for Transcendence in the Postmodern World," Václav Havel was the first president of the Czech Republic (1993–2003). The speech was made in Independence Hall, Philadelphia, July 4, 1994; Vaclav Havel, "The Search for Meaning in a Global Civilization," in *The Truth About the Truth: De-confusing and Re-constructing the Postmodern World*, ed. Walter Truett Anderson, 232–38 (New York: G. P. Putman and Sons, 1995); James H. Mittleman, *The Globalization Syndrome: Transformation and Resistance* (Princeton, N.J.: Princeton University Press, 2000), 165–78; William Robinson, "Reamapping Development in Light of

Globalization: From a Territorial to a Social Cartography," *Third World Quarterly* 23, No. 6 (2002): 1047–71.

23. Havel, 1994, Havel 1995, 232–38; Sorokin, 623–28, 699–704; Walter Truett Anderson, 7; Johann P. Arnason, "Nationalism, Globalization and Modernity," in *Global Culture: Nationalism, Globalization, and Modernity*, ed. Mike Featherstone (Thousand Oaks, CA.: Sage Publications, 1990), 220; Eisler, 42–44, 66–69, 73–77; Featherstone, 11; Ulf Hannerz, "Cosmopolitans and Locals in World Culture," in *Global Culture: Nationalism, Globalization, and Modernity*, ed. Mike Featherstone, 237–53 (Thousand Oaks, CA.: Sage Publications, 1990), 237; Pauline Rosenau, *Postmodernism and the Social Sciences* (Princeton: Princeton University Press, 1995), 54.

24. Ken Wilber, *A Brief History of Everything* (Boston, MA.: Shambhala Publications, 1996), 27–32, 332; Havel, 1994; Havel 1995, 232–38.

25. Shohat and Stam, 39.

26. Ibid., 1–54.

27. Ibid.

28. Ibid.

29. Ibid.

30. Ibid.

21. Ibid.

32. Robert J. C. Young, *Colonial Desire: Hybridity in Theory, Culture, and Race* (New York: Routledge, 1995), 10; Robert J. C. Young, "Egypt in America: Black Athena, Racism, and Colonial Discourse," in *Racism, Modernity and Identity: On the Western Front*, ed. Ali Rattansi and Sallie Westwood, 150–169 (Cambridge: Polity Press, 1994).

33. Shohat and Stam, 42.

34. Williams and Chrisman, 1–19.

35. G. Reginald Daniel, *More Than Black? Multiracial Identity and the New Racial Order*, (Philadelphia: Temple University Press, 2001), 178–79.

36. Omi and Winant, 55–61.

37. Shohat and Stam, 1–54.

38. Chela Sandoval. *Methodology of the Oppressed* (Minneapolis, Minnesota: University of Minnesota Press, 2000), 72.

39. Jan Nederveen Pieterse, "Unpacking the West: How European Is Europe?," in *Racism, Modernity and Identity: On the Western Front*, ed. Ali Ratanssi and Sallie Westwood, 129–150 (Cambridge: Polity Press, 1994b), 144.

40. Pieterse, 1994b, 146.

41. Shohat and Stam, 1–54; Pieterse 1994b, 146.

42. The one-drop rule of hypodescent designates as black everyone with any amount of African American ancestry ("one-drop of blood"). It precludes any choice in self-identification and ensures that all future offspring of African American ancestry have been socially designated as black. Though rules of hypodescent have been applied elsewhere to individuals with varying degrees of African ancestry (such as in Brazil and South Africa), the one-drop rule is unique to the United States. It emerged between the late-seventeenth and early-eighteenth centuries and had the benefit of exempting white landowners (particularly slaveholders) from the legal obligation of passing on inheritance and other benefits of paternity to their multiracial offspring. By the 1920s, the one-drop rule had become the common sense definition of blackness, and had been internalized among the vast majority of African-descent Americans. Generally, rules of hypodescent have relegated the racial group membership of the offspring of unions between European Americans and Americans of color exclusively to their background of color (e.g., Native American, Asian American, Pacific Islander American, Latina/o American, African American, etc.). Historically, this rule has been such an accepted part of United States racial common sense that its oppressive origins have often been obscured. European Americans began enforcing rules of hypodescent in the late-1600s in order to draw social distinctions between themselves and subordinated groups of color. These were implemented primarily to regulate interracial sexual relations, and more specifically, interracial marriages, in order to preserve so-called white racial purity. However, hypodescent

has also helped maintain white racial privilege by supporting other legal and informal barriers to racial equality in most aspects of social life, reaching extreme proportions at the turn of the twentieth century with the institutionalization of Jim Crow segregation. These barriers have existed in public facilities and other areas of the public sphere, such as the educational, occupational and political structure, as well as in the private sphere (e.g., neighborhoods, associational preferences and interpersonal relationships).

The rule of hypodescent typically has been applied most stringently (depending upon the background of color) to the first-generation offspring of European Americans and Americans of color. Meanwhile, successive generations of individuals with European ancestry and a background of color have typically have not been designated exclusively, or even partially, as members of that group of color if the background is less than one-fourth of their lineage. For these multigenerational individuals, self-identification with the background of color has been more a matter of choice. However, this flexibility has not been extended to individuals of African American and European American descent. Both the first-generation offspring of interracial relationships between African Americans and European Americans and later generation descendants have experienced the most restrictive rule of hypodescent: the one-drop rule.

United States attitudes toward the offspring of unions between African Americans and other groups of color (e.g. Native Americans) have varied. More often than not, these individuals have been subject to the one-drop rule. However, there has been greater ambivalence regarding the classification of offspring whose ancestry reflects the combination of groups of color other than African Americans. This is partially due to the fact that these other groups of color have occupied a more ambiguous position in the United States racial hierarchy. For example, individuals of Mexican or Asian Indian ancestry have been alternately classified as either white or nonwhite, according to federal court decisions, state legislation, and policies of government bureaucracies (such as the Census Bureau). Also, membership in these groups—except perhaps in the case of Native Americans—has been less clearly defined in United States law. Consequently, the racial subordination of Americans of color by European Americans, while oppressive, has not been the same as that of African Americans. Some members of these groups have sought a more intermediate position in the racial hierarchy by avoiding contact with what they perceived as more subordinate groups of color. Still others have forged multiethnic communities of color. For example, Karen Leonard (*Making Ethnic Choices: California's Punjabi Mexican Americans*, 1992) has traced the formation of Punjabi Mexican American communities in California's agricultural valleys, while Rudy Guevarra ("Burritos and Bagoong: Mexipinos and Multiethnic Identity in San Diego, California," 2003) has researched the Mexipino (Mexican and Filipino) community in San Diego.

43. Rhett S. Jones, "The End of Africanity?: The Bi-Racial Assault on Blackness," *The Western Journal of Black Studies* 18, no. 4 (1994): 201–10; Donna Landry and Gerald Maclean, ed. *The Spivak Reader: Selected Works of Gayatri Chakravorty Spivak* (New York: Routledge, 1995), 7, 54–71, 159, 204, 295.

44. Pedro Pérez-Sarduy and Jean Stubbs, ed. *No Longer Invisible: Afro-Latin Americans Today* (London, Minority Rights Group Publications, 1995; Jorge Fortes and Diego Ceballos, *Afroargentines (Afroargentinos)* Filmagen Producciones, Lagartija Muda Producciones (New York: Latin American Video Archives, 2002). G. Reginald Daniel, *Race and Multiraciality in Brazil and the United States: Converging Paths?* (University Park, PA.: Pennsylvania State University Press, 2006), 292–3; Peter Fry, "Politics, Nationality, and the Meaning of Race," *Daedalus* 129, no. 2 (2000): 83–118; Ali Kamel, *Não Somos Racistas: Uma Reação Aos Que Querem Nos Transformar Numa Nação Bicolor*. 2a impressão (Rio de Janeiro: Editora Nova Fronteira, 2006), 17–41, 49–57; Peter Fry and Yvonne Maggie, "Política Social de Alto Risco," in *Divisões Perogosas: Políticas Racias no Brasil Contemporâneo*, ed. Peter Fry and Yvonne Maggie, Marcos Chor Maio, Simone Monteiro, and Ricardo Ventura Santos, 277–81 (Rio de Janeiro: Civilização Brasileira, 2007); Antonio Risério, *A Utopia Brasileira e Os Movimentos Negros* (São Paulo: Editora 34 Ltda, 2007), 19, 24, 55, 67; G. Reginald Daniel, "Multiracial Identity in Global Perspective: The United States, Brazil and South Africa," in

.Loretta Winter and Herman Dubose, ed. *New Faces in a Changing America: Multiracial Identity in the 21st Century* (Thousand Oaks, CA.: Sage Publications, 2002), 247–86.

45. Pierre Bourdieu and Loïc Wacquant, "On the Cunning of Imperialist Reason," *Theory, Culture, and Society* 16, no. 1 (1999), 47–48.

46. Ibid.

47. ibid.

48. Bell Hooks, *Yearning: Race, Gender, and Cultural Politics* (Boston: South End Press. 1995), 23–31; Manning Marable, *Beyond Black and White: Transforming African American Politics* (New York: Verso, 1995), 121–22.

49. Sarduy and Jean Stubbs, 1995; Fortes and Ceballos, 2002; Daniel 2002, 247–86; Daniel 2006, 292–3; Fry, 83–118; Kamel, 17–41, 49–57; Fry and Maggie, 277–81; Risério, 19, 24, 55, 67.

50. Prior to the late 1960s sociological definitions of racism relied heavily on notions of individual psychological biases and discriminatory attitudes. Since the 1960s racism has been viewed as more than simple antipathy and discrimination toward individuals based on individual racial prejudice. It is now defined as an overarching and more systematic implementation of discrimination based on the desire and power of dominant groups to maintain advantages for themselves at the expense of racialized "others." According to this view, racially subordinate groups—which by definition lack structural power—are not capable of "racism." Others make a distinction between individual racism, which is defined as everyday individual antipathy based on race, and institutional racism, which has larger social structural implications in terms of the distribution of wealth, power, privilege, and prestige. Molefi Asante, *Kemet, Afrocentricity, and Knowledge* (Trenton, N.J.: Africa World Press, 1992), 17–22; Ali Rattansi, "'Western' Racisms, Ethnicities and Identities in a 'Postmodern' Frame," in *Racism, Modernity and Identity: On the Western Front*, ed. Ali Rattansi and Sallie Westwood (Cambridge: Polity Press, 1994), 57; Christie Farnham Pope, "The Challenge Posed by Radical Afrocentrism: When a White Professor Teaches Black History," *Chronicle of Higher Education*, (March 30, 1994), B1; Gerald Early, "Understanding Afrocentrism: Why Blacks Dream of a World without Whites," *Civilization* (July/August 1995): 31–9; Stephen Howe, *Afrocentrism: Mythical Pasts and Imagined Homes* (New York: Verso, 1998), 215–58.

51. Howe, 215–58.The contrast between these two types of pluralism is captured in Figure 1.e and 1.f. The pluralistic relationship is indicated by the fact that the circles are separated, as opposed to being linked, as they are in the integrationist half of the chart. The relationship in Figure 1.e is not only vertical (inegalitarian) and thus hierarchical, but also the positions of the previously subdominant black and dominant white circles in Figure 1.f are reversed. However, both Figure 1.e and 1.f differ significantly from the premises and goals of the black consciousness movement that are best captured in Figure 1.c. The black and grey circles are bracketed by virtue of their shared dissimilarities to the white. The goal is to establish a horizontal (as opposed to hierarchical) and thus egalitarian relationship that valorizes the two previously subdominant and excluded circles.

52. Molefi Asante, *Afrocentricity: The Theory of Social Change* (Buffalo: Amulefi, 1980), 4; Rattansi, 57; Marable, 121–22.

53. Mahgan Keita, "Deconstructing the Classical Age: Africa and the Unity of the Mediterranean World," *Journal of Negro History*, LXXIX, no. 2 (Spring 1994): 146–66; Molly Myerowitz Levine, "Review Article, The Use and Abuse of Black Athena," *American Historical Review* (April 1992): 440–64; Mary Lefkowitz, *Not Out of Africa: How Afrocentrism Became an Excuse to Teach Myth As History* (New York: Basic Books, 1996), 161; George Will, "Intellectual Segregation: Afrocentrism's Many Myths Constitute Condescension toward African-Americans," *Newsweek* (February 19, 1996), 78.

54. Will 78; Lefkowitz, 161.

55. Marable 1995, 117–24; G. Reginald Daniel, "Eurocentrism, Afrocentrism, or Holocentrism?" *Interrace Magazine*, 3, no. 2 (1992): 33; Cornel West, *Beyond Eurocentrism and Multiculturalism.* vol. I. (Monroe, Maine: Common Courage, 1993), 1–30.

56. Rattansi, 15–86; Marable, 117–24.

57. Daniel 1992, 33; Hooks, 23–3.

58. These dynamics are also captured in Chela Sandoval's concept of "radical mestizaje." Sandoval, 72.

59. John Michael Spencer, "Trends of Opposition to Multiculturalism," *The Black Scholar* 23, no. 2 (1993): 2–5; Jones, 201–10; Charles Lemert, *Sociology After the Crisis* (Boulder Colorado: Westview Press, 1996), 86.

60. Victor Anderson, 11–19.

61. Hooks, 23–31; Collins, Patricia Hill. "Setting Our Own Agenda." *The Black Scholar* 23, no. 3 & 4 (1993): 52–5.

62. Collins, 22–55; Hooks, 23–31.

63. Jerome H. Schiele, "Afrocentricity for All," in *Black Issues in Higher Education* (September 26, 1991), 27; Jerome H. Schiele, "Rethinking Organizations From an Afrocentric Viewpoint," in *Afrocentric Visions: Studies in Culture and Communication*, ed. Janice D. Hamlet, 73–88 (Thousand Oaks, CA.: Sage Publications, 1998).

64. Asante 1987, 3–18; Norman Harris, "A Philosophical Basis for an Afrocentric Orientation," in *Afrocentric Visions: Studies in Culture and Communication*, 15–26; Terry Kershaw, "Afrocentrism and the Afrocentric Method," in *Afrocentric Visions: Studies in Culture and Communication*, 27–44; Linda James Myers, "The Deep Structure of Culture: Relevance of Traditional African Culture in Contemporary Life," in *Afrocentric Visions: Studies in Culture and Communication*, 1–14; Schiele 1991, 27; Asante 1987, 3–18; Harris, 15–26; Kershaw, 27–44; Myers, 1–14.

65. Asante 1987, 3–18; 1992, 17–22; Jennifer Hochschild, *Facing Up to the American Dream* (Princeton: Princeton University Press, 1996), 137–38; Kershaw, 27–44; Myers, 1–28; Schiele 1992, 27; Schiele 1998, 73–88.

66. Daniel 2002, 180, 189; Stanley Teitelbaum, "Making Everything Perfectly Fuzzy," *Los Angeles Times Magazine* (April 1 1990), 24–42.

67. George Lipsitz, "Noise in the Blood: Culture, Conflict, and Mixed Race Identities," in *Crossing Lines: Race and Mixed Race Across the Geohistorical Divide*, ed. Marc Coronado, Rudy P. Guevarra Jr., Jeffrey Moniz, and Laura Furlan Szanto, 32–35 (Santa Barbara, CA.: Multiethnic Student Outreach, in collaboration with the Center for Chicano Studies, University of California, Santa Barbara, 2003).

68. Emmanuel Chukwudieze Eze. *Achieving Our Humanity: The Idea of the Postracial Future* (New York: Routledge, 2001), 159–63; Manthia Diawara, "Pan-Africanism and Pedagogy." *Black Cultural Studies*. org. http://www.blackculturalstudies.org/m_diawara/panafr.html, 1996; Jean-Paul Sartre, *Black Orpeheus*. Translated by S. W. Allen (Paris, Présence Africaine, 1963), 17.

69. Diawara 1996.

70. Sartre 10, 12, 43–8; Howe, 26–7.

71. Lilyan Kesteloot, *Les Écrivains Noirs de Langue Française: Naissance d'une Littérature*. Brussels: Université de Bruxelles, 1965, 122; Eze, 159–63.

72. Frantz Fanon, *Black Skin, White Masks*. Translated by Charles Lam Markmann (New York: Grove Press, Inc., 1967/1952), 138; Sartre 1963, 57, 60–2. In this context, it should be pointed out that transcendence, which is premised on a more inclusive egalitarian integration, should not be confused with the denial, deracination, and deculturation associated with inegalitarian integration (or assimilation). Indeed, the vision expressed by Negritude's most preeminent voices—Leopold Sénghor, Léon Damas, and Aimé Césaire—has less of an affinity with either the assimilationist premises and goals of French colonial policy or the rigid essentialism and pluralism that underpins radical Afrocentrism. Rather, it is more akin to integrative pluralism, which sought to borrow on the most useful aspects of both traditional African and modern West European societies to forge a new synthesis that was uniquely African. Howe, 24; Eze 134–40.

73. Asante 1980, 105–8; 1992, 17–22; Marable 122; Rattansi, 57.

74. Rattansi, 30; Rosenau, 5–7; Steven Seidman, "Introduction," in *The Postmodern Turn: New Perspectives on Social Theory*, ed. Steven Seidman, 8–9 (New York: Cambridge University Press, 1994).

75. Victor Anderson 1995, 13.

76. Hooks, 23–31.

77 Howe, 275–86.

78. Eze. 275–86.

79. "An Overview of the Human Genome Project (HGP)," http://www.genome.gov/12011238; "Human Genome Project Goals", http://www.genome.gov/11006945; L. Luca Cavalli-Sforza, Paolo Menozzi, and Alberto Piazza, *The History and Geography of Human Genes* (Princeton, New Jersey: Princeton University Press, 1994), 377–78; Mark A. Jobling, Matthew Hurles, and Chris Tyler-Smith, *Human Evolutionary Genetics: Origins, Peoples, and Disease* (New York: Garland Publishing, 2004), 274–75; Ricardo Ventura Santos and Marcos Chor Maio, "Race, Genomics, Identities and Politics in Contemporary Brazil," *Critique of Anthropology* 24, 4 (2004): 363–4; Ricardo Ventura Santos and Marcos Chor Maio, "Antropologia, Raça e os Dilemas das Identidades na Era da Genômica," *História, Ciências, Saúde—Manguinhos*, 12, no. 2 (May–August 2005): 447–68.

80. These data from the Human Genome Project reaffirm arguments made during the early 1970s by Richard Lewontin in his landmark research, which determined that most of the variation (80–85%) within human populations is found within local geographic groups and differences attributable to traditional "racial groups" are an insignificant part of human genetic variability (1–15%); Richard Lewontin, "The Apportionment of Human Diversity," *Evolutionary Biology* 6 (1972): 391–98; Mildred K. Cho and Pamela Sankar, "Forensic Genetics and Ethical, Legal, and Social Implications Beyond the Clinic," *Nature Genetic Supplement* 36, no. 11(November 2004): s8–s12.

81. Robin Marantz Henig, "The Genome in Black and White (and Gray)," *New York Times Magazine*, October 10, 2004, http://www.nytimes.com/2004/10/10/magazine/10GENETIC .html/; Kristen Philipkoski, "Gene Map Presents Race Concerns," *Wired*, http://www.wired.com/science/discoveries/news/2001/02/41619; Santos and Maio 2004, 361–62; "Science," DNAPrint Genomics, http://www.dnaprint.com/welcome/science/; Lee Herring and Mercedes Rubio, "Scientists Warn of Conceptual Traps Concerning 'Race' in New Genetic Map of Human Populations," *Footnotes* (April 2005 http://www2.asanet.org /footnotes/apr05/indextwo.html; Lynn B. Jorde and Stephen B. Wooding, "Genetic Variation, Classification, and Race," *Nature Genetic Supplement* 36, no. 11 (November 2004): s28–s33.

82. Amy Harmon, "The DNA Age: DNA Era, New Worries About Prejudice," *The New York Times*, November 11, 2007. http://www.nytimes.com/2007/11/11/us/11dna.html?_r=1&ei=5070&en=4bc0f4e574c203e6&ex=1195534800&adxnnl=1&oref=slogin&emc=eta1&adxnnlx=1204484787-Poyet6NwP5uei32GekcxEw.

83. Sarah A. Tishkoff and Kenneth K Kidd, "Implications of Biogeography of Human Populations for 'Race' and Medicine," *Nature Genetic Supplement* 36, no. 11 (November 2004): s21–s27, s34–s41.

84. Henig 2004; Jorde and Wooding, s28–s33.

85. Steven Epstein, *Inclusion: The Politics of Difference in Medical Research* (Chicago, Ill.: University of Chicago Press, 2007), 74–93.

86. Herring and Rubio 2005; Ari Patrinos, "Race and the Human Genome," *Nature Genetic Supplement* 36, no. 11 (November 2004): s1–s2.

87. Epstein, 94–114; Duana Fullwiley, "The Molecularization of Race: Institutionalizing Human Difference in Pharmacogenetics Practice," *Science as Culture* 16, no. 1 (March 2007): 1–30; Ziba Kashef, "Genetic Drift," *ColorLines*. no. 40 (Sept/Oct 2007) http://www.colorlines.com/article.php?ID=245.

88. Fullwiley 1–30; Harmon 2007; Epstein, 4; Francis S. Collins, "What We Do and Do Not Know About 'Race,' 'Ethnicity,'" Genetics, and Health at the Dawn of the Genome Era," *Nature Genetic Supplement* 36, no. 11 (November 2004): s13–s15.89. Epstein, 116–134; Duana Fullwiley, 1–30; Kashef, **2007**.

90. Kashef, 2007.

91. Troy Duster, *Back Door to Eugenics* (New York: Routledge, 2003), 47; Epstein, 4; Sarah K. Tate, "Will Tomorrow's Medicines Work for Everyone," *Nature Genetic Supplement* 36, no. 11 (November 2004): s34–s41.

92. Duster 147; Epstein 2007, 4.

93. Henig 2004.

94. For a more detailed discussion, see Part III, Chapter 1 in this book; Henig 2004; Duster, 147; Epstein, 2, 180, 204, 214–30; Malorye Allison Branca, "BiDil Raises Questions About Race As A Marker," *Nature Reviews Drug Discovery* 4, 615–616 (August 2005)|doi:10.1038/nrd1812.

95. Philipkoski 2001.

96. Keith Wailoo and Stephen Pemberton, *The Troubled Dream of Genetic Medicine: Ethnicity and Innovation in Tay-Sachs, Cystic Fibrosis, and Sickle Cell Disease* (Baltimore, MD.: The Johns Hopkins University Press, 2006), 78–9; Duster, 154; Herring 2005.

97. Duster, 47–52, 154; Wailoo and Pemberton, 78–79; Henig 2004; Charles N. Rotimi, "Are Medical and Nonmedical Uses of Large-Scale Genomic Markers Conflating Genetics With 'Race,'" *Nature Genetic Supplement* 36, no. 11 (November 2004): s43–s47.

98. Henig 2004.

99. Ibid.

100. Ziba Kashef, 2007.

101. Henig ,2004; Duster, 117–18 ; Collins 2004, s13–s15.

102. Duster 117–8; Kashef, 2007; Henig 2004; Collins, 2004, s13–s15.

103. Wailoo and Pemberton, 78–79; Henig 2004.

104. Kashef 2007.

105. Duster, 56–9; Kashef 2007; Henig 2004; Collins 2004, s13–s15.

106. Kashef,2007; Henig 2004.

107. Duster, 45–47, 153–4; Wailoo and Pemberton, 78–79; Sarah K. Tate, "Will Tomorrow's Medicines Work for Everyone," *Nature Genetic Supplement* 36, no. 11 (November 2004): s34–s41.

108. Kashef, 2007; Tate, s34–s41.

109. Herring 2005.

110. Philipkoski 2004; Cho and Sankar, s8–s12.

111. "About the Innocence Project" http://www.innocenceproject.org/about/; Kashef 2007; Robert Bazell, "DNA Acquittals Shaking Up Forensic Science, Current Methods Questioned As More Wrongful Convictions Emerge," February 12, 2008, http://www.msnbc.msn.com/id/23113417/.

112. Nancy Touchette, "Genome Test Nets Suspected Serial Killer." http://www.genomenewsnetwork.org/articles/06_03/serial.shtml June 13, 2003; "DNAPrint's DNA Witness Test Provided Break in the Louisiana Multi-Agency Homicide Task Force Serial Killer Case," http://www.dnaprint.com/welcome/press/press_recent/ June 5, 2003; Richard Willing, "DNA Tests Offer Clues to Suspect's Race." *USA TODAY* 8/16/2005; http://www.usatoday.com/news/nation/2005-08-16-dna_x.htm;   Dana   Hawkins   Simons, "Getting DNA to Bear Witness Genetic Tests Can Reveal Ancestry, Giving Police a New Source of Clues," http://www.usnews.com/usnews/culture/articles/030623/23dna.htm. June 15, 2003

113. "DNAWitness™ 2.5" http://www.forensic.e-symposium.com/humid/dnaprint/DNA_Forensic_Flyer.pdf.; Kashef **2007.**

114. Duster, 152–63; Kashef 2007.

115. Kashef 2007.

116. Kashef 2007.

117. Duster, 152–63; Kashef 2007.

118. Kashef 2007.

119. "About Us," DNA Print, http://www.dnaprint.com/welcome/corporate/; Coleen Fitzpatrick and Andrew Yeiser, *DNA and Genealogy* (Fountain Valley, CA.: Rice Book Press, 2005), 1–20; *60 Minutes*—"Roots," CBS DVD recording (October 7, 2007); Kashef 2007. Despite denials from Jefferson's European American descendants, recent DNA evidence

confirms the long-disputed contention that Thomas Jefferson—one of the founding fathers and third President of the United States—fathered several children with a slave mistress, Sally Hemings, who was of partial African descent. The DNA evidence indicates that Jefferson most likely fathered at least one of Sally Hemings's sons (Eston). Eston and some of his descendants apparently passed as European American (Daniel 2006, 282).

120. Spencer Wells, *Deep Ancestry: Inside the Genographic Project* (Washington D.C. National Geographic, 2006), 1–9.

121. Wells, 58, 233; *60 Minutes*—"Roots."

122. Megan Smolenyak Smolenyak and Ann Turner, *Trace Your Roots with DNA: Using Genetic Tests to Explore Your Family Tree* (Holtzbrinck Publishers, 2004), 35–7, 59–74; Fitzpatrick and Yeiser, 1–20; Ziba Kashef, 2007; *60 Minutes*—"Roots."

123. Smolenyak and Turner, 1–20; Kashef 2007.

124. African Ancestry.com is a company devoted to tracing ancestry specific to geographic areas on the African continent through DNA analysis. It has compiled a DNA database containing 11,747 samples of paternal lineages and samples of 13,690 maternal lineages from 30 countries and over 200 ethnic groups from Africa. Like many other similar companies African Ancestry.com can provide both Y-chromosome and mitochondrial tests. However, the former test poses special challenges for African-descent Americans seeking to trace an ancestral link to diasporic Africa. Y-chromosome analysis is more likely to reveal European ancestry by virtue of plantation dynamics that involved sexual relations between European American male slave owners and/or overseers and African female slaves. Consequently, the company's most common test tracks mitochondrial DNA. Paul Elias, "DNA Offers Avenue to Black Ancestry Genetic Analysis Provides New Options, But Also Raises Questions," Sept. 15, 2003 http://www.msnbc.msn.com/id/3077132/; "Our Exclusive African Lineage" http://www.africanancestry.com/

125. F. James Davis, *Who Is Black?: One Nation's Definition* (University Park, PA.: Pennsylvania State University, 1991), 19–23.

126. Kashef, 2007.

127. Kashef, 2007; *60 Minutes*—"Roots."

128. Herring 2005; Kashef 2007; Rotimi, s43–s47.

129. Herring 2005; Kashef 2007.

130. Wells, 20–1; Kashef 2007; Philipkoski 2001.

131. Harmon 2007. Such discussions are among thousands that followed geneticist and Nobel Prize winner James D. Watson's assertion that individuals of Africans are inherently less intelligent than individuals of European descent. He subsequently apologized and resigned from his position at the Cold Spring Harbor Laboratory on Long Island. Cornelia Dean, "James Watson Quits Post After Remarks on Races," *New York Times* http://www.nytimes.com/2007/10/26/science/26watson.html, October 6, 2007.

132. Harmon 2007.

133. Ibid.

134. Ibid.

135. Ibid.

136. Santos and Maio 2004, 363–4; 2005, 447–68.

137. Lewontin, 391–98; Philipkoski 2001; Santos and Maio 2004, 363–4; 2005, 447–68.

138. Harmon 2007.

139. This title borrows on research coordinated by geneticist Sérgio Pena at the Universidade Federal de Minas Gerais (UFMG) in Brazil. The findings of the studies, known as "Retrato Molecular do Brazil" ("Molecular Portrait of Brazil)," were published in 2000. By sequencing portions of mitochondrial DNA and the Y chromosome, geneticists sought to map out the geographical distribution and patterns of the Brazilian population's respectively matrilineal and patrilineal ancestry, paying special attention to the social and demographic reality of the nation in terms of miscegenation. The findings thus reiterate the limited significance and utility of race as a biological concept and portray Brazilians as the end products of pervasive blending, which underscores the fluidity, instability, and ill-defined nature of racial categories. In particular, these new bio-historical narratives reinforce a long-standing and deeply rooted

social imagination that considers miscegenation a positive and defining element of Brazil's national identity. Sérgio D.J. Pena, Denise R. Carvalho-Silva, J. Alves-Silva, Vania Ferreira Prado, and Fabríco R. Santos, "Retrato Molecular do Brasil," *Ciência Hoje* 159 (2000): 16–25; See Part II, Chapter 7 in this book.

140. This title borrows on the research coordinated by geneticist Sérgio Pena at the Universidade Federal de Minas Gerais (UFMG) in Brazil. The findings of these studies, which sequenced portions of mitochondrial DNA and the Y chromosome among Brazilians, were published in 2000 and are known as "Retrato Molecular do Brazil" ("Molecular Portrait of Brazil)." See Part II, Chapter 7 in this book.

141. Pena et al., 2000, 25.

142. Santos and Maio 2004, 363–4; 2005, 447–68; Pena et al., 2000: 25.

143. Paul Brodwin, "Genetics, Identity, and the Anthropology of Essentialism," *Anthropological Quarterly*. 75, no. 2. (Spring, 2002), 324; Carl Elliott and Paul Brodwin, "Identity and Genetic Ancestry Tracing," *BMJ* (*British Medical Journal*) 325 (December 21, 2002: 1469–71.

144. Omi and Winant, 55–6; Santos and Maio 2005, 16.

145. Santos and Maio 2005, 16.

146. Santos and Maio 2004, 464–65.

147. Paul Gilroy, *Against Race: Imagining Political Culture Beyond the Color Line* (Cambridge, Mass.: The Belknap Press of Harvard University, 2000), 12.

148. Gilroy 2000, 17; Santos and Maio 2004, 363–4; 2005, 447–68.

149. José Vasconselos, *La Raza Cósmica: Misión de la Raza Iberoamericana* (Mexico D.F., Espasa Calpe, S.A., 1948), 65–6.

150. Vasconselos, 39, 65–6; Marco Polo Hernández Cuevas, *African Mexicans and the Discourse on Modern Nation* (Lanham, Maryland: University Press of America, 2004), xvi, 1–30.

151. Vasconselos, 4, 14–33; Cuevas, xvi, 1–30.

152. Emily Monroy, "Whither Miscegenation?" *Interracial Voice* http://www.webcom.com/intvoice/emily29.html. 2003; *The Dialogues of G. de Purucker* KTMG Papers: Thirteen Meeting of May 28, 1930. Pasadena, CA.: Theosophical University Press, 1997. http://www.theosociety.org/pasadena/dialogue/dial-hp.htm; Jan Nederveen Pieterse, *Globalization and Culture: Global Mélange* (Lanham, MD.: Rowman and Littlefield Publishers, Inc., 1994), 38, 100–17.

153. Monroy, 2003; Jan Nederveen Pieterse, *Globalization and Culture: Global Mélange* (Lanham, MD.: Rowman and Littlefield Publishers, Inc., 1994), 38, 100–17.

154. Cuevas, xvi, 1–30.

155. Rattansi, 30; Seidman 8–9; Rosenau, 5–7.

156. Ibid.

157. Hooks, 23–31.

158. Broadly speaking, the African Diaspora refers to the dispersal of Africans and their descendants across the globe. However, more specifically it refers to the massive importation of slaves, particularly into the Americas, during the Atlantic Slave trade between the 16th and 19th centuries.

159. Eze, 222–23; Wilber, 166, 187–92, 261–72; Rattansi, 30; Seidman, 8–9; Rosenau, 5–7.

References

Anderson, Victor. *Beyond Ontological Blackness: An Essay on African American Religious Criticism.* New York: Continuum, 1995.

Anderson, Walter Truett. "Introduction: What's Going on Here?." In *The Truth About the Truth: De-confusing and Re-constructing the Postmodern World*, ed. Walter Truett Anderson, 1–17. New York: G. P. Putman and Sons, 1995.

"An Overview of the Human Genome Project (HGP)" http://www.genome.gov/12011238

Arnason, Johann P. "Nationalism, Globalization, and Modernity." In *Global Culture: Nationalism, Globalization, and Modernity*, ed. Mike Featherstone, 207–36. Thousand Oaks, CA.: Sage Publications, 1990.

Asante, Molefi. *Afrocentricity: The Theory of Social Change*. Buffalo: Amulefi, 1980.

_____. *Kemet, Afrocentricity, and Knowledge*. Trenton. N. J.: Africa World Press, Inc., 1992.

_____. *The Afrocentric Idea*. Philadelphia, PA.: Temple University Press, 1987.

Bazell, Robert. "DNA Acquittals Shaking Up Forensic Science, Current Methods Questioned As More Wrongful Convictions Emerge," February 12, 2008, http://www.msnbc.msn.com/id/23113417/.

Bourdieu, Pierre and Loïc Wacquant. "On the Cunning of Imperialist Reason." *Theory, Culture, and Society* 16, no. 1 (1991): 41–58.

Branca, Malorye Allison. "BiDil Raises Questions About Race As A Marker," *Nature Reviews Drug Discovery* 4, 615–16 (August 2005)|doi:10.1038/nrd1812.

Brodwin, Paul, "Genetics, Identity, and the Anthropology of Essentialism," *Anthropological Quarterly*. 75, no. 2 (Spring 2002): 323–30.

Cavalli-Sforza, L. Luca, Paolo Menozzi, and Alberto Piazza. *The History and Geography of Human Genes*. Princeton, New Jersey: Princeton University Press, 1994.

Cho, Mildred K. and Pamela Sankar. "Forensic Genetics and Ethical, Legal, and Social Implications Beyond the Clinic," *Nature Genetic Supplement* 36, no. 11 (November 2004): s8–s12.

Collins, Francis S. "What We Do and Do Not Know About 'Race,' 'Ethnicity,'" Genetics, and Health at the Dawn of the Genome Era," in *Nature Genetic Supplement* 36, no. 11 (November 2004): s13–s15.

Collins, Patricia Hill. "Setting Our Own Agenda." *The Black Scholar* 23, 3 & 4 (1993): 52–5.

Cuevas, Marco Polo Hernández. *African Mexicans and the Discourse on Modern Nation* (Lanham, Maryland: University Press of America, 2004.

Daniel, G. Reginald. "Eurocentrism, Afrocentrism, or Holocentrism?" *Interrace Magazine*. 3, 2(1992): 33.

_____. *More Than Black? Multiracial Identity and the New Racial Order*. Philadelphia: Temple University Press, 2002.

_____. "Multiraical Identity in Global Perspective: The United States, Brazil, and South Africa." In *New Faces in a Changing America: Multiracial Identity in the 21st Century*, ed. Loretta Winter and Herman Dubose, 247–86. Thousand Oaks, CA.: Sage Publications, 2002.

_____. *Race and Multiraciality in Brazil and the United States: Converging Paths?* University Park, PA.: Pennsylvania State University Press, 2006.

Davis, F. James. *Who Is Black?: One Nation's Definition*. University Park, PA.: Pennsylvania State University, 1991.

Diawara, Manthia. 1996. "Pan-Africanism and Pedagogy." *Black Cultural Studies*. org. http://www.blackculturalstudies.org/m_diawara/panafr.html

Duster, Troy. *Backdoor to Eugenics*. New York: Routledge, 2003.

Early, Gerald. "Understanding Afrocentrism: Why Blacks Dream of a World Without Whites," *Civilization* (July/August 1995): 31–9.

Eisler, Riane. *The Chalice and the Blade: Our History, Our Future*. San Francisco: Harper and Row, 1988.

Elias, Paul. "DNA Offers Avenue to Black Ancestry Genetic Analysis Provides New Options, But Also Raises Questions." Sept. 15, 2003 http://www.msnbc.msn.com/id/3077132/

Elliott, Carl and Paul Brodwin. "Identity and Genetic Ancestry Tracing," *BMJ (British Medical Journal)* 325 (December 21, 2002): 1469–71.

Epstein, Steven. *Inclusion: The Politics of Difference in Medical Research*. Chicago, Ill.: University of Chicago Press, 2007.

Eze, Emmanuel Chukwudieze. *Achieving Our Humanity: The Idea of the Postracial Future*. New York: Routledge, 2001.

Fanon, Frantz. *Black Skin, White Masks*. Translated by Charles Lam Markmann. New York: Grove Press, Inc., 1967/1952.

Featherstone, Mike. "Introduction." In *Global Culture: Nationalism, Globalization, Modernity*, ed. Mike Featherstone, 1–13. Thousand Oaks, CA.: Sage Publications, 1990.

Fitzpatrick, Coleen and Andrew Yeiser. *DNA and Genealogy*. Fountain Valley, CA.: Rice Book Press, 2005.

Fortes, Jorge and Diego Ceballos. *Afroargentines (Afroargentinos)* Filmagen Producciones, Lagartija Muda Producciones. New York: Latin American Video Archives, 2002.

Fry, Peter. "Politics, Nationality, and the Meaning of Race." *Daedalus* 129, no. 2 (2000): 83–118.

Fry, Peter and Yvonne Maggie, "Política Social de Alto Risco." In *Divisões Perogosas: Políticas Racias no Brasil Contemporâneo*, ed. Peter Fry and Yvonne Maggie, Marcos Chor Maio, Simone Monteiro, and Ricardo Ventura Santos, 277–8. Rio de Janeiro: Civilização Brasileira, 2007.

Fullwiley, Duana. "The Molecularization of Race: Institutionalizing Human Difference." *Pharmacogenetics Practice* 16 no. 1 (March 2007): 1–30.

Gilroy, Paul. *Against Race: Imagining Political Culture Beyond the Color Line*. Cambridge, Mass.: The Belknap Press of Harvard University, 2000.

Guevarra, Rudy P. Jr. "Burritos and Bagoong: Mexipinos and Multiethnic Identity in San Diego, California." In *Crossing Lines: Race and Mixed Race Across the Geohistorical Divide*, ed. Marc Coronado, Rudy P. Guevarra, Jr., Jeffrey Moniz, and Laura Furlan Szanto, 73–96. Santa Barbara, Calif.: Multiethnic Student Outreach in collaboration with the Center of Chicano Studies, University of California, Santa Barbara, 2003.

Hardt, Michael and Antonio Negri. *Empire*. Cambridge, Massachusetts: Harvard University Press, 2000.

Harmon, Amy. "The DNA Age: In DNA Era, New Worries About Prejudice," November 11, 2007.

Havel, Václav. "The Need for Transcendence in the Postmodern World." Václav Havel was the first president of the Czech Republic (1993–2003). The speech was made in Independence Hall, Philadelphia, July 4, 1994.

_____. "The Search for Meaning in a Global Civilization." In *The Truth About the Truth: De-confusing and Re-constructing the Postmodern World*, ed. Walter Truett Anderson, 232–238. New York: G. P. Putman and Sons, 1995.

Henig, Robin Maranyz. "The Genome in Black and White (and Gray)." *New York Times Magazine,* October 10 2004.
http://www.nytimes.com/2004/10/10/magazine/10GENETIC.html/

Hernández Cuevas, Marco Polo. *African Mexicans and the Discourse on Modern Nation*. Lanham, Maryland: University Press of America, 2004.

Herring, Lee and Mercedes Rubio, "Scientists Warn of Conceptual Traps Concerning "Race" in New Genetic Map of Human Populations," Footnotes," April 2005 American Sociological Association
http://www2.asanet.org/footnotes/apr05/indextwo.html

hooks, bell. *Yearning: Race, Gender, and Cultural Politics*. Boston: South End Press. 1995.

Hochschild, Jennifer L. *Facing Up to the American Dream: Race, Class, and the Soul of the Nation*. Princeton, New Jersey: Princeton University Press, 1995.

Howe, Stephen. *Afrocentrism: Mythical Pasts and Imagined Homes*. New York: Verso, 1998.

"Human Genome Project Goals." http://www.genome.gov/11006945

Jobling, Mark A., Matthew Hurles, and Chris Tyler-Smith. *Human Evolutionary Genetics: Origins, Peoples, and Disease* (New York: Garland Publishing, 2004

Jones, Rhett S., "The End of Africanity?: The Bi-Racial Assault on Blackness. *The Western Journal of Black Studies*, 18, 4 (1994): 201–210.

Jorde, Lynn B. and Stephen B. Wooding, "Genetic Variation, Classification, and Race," in *Nature Genetic Supplement* 36, no. 11 (November 2004): s28–s33.

Kamel, Ali. *Não Somos Racistas: Uma Reação Aos Que Querem Nos Transformar Numa Nação Bicolor*. 2a impressão. Rio de Janeiro: Editora Nova Fronteira, 2006.

Kashef, Ziba. "Genetic Drift," *ColorLines*. no. 40 (Sept/Oct 2007).

Keita, Mahgan, "Deconstructing the Classical Age: Africa and the Unity of the Mediterranean World." *Journal of Negro History*, LXXIX, 2 (Spring 1994): 146–166.

Kesteloot, Lilyan. *Les Écrivains Noirs de Langue Française: Naissance d'une Littérature*. Brussels: Université de Bruxelles, 1965.

Kershaw, Terry. "Afrocentrism and the Afrocentric Method." In *Afrocentric Visions: Studies in Culture and Communication*, ed. Janice D. Hamlet, 27–44. Thousand Oaks, CA.: Sage Publications, 1993.

Lefkowitz, Mary. *Not Out of Africa: How Afrocentrism Became an Excuse to Teach Myth As History*. New York: Basic Books, 1996.

Landry, Donna and Gerald Maclean, ed. *The Spivak Reader: Selected Works of Gayatri Chakravorty Spivak*. New York: Routledge, 1995.

Lemert, Charles. *Sociology After the Crisis*. Boulder: Westview Press, 1996.

Leonard, Karen Isaksen. *Making Ethnic Choices: California's Punjabi Mexican Americans*. Philadelphia, PA.: Temple University Press.

Levine, Molly Myerowitz. "Review Article, The Use and Abuse of Black Athena." *American Historical Review* (April 1992): 440–64.

Lewontin, Richard. "The Apportionment of Human Diversity," *Evolutionary Biology* 6 (1972): 391–98.

Lipsitz, George. "Noise in the Blood: Culture, Conflict, and Mixed Race Identities." In *Crossing Lines: Race and Mixed Race Across the Geohistorical Divide*, ed. Marc Coronado, Rudy P. Guevarra, Jr., Jeffrey Moniz, and Laura Furlan Szanto, 32–5. ESanta Barbara, Calif.: Multiethnic Student Outreach in collaboration with the Center of Chicano Studies, University of California, Santa Barbara, 2003.

Mittleman, James H. *The Globalization Syndrome: Transformation and Resistance*. Princeton, N.J.: Princeton University Press, 2000.

Marable, Manning. *Beyond Black and White: Transforming African American Politics*. New York: Verso, 1995.

Monroy, Emily. "Whither Miscegenation?" *Interracial Voice* http://www.webcom.com/intvoice/emily29.html. 2003.

Myers, Linda James. "The Deep Structure of Culture: Relevance of Traditional African Culture in Contemporary Life." In *Afrocentric Visions: Studies in Culture and Communication*, ed. Janice D. Hamlet, 1–14. Thousand Oaks, CA.: Sage Publications, 1998.

Omi, Michael and Howard Winant. *Racial Formation in the 1980s and 1990s*. New York: Routledge, 1994.

"Our Exclusive African Lineage." *African Ancestry*. com http://www.africanancestry.com/

Patrinos, Ari. "Race and the Human Genome," *Nature Genetic Supplement* 36, no. 11 (November 2004): s1–s2.

Pena, Sérgio D. J. "Há Uma Base Objetiva Para Definir o Conceito de Raça?," *Folha de São Paulo*, (December 21, 2002): A3.

Pena, Sérgio D.J., Denise R. Carvalho-Silva, J. Alves-Silva, Vania Ferreira Prado, and Fabríco R. Santos, "Retrato Molecular do Brasil," *Ciência Hoje* 159 (2000): 16–25.

Pérez-Sarduy, Pedroand Jean Stubbs, ed. *No Longer Invisible: Afro-Latin Americans Today*. London, Minority Rights Group Publications, 1995.

Philipkoski, Kristen. "Gene Map Presents Race Concerns," http://www.wired.com/science/discoveries/news/2001/02/41619.

Pieterse, Jan Nederveen. *Globalization and Culture: Global Mélange*. Lanham, MD.: Rowman and Littlefield Publishers, Inc., 1994a.

_____. "Unpacking the West: How European Is Europe?" In *Racism, Modernity and Identity: On the Western Front*, ed. Ali Ratanssi and Sallie Westwood, 129–150. Cambridge: Polity Press, 1994b.

Pope, Christie Farnham. "The Challenge Posed by Radical Afrocentrism: When a White Professor Teaches Black History," *Chronicle of Higher Education*, (March 30, 1994), B1.

Rattansi, Ali. "'Western' Racisms, Ethnicities and Identities." In *Racism, Modernity and Identity: On the Western Front*, ed. Ali Ratanssi and Sallie Westwood, 15–86. Cambridge: Polity Press, 1994.

Risério, Antonio. *A Utopia Brasileira e Os Movimentos Negros*. São Paulo: Editora 34 Ltda, 2007.

Robinson, William. "Reamapping Development in Light of Globalization: From a Territorial to a Social Cartography," *Third World Quarterly* 23, no. 6(2002): 1047–1071.

Rosenau, Pauline Marie. *Postmodernism and the Social Sciences: Insights, Inroads, and Intrusions*. Princeton, N.J.: Princeton University Press, 1992.

Rotimi, Charles N. "Are Medical and Nonmedical Uses of Large-Scale Genomic Markers Conflating Genetics With 'Race,'" in *Nature Genetic Supplement* 36, no. 11 (November 2004): s43–s47.

Sandoval, Chela. *Methodology of the Oppressed*. Minneapolis, Minnesota: University of Minnesota Press, 2000.

Santos, Ricardo Ventura and Marcos Chor Maio. "Antropologia, Raça e os Dilemas das Identidades na Era da Genômica," *História, Ciências, Saúde—Manguinhos* 12, no. 2 (May–August 2005): 447–68.

Santos, Ricardo Ventura and Marcos Chor Maio. "Race, Genomics, Identities, and Politics in Contemporary Brazil," *Critique of Anthropology* 24, no. 4 (2004): 363–4.

Sartre, Jean-Paul. *Black Orpheus*. Translated by S. W. Allen. Paris, Présence Africaine, 1948/1963.

Schiele, Jerome H.1991. "Afrocentricity for All," *Black Issues in Higher Education* (September 26): 27.

_____. "Rethinking Organizations From an Afrocentric Viewpoint" In *Afrocentric Visions: Studies in Culture and Communication*, ed. Janice D. Hamlet, 73–88. Thousand Oaks, CA.: Sage Publications, 1998.

Seidman, Steven. 1994. "Introduction." In The Postmodern Turn: New Perspectives on Social Theory, ed. Steven Seidman, 1–21. New York: Cambridge University Press.

Shohat, Ella and Robert Stam. *Unthinking Eurocentrism: Multiculturalism and the Media*. New York: Routledge, 1994.

Simons, Dana Hawkins. "Getting DNA to Bear Witness Genetic Tests Can Reveal Ancestry, Giving Police a New Source of Clues." June 15, 2003. http://www.usnews.com/usnews/culture/articles/030623/23dna.htm.

60 Minutes—"Roots." CBS DVD recording (October 7, 2007).

Slater, David. "Exploring Other Zones of the Postmodern: Problems of Ethnocentrism and Difference Across the North-South Divide." In *Racism, Modernity and Identity: On the Western Front*, ed. Ali Rattansi and Sallie Westwood, 87–126. Cambridge: Polity Press, 1994.

Smedley, Audrey. *Race in North America: Origin and Evolution of a Worldview*. Boulder, Colorado: Westview Press, 1993.

Smolenyak, Megan Smolenyak and Ann Turner. *Trace Your Roots with DNA: Using Genetic Tests to Explore Your Family Tree*. Holtzbrinck Publishers, 2004.

Snowden, Frank M. Jr. *Before Color Prejudice: The Ancient View of Blacks*. Cambridge, Mass.: Harvard University Press, 1983.

Sorokin, Pitirim. *Social and Cultural Dynamics: The Study of Change in Major Systems of Art, Truth, Ethics, Law and Social Relationships*. Revised and Abridged. Boston: Porter Sargent Books, 1957/1985.

Spencer, John Michael. "Trends of Opposition to Multiculturalism." *Black Scholar* 23 (1993): 2–5.

Spivak, Gayatari Chakrovorti. *The Post-colonial Critic: Interviews, Strategies, Dialogues*. New York: Routledge, 1990.

Tate, Sarah K. "Will Tomorrow's Medicines Work for Everyone." *Nature Genetic Supplement* 36, no. 11 (November 2004): s34–s41.

Teitelbaum, Stanley. 1990. "Making Everything Perfectly Fuzzy." *Los Angeles Times Magazine*, April 1, 24–42

Tiffin, Helen. "Introduction." In *Past the Last Post: Theorizing Post-Colonialism and Post-modernism*, ed. Ian Adam and Helen Tiffin, vii–xvi. Calgary, Albert, Canada: University of Calgary Press, 1990.

Tishkoff, Sarah A. and Kenneth K Kidd. "Implications of Biogeography of Human Populations for 'Race' and Medicine," in *Nature Genetic Supplement* 36, no. 11 (November 2004): s21–s27, s34–s41.

Touchette, Nancy. "Genome Test Nets Suspected Serial Killer" http://www.genomenewsnetwork.org/articles/06_03/serial.shtml, June 13, 2003.

Vasconselos, José. *La Raza Cósmica. Misión de la Raza Iberoamericana*. Mexico D.F., Espasa Calpe, S.A., 1948.

Wailoo, Keith and Stephen Pemberton. *The Troubled Dream of Genetic Medicine: Ethnicity and Innovation in Tay-Sachs, Cystic Fibrosis, and Sickle Cell Disease*. Baltimore, MD.: The Johns Hopkins University Press, 2006.

Wells, Spencer. *Deep Ancestry: Inside the Genographic Project*. Washington D.C. National Geographic, 2006.

West, Cornel. *Beyond Eurocentrism and Multiculturalism*. vol. 1. Monroe, Maine: Common Courage, 1993.

Wilber, Ken. *A Brief History of Everything* (Boston, MA.: Shambhala Publications. Inc., 1996.

Will, George. "Intellectual Segregation: Afrocentrism's Many Myths Constitute Condescension toward African-Americans." *Newsweek* (February 19, 1996): 78.

Williams, Patrick and Chrisman, Laura. "Colonial Discourse and Post-Colonial Theory: An Introduction." In *Colonial Discourse and Post-Colonial Theory: A Reader*, ed. Patrick Williams and Laura Chrisman, 1–19. New York: Columbia University Press, 1994.

Willing, Richard. "DNA Tests Offer Clues to Suspect's Race." *USA TODAY* (August 16, 2005) http://www.usatoday.com/news/nation/2005-08-16-dna_x.htm.

Wilson, Carter. *Racism: From Slavery to Advanced Capitalism*. Thousand Oaks, CA.: 1996.

Young, Robert J. C. *Colonial Desire: Hybridity in Theory, Culture, and Race*. New York: Routledge, 1995.

_____. "Egypt in America: Black Athena, Racism, and Colonial Discourse." In *Racism, Modernity and Identity: On the Western Front*, ed. Ali Rattansi and Sallie Westwood, 150–169. Cambridge: Polity Press, 1994.

Part III

Race, Ethnicity, and Conflict in Contemporary

Societies

Chapter 17

Black No More: African Americans and the 'New' Race Science

Hettie V. Williams

Discussions about race[1] and racial categorization in contemporary American society have become increasingly complex as coupled with developments in the study of human genetics. The Human Genome Project (HGP) and the rise of genomics have come to influence our understanding of race in terms of both historical and social relationships between and within human populations. This chapter examines race in American society in the post-genomic era as related to the historical experience of African Americans.

Introduction

"Ever since the first sanitarium of Black-No-More, Incorporated, started turning Negroes into Caucasians, the National Equality League's income had been decreasing," states George Schuyler in his fantastical satire entitled *Black No More* published in 1931.[2] The idea of race as biology is embedded in the social psyche of America. Although race as a biologic category of human difference has been vociferously challenged by social scientists for decades, race as an "idea" has a social and cultural history that evolved with slavery. Race as a "social construction" was informed by stereotypes of black Africans manufactured to sustain economic advantage and to justify white supremacy before, during, and after slavery. Historically, race in American society has been defined as color, physical appearance, blood, culture, ancestry, and sometimes by association. This was reinforced in law and social custom. Interracial liaisons have been a constant throughout the history of America. The binary American color-line has proven to be fluid, counterfactual, and ultimately contradictory as those with "black" blood and an ambiguous appearance have sometimes passed for "white."

The findings of the Human Genome project (HGP) have concluded that physical variation between one human and another is numerically miniscule (DNA is 99.9% identical in the human species and differs at 0.1% between individuals).[3] In fact, the science of DNA mapping indicates that African DNA is the most diverse and consequently present within the DNA of all modern humans.[4] Does George Schuyler's fanciful spoof postulating the end of blackness through a new race science inadvertently reflect the present and future of race and race science in America? Schuyler's *Black No More* characters become *whiter than white* thereby ensuring a reconstructed racism as a result of the new race science developed by Black-No-More-Incorporated. Race construed as *biology* has been largely hazardous to African Americans in American history.

Given the complex history of race in America, along with the most recent developments in the study of human genetics, is it plausible that America will consider "black no more" or will race be reified as a biological category of human difference? Race is still with us. In fact, a vociferous reification of race as a biologic category of human difference is in progress *despite* the scientific discovery of the "miniscule" physical variation between humans. Although race and racism *in* American society is not the same thing as racial genetics, there is an interrelationship between the social reality of race and the scientific debates that emanate from the racial genetics discourse. Scientific inquiry is influenced by race as a pervasive social phenomenon shaped by perceptions about the supposed biological inferiority of African Americans. This is reflected in the clinical approach to the consideration of race as science in medical practices and experimentation.[5] Historically, African Americans have been the most vulnerable group as related to *any* discussion of race as biology. The new business of race in America is primarily detrimental, exploitative, and dangerous to African Americans as has been the history of race science in America. This chapter will demonstrate how "dangerous" a business the new race science is to African Americans through a discussion of (1) the new genomics and the capitalist imperative, (2) race, disease, and medical remedies, (3) and lastly, race and the criminal justice system.

The dialogue on race in contemporary America involves a discussion of a confusing labyrinth of congruent and sometimes contradictory notions. Delineation between the two more commonly used definitions of race is first necessary: social race and biological race. This is also compulsory to illustrate that race as a social construct (expressed in social experience) and the premise of race as biology work in tandem to reinforce biology as a metonym for race that helps to engender dangerous biomedical circumstances that may negatively impact the lives of African Americans. Social scientists debating race in the U.S. generally fall into three categories including those who argue that race is an illusion, others who argue that race is becoming increasingly obsolete and those who merely argue for transcendence beyond the binary paradigm while some biological scientists and geneticists continue to promote the validity of race as a useful category of human difference. The heated exchanges among scholars across disciplines often hinge upon disputes about race either as social construct, biological reality, or both.

The great "labyrinth" of race is that humans have used science (particularly genetics) to both explain *and* denounce the race concept thereby continuously "naturalizing the social order" in the United States as one historian explains that race has served as a "dense transfer point between nature and society."[6] Many scholars interrogating race often fall into the problem of language as they seek to explain what race is and what race is not. To say race is a social construct and therefore no longer a potent force in human society is inexact because race does exist as a profound *social reality* yet it is not a discrete biological unit in terms of defining human differences. Race is not an inextricable biosocial unit but social race conflated as color, culture, and ancestry does have an impact on biomedical decision-making. In fact, social race has a tremendous sway over the human psyche in America particularly as it is associated with institutionalized power structures and this is evidenced with the rise of social race in the history of the American Republic. Those who "confuse" race with biology as a category of human classification, to justify social group identification, for medical purposes, or to advance socio-political agendas, must also recognize that such pronouncements only help to propagate a faulty concept with a volatile history. Those who utilize race to explain human illness and social problems as determined by genetics or biology often confuse a "social construct" with natural science.

Race has a socio-cultural history rooted in both the ancient and medieval imagination of European civilization while race as biology is a relatively modern idea. The rise of European expansion and the Atlantic Slave Trade through the fifteenth century solidified the social construction of race in the Americas as part of a justification for black servitude. This binary racial system was connected to the rise of politico-economic power structures in North America dominated by Europeans and defined through legally constructed concepts of race such as with the colloquial and socio-legal phrase "one drop rule."[7] Race emerged as a result of a historical process determined by both the macro forces of politico-economic structures and the micro social experiences of human groups. These unique "social experiences" have been shaped by perceptions about physical differences between human populations. Social race should be seen as an ongoing historical process involving constantly shifting contested systems of meaning as negotiated between and within social racial groups in American society. As a mechanism of power, the dominant social racial group may often manipulate concepts of social race to justify the subjugation of the racialized "Other" while the marginalized group may often embrace "race" based on common history and social experience to circumvent trespass. Paradoxically, African Americans, as has been the case with several ethnic groups in America, have historically embraced concepts of race as color to gain redress in a society dominated by a color struck (white supremacist) belief system.

Africans first came to the Americas as Igbo, Mandinka, or Fulani, among other ethno-linguistic formations, and *became* black as a result of a socialization process defined by racial slavery. The advent of sociological jurisprudence in Progressive Age America (1890-1920) as championed by such legal minds as Louis B. Brandeis subsequently gave rise to the concept of "protected groups" based not only on sociological data regarding groups seeking special protections under the law but socio-cultural perceptions of race and gender. Therefore, social race has been used as a legal strategy by disenfranchised ethnic groups in America to demand redress and gain civil rights. The enculturation of the social racial binary has become embedded in the psyche of both the dominant culture and the sub-culture. The psycho-social development of the self in American society is heavily shaped by concepts of social race.

The construction, negotiation, and reconfiguration of social race in American society are intrinsically bound to what sociologist Patricia Hill Collins has aptly labeled a "matrix of power" with intersecting hierarchies defined through the socially contrived categories of gender, race, and class. Racial slavery in American history after the seventeenth century ensured that negative concepts of "blackness" became institutionalized during and after slavery within the politico-economic power structures of U.S. society, including the medical establishment. Our understanding of race has been continuously reconfigured, but race has yet to be dismantled as a categorical system of power. We must not exchange "old" racial paradigms for "new" ones, as has been the case in this reconfiguration, and be satisfied. Transcendence beyond the binary to the ternary is not enough. The current "reconfiguration" while presenting a challenge to old ideas also helps to perpetuate a new system of racial classification that is primarily harmful to African Americans as Americans remain color struck. Indeed, the colors of multiethnic and multiracial America have been expanded from the black-white binary to include tan and brown. Colors belong in the crayon box. Social race must be un-learned and yet it is just as *real* as the *idea* of biological race. Race has become a great paradox in the social arena [in part] because disadvantaged groups have historically used concepts of social race *as agency* to demand redress and "special protections" thereby contributing, however overtly or inadvertently, to the continuous reification of race as biology.

Biological race as a distinct category of human difference is an illusory concept because it is impossible to organize human groups into neat categories based on physical appearance or genetic material (including simple notions of ancestry conflated as "mixed race"). Human populations share ancestry and genetic material as indicated by the most recent findings of paleobiologists. The *human species* first walked out of Africa. Human groups exhibit visibly recognizable physical traits but these characteristics are largely superficial and do not represent the genetic totality of an individual or group and are shaped by multiple factors such as environment. The genetic characteristics present in one population are not necessarily absent in another. The idea of mixed race as ancestry may be explained away quite succinctly as Pilar Ossorio and Troy Duster assert:

> People whose skin color is perceived as white can have genetic profiles indicating that 80% of their recent ancestry is West African, and people whose skin color is perceived as black can have genetic profiles indicative of predominantly European ancestry. A person with substantial, recent African ancestry may pass as White and may have medically and psychologically consequential social advantages of whiteness. On the other hand, a person may

pass as White but possess medically relevant alleles more commonly associated with Blacks or with African ancestry.[8]

Ancestry fails to serve as a firm moniker for race or "mixed race," from one generation to the next, despite arguments to the contrary made by mixed race studies theorists.

Biological race became a popular idea in the late nineteenth century as a major justification for European imperialism in such places as Africa and Asia. Because superficial physical traits have been historically used to determine membership in a social racial group, the concept of social race and the *idea* of biological race as constructs often overlap and work in tandem. The enculturation of the binary racial paradigm as a point of reference in understanding race remains pervasive and continues to shape profoundly considerations of race in American society. Social attitudes about race as "color" or other physical traits continue to significantly influence political and economic decision making such as the case with the new race science in America.

Throughout this discourse, the rubric utilized by biological anthropologist Alan H. Goodman to demonstrate the incongruent relationship between genetic variation and race in understanding human disease is applied to illustrate the fallacy of race when associated with genetic differences in the medical sciences:

1. Race as a concept is based on fixed and unchanging types.
2. Human variation is continuous; therefore there is no clear place to designate where one race begins and another ends.
3. Human variation is nonconcordant-traits tend to vary independently of other traits.
4. Within-group genetic variation is much greater than variation among "races."
5. There is no way to consistently classify by race.
6. There is no clarity as to what race is and what it is not.[9]

Although reconfigured from the binary to an ever emergent ternary racial paradigm, social race is as dangerous as the idea of race as biology and continues to exist as a sort of strange alchemy in American society. To concur once again with Goodman, the "old race is the new race" and this is exemplified in the fallacious arguments about human disease as associated with "race" as word and idea.[10]

The New Race Science and the Capitalist Imperative

Human organisms acquire physical traits and characteristics through a biological hereditary unit called a gene thus producing a genotype (an organism's genetic inheritance). DNA is found in the control center (nucleus) of a cell where it constitutes the genetic code. A gene as a segment of the DNA molecule and a hereditary unit located on a chromosome (linear strand of DNA) determines the characteristics of an organism. Genes carry proteins that determine physical traits. These biologically inherited traits and characteristics interact with the physical environment thereby producing a phenotype (physical expression of the gene). The phenotype is both environmentally and genetically determined. Genes operate in concert with environmental pressures *not* as independent determinants. The Human Genome (the whole genetic material of an organism encoded on the DNA) Project, as the largest scientific endeavor in history, accomplished the mapping of human DNA and thereby proving that the genetic code of humans has greater biological similarities than disparities.[11] In fact, the genetic variation within groups has been proven to be more diverse than the genetic variation between human groups exhibiting distinct phenotypes. Genomics (science of genetics) is the study of an organism's genome.

The findings of the HGP have led to both the Human Genome Diversity Project (HGDP) and the Hap-Map Project. These initiatives have both yielded scientific discoveries that have furthered advances in genetics as related to human variation (the Hap-Map Project involves scientists who use genetic sequences to map and catalog human genetic variation) and genetic sequences within the context of genome wide association studies. Much of the new race science is based on discoveries related to the examination of human variation in conjunction with DNA sequencing. Genetic variations in humans and between groups are important because they can help to determine an individual's predisposition for disease.

The science of genetics has reduced the body to discussions of genotype, phenotype, alleles (variant form of a gene or genetic sequences that code for a gene that arise as a result of mutation) and now single nucleotide polymorphisms (SNPs) often pronounced as "snips." SNPs are DNA sequence variations[12] that occur when a single nucleotide[13] in the genome sequence is altered that make up 90% of all human genetic variation, are evolutionarily stable, and may have a significant impact in how scientists study disease. Alleles and SNPs are measured in populations not in individuals; SNPs are sometimes assigned as minor allele frequencies in a population. Allele frequencies represent the frequency of an allele on a genetic locus in a population measured in a proportion or percentage.

Can we now say that race as a barometer for the classification of human groups into separate sub-categories is at best a specious hypothesis and lacks serious taxonomic integrity? If phenotype is determined by both genetics and environment, race conflated as color, culture, or appearance has been historically a fluctuating phenomenon given the history of human migration patterns alone. Human evolution and human biological diversity are determined by a variety of factors including genetic drift, mutation, continuous interbreeding, and migration as Alexander Alland States:

> Migration and gene flow have spread human genes around the world in myriad ways. Successive migrations, conquests, absorptions, intermarriage, alliances, and extinctions of populations have produced a constant, never-ending shuffling of human genetic material.[14]

This is *not* to say the *belief* that race is a category of human difference no longer exists in American society. It does. While race literally has only a fractional merit as a biological concept, race exists as a very present social and cultural idea in American history and society. It is race as multiple conflicting *ideas* fueled by capitalist imperative that helps to propel the new science of racial genetics. While some may correctly argue that the broad science of genetics (or genomics) has profound beneficial qualities, the new science of *racial* genetics, as buttressed by the capitalist imperative and regulatory procedure, coupled with negative socio-cultural perceptions of blackness, is proving harmful to African Americans.

The exploitation of difference for profit has a long history in America. The American South became economically and politically dependent on slavery by the late eighteenth century just as medical practitioners developed a dependency for the use of black subjects as guinea pigs shaped by commonly held beliefs about the biological inferiority of African Americans.[15] Historically, African Americans have been targeted for abominable medical practices. African Americans deemed "afflicted" in slavery with such ailments as chronic dysentery were used as specimens to dissect and sometimes simply bled to death for the sheer purposes of medical experimentation. Now the new science of race claims to offer race specific remedies for ailments "commonly known" to have a greater impact on the health of African Americans such as heart disease, diabetes, asthma, and schizophrenia.

Statistics indicate that African Americans make up a disproportionate number of those with ailments such as heart disease. These statistics have as much to do with environmental, economic, social, and cultural factors, as they have to do with genetics. An appropriate correlation between race and disease is that *racism* [produced as a result of socially constructed perceptions about the black body] causes or at the least contributes to diseases "commonly known" to afflict African Americans. Harvard psychiatrist Alvin Pouissaint made such an association:

> The well-documented high rates of heart disease, hypertension, and other stress related illnesses found in African-Americans are traceable in part to social factors, including most prominently the long history of blacks being required to endure racism, poverty, discrimination, and the lack of adequate health services-including mental health care-in America. The persistent presence of racism, despite the significant legal, social, and political progress made during the last half of the twentieth century, has created a physiological risk for black people that is virtually unknown to white Americans.[16]

Racism acts as a stressor upon the body that may contribute to such illnesses as hypertension and diabetes. While rates of hypertension among native Nigerians are relatively low, rates of hypertension among African Americans in the U.S. and Africans living abroad in Europe are characteristically high; given the shared genetic heritage between these groups [75% in this particular study as based on the genetic make-up of the participants], researchers have come to infer that racism may be a key factor in the common rates of high blood pressure in these two groups.[17] It is much easier for those in power to explain away healthcare disparities, social problems, and discriminatory practices by confusing social race with human biology. Those deemed physically vulnerable to disease and therefore "genetically inferior," or those defined as "genetically predisposed" to commit crime help to explain the "natural order" of the social world as conceived by the dominant social group. This is a practice that also helps to assuage guilt within the self-imposed dominant group *when social race is strategically confused as biology to explain away social problems and disease.*

Race continues to have a profound economic utility when associated with vulnerable groups in the U.S. and can even be made to seem attractive when associated with diseases "known" to afflict one group more than another as explained through racial genetics. The mechanizations of the FDA help to facilitate circumstances in which the U.S. pharmaceutical industry finds it necessary to promote drug combinations specific to "race."

It is important to briefly examine the history, regulatory procedures, and basic operations of the Food and Drug administration as related specifically to the introduction of new drugs and medications. The U.S. Food and Drug Administration (FDA) is an agency of the United States Department of Health and Human Services responsible for regulating food, dietary supplements, drugs, and biological medical products. The modern FDA can be traced back to the Food and Drug Act of 1906. The term Food and Drug Administration or FDA was first used in 1930. The agency remained within the Department of Agriculture until 1940 when it was transferred to the Federal Security Agency later it became a part of the Department of Health, Education, and Welfare (HEW) in 1953 until 1980 when the Department of Health and Human Services was created. Currently, it is an agency engaged in the evaluation of applications for new human drugs and biologics along with such items as infant formulas, food, and food additives comprising more than 9,000 employees in 150 field offices with a budget of more than 1 billion dollars including various subdivisions.

Through operations of its multiple subdivisions, the FDA has the power to regulate, control, or ban marketed food, medical, and cosmetic products. The two most important subdivisions involved in the regulation of medical substances include the Center for Biologics Evaluation and Research (CBER) and the Center for Drug Evaluation and Research (CDER). The CBER monitors the purity and potency of biological products such as blood, vaccines, and those that are related to gene therapy and transplants. New drugs and drug combinations, including the approval, labeling, marketing, packaging and manufacture of new medications, are overseen by the CDER. Patents for new drugs are not secured through the FDA but are approved through the United States Patent and Trademark office. Patents are typically applied for before clinical trials of new drugs begin. The patent "life" of an investigational new drug is generally twenty years but the time limitation on drug patents typically begins *before* the drug even arrives on the shelf after FDA approval. Often, the patent life of a new drug, if one factors in clinical trials coupled with the general FDA approval process, is customarily less than a dozen years *if* the drug surpasses FDA regulatory procedures without significant delay. A brief outline schedule of the standard drug approval process is as follows:

1. U.S. based researcher or company submits investigational new drug (IND) including pre-clinical trial data.
2. Drug approved for travel across state lines.
3. Clinical trials conducted by drug sponsor that demonstrate the efficacy and safety of the drug (may take years costing as much as $800 million).
4. Application for New Drug Application submitted (NDA).
5. FDA review process (involving physicians, statisticians, chemists, and pharmacologists).
6. FDA approval, approvable, or rejected.

The history, operations, and mechanizations of the FDA obviously represent an intricate web of bureaucracy however necessary to ensure safety measures. The expenses incurred in the development of new drugs and clinical trials can be astronomical. Therefore, the American pharmaceutical industry has devised not only the research and development of new drug combinations as coupled with developments in the science of genetics (as much through the use of public funds coupled with private) but also strategies to circumvent regulatory procedure as will be discussed.

The emergence of pharmacogenomics (science of associating genetic markers with drug efficacy) has helped to facilitate developments related to the exploitation of select population groups in medical experimentation. The very attractive idea of *individualized* medicine including new investigational drugs and clinical trials designed with the specific purpose of targeting select ethno-racial groups was produced as a result of this expanding field of scientific inquiry. Color is not a sound genetic marker yet race conflated as color has been employed in these biomedical processes. We see the capitalist imperative demonstrated in this emergent field, as the "idea" of race continues to have a tremendous economic utility in U.S. society and particularly within the pharmaceutical industry.

Vulnerable communities, as aforementioned, such as the learning disabled and ethnic minorities, including African Americans, have long been exploited for the purpose of medical experimentation in the name of profit. Inmates in forty-two prisons around the country by 1969 made up 85% of the test subjects used in medical experimentation throughout the U.S. including tests encompassing everything from cosmetics to harsh chemicals such as dioxin and radioactive agents.[18] The poor, disadvantaged, and disenfranchised have sometimes been willing subjects in that the "testers" have often induced participants with the promise of everything from a warm bed to monetary compensation, "To fill beds [in early American medical school programs] it became essential to use the poor and the enslaved. Medicine thus capitalized on the need of the indigent and the helpless for medical care."[19]

African Americans [prisoners in particular] from Alabama to Washington State, and Pennsylvania were made subject to heinous medical experimentation during a time period that has been labeled the dark ages of medical experimentation from 1932 through 1972. This "dark age" began of course with the now infamous Tuskegee syphilis study when the U.S. Public Health Service in Tuskegee, Alabama allowed an estimated 400 African American men to grow progressively ill from syphilis until death. In the NIH sponsored Ohio State prison study of 1952, live cancer cells were injected into prisoners. A significant number of these prisoners were African American men. Black male prisoners at Washington State prison, between the years 1963-1973, had their testicles sliced and irradiated during this "dark period" of experimentation. These men were subsequently awarded 2.4 million dollars in damages in 2000. African American prisoners were exposed to radio-active, carcinogenic, and hallucinogenic substances at Holmesburg prison in Philadelphia from 1951 to 1974 as documented in urban studies scholar Allen M. Hornblum's book *Acres of Skin: Human Experiments at Holmesburg Prison* (1998).

A series of reforms were introduced in the U.S. to protect human subjects in the early 1970s. The National Research Act became law in 1974. This act led to the creation of the National Commission for the Protection of Human Subjects of Biomedical and Behavioral Research. The Belmont Report (1979) led to a statement of basic ethical principles regarding human subjects in medical experimentation. In 1981, the Department of Health and Human Services (DHHS) issued regulations based on the Belmont Report that led to the creation of Institutional Review Boards (IRBs) to further protect human subjects. By the 1990s, the U.S. federal government implemented specific guidelines limiting the use of prisoners as human subjects.

There has recently been a call for more lenient procedures in regards to the use of human subjects under penal supervision in medical experimentation in the post 9/11 world. The DHHS office for human research protections commissioned the Institute of Medicine to review the ethical considerations concerning the resumption of medical experiments involving prisoners in 2004. The Institute delivered its findings in 2006 that the use of prisoners should be reconsidered. The prison population has quadrupled in the time period since "the dark ages" of medical experimentation. Prison populations have the highest concentration of hepatitis C while 17% of all new HIV/AIDS cases have spent time incarcerated. Let us be clear with this association: of the more than 2 million prisoners in the American penal system (64% of whom were racial minorities by 2001 according to the U.S. Department of Justice) more than 50% of the American prison population today consists of African American men. According to the 1980-2006 annual reports of the U.S. Bureau of Justice, in roughly three decades, the prison population has grown by 362% from 0.5 million to 2.3 million. African Americans have been progressively more likely to be incarcerated through these decades from four times likely in the 1970s to seven times more likely to be incarcerated by 1989.[20] Incidentally, flagrant violations of federal standards regarding human subjects in prisons have been committed in states from Florida to Texas since 2001.

The juxtaposition of profit motive and the need for regulatory "short-cuts" has helped to perpetuate the rise of racial genetics and the reemergence of the exploitation of vulnerable subjects. FDA regulations have also been relaxed (given the juggernaut that is the pharmaceutical industry lobby) with the rise of the AIDS pandemic through the 1990s evidenced with the Abbreviated New Drug Application (ANDA) that works to expedite the approval process when investigational new drugs can be linked to cures for catastrophic illnesses. The prison population with its high concentration of potentially catastrophic diseases has become an ever more attractive bio-colony.

The practice of research and development in the U.S. pharmaceutical industry are propelled by a vociferous profit motive. The pharmaceutical industry has routinely occupied a top tier position on the list of profitable U.S. industries for more than a decade through the 1990s to 2005. During these years, it was positioned as the most profitable industry in the U.S more than once. The median profit margin for major U.S. drug companies in 2002 was at 17% this compared to 3.1% for other industries included on the Fortune 500 list; the ten major companies with the highest profits outdistanced the profits made by the remaining 490 industries *combined*.[21] As for research and development, the American pharmaceutical industry relies heavily on drugs or drug combinations that are already on the market and have established profitability to determine research and development strategies and expenditures:

> Because me-too drugs [minor variations of already profitable drugs] are cheaper and less risky to develop and have ready-made markets, the industry increasingly relies on them. From 1998 through 2003, 487 drugs were approved by the US Food and Drug Administration (FDA). Of those, 379 (78%) were classified by the agency as "appearing to have therapeutic qualities similar to those of one or more already marketed drugs," and 333 (68%) weren't even new compounds (what the FDA calls "new molecular entities"), but were new formulations or combinations of old ones.[22]

This is a practice utilized to circumvent government policies related to patents and patent extensions as well as a way to minimize financial risk in terms of developing new products. The industry has routinely spent more money on marketing at 35% (a staggering $67 billion dollars of $217 billion in sales) of its revenue since the 1990s than it does on research and development spending only about 11% to 14% in this area.[23] As collectively one of the most powerful industries in the U.S., pharmaceutical companies occupy an extraordinary position through which to place pressure on lawmakers in Washington, D.C. The release of the federal lobbying disclosure records for 2002 indicated that U.S. pharmaceutical companies spent millions on federal lobbying activities including 675 lobbyists (more than the total number of members in Congress and equivalent to almost seven lobbyists per senator).[24] How profound are the possibilities for profit and FDA approval of a drug marketed as "race specific" using a combination of pre-existing drugs?

DNA ancestry tracing is also propelled by the capitalist imperative. Dozens of companies now offer DNA ancestry tests based on population-based research. Many such as Ancestry.com and African Ancestry specifically target African Americans in their marketing schemes. These companies claim the ability to reconstruct links to one's genetic heritage as determined by tests based on mtDNA (passed only from mother to child and used to test a direct maternal line) and y-chromosome (used to test paternal ancestry). DNA ancestry testing illustrates how social understandings of race are conjoined with an individual's genetic markers in an attempt to present a picture of one's genealogy thus reifying race as a biologic category of human difference. The percentage of variations found in groups is being used to make claims about individual ancestry without delivering a complete analysis of all ancestral links. DNA ancestry tracing is a booming business. There is much money to be made.

Race, Disease, and Medical 'Remedies'

The human DNA exists as a 3 billion long unit string; the 0.1% genetic difference, as opposed to the 99.9% similarity in humans, between humans represents 3 million variations that help to make each individual's DNA a unique composite with the exception of identical twins. This is obviously a vast amount of genetic material to scientifically investigate, reformulate, or reify race as a biologic category of human difference. Scientific investigations have continuously affirmed that genetic variability is greatest within human populations of a common geographic locale at 85% and variation between human populations inhabiting divergent locales is significantly less, comprising the remaining 15% between the previously 'defined' racial groups (including a slight percentage within the formerly defined racial groups and the final percentage between these groups at 6% to 10%).[25]

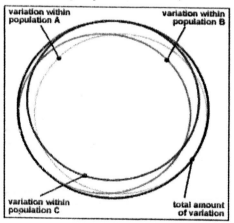

Figure 17.1-Genetic variation within and between groups. *Human Genetic Variation.* Copyright © 1999 by BSCS and Video Discovery. All Rights Reserved (Used with Permission).

A new race science arose out of scientific inquiries related to the percentages of the existent variations between human groups. Although there exists percentages of difference between each individual human, and human groups, conclusions about the nature of these variations as related to race among the biological sciences are incongruent. While social scientists have decreed race as nothing more than a social construction, there is *no consensus among the biological sciences as to what race actually is beyond its socio-cultural implications.*

> In fact, a strict biological definition of race among humans does not exist, and most useful definitions of race involve social or cultural parameters as well as referring to specific continental populations such as Europeans, Asians, and Africans. There are no good biological criteria on a phenotypic level to determine the race of any individual, or even to determine with any precision exactly how many races exist.[26]

Biologists, anthropologists, and geneticists have yet to agree upon how many races exist! Numbers range from the original three (Caucasian, Asian, and African) to several dozen and this imprecision only reflects the complex nature of human biodiversity. Despite this profound lack of consensus, *there is* a rising industry of race specific remedies and, more disturbingly, clinical trials and experimentations on African Americans to support the new racial genetics. As aforementioned, genetic variation is most profound within groups and this is most expressly in people of African descent around the world. Therefore, Black people have the greatest in-group genetic variability. With the rise of race science used to justify European expansion and imperialism through the nineteenth century, Black people have ironically become the most likely to be classified as a *homogeneous* group despite the greatest in-group variability.

> Around the globe, Blacks have the most internal genetic variation of any racialized population group yet are most likely to be treated as if they were genetically homogeneous. Although not genetically homogeneous, Black people are often placed at the bottom of the social hierarchy, and this fact has practical, biomedical consequences.[27]

Perceptions about African Americans as the racialized "Other" are a product of historical circumstance that impacts profoundly scientific considerations about the nature of the biological relationship between genotype and phenotype. These notions are of course reinforced by the now documented scientific potentiality of the points of variation between humans and human groups; specifically, with the focus on the propensity within the sequence of the human DNA for discontinuous genetic variation (polymorphisms) that may or may not affect the phenotype.

Alleles are an alternative form of the same gene at a specific location on a chromosome that produce variation in inherited physical traits such as hair color, eye color, or blood type. This is known as allelic variation, which does indicate that there are indeed genetic sequences in populations that reflect a significant difference between the formerly recognized major racial groups.[28] Much of the basis for the new racial genetics comes from the scientific study of alleles. Alleles can be considered the fundamental unit of genetic diversity in humans. There is no firm consensus among scientists as to how great a role environmental factors play in allelic variations within and between human groups. Geneticists who have discovered specific variations in allele frequencies between the former three major groups of humans must contend with the findings of population biologists who have come to opposite conclusions about genetic variation between human groups.[29] Some of the same allele frequencies found within specific human population groups have also been found *between* human groups. Geneticists tend to focus on a fraction of the 0.1% locations that alleles vary in frequency between human groups from different continents to make claims about race.[30]

There are a series of race specific remedies and medical experiments that are associated with the African American community in the post-genomic era. These remedies and experiments targeting the community at the bottom of the social hierarchy are driven by both a folkloric understanding of race fused with an imprecise scientific definition of race by an American pharmaceutical industry that spends more money on marketing than on research and development. Studies in allelic variation have certainly yielded findings related to diseases such as cancer, AIDS, and heart disease as related to genetic disparities between human groups. Human diseases have both a genetic and environmental component. Diseases such as cancer, diabetes, and heart disease are characteristically diseases with smaller genetic components than others. The environmental component in these diseases is far greater as compared to the genetic component. Of course, there are specific diseases with larger genetic components as compared to other disorders.

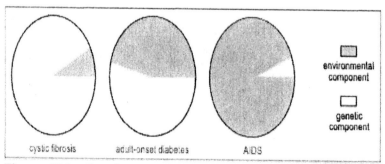

Figure 17.2 -Genetic and environmental components of specific diseases. *Human Genetic Variation.* Copyright © 1999 by BSCS and Video Discovery. All Rights Reserved (Used with Permission).

Although the widely studied sickle cell allele present in hemoglobin that affords an individual with protection against malaria, known to be present primarily in individuals living in regions where malaria is more common (this includes white as well as black people), is largely a result of the interaction between the genotype and specific environmental conditions that influence the behavior of the allele.[31] It is difficult to predict how and why different alleles react as a result of environmental pressures and furthermore allelic variation is *more common* within human groups and not between populations. The amount of melanin in one's skin is not a determinate for the causes of disease. Tay Sachs as a disease "commonly known" to afflict people of Jewish descent is highly prevalent among French Canadians of South Eastern Quebec and Cajuns of Southwest Louisiana.[32] Race conflated as color is not an exact lens through which to study human biology. This approach to the study of human genetics is positively medieval. Why then did the U.S. Food and Drug Administration (FDA) approve a "race specific" drug called BiDil to combat heart disease in African Americans?

There is great controversy surrounding a series of clinical trials related to ethnic minorities. Why are these groups made more readily subject to the most rudimentary forms of medical experimentation? The chimpanzee has more protection under federal law than the disproportionate number of black men incarcerated in the American Gulag otherwise known as the U.S. penal system. It seems that race, construed as biology, has become a convenient strategy through which to circumvent rigorous regulatory procedure. It seems that the rise of "prison bio-colonies" is a highly plausible outcome of the capitalist imperative and not merely the product of science fiction.

BiDil is not a new drug. It is a combination of two preexisting drugs, isosorbide dinitrate (blood vessel relaxant) and hydralazine (anti-hypertension drug), that had already been on the market as generics. BiDil, in its combined form, was denied approval by the FDA twice (without using race as a consideration) before it was eventually accepted as a race specific drug in 2005. The transformation of BiDil as an "ethnically targeted" therapeutic is new. It is not surprising that many involved in medical science have now come to believe that African Americans are more prone to schizophrenia, depression, low-birth weight, certain types of cancer, obesity, diabetes, hypertension, and Alzheimer's disease (just to name a few) because of race *conflated* as biology given the history of race science in America. Certainly, NitroMed conducted clinical trials involving more than 1,000 "self-identified" African Americans but given the in-group variability of those with African genetic inheritance such a sweeping conclusion on BiDil as a drug for African Americans seems simplistic. It is also pertinent to note that the NAACP and the Association of Black Cardiologists, serving as a co-sponsor, endorsed BiDil. The NAACP was given 1.5 million dollars to "develop health advocacy initiatives" from NitroMed while the Association of Black Cardiologists were given $200,000.[33]

Predictions related to the health of African Americans (allelic variations within groups are often profound) are faulty if not based on a vast continental and transcontinental clinical study involving multiple population groups given the nature of allele frequencies. Also, the genetic inheritance of African Americans includes alleles that are common to European Americans as well. It is impossible to consider race as anything *without* also considering geographic, environmental, social, genetic, and cultural factors holistically. Once these factors are considered race as a stand alone basis of human classification becomes suspiciously untenable as word and idea in both the social and biological sense. Yet studies on other diseases such as breast cancer continue to invoke race as an important factor without considering other factors holistically. Several other clinical "experiments" if understood within the context of the history of African Americans and race science in America, along with the discovery of the "metabolic syndrome," also raise questions about the dangers of racial genetics.

The metabolic syndrome, also known as the insulin resistant syndrome, or syndrome x, is explained as a group of risk factors in one person for specific diseases related to plaque buildup in the artery walls and obesity. This "syndrome" is essentially a new biomedical concept that represents multiple disease biomarkers for specific disorders that may or may not be rooted in profound genetic causation. Individuals with metabolic syndrome are at increased risk for diseases such as coronary heart disease, type II diabetes, and hypertension. Race conflated as biology has become an integral factor in the study of syndrome x in African Americans. The use of social race in biomedical research, such as with BiDil and syndrome x, allows for corporate, educational, and government entities to gain market opportunities to increase profit potential. This may also open the door to a new era of sophisticated eugenics.

The commodification and commercialization of social race as buttressed by the new racial genetics is leading to a vociferous reification of race in American life. There are now twenty private companies that offer genetic ancestry testing. The makers of Pantene Pro-V offer a race specific hair care solution for African Americans. The National Institute of Mental Health [NIMH] has given $21.7 million dollars in funding to the PAARTNERS [Project among African Americans to Explore Risks for Schizophrenia] program to explore genetic risk factors for schizophrenia in African Americans. Scientific discoveries in the field of genetics have in fact helped to reify race as a biologic category of human difference despite the wealth of evidence to the contrary; and this is largely due to the fact that race as an "idea" continues to have a profound economic utility in American society.

Race, Genetics, and the Criminal Justice System

Human behavioral genetics is an emergent field associated with the criminal justice system that may also come under the influence of the new race science along with DNA forensics. Human behavioral genetics as a field seeks to illustrate the correlation between human genetic variation, environment, and human behavior among individuals in a specific population group. Studies in behavioral genetics have primarily focused on attempts to understand the connection between genetics and characteristically anti-social behaviors such as aggression, violence, hyperactivity, impulsivity, along with drug and alcohol abuse. Forensics is a sub-field of criminology that uses methods such as fingerprinting, ballistics, and toxicology to investigate crime. DNA forensics involves the use of genetic material from DNA databases to investigate crime. The collection of DNA samples from crime scenes and those incarcerated for crimes have become routine practice. The Combined DNA Index System includes an estimated 2.5 million DNA profiles of persons convicted for crimes collected from all fifty states, the U.S. Army and FBI.[34] Given that African American and Hispanic men make up a disproportionate number of those incarcerated, as aforementioned, these existing DNA profiles are over-balanced with samples from racial minorities. This presents a potential for danger in terms of researchers seeking to utilize these samples for the purpose of understanding criminal behavior. The findings of human behavioral geneticists have already been utilized in criminal trials for the purpose of supporting pre-existing legal defenses, as mitigating evidence during sentencing or as exculpatory evidence.[35] The intersections between studies related to human genetics, race, and crime are profound.

One may argue that the use of DNA evidence in criminology has yielded significant gains while human behavioral genetics may indeed provide important insight into understanding criminal behavior and the causes of crime. Therefore, the plausible negative impact that both may have on minority communities [particularly African Americans] must be carefully explored. This author acknowledges the beneficial qualities of human behavioral genetics and DNA forensics in criminal justice but remains abundantly aware of the detrimental implications of both to minority communities. It is necessary to examine the pros and cons of genetics in the criminal justice system to elucidate these implications.

Human developmental biology and DNA science have both been used in the American legal system for some time. Historically, human developmental biology has been taken into account by American law on the basis of age, mental health disorders such as schizophrenia, epilepsy, and injuries causing serious brain damage.[36] Attorneys throughout history, in defense of their clients, have used these and other human developmental circumstances. In the case of age, the American legal system has routinely recognized age as a "developmental circumstance" that may shield a defendant from harsh penalty. States have collected DNA samples from those arrested, convicted, and from crime scenes. DNA collected from a crime scene can be used to match a DNA profile already in a database. DNA has also been collected voluntarily through periodic "dragnets" following heinous crimes. These profiles are based on samples generated from tests based on variable regions of the human genome that are used to create a genetic profile that is uniquely identified with a specific individual. Profiles are stored on computers as a series of numbers that illustrate a unique pattern of DNA variants. The use of DNA forensics has led to 232 post-conviction exonerations in U.S. history; 70% of those exonerated have been members of minority groups.[37] Those exonerated have included more than a dozen people on death row.

DNA testing is not infallible. Indeed, the collection of DNA evidence is open to contamination, misreading, clerical errors, false matches, and may ultimately jeopardize civil liberties. The use of DNA evidence is not always an absolute and the random collection of samples is not always a full-proof method to catch a criminal. DNA dragnets conducted in England (292 in total) have yielded successful convictions at a 20% rate while of the nineteen "dragnets" conducted in the U.S. only one has led to a successful conviction. Roughly 5% of the population in England, as a result of both dragnets and arrests, has their DNA in a database. The probability of false matches grows exponentially as the DNA database expands as civil liberties are jeopardized by the very nature of these "voluntary" sweeps. By 2009, California law will require mandatory DNA samples from every person arrested for a felony and some misdemeanors.

Conclusion

Race remains with us although discourses on hybridism and the mixed race consciousness movement may help American society to move beyond the racial binary in American life. The election of the first self-identified African American president has prompted some to postulate that America is now a "post-racial" society. Indeed, it is plausible that the future of America will be that of a society "all mixed up" about race both socially and biologically. The discussion of mixed race identities of course has been shaped by contemporary global migration patterns with the influx of non-western peoples into the U.S. and not merely on the gains of civil rights activism in the 1960s that culminated in the *Loving* decision of 1967 that made anti-miscegenation laws illegal. There has also been the expansion of whiteness amid this influx and a continuous disdain for blackness. Black remains with us and the recent discovery in 2005 of the gene variant most instrumental in human skin pigmentation (SLC24A5), as a result of findings related to the Hap-Map Project, has prompted some scientists to postulate the viability of the genetic manipulation of skin color. Perhaps George Schuyler's story is not so fanciful a "spoof" after all.

America is not a post-racial society. Race specific medicines, DNA forensics, human behavioral genetics, and genetic ancestry tests all help to reify race as a biologic category of human difference. Although America has elected a bi-racial man self-identified as "Black" to the office of president, while those of mixed race ancestry claim to be "more than black," race remains with us. In fact, sociologist Troy Duster argues that because race continues to be employed for practical clinical purposes [and sometimes can be empirically "apprehended"] it is ultimately impossible to disentangle the biological from the social.[38] What is race? There is no either/or answer contends Duster.[39] The notion of "black no more" is simply a whimsical fantasy.

Notes

1. This author rejects race as a biological category of human difference yet understands that historically race has been defined in several ways (but ultimately is a flawed concept). In his book *The Ethics of Identity* the African American Studies scholar Kwame Appiah has argued that race belongs in the category of "irrational identity" because the criteria often used (across time, space, and place) to define social racial categories fluctuate and are many times inconsistent with basic facts and therefore "offend against reason." Harvard historian Louis Gates, Jr. in his PBS documentary *African American*

Lives illustrated the potential impact of DNA Ancestry tracing on those "self-identified" as a particular "race" in terms of factual consistency if one were to rely on simple notions of ancestry in conjunction with genetic testing; DNA Ancestry helps to reinforce the fact that human ancestry is shared the further one interrogates ancestry through multiple generations.

2. George Schuyler, "Black No More," in *The Portable Harlem Renaissance Reader*, ed. David Levering Lewis (New York: Penguin Books, 1995), 655-666.

3. The term DNA is defined as deoxyribonucleic acid one of two major classes of molecules found in the nucleus of a cell that constitute the genetic code consisting of two elaborate chains of nucleotides arranged in a double helix. A gene as a segment of DNA and hereditary unit located on a chromosome exists as a component of a genome which is the totality of an organism's genetic material.

4. Nancy Shute, "Where We Come From," *U.S. News & World Report*, Jan. 29, 2001, 36-41.

5. Such has been the case with the race specific heart health drug BiDiL and the clinical trials surrounding its development orchestrated by Nitromed. This and a series of other clinical trials in the interest of developing race specific medications raise some serious questions about race as science.

6. Evelyn Hammonds, "Straw Men and their Followers: The Return of Biological Race," *Is Race Real? Web Forum of the Social Science Research Council*, (2006) http://raceandgenomics.ssrc.org/Hammonds/printable.html

7. In the 1640s Colonial governments, beginning with Virginia's planter elite, first began to regulate human bondage based on socio-cultural concepts of race and interracial relations. By the 1700s with the signing of the U.S. Constitution black servitude was etched in American law. The Supreme Court decision in the Dred Scott case (1854) defined African Americans as "non-citizens" free or enslaved. The doctrine of "separate but equal" created a distinct social barrier or color line between the perceived races with the rise of Jim Crow Laws after 1896. The twentieth century brought the legal entrenchment of the "one drop rule" implying one drop of black blood made one black.

8. Pilar Ossorio and Troy Duster, "Race and Genetics: Controversies in Biomedical, Behavioral, and Forensic Sciences," *American Psychologist* 60 (January 2005), 116-118.

9. Alan H. Goodman, "Why Genes Don't Count (for Racial Differences in Health)," *American Journal of Public Health*, November 90 (2000): 1699-1702.

10. Ibid.

11. An undertaking that took 13 years to complete as supported by the U.S. Department of Energy and the National Institutes of Health along with the support of several other nations, the stated goals of the HGP were to identify all of the 20,000 to 25,000 genes in the human DNA and the 3 billion chemical base pairs that make up the DNA.

12. A DNA sequence consists of a succession of letters representing the primary structure of a DNA molecule. The DNA strand is made up of four nucleotide subunits.

13. The structural units of DNA, RNA, and several co-factors that have important roles in metabolism; thousands of nucleotides are joined in a long chain to form a DNA or RNA molecule. The human genome is made up of billions of nucleotides this includes both the genes and the non-coding sequences of DNA.

14. Alexander, Alland, Jr., *Race in Mind: Race, I.Q., and Other Racisms* (New York: Palgrave Macmillan, 2001), 46.

15. Harriet A. Washington, *Medical Apartheid: The Dark History of Medical Experimentation on Black Americans from Colonial Times to the Present* (New York: Doubleday Publishing, 2007), 1-5.

16. Alvin Pouissaint and Amy Alexander, *Lay My Burden Down: Suicide and the Mental Health Crisis among African Americans* (Boston: Beacon Press, 2000), 15.

17. Brenda Lane Richardson and Brenda Wade, *What Mama Couldn't Tell Us About Love: Healing the Emotional Legacy of Racism by Celebrating Our Light* (New York: Perennial, 1999), 117.

18. David Kinney, "The Republic of No Conscience: How the United States Committed Atrocities Against Its Own Citizens," *Los Angeles Times*, June 21, 1998.

19. Todd L. Savitt, "The Use of Blacks for Medical Experimentation and Demonstration in the Old South," *The Journal of Southern History,* Vol. 48, No. 3 August (1982): 331-348.

20. Ossorio and Duster, 122.

21. Marcia Angell, "Excess in the Pharmaceutical Industry," *Canadian Medical Association Journal* 171, No. 12, December (2004): 1451-1453.

22. Ibid.

23. Angell, 1451-1452.

24. Craig Aaron, Taylor Lincoln, "The Other Drug War 2003: Drug Companies Deploy an Army of 675 Lobbyists to Protect Profits," *Public Citizen Congress Watch* June (2003): 1-43.

25. R.C. Lewontin, "Confusions About Human Races," *Is Race Real? Web Forum of the Social Science Research Council,* (2006), http://raceandgenomics.ssrc.org/Lewontin/printable.html

26. Seymour Garte, "The Racial Genetics Paradox in Biomedical Research and Public Health," *Public Health Reports* September-October 117 (2002): 421-425.

27. Pilar Ossorio and Troy Duster, "Race and Genetics: Controversies in Biomedical, Behavioral, and Forensic Sciences," *American Psychologist* 60, No. 1, January (2005): 115-128.

28. Garte, 421-422.

29. Garte, 422.

30. Ossorio and Duster, 118.

31. Garte, 423.

32. Peter Hectman, Faige Kaplan, Janet Baylenan, et.al, "More Than One Mutant Allele Causes Infantile Tay-Sachs Disease in French Canadians," *The American Journal of Human Genetics.* Vol. 47 No. 5 Nov. 1990, 815-822.

33. Osagie K. Obasogie, "Playing the Gene Card: A Report on Race and Human Biotechnology" (Oakland: Center for Genetics and Society, 2008), 11.

34. Karen Rothenberg and Alice Wang, "The Secret Gene: Behavioral Genetics, Criminal Law, AND Racial and Ethnic Stigma," *Law and Contemporary Problems,* 59 (Winter/Spring 2006): 343-365.

35. Owen D. Jones, "Behavioral Genetics and Crime, In Context," *Law and Contemporary Problems* 59 (Winter/Spring 2006): 80-100.

36. Jones, 85.

37. "Innocence Project Case Files,"   www.innocenceproject.org/know/ February 10, 2009.

38. Troy Duster, "Buried Alive: The Concept of Race in Science," eds. Alan H. Goodman, Deborah Heath, and M. Susan Lindee (Berkeley: University of California Press, 2003), 262-273.

39. Ibid.

References

Aaron, Craig, and Taylor Lincoln, "The Other Drug War 2003: Drug Companies Deploy an Army of 675 Lobbyists to Protect Profits." *Public Citizen Congress Watch* (June 2003): 1-43.

Alland, Alexander, Jr., *Race in Mind: Race, I.Q., and Other Racisms*. New York: Palgrave-Macmillian, 2001.

Angell, Marcia, "Excess in the Pharmaceutical Industry." *Canadian Medical Association Journal* 12 (December, 2004): 1451-1453.

Duster, Troy, "Buried Alive: The Concept of Race in Science," *Genetic Nature/Culture: Anthropology and ScienceBeyond the Two-Culture Divide*, ed., Alan H. Goodman, Deborah Heath, and M. Susan Lindee. Berkeley: University of California Press, 2003.

Faranany, Nita A, and James E. Coleman Jr., "Genetics and Responsibility: to Know the Criminal from the Crime." *Law and Contemporary Problems* 69 (Winter-Spring 2006): 344-365.

Garte, Seymour, "The Racial Genetics Paradox in Biomedical Research and Public Health." *Public Health Reports* 117, (September 2002): 421-425.

Goodman, Alan H., "Two Questions About Race," *Is Race Real: Web Forum of the Social Science Research Council*. raceandgenomics.ssrc.org, December 5, 2007. http://raceandgenomics.ssrc.org/Goodman/printable.html

Goodman, Alan H., "Why Genes Don't Count for Racial Differences in Health." *American Journal of Public Health* 90, (November 2000): 1699-1702.

Hammonds, Evelyn, "Straw Men and their Followers." *Is Race Real: Web Forum of the Social Science Research Council*. raceandgenomics.ssrc.org. December 7, 2007. http//raceandgenomics.ssrc.org/Hammonds/printable.Html

Hectman, Peter, Faige Kaplan, and Janet Baylenan. "More than One Mutant Allele Causes Infantile Tay-Sachs Disease in French Canadians." *The American Journal of Human Genetics* 47 (November 1990): 815-822.

Jones, Owen, "Behavioral Genetics and Crime in Context." *Law and Contemporary Problems* 69 (Winter-Spring 2006): 82-100.

Kaye, D.H., "Behavioral Genetics Research and Criminal DNA Databases." *Law and Contemporary Problems* 69 (Winter-Spring 2006): 260-299.

Kinney, David, "The Republic of No Conscience: How the United Sates Committed Atrocities Against its Own Citizens." *Los Angeles Times,* June 21, 1998.

Lane Richardson, Brenda, and Brenda Wade, *What Mama Couldn't Tell Us About Love: Healing the Emotional Legacy Of Racism by Celebrating Our Light*. New York: Perennial, 1999.

Lewontin, R.C., "Confusions about Human Races." *Is Race Real? Web Forum of the Social Science Research Council,* raceandgenomics.ssrc.org December 8, 2007. http//raceandgenomics.ssrc.org/Lewontin/printable.html

Obasogie, Osagie K., "Playing the Gene Card: A Report on Race and Human Biotechnology." Oakland: Center for Genetics and Society, 2009.

Ossorio, Pilar, and Troy Duster, "Race and Genetics: Controversies in Biomedical, Behavioral, and Forensic Sciences."*American Psychologist* 60 (January 2005): 115-128.

Pouissant, Alvin, and Amy Alexander, *Lay My Burden Down: Suicide and the Mental Health Crisis Among African Americans*. Boston: Beacon Press, 2000.

Rothenberg, Karen, and Alice Wang, "The Scarlet Gene: Behavioral Genetics, Criminal Law, and Racial and Ethnic Stigma." *Law and Contemporary Society* 69 (Winter-Spring): 344-365.

Savitt, Todd L., "The Use of Blacks for Medical Experimentation and Demonstration in the Old South." *The Journal of Southern History* 48 (August 1982): 331-348.

Schuyler, George, "Black No More," *The Portable Harlem Renaissance Reader,* ed., David Levering Lewis (New York: Penguin Books, 1995. 655-666.

Shute, Nancy, "Where We Come From." *U.S. News and World Report* (January 2001): 36-41.

Chapter 18

Contesting Identities of Color: African Female Immigrants in the Americas

Phil Okeke-Ihejirika

Alberta, one of the most economically viable of Canada's ten provinces, records its black population as largely immigrant; a significant portion coming from the more recent African immigration stream that followed the continent's economic decline since the 1980s.[1] African women in Alberta, a part of this continental outflow and the focus of my study, are dealing with very interesting challenges: as newcomers in a new homeland, seeking out any available means to adjust, adapt, and integrate; as the gender mostly responsible for community building and enculturation. Their lives also reflect a struggle to sustain old identities within and outside ethnic boundaries even as they are confronted with new ones they cannot ignore. It is argued in this chapter that, for these women and their families, the assumption of identities in the new world is problematic given their collective diversity, the different reasons which propelled them to migrate, and the various challenges they face in their new homeland. Vividly captured in qualitative interviews and a province-wide survey, African women's experiences in Alberta not only expose the limitations of color identities, but also raise serious questions about their role in the political mobilization of "new" populations in the Americas.

Introduction

Since the mid 1980s when Africa's economic decline and political crises began to propel individuals and groups within its teeming population to leave the continent in search of a better life, significant numbers have settled in North America, particularly, the United States and Canada. Unlike the case before the 1980s when the majority of Africans traveled to North America in pursuit of higher education, the seemingly unending economic decline as well as the growing political unrest across the continent, have initiated and sustained a steady migratory outflow. Very little is known about these migrants and their struggles for self-definition in the vast North American political and cultural mosaic. The terms 'Black' and 'African' continue to be bandied about as uncontroversial and uncontested identities that could encompass any group as long as a reasonable elimination from other non-Caucasian ones could be made. This huge umbrella also tends to blur any distinctions between the black Diaspora and new African settlers in the Americas who still have an unbroken regional, national and ethnic attachment to Africa. The vague spread of 'blackness,' as will become obvious in the experiences of women in this study, envelopes other identities of color within this new population in that it redefines what it means to be African for millions of people North and South of the Sahara, including the outlying Islands.

It seems, however, that the growing presence of these Africans in North America could increasingly expose the ambiguity, inconsistencies and in some cases, absurdity of this unquestioned expression of 'Black' and 'African as well as the inter-change of one with the other. In a diversity of voices and stripes, new Africans in the new world are struggling with both the challenge of sustaining, for very good reasons, their unique identities as they are forced to embrace broader ones that already label and place them within the North American cultural and political landscape. The latter has found it very convenient and less demanding sometimes to label them Blacks and at other times, Africans. As Blacks, they are lumped together with peoples of different histories and cultures, who share only the similarity of skin tones. As Africans, they are homogenized with little or no regard for their different ethnic origins, languages, religions, colonial histories, and nationalities (fifty-four, at present, with their diverse social, political and economic development history).

People who knew very little about one another 'back home' are now forced to share an illusive African identity. But this is only an initial stage in the process of amalgamation. As Africans, they must also pull together whatever commonality binds them together to join the Black Diaspora in the Americas. The latter may not necessarily be prepared at all times and places to embraces their brothers and sisters from the "Dark Continent" whose backwardness is characterized by political strife, war, poverty, and ill health. While the social and cultural implications of loosing oneself among a diversity of 'strangers' makes these new settlers reluctant to 'reach out,' the political urgency of building platforms that could command a firmer response to the challenges of settlement, compel them to embrace amalgamated identities at certain levels and in some situations. The question arises as to how their circumstances in the new world fit into these already constructed labels. This analysis undertakes a brief but critical exploration of the latter starting with the Diasporic construction of blackness.

Blacks in Diaspora: Contesting a Definition 'Given'

The Greek term, diaspora, means "scattering, as in the sowing of grain."[2] Obviously, the prophetic "dispersal"[3] of Jews on the face of the earth and the subsequent transplanting of Africans through the transatlantic slave trade, have to a great extent, provided a benchmark for assessing the experiences and prospects of other populations described as Diasporas. Regardless of the specificities of its history, present constitution, and struggles faced, each diasporic community embraces "an inescapable link with . . . [its] past migration history and a sense of co-ethnicity with others of a similar background."[4] Endowed in members with differing levels of intensity, this 'adherence' to an original homeland with its cultures, politics, and social relations significantly frames that sense of who they are. Characterized in such conventional terms, the notion of an African Diaspora could then easily be summed up as "the global dispersion (voluntary and involuntary) of Africans throughout history; the emergence of a cultural identity abroad based on original and social condition; and the psychological or physical return to the homeland."[5] Evidently, the strong presence of people of African descent throughout the Americas, appear to have provided a rich history for a substantive exploration of such an adherence linked to identity. Research on the history and treatment of African populations in the New world, have not only exposed their contributions to social progress, but has also shed light on the specificities of African identities nestled among other social groups abroad. The impact of slavery entrenched in transatlantic trade and the treatment of African's in the New world, therefore, place generations of this huge historical stream at the mainstream of any discourse about Africans in diaspora. This Diaspora had little problem forging their identities wherever fate and, when possible, own assertion, took them across the Americas.

But annexed to this historical stream, the origins and experiences of new Africans in the Americas wholly defy the diasporic construction. The expansion of transatlantic immigration over the past three decades has not only given new meanings to the term Diaspora but also convoluted the identities of many other groups under its rubric.[6] In his analysis of national and ethnic diasporas, Richard Robert acknowledges that "the concept of a unified African experience in the New world is very attractive to members of the [African] diaspora . . . especially those who see in the experience of enslavement, the slave trade, and working on plantations a common and determinative experience."[7] While the transatlantic trade made the largest contribution to what may be loosely termed the 'contemporary' Africa diaspora, he argues that other African groups did form (and many continue to arrive in more recent times, establishing themselves as communities of) 'voluntary diasporas.'[8] It seems that these newer groups are not recognized as unique entities, but annexed as part of that "dynamic, continuous, and complex phenomenon stretching across time, geography, class, and gender."[9] As Isidore Okpewho, a major contributor to the debate on black identities argues instead:

> The growing presence of the new migrants has (let's face it) brought some stresses into the solidarity that we have generally assumed binds all black people together...The newcomers have left their homelands under circumstances that qualify their relations with [the new world]...since they still have social and cultural roots back [home]...These circumstances have implications for the ways in which members of the new African diaspora have been inclined to define themselves.[10"]

It is arguable therefore if the stream of African immigration to North America can easily and quickly be subsumed into a Diasporic phenomenon which does not relate in any way to both their diverse continental history and the various experiences as new settlers. These new populations are arriving under different circumstances, facing unique challenges of resettlement, adjustment, and adaptation.

Africans as Trans-nationals

It is not surprising that the presence of new African settlers seems to have received more attention not in the now almost mundane discussion of black racism and comparisons of living standards with mainstream and less privileged populations, but in the parallel discourse on trans-nationalism, a much smaller but growing literature. It needs to be said that although discourses of transnational experiences have grown over the past decade, the study of emerging African populations is relatively a new development.[11] Much of that sparse literature has focused on men's experiences with a unique focus on brain drain.[12] Studies of African women are also still few and far between. This is not particularly surprising since women's experiences of migration have often been regarded as ancillary to the movement of men.[13] Earlier contributors to transnational discourses in the early 1990s noted a distinct trend in the manner in which groups cut in the waves of migration from the developing world to advanced industrial countries are increasingly organizing their lives.[14] Unlike previous groups of immigrants, who leave their original homelands to establish a new life in another society, they observed, "a new kind of migrating population is emerging, composed of those whose networks, activities and patterns of life encompass both their host and home societies. Their lives cut across national boundaries and bring two societies into a single social field."[15] As newer settlers in industrial societies, they struggle to carve out identities that distinguish them from a larger mainstream that attempts to qualify their sense of belonging in social, political and economic terms. According to Glick Schiller, Basch, and Blanc-Szanton:

> By maintaining many different racial, national, and ethnic identities, trans-migrants are able to express their resistance to the global political and economic situations that engulf them, even as they accommodate themselves to living conditions marked by vulnerability and insecurity. These migrants express this resistance in small, everyday ways that usually do not directly challenge or even recognize the basic premises of the systems that surround them and dictate the terms of their existence.[16]

Admittedly, the experiences of new African settlers wrestle with reflect some of these characteristics of 'home-away-from-home.' Obviously, the globalization of advanced technologies of transportation, information and communication has made conceivable the plausibility of populations endowed with multiple identities connected to multiple social and physical locations.[17] But the virtually uncontroversial expression of trans-nationalism ignores the definition and constructions of social fields, which subject some migrants to ambiguous responses. The experiences of women in this study mirror Ruba Salih's contention that, "transnational relations may not always seem to forge the sense of belonging to two countries. On the contrary, they may paradoxically reinforce migrants' feelings of living in more than one country and belonging to neither place."[18] A crucial element of building a home-away-from-home for these women and their families is that of making the transition from new comers to members of defined and recognized group(s). It is both an interesting as well as an arduous challenge because they are not really recognized as *trans-nationals* but as Blacks and *trans-continentals*. In many cases, as these women point out, their ethnicity, language or even countries of origin are hardly known to the populations around them. While they lament the fact that the African and Black labels they are smacked with on arrival subsume the uniqueness of a multiplicity of identities (including *color*, which they previously had no reason to question), they are also waking up to the fact that these labels, with their broad sweeps, are somewhat crucial to the task of reconstituting and rebuilding building 'their' peoples.

Settling Continental Africans: Gender Matters

Canadian immigration literature clearly shows that women constitute a larger proportion of immigrants but still remain the more vulnerable gender due, in part, to immigration policies that define them as dependants to men. Regardless of their individual educational and professional status, these women are given only limited access to support services that could quicken their settlement.[19] As new comers to a new homeland, they are expected not only to prepare themselves for the challenges of a new environment, but also to help establish their families as part of a larger society. Regardless of their educational and professional status, female migrants are expected to care for family members as their primary responsibility. They are responsible for enculturating the next generation, defining the boundaries of social integration to protect this enculturation, building the necessary connections between the family and important social institutions such as schools and churches. Further, female immigrants are expected to wrap a sense of community around these linkages in order to exploit the necessary support they could yield. Even though their income and quality of employment reflect hardly this, most of these women are highly qualified, many engaged in paid work; defying two common myths about immigrant women as uneducated and unemployed outside the home.[20] As their responses below show, it is perhaps these women's struggles to settle self and family that vividly expose the importance of identity, especially with regards to color.

The African Women's Project

The experience of African immigrants in Canada, especially the females, is still considerably understudied.[21] According to the 2001 Canadian census, Africans make up about 5.2 % and 5.3% of immigrants in Canada and Alberta, respectively. The population of Africans in Canada grew from 229,600 in 1996 to 282,600 in 2001. In the Alberta province, this population grew from 17,075 to 22,975 over the same period.[22] Women make up about x% (Change to 2006). Research on migrant women in Canada has tended to focus on the intersections of gender, ethnicity and class in the context of work, health and citizenship. African women tend to be homogenized within a "Black pool" of Caribbean and/or older diasporic communities that subsumes "the different meanings [migration has]... for different people at different times of their lives."[23] To begin to address this gap in our understandings of experiences of migration, the project entitled, *In Search of Identity, Longing for Homelands: African Women in Alberta,* set out to identity and examine the challenges African women face as new settlers. Data collection for the four year study (2002-2005) comprised of six focus group interviews of African women 15 years and over (including a youth forum); in-depth interviews of African women identified as community leaders, and a province-wide survey of African women in Alberta which yielded 873 questionnaires for analysis. The research targeted women from West, Southern, Eastern, Central, and Horn of Africa. The rationale was to encompass a purposively representative sample that would include those outside Sub-Saharan Africa, the region enfolding most of 'Black' Africa and the 'Africa' outsiders know about. This chapter is based on the responses of women from the five adult focus groups. Most are married with children and arrived in Canada with their families.

Black, African and in-Between: Where Do You Fit in?

The experience was nearly the same for a good number of women in every focus group meeting; that feeling of being among strangers. There was some degree of reluctance to reach out. The yearning to connect was there; that urge to find out where the migration journey started back home. The connection was crucial because it opens the door to information that could address immediate anxieties that dwell above an eroding sense of belonging: what to do with teenage daughters in the summer, a list of good elementary schools, directions to those 'ethnic' food stores which carry the family's staple. As soon as the connection was made with initial personal introductions, everybody was talking at the same time. The 'informal' meeting comes to an end and the focus group emerges for discussion with a sense of familiarity. Even as the familiarity grew and the focus group meeting progressed, individual women would look around the room, taking in the overwhelming diversity of color, language, and African origin. The separation of Francophone and Anglophone women; those from Sub Saharan Africa and their Northern sisters greatly facilitated the coordination of the interviews. For a research project that spanned fours years, many of the women came to know one another. This was the first time they were engaged in discussions about collective interests with others outside their ethnic group, country and region in Africa. The eruption in North America of the North -South Saharan divide, which roughly separated Blacks and 'Non Black' was, perhaps, the most overwhelming.

Identity was something that became a 'problem' only with their arrival in Canada. As many of them pointed out, there was no time in their 'previous' lives that the question of identity presented itself. Even those of them who accompanied their 'student' husbands to Canada over three decades ago did not have to deal with the contestations of identity African women are engaged in at present. Effie, for instance, came with her husband from Ghana in 1975. She easily identified with an almost negligible black population that welcomed them, accepting a label that would never have made any meaning in Ghana where virtually everybody is black. Effie expected to go home to Ghana and resume her 'normal' life as soon as her husband finished his studies. On a similar note, other African women who came with working husbands before the mid 1980s, the period when Africa's economic decline became increasingly obvious, life in Canada was still a temporary sojourn. Martha, a Ghanaian whose husband accepted a job in Canada after graduation in a German university in 1983, also felt at home among members of a tiny black majority. On her experience hanging out with blacks from various parts of the world, Martha has this to say: ". . . I felt like one of the very few . . . [s]ince at that time, you can put all black people in Edmonton in one room for [a] . . . party. So I think I felt like everyone else, since we were not many. I did not feel different from the rest."

Both the older and, even more so, the newer settlers now find themselves in a world where they cannot easily respond to questions such as 'Where are you from?' What are you?' (in terms of ethnicity). These are the questions posed to them from within and without. These are questions they did not have to think about before answering back home. And because the question is regularly posed (in the mall, in city buses, at work, on numerous forms, etc) they must continuous think about an appropriate answer. As Mercer, one of the early contributors to this discourse, points out, "identity only becomes an issue when it is in crisis, when something assumed to be fixed, coherent and stable is displaced by the experience of doubt and uncertainty."[24]

Unlike Effie and Martha, the newer settlers within the group of women interviewed, were confronted at the onset, with the problem of 'who are you?' something they never gave a thought to back in Africa. There lives as settlers in a new homeland have necessitated both a reassertion as well as a reformulation of their identities. On a daily basis they are faced with scenarios in their lives, which demand a rethink of their identity. They must confront that integrate view of self which before immigration assumed its place among people of race, nation, ethnic, gender and other social groupings without any question. Being identified as black and African, for Maria, a Rwandan was both a shock and an eye opener, ". . . It's funny but I never thought of myself as an African or a Black woman before coming to Canada. I'm from Rwanda. As I settled in, I started to identify myself with something other than Rwandan, African or Black; in other words, as being part of... minority groups."

It is often surprising to most new African arrivals to discover that they are black. It is even more fascinating or scary depending on the circumstance to take in the diversity of peoples they are sharing this 'new' identity with. The racist implications of this label often follow. For many of the women who grew up in African countries with indigenous and colonial histories that maintained a dark skinned population, black has no bearing on their identity. Within such countries, peoples and groups might be described as 'fair' (white) or dark (black) with adjectives such as very, a little and minimal, used to punctuate the gradations of skin tone. Admittedly, these descriptions could also embody racial, class and rendered gradations of acceptability in society. As Carla Rice notes in her analysis of global interconnections of color and beauty, "though rarely officially sanctioned, colorist beauty standards are deeply sanctioned in the economic and cultural fabric of many nations"[25] with even stronger historically racist divides in places like India, Brazil, and Mexico. Indeed, the geo-historically blurred but still portent Christian/Islamic and Anglo/Persian divides in Africa are also laced with racial (and in many cases racist) color connotations. Globalization has further internationalized in many places, what may be considered originally Caucasian standards of acceptance. Except for South Africa with its history of Apartheid, differentiations of skin tones within the Sub Sahara do not convey the heavily racist connotations they carry today in the Americas. In any case distance, a much lower capacity for migration earlier on and a slower pace of technological growth may have rendered these potentially divisive characteristics less effective in the continent. For many of the women in the study therefore, to be labeled Black upon arrival in North America was therefore derogatively baffling. It takes months and years for them to begin to understand and juggle the racist implications of this identity with the agency it creates for the empowerment struggle with their brothers and sisters in Diaspora.

Unlike the women from dark skinned national populations, the reaction was different for South African women, like Linzi who were born and raised in a racially divided society, blackness was a familiar label, one they wore for very important reasons:

> I don't think I had any problem with identity. Because I already knew I'm Black and I am African. That thing was heightened or embedded in our mentality from the time we were young.... It gave us the incentive to do what it needed to be done. Because the moment we had any hesitation about who we are, we are lost.

Often, Jambo the immigrant service provider explains, Africa women find themselves embracing the 'black' identity as the first level of recognition. According to her, it is when people probe further "... that is when you say ... I am African ... I am Malawian ... But, more and less, everybody just looks at ... you [as] ... Black." Among people of the same nationality, women in this study also point out, it was important to claim ethnic identities, especially in safe social spaces (e.g., parties) where they can comfortably speak in their native languages).

While individual women emphasized their need to be identified as members of specific nationalities and ethnicities, they also recognize the increasing need to forge a common identity with other African women outside the black label. Linzi who have lived in Canada for over twenty-five years explains:

> I have always identified my self as a black person. But I became more conscious of being African . . . when I meet my fellow black people from other places, like the West Indies or North America . . . say the USA, they had the thing, that you are African . . . . The black identity is universal one, everybody who walks in the street. . . looks at me and say you are . . . you're Black. They won't say African . . . .

Forging an African identity is crucial not only as a mark of distinction from a black pool that could be dominated by those of Caribbean origin, but also imperative in order to identify with their 'non-black' African sisters whose voice is also crucial in the struggle to strengthen social presence and political clout. Women who are not from 'Black' Africa could not identify with the black label. Saoussen, for instance, is from Tunisia. She came to Canada to join her already established husband only a few months before the focus group interviews took. Saoussen was blunt about where she sees herself in all the discussions about blackness and African-ness, "I see my self as an Arab and African woman. I don't think in terms of skin color." Similarly, Maxine is from Mauritania, a multi-ethnic country with a population of mostly non-blacks has strong ties with her black sisters but does not share their blackness. She came to Canada over thirty years ago with her husband, stayed in academia for many years, and finally moved on to a social work career. In Maxine's view:

> being Mauritian stands for being francophone...;[b]eing born and raised in a diversified culture (Indian, Chinese, French and English). I always felt at ease in that environment. I had a lot of friends from all over the world. Besides, I had a lot of responsibilities as well as in my workplace and at home. I used to dress in Indian attire. I worked in every kind of environment: office work, academic, international organizations. I brought along with me a rich cultural background that really helped me deal with the Canadian society.

Women like Maxine and Saoussen's were somewhat 'distanced' from their Sub-Saharan African sisters in the focus groups. Besides their 'different' features and view of life, this distance could also be a response to new hierarchies everyone is gradually adjusting to. Unlike those from South Africa who had a longer history of white domination, Maxine's Indian background gave her a valuable backing to assert herself within the Mauritian society. Besides her educational and professional advantage, this ethnic position certainly made her experience significantly different from that of black African women.

Similarly, African women of Francophone background, the focus group discussions clearly showed, emphasized their French background while the Anglophone women did not even consider the fact that they spoke English something of a notable identity. Indeed, most of the women situated themselves within specific organizations as communities in which their identities are rooted. These include religious (Christian, Moslem) and national associations. Interestingly, the francophone African's include specific French groups and organizations, as part of their community of family and friends. Evidently, these women unlike their Anglophone sisters, must deal with the language barrier in a province dominated by English speaking populations. Thus, their identification with other French speaking minorities is not only necessary but also strategic.

They point out that beside race, continent of origin and other identities do come into play in specific situations. Nationality or ethnicity is a better way of situating their 'African-ness,' to avoid being lumped into another pool–the pan-African one. Among members of the same nationality, for instance, ethnicity, language, and part of the country resided in before emigration, become crucial identities for situating individuals. It seems, therefore, that black is associated with the larger 'kindred,' African a distinct form of blackness, and nationality, language, ethnicity as more distinguishing features for situating oneself both within Africa. As Almaz notes, it depends on the situation. She has described herself at various instances as "Black, African, Eritrean. . . and, sometimes, yeah Muslim . . ." within Canada, and as ". . . a Canadian everywhere else." On the whole, however, all the women agree that how one defines her identity and social space depends on the circumstance.

Juggling Identities in a New Homeland

The experiences of these African women provide very useful insights into the process of adjustment, adaptation, and integration in the new world. Their connections with both the Canadian mainstream and minorities groups; with both the old homeland and the international community, unveil aspects of transnationalism as well as diaspora relations. For refugees like Katya and Tuggy, the process of settling down, at present, could be seen as an experience they are still immersed in and therefore not in a position to reflect on. Those who have stayed longer in Canada, such as Effie, Martha and Linzi, however, have come to accept the fluidity of social status, identities and community. As the experiences of these women clearly show, life with the various communities they belong to exhibits its own peculiarities, which cannot easily be fitted into the diasporic construction as presently defined. It might also be argued that these are simply the 'teething troubles' of yet another group in the throes of forming a Diaspora. In this sense, the *kind* of Diaspora that will eventually emerge remains uncertain. As Richard Roberts argues in his analysis of African New World experiences,'

There is no such thing as an African diasporas in the New world. There are instead many African New world diasporas. . . When examined in terms of the historical dynamic of cultural production, the same would hold true for any Diaspora anywhere. Efforts to mobilize diasporic communities toward common political goals . . . will invariably confront the fiction of the diaspora as a coherent unit of analysis."[26]

But the incoherency of Diaspora as a historical construction points to its inadequacy in arresting the collectivity of experiences lumped under the label. This is even so in the African case where even the definition of Diasporic identities is already proving to be a difficult task. Across the African Diaspora in the US and Canada, for instance, the use of terms like 'African Americans,' 'African Canadians,' 'Blacks,' and 'People of African Descent' are seemingly inclusive because they attempt to enlarge the rubric at any point to acknowledge every in-coming group. As inclusive as these terms may seem, the homogenization of populations of Africans in Diaspora, who beyond the commonality of skin color, have inherited different histories that shape their identities. In such a context, blackness and African-ness over time and space, complicated by national, gendered and class identities, do not only take on different meanings but eliminate a colossal number of Africans outside the Suh Sahara, who cannot embrace blackness as a mark of identity. It is also debatable if whatever groupings eventually emerge can be expected to punctuate the typical features of previous Diasporas. For one thing, the potential for linkages made possible by globalization means that ties with the old homelands may not gradually loosen. For another, the bleak social conditions across Africa, unyielding so far to a multiplicity of policy actions, may sustain both the ties settlers in the Americas have with their homelands as well as nurture a continuous outflow that builds newer ties.

As women in this study declare, the struggle to redefine self and selves in order to fit into a new society now necessitates the juggling of identities. Despite the challenges this struggle presents, they now realize that identity can no longer be assumed a simple, definite, and immovable posture. Who they are can no longer be understood in those conventional terms that called for a rethink. For one thing, identity now has multiple options. These options may appear dispersed in certain instances, but as these women emphasize, there are social, cultural, and political relations, which connect these identities. The challenge now lies in how to juggle a multiplicity of identities. Juggling them calls for a good deal of strategizing in order to produce the most appropriate one(s) in a particular context. Strategizing is greatly facilitated by the fluidity with which these women move from one set of identities to another. With little thought given to the process they are engaged in continually, each woman appears to be juggling a multiplicity of identities in various social contexts. Their experience vividly captures Hall's piercing rendition, "the subject previously experienced as having a unified and stable identity, is becoming fragmented; . . . The very process of identification, through which we project ourselves into our cultural identities, has become more open-ended, variable and problematic."[27] In essence, trans-migrants are forced to generate a multiplicity of identities, some of them quite fluid, in strategic response to new circumstances. It is also obvious that the different 'modalities of power' such as racialization, gender, class, and ethnic, also impact the currency held by specific identities in particular instances.[28]

Given the fluidity of personhood and group relations, which new settlers in North America navigate today, labels of identity must be applied with caution. As Bramadat (2001, 2) notes, identity in the present context is ". . . a highly fluid state of mind or set of assumptions regarding selfhood or group definition . . . [and] while no one constitutes his or her identity exnihilo, it is important to resist the simply lucidity of "essentialist" assumptions about the way members of a given group really and irreducibly are. In other words, identities are human constructions that are conditioned by resilient communal meta-narratives about the history and nature of a group." As the experiences of women in this study clearly show, the identity [ies] of new African settlers in the new world is [are] still under construction.

Negotiating the Continental Color Divide

Perhaps, the more difficult challenge women in this study as well as other African women in the Americas face is that of juggling their identities *collectively*, aggregating and disaggregating themselves in order to strategize for political action. The transition to a new homeland has placed them in a situation where they must learn to juggle their collective identities strategically. Depending on what each context demands, they must work on embracing aggregations that create stronger political and cultural platforms; resist amalgamations that bury their unique identities or assert their place within the mainstream. For people who have share only the basic commonality of coming a continent, African women may also consider creating new and competing identities to assert themselves.[29]

Conclusion

It is therefore debatable if any "pre-made" identities would suffice for these African women, given the changes they and their families are undergoing at present. This is because the process of evolving as a people has only begun. The women in this study recognize the need to forge an African identity in order to nurture a sense of belonging and, where the occasion demands, a political presence. While they are not prepared to shed off their "group" identities, they recognize the fact that the responsibility for enculturation and community building enforce a sense of urgency to harness any collective support, agency and power that could be mustered by building an African identity. As they strongly expressed at the celebration of the completion of this project in the spring of 2006, the need for new kinds of African women's organizations is long overdue. At present, their involvement with Canadian social organizations as provides a good deal of support in the journey towards adjusting and adapting to a new life. These associations are not necessarily equipped to convey that sense of belonging that comes with knowledge and pride in one's social location. Even their status in ethnic and national organizations, the women point out, still mirrors the gendered arrangements characteristic of the social organizations they left behind. With their minimal immigrant representations in national groups, attempts to form their own women only organizations are usually threatened by even smaller numbers. Connecting women who trace their origins across the continent appears to be one potentially path in the search for social identities that could produce a strong collectivity. As the women emphasized during the celebration, the vision is not to repeat the organizations many of which for socializing. They envision, instead, organizations that would undertake the task of 'bringing African women' to begin the difficult journey of getting to know one another. They yearn for unique associations that would strongly impress upon them the urgency to come together for the main purpose of building a firm ground to stand on. They recognize the huge costs of ignoring identity barriers that stayed unchallenged in Africa but must now give way to a much-needed political mobilization.

While they brace themselves for the task ahead, these women do not underestimate the challenges involved in building this unified space. As the lives of women portray, a range of social hierarchies, including color, is already emerging. Apart from the removal of distance and all protocols, the move from Africa to Canada has also overturned all forms of hierarchies. The different circumstances of migration and the opportunities presented to different groups and individuals have in many cases rearranged living conditions and social positions. In a world where, according to these women's testimonies, the majority is struggling to reestablish itself as persons and as peoples, what they evolve to become is, at best, still under construction. As a crucial element of identification and recognition in the Americas, color is very likely to continue to play a role in this struggle. If that is the case, it will be safe to assert that being color-struck at the beginning of the journey is merely an initial stage of an interesting challenge.

Notes

1. Indeed, Black immigrants constitute the majority among Blacks, recording even higher proportions in provinces such as Alberta, which has a minimal history of slavery and black settlement, Philomina, P. Okeke, et al. *Black Women and Economic Autonomy in Edmonton, Alberta: Barriers to Accessing Equal Opportunities.* Report prepared for Status of Women, Canada (2000).
2. Philip D. Curtin, *Cross-Cultural Trade in World History* (New York: Cambridge University Press, 1984), 2.
3. Holy Bible, Deut. 28: 25.
4. Robin Cohen, *Global Diasporas: An Introduction* (Seattle: University of Washington Press, 2003), ix.
5. Ibid., 3-4.
6. Cohen, 2003.
7. Richard Roberts, "The Construction of Cultures in Diasporas: African and African New World Experiences," *The South Atlantic Quarterly* 98 (1/2): 184, 1999.
8. Ibid., 182.
9. Joseph Harris, ed., "Introduction," in *Global Dimensions of the African Diaspora* (Washington, D.C.: Howard University Press, 1992), 3.

10. Isidore Okpewho, "Introduction," in *The African Diaspora: African Origins and New World Identities*, ed., I. Okpewho, D. Boyce and Ali Mazrui (Bloomington: Indiana University Press, 1999), xxiv.

11. Okeke, et al. 2000; Elabor-Idemudia, Patience, "Gender and the New African Diaspora: African Immigrant Women in the Canadian Labor Force," in ed., Okpewho, Boyce Davies, and Mazrui, 234-271.

12. T. Mkandawire, "The Social Sciences in Africa: Breaking Local Barriers and Negotiating International Presence." The Bashorun M. K. O. Abiola Distinguished Lecture Presented to the 1996 African Studies Association Annual Meeting. *African Studies Review 40*(2): 15-36, 1997; D. McDonald, and J. Crush, eds. *Destinations Unknown: Perspectives on the Brain Drain in Southern Africa* Pretoria: African Institute of South Africa, South African Migration Project, 2002).

13. P. Boyle and Halfacree K., eds. *Migration and Gender in the Developed World* (New York: Routledge Press, 1999).

14. S. Hall, "Cultural Identity and Diaspora," in *Identity*, ed., J. Rutherford (London: Lawrence and Wishart, 1990); R. Cohen, 2003; A. Portes, "Immigration Theory for a New Century: Some Problems and Opportunities," *International Immigration Review* 31:799-825, 1997.

15. Nina Glick-Schiller, Linda Basch and Cristina Blanc-Szanton, "Transnationalism: A New Analytical Framework for Understanding Migration," in *Towards a Transnational Perspective on Migration: Race, Class, Ethnicity, and Nationalism Reconsidered*, ed., Glick-Schiller, Basch and Blanc-Szanton (New York: The New York Academy of Sciences, 1992), 1-24.

16. Ibid, 10.

17. R. Cohen, 2003, R. Cohen and Vertovec, eds. *Conceiving Cosmopolitanism: Theory, Context and Practice* (London: Oxford University Press, 2002).

18. Salih Ruba, "Shifting Means of 'Home': Consumption and Identity in Moroccan Women's Transnational Practices between Italy and Morocco," in *Transnational Communities and the Transformation of Home*, ed., Nadje Al-Ali and Khalid Koser (London: Routledge, 2002), 52.

19. CRIAW. Canadian Research Institute for the Advancement of Women: Fact Sheet. 5, 2003; Evangelia Tastsoglou, Brian Ray, and Valerie Preston, "Gender and Migration Intersections: In a Canadian Context." Canadian Issues, Spring, 91-93. 2005.

20. Marlene Mulder and Bojan Korenic, *Portraits of Ethnic Minorities in Canada: Regional Comparisons* (Edmonton: Prairie Centre of Excellence for Research in Immigration and Integration, 2005).

21. Elabor-Idenmudia 1999, D. Spitzer and P. Okeke, "African Women in Alberta on Identity and Homelands." Presentation to the 9th International Metropolis Conference, Geneva, Switzerland, 2004).

22. Collated from *A National Overview – Population and Dwelling Counts*, 2001 Census (Ottawa: Statistics Canada, 2002).

23. N. Al-Ali, and K. Koser, "Transnationalism, International Immigration and Home," in *Transnational Communities and the Transformation of Home*, eds., Al-Ali and Koser (London: Routledge, 2002), 1.

24. Mercer, K. , "Welcome to the Jungle," in ed., Rutherford., 43.

25. Carl Rice, "Between Body and Culture: Beauty, Ability, and Growing Up Female," in *Gender, Race and Nation: A Global Perspective*, eds., Vanaja Dhruvarajan and Jill Vickers (Toronto: University of Toronto Press, 2002), 147-181.

26. Robert, 188.

27. C. Hall, *White, Male and Middle Class: Explorations in Feminism and History* (Cambridge: Polity Press, 1992), 276-277.

28. Stuart Hall, David Held and Tony McGrew, eds., *Modernity and its Futures* (Cambridge: Polity Press, 1992), 19.
29. A. Giddens, *The Consequences of Modernity* (Cambridge: Polity Press, 1990); D. Harvey, *The Condition of Post-Modernity* (Oxford: Oxford University Press, 1989).

References

Al-Ali, N. and K. Koser, eds. *Transnational Communities and the Transformation of Home.* London: Routledge, 2002.

Boyle, P. and Halfacree K., eds. *Migration and Gender in the Developed World.* New York: Routledge Press, 1999.

Cohen, Robin. *Global Diasporas: An Introduction.* Seattle: University of Washington Press, 2003.

Cohen, R and Vertovec, eds. *Conceiving Cosmopolitanism: Theory, Context and Practice.* London: Oxford University Press, 2002.

CRIAW. Canadian Research Institute for the Advancement of Women: Fact Sheet. 5, 2003.

Evangelia Tastsoglou, Brian Ray, and Valerie Preston, "Gender and Migration Intersections: In a Canadian Context." *Canadian Issues,* (Spring 2005).

Elabor-Idemudia, Patience. "Gender and the New African Diaspora: African Immigrant Women in the Canadian Labor Force," in Okpewho, Boyce Davies, and Mazrui, eds., *The African Diaspora: African Origins and New World Identities.* Bloomington: Indiana University Press, 1999.

Glick-Schiller, Nina, Linda Basch and Cristina Blanc-Szanton, ed. *Towards a Transnational Perspective on Migration: Race, Class, Ethnicity, and Nationalism Reconsidered.* New York: The New York Academy of Sciences, 1992.

Hall, C. *White, Male and Middle Class: Explorations in Feminism and History.* Cambridge: Polity Press, 1992.

Hall, Stuart, David Held and Tony McGrew, eds. *Modernity and its Futures.* Cambridge: Polity Press, 1992.

Hall, S. "Cultural Identity and Diaspora." In J. Rutherford, ed. *Identity: Community, Culture, Difference.* London: Lawrence and Wishart, 1990.

Harris, Joseph, ed. *Global Dimensions of the African Diaspora.* Washington, D.C.: Howard University Press, 1992.

Harvey, D. *The Condition of Post-Modernity.* Oxford: Oxford University Press, 1989.

McDonald, D. and J. Crush, eds. *Destinations Unknown: Perspectives on the Brain Drain in Southern Africa.* Pretoria: African Institute of South Africa, South African Migration Project, 2002.

Mercer, K. "Welcome to the Jungle.' In J. Rutherford, ed. *Identity: Community, Culture , Difference.* London: Lawrence and Wishart, 1990.

Mulder, Marlene and Bojan Korenic, *Portraits of Ethnic Minorities in Canada: Regional Comparisons.* Edmonton: Prairie Centre of Excellence for Research in Immigration and Integration, 2005.

Mkandawire, T. "The Social Sciences in Africa: Breaking Local Barriers and Negotiating International Presence." The Bashorun M.K.O. Abiola Distinguished Lecture Presented to the 1996 African Studies Association Annual Meeting. *African Studies Review* 40(2): 15-36, 1997.

Okeke, Philomina, et al., "Black Women and Economic Autonomy in Edmonton, Alberta: Barriers to Accessing Equal Opportunities." Report Submitted by the Black Women Working Group to the Status of Women Canada: Status of Women, 2000.

Okpewho, Isidore, D. Boyce and Ali Mazrui, eds. *TheAfrican Diaspora: African Origins and New World Identities.* Bloomington: Indiana University Press, 1999.

Portes, "Immigration Theory for a New Century: Some Problems and Opportunities," *International Immigration Review* 31 (1997).

Rice, Carl. "Between Body and Culture: Beauty, Ability, and Growing Up Female," in Vanaja Dhruvarajan and Jill Vickers eds. *Gender, Race and Nation: A global Perspective* (Toronto: University of Toronto Press, 2002).

Richard Roberts, "The Construction of Cultures in Diaspora's: African and African New world Experiences." *The South Atlantic Quarterly* 98 (1/2) (1999).

Salih Ruba, "Shifting Means of 'Home': Consumption and Identity in Moroccan Women's Transnational Practices between Italy and Morocco." In Nadje Al-Ali and Khalid Koser, eds. *Transnational Communities and the Transformation of Home.* London: Routledge, 2002.

Tastsoglou, Evangelia, Brian Ray, and Valerie Preston, "Gender and Migration Intersections: In a Canadian Context." *Canadian Issues,* (Spring 2005).

Chapter 19

Burdened Intersections: Black Women and Race, Gender, and Class

Marsha J. Tyson Darling

Scholars of the social construction of race in the United States have the ambitious, if daunting task, of interrogating the past as a means of identifying and examining the burdened social and political lives the majority of Black women have experienced to date. Black in a society that has always valued whiteness, female in a society that has always prized maleness, and financially poor and impoverished in a society that has through public and private discrimination marginalized all women of color, women of African descent and indigenous women have been pushed the farthest from the exercise of constitutional rights. Hence, women of African descent, Black women and indigenous women have and continue to experience the greatest range of burdens and obstacles to equality and justice. This chapter examines the multiple and intersecting burdens dating from the creation of the Atlantic World Trade System that have hampered, restricted or prevented the greater exercise of human rights for Black women, and since the passage of the Thirteenth and Fourteenth Amendments to the Constitution, Black women's access to the exercise of rights and privileges set out in the social contract that governs the United States.

Introduction

One of the most pressing and persistent challenges we face as a nation that extends the promise of constitutional protection to all citizens through the letter of the law, is related to unraveling the unique burdens that the intersections of race, gender, and class have presented for women of the African diaspora in the United States. This chapter notes the unique burdens Black women have endured in the United States as a consequence of living experiences at the intersection where race, gender, propertied status, class and sexuality have met medical and scientific racism, and adverse social policy. Stated simply, no other group of American women lived the unique burdens embedded in Black women's herstories. Black women, more so than any other group of American women (except indigenous women), have experienced multiple and intersecting discriminations—initially those rooted in social customs in the British Atlantic colonies of North America during the colonial era, but over time the discrimination has codified into property law, unethical medical practice, scientific racism, state sponsored involuntary sterilization under Eugenics (population control), and expropriation of reproductive autonomy.

Intersectionality and Black Women's Historical Experiences

Intersectionality, a theoretical tool that exposes socially imposed marginalizing identities that derive from multiple and intersecting discriminations that are often difficult to discern and measure even as they stigmatize is a useful paradigm. For a very long time the intersecting and even compounding discriminations that have burdened Black women too often have been missing from public and even scholarly discourses. Intersectionality is not a new paradigm for delineating multiple, intersecting, and compounding identities, especially identities marked for discrimination, subordination, and marginalization. Theorists argued that through socially constructed identities, women belong concurrently to more than one community, and experience more than one identity. As a theoretical approach, Intersectionality has emerged as an analysis of the impact of the intersection of race, gender, sexuality, and class on the lives of Black women. Over the course of the past several decades Black feminist theorists have enjoined intersectional analyses in providing discourses regarding critical race feminism. This essential multidisciplinary work has been critical to domestic and international efforts to promote advancement and equity for marginalized women, including Black women and other women of color.[1]

In the context of Black women's historical experiences as producers and reproducers, as workers, mothers, wives, concubines, healers and social change agents, here we examine several historically complex legacies that are unique to Black women's lived experiences. Focusing on the historical factors that have set Black women's relationships apart from other women's experiences in the United States, it is important to identify several key ways in which Black women's relationships with American society have created enduring and burdened obstacles to the exercise of human rights and reproductive autonomy, including: the historical dimensions of Black women experiences as chattel property dating to the beginning of the Atlantic World Trade System; Black women bodies as sexual property and reproductive containers under the control of men outside of their ethnic group or "race" under slavery; Black women as medical and surgical objects of curiosity and experimentation in the nineteenth century; Black women's wombs as prohibitive gateways undergoing Eugenics intervention and control in the twentieth century; Black women's bodies as sites of excess fertility and hence population control that warrant expropriation of reproductive autonomy; and Black women's wombs as useful for contract surrogacy and tissue and ova donation.

Burdened Intersections

Why has the exercise of reproductive rights and reproductive justice for poor and working class Black women been so complicated and burdened a public policy challenge at all levels of government? Whether we are reflecting on the explicit sexual exploitation of Black women by white males in the seventeenth, eighteenth, and nineteenth centuries, or the trashing of Black women through destructive iconic level stereotypes of Jezebel, Sapphire, and Welfare Queens, or control of Black women's reproductive choices through austere welfare policy and abortion restrictions in the Hyde Amendment, or the criminal prosecutions of impoverished pregnant Black women culminating at the Supreme Court level in *Ferguson vs. Charleston* in the 1990s, Black women have experienced, endured and struggled against challenges unique to the multiple and intersecting identities they have grappled with for centuries.

By way of dating a point of origin linked to the social justice issues that this work references, it is important to implicate the historical roots of contemporary civil rights and distributive justice challenges regarding reproductive rights and reproductive justice for poor and working class Black women. The marginalization that Black women have endured comes into focus more clearly as we explore the social construction of 'race,' sex, sexuality and gendered notions of femininity and motherhood, patriarchy, white supremacy, and class dating back to the formation of the Atlantic World Economy.

The Social Construction of Captive African Women's Identities

It is important to begin with the social construction of captive African women's identities in the North Atlantic British colonies, as their status and treatment at the hands of white males departed radically from the treatment accorded women under English customary notions of femininity and motherhood. Captive African women's subjugation under the idea and illusion of race was also always simultaneously peculiar and perverse gender subjugation. Because captive African women had female genitalia, their female sexuality immediately marked them as sexual prey, and their physical possession by the men who held them in captivity forced them into serving the sexual interests of those whose predatory behavior can be summed up in one word—rape. In addition to having been the sexual possession of men with little interest in courtship, marriage, protected motherhood, or the spacing of pregnancies or childbirths, the property status of enslaved African women's bodies marked them not only for concubinage, but also the objectification of their wombs. Enslaved Black women's wombs reproduced only "slaves," thereby serving the economic interests of White men by reproducing the next generation of slaves free of cost. North Atlantic English colonial law dating from 1662 insured the intergenerational transmission of slavery through Black women's wombs, thereby codifying intersecting subordinations.

Black women are the only group of North American women ever owned as chattel property; that is, owned in their person entirely as the private property of white males, beyond the reach of ameliorating social arrangements, religious or cultural conventions. It is argued that:

> The word slavery is used to describe a number of related conditions involving control of a person against their will, enforced by violence or other clear forms of coercion. It almost always occurs for the purpose of securing the labor of the person or people concerned. A specific form, chattel slavery, involves the legal ownership of a person or people. In the strict sense, slaves are people who have no rights. Therefore, serfdom does not usually mean slavery because serfs almost always have some rights.[2]

Thus, as legally chattel property, Black women are the only group of American women ever to live under the doctrine of "absolute authority," a legal doctrine established in the colonial era that granted white males absolute authority in all matters, at every level, even the right to kill the enslaved without any felony charge. According to primary documents, as early as 1669, lawmakers in the Virginia House of Burgesses enacted a statute notifying slave owners that the casual killing of enslaved Black women or men by white men occasioned no felony charge.[3] In essence, the legal doctrine of absolute authority accomplished its legal purpose, namely, it summarily extinguished the exercise of human rights for enslaved Black women and men until the end of the Civil War.

A few decades later, in 1705 Virginia lawmakers enacted Legislative Act 38 which stated, "Provided always, and it is further enacted, that for every slave killed, in pursuance of this act, or put to death by law, the master or owner of such slave shall be paid by the public."[4] In the now classic nearly 700 page tome entitled *Race, Racism and American Law*, Derrick Bell, former Harvard law professor, notes:

> They were property subject to ownership; and the law, reflecting as it did then the prevailing belief in the inherent inferiority of all blacks, experience little difficulty in treating them as 'chattels personal.' There were contradictions involved in holding 'chattels personal' responsible for acts requiring the free will of humans, while at the same time denying to those 'chattels' the basic due process rights the law guaranteed to all humans.[5]

In considering the unique problems women confronted under patriarchal dominion, it is important to consider that while women of European ancestry were subordinated, they nonetheless enjoyed basic human rights protections as most, even the very poor women had been baptized as Christians, and all, even those who remained unmarried, were viewed through a cultural lens that valued their role in motherhood as inextricably linked with the reproduction and raising of successive generations of white children. White men's survival depended on white wombs, and as such, white women were always accorded basic human rights protections. Indeed, no other race of men was ever allowed to capture, rape, or sexually coerce, and colonize through breeding American white women as a corporal entity.

In British North America and still later in the new American republic, neither were white children ever inheritable as anyone else's chattel, nor personal property; for whites, blood inheritance and ancestral or familial association delineated the "place" where white children belonged. But, dating from the Atlantic World colonial era enslaved Black women increasingly lived under a system of racial patriarchy in which, according to Barbara Omolade:

> Usually the patriarch in a society is the father, husband, brother, or son of a woman. These men protect, take care of, subjugate, and dominate women, but these are also men with whom women have a primary emotional, biological, and social attachment. . . . The racial patriarch has no primary relationship with women of color, and therefore, no interest in protecting women of color. It has only an interest in exploiting these women and their men.[6]

This dimension of white supremacy focused on the social construction of race as the important marker for ancestral bloodline transmission. Race was not just skin color, the invention of race and its inheritance within and across generations was assessed by the percentage of African blood thought to be transmitted from one generation to the next. Hence, then and now, race was used to divide and categorize people in order to naturalize domination and marginalization. This aspect of white supremacy is important to assess as the United States is one of the countries bearing a legacy of a one-drop rule, meaning that one-drop of African blood anywhere in one's ancestry, even if it was physically indiscernible, rendered a child ineligible to belong to the white race.[7]

In terms of the evolution of the enslavement of African women, men, and children in the Atlantic British colonies and later in the United States, slavery functioned as a production system based on the relationship between production and markets, the evolution of a corpus of slave law to dictate the nature of authority over captives of African descent, delineate the structure of labor, and codify as law the sexual exploitation of enslaved Black women so as to establish and perpetuate inheritable, intergenerational race based servitude. In terms of plantation labor, Darlene Clark Hine asserts that, "during the late seventeenth and eighteenth centuries, approximately 90 % of southern Black women worked in the fields . . ." cultivating tobacco, rice, and indigo. In the nineteenth century, King Cotton cultivation took over.[8]

In an article entitled "Black Women and the Constitution," legal scholar Judy Scales-Trent argues that " . . .Black women, unlike white women, were often grouped along with white and Black men as persons who were to till the soil. A 1643 Virginia statute, for example, stated that 'tithable persons'—those who worked the ground, whether slave or free—included all adult men and Black women. Maryland enacted a similar statute in 1664."[9] Overall, enslaved Black women's typical work day can aptly be referred to as a double duty, as Black women were agricultural laborers, and also did the work of birthing, nursing, feeding, and taking care of enslaved children, cooking for their family or kin, including going to get firewood and water needed for drinking and preparing food and bathing, sewing, attending to the conjugal needs of sexual partners, and attending to whatever small garden areas the enslaved might have been permitted to cultivate. In addition, enslaved Black women worked as midwives and birth attendants, and served as wet nurses for planter's children. Some women became house servants, cooks, and body servants, and a number of enslaved women learned about and used medicinal herbs and flowers for healing in the slave quarters, and sometimes in the planter's house as well.[10]

The Legal Ownership of Black Women's Reproductive Sexuality

Second, Black women are also the only group of North American women whose reproductive sexuality was legally owned and used by men of a race other than their own. Enslaved Black women's fertility was the property of white males, who themselves, often sired the large mixed race population of children who could not lay claim to their white father's free status. Enslaved Black women also bore the children of enslaved Black and mulatto men. In this vein, enslaved Black women are the only group of American women whose reproductive capacity was folded into an agricultural production process as an integral and financially valuable component of production that many white planters continually sought to exploit. In "Reproductive Choice," Amy Leipziger wrote:

> While slave masters held little interest in caring for pregnant slaves, they went to great lengths to protect her womb. To whip pregnant slaves, the White folks would dig a hole in de ground just big enough for her stomach, make her lie face down and whip her on the back to keep from hurting the child. The master was thus able to punish and control his female slave while preserving his future investment.[11]

Black women's wombs were put to work transmitting intergenerational servitude on a massive scale. The slave law that established white males as breeders over enslaved Black women dates to the colonial era, and was one of the earliest colonial statutes crafted by colonial lawmakers, extending from the mid-1600s to the demise of the peculiar institution in the South. In the painstakingly researched study of colonial legislation in the British North Atlantic colonies, *In the Matter of Color*, Judge A. Leon Higginbotham demonstrates that Virginia statutes were important in their own right, but they also served as the foundation for colonial statutes enacted in neighboring colonies. White men of property who oversaw the creation of Virginia dynasties used the legislative reach of the Virginia House of Burgesses to craft slave law that broke away from conventions and traditions embedded in English Common Law, thereby establishing colonial Virginia law as the leader for other slaveholding colonies. Where children followed the legal status of their father under English customary law, slave law tacitly condoned interracial sex between white men and captive African women, while insuring that all children born to any enslaved Black women, regardless of paternity, remained the property of white men.

Virginia Statute, Act 12 enacted in 1662, just a few decades following the arrival of twenty captive Africans in the nearby Jamestown, attempted to legislate white male private action, and dealt explicitly with interracial sex between White men and captive African women. It bears noting that usually new laws follow or respond to existing social behavior or patterns embedded in social custom, thereby attempting to influence, shape, or mold future social behavior. While it appears that interracial relationships occurred from the earliest interactions between whites, blacks and indigenous peoples, the records show that white male lawmakers were particularly concerned with establish statutory prohibitions of interracial sex between black and indigenous males and white women, while tacitly condoning interracial sex between white males and captive African females. The language of the 1662 statute is as follows: "Children got by an Englishman upon a Negro woman shall be bound or free according to the condition of the mother . . ."

Dating from the colonial era each child born to an enslaved woman, no matter it white, mulatto or African father followed the status of its enslaved mother. The 1662 statute conferred an immediate economic advantage to white planters who sought to extend servitude and slavery. It allowed them to reproduce the slave force from the fertility capacity of captive African women, as White planters eliminated the cost of purchasing an enslaved infant. The law implicitly assessed whiteness as racially exclusive, as any child born to African sexual concubines even if their mulatto color and/or features marked it them as mixed race could not be free or belong to a white family with a male surname. Such mulatto children were immediately the chattel property of white males, legally not their children, but their slaves, humans to be used as laborers in agricultural production. Hence, White planters who sired interracial children themselves became slave breeders.[12]

By this act and a number of other restrictive laws enacted in the mid to late 1600s Virginia lawmakers established the legal foundation of whiteness, for it was not enough to look white. Whiteness as an inherited status rested not alone on paternity, but on whether a child was born from within a white womb, sired by a white male. In establishing a sexual double standard in the restrictive miscegenation statutes that dated from 1691 lawmakers punished white women for engaging in interracial sex, as white males clearly intended to insure that white women, no matter how poor only had sex with white males, while white males were unrestricted in their access to white, black, mulatto and indigenous females. In the context of this article, in the 1662 statute, Virginia lawmakers established the wombs of captive African women as the nexus point for the transmission of multi-racial intergenerational servitude, as captive mother and all of the offspring of her fertility, and their offspring born into slavery were to be enslaved perpetually.

Under plantation slavery in the South white planters called on white male doctors to assist them in furthering the goals of the plantation economy, namely, treating the health maladies that afflicted the enslaved, and increasing the reproductive capacity of enslaved Black females. Planters consulted Southern doctors, who were eager to further the visibility of their professional careers, in their attempts to monitor and control enslaved women's reproduction, especially because some enslaved Black women, experienced very low fertility or infertility, or were so weary from not only multiple pregnancies, but pregnancies too close to one another, that they sought to exert some measure of control of their reproduction. In a recent path-breaking book Marie Jenkins Schwartz argues:

> The importance of their wombs and breasts for the future of slavery meant that the struggle for domination centered on their bodies. The women suffered a peculiar form of violence as slaveholders and doctors exploited female anatomy for their own purposes. Thus, women experienced slavery differently from men precisely because of their childbearing experiences."[13]

Enslaved Black women sometimes practiced alternative medicinal interventions. In her well regarded monograph on enslaved Black women in the plantation South, entitled *Ar'n't I A Woman: Female Slaves in the South,* Deborah White examined Black women's use of contraception, miscarriage and abortion and concluded that: "It is almost impossible to determine whether slave women practiced birth control and abortion. These matters were virtually exclusive to the female world of the quarters, and when they arose they were attended to in secret and were intended to remain secret."[14] Further, Liese M. Perrin of the University of Warwick at Coventry in the U.K. has undertaken an extensive examination of extant slave narratives in her article, "Resisting Reproduction: Reconsidering Slave Contraception in the Old South." She notes that according to details contained in oral history narratives in the WPA Slave Narratives, mention of cotton root by formerly enslaved women suggests it use as a very effective contraceptive. Gossypol is one of the substances found in all parts of the cotton root plant, and it curtails reproductive rates. Cotton root's properties appear to be a contraceptive; it has been used as a male contraceptive in China since 1980.[15]

Enslaved Black women experienced the traumas associated with non-existent prenatal care, the physical controls based on cruelty associated that came with their bondage, and the deteriorating impact constant work exerted on their well-being and the survival rates of young infants. According to Hine:

> Since enslaved Black women worked up to the moment of birth delivery they experienced many more birth complications than white women and because of the combination of a nutritionally poor diet, often hard physical labor, and beatings, Black women gave birth to far many more low birth weight babies. Because the stereotypes that white male planters in particular crafted about enslaved Black women, images of Black women as polygamous and promiscuous, indifferent to pain and sassy covered their indifferent or callous treatment of enslaved Black women, most enslaved women received very little

concern during pregnancy and labor. Many enslaved pregnant or nursing Black women lived with chronic back-pain, uterine pain and hernias. It should come as no surprise that even though white planters valued the cash price that could be asked for all children born to enslaved women, known legally as "issue," more than 50% of enslaved Black infants never reached five years old, as they were far more likely to subjected to irregular feeding, poor hygiene, improper care, and to suffer rickets, tetany, tetanus, high fevers that often killed them, intestinal worms, and influenza.[16]

The Bodies of Black Women and the Medical Establishment

A third historical burden that has challenged Black women is that Black women are the only group of American women ever used for risky, invasive, painful and at times unethical medical and especially surgical procedures dating from the nineteenth century. Southern white male doctors eager to prove themselves as pioneering men of science and medicine used enslaved women brought to them by white planters as well as enslaved women who they purchased for risky, invasive, and painful medical and surgical procedures. While there are several southern white male doctors whose antebellum medical practices were ethically suspect, the doctor referred to as the father of gynecology J. Marion Sims conducted unethical experiments on enslaved Black women.

Sims, a southern doctor, moved his practice from Alabama to the New York City area. There he was widely acclaimed and eventually awarded the presidency of the American Medical Association, and still later the American Gynecological Association. Today, Sims is often referred to as the father of gynecology. Yet, while Sims is credited with pioneering a successful surgical solution for treating vesico-vaginal fistula in women, a procedure he performed on many women, a little known fact is that he pioneered the procedure on enslaved Black women without the use of anesthesia. According to sources, Sims performed multiple experimental surgical procedures on enslaved women for four or more years. When Sims later wrote about his surgical successes, he obscured the fact that he had used [who were not anaesthetized] enslaved women to pioneer risky surgical procedures. By his own admission Sims acknowledged the harm he caused, "When he first attempted an operation upon [an enslaved woman] Lucy, a sponge he was using adhered to her bladder. Sims forcibly pulled it away. In Sims' words, the patient's agony was extreme; she was much prostrated, and I thought she was going to die." Later, when Sims performed gyn procedures on white women they were offered chloroform or other anesthetics. In addition, elsewhere in the South, the *Nashville Journal of Medicine and Surgery* reported on the following, quote, "Successful Case of Extraction of Living Child by the Caesarian Section, after the Death of the Mother," and in New Orleans in the 1820s and 1830s, Dr. Francois Prevost and Dr. Charles Luzenberg, antebellum southern doctors performed risky Caesarean sections on enslaved Black women without anesthesia.[17]

Decades later, Black women's bodies remained marked for control by white males, as thousands of poor Black women were among the approximately 70,000 American citizens who were involuntarily sterilized by Eugenics directives in states across the country between 1910 and 1970. In a number of southern states governors have recently officially apologized for their states Eugenics legacies. While Eugenicists who were concerned to translate science into social policy initially targeted disability, as the infamous Supreme Court decision *Buck vs. Bell* illustrates, in a number of states officially mandated Eugenics sterilizations based on alcoholism, anger, vagrancy, criminal behavior, sexual orientation and behaviors associated with poverty were aggressively pursued. Hence, deeply embedded racialized and sexualized beliefs about Black inferiority and racial degeneracy under cover of Jim and Jane Crow segregation furnished the impetus for the Eugenics attack on Black women's wombs, in the many states where Eugenics laws and practices prevailed.[18]

The lasting negative stigma that has surrounded Black women's reproductive sexuality, namely, that white men must intervene to control and bring order to Black women's sexuality and reproductive behavior has surfaced again in population control programs that derive their emotional fuel from sentiments that Black women and other women of color have excess fertility and birth too many babies for the well being of the planet. Everywhere in our public life, the wombs of women of color are faulted for the planet's population challenges and problems. As a matter of fact, these popularized perceptions have provided cover for the Eugenics influenced policies and practices proffered by the Population Council and other powerful political interests that have chosen the bodies of poor women of color: Black, Puerto Rican, Asian Indian, Vietnamese, and African women either for population control programmatic activities, or for clinical testing of all of the successful and failed contraceptive drugs, devices, and products in the global pipeline since WWII.[19]

Most recently, the global ova trade is in full stride, with the issue of egg donation firmly at the center of *In Vitro Fertilization* procedures and the quest for women's ova for infertility and research. What is seldom mentioned is that egg donation for stem cell research will require large quantities of embryos from which stem cells can be taken. Researchers want an abundant supply of free or cheap embryos, and since the legacy of contract motherhood surrogacy and more recently womb renting in reproductive tourism already implicates the wombs of marginalized women, including poor Black women and poor women of color, we can expect that a recent burden that Black women will confront is the view that Black wombs are apt baby containers for hire.[20]

Conclusion

There have been a number of historical developments, spanning decades that have shaped popular perceptions of Black women's bodies, especially their wombs and their reproductive sexuality. This article has explored marginalizing burdens imposed on Black women. These issues bear significance for deepening our understanding of the unique and complex challenges that have and continue to burden Black women's exercise of human rights, civil rights and reproductive autonomy. Margaret M. Russell of the Santa Clara School of Law, who is also a former board member of the American Civil Liberties Union has offered an important insight about the connections between the historical experiences of Black women and the social construction of reproductive liberty for racially, socially, economically and politically marginalized women. She noted:

> For women with race and class privilege, the struggle for reproductive autonomy in the United States historically has meant emancipation from stereotypical assumptions that motherhood is both their destiny and their primary societal mission. Black women endure a more complex set of burdens. These burdens are rooted in the lasting belief that Black women's reproductive choices – including motherhood – warrant neither legal protections nor social respect. Therefore, the struggle for the reproductive rights of Black women has focused on liberation from government policies that at various points either compelled or punished childbearing.[21]

The burdens confronting Black women's full exercise of constitutional rights implicate the lasting effects of historic barriers to the exercise of human rights, civil rights, reproductive autonomy and protection for bodily integrity. Those marginalized because of discrimination have been and continue to be pushed the furthest from the protection of progressive laws. Those marginalized have the greatest distance to travel to actualize the exercise of their rights. In the United States, that means that poor Black women still have a long road to travel.

Notes

1. Patricia Hill Collins, "Black Feminist Thought," and Patricia J. Williams, "Race and Rights," in *Theories of Race and Racism: A Reader*, ed., Les Back & John Solomos, eds. (New York: Routledge, 2000); Kimberlé Crenshaw, "Mapping the Margins: Intersectionality, Identity Politics, and Violence against Women of Color," in *Critical Race Theory: The Key Writings that Formed the Movement*, ed., Kimberlé Crenshaw, Neil Gotanda, Gary Peller & Kendall Thomas (The New Press, 1995); and a number of the articles in *Critical Race Feminism: A Reader*, ed., Adrien Katherine Wing.
2. See www.downbound.com (USA).
3. A. Leon Higginbotham, Jr., *In the Matter of Color: Race and the American Legal Process: The Colonial Period* (New York: Oxford University Press, 1978).
4. Ibid., 57.
5. Derrick Bell, *Race, Racism and American Law* (Boston: Little, Brown & Co., 1980), 11.
6. Mary Joe Frug, *Women and the Law* (Westbury, NY: Foundation Press, 1992), 511.
7. F. James Davis, *Who is Black?: One Nation's Definition* (University Park, PA: Pennsylvania State University Press, 1991); and Ian F. Haney Lopez, *White By Law: The Legal Construction of Race* (New York: NYU Press, 1996).
8. Darlene Clark Hine, William C. Hine and Stanley Harrold, *The African-American Odyssey*. Fourth Edition (Upper Saddle River, NJ: Pearson Prentice Hall, 2008), 73.
9. Judy Scales-Trent, "Black Women and the Constitution: Finding Our Place, Asserting Our Rights," in *Feminist Jurisprudence*, ed., Patricia Smith, ed. (New York: Oxford University Press, 1993).

10. Angela Y. Davis, "Reflections on the Black Woman's Role in the Community of Slaves," *Black Scholar* 3 (December 1971): 2-15; and Deborah Gray White, *Ar'n't I a Woman? Female Slaves in the Plantation South* (New York: Norton, 1985 and 1999).

11. Amy Leipziger, "Reproductive Choice," at http://www.gwu.edu/~medusa/reproductive.html (accessed 3/17/2008), 3.

12. Dorothy Roberts, *Killing the Black Body: Race, Reproduction, and the Meaning of Liberty* (New York: Pantheon Books, 1997); Thelma Jennings, "Us Colored Women had to go Through a Plenty: Sexual Exploitation of African-American Slave Women," *Journal of Women's History* 1 (1989-1990) 3, 45-74; Edward E. Baptist, "Fancy Maids, and One-Eyed Men: Rape, Commodification, and the Domestic Slave Trade in the U.S.," *American Historical Review* 106 (2001) 5, 1619-1650; and Herbert Gutman, *The Black Family in Slavery and Freedom, 1750-1925* (New York: Vintage Books, 1976).

13. Marie Jenkins Schwartz, *Birthing A Slave: Motherhood and Medicine in the Antebellum South* (Cambridge, MA: Harvard University Press, 2006), 5; Todd L. Savitt, *Medicine and Slavery: The Diseases and Health Care of Blacks in Antebellum Virginia* (Urbana: University of Illinois Press, 1978); Richard Follet, "Heat, Sex, and Sugar: Pregnancy and Childbearing in the Slave Quarters," *Journal of Family History* 28 (2003) 4, 510-539; and Jennifer L. Morgan. *Laboring Women: Reproduction and Gender in New World Slavery* (Philadelphia, PA: The University of Pennsylvania Press, 2004).

14. White, 84.

15. Liese M. Perrin, "Resisting Reproduction: Reconsidering Slave Contraception in the Old South," *Journal of American Studies*, 35 (2001), 2, 255-274; Schwartz, 239; Stephanie M. H. Camp. *Closer to Freedom: Enslaved Women and Everyday Resistance in the Plantation South* (Chapel Hill: University of North Carolina Press, 2004); Sharla M. Fett, *Working Cures: Healing, Health, and Power on Southern Slave Plantations* (Chapel Hill: University of North Carolina Press, 2002); Kirsten Fischer, *Suspect Relations: Sex, Race, and Resistance in Colonial North Carolina* (Ithaca: Cornell University Press, 2002).

16. Hine, Hine and Harrold, 153.

17. Harriett A. Washington, *Medical Apartheid: The Dark History of Medical Experimentation on Black Americans from Colonial Times to the Present* (New York: Harlem Moon Broadway Books, 2006).

18. Daniel J. Kevles, *In the Name of Eugenics: Genetics and the Uses of Human Heredity* (Cambridge: Harvard University Press, 1985 and 1995); John S. Haller, *Outcasts from Evolution: Scientific Attitudes of Racial Inferiority, 1859-1900* (Urbana: University Of Illinois Press, 1971); and Allan Chase, *The Legacy of Malthus: The Social Costs of the New Scientific Racism* (New York: Alfred A. Knopf, 1980).

19. Betsy Hartmann, *Reproductive Rights or Wrongs? The Global Politics of Population Control* (Cambridge, MA: South End Press, 1995); and Nilanjana Chatterjee and Nancy E. Riley, "Planning and Indian Modernity: The Gendered Politics of Fertility Control," *Signs* 26 2001; 3: 812-845; and Bonnie Mass, "Puerto Rico: A Case Study of Population Control," *Latin American Perspectives* 1977; 4: 66-81; and Jurema Werneck, Fernanda Carneiro, Alejandra Ana Rotania, Helen B. Holmes and Mary R. Rorty, "Autonomy and Procreation: Brazilian Feminist Analyses," in *Globalizing Feminist Bioethics*, ed., Rosemarie Tong, et.al. (Boulder, CO: Westview Press, 2000); and S. Correa. *Population and Reproductive Rights: Feminist Perspectives from the South* (London: ZED Press, 1994).

20. Donna Dickenson. "Who Owns Embryonic and Fetal Tissue." *Ethical Issues in Maternal-Fetal Medicine* 2002; Donna Dickenson. "Property and Women's Alienation from Their Own Reproductive Labour." *Bioethics 2001;* 15:205-217; J. G. Raymond. *Women as Wombs: Reproductive Technologies and the Battle Over Women's Freedom* (Melbourne, Australia: Spinifex, 1993); SAMA. *Consultation on New Reproductive and*

Genetic Technologies (NRGTs) and Women's Lives (New Delhi, India: SAMA Resource Group for Women and Health, 2006); and SAMA. *Assisted Reproductive Technologies (ARTs) and Women: Assistance in Reproduction or Subjugation?* (New Delhi, India: SAMA Resource Group for Women); and K. Ahuja, E. Simons & R. Edwards, "Money, Morals and Medical Risks: Conflicting Notions Underlying the Recruitment of Egg Donors," *Human Reproduction*, 14, 2: 279-284; and M. Mukherjee, M. & S. B. Nadimipally, "Assisted Reproductive Technologies in India," Special Issue: New Technologies and Development, *Development, 2006;* Marsha J. Tyson Darling, "Gender, New Technologies and Development," Special Issues: New Technologies and Development, *Development, 2006,* 49, 4:23-28; and Marsha J. Tyson Darling. "Reproductive and Genetic Bio-Technologies: Taking up the Challenge," *Development 2006;* 49, 1: 18-22.
21. Margaret M. Russell, "African American Women and Reproductive Rights," in *Historical and Multicultural Encyclopedia of Women's Reproductive Rights in the United States*, ed., Judith A. Baer (Westport, CT: Greenwood Press, 2002).

References

Bell, Derrick. *Race, Racism and American Law*. Boston: Little, Brown & Co. 1980.

Clark Hine, Darlene, and William C. Hine. *The African-American Odyssey*. Upper Saddle River: Pearson Prentice Hall, 2008.

Davis, Angela Y. "Reflections on the Black Woman's Role in the Community of Slaves." *Black Scholar* 3 (1971): 2-15.

Davis, F. James. *Who is Black? One Nation's Definition*. University Park: Pennsylvania University Press, 1991.

Dickson, Donna. "Who Owns Embryonic and Fetal Tissue." *Ethical Issues in Maternal-Fetal Medicine*. (2002).

Frug, Mary Joe. *Women and the Law*. Westbury: Foundation Press, 1992.

Gray White, Deborah. *Ar'n't I a Woman? Female Slaves in the Plantation South*. New York: Norton, 1985.

Haney Lopez, Ian F. *White by Law: The Legal Construction of Race*. New York: New York University Press, 1996.

Hartmann, Betsy. *Reproductive Rights or Wrongs? Global Politics of Population Control*. Cambridge: South End Press, 1995.

Higginbotham, A. Leon, Jr. *In the Matter of Color: Race and the American Legal Process: The Colonial Period*. New York: Oxford University Press, 1978.

Hill Collins, Patricia. "Black Feminist Thought." In *Theories of Race and Racism: A Reader*, edited by Les Black and John Solomons. New York: Routledge, 2000.

Jenkins Schwartz, Marie. *Birthing A Slave: Motherhood and Medicine in the Antebellum South*. Cambridge: Harvard University Press, 2006.

Leipziger, Amy. "Reproductive Choice." Accessed March 17, 2008, http:www.gwu.edu http://www.gwu.edu/~medusa/reproductive.html

Kevles, Daniel J. *In the Name of Eugenics: Genetics and the Uses of Human Heredity*. Cambridge: Harvard University Press, 1985.

Perrin, Liese M. "Resisting Reproduction: Reconsidering Slave Contraception in the Old South." *Journal of American Studies* 35 (2001): 255-274.

Roberts, Dorothy. *Killing the Black Body: Race, Reproduction, and the Meaning of Liberty*. New York: Pantheon Books, 1997.

Russell, Margaret M. "African American Women and Reproductive Rights." In *Historical and Multicultural Encyclopedia of Women's Reproductive Rights in the United States*, edited by Judith A. Baer. Westport: Greenwood Press, 2002.

Scales-Trent, Judy. "Black Women and the Constitution: Finding Our Place, Asserting Our Rights." In *Feminist Jurisprudence*, edited by Patricia Smith. New York: Oxford University Press, 1993.

Washington, Harriet A. *Medical Apartheid: The Dark History of Medical Experimenttion on Black Americans from Colonial Times to the Present*. New York: Harlem Moon Broadway Books, 2006.

Chapter 20

Ethnic Conflicts in the Middle East: A Comparative Analysis of Communal Violence within the Matrix of the Colonial Legacy, Globalization, and Global Stability

Magid Shihade

In mainstream social sciences and the field of ethnic/communal conflicts and resolution, scholars have often explained the phenomenon either in ahistorical historicization, that is, explaining these conflicts in terms of ancient hatred between groups, or through a Western centric a-geographical racism, which argues that Third World states and societies are unable to catch up with modernity. This chapter argues against the grain of such pervasive theories as we see now in the debates about Iraq for example, and suggests contextualizing modern day conflicts in their modern times contexts. Furthermore, the chapter argues that this phenomenon which is caused by the forming of modern nation states in the Third World is a result of European/Western colonialism whose racist basis has not only plagued the Third World during colonization, but Western societies as well. Finally, this racist colonial structure is not to be seen as a historic event that took place in the past and no longer at work, but rather as a structure that continues to shape modern day states and societies in both Third World-Global South as well as in the Global North. The chapter ends with a proposal to adopt a non-Western approach to deal with this phenomenon.

Introduction

The topic of race and human origins is indeed an ancient one. Ibn Khaldoun, the great fourteenth century Arab philosopher, argued that the obsession with origins and race was a fallacy and an illusion by those who tried to present themselves as superior to others. He argued that since the beginning of the human race, people mixed with each other and lived together in different civilizations, which made the purity of blood or race impossible. He also argued against those who pointed to skin color as an indication of race. By observing an ethnic group in North Africa, whose branch moved to live in Spain, and after many decades this looked much lighter than the original group's color that remained in North Africa. Observing this, Ibn Khaldoun argued that only geography and environment could explain skin color, not race.[1]

This progressive thought of the supposedly non-modern world of the Arabs, was overcome by the Western rhetoric of modernity that used race as a tool to justify its hegemony over the rest of the world. Western modernity's rhetoric argued that nation-states according to the Western model are the only solution for political organization that can solve the problems faced by people in the West and the rest, including the question of war and violence.

The West embarked on creating states in its own image around the world during the period of colonization. In most of these created states race, religion, and or ethnic identity, were part and parcel of the creation and shaping of the nation states. This nation state as political entity that is central in the global strategy of the West to run and organize international relation was essential and continues to be so to this day.

The nation state is the ultimate example of modernity's political organization and structure. Through the rhetoric and action of modernity enforced and replicated all around the world, which is based on exclusion as much on inclusion, on differentiation as much as on homogenization, based on ethnic, religious, class, and gender categories, which is the source of racism, conflict and violence. Nation state did not bring harmony and peace but rather manipulated identities, violence, used and utilized violence between groups and against groups in order to maintain territory, and maintain global structure of hegemony by the West.

Globalization is not an end of the nation-state; in fact, it depends on it. The nation state is needed to keep the image of independence rather than brute imperialism, and Empire. Nation states are so weak and are dependent in their relationship with the Empire's center. Globalization is a nice game adopted by the powerful to hide the brute reality of imperial global system of domination, and hegemony, and exploitation. It is a new face of an empire that works through a matrix of economic, political, and military control.

Analyzing the current state of affairs in the "Middle East," Robert Dreyfuss has shown in his book, *Devil's Game* how the religious/secular identities and the development of the region were the making of European colonialism, and how the region remained hostage to U.S., and Western powers to manipulate religious and ethnic identities of people loving there, and how this affected social, economic, and political disruption rather than development and peace in the region.[2]

Similarly, Mamdani argues that Rwanda's ethnic classification was constructed by European colonialism and adopted by native and colonized Africans—Tutsis and Hutus, who were both black skinned. It was colonial European constructed theories and practices in ideology, and practice of racism and race, ethnicity and manipulation of thereof in a country, which remained hostage to neocolonial relations with the West, and was a major factor in the genocide that took place there in 1994.[3]

Despite these and many other studies in support of such arguments, mainstream social sciences and the field of ethnic/communal conflicts and resolution continue to evade the culpability of the West in what has happened in the rest, and continue to happen today in the global structure of neocolonial domination and interventions. These western centric theories and scholars continue to dominate the field and thus warrant some discussion and reconstruction, which will be explored in the next part of this chapter, and will conclude by expanding on the structural framework that is discussed here briefly as an alternative paradigm that can help us explain and understand communal and ethnic conflicts, violence, and racism in the West and the rest.

Methodology

Warning against taking the hegemony of dominant discourses and paradigms at their face value, Ibn Khaldoun proposed that a sound scholarly inquiry should avoid these pitfalls by using three tools: first, logical deduction based on analytic reasoning; second, field work in the location of inquiry and empirical research; and third, engagement with other scholarly works and sources that deal with the subject, while utilizing logical deduction at and in every step of the work as will be illustrated throughout this chapter.[4]

The primary research is on sectarian violence among Arabs-Palestinians in Israel, drawing on Ian Lustick's work,[5] which analyzes the policies of the Israeli state towards its Arab Palestinian citizens. Lustick describes these as a general policy of control—in other words, the state's policy of divide and rule. The analysis of the Israeli state's mechanism of control of its Arab Palestinian citizens has been extended to include issues of internal sectarian violence. My own research develops Lustick's descriptive analysis of the relationship between the state of Israel and its Palestinian Arab citizens by examining the causes of that relationship and what structure creates it, not just describing what it is.

Initially, my research dealt with Druze-Christian violence among Arab Palestinians in Galilee and, specifically, a case study of an attack by Druze on the village of Kafr Yassif in 1981, in which Kafr Yassif was the target of an attack by Druze mob many of which were dressed in Israeli military uniforms and equipped with its weapons. It is based on fieldwork, interviews, and archival research in the local council and local press, thus supplementing the narrative of the state about these events, in addition to secondary sources on the relationship between the state of Israel and its Arab Palestinian citizens.[6]

The research demonstrates that the state has sanctioned and encouraged Druze attacks against Christians, and group violence among Arabs in general. This conclusion is supported by a pattern of repeated group violence among Arabs, which is not prevented by the state, despite the presence of Israeli security at many of these incidents. Furthermore, Israeli security forces have sometimes participated in the attacks along with the Druze perpetrators, and at times the state authorities have blocked intervention to prevent or stop the violence by third parties. The state has not punished the perpetrators, thus sanctioning such behavior and giving a green light for the perpetrators of violence to act with impunity.

During my fieldwork, I discovered interesting historical material about my village—Kafr Yassif—that sheds new light on the relationship between the state and the village, and also on the issue of Palestinian Arab mobilization inside Israel. In an article in the *Arab Studies Quarterly*, Ahmad Sa'di[7] documented a little known history of coalition building and politics of resistance by the residents of Kafr Yassif against discrimination and oppression by the state of Israel, and government retaliation against local activists including the funding of religious parties to undermine the coalitions in the village and under funding of the local council in Kafr Yassif. I also found that the village's history of resistance came to the attention of scholars and activists in Europe, including Simone de Beauvoir and Jean Paul Sartre, who visited Kafr Yassif after hearing about the non-violent strategy used by the village leaders and residents in 1952. In one incident, for example, they engaged in non-violent resistance to prevent the Israeli Army from entering the village to deport internal Palestinian refugees who had found sanctuary in Kafr Yassif after being displaced by Israeli Army in the 1948. This incident, as well as others, is barely known outside the Palestinian community in Israel but has important implications for they counter the Israeli state's narrative about the culture of violence among Arabs as the cause of conflicts within the community, which was also the official line regarding the events in Kafr Yassif in 1981.

It is argued in this chapter that it is important to consider the origin of the state as a settler colonial state and its relationship to the indigenous population in order to explain this phenomenon. As a settler colonial state, Israel has worked to divide the indigenous community in various ways, exploiting differences and at times creating new ones to undermine the mobilization by the Arab Palestinian community against the state's policies of discrimination and marginalization. In the case of the Druzes, an Islamic sect that, like the Shi'a, was not recognized by mainstream Sunni Islam, the Ottomans, or the British Colonial government in Palestine as a separate religion. The Israeli state, on the other hand, not only classified them as a separate religious group, but also an ethnic group for the first time in history. The state created for the Druze a separate educational system, drafted them into the Israeli army, and co-opted leaders of the Druze community in Israel effectively separating them from the rest of the Palestinian Arab community in Israel.[8]

Analyzing Communal Violence: Theoretical Debates and an Alternative Approach

A fundamental aspect of most theories of communal violence, or violence between ethnic or religious groups is that they examine this phenomenon from a perspective external to the concerned communities, generally from the perspective of the state that does not question its power. My own concern is not the stability and future of the state of Israel, or any other state for that matter, but rather the well being of the community itself—of the people, a project aimed at providing an indigenous perspective with the aim of decolonization, scholarly as well as political.

Although my research provides information on the communities under study, their history, and their inter-communal relationship, in order to examine the claims about the "violent nature of Arab society" and other societies to test the different theories in the field dealing with historical antipathy and the like, I believe the state is the most important issue/variable in studying issues of racism and sectarian violence. The state, as analytical unit and more so as the cause of this phenomenon, has been largely marginalized in the field of ethnic conflict and resolution. Instead, there has been too much focus on the communities involved; their mindset, their religion, culture, and identity. In a way, in my view, to provide the state with tools to control them, or maybe because it is really thought of as the right way to examine causes of sectarian conflicts. In my view, this is a problematic approach to say the least, and underlies parochial and patriarchal predispositions of such scholars, even though many of them might be not aware of it. To assume that cultures, identities of groups are the cause of conflict is in fact to argue that wherever we do not see conflicts/violence (at least on the surface) there are more tolerant and flexible identities. Thus, it is a problem of culture. Against that, it is argued that people are people regardless of where they live and what "group" they belong to. Rather, than looking at that, it is better to look at the state; its nature, origin, and development, structure and policies that create and bring about racism, inter-group conflicts and violence. It is true that people have their own agency, but people act freely to an extent and within the limits of the structure of the state that they live under. Most people around the world did not create these structures, but often, especially in the so called Third World, was imposed on them by the dynamic of colonial, and neo colonial dictates and resistance to it, which ended up producing the state system that we have today around the world.

Instead of being critical of state power and actions, scholars have often concerned themselves with the status quo and the preservation of the state power, and often provided the state with pretexts to act violently within and without its borders. This is a familiar concept in the U.S. since September 11, 2001 and the surge of homeland security studies, and before 9/11 and the theories of "just" wars, which the neocons took to the extreme. Many scholars have attached themselves to power, rather than being concerned with creating a better world, which can only happen through critical thinking and the critique of power and by exposing the hypocrisy and contradictions that lie at the heart of the racist structure of the nation state. This is for example is evident in the field of Middle Eastern studies, in which the role of the West and their allies in the region, mainly Israel, in promoting sectarian politics and terror as, for example, Robert Dreyfuss has shown in his work, remains marginalized.[9]

Similarly, scholars who write about Israel, instead of being objective and apply theories and test them on Israel, create specific theories to confuse readers and normalize an abnormal case. For example, they fail to expose that Israel does not fit the theory and category of a liberal democracy, and that it is better described as a settler colonial state, an apartheid system as Uri Davis has argued. Instead, they create new theories to obscure what is taking place in that country, and furnish it with all different "scientific" studies such as the theories of "ethnic democracy," "theo-democracy" and the like. These theories help Israel in its international public relations campaigns that present Israel as the "only democracy in the Middle East" rather than "the only settler-colonial and apartheid state in the region."

As will be shown later, the labeling/categorizing the Israeli state, or any other for that matter, as democratic or otherwise is secondary to the real meaning of these labels. This can be better understood from the stand point of the application of the policies of the state, and how groups under its control, as the receiving end of these policies, labels, and justifications, feel about them, and what concrete results the application of these policies on them means, and what structure these policies create that imposes itself on these people-citizens.

The larger question is how to study the causes of communal violence within the nation-state and how this phenomenon is linked to structures of colonialism, settler-colonialism, and nationalism and to Western notions of modernity informed by racism. It is not historically accurate to argue here that violence was absent in pre-modern times, and that religious groups coexisted in harmony with each other; in fact one can argue that violence is as old as humans. One needs only to look at ancient scriptures such as the Old Testament (the Torah) and find that violence was justified in the name of "Chosennes" and in the name of God; all religions and cultures justified violence. Thus violence is not new. The objective here is to counter the rhetoric of modernity that claims that organizing our lives according to "secular," modern, rational, democratic, and liberal principles and free market theories is the road to better harmony and peace. The argument is that the very origins of this discourse is racist in its universalizing outlook and breaching—the supposedly rational West found a political and economic formula for the rest of the world to follow, which continues to mask the imperialist and patriarchal hegemony of the world we live in. Western colonial and neo-colonial powers claimed their notions of democracy and nation-state building would create equality among peoples and nations and equality of individuals within them but instead they created marginalization and hegemony; they exploited existing differences and created new categories of social difference endowed with political and economic powers in the name of modernity and liberalism of the "civilized" world. Modern conflicts, including ethnic and communal violence, that were generated within the modern systems of the nation-state, colonialism, imperialism, and neocolonialism, ought be explained not through discourses of "ancient" cultural differences but situated in the context of the modern mechanisms and factors that caused them.

As Laura Nader argues,[10] the rhetoric of modernity in the West has been used to achieve two goals; first, to justify Western interventions abroad, and second, to safeguard the status quo at home, included gendered and racialized relations of power. Although Nader's argument focuses primarily on the ways patriarchy is maintained through a discourse about the comparative status of women within and outside the West, this argument can also be extended to other discourses about notions of democracy, political systems, "culture," free markets, liberalization, violence, and modernity. A thematic extension of Nader's argument helps to deconstruct the rhetoric of modernity, civilization, and culture. Mahmood Mamdani[11] cautions on such discourses because imperialist and colonialist powers have used them to justify their so-called humanitarian interventions and or civilizational missions, which in reality were selective and politically motivated, and inevitably devastating for colonized societies. Mamdani explores how the "politics of naming" underlies the selective classification of certain events as genocide, ethnic cleansing, war crimes especially in the United States, by the government and media alike. This analysis draws attention to the power of naming—that is, the power to make hegemonic the significance of some historical occurrences of violence while marginalizing and ignoring others. It also calls into question the powers behind the naming—for example, the ways the U.S. (government or media) forced a global acceptance of the designation of the Iraqi regime before 2003 as guilty of committing war crimes; the events in the Sudan as genocide; and the events in the former Yugoslavia as ethnic cleansing. Iraq cannot create a global consensus that U.S. atrocities committed in Iraq before and after 2003 are acts of terrorism, war crimes, or genocide, nor can the Palestinians force the international community to recognize Israeli actions before and after 1948 as terror, war crimes, ethnic cleansing, or apartheid.

In addition to the politics of naming that Mamdani emphasizes, there is the politics of theorizing that is crucial to the process of decolonization, in the process of exposing the linkage between knowledge and power and hegemony, concepts that were developed by Foucault, Gramsci, and Edward Said, and which Ibn Khaldoun warned us against. The U.S. academy serves largely the status quo instead of producing knowledge for social change and speaking truth to power, by largely evading the atrocities committed by certain states, regimes, and groups, sometimes providing them with pretexts and other times a cover up for their actions. Israel is rarely acknowledged to be a racist, colonial state and, in certain fields, neither is the U.S. Israeli and U.S. wars at home and abroad are justified by the governments of these states with different rationales and the academy has, to a large degree, either been silent, or even provided these states with theories of "security," "deterrence," or "just wars" that justify their wars and mask their crimes. In the field of ethnic and communal conflict and violence, there has been strong reluctance to theorize how racism, colonialism, and neocolonialism are at the heart of communal violence. Little attention is given to how these conflicts are the making of Western colonial and neocolonial practices that continue to impact dependent regions and groups around the world as long as theorizing largely evades this issue.

My research offers an intervention into the larger literature on communal and ethnic violence and the field of "conflict resolution," examining theoretical approaches in the field and various cases from around the world. This comparative theoretical approach goes beyond a critique of a single state or analyses that claim to speak on behalf of a specific people, providing a deeper understanding of communal violence. It is believed that a comparative approach is the best way to avoid the pitfalls of political loyalty, which Ibn Khaldoun also warned against, and which can contaminate scholarship and knowledge.

Before discussing my approach to the field of sectarian conflict and violence, it is imperative to discuss four dominant paradigms in the field of conflict resolution, and suggest an alternative approach to the understanding of this phenomenon using various examples of violent conflicts from around the world, including that of the current violence in Iraq.

The Four Dominant Paradigms

Peaceful Democracy

One of the widely accepted theories in the field of politics is the paradigm of peaceful democracy, which argues that democratic states are more peaceful than non-democratic states, internally and externally—for the groups living within the state as well as for other states. Despite the general acceptance of this paradigm, it does not hold ground when examined through research. The logical inference that Ibn Khaldoun advised contradicts commonly held assumptions. One of the commonly held assumptions is that certain nation-states are democracies, for example: the US, Great Britain, India, and Israel; these states are considered models of democracy to be emulated regionally and globally. These states have been no less, if not more, violence at home and abroad than many other states that are not considered democratic, such as Iran, Syria, North Korea, China, or Cuba, to name just a few.

Some scholars have challenged this paradigm and argued that democracy is not actually a guarantee to peace, in contradiction of the dominant paradigm.[12] John Keane suggests paying attention to the exporting of violence by democracies to their colonies; for example, by Britain, France, and the USA to Asia, Africa, and the Americas. Britain, like many states in the West, is not that peaceful internally and has had its share of communal and ethnic violence, as will be discussed later. In his *Violent Democracy*, Daniel Ross argues that the very origin of democracy lies in violence, as evident from studying the historical development of liberal democratic states.[13] Ross shows that democracies such as Australia and the USA were built on the slaughtering of the natives, which is part of the violent foundational history of these two countries. The paradigm of peaceful democracy needs to be reexamined or at least further qualified. Therefore, the cause of violence lies in factors other than the type of political system.

Another argument that is often used, especially in the case of Iraq, is that the authoritarian (non-democratic) regime of Saddam Hussein has managed to suppress ethnic and communal violence in Iraq. There are two reservations on this argument. First, is that it lacks any evidence. People are just supposed to believe that there were sectarian conflicts in Iraq prior to 2003, and that their suppression by the regime made us blind to their existence. Second, this argument, which presumes, or wants us to believe, that the American occupation regime in Iraq is somehow democratic, and that is why there are sectarian violence in Iraq among Shi'a and Sunni Iraqis today. It is important to mention that the occupation of Iraq and its colonization is the ultimate authoritarianism that can exist in that country, which robs the Iraqis of a fundamental right (self determination), which is central to democracy and self government. It is worth adding that Balkanization, rape, mass murder, lynching, Fallujah, Abu-Ghraib, and death squads are the tools and realities of U.S. occupation of Iraq, which is the farthest that Iraqis had from democracy. The cause for sectarian violence in Iraq is largely because of U.S. occupation (as will be discussed later in the chapter).

Weak States

A second major paradigm in the field of ethnic and communal violence is that of "weak states." For example, David Laitin and James Fearon have argued in much of their work that the defining factor in keeping internal peace is the strength of the state under consideration, rather than the type or form of the political system. They argue that the weakness of particular states is the cause for ethnic and communal violence.[14] While this theory has much merit, it is still limited in content and scope for it does not shed light on ethnic and communal violence in "strong" states, such as Israel. Even more importantly, this approach explains only the surface, and not the core, of the problem of communal violence.

For example, it is plausible to argue that the weakness of the state, especially the security branch, has been partly responsible for the ethnic, communal, and sectarian violence among Iraqis since 2003. But such an explanation, if it stops there, skims just the surface of the issue, failing to address why the state became weak in the first place, when it became weak, and who is the state under the present circumstances. It is now common knowledge that the U.S. has since its invasion of Iraq destroyed the pre-2003 state apparatus, armed the militias, and empowered certain Iraqi groups (e.g. Kurdish and Shi'a militias) with the aim of undermining other groups (Sunnis and Ba'thists). This process has created many state-like groups in Iraq who take the law in their hands when they wish to, without any serious attempt by the U.S. to change that reality. How, then, could the notion of the weak state explain the situation in Iraq and what can even be considered the state at such a moment, when the sovereignty of Iraq and its people has been hijacked by the U.S. and its military? My argument here is that the current ethnic and communal violence in Iraq cannot be explained without situating it in the context of the U.S. occupation and colonization of the country.

Theories of weak states are generally applied to examples of states in the global South as if this phenomenon prevails only in the South and states in the North are orderly and peaceful. Such approaches ignore historic conflicts in the USA, France, Britain, Spain, Ireland, Australia, and many other states in the North that have witnessed, and still witness, violence against ethnic and religious groups, particularly minorities, for a very long time. Although these minority groups are often used as enablers of their nation-building project—

economically, politically, and in other ways—they are always the targets of violence when the national project fails or seems, to some, to be failing or is threatened.

Even the so-called weak states are not truly impartial in their responses to ethnic and communal violence. One example of this is the current conflict that has been brewing in the Darfur region of the Sudan. Even though the state has been described as weak by many scholars, it has not been neutral in the violence in Darfur, at times directly taking part in the killings, and at others supplying support or allowing one party to attack another in order to achieve the Sudanese government's primary goal of controlling the region and its resources. Furthermore, the weakness of the Sudanese state should be assessed in relation to the external, regional and global, powers that are involved and their relative strength and role in affecting the unfolding conflict in Darfur. To explain the situation in the Sudan chiefly in terms of the weakness or strength of the state is to ignore the many external factors affecting the conflict there.[15] A situation such as this cannot be explained in isolation, as is also the case for conflicts in Iraq, Lebanon, or other countries around the world that are highly dependent in the world system. Even though many of these states are no longer subject to direct colonial control by Western powers, indirect control and influence operates economically and politically. The hegemony of global and regional powers cannot to be freed from responsibility for the outbreaks of violence in the so-called "weak" states.

Manipulative Leaders

A third common paradigm in the field is theories that focus on the manipulation of leaders, for example, in Paul Brass' work on communal violence in India.[16] Brass argues that a primary reason for violence is the role of community leaders who utilize violence in order to gain greater support from their communities, especially during election campaigns; this was a factor in the rise to power of the rightwing, Hindu nationalist Bharatiya Janata Party (BJP) in India. This theory has a kernel of truth for it is evident that leaders of ethnic and religious groups could benefit from ethnic and communal violence that bolsters communal identities and compels members of these communities to turn to leaders for protection, especially when they believe that the state is unwilling or unable, to protect them in times of internal violence. However, this same perspective on the belief in the state's ineffectiveness is also the weak point in this explanation. The question ought to be why the state is unwilling or unable to intervene in violent conflicts, punish harshly those who commit such acts, and hold officials accountable for such incidents, when the state is ultimately responsible for the safety of the public. Thus the state is let off the hook according to such explanations, but the role of the state is the primary analytical tool in studying communal violence.

Brass' theory fails to account for the lack of violence in many regions and localities in India where mixed religious communities lived for years in close proximity without experiencing violence, even during election campaigns. Thus, the particular case or two that Brass uses from India seem to be the exception, not the rule, and so there must be other reasons more primary than the role of community leaders. Even more problematic is the implication that ordinary people who participate in these incidents are passive subjects manipulated by their leaders and lacking any agency of their own.

If the manipulation of ethnic or religious violence is a strategy by political leaders to increase their standings in the polls, why would that strategy not be used, to varying degrees in other countries, such as the United States or Canada, given that violent conflicts do occur in these countries at various moments? Or is this communalization of politics and violence just an Indian phenomenon? It is very apparent that political parties in various Western states do attract particular religious constituencies. For example, the Republican Party in the U.S. tends to draw its supporters heavily from the Christian right and it is well known that the Conservative party in Canada draws its political power mainly from Catholics, especially in the Quebec region. This is also true for many parties in Israel and Europe that have religious bases or followings, but it seems that the manipulation of leaders for vote banks is not related to violent conflicts in discussions of these other cases. Is this strategy of communalizing politics, then, a cultural explanation? In my view, the theory of manipulative leaders cannot be used in many other cases from around the world because it fails to offer a sufficiently complex account of communal violence and ignores the role of the state, which is after all the only legitimate source of power and perpetrator of violence.

Historical Antipathies

The fourth and most commonly used explanation in the field is the "historical antipathy" paradigm, which is offered by scholars such as Donald Horowitz, who argues that the primary cause of ethnic and communal violence is historical antipathy—economic and/or political.[17] Liberal and conservative scholars alike often use this paradigm to explain violent conflicts in the Middle East, thus it is a significant approach to consider in relation to the cases I use in this chapter. Historical antipathy might be a factor that comes into play after a conflict begins to unfold, this, however, is not the chief cause of conflict and violence and should not be used as a totalizing, ahistorical framework. Thus, when mainstream analysts suggest that the sectarian violence in Iraq is due to deeply ingrained antipathies, real or imagined, between Muslim sects that stretch back in time to the seventh century, they forget that if this were the case, there should have been Shi'a-Sunni violence in Iraq based on religious beliefs for hundreds of years. But there is no evidence for this argument. It is important to historicize conflicts in the region rather than resorting to Orientalist explanations of ancient hatreds that evade analysis of specific temporal and political contexts and frame the problem in primordial views of culture and essentialist constructions of history. The current seemingly "religious" conflict simmering in Iraq is, in fact, is a political conflict between various segments of Iraqi society (Shi'a, Sunni, and Kurdish) that is born of the U.S. occupation and colonization of Iraq. As history of colonialism shows, the main principle of colonizing projects is to divide—not unite—and rule, and divide and quit when rule becomes too costly.

A simple question that can be easily answered and help shed light on the internal violence in Iraq is: who armed the Iraqi religious factions currently fighting one another? Who sanctioned the political power of their leaders and damaged not only the economic, but also the social and political, fabric of Iraq? It would be more accurate to conclude that the violence in Iraq is waged mainly by an insurgency that is fighting U.S. occupation and colonization of Iraq and their local enablers, who tend to be heavily from among the Shi'a. Thus, the focus on historical antipathy seems to treat historical actors as permanently static subjects that do not change and evolve; according to which, a Shi'a-Sunni conflict that took place in the seventh century remains the primary explanatory paradigm for Shi'a-Sunni relations in the twenty-first century. Such explanations tend to frame historical events through an essentialist and primordialist cultural lens, often providing ahistorical explanations. As Mamdani has rightly argued, such culturalist explanations are superficial, simplistic, and tend to obscure political and historical contexts.[18] Furthermore, such totalizing theories lump various groups of people together in certain categories without seeing through the differences in time, space, and context to the diversity within such categories, homogenizing Muslims, Druzes, Christians, Jews, and Hindus.

This perspective emphasizing ancient hatred and the culture of violence is exposed in a recent chapter in the U.S. media[19] about a massacre in Iraq of Shi'a tribes in southern Iraq in January 2007. These Shi'a tribes are actually opposed to the Shi'a led government in Baghdad and have been building coalitions with Sunni Iraqis, who have been the target of Shi'a (Al-Badr and Al-Mahdi militias) militias who dominate the Iraqi army and police under U.S. occupation. When these militias were unable to suppress these Shi'a tribes, despite assassinating many of their members and leaders, they engaged in a direct, full-fledged confrontation with them near the city of Najaf. They were unable to defeat the tribes, so the Iraqi army and militias called on the U.S. and British forces that came to their aid and bombed the two tribes, killing and injuring hundreds of their members. The U.S. media, reporting the official line of the U.S. and Iraqi governments (that the battle was against a fanatic religious group) covered up this massacre. The media has echoed the U.S. government's focus on Shi'a-Sunni tensions, obscuring the reality of the situation in Iraq and presenting the violence in Iraq as a conflict between two groups with ancient antagonism.

An Alternative Approach

A Structural Approach as an Alternative Paradigm

Having discussed a few dominant paradigms in the field, attention will be focused on an alternative paradigm, called the structural paradigm. The structural paradigm helps explain communal violence by contextualizing its temporal, political, and materialist dimensions and addresses the weaknesses and limitations of the approaches discussed previously. This framework contextualizes the inter-ethnic/inter-communal relations in the context of the policy of the nation-state towards its minority groups—native or non- native— through an analysis of the nature of the state and its historical development, taking into account which groups were included and excluded from the national project at its origin. This structural framework helps focus on the attitude of state's authorities towards those who are not included within the nation-building agenda. This paradigm is built on the work of scholars who discuss cases from around the world and thus provide a basis for my argument.

Aijaz Ahmad, in his work on India and Muslim-Hindu violence, argues that this communal violence is a consequence of the partition of India into two states—Pakistan and India--in 1947 by Britain at the end of its colonial rule of the subcontinent.[20] Ahmad suggests that partitioning India, and creating Pakistan as a state for Muslims by the British, placed the Muslims who remained in India in an ambiguous position. The partition implied that the more suitable national home for Muslims in post-1947 India was Pakistan, since the basic rationale for its creation was to "create a safe and secure place for Muslims." This logic suggested that Muslims did not completely belong in independent India, and their marginalization after 1947 was a corollary of the partition, even if Indian leaders and governments aimed at their integration. The growth of violence against Muslims by Hindu nationalists after 1947, and especially since the 1980s, is a natural consequence of the politics of communal partition imposed on the Indian subcontinent by Britain and of neo-liberal globalization or neo-colonialism.

Hindu-Muslim violence in India is not an issue that can be simply attributed to the manipulation of some leaders, as Brass argues, even though leaders could certainly foster communal divisions to some extent. Rather, it is an issue that goes to the heart of the British colonial project in India that created two states— one for Muslims and one implicitly, if not explicitly, for Hindus. The manipulation of Hindus by right-wing leaders in India was easier under British colonial rule and, even more so, after 1947 where Muslims became seen as illegitimate group who were often associated with an enemy state, Pakistan. The violence against Sikhs in India, as well as Christians, can also be better understood as a result of the origin of the post-colonial state and the partition, a legacy of the politics of confessions long practiced by British colonizers in India. As a result of these colonial policies, the Muslim-Hindu divide was widened, emphasized, and made official, for example, through the history textbooks produced for Indians by the British colonial government, according to which all ills in India were attributed to the Muslim invasion and influence since the eleventh and twelve centuries.[21]

Many works on the subject of communal relations in India and other decolonized states in one way or the other blame the national leadership for failing to overcome the communal divide and the communal nature of the state created by colonial regimes. While some scholars acknowledge the role of colonialism's legacy, they overlook the fact that communal and ethnic classifications were officially established as the framework for belonging in the postcolonial nation the moment that colonized states were partitioned or created based on politicized communal and ethnic lines. There is hardly any way out of this communalized framework other than turning back the clock of history to the time before colonization invented, or at least politicized, communal and ethnic boundaries. Colonial rulers invested these categories with varying political and economic power, sowing the seed for the communal ills that later plagued these nation-states. Violence that took place under such circumstances takes life of its own. Thus, "modernization" rather than creating a harmonious developed and unified political entities that can govern themselves and live in peace with themselves as well as with other states, created polities according to communal lines that made these entities less peaceful within and without as the history of India and Pakistan show.

After decolonization, nation-states remained hostage to global powers and dependent on them economically, politically, and for security. The theory of dependency is often discussed in terms of economic and political development in Latin America, but it also applies to other regions of the global South that were never left alone, not just marginalized, by the great powers, who often intervened politically and economically in their affairs, and still do for weaker, dependent states. Colonialism and neo-colonialism created patterns of governance in Africa and Asia designed to either divide and rule directly (colonialism), or "divide and quit," keeping formerly colonized states weak, unstable, and dependent (neo-colonialism). Setting aside the issue of the intentionality of these colonial policies, they undoubtedly created conditions of instability and divisiveness in these nation-states that are difficult to overcome.

While many scholars blame postcolonial states and their leadership for not being able to resolve the messy conflicts whose structures were put in place during the colonial period, other scholars assign blame both to the colonial legacy and the postcolonial national leadership. For example, in *When Victims Become Killers*, Mamdani is critical of the colonial regime as well as the Rwandan state and its leadership after decolonization for being unable to break out of the categories created by European colonization. Furthermore, he argues that post-colonial Rwanda used the same invented ethnic categories, which were invested with political and economic powers leading to the Tutsi-Hutu confrontation and the bloodshed in Rwanda. Mamdani suggests that there is a need to rethink the frameworks created by colonialism, which have caused ethnic and communal violence in Rwanda and other postcolonial states. However, asking postcolonial nations to rethink categories that are a major source of their internal conflicts is easier said than done. In my view, it is not so easy to rethink these categories, and even harder to undo structures have been in place for decades and, in some cases, for centuries.

It is assumed in many postcolonial analyses that colonialism has ended, and neo-colonial interventions are absent. Rather, as Gerard Prunier[22] argues, even if European colonialism has officially ended in the case of Rwanda as elsewhere in Africa, European states such as France, and also the U.S., remain deeply involved in these postcolonial states. These Western states have in many ways helped shape conflicts in Rwanda and elsewhere in Africa and Latin America, often through proxy arm suppliers such as Israel. Similarly, Mamdani[23] argues in a later chapter that the Rwandan genocide was partly the making of the U.S. since it supported the Rwanda Patriotic Front (PRF), a dominantly Tutsi political group, and its military arm; instead of being pressured for compromise, they were encouraged to pursue a victory, and thus acted with impunity in the massacre that ensued. It needs to be kept in mind that there is a pattern of U.S. and other Western states selectively calling for UN and non-UN involvement and non-involvement at different times, such as the push for intervention in Yugoslavia in the shape of NATO, and for UN non-involvement in the case of the U.S.-British invasion of Iraq. Thus, the role of the postcolonial state and its leadership is only part of the story of communal violence, and in my view, less significant than that of the structures created by colonial and neo-colonial regimes. These formerly colonized states ought to be analyzed and considered not as post-colonial states, but as still colonized in one form or another, and hence the burden is on those states that hold power in the international system. This structure of communal boundaries is informed by racist notions of modernity transplanted by Western powers through colonialism around the world, creating states in their own image—that is tribal, ethnic, and religious, despite the rhetoric of secularism and modernity. This is not only a one-way structure that impacts only the colonized or ex-colonized societies, but also a two-way structure that plagues the colonial states and societies themselves to this day.

Racism against Arabs and Muslims in the U.S. after 9/11 should be situated within the structures that were created in the U.S. (in its own national formation and understood in this context). Steven Salaita[24] argues that racism against Arabs and Muslims in post-9/11 USA needs to be understood not simply as a reaction to the events of 9/11 but as a reflection of the nature of the U.S. state, its origins and historic development. Salaita suggests that the post-9/11 violence and racism against Arabs and Muslims in the U.S. and abroad after 9/11 has to be contextualized in the structural racism that is embedded in the origins of the U.S. settler colonial state. The state was built on the cleansing of the Native Americans and conquest of their territories, on slavery, and on colonialist expansion and imperialist interventions around the world. In this analysis, violence and racism against Arabs and Muslims in the USA is a part of a pattern that has been present in the USA since its inception, and according to which different groups throughout U.S. history experienced a similar fate of racialization and subordination.

Colonialist processes of racialization and subordination are a consequence of the creation of the European nation-state and its historic development through the colonial period and the racist thought underlying this adventure that was disseminated around the world. This racist outlook sees the world through politicized identities based on race, ethnicity, or religion. This framework has created economic and political structures of exclusion, domination and marginalization of groups who are seen as not belonging to the colonizing as well as the colonized states, which leads to conflict and possible violence between those included and excluded as well as among them. This phenomenon has not only plagued the colonized but the colonizer as well, since racism is dynamic and affects the outside and the inside of the colonial state.

According to Caroline Elkins and Susan Pedersen,[25] settler colonialism, and in my view colonialism in general, is not simply an event contained within the past but rather as a structure with long-lasting ramifications on both colonizer and colonized, that are still present on both sides of the colonial equation. In colonial and settler colonial structures, the marginalization of the colonized is central and is sought in every aspect of the lives of those colonized: economic, political, and social. Through the principle of divide and rule, as well as divide and quit, as often happened when direct colonization was no longer possible, this marginalization has been historically achieved. Internal politicized divisions along ethnic and or religious lines remained intact, even after colonization officially ended, and became the hallmark of the post-colonial state. The ramifications of colonialism are at the heart of all ethnic and religious conflicts and violence in postcolonial nation-states. Racism as it informed Western adventure abroad plagues the West as well and manifests itself in violence against minorities, immigrants, and violence abroad.

Karen Armstrong rightly argues that the remarks made in 2006 by the British ex-foreign minister, Jack Straw, condemning the hijab used by Muslim women in the UK is not an exception, but rather the rule of British communalism, even if communal politics is hardly ever named as such for Western "liberal democracies."[26] She observed that when Catholic nuns started appearing in Britain wearing head covers they were also attacked and were portrayed as a threatening fifth column connected to despotic foreign regimes— not loyal British, not belonging. Thus, the violence that took place in Britain against South Asians in the 1980s, or against Turks in Germany in the 1990s, or in France against North Africans and Africans in general, is at root a reflection of the state's nature and historical policies of inclusion and exclusion. This is one of the main problems of the nation-state, colonizing and colonized alike, and it is at the heart of communal and ethnic conflicts and violence.

This chapter has argued that the problem of communal violence and racism is fundamentally a structural problem. This analytic approach is needed in the field of ethnic conflict in order to better understand the phenomenon and move away from blaming the victims of historical structures of colonialism and, by extension, postcolonial nationalism, as well as neocolonial global structures.

Many scholars agree that the modern nation-state is the cause for most ethnic and communal conflicts since there is hardly any state that is uniform in either category—race or religion—and thus by nature it must exclude while it includes. Most scholars agree also that the nation-state is a modern European phenomenon created and replicated by European colonialism and imperialism around the globe. Yet, there is less theoretical emphasis on the fact that the root of ethnic and communal conflicts and violence is in the structures linked to European and Western colonialism and imperialism, which has created and still creates the same problem over and over again, as we now see in Iraq. Behind this universalizing mechanism of political systems around the world lies at the heart a racist mindset that sees itself as a model that other need to follow.

Furthermore, European and Western colonialism is still continuing in many different forms in Africa, Asia and the Americas.

The suggestion here is to stop ignoring the elephant in the room—the colonial structures that are informed by racism and that had and still have a two-way effect, on the colonized as well as the colonizer. A focus on the role of racism in communal conflicts and its modern colonial structure is central to a discussion about how to undo its effects, if that is possible. This is much needed in order to analyze and try to find a solution to the phenomenon of communal violence. At the same time, we need to keep in mind that neo-colonial interventions disguised under slogans of "reform," open markets, "liberalization," "democratization," "war on terror," and globalization are all structures that reinforce colonial mechanism of subjugation, control, marginalization, and hegemony affecting dependent states in the global economic and political system.

As this chapter shows, the state, regardless of whether weak or strong, colonial, settler colonial or post-colonial ought to be the center of analysis on the question of ethnic and communal conflict and violence. How the state was created, who excluded and who included, who was empowered and who was marginalized, come to determine and shape the relationship between the different religious and ethnic groups in that state. The historical development of the state also helps shape these relationships.

When dealing with the question of the state, that is the nation state, and the problems that come as a result of its creation, it is crucial to keep in mind that it is a modern construct that came as a result of the theories of nationalism and racism emanating from Europe, and that was transplanted all around the world through European colonialism, which created political entities around the globe in their own image, that is religious, ethnic, and tribal, despite the rhetoric of secularism, cosmopolitanism, and universalism that is often veils the origin and reality of modernity shaped by European powers mainly and the west in general. Iraq is a living example on that. Created in its current borders by British colonialism, challenged since then by Western imperialism, colonized again by the U.S., divided and controlled through the politics of ethnicity and sectarianism, its development is seen through a security lens that focuses on military and police institutions' building, the violence that has been taking place there as a result, which will have a life on its own for very long even after decolonization, Iraq, even if liberated will be defined by sectarianism, ethnicity politics, and militarism. This will be further complicated by the politics of neocolonial interventions in that country by the U.S and others. No one should wonder what the plague of internal relations in that country are and will be for long time to come.

Conclusion

This question is not an event in the past, but a structure that is hard to undo, more so in places where colonialism is still directly involved, but in general as well all around the world that is under a global structure of neo-colonialism and imperialism, which is often veiled under the rhetoric of spreading democracy, free market, human rights, structural adjustment, and globalization, and which are all tools in the hand of powerful states and empires such as the United States and other European countries, who, despite resistance here and there, attempt to utilize these tools to dominate global political, military, and economic organizations, such as the United Nations, World Bank, and the International Monetary Fund (IMF), and intervene in the lives of billions of peoples around the world. Until colonialism, neo colonialism, and imperialism are defeated there is no way to get out of this global problem of ethnic and communal violence. Maybe then, when that time comes, we can try to rethink the racist origins of the nation state and possibly undo them through a new form of political entities that can be based on equality for all regardless of any ethnic or religious differences. This is only possible when such future political entity also enjoys global equality and respect regardless of economic and military power. Perhaps, as the Venezuelan president Hugo Chaves suggested, global democracy is possible to reach when the undemocratic global structure embodied in the UN and other global organizations is reformed to reflect democracy in which equality is at the core of any political organizing.

Until then, those states who assume power in this global structure, and reap the benefits that come from that role, ought to be the ones responsible for global security, and global justice, and they are to blame and be held responsible for what is taking place and the suffering that is evident in countries around the world that is plagued by ethnic and communal violence. This is true for countries in the Middle East such as Iraq, Lebanon, and Palestine, but also elsewhere around the world.

It is worth bringing here the issue of traditional Arab conflict resolution method-Sulha,[27] which these big powers—colonial, ex-colonial, and neo colonial alike must adhere to if we want to end this problem-sectarianism. According to this method, to bring about a resolution to a conflict, two essential conditions are needed. First is the admitting of wrong doing by the aggressor party with an open, clear-cut, public apology for the wrongdoing, which serves to bring closure to the offended party. Second is that those who committed the offense and caused harm to others must pay reparation for their wrongdoing. In this case, Britain, France, the U.S., for example, will be forced to pay reparation for many countries and societies around the world. Making those states apologize publicly and pay reparations to people in Africa, Asia, and the Americas can help appease those states and groups that were wronged by global powers, who will be more hesitant to keep doing the same thing to different groups, societies around the world if they are held responsible and made to pay for their misdeeds. Those states that continue to transgress against others and cause so much harm will continue to do so if they feel they can act with impunity. This is evident if one takes the U.S. as an example that has been going to wars against others since its inception as a nation state. Similarly, France that was the cause of communal-sectarian politics in Lebanon, and because it never apologize for what it did there since eighteenth century, and because it never paid reparation for Lebanon, feels that it can act with impunity and keep interfering in internal Lebanese politics.

Only then such states will realize that colonization, promoting sectarian politics around the world, and neocolonialism must have consequences—financial and political—which might deter these states in check rather than keep acting with impunity. Perhaps then, there will occur a better chance to proceed with a resolution and future where sectarianism will be less deadly, more contained, and presumably eliminated.

Notes

1. Ibn Khaldoun, *The Muqaddimah: An Introduction to History*, translated and introduced by Franz Rosenthal, abridged, ed., N.J. Dawood, with a new introduction by Bruce B. Lawrence, Bollingen Series (New York and Oxford: Princeton University Press, 2005).
2. Robert Dreyfuss, *Devil's Game: How the United States Helped Unleash Fundamentalist Islam* (New York: Owl Books, 2005).
3. Mahmood Mamdani, *When Victims Become Killers: Colonialism, Nativism, and the Genocide in Rwanda* (Princeton, NJ: Princeton University Press).
4. Ibn Khaldoun, 2005.
5. Ian Lustick, *Arabs in the Jewish State: A Study in the Control of a National Minority* (Austin: University of Texas Press, 1980).
6. For details of the incident see, Magid Shihade, *"Internal Violence: State's Role and Society's Reponses,"* Arab Studies Quarterly (ASQ)Volume 27, Number 4, Fall 2005, 31-43.
7. Ahmad H. Sa'di, "Control and Resistance at Local-Level Institutions: A Study of Kafr Yassif's Local Council Under the Military Government," *Arab Studies Quarterly* (ASQ) 23.3 (Summer 2001).
8. For more information on the Druzes in Israel see: Robert B. Betts, *The Druze* (New Haven, CT: Yale University Press, 1988), also Kais Firro, *The History of the Druzes* (Leiden, The Netherlands: E. J. Brill, 1992), and Laila Parson, *The Druze Between Palestine and Israel 1947-1949* (London: Macmillan Press, 2000).
9. Robert Dreyfuss, Devil's Game: How the United States helped unleash Fundamentalist Islam (New York: Owl Books, 2005).
10. Laura Nader, "Orientalism, Occidentalism and the Control of Women," *Cultural Dynamics*, 1989, Issue 2; 323.
11. Mahmood Mamdani, "The Politics of Naming: Genocide, Civil War, Insurgency," *London Review of Books*, Vol. 29, No. 5, 8 March 2007.
12. John Keane, *Violence and Democracy* (Cambridge, UK: Cambridge University Press, 2004).
13. Daniel Ross, *Violent Democracy* (Cambridge, UK: Cambridge University Press, 2004).
14. Among many of their work see a short chapter in: Laitin, D and James Fearon, "End of Cold War is not the Cause (Civil War)," *USA Today* (Magazine), 131.2691 (Dec. 2002): 6(1).
15. A better explanation of it is happening in the Sudan can be found in Mahmood Mamdani's article, "The Politics of Naming," *London Review of Books*, Vol. 29, No 5, 8 March 2007.
16. Paul Brass, *The Production of Hindu-Muslim Violence in Contemporary India* (Seattle, WA: University of Washington Press, 2003).

17. Donald L. Horowitz, *Ethnic Groups in Conflict.* (Berkeley, CA: Berkeley University Press, 1985), and *The Deadly Ethnic Riot*, (Berkeley: University of California Press, 2001).

18. Mahmood Mamdani, *Good Muslim, Bad Muslim: America, The Cold War, and the Roots of Terror* (New York: Pantheon Books, 2004).

19. Conn Hallinan, "Anatomy of Massacre," *The Berkeley Daily Planet*, Weekend Edition, February 16-19, 2007, 8.

20. Aijaz Ahmad, *Lineages of the Present: Ideology and Politics in Contemporary South Asia* (London and New York: Verso, 2000).

21. For more on the policies British colonial rule in India see, Bernard S. Cohn, in *"The Command of Language and the Language of Command,"* in *Subaltern Studies IV: Writing on South Asian History and Society*, ed., Ranajit Guha (New Delhi: Oxford University Press, 1994).

22. Gerard Prunier, *The Rwanda Crisis: History of a Genocide* (New York: Columbia University Press, 1997).

23. Mahmood Mamdani, "The Politics of Naming."

24. Steven Salaita, *Anti-Arab Racism in the USA: Where it Comes from and What it Means for Politics Today* (London: Pluto Press, 2006).

25. Caroline Elkins and Susan Pedersen, eds., Settler *Colonialism in the Twentieth Century: Projects, Practices, and Legacies* (New York and London: Routledge, 2005).

26. Talk at Washington, D.C. National Press Club broadcasted on C-SPAN2-BookTV, November 20, 2006.

27. For more information about this method of conflict resolution, see Elias J. Jabbour, *Sulha: Palestinian Traditional Peacemaking Process* (Montreat, NC: House of Hope Publications, 1996).

References

Aijaz Ahmad. *Lineages of the Present: Ideology and Politics in Contemporary South Asia.* London and New York: Verso, 2000.

Dreyfuss, Robert. *Devil's Game: How the United States Helped Unleash Fundamentalist Islam.* New York: Owl Books, 2005.

Elkins, Caroline, and Susan Pedersen, eds., *Settler Colonialism in the Twentieth Century: Projects, Practices, and Legacies.* New York and London: Routledge, 2005.

IKhaldoun, Ibn. *The Muqaddimah: An Introduction to History*, translated and introduced by Franz Rosenthal, abridged and edited by N.J. Dawood, with a new introduction by Bruce B. Lawrence, Bollingen Series. New York: Princeton University Press, 2005.

Keane, John. *Violence and Democracy.* Cambridge, UK: Cambridge University Press, 2004.

Lustick, Ian. *Arabs in the Jewish State: A Study in the Control of a National Minority.* Austin: University of Texas Press, 1980.

Mamdani, Mahmood. *When Victims Become Killers: Colonialism, Nativism, and the Genocide in Rwanda.* Princeton, NJ: Princeton University Press, 2002.

Sa'di, Ahmad H. "Control and Resistance at Local-Level Institutions: A Study of Kafr Yassif's Local Council Under the Military Government," *Arab Studies Quarterly* (ASQ) 23.3 (Summer 2001).

Salaita, Steven, *Anti-Arab Racism in the USA: Where it Comes from and What it Means for Politics Today.* London: Pluto Press, 2006.

Shihade, Magid, "Internal Violence: State's Role and Society's Reponses," *Arab Studies Quarterly* (ASQ) vol. 27, no. 4, Fall 2005, 31-43.

Chapter 21

Ethnic Identity in China:
The Politics of Cultural Difference

Dru C. Gladney

Foreigners and the Chinese themselves typically picture China's population as a vast monolithic Han majority with a sprinkling of exotic minorities living along the country's borders. This understates China's tremendous cultural, geographic, and linguistic diversity—in particular the important cultural differences within the Han population. This ignores the fact that China is officially a multi-national country with 56 recognized "nationalities." China argues that its minorities are involved in local and national governance, proving that China has a socialist system that represents the many peoples of the People's Republic in a democratic system. More importantly, recent events suggest that China may well be increasingly insecure regarding not only these nationalities, but also its own national integration. The World Trade Center and Pentagon attacks of September 11, 2001 actually brought China and the United States closer together in an anti-terrorism campaign that has made the case of Uyghur separatism in China much more prominent in the Western press.

Introduction

China is now seeing a resurgence of local nationality and culture, most notably among southerners such as the Cantonese and Hakka, who are now classified as Han. These differences may increase under threats from ethnic separatism, economic pressures such as inflation, the growing gap between rich and poor areas, and the migration of millions of people from poorer provinces to those with jobs. Chinese society is also under pressure from the officially recognized minorities such as Uyghurs and Tibetans. For centuries, China has held together a vast multicultural and multiethnic nation despite alternating periods of political centralization and fragmentation. But cultural and linguistic cleavages could worsen in a China weakened by internal strife, inflation, uneven growth, or a struggle over future political succession. The National Day celebrations in October 1999, celebrating fifty years of the Communist Party in China, underscored the importance of China's many ethnic peoples in its national resurgence. Recent crackdowns on anti-separatism and anti-terrorism underscore China's increasing concern regarding national security and the integrity of its border areas.

Just as the legitimacy of the Communist Chinese government has always rested on the construction of Han majority and of selected minority nationalities out of Sun Yat-sen's shifting "tray of sand," the prospects for and implications of democratization in China are closely tied to the ongoing constitution of collective identities. In China's increasingly assertive cultural diversity—intensely sharpened by economic liberalization—lies a new and perhaps precarious pluralism. It is too early to claim that this tolerance of diversity within authoritarian political unity carries the seeds of democracy. Nevertheless, it does reflect a heightened search for party-state legitimacy in the face of the increasing social, economic, and cultural strains brought on by globalization.

The Soviet Union as China's Prologue

At the beginning of the last decade, not a single observer of international politics predicted that the former Soviet Union would now be fragmented into a mélange of strident new nations and restive ethnic minorities. When Russian troops marched on Chechnya in hopes of keeping what remains of its former empire together, few analysts drew parallels to China's attempts to reign in its restive Muslim Uyghur minority. Considering worldwide Muslim support for the liberation struggles of Muslims in Bosnia and Kosovo, and with growing support among world—notably Asian—Muslims for the Palestinian "anti-colonial" struggle against Israel, it is not surprising to find growing Muslim concern regarding the "plight" of China's Muslims.[1]

China is thought to be different because it is not shaken by ethnic or national disintegration.[2] Cultural commonality and a monolithic civilization are supposed to hold China together. While ethnic nationalism has generally been absent from Western reporting and perspectives on China, the peoples of the People's Republic have often demonstrated otherwise. Continuing separatist activities and ethnic unrest have punctuated China's border areas since a major Muslim uprising in February 1996, which led to bombings in Beijing, and frequent eruptions on its periphery.[3] Quick and violent responses to thwart localized protests, with twenty seven "splittists" reportedly killed in an uprising in December 1999 outside of Khotan in southern Xinjiang Uyghur Autonomous Region, indicates rising Chinese concern over the influence of separatist sentiment spilling over from the newly independent Central Asia nations into China's Muslim areas. The more than 20 million Turkic Uyghurs, Kyrgyz, Kazakhs and other Muslims who live in these areas are a visible and vocal reminder that China is linked to Eurasia. For Uyghur nationalists today, the direct lineal descent from the Uyghur Kingdom in seventh century Mongolia is accepted as fact, despite overwhelming historical and archeological evidence to the contrary, and they seek to revive that ancient kingdom as a modern Uyghuristan.[4] Random arrests and detentions continue among the Uyghur, who are increasingly being regarded as China's Chechens. A report in the Wall Street Journal of the arrest on 11 August 1999 of Rebiya Kadir, a well-known Uyghur businesswoman, during a visit by the United States Congressional Research Service delegation to the region, indicates China's suspicion of the Uyghur people continues. Rebiya was sentenced to eight years imprisonment, and after several governments put pressure, her sentence was reduced by one year in 2003.[5] In the face of pressure from Condoleezza Rice, she was released in March 17, 2005, and has since become the leading voice for Uyghur human rights activities in Washington, DC and elected President of the World Uyghur Congress.

China is also concerned about the "Kosovo effect," fearing that its Muslim and other ethnic minorities might be emboldened to seek outside international (read Western) support for continued human rights abuses. Just prior to its fifty-year National Day celebrations in October 1999, the State Council hosted its first three-day conference on 'the nationalities problem' in Beijing and issued a new policy paper, "National Minorities Policy and its Practice in China."[6] Though this White Paper did little more than outline all the "good" programs China has carried out in minority areas, it did indicate increasing concern and a willingness to recognize unresolved problems, with several strategic think tanks in Beijing and Shanghai initiating focus groups and research programs addressing ethnic identity and separatism issues.[7]

But ethnic problems in Hu Jintao's China go far deeper than the "official" minorities. Sichuanese, Cantonese, Shanghainese, and Hunanese cafes are avidly advocating increased cultural nationalism and resistance to Beijing central control. As the European Union experiences difficulties in building a common European alliance across these linguistic, cultural, and political boundaries, we should not imagine China to be less concerned about its persistent multi-culturalism.

If the Holy Roman Empire were around today, it would look much like China. Two millennia ago, when the Roman Empire was at its peak, so was the Han dynasty—both empires barely lasted another 200 years. At the beginning of the last millennium, China was on the verge of being conquered by the Mongols, and divided by a weakened Song dynasty in the south and the Liao dynasty in the north, whose combined territory was equal only to the five northern provinces in today's PRC. Indeed, it was the Mongols who extended China's territory to include much of what is considered part of China today: Tibet, Xinjiang, Manchuria, Sichuan, and Yunnan. Over the last two millennia China has been divided longer than it has been unified; can it maintain national unity until the next century? History suggests otherwise. Indeed, with the reacquisition of Macao in late 1999, China is the only country in the world that is *expanding its territory* instead of reducing it. Will China be able to continue to resist the inexorable forces of globalization and nationalism?

Just as linguistic diversity within China leads Chinese linguists such as John DeFrancis to speak of the many Chinese languages, attention to cultural diversity should force us to give further weight to the plurality of the Chinese peoples in national politics. A former American President once claimed to know the mind of "the Chinese." This is as farfetched as someone claiming to know the European mind. Have any U.S. policy-makers spent time talking to disgruntled entrepreneurs in Canton and Shanghai, impoverished peasants in Anhui and Gansu, or angry Central Asians in Xinjiang, Mongolia and Tibet? While ethnic diversity does not necessitate ethnic separatism or violence, growing ethnic awareness and expression in China should inform policy that takes into account the interests of China's many ethnic groups, not just those in power. China policy should represent more than the interests of those in Beijing.

Nationality in China

Officially, China is made up of fifty-six nationalities: one majority nationality, the Han, and fifty-five minority groups. Initial results from the 2000 census suggest a total official minority population of nearly 104 million, or approximately 9% of the total population. The people, identified as Han, comprise 91% of the population from Beijing in the north to Canton in the south and include the Hakka, Fujianese, Cantonese, and other groups.[8] These Han are supposedly united by a common history, culture, and written language; differences in language, dress, diet, and customs are regarded as minor and superficial. The rest of the population is divided into fifty-five official "minority" nationalities that are mostly concentrated along the borders, such as the Mongolians and Uyghurs in the north and the Zhuang, Yi, and Bai in southern China, near southeast Asia. Other groups, such as the Hui and Manchus, are scattered throughout the nation, and there are minorities in every province, region, and county. An active state-sponsored program assists these official minority cultures and promotes their economic development (with mixed results). The outcome, according to China's preeminent sociologist, Fei Xiaotong, is a "unified multinational" state.[9] Even this recognition of diversity understates the divisions within the Chinese population, especially the wide variety of culturally and ethnically diverse groups within the majority Han population.[10] These groups have recently begun to rediscover and reassert their different cultures, languages, and history.[11] As the Chinese worry and debate over their own identity, policymakers in other nations still take the monolithic Han identity for granted.

The notion of a Han person (*Han ren*) dates back centuries and refers to descendants of the Han dynasty that flourished at about the same time as the Roman Empire. But the concept of Han nationality (*Han minzu*) is an entirely modern phenomenon that arose with the shift from the Chinese empire to the modern nation-state.[12] In the early part of this century, Chinese reformers had been concerned that the Chinese people lacked a sense of nationhood, unlike Westerners and even China's other peoples such as Tibetans and Manchus. In the view of these reformers, Chinese unity stopped at the clan or community level rather than extending to the nation as a whole. Sun Yat-Sen, leader of the republican movement that toppled the last imperial dynasty of China (the Qing) in 1911, popularized the idea that there were "Five Peoples of China"—the majority Han being one and the others being the Manchus, Mongolian, Tibetan, and Hui (a term that included all Muslims in China, now divided into Uyghurs, Kazakhs, Hui, etc.). Sun was a Cantonese, educated in Hawaii, who feared arousing traditional northern suspicions of southern radical movements. He wanted both to unite the Han and to mobilize them and all other non-Manchu groups in China (including Mongols, Tibetans, and Muslims) into a modern multiethnic nationalist movement against the Manchu Qing state and foreign imperialists. The Han were seen as a unified group distinct from the "internal" foreigners—within their borders the Manchus, Tibetans, Mongols, and Hui—as well as the 'external' foreigners—on their frontiers, namely the Western and Japanese imperialists.

Dikotter has argued a racial basis for this notion of a unified Han *minzu*, but perhaps the rationality was more strategic and nationalistic—the need to build national security around the concept of one national people, with a small percentage of minorities supporting that idea.[13] The Communists expanded the number of "peoples" from five to fifty six but kept the idea of a unified Han group. The Communists were, in fact, disposed to accommodate these internal minority groups for several reasons. The Communists' 1934-1935 Long March, a 6,000-mile trek across China from southwest to northwest to escape the threat of annihilation by Chiang Kai-shek's Kuomintang (KMT) forces, took the Communists through some of the most heavily populated minority areas. Harried on one side by the KMT and on the other by fierce "barbarian" tribesmen, the Communists were faced with a choice between extermination and promising special treatment to minorities—especially the Miao, Yi (Lolo), Tibetans, Mongols, and Hui—should the party ever win national power. The Communists even offered the possibility of true independence for minorities. Chairman Mao frequently referred to Article 14 of the 1931 Chinese Communist Party (CCP) constitution, which "recognizes the right of self-determination" of the national minorities in China, their right to complete separation from China, and to the formation of an independent state for each minority. This commitment was not kept after the founding of the People's Republic.[14] Instead, the party stressed maintaining the unity of the new nation at all costs. The recognition of minorities, however, also helped the Communists' long-term goal of forging a united Chinese nation by solidifying the recognition of the Han as a unified "majority." Emphasizing the difference between Han and minorities helped to de-emphasize the differences within the Han community.

The Communists incorporated the idea of Han unity into a Marxist ideology of progress with the Han in the forefront of development and civilization, the vanguard of the people's revolution.[15] The more "backward" or "primitive" the minorities were, the more "advanced" and "civilized" the so-called Han seemed and the greater the need for a unified national identity. Cultural diversity within the Han has not been admitted because of a deep (and well-founded) fear of the country breaking up into feuding warlord-run kingdoms as happened in the 1910s and 1920s. China has historically been divided along north/south lines, into Five Kingdoms, Warring States, or local satrapies, as often as it has been united. Indeed, China as it currently exists, including large pieces of territory occupied by Mongols, Turkic peoples, Tibetans, etc., is three times larger than China was under the last Chinese dynasty, the Ming, which fell in 1644. Ironically, geographic "China" as defined by the People's Republic was actually established by foreign conquest dynasties, first by the Mongols and finally by the Manchus. A strong, centralizing Chinese government (whether of foreign or internal origin) has often tried to impose ritualistic, linguistic, and political uniformity throughout its borders. The modern state has tried to unite its various peoples with transportation and communications networks and an extensive civil service. In recent years these efforts have continued through the controlled infusion of capitalistic investment and market manipulation. Even in the modern era, these integrative mechanisms have not produced cultural uniformity.

Han Nationality as Invented National Unity

Although presented as a unified culture—an idea also accepted by many Western researchers—Han peoples differ in many ways, most obviously in their languages. The supposedly homogenous Han speak eight mutually unintelligible languages (Mandarin, Wu, Yue, Xiang, Hakka, Gan, Southern Min, and Northern Min). Even these subgroups show marked linguistic and cultural diversity; in the Yue language family, for example, Cantonese speakers are barely intelligible to Taishan speakers, and the Southern Min dialects of Quanzhou, Changzhou, and Xiamen are equally difficult to communicate across.[16] Chinese linguist Y. R. Chao has shown that the mutual unintelligibility of Cantonese and Mandarin is as great as that of Dutch and English or French and Italian.[17] Mandarin was imposed as the national language early in the twentieth century and has become the lingua franca, but, like Swahili in Africa, it must often be learned in school and is rarely used in everyday life in many areas.

Cultural perceptions among the Han often involve broad stereotypical contrasts between north and south.[18] Northerners tend to be thought of as larger, broader-faced, and lighter-skinned, while southerners are depicted as smaller and darker. Cultural practices involving birth, marriage, and burial differ widely; Fujianese, for example, are known for vibrant folk religious practices and ritualized re-burial of interned corpses, while Cantonese have a strong lineage tradition, both of which are far almost non-existent in the north. One finds radically different eating habits from north to south, with northerners consuming noodles from wheat and other grains, open to consuming lamb and beef, and preferring spicy foods, while the southern diet is based upon rice, eschews, such meats in favor of seafood, and along the coast is milder. It is interesting in this regard that Fei Xiaotong[19] once argued that what made the Han people different from minorities was their agricultural traditions (i.e., minorities were traditionally not engaged in farming, though this failed to take account of groups like the Koreans and Uyghur who have farmed for 1400 years). Fei never considered the vast cultural differences separating rice-eaters in the South from wheat-eaters in the North. This process of national unification based on an invented majority at the expense of a few isolated minorities is one widely documented in Asia and not unique to China.[20]

Identity Politics and National Minorities

China's policy toward minorities involves official recognition, limited autonomy, and unofficial efforts at control. The official minorities hold an importance for China's long-term development that is disproportionate to their population. Although totaling only 8.04% of the population, they are concentrated in resource-rich areas spanning nearly 60% of the country's landmass and exceed 90% of the population in counties and villages along many border areas of Xinjiang, Tibet, Inner Mongolia, and Yunnan. While the 1990 census recorded 91 million minorities, the 2000 census is estimated to report an increase of the minority population to be 104 million.[21]

Shortly after taking power, Communist leaders sent teams of researchers, social scientists, and party cadres to the border regions to "identify" groups as official nationalities. Only forty-one of the more than 400 groups that applied were recognized, and that number had reached only fifty-six by 1982. For generally political reasons, most of the nearly 350 other groups were identified as Han or lumped together with other minorities with whom they shared some features. Some are still applying for recognition. The 1990 census listed almost 750,000 people as still "unidentified" and awaiting recognition—meaning they were regarded as ethnically different, but did not fit into any of the recognized categories. In recognition of the minorities' official status as well as their strategic importance, various levels of nominally autonomous administration were created: five regions, thirty-one prefectures, ninety-six counties (or, in Inner Mongolia and Manchuria, banners), and countless villages. Such "autonomous" areas do not have true local political control, although they may have increased local control over the administration of resources, taxes, birth planning, education, legal jurisdiction, and religious expression. These areas have minority government leaders, but the real source of power is still the Han-dominated Communist Party. As a result, they may actually come under closer scrutiny than other provinces with large minority populations such as Gansu, Qinghai, and Sichuan. While autonomy seems not to be all the word might imply, it is still apparently a desirable attainment for minorities in China. Between the 1982 and 1990 censuses, eighteen new autonomous counties were established, three of them in Liaoning Province for the Manchus, who previously had no autonomous administrative districts. Although the government is clearly trying to limit the recognition of new nationalities, there seems to be an avalanche of new autonomous administrative districts. Besides the eighteen new counties and many villages whose total numbers have never been published, at least eight more new autonomous counties are to be set up. Five will go to the Tujia, a group widely dispersed throughout the southwest that doubled in population from 2.8 to 5.8 million from 1982 to 1990.

The increase in the number of groups seeking minority status reflects what may be described as an explosion of ethnicity in contemporary China. Indeed, it has now become popular, especially in Beijing, for people to "come out" as Manchus or other ethnic groups, admitting they were not Han all along. While the Han population grew a total of 10% between 1982 and 1990, the minority population grew 35% overall—from 67 million to 91 million. The Manchus, a group long thought to have been assimilated into the Han majority, added three autonomous districts and increased their population by 128 percent from 4.3 to 9.8 million, while the population of the Gelao people in Guizhou shot up an incredible 714% in just eight years. Clearly these rates reflect more than a high birthrate; they also indicate "category-shifting," as people redefine their nationality from Han to minority or from one minority to another. In interethnic marriages, parents can decide the nationality of their children, and the children themselves can choose their nationality at age 18. One scholar predicts that if the minority populations' growth rate continues, they will total 100 million in the year 2,000 and 864 million in 2080.[22] Recent reports regarding the 2000 census have suggested that minority population will have increased to 104 million, amounting to 9.1% of the total population. China has recently begun to enforce the limits on births among minorities, especially in urban areas, but it is doubtful that authorities will be able to limit the avalanche of applications for redefinition and the hundreds of groups applying for recognition as minorities. In an important volume, Ralph Litzinger[23] has suggested that the "politics of national belonging" have led the Yao to willingly participate in the process of Chinese nationalization. Similarly, Louisa Schein's[24] book on the Hmong minority, argues that "internal Orientalism" has led to a resurgence of interest in the exoticized minority other.

Why was it popular to be "officially" ethnic in 1990s China? This is an interesting question given the negative reporting in the Western press about minority discrimination in China. If it is so bad to be a minority in China, why are their numbers increasing? One explanation may be that, in 1982, there were still lingering doubts about the government's true intent in registering the nationalities during the census. The Cultural Revolution, a ten-year period during which any kind of difference, ethnic, religious, cultural, or political, was ruthlessly suppressed, had ended only a few years before. By the mid-1980s, it had become clear that those groups identified as official minorities were beginning to receive real benefits from the implementation of several affirmative action programs. The most significant privileges included permission to have more children (except in urban areas, minorities are generally not bound by the one-child policy), pay fewer taxes, obtain better (albeit Chinese) education for their children, have greater access to public office, speak and learn their native languages, worship and practice their religion (often including practices such as shamanism that are still banned among the Han), and express their cultural differences through the arts and popular culture. Indeed, one might even say it has become popular to be "ethnic" in today's China. Mongolian hot pot, Muslim noodle, and Korean barbecue restaurants proliferate in every city, while minority clothing, artistic motifs, and cultural styles adorn Chinese bodies and private homes. In Beijing, one of the most popular new restaurants is the Thai Family Village (*Dai Jia Cun*). It offers a cultural experience of the Thai minority (known in China as the Dai), complete with beautiful waitresses in revealing Dai-style sarongs and short tops, sensually singing and dancing, while exotic foods such as snake's blood are enjoyed by the young Han *nouveau riche*. As predicted, it is not unusual to learn of Han Chinese prostitutes representing themselves as Thai and other minorities to appear more exotic to their customers.[25] Surprisingly, the second-most popular novel in China in 1994 was *The History of the Soul (Xin ling shi)*, which concerned personal and religious conflicts in a remote Muslim region in northwest China and was written by Zhang Chengzhi, a Hui Muslim from Ningxia. This rise of 'ethnic chic' is in dramatic contrast to the anti-ethnic homogenizing policies of the late 1950s anti-Rightist period, the Cultural Revolution, and even the late-1980s 'spiritual pollution' campaigns.

Foreign policy considerations have also encouraged changes in China's treatment of minority groups. China has one of the world's largest Muslim populations—nearly 20 million, more than the United Arab Emirates, Iraq, Libya, or Malaysia—and has increasing contacts with trade partners in the Middle East and new Muslim nations created on its borders. China provides the Middle East and Central Asia with cheap labor, consumer goods, weaponry— and increasing numbers of Muslim pilgrims to Mecca.[26] These relations will be jeopardized if Muslim, especially Uyghur, discontent continues over such issues as limitations on mosque building, restrictions on childbearing, uncontrolled mineral and energy development, and continued nuclear testing in the Xinjiang region. Foreign policy considerations also argue for better treatment of Korean minorities, since South Korean investment, tourism, and natural resources have given China's Koreans in Liaoning and Manchuria a booming economy and the best educational level of all nationalities (including the Han). Another factor has been international tourism to minority areas, including the "Silk Road" tourism to Xinjiang and marketing of package tours to the "colorful" minority regions of Yunnan and Guizhou for Japanese, Taiwanese, and Southeast Asian Chinese tour groups. The most striking change in China's policy toward a single minority as a result of international relations has been the initiation, just after the improvement in Sino-Israeli relations in 1992, of discussions about granting official nationality status to the Chinese Jews (*Youtai ren*), once thought to have disappeared entirely. As Sino-Israeli relations improve, and China seeks increased tourism dollars from Tel Aviv and New York, one might imagine that the Chinese Jews will once again reappear as an official nationality in China.

The creation of several new nations on China's Central Asian frontier with ethnic populations on both sides of the border has also made ethnic separatism a major concern. The newly independent status of the Central Asian states has allowed separatist groups in Xinjiang to locate some sources of support, leading to over 30 reported bombing incidents in the Xinjiang Region in 1999, claimed by groups militating for an "Independent Turkestan." At the same time, freer travel across the Central Asian borders has made China's Muslims well aware of the ethnic and political conflicts in Azerbaijan and Tajikistan, and also that many of them are better off economically than their fellow Muslims across the border. Several meetings of the "Shanghai Five" (PRC, Kazakhstan, Kyrgyzstan, Tajikistan, and Russia) since April 1997 have concluded treaties strengthening border security and the refusal to harbor separatist groups. In April 1999, Kazakhstan returned three Uyghurs accused of separatism to China. Beijing's challenge is to convince China's Muslims that they will benefit more from cooperation with their national government than from resistance. In the south, a dramatic increase in cross-border relations between Chinese minority groups and Myanmar (Burma), Cambodia, and Thailand has led to a rising problem of drug smuggling. Beijing also wants to help settle disputes in Cambodia, Vietnam, and Myanmar because of the danger of ethnic wars spilling over the border into China. In Tibet, frequent reports of ongoing resistance and many arrests continue to filter into the media despite the best efforts of Beijing spin control.

Internal Divisions among the Han Majority

Not only have the "official" minorities in China begun to assert their identities more strongly, pressing the government for more recognition, autonomy, and special privileges, but different groups within the so-called Han majority have begun to rediscover, reinvent, and reassert their ethnic differences. With the dramatic economic explosion in South China, southerners and others have begun to assert cultural and political differences. Cantonese rock music, videos, movies, and television programs, all heavily influenced by Hong Kong, are now popular throughout China. Whereas comedians used to make fun of southern ways and accents, southerners now scorn northerners for their lack of sophistication and business acumen. As any Mandarin-speaking Beijing resident will tell you, bargaining for vegetables or cellular telephones in Guangzhou or Shanghai markets is becoming more difficult for them due to growing pride in the local languages: non-native speakers always pay a higher price. Rising self-awareness among the Cantonese is paralleled by the reassertion of identity among the Hakka, the southern Fujianese Min, the Swatow, and a host of other generally ignored peoples now empowered by economic success and embittered by age-old restraints from the north.

Interestingly, most of these southern groups traditionally regarded themselves not as Han but as Tang people, descendants of the great Tang dynasty (618-907 A.D.) and its southern bases.[27] Most Chinatowns in North America, Europe, and Southeast Asia are inhabited by descendants of Chinese immigrants from the mainly Tang areas of southern China and built around Tang Person Streets (*tang ren jie*). The next decade may see the resurgence of Tang nationalism in southern China in opposition to northern Han nationalism, especially as economic wealth in the south eclipses that of the north. There is also a newfound interest in the ancient southern Chu kingdom as key to modern southern success. Some southern scholars have departed from the traditional Chinese view of history and begun to argue that, by the sixth century B.C., the bronze culture of the Chu spread north and influenced the development of

Chinese civilization, rather than this culture originating in the north and spreading southward. Many southerners now see Chu as essential to Chinese culture, to be distinguished from the less important northern dynasties—with implications for the nation's economic and geopolitical future. Museums to the glory of Chu have been established throughout southern China. There is also a growing belief that northerners and southerners had separate racial origins based on different histories and contrasting physiogenetic types that are influenced by highly speculative nineteenth century notions of race and Social Darwinism.[28] There has also been an outpouring of interest in Hakka origins, language, and culture on Taiwan, which may be spreading to the mainland. The Hakka, or 'guest people', are thought to have moved southward in successive migrations from northern China as early as the Eastern Jin (317-420 A.D.) or the late Song dynasty (960-1279 A.D.) according to many Hakka (who claim to be Song people as well as Tang people). The Hakka have the same language and many of the same cultural practices as the She minority, but never sought minority status themselves—perhaps because of a desire to overcome their long-term stigmatization by Cantonese and other southerners as "uncivilized barbarians."[29] This low status may stem from the unique Hakka language (which is unintelligible to other southerners), the isolated and walled Hakka living compounds, or the refusal of Hakka women during the imperial period to bind their feet. Nevertheless, the popular press in China is beginning to more frequently note the widely perceived Hakka origins of important political figures (including Deng Xiaoping, Mao Zedong, Sun Yat-sen, former party general secretary Hu Yaobang, and former president Ye Jianying). People often praise Zhou Enlai by stressing his Jiangnan linkages, Lee Kuan-yew as a prominent Hakka statesman. Even Chiang Kai-shek is lauded as a southerner who knew how to get money out of the United States.

Internet Cafes, Discos, and Democratization?

China's very economic vitality has the potential to fuel ethnic and linguistic division, rather than further integrating the country as most would suppose. As southern and coastal areas get richer, much of central, northern, and northwestern China is unlikely to keep up, increasing competition and contributing to age-old resentments across ethnic, linguistic, and cultural lines.[30] Southern ethnic economic ties link wealthy Cantonese, Shanghainese, and Fujianese (also the majority people in Taiwan) more closely to their relatives abroad than to their political overlords in Beijing. Already provincial governments in Canton and elsewhere not only resist paying taxes to Beijing, but also restrict the transshipment of goods coming from outside across provincial—often the same as cultural—lines. Travelers in China have seen an extraordinary expansion of toll roads, indicating greater interest in local control. Dislocations from rapid economic growth may also fuel ethnic divisions. Huge migrations of 'floating populations,' estimated to total over 150 million nationally, now move across China seeking employment in wealthier areas, often engendering stigmatized identities and stereotypical fears of the 'outsiders' (*wai di ren*) within China. Crime, housing shortages, and lowered wages are now attributed most to these people from Anhui, Hunan, or Gansu who are taking jobs from locals, complaints similar to those in West Germany about the influx of Easterners after reunification. Reports that 70% of those convicted of crimes in Beijing were 'outsiders' have fueled criticisms of China's increasingly open migration policy.[31] Eric Harwit has noted that the "digital divide" in China is closing, and the rapid expansion of Internet usage (up to 27% of all households are on-line in Beijing), has fostered wider communication and dissemination of news and information.[32]

The result of all these changes is that China is becoming increasingly de-centered. This is a fearsome prospect for those holding the reins in Beijing and, perhaps, was a factor in the decision to crack down on the June 1989 demonstrations in Tiananmen Square. At that time central authorities had begun to lose control of a country they feared could quickly unravel. That such fears have not eased is shown by the increased calls during the National Day celebrations for National Unity and the efforts to reduce corruption. Worker and peasant unrest reported throughout China cut across and may at times exacerbate cultural and ethno-linguistic differences between the haves and the have-nots, who in today's China are often and increasingly interacting along lines marked by multiethnic diversity.

Studies of democracy and democratization in China suggest that, at least at the village level, legitimate local elections are leading to a rising civil society and increasing pluralization.[33] Nevertheless, few see this process advancing to the level of actually posing a serious threat to the rule of the Communist Party.[34] Most scholars locate China's increasing civil society, not in the political domain, but in those spaces created by the market economy that the state has difficulty controlling, such as the dance halls and discos,[35] the karaoke bars, massage parlors, and private businesses,[36] and the free marketplace.[37]

Interestingly, scholars of Taiwan democratization were equally skeptical of the democratic process ever dislodging the Nationalist Kuomintang Party, the wealthiest and most entrenched Chinese political party in history.[38] The recent re-election of Chen Shui-bian, suggests that local politics were the key to his winning the narrow vote, despite continuing controversy over the assassination attempt.[39] Comparisons between China and Taiwan suggest that democratization will never happen as a result of encouragement from the top, as it would only dislodge those in power, but only as an uncontrollable coalition of marginal groups.[40] Bruce Dickson[41] coherently argues that the Leninist system, though theoretically open to participatory governance, is inherently resistant to pluralist democratic processes due to the role of the Communist Party leadership as permanent leader of the proletariat. Nevertheless, it was the Leninist system that created a system of recognizing and legitimating separate nationalities, what many scholars suggest was the Soviet Union's ultimate undoing.[42]

In the Taiwan case, Shelley Rigger[43] has argued forcefully for the role of marginal coalition politics in the rise of the Democratic Peoples Party (DPP), which Chen Shu-ibian masterfully united to unseat the ruling Nationalist Party. The successful mobilization of women, temple organizations, Taiwanese nationalists, environmentalists, aboriginals, and disenfranchised workers helped to unseat a well-organized political machine. Rigger pays scant attention to the role of the minority aboriginal peoples in this process of "Taiwanization." Though small in number (about 2% of the total population), the Taiwan aboriginals (*yuanzhu min*) were a significant emblem of Taiwanese separate identity from mainland China, and enlisting their support was a pivotal symbolic move on the part of the DPP. Might not China's indigenous minority groups (numbering about 9%) also play a role in China's future democratization? Certainly, many of them are pushing at the seams of Chinese rule, and some, like the Uyghurs and Tibetans, are receiving increasing international support. Only time will tell if they play an increasing role in Chinese affairs.

Conclusion

While ethnic separatism on it own will never be a serious threat to a strong China, a China weakened by internal strife, inflation, uneven economic growth, or the struggle for succession after Deng's death could become further divided along cultural and linguistic lines. China's separatists such as they are could never mount such a coordinated attack as was seen on September 11, 2001 in the United States, and China's more closed society lacks the openness that have allowed terrorists to move so freely in the West. China's threats will most likely come from civil unrest, and perhaps internal ethnic unrest from within the so-called Han majority. We should recall that it was a southerner, born and educated abroad, who led the revolution that ended China's last dynasty; and, when that empire fell, competing warlords—often supported by foreign powers—fought for local turf occupied by culturally distinct peoples. Moreover, the Taiping Rebellion that nearly brought down the Qing dynasty also had its origins in the southern border region of Guangxi among so-called marginal Yao and Hakka peoples. These events are being remembered as the generally hidden and overlooked 'Others' within Chinese society begin to reassert their own identities, in addition to the official nationalities. At the same time, Chinas leaders are moving away from the homogenizing policies that alienated minority and non-northern groups. Recent moves to allow and even encourage the expression of cultural diversity, while preserving political unity, indicate a growing awareness of the need to accommodate cultural diversity. Further evidence of this trend was the 1997 incorporation of Hong Kong, a city that operates on cultural and social assumptions very different from those of Beijing, and that was granted an unprecedented degree of autonomy within China.

The construction of Chinese national identity has always been tentative. In June 1989, while China's future hung in the balance, there was significant concern over which armies would support Deng's crackdown: those based in Sichuan, Hunan, Canton or Beijing, all with their own local concerns. The military has since been reshuffled and somewhat downsized, attempting to uproot any local attachments and professionalize the command structure.[44] However, this only underlines the growing importance of regional and local ties.

China, as of now, is a unified country militarily and, perhaps, politically. As a result of Hu Jintao's and Jiang Zemin's continuance of the Deng Xiaoping reforms, it is increasingly less unified economically. How can China continue to withstand the forces of globalization and nationalism without a government legitimated through popular elections, transparency in the political process, adherence to the rule of law, and good governance?

In November 2000, an ambassador from one of China's friendliest Muslim nations remarked privately to this writer that by the end of the next decade China would be divided into nine republics. Historians debate whether a foreign threat has been the only thing that has held China together. Now that the encirclement doctrine, upon which Nixon and Kissinger built the Sino-American alliance, is no longer valid, and containment has been replaced by improving US-China relationship based on an 'engagement' policy, China faces its only enemies from within. Certainly, the events of September 11, 2001 and China's participation in the war on terrorism have helped to further reign in China's separatist groups and further secure its borders.[45]

The Chinese press reported more than 5000 organized social protests in 1998 alone, with many more in 1999, culminating in the widespread Falun Gong uprising and crackdown. Labor groups and peasant associations have organized many of these protests, but ethnic and religious groups, such as the Falun Gong, have begun to speak out.[46] Provincial governments in Canton and elsewhere have continued to resist paying taxes to Beijing, as well as restrict the transshipment of outside goods across provincial, and often cultural lines, to the extent that China is becoming dangerously decentered—a fearsome prospect for those holding the threads in Beijing, and perhaps the main reason for the rush to finalize international border agreements with Russia, Kazakhstan, Kyrgyzstan, Tajikistan, and Vietnam.

Senator Daniel Patrick Moynihan once predicted that there would be fifty new countries in fifty years. The trend began with the Soviet Union in 1991 and has continued throughout much of Africa and Asia, particularly Indonesia. Why should China be immune from such global diversification? While ethnic separatism alone will never be threatening enough to pull a strong China apart, a China weakened by internal strife, inflation, uneven economic growth, or the struggle for (un)democratic succession, could certainly fragment along cultural and linguistic lines. Ethnic strife did not dismantle the former Soviet Union; but it did come apart along boundaries defined in large part by ethnic and national difference. The generally hidden and over-looked "Others" within Chinese society, the Cantonese, Shanghainese, Sichuanese, and Fujianese, are beginning to reassert their own identities in addition to the 'official' nationalities on China's borders. Increasing Taiwanese nationalism has caused great consternation in Beijing; an 'internal' ethnic nationalism that few Chinese nationalists can understand.

The rising politics of difference are of concern not only in Lhasa and Urumqi, but in Canton and Shanghai as well. The "Kosovo effect" may very well turn into the "Chechnya effect" where ethnic groups, especially Muslims in general (not just the Uyghur), become stereotyped as internal threats and as separatists, and 'cleansing' is launched as an internal affair. China also may link Uyghur separatist actions to the issue of Tibet and Taiwan, leading to broader international ramifications of any crackdown. The problem for China, however, is that many of its internal threats may not come from official nationalities, who are more easily singled out by race or language. China's Chechnya, like Indonesia's Aceh, may very well come from within its own people who seek economic and political advantage. The admission of China into the WTO will mean an even further enrichment of the largely coastal and urban developed areas over the more rural central provinces and peripheral minority areas, exacerbating underlying tensions and cultural fault lines. The next decade promises to be as momentous for China as the last decade was for the United States, Europe and Russia.

Notes

1. See the statements by Zainuddin, spokesman for the Indonesian Islamic Defenders Front: 'Israelis are not welcome in Indonesia because their illegal colonization has killed thousands of Muslim people.... We are ready to go to war, a holy war, to defend Islam.... The Israelis are colonialists, and we are against what they have done to the Palestinians, therefore they should have been barred from coming to Indonesia' (Calvin Sims, 'Islamic Radicals in Indonesia Vow Vengeance on Israelis' *New York Times* 15 October 2000: 11). For Xinjiang as an 'internal colony of China' see Gladney (1998b: 47).
2. David Shambaugh's (2000) collection of essays entitled, *Is China Unstable*, dismisses the ethnic issue as minor and completely unlike the troubles encountered by the former Soviet Union. For a recent work on the way's in which marginalized peoples help us to understand China in different ways, see Dru C. Gladney, *Dislocating China: Muslims, Minorities, and Other Subaltern Subjects* Chicago: University of Chicago Press, 2004.
3. See the critical report, Amnesty International, *Peoples Republic of China: Gross Violations of Human Rights in the Xinjiang Uighur Autonomous Region* (London, 21 April 1999).
4. The best 'Uyghur nationalist' retelling of this unbroken descent from Karakhorum is in the document 'Brief History of the Uyghers', originating from the Eastern Turkestani Union in Europe, and available electronicallyat<www.geocites.com/CapitolHill/1730/buh.html>. For a review and critique, including historical evidence for the multi-ethnic background of the contemporary Uyghur, see Dru C. Gladney, 'Ethnogenesis and Ethnic Identity in China: Considering the Uygurs and Kazakhs' in Victor Mair (ed.), *The Bronze Age and Early Iron Age People of Eastern Central Asia: Volume II* (Washington DC: Institute for the Study of Man, 1998), 812-34. For a discussion of the recent archeological evidence derived from DNA dating of the dessicated corpses of Xinjiang, see Victor Mair, 'Introduction' in Victor Mair (ed.), Ibid., 1-40.
5. *Wall Street Journal*, Ian Johnson, 'China Arrests Noted Businesswoman in Crackdown in Muslim Region', 18 August 1999.
6. China State Council, 'National Minorities Policy and its Practice in China', Beijing, October 1999.
7. The China Institute for Contemporary International Relations (CICIR), under the State Council, has initiated a 'Nationality Studies Project' in order to examine security implications of China's minority problems (Chu Shulong interview, November 14, 1999).

8. Colin MacKerras, *China's Minorities: Integration and Modernization in the Twentieth Century* (Ann Arbor: University of Michigan Press, 1994), 25.

9. Xiaotong Fei, "Ethnic Identification in China," in *Toward's a People's Anthology*, ed. by Xiaotong Fei (Beijing: New World Press, 1981), 20.

10. Emily Honig's *Creating Chinese Ethnicity* (1992).

11. Dru C. Gladney *Ethnic Identity in China: The Making of a Muslim Minority Nationality* (1998).

12. Prasenjit Duara, *Rescuing History from the Nation* (Chicago: University of Chicago Press, 1995), 47.

13. Frank Dikotter *The Discourse of Race in Modern China* (1992).

14. Dru C. Gladney, *Muslim Chinese: Ethnic Nationalism in the Peoples Republic* (Cambridge: Harvard University Press, 1996), 60-75.

15. Dru C. Gladney, "Representing Nationality in China: Refiguring Majority/Minority Identities," *The Journal of Asian Studies* No. 1 (1994): 97.

16. Jerry Norman, *Chinese* (Cambridge: Cambridge University Press, 1988), 27.

17. Ren Yuen Chao, *Aspects of Chinese Sociolinguistics* (Stanford: Stanford University Press, 1976), 83.

18. Fred C. Blake *Ethnic Groups and Social Change in a Chinese Market Town* (1981).

19. Xiaotong Fei, "Plurality and Unity in the Configuration of the Chinese Nationality," *Beijing Daxue Xuebao* No. 4, (1989): 12.

20. Gladney *Ethnic Identity in China: The Making of a Muslim Minority Nationality* (1998).

21. Tianlu Zhong, "Analysis of the Contemporary China Minority Nationality Population Situation," Paper presented at the Conference on Contemporary Migration and Ethnicity in China, 7-8 October, 1999, Institute of Nationality Studies, Chinese Academy of Social Science, in Beijing.

22. Ibid.

23. Ralph Litzinger, *Other Chinas: The Yao and the Politics of National Belonging* (Durham: Duke University Press, 2000), 238.

24. Louisa Schein, *Minority Rules: The Miao and the Feminine in China's Cultural Politics* (Durham: Duke University Press, 2000), 30-31.

25. Dru C. Gladney "Representing Nationality in China."

26. Ibid.

27. Leo J. Moser *The Chinese Mosaic: The Peoples and Provinces of China* (1985).

28. Victor Mair's *The Bronze Age and Early Iron Age People of Eastern Central Asia* (1999).

29. Fred C. Blake *Ethnic Groups and Social Change in a Market Town* (1981).

30. Shaoguang Wang, et. al., *The Political Economy of Uneven Development: The Case of China* (2000).

31. Fei Guo "Beijing's Policies towards Ethnic Minorities/Rural Migrant Villages," Paper presented at the Conference on Contemporary Migration and Ethnicity in China, 7-8 October, 1999, Institute of Nationality Studies, Chinese Academy of Social Sciences, Beijing.

32. For a critical discussion of China's "digital divide" and the often surprising accessibility of many internet sites, see Eric Harwit, "The Digital Divide of China's Internet Use" Paper presented at the Association for Asian Studies Annual Meeting, New York, 28 March 2003. See also his co-authored article, Eric Harwit and Duncan Clark, "Shaping the Internet in China: Evolution of Political Control over Network Infrastructure and Content," *Asian Survey* 41, no. 3 (2001): 378-381.

33. Timothy Brook, ed., *Civil Society in China* (Armonk: M.E. Sharpe, 2000), 12.

34. Shao-hua Hu *Explaining Chinese Democratization* (2000).

35. Orville Schell *Discos and Democracy: China in the Throes of Reform* (1989).

36. Xin Liu *The Otherness of Self: A Genealogy of the Self in Contemporary China* (2001).
37. Ann Anagnost *National Post-Times: Narrative, Representation, and Power in Modern China* (1997).
38. Shelley Rigger, *Politics in Taiwan: Voting for Democracy* (London and New York: Routledge Press, 1999), 23.
39. For an excellent discussion, see the 23 February 2004 Brookings Institute report, "Taiwan Elections 2004" http://www.brookings.edu/dybdocroot/comm/events/20040223 .pdf.
40. Bruce Dickson, *Democratization in China and Taiwan: The Adaptability of Leninist Parties* (New York and London: Clarendon Press, 1998), 82.
41. Ibid., 26.
42. Helene Carrere d' Encausse, *The End of the Soviet Empire: The Triumph of the Nations* (New York: Basic Books, 1993), 31-47.
43. Rigger, 80-93.
44. James Lilley, and David L. Shambaugh, *China's Military faces the future* (Armonk: M.E. Sharpe, 1999), 28.
45. Dru C. Gladney *Dislocating China: Muslims, Minorities, and other Subaltern Subjects* (2004).
46. Nancy Chen, "Healing Sects and Anti-Cult Campaigns," in *Religion in China Today,* ed. by Daniel L. Overmyer (Cambridge: Cambridge University Press, 2003), 206-213.

References

Anagnost, Ann S. *National Past-Times: Narrative, Representation, and Power in Modern China.* Durham, NC: Duke University Press, 1997.

Blake, Fred C. *Ethnic Groups and Social Change in a Chinese Market Town.* Honolulu: University of Hawaii Press, 1981.

Brook, Timothy, ed., *Civil Society in China.* Armonk: M.E. Sharpe, 2000.

Chao, Yuen Ren. *Aspects of Chinese Sociolinguistics.* Stanford: Stanford University Press, 1976.

Chen, Nancy N. "Healing Sects and Anti-Cult Campaigns," 199-214. In *Religion in China Today,* ed., Daniel L. Overmyer. Cambridge: Cambridge University Press, 2003.

Dickson, Bruce. *Democratization in China and Taiwan: The Adaptability of Leninist Parties.* New York and London: Clarendon Press, 1998.

Dikotter, Frank. *The Discourse of Race in Modern China.* Stanford: Stanford University Press, 1992.

Duara, Prasenjit. *Rescuing History from the Nation.* Chicago: University of Chicago Press, 1995.

Encausse, Hélène Carrère d'., *The End of the Soviet Empire: The Triumph of the Nations.* Franklin Philip, Trans. New York: Basic Books, 1993.

Fei Xiaotong. 'Ethnic Identification in China.' *In Toward a People's Anthropology,* ed., Fei Xiaotong. New World Press: Beijing, China, 1981.

_____. 'Zhonghua minzu de duoyuan jiti juge' (Plurality and Unity in the Configuration of the Chinese Nationality), *Beijing Daxue Xuebao,* 1989, 4:1-19.

Gladney, Dru C. *Dislocating China: Muslims, Minorities, and Other Subaltern Subjects.* Chicago: University of Chicago Press, 2004.

_____*Ethnic Identity in China: The Making of a Muslim Minority Nationality.* New York & London: Wadsworth Publishers, 1998.

_____*Muslim Chinese: Ethnic Nationalism in the People's Republic*, 1ˢᵗ edition. Cambridge: Harvard University Press, 1996.

_____"Representing Nationality in China: Refiguring Majority/Minority Identities," *The Journal of Asian Studies* vol. 53, no. 1: (1994a): 92-123.

_____"Sino-Middle Eastern Perspectives and Relations Since the Gulf War: Views from Below," *The International Journal of Middle Eastern Studies*, Forthcoming November (1994b).

_____ed., *Making Majorities: Constituting the Nation in Japan, Korea, China, Malaysia, Fiji, Turkey, and the United States*. Stanford: Stanford University Press, 1998.

_____"Internal Colonialism and the Uyghur Nationality: Chinese Nationalism and its Subaltern Subjects' *CEMOTI: Cahiers d'études sur la Méditerranée Orientale et le Monde Turco-Iranien* no. 25: (1998b): 47-64.

Guo, Fei. 'Beijing's Policies towards ethnic minority /rural migrant villages' Paper presented at the Conference on Contemporary Migration and Ethnicity in China, 7-8 October 1999, Institute of Nationality Studies, Chinese Academy of Social Sciences, Beijing.

Harwit, Eric and Duncan Clark. "Shaping the Internet in China: Evolution of Political Control over Network Infrastructure and Content," *Asian Survey* 41, no. 3: (2001): 377-408.

Honig, Emily. *Creating Chinese Ethnicity*. New Haven: Yale University Press, 1992.

Hu, Shao-hua, *Explaining Chinese Democratization*. New York: Praeger Publishers, 2000.

Lilley, James R. and David L. Shambaugh, eds. *China's Military Faces the Future*. Armonk: M.E. Sharpe, 1999.

Litzinger, Ralph A. *Other Chinas: The Yao and the Politics of National Belonging*. Durham: Duke University Press, 2000.

Liu, Xin, *The Otherness of Self: A Genealogy of the Self in Contemporary China*. Ann Arbor: University of Michigan Press, 2001.

Mackerras, Colin. *China's Minorities: Integration and Modernization in the Twentieth Century*. Hong Kong, Oxford, New York: Oxford University Press, 1994.

Mair, Victor. Editor. *The Bronze Age and Early Iron Age People of Eastern Central Asia*. Washington, D.C.: Institute for the Study of Man, Inc., 1999.

Moser, Leo J. *The Chinese Mosaic: the Peoples and Provinces of China*. Boulder: Westview Press, 1985.

Norman, Jerry. *Chinese*. Cambridge: Cambridge University Press, 1988.

Rigger, Shelley. *Politics in Taiwan: Voting for Democracy*. London and New York: Routledge Press, 1999.

Schein, Louisa. *Minority Rules: The Miao and the Feminine in China's Cultural Politics*. Durham: Duke University Press, 2000.

Schell, Orville. *Discos and Democracy: China in the Throes of Reform*. New York: Anchor Books, 1989.

Shambaugh, David, Ed. *Is China Unstable: Assessing the Factors*. Armonk: M.E. Sharpe, 2000.

Wang Shaoguang, Hu Angang, Kang Xiaoguang. *The Political Economy of Uneven Development: The Case of China*. Armonk: M.E. Sharpe, 2000.

Zhang Tianlu. 'Xiandai Zhongguo Shaoshu minzu renkou zhuangkuang' (Analysis of the Contemporary China minority nationality population situation). Paper presented at the Conference on Contemporary Migration and Ethnicity in China, 7-8 October 1999, Institute of Nationality Studies, Chinese Academy of Social Sciences, Beijing.

Chapter 22

Shangri-la has Forsaken Us: China's Ethnic Minorities, Identity, and Government Repression

Reza Hasmath

In China, unlike most nations, the term ethnic minorities, refers to specific groups officially identified as minority nationalities by the Communist Party of China. This chapter traces the historical development of the classification of ethnic minorities in the nation and discuss how ethnic identity is presently understood in an environment of assimilation.

Introduction

China is one of the largest and most ethnically diverse nations in the world. Yet, this may not seem apparent to the casual observer, which is startling when placed in perspective. If China's ethnic minority population alone was a nation-state, the nearly 90 million ethnic minorities would be the twelfth most populous nation or 1.34% of the world's population.[1] Even in broader academic and mainstream literature, discussions of China generally take ethnic uniformity for granted, whereby China is often tacitly portrayed as a homogeneous, mono-ethnic, Han dominated state; at the very least, perhaps mentioning there are few ethnic minorities in the bordering areas.

Ethnic minority management in China is operated by a combination of Central government decrees, social policy protections and local attempts to promote ethnic minority culture such as festivals, food, sport or dance in the mainstream. For example, in Beijing, government officials stress a loud confidence that China and the municipality actively promotes and respects the religious affairs, education, culture, and sport of the official fifty five ethnic minority groups. When interviewing officials from the Beijing Municipal Commission of Ethnic Affairs, they pointed out the Muslim population—

numbering upwards of 300,000 and comprising followers among more than ten ethnic groups, including the Hui, Uyghur, Uzbek and Kazak—peacefully practiced their religion in the city's eighty-odd mosques. The officials argued this illustrated that policies, from the local to the national level, were successful in promoting ethnic tolerance and managing ethnic difference.

Upon closer examination of several mosques one is struck by an older age demographic that visits the mosques regularly. In fact, several members of the mosque revealed that their children do not practice or adopt the Islamic culture. They assert their children are Beijingers, educated within a Han dominated community. Their female children do not wear headscarves; the males do not wear Islamic topees. They do not eat traditional foods, save to occasionally go to "ethnic" restaurants which are increasing in popularity among Beijingers. But even moving away from the obvious (ceremonial) cultural rituals, their children do not speak the minority language, they are products of an education system that promote a Han dominated culture. Although from the local to the national level (most prominently the 1999 National Minorities Policy), government policy documents do on paper promote and preserve ethnic minority rights and traditions, empirical evidence does seem to suggest assimilation among members of ethnic minority groups.

This chapter examines the modern development of the classification of ethnic minorities in China. In the People's Republic, the term "ethnic minorities" refers to fifty five specific ethnic groups who are officially identified as minority nationalities by the Communist Party of China (CPC). Moreover, drawing partially from interviews in 2006, it becomes evident throughout the chapter, assimilation defined at the level of ideology, plays a burgeoning role in shaping ethnic identity.

Ethnic Identification

In the most simplistic form, ethnic groups can be viewed in two lights, which are not necessarily exclusive from each other. The first, as a primordial occurrence that is unchanging and universal, meaning certain ethnic traits can be ascribed at birth, for example one's skin pigmentation.[2] The second understanding sees ethnic groups as socially constructed, forged on the basis of a particular history. In other words, ethnic identity is achieved after birth, for instance ethnic groups may be identified by the language spoken;[3] by ancestry— either by place of birth or the ancestors of the individual who form the group[4]; by religious affiliation;[5] and more broadly, by cultural artefacts, i.e. foods, traditions. Although innumerable theories have been developed to describe ethnicity and ethnic group boundaries, each serving different analytical purposes, including primordialist theory;[6] modernization theory;[7] neo-Marxist or class approach to ethnicity – including class segmentation;[8] split-labor market;[9] internal colonialism;[10] and, world systems theory,[11] they all allow that the concept is a potent force under certain conditions.[12] Moreover, all theories ultimately point to different mechanisms and accuse different social actors of using ethnic division to their advantage. In essence, they generally emphasize that ethnicity is a constructed social and/or political relation rather than an immutable force. At an even more basic level, all approaches nevertheless agree that ethnicity has something to do with the classification of people and group relationships. They emphasize the sharing of social ties by reference to common origins and a historical past (whether real or perceived); shared cultural heritage; and/or language.[13] But then there is power factor, and this is where it gets muddy as demonstrated in the case of China.

In many respects, ethnicity in China is seen as one of several outcomes of group interactions in which there is a differential power between dominant and minority groups.[14] In Schermerhorn's work on ethnic stratification he describes a paradigm that uses size and access to power to determine whether ethnic groups are dominant or subordinate, which is useful to understanding the reality in China.[15] According to this characterization, as illustrated in Table One, if an ethnic group has both power and size it is the *dominant majority*. If it has power, but not size, they are the *dominant elite*. If it has size, but does not have power, it is classified as *mass subjects*. And, if the group has neither size nor power, it is classified as a *minority group*. It is important to note each of the four types of stratified groups can be multi-ethnic or homogeneous. As such, any of the group types could be made up of several ethnic groups or just one. Through situations of social change and increased mobility they may start to crosscut one another so that members of all ethnic groups are found in all strata.[16] In this vein, Schermerhorn's model opens the door to discuss power relations between the *dominant majority* Han and *minority groups* in China. From this perspective, as we shall see, ethnicity in China is an aspect of stratification, as well as a criterion of group delineations.[17]

Table 22.1: Majority and Minority Relations[18]

Type of Stratified Grouping	Power		Size	
Dominant Majority		+		+
Dominant Elite(s)	+		-	
Mass Subjects		-	+	
Minority Groups		-	-	

Source: Schermerhorn's (1970)

Before continuing, it should be noted when studying ethnic groups in this fashion there is still an invariable risk of "tribalizing people instead of listening to them . . . [and] studying communities of the researcher's own making."[19] Coiled in the heart of this concern is the modern obsession of defining the boundaries of what "people" are members of a particular ethnic group or culture. In practice, there appear to be two fundamental forms of identification. The first is self-identification. This is perhaps the most accepted normative form of identifying membership into an ethnic group, especially in Western nations, as it provides the freedom of the individual to define himself/herself.[20] Given our nominal repertoire of identities, individuals are able to choose their ethnic group category(-ies) that defines them.[21] The second form is fixed ethnic identification as presently utilized in China. This form of identification essentially narrows the ability of the individual to define themselves outside the boundaries of accepted ethnic group categories. So for example, the state may provide a list of "official" ethnic groups based on pre-defined categories of understanding. In effect, for the most part, each individual will be born into a particular ethnic category and is seen as a member of that ethnic group for life.

In the People's Republic of China, the concept of ethnicity appears to be straightforward, definitive, and perhaps rigid. Although relative to East Asia, China is at the forefront for providing specific minority rights that are enshrined in its Constitution, and is a leader, at least on paper, for providing allowances for ethnic autonomy in parts of the nation, the system of categorizing and delineating minority groups is ripe with difficulties. The term "ethnic minorities" refer to individuals officially identified as minority nationalities (*shaoshu minzu*)[22] by the CPC. When the CPC came into power in 1949 they commissioned studies to categorize ethnic groups within the boundaries of the People's Republic. Teams were sent into regions heavily populated with ethnic minorities to conduct research and fieldwork, investigating minorities' social history, economic life, language and religion. Although 400 plus separate groups applied to be formally recognized, after detailed study they found that there was a lot of overlapping, and that a significant number of groups that claimed to be separate actually belonged to existing groups (albeit with different names). As a result, 39 ethnic groups were officially recognized in 1954; and by 1964, another fifteen were identified, with the Lhoba ethnic group added in 1965.[23] The Jino, were added in 1979, bringing the present-day count to fifty-six official ethnic groups. All Chinese citizens were subsequently registered by "nationality" status in household registration and personal identification—a practice that still remains today. In Table 22.2 the population demographics by 'nationality' status is listed.

In determining what constituted an ethnic group, the CPC leaders, who were extremely inexperienced in administrative matters, followed the Soviet model, which politicized and institutionalized the identification and categorization of ethnic minority groups.[24] Inspired by Joseph Stalin's "four commons,"[25] the criterion is: 1) Distinct Language—while there are virtually hundreds, perhaps thousands, of dialects spoken across China, a minority language is not simply a dialect. It is a language with distinct grammatical and phonological differences. In fact, among the 56 official ethnic groups identified, four of the world's largest language families are covered, including Sino-Tibetan (e.g. Tibetan), Altai (e.g.

Table 22.2: Population Demographics by Nationality Status in China, 2000[26]

Nationality	Population	%	Nationality	Population	%
Han	**1,136,703,824**	**92.6961**	Du	192,600	0.0157
Ethnic			Xibo	172,900	0.0141
Minorities	**89,367,200**	**7.2877**	Mulam	160,600	0.0131
			Kirgiz	143,500	0.0131
Zhuang	15,555,800	1.2685	Daur	121,500	0.0117
Manchu	8,846,800	0.7214	Jingpo	119,300	0.0097
Hui	8,612,000	0.7023	Salar	87,500	0.0071
Miao	7,383,600	0.6021	Bulang	82,400	0.0067
Uyghur	7,207,000	0.5877	Maonan	72,400	0.0059
Yi	6,578,500	0.5365	Tajik	33,200	0.0027
Tujia	5,725,000	0.4669	Pumi	29,700	0.0024
Mongolian	4,802,400	0.3916	Achang	27,700	0.0023
Tibetan	4,593,100	0.3746	Nu	27,200	0.0022
Bouyei	2,548,300	0.2078	Ewenki	26,400	0.0022
Dong	2,506,800	0.2044	Jing	18,700	0.0015
Yao	2,137,000	0.1743	Jino	18,000	0.0015
Korean	1,923,400	0.1568	De'ang	15,500	0.0013
Bai	1,598,100	0.1303	Uzbek	14,800	0.0012
Hani	1,254,800	0.1023	Russian	13,500	0.0011
Li	1,112,500	0.0907	Yugur	12,300	0.0010
Kazak	1,110,800	0.0906	Bonan	11,700	0.0010
Dai	1,025,400	0.0836	Menba	7,500	0.0006
She	634,700	0.0518	Oroqin	7,000	0.0006
Lisu	574,600	0.0469	Drung	5,800	0.0005
Gelao	438,200	0.0357	Tatar	5,100	0.0004
Lahu	411,500	0.0336	Hezhen	4,300	0.0004
Dongxiang	373,700	0.0305	Gaoshan	2,900	0.0002
Wa	352,000	0.0287	Lhoba	2,300	0.0002
Shui	347,100	0.0283			
Naxi	277,800	0.0227	**Total**	**1,226,269,624**	**100**
Qiang	198,600	0.0162	**Population**		

Source: National Bureau of Statistics and Ethnic Affairs Commission (2003) Kazak, Uyghur, Mongolian, Manchu, Korean), Austro-Asiatic (e.g. Miao), and Indo-European (e.g. Tajik, Russian). Twenty-one ethnic groups have unique writing systems. (2) A recognized indigenous homeland—a common territory—

within the boundaries of China. For example, the majority of the nation's 4.8 million Mongol ethnic population lives in the Inner Mongolia Autonomous Region in Northern China. (3) A common economic life, and (4) a strong sense of identity and distinctive customs, ranging from dress, religion, foods.

Even the *dominant majority* Han nationality, which has a population of 1.136 billion persons,[27] groups together a wide array of culturally diverse populations, including eight vastly different linguistic groups (Mandarin, Gan, Hakka, Southern and Northern Min, Wu, Xiang, Yue). There is even great diversity within the linguistical sub-groups. Among the Yue language family, Cantonese and Taishan are difficult to be understood between them. Few commentators on China seemingly question the validity of a unified Han nationality and often they accept Han is representative of 'Chinese' in general. While the notion of the Han *ren* (person) has existed since the time of the Han dynasty (206 BC – 220 AD), the Han nationality is an entirely modern phenomenon, which arose with the shift from Chinese Empire to modern nation-state. The notion of a unified Han nationality – a Pan-Hanism – gained its modern popularity under Sun Yat-sen, the leader of the Guomindang (GMD), who were instrumental in overthrowing the last dynasty of China, the Manchurian-led, Qing Dynasty in 1911. In order to mobilize all Chinese against Qing imperial rule, the GMD promoted an argument that the vast majority of people in China were Han and thus should rally together to remove all "foreign occupiers." Central to their argument was the idea of the "Five Races of China" (*wuzu gonghe*): the Han, Manchu, Mongolian, Tibetan and Hui (which was used to refer to all Muslims), which promoted an idea of a quinque-racial republic. The new Republican government sought to emphasize the idea that Han and the four other nationalities belonged to a supra-ethnic, nation-state that had been in existence as this entity from time immemorial[28] – which was then and continues to be proven flawed.[29] Yet, by employing the term Han minzu, Sun Yat-sen and the GMD essentially brought together northern Mandarin speakers, the southern Cantonese and the economic power of Shanghai, into one superimposed nationality. In effect, a new identity or in Benedict Anderson's terms, a new "imagined community" was formed for Hans.

The Historical Factor

Of course, the purpose of officially classifying ethnic minority groups in China rather than adopting self-identification style used in many Western nations lies in the history of the CPC and the modern-day public benefits that are afforded to minorities. During the "Long March" of 1934-1935, Chinese Communist leaders became aware first-hand, of the sheer ethnic diversity and cultures of China as they moved from the southwest to northwest of China. Facing near defeat by the Japanese and the Guomintang on one side, and barbarian tribesmen on the other, the Communists made promises of special treatment, recognition and the promise of establishing autonomous regions for minorities – notably the Miao, Yi, Tibetans, Mongols and Hui – in exchange for their support. [30] It is thus from this modern legacy that ethnic nationality identification and ethnic minorities policies have emerged.

It can also be suggested that a minority identification policy has allowed the new People's Republic to forge a nation-building project under the leadership of the *dominant majority*, Han nationality. Projecting the image of Han superiority became useful for the Communists who incorporated it into Marxist ideology of progress. Recognized minority nationalities were categorized according to five major modes of production: primitive, slave, feudal, capitalist, and socialist. The Hans were ranked the highest on this scale, reinforcing the Han idea that minorities are backward[31] and perpetuating the Communists' portrayal of Hans as the "vanguard" of the people's revolution. Ethnic minorities were thus encouraged to follow the Han example.

Prior to the founding of the People's Republic, it was out of political necessity by the Communists to secure the support of ethnic minorities to ensure their very survival against the Republican Guomintang and Japanese forces. However, with China no longer facing these "foreign" threats, the CPC turned its attention to "modernizing" and "improving the livelihoods" of ethnic minorities through public policies. As a consequence, ethnic minorities today are guaranteed systematic and procedural "special rights" and preferential treatment under China's constitution, reaffirmed in various national (e.g. 1999 National Minorities Policy) and local (e.g. Beijing Minority Rights Protection Policies) public policies. The "one-child" policy typifies such a preferential treatment. Since 1982, and reinforced by the Population and Family Planning Law in 2002, China's population policy seeks to control the size of the population, calling for late marriages and fewer births. It strongly encourages couples to have only one child. Special exemptions in the population policy have however been afforded to ethnic minorities, whereby couples from ethnic minorities are usually exempt or have a higher quota for children.[32] In Beijing, for example, ethnic minorities can often have two children. Other special exemptions vary by province, autonomous region or even municipalities. They include paying lower taxes; lower required scores for entry into university; easier access to public office; freedom to practice their religions; and funding to express their cultural difference through the arts and sports. Due to these advantages and preferential treatments afforded to ethnic minorities in China, the status of an ethnic citizen cannot be altered at his/her discretion.[33]

Ethnic minorities are also well represented in the National People's Congress, as well as regionally. Regional autonomy is given in areas heavily populated by ethnic minorities. There are currently six autonomous regions which have political autonomy in theory – among them Inner Mongolia, Tibet and Xinjiang. Moreover, autonomous cities, prefectures and municipalities where minority nationalities are territorially concentrated are still present. In practice, the system remains subject to the political control of the CPC. A case in point: the Constitution stipulates that the leaders of an autonomous area and most of its representatives to the People's Congress must be members of the area's main ethnic nationality. However, the CPC, which controls the government and holds all final decision-making powers are exempt from these stipulations. Notwithstanding, the People's Daily proudly boasts there are over 2.824 million ethnic minority government officials, or 6.9 percent of the national total, the majority residing in the Western Provinces.[34] Thus, if the CPC were to add further ethnic minority groups to the list, a greater population will be subjected to preferential treatment alienating the harmony of the nation. In other words, for the sake of not alienating the Han majority and by ensuring that the "strategically important" regions (in terms of military and trade) that are heavily populated by ethnic minorities (mostly in Western Provinces) are kept at bay, the CPC have not expanded the official list of ethnic minorities, although this is not without controversy.

Debating the Categories of Ethnic Groups

Although the categorization of fifty five ethnic minority groups by the CPC was a step forward from Sun Yat-sen Nationalist Party's denial of the existence of a wide variety of different ethnic groups in China; and from the derogatory names commonly used to refer to ethnic minority groups (officially abolished in 1951), the process of modern-day official ethnic group recognition has sparked intense debate. For example, Chinese sociologist Fei Xiao Tong points to the Chuanqing Blacks, who although had a close relationship with Hans, had unique features in language, location and economic life that would warrant *minzu* recognition based on the four criteria.[35] However, it was determined by CPC researchers that the Chuanqing Blacks were not a separate nationality, but rather descendants of Han garrison troops who intermarried with the local population during the Ming dynasty. Thus they are to be categorized as Han Chinese.

In a contrasting example, in 1978, 30,000 Fujianese who no longer practice Islam, were recognized as members of the Hui (Islamic) nationality using historical records of foreign ancestry.[36] They were able to prove descent from foreign Muslim officials and traders who settled in their area between the nineth and fourteenth centuries. This practice would appear to create precedence for many groups to seek nationality recognition based on historical records of foreign ancestry. However, the CPC has not recognized a "new" ethnic group in nearly thirty years. In fact, among the 350 plus groups who were not originally classified as a separate ethnic group, only fifteen groups are still officially being considered for nationality recognition. The *wei shibie minzu*, literally the "undistinguished ethnic groups," total around 730,000 people.[37] Examples of these groups include the Gejia, Khmu, Kucong, Mang, Deng, Sherpas, Bajia, Yi and Youtai (Jewish). In other words, these individuals are regarded as ethnically different, but do not currently fit into the CPC's official ethnic minorities' framework.

Certain official ethnic groups are even near extinction or borderline assimilated into Han, which begs whether a re-categorization or abolition of official ethnic minority groups is needed in the near future. For example, typical of many interview responses when asked, "what does it mean to be an ethnic minority?" Joanna, an ethnic Xibo, replies, "We don't eat dogs or horses. Otherwise we are the same as Han." Elaborating further, her explanation was her grandparents will wear traditional clothing during festivals, otherwise, their cultural and social lives are virtually the same as other Han. Few Xibos she knows can speak the traditional dialect fluently; a trend that will continue as the numbers of elders diminish. Joanna, like many young ethnic minorities interviewed, can barely speak their ethnic language or dialect, and does not practice it everyday. While officially she is considered a member of an ethnic minority, her way of life are indistinguishable from a Han. This situation has vivid resemblance to Moerman's study[38] on ethnic relations in Thailand, where he pondered "Who are the Lue?" While attempting to describe who the Lue were in his research, in ways that were distinctive for other ethnic groups, he encountered numerous problems. When querying individual Lues what were their typical characteristics they would mention cultural traits, which they in fact shared with other (often dominant) neighbouring groups. They lived in close interaction with other groups in the area; they had no exclusive livelihood, language or customs. Why was it appropriate to describe them as an ethnic group? This problem, concerned with the boundaries of a group, is becoming increasingly common among many of the ethnic groups in China. Many Chinese scholars interviewed believed that a "multi-ethnic" environment will not last long in many parts of urban China, because, in the words of the current Minister in Charge of the State Ethnic Affairs Commission, an ethnic Korean, Li Dezhu "like a grinding shed, the city will grind off ethnic [minority] features."[39] Ethnic minority features slowly were assimilated into the *dominant majority* Han culture.

Ethnic Assimilation

Assimilation is prominent in many (perhaps most) communities around the world. If we search for an official assimilation policy in China it will be difficult to find in the present time. Assimilation in China is accelerated due to the political climate in China and is often seen in the outcomes of CPC public policies, rather than a distinct, singular policy statement, which calls for assimilation. Pardoning their vagueness, Park and Burgess provide a definition of assimilation that is still useful in the modern context:

> Assimilation is seen as a process of interpenetration and fusion in which persons and groups acquire the memories, sentiments, and attitudes of other persons and groups ... by sharing their experience and history, are incorporated with them in a common cultural life.[40]

In many regards, assimilation can be viewed as the process of the "they" becoming part of the "we." In other words, it revolves around deep layers of ethnic superiority and ethnocentric pretensions.[41]

Suffice to say, assimilation can have negative implications for ethnic minority groups. After assimilation the distinctive features of the original ethnic minority group can be minimized and can disappear altogether,[42] such as the case of the Chuanging ethnic group mentioned earlier, who have been virtually assimilated and are now categorized as Han. Whatever deficiencies we may find in assimilation we cannot deny that it has and continues to play a major role in the development and destruction of communities. This is certainly the case throughout China's history, which is littered with diverse ethnic groups interacting with one another and ultimately assimilating into the dominant culture. Over the last two thousand years the Hans have prospered in spite of invasion by ethnic empires, such as the Mongols and Manchurians. With every invasion, many ethnic groups appear to successfully assimilate into Han culture. The example of the Manchus who ruled during the Qing Dynasty from 1644 to 1911 best illustrates this case. For political purposes, the early Manchurian emperors often inter-married with Mongols, so that their descendants would also be seen as legitimate heirs of the previous Mongolian-dominated, Yuan Dynasty. However, it was the interaction between Hans and Manchus throughout the Qing Dynasty that tested the resolve of Manchurian ethnic management. On the one hand, the Manchu rulers sought to preserve a distinct Manchurian ethnic identity, however, to keep power, they had to respect the existence of various ethnic groups, notably the Han, who were the majority population. One tactic the Manchus utilized was to maintain a system of dual appointments in which all major imperial offices would have a Manchu and a Han member. In the late nineteenth century, it became apparent that Manchus were beginning to largely assimilate with Hans, to the extent that they began adopting their customs and language. Spoken Manchu began to be rarely used in the Imperial Court or in local streets. Scholars have pointed out that it is this shift in assimilation towards Han culture that played a major role in overthrowing Manchurian control of Beijing in 1912; and ultimately, to the creation of the Republic of China led by Sun Yat-sen.[43]

The legacy of such ethnic minority groups today, notably in the capital city, can be seen in the wider Han cultural context. For example, although 43% of the ethnic minority population in Beijing officially belongs to the Manchu group, this number can be significantly higher as many with Manchurian ancestry choose to identify themselves as Han in order to protect themselves from the stigma of being seen as "outside colonizers" (as Manchus were initially portrayed by Sun Yat-sen) or "imperialists" (as portrayed by the CPC). Certain groups in the capital such as the Zhuang and ethnic Koreans are well adapted into urban milieu. The ethnic Korean population in particular can be seen as one of the most successful minority groups in terms of economic capital and social assimilation. Their history in migrating to the city was often due to famine and war in the Korean peninsula from the 1860s onwards. Most famously, the Japanese, who occupied Manchuria in the 1930s, organized a series of collective migration from southern Korea to parts of Northeastern China, which eventually lead to thousands of ethnic Koreans settling in Beijing.[44] After the Sino-Japanese war and civil war between the Communists and GMD during 1945-1949, Koreans in China who allied with the Communists were granted formal citizenship and were encouraged to maintain their ethnic language, education, and culture. During the Cultural Revolution (1966-1976), Koreans encountered setbacks as an ethnic minority group when the Communists sough to abolish bureaucracy and feudalistic elements of society. After having realized the vulnerability of being a minority group and the danger of nationalism, many ethnic Koreans in Beijing seemingly adopted a strategy of full accommodation to the authority of the Central and local Beijing government. They even obeyed the population control policy so enthusiastically that most ethnic Korean families in the capital city have opted to have just one child, even though they are allowed to have two children. As a result, their birth rates and population growth statistics are much lower than Han and all other ethnic minorities.

The reality for other ethnic minority groups in the capital city, notably Tibetans and Uyghurs, is quite the opposite. These groups tend to resist assimilation and often harbour deep resentment against the *dominant majority* Han due to the CPC's treatment of their large populations in the Western provinces. In many regards, assimilation in the P.R.C. is defined at the level of ideology and seen in the outcomes of public policy; it is the acceptance of a universal belief structure, which many Tibetans and Uyghurs seemingly do not subscribe too, especially the older generations. Nevertheless, there is seemingly an implicit deficit model that is inherent in the formulation and implementation of public policies that affect ethnic minority groups. As Zhou and Lin argue, in the P.R.C, an ethnic minority group must learn how to become more like the dominant Han group to overcome their "deficits" with respect to the dominant group's values, beliefs and language.[45] Lin's study on the situation of ethnic minority groups concluded that among the Han majority, a "great Han mentality" has long existed, and biases against minorities groups persist. In short, the promotion of a "culturally advanced" Han Chinese community is preferred, and reflected in numerous public policies.

Not surprisingly, China's National Minorities Policy (1999) articulates a different picture. In the preamble it writes, China is "a united multi-ethnic state founded jointly by the people of all its ethnic groups;" fifty six ethnic groups as stipulated by policy.[7] The CPC has noted they have adopted special policies and measures to effectively realize and guarantee equality of opportunity for all ethnic groups. This is prescribed by the current Chinese Constitution and reaffirmed in the National Minorities Policy:

> All ethnic groups in the People's Republic of China are equal. The state protects the lawful rights and interests of the ethnic minorities and upholds and develops a relationship of equality, unity and mutual assistance among all of China's ethnic groups. Discrimination against and oppression of any ethnic group are prohibited (Section II, Paragraph 3).

The National Minorities Policy continues to articulate China's official policy toward ethnic minority groups. It presents five basic principles that should be adhered to in public policy when managing ethnic difference:

1. Adherence to Equality and Unity Among Ethnic Groups (Section II, Paragraph 1)

Equality among ethnic groups means every ethnic group is a part of the Chinese nation, having equal status and enjoying the same rights and duties in every aspect of political and social life according to law, and ethnic oppression or discrimination of any form is firmly opposed. To achieve such unity, the various ethnic groups are required to: promote the development and prosperity of the nation; oppose ethnic splits; and, safeguard the unification of the country.

2. All Ethnic Groups Participate in State Affairs (Section II, Paragraphs 8-10)

Minority and Han peoples will participate as equals in the management of affairs of the state and local governments at various levels and the rights of the minority ethnic groups to take part in the management of state affairs are guaranteed.

3. Use and Development of Spoken and Written Languages of Ethnic Minorities (Section II, Paragraphs 18-20)

All ethnic groups in China have the freedom and right to use and develop their own spoken and written languages.

4. Development of Education for Minorities (Section IV, Paragraphs 23-26)

Education among national minorities is an important part of education of China. The development of education among national minorities is of paramount importance to the improvement of the quality of the minority population and the promotion of economic and cultural development in ethnic minority areas.

5. Preservation of the Cultural Heritage of Ethnic Minorities (Section V)

Preserve the traditional cultures of the ethnic minorities and the protecting their famous historical monuments, scenic spots, rare cultural relics and other important items of the historical and cultural heritage.

The end goal of the National Minorities Policy is to create "a favorable social environment for ethnic groups ... to treat each other on an equal footing and to develop a relationship of unity, harmony, friendship and mutual assistance among them" (Section II, Paragraph 1).

Evaluations on China's National Minorities Policy and its application on public policy provide mixed reviews. Zhou and Lin have argued that in spite of the National Minorities Policy, when applied to public policies, assimilation has become more prevalent. The reason for assimilation is practical. In China, large minority populations have been a significant cause of political and social instability. In the hope of maintaining unity, the CPC has used public policies to encourage assimilation. This becomes evident when examining China's policies on minority languages and education.

Although minority languages are granted equal status with the Han language since Article fifty three of the Common Program of the Chinese People's Political Consultative Conference in 1949, reaffirmed with every version of the Chinese Constitution, and further by the National Minorities Policy, historical circumstances and inequities in social and economic development, have impacted the use and accessibility of various minority languages in the community. As a result, Mandarin Chinese remains the dominant, official language spoken in government agencies and media. It is the language used in most forms of business, to the point that even at the Beijing Municipal Commission of Ethnic Affairs, the majority of employees can only speak Mandarin Chinese. This has created what Stites coins as "reward mechanisms" that have been set up by and for the Han.[46] The Mandarin language is the avenue to opportunities and social acceptance, whilst minority languages are limited in use and [are] of low social status.[47] This may explain why in conversation with members of the Muslim community in Beijing, they have expressed disappointment that their children cannot speak their minority language(s) and have assimilated fully into the Han culture in order to have more opportunities.

Education policy suggests an even more pronounced assimilation strategy. Article 7 of Order No.45 of the President of the People's Republic of China on March 18, 1995 (referred thereafter as the Education Law) stipulates: "Education shall be carried out in the spirit of inheriting and expanding the fine historical and cultural traditions of the Chinese nation . . . and assimilating all the fine achievements." Lin's examination of the common centralized curriculum illustrates the effect of this stipulation. Designed by the State Education Commission for all schools to follow, the common curriculum seldom stresses a concern for knowledge about ethnic minority groups to be incorporated. It instead focuses on the Han Chinese experiences thus the curriculum tends to be very impractical for meeting the needs of local ethnic minority groups. For example, textbooks at the secondary-school level are filled with Han classic canons, which are remote from students' lives and the languages they use daily. In order to understand, ethnic minority groups have to go through a "dual translation" —a cultural and intellectual assimilation – to comprehend the content.

Alba and Nee can be used to explain the Chinese approach in a more sociological slant.[48] Assimilation among ethnic minority groups, they argue, can take place due to an intimate and intense social contact with the dominant group. Since the nature of the social contact is what is decisive, it follows that a "common language is indispensable for the most intimate associations of the members of the group."[49] With a nation of fifty-five official ethnic minority groups, and even more languages and dialects, installing Mandarin Chinese as the dominant language of instruction for all ethnic groups is prudent for all ethnic minority groups to interact with one another, however, it comes at the high cost of eroding ethnic minority cultures and languages. Underneath the policy rhetoric of the CPC, assimilation is still strong in China. From language to education practices, ethnic minority groups face a downhill struggle to retain their ethnic groups' "essential characteristics."

Conclusion

This chapter has illustrated how ethnicity can be a malleable concept in China.The main reason for China's strategy for identifying and classifying ethnic groups lies in historical circumstances. In China, the identification of certain groups within China as "minorities" and the recognition of the Han as a unified "majority" have played a fundamental role in forging the People's Republic of China. Rarely has serious attention been paid to ethnic differences in the nation unless it is concerned with the "exotic" minority border peoples or "those ethnics" living in the "mountains"—almost always regarded as marginal in power and socio-economic stature. Traditionally, China has been studied as one civilization and one culture. This chapter has illustrated that is far from the reality. However, ethnic minorities are facing a downward struggle to retain their 'essential' ethnic group characteristics. As the older members of the Mosque in Beijing remarked, in time, their grandchildren may not remember the traditional ethnic traditions and language. They will lose part of themselves. In the case of Joanna, officially an ethnic Xibo, this trend has already occurred, as she cannot speak her ethnic language and finds it difficult to relate to her "ethnic" customs. Paraphrasing Li Dezhu, like a grinding shed, the effects of the CPC's public policies, especially in education, may slowly grind off ethnic features of most ethnic minority groups, to a point where history may be the only record of their existence.

Notes

1. National Bureau of Statistics and Ethnic Affairs Commission, *Tabulation on Nationalities of 2000 Population Census of China,Vols. 1 and 2 (Beijing*: The Ethnic Publishing House, 2003), in Chinese.
2. See L. Kriesberg, "Identity Issues," *Beyond Intractability Online* (USA:University of Colorado, 2005), available at: http://www.beyondintractability.org.
3. J. Fishman, "Social Theory and Ethnography", in *Ethnic Diversity and Conflict in Eastern Europe,* ed. P. Sugar, (USA: ABC-Clio, 1980).
4. R.A. Schermerhorn, *Comparative Ethnic Relations* (New York: Random House, 1970).
5. G.Goldman, "Defining and Observing Minorities: An Objective Assessment", IAOS Conference (4-8 September, 2000).
6. C. Geertz, *The Interpretation of Cultures* (New York: Basic Books, 1973); E. Shils "Primordial, Personal, Sacred and Civil Ties." *British Journal of Sociology* 8 (1957): 130-145.
7. B. Hettne, "Ethnicity and Development: An Elusive Relationship", in *Ethnicity and Development: Geographical Perspectives*, ed. D. Dwyer and D. Drakakis-Smith, (UK: John Wiley & Sons, 1996).
8. M. Reich et al., "A Theory of Labour Market Segmentation", *American Economic Review* 63 (1973): 359-365.

9. E. Bonacich, "A Theory of Ethnic Antagonism: The Split Labour Market", *American Sociological Review* 37 (1972): 547-559.

10. P. Gonzalez-Casanova, "Internal Colonialism and National Development", *Studies in Comparative International Development* 1, No. 4 (1965): 27-37.

11. I. M. Wallerstein, *The Capitalist World Economy* (Cambridge: Cambridge University Press, 1979).

12. B. Anderson, *Imagined Communities: Reflections on the Origin and Spread of Nationalism* (UK: Verso Publishers, 1991).

13. K. Chandra, "What is Ethnic Identity and Does it Matter?", *Annual Review of Political Science* 9 (2006): 397-424.

14. I. M. Young, *Justice and the Politics of Difference.* (USA: Princeton University Press, 1990).

15. Schermerhorn, 13.

16. R. Cohen, "Ethnicity: Problem and Focus in Anthropology", *Annual Review of Anthropology* 7 (1978): 379-403

17. T. Shibutani and J. Kwan, *Ethnic Stratification: A Comparative Approach* (New York: Macmillan, 1965).

18. "+" denotes having this attribute; likewise "-" means the absence of this attribute. It should also be noted that majority/minorities may be defined on the basis of a variety of factors such as ethnic characteristics (e.g. ethnic minority group), demographic characteristics (e.g. elderly), socio-economic status (e.g. working poor) and relationship to the political structures, to name a few. Although the discussion in this essay will focus primarily on ethnic characteristics, invariably it will also include elements of the other factors mentioned above.

19. G. Baumann, *Contesting Culture. Discourses of Identity in Multi-Ethnic London* (Cambridge: Cambridge University Press, 1996), 8.

20. It should be obvious that no one is completely free to define his/her ethnic membership. Constraints may be imposed be numerous circumstances, family and genetic markers to name a few. The point nevertheless remains, that within reason, self-identification of ethnicity provides a relative freedom to choose one's ethnic membership both in a legal sense and in daily life.

21. K. Chandra and M. Htun (2007) "How Should Democratic Societies and States Respond to Diversity?", APSA Annual Meeting (30 August – 2 September, 2007).

22. The term *minzu* is directly translated into English as 'nation'. In recent years, another word *zuqun* has slowly appeared in scholarly literature often referring to 'ethnic groups' or 'ethnicity' in the Western sense. While officially there are 55 *shaoshu minzu* in the P.R. China, Ma (*infra* note 24) have suggested, it may be prudent to officially change reference to these groups from 'nationalities' to 'ethnic groups' or 'ethnic minorities' for two reasons. First, the social and cultural connotations of minority groups such as Mongolians, Manchus, Tibetans, Uyghurs and Hui are approximate to 'ethnic minorities' in other countries. Thus, the term 'ethnic groups' reflects the structure of ethnicity in China more accurately. Second, conceptual confusion of both terms *minzu* and *zuqun* will be avoided. There is a potential for wrongful confusing the 55 minority 'nationalities' as independent political entities whom have unique interests based on Western ideals of 'nationalism'. Notwithstanding, until academic consensus is reached on these conceptual differences, for the purposes of this essay, when referencing Chinese ethnicity, 'nationalities' and 'ethnic groups' will be used interchangeably.

23. By early 1965, there were 183 nationalities registered (based on the 1964 census), among which the government recognized only 54.

24. R. Ma, "A New Perspective in Guiding Ethnic Relations in the 21st Century: De-Politicalization of Ethnicity in China", Discussion Paper 21 (China Policy Institute, 2007).

25. J. V. Stalin, *Works 1907-1913, Volume XI*. (Moscow: Foreign Languages Publishing House, 1953).

26. There are alternate spellings for many minority groups in China. Most common alternatives are Bonan (Bao'an); Bouyei (Bouyi or Buyi); Bulong (Blang); De'ang (Deang); Drung (Dulong); Du (Tu); Gelao (Gelo); Hani (Ahka or Hakka – especially outside of PRC); Hezhen (Hezhe); Jingpo (Kachin); Jino (Junuo); Kazak (Kazakh); Kirgiz (Kirghiz); Korean (sometimes referred to as Chaoxian especially among the elder population); Lhoba (Loba or Luoba); Menba (Moinba or Mongba); Miao (sometimes referred to as Hmung); Mulam (Mulao); Naxi (Nakhi or Nahi); Oroqin (Orogen); Tatar (Tartar); Uyghur (Uygur or Uigur); Uzbek (Ozbek); Wa (Va); Yugur (Yugu) and Xibo (Xibe or Sibe).

27. National Bureau of Statistics and Ethnic Affairs Commission, *supra* note 1.

28. T- K. Hon, "Ethnic and Cultural Pluralism: Gu Jiegang's Vision of a New China in His Studies of Ancient History", *Modern China* 22, No. 3 (1996), 332.

29. In response to Pan-Hanism, the Chinese historian Jiegang Gu, a contemporary of Sun Yat-Sen and Dai Jitao, argued that China before the Qin Dynasty (221 – 206 BC) were ruled by groups with different ethnic backgrounds. Gu continued to prove that a unified China was not only a relatively late development, but also the result of a long process of conquest by stronger ethnic tribes (See *supra* note, 322). In effect, Gu's efforts unmasked the political agenda behind the GMD attempt to promote a Pan-Hanism.

30. E. Snow. *Red Star over China: The Classic Account of the Birth of Chinese Communism* (USA: Grove Press, 1994).

31. T. Heberer, *China and its National Minorities: Autonomy or Assimilation?*. (USA: M.E. Sharpe, 1989).

32. Since ethnic minorities are exempt from the one-child policy, Ma (*supra* note 24) suggests this is one of the main reasons why many farmers tried to change their nationality status from Han to a minority group. From 1982 to 1990, several minority groups doubled their population size mainly by re-registration (e.g. the Manchu population increased from 4.3 million to 9.8 million, and Tujia increased from 2.8 million to 5.7 million during an 8 year period.

33. Save in the situation where a child is born by mixed parents due to inter-ethnic marriage. Here the ethnic status will be determined by the parents before the child reaches 18 years of age. However, when the child reaches 18, s/he can choose which parent's ethnic status s/he chooses to adopt. By the age of 20 no alteration can be made. In practice, the large majority adopts the ethnicity of their father. Also, in cases where the CPC were mistaken in nationality status recognition, an individual can to apply for "correction" of their status. In practice, most individual apply to correct their status due to nationality recognition "errors" during the Cultural Revolution. The present-day CPC have been active in "addressing" the mistakes made during the Revolution.

34. People's Daily, "Number of Ethnic Minority Cadres Soaring up," June 28, 2000. http://english.people.com.cn/english/200006/28/ eng20000628_44161.html.

35. F. X. Tong, *Toward a People's Anthropology* (Beijing: New World Press, 1981). 36. D. Gladney, "Ethnic Identity in China: The New Politics of Difference", in *China Briefing*, ed. W. Joseph (USA: Westview Press, 1994).

37. Minority Rights International, *State of the World's Minorities 2007*. Available at: http://www.minorityrights.org.

38. M. Moerman, "Who are the Lue?", *American Anthropologist* 67 (1965): 1215-1230.

39. D. Li "City: An Important Arena to Display Ethnic Cultures and Ethnic Development," in *Urban Culture and Urban Ecology in China*, ed. H. Yang (Beijing: China Urban Anthropology Association, 1998), 109.

40. R. Park and E. Burgess, *Introduction to the Science of Sociology*. Chicago: University of Chicago Press, 1969), 735.

41. R. Rumbaut, "Assimilation and Its Discontents: Between Rhetoric and Reality", *International Migration Review* 31, No. 4 (1997): 923-960., 2. K. Deutsch, *Nationalism and Social Communication: An Inquiry into the Foundations of Nationality* (USA: Massachusetts Institute of Technology Press, 1953).

43. E. Rawski, *The Last Emperors: A Social History of the Qing Imperial Institutions* (USA: University of California at Berkeley Press, 2001).

44. S. J. Kim, "The Economic Status and Role of Ethnic Koreans in China", in *The Korean Diaspora in the World Economy*, eds.
C. F. Bergsten and I.B. Choi (Washington, DC: Institute for International Economics, 2003).

45. J. Lin "Policies and Practices of Bilingual Education for the Minorities in China", *Journal of Multilingual and Multicultural Development* 18, No. 3 (1997): 193-205; M.L. Zhou, "Language Policy and Illiteracy in Ethnic Minority Communities in China", *Journal of Multilingual and Multicultural Development* 21, No, 2 (2000): 129-148.

46. R. Stites, *China's National Minority Education* (New York: Routledge Publishers, 1999).

47. See *supra* note 43.

48. R. Alba and V. Nee, "Rethinking Assimilation Theory for a New Era of Immigration," *International Migration Review* 31, No. 4 (1997): 826-874.

49. Alba and Nee, 827.

References

Alba, R., and Nee, V. "Rethinking Assimilation Theory for a New Era of Immigration." *International Migration Review* 31, no. 4 (1997), 826-874.

Anderson, Benedict. *Imagined Communities: Reflections on the Origin and Spread of Nationalism.* United Kingdom: Verso Publishers, 1991.

Bonacich, Edna. "A Theory of Ethnic Antagonism: The Split Labor Market." *American Sociological Review* 37, (1972), 547-559.

Baumann, Gerd. *Contesting Culture: Discourses of Identity in Multiethnic London.* Cambridge: Cambridge University Press, 1996.

Chandra, K. "What is Ethnic Identity and Does it Matter?" *Annual of Political Science* 9 (2006): 397-424.

Chandra, K., and M. Htum. "How Should Democratic Societies and States Respond to Diversity?" APSA Annual Meeting, September 2007.

Cohen, Ronald. "Ethnicity: Problem and Focus in Anthropology." *Annual Review of Anthropology* 7 (1978): 379-403.

Deutsch, Karl W. *Nationalism and Social Communication: An Inquiry into the Foundations of Nationality.* Cambridge: MIT Press, 1953.

Fishman, Joshua. "Social Theory and Ethnography." In *Ethnic Diversity and Conflict in Eastern Europe.* ed. P. Sugar. Santa Barbara: ABC-Clio, 1980.

Geertz, Clifford. *The Interpretation of Cultures.* New York: Basic Books, 1973.

Gladney, Dru C. "Ethnic Identity in China: The New Politics of Difference." In *China Briefing*, edited by W. Joseph. New York: Westview Press, 1994.

Goldman, Gustave. "Defining and Observing Minorities: An Objective Assessment." LAOS Conference (September 2000).

Gonzalez-Casanova, Pablo. "Internal Colonialism and National Development." *Studies in Comparative International Development* 1, no. 4 (1965): 27-37.

Heberer, Thomas. *China and its National Minorities: Autonomy or Assimilation?* New York: M.E. Sharpe, 1989.

Hettne, Bjorn. "Ethnicity and Development: An Elusive Relationship." In *Ethnicity and Development: Geopolitical Perspectives,* ed. D. Dwyer and D. Drakakis- Smith. London: John Wiley & Sons, 1996.

Hon, Tze-ki. "Ethnic and Cultural Pluralism: Gu Jiegang's Vision of a New China." *Modern China* 22, no. 3 (1996): 332-352.

Kriesberg, Louis. "Identity Issues." In *Beyond Intractability,* edited by Guy Burgess. Boulder: Conflict Research Consortium, 2005. Available at: http://www.beyondintractability.org

Kim, S.J. "The Economic Status and Role of Ethnic Koreans in China." In *The Korean Diaspora in the World Economies,* edited by C.F. Bergsten and I.B. Choi. Washington, D.C.: Institute for International Economics, 2003.

Li, D. "City: An Important Arena to Display Ethnic Cultures and Ethnic Development." In *Urban Culture and Urban Ecology in China,* ed. H. Yang. Beijing: China Urban Anthropology Association, 1998.

Lin, J. "Policies and Practices of Bilingual Education for the Minorities in China." *Journal of Multilingual and Multicultural Development* 18, no. 3 (1997): 193-205.

Moerman, Michael. "Who are the Lue?" *American Anthropologist* 67, (1965): 1215-1230.

Minority Rights International. *State of World's Minorities* 2007. Found at: http://www.minorityrights.org

National Bureau of Statistics and Ethnic Affairs Commission. *Tabulation on Nationalities of 2000 Population Census of China, Vol. 1 and 2.* Beijing: The Ethnic Publishing House, 2003.

Park, R., and E. Burgess. *Introduction to the Science of Sociology.* Chicago: University of Chicago Press, 1969.

People's Daily. "Number of Ethnic Minority Cadres Soaring Up." June 28, 2000. http://www.english.people.com.cn/english/20006/28/eng20000628_44161.html

Rawski, E. *The Last Emperors: A Social History of the Qing Imperial Institutions.* Berkeley: University of California Press, 2001.

Reich, Michael, David M. Gordon, and Richard C. Edwards. "A Theory of Labor Market Segmentation." *American Economic Review* 63 (1973): 359-365.

Rumbaut, R. "Assimilation and Its Discontents: Between Rhetoric and Reality." *International Migration Review* 31, no. 4, (1997): 923-960.

Schermerhorn, Richard A. *Comparative Ethnic Relations.* New York: Random House, 1970.

Stites, R. *China's National Minority Education.* New York: Routledge Publishers, 1999.

Tong, F. X. *Toward a People's Anthropology.* Beijing: New World Press, 1981.

Wallerstein, Immanuel. *The Capitalist World Economy.* Cambridge: Cambridge University Press, 1979.

Young, Iris M. *Justice and the Politics of Difference.* Princeton: Princeton University Press, 1990.

Chapter 23

The Russian/Chechen Conflict and Its Consequences

Mariana Tepfenhart

The purpose of this chapter is to present a short history of the conflict between Russia and Chechnya that led to a vicious action-reaction cycle that reinforced the prejudices and hatreds of both sides. The history of prejudice on the part of Russians is justified by the terrorist methods used by the Chechens. The history of abusive treatment by the Russians justifies the Chechens in adopting brutal tactics to resist the Russians. With violence begetting violence on both sides of the conflict, a peaceful solution has been difficult to achieve. This conflict remains one of the best examples where history interacts between the past and the present.

Introduction

For three hundred years, the Russian government has tried to subdue and impose its rule on a tiny place in the Caucasus Mountains called Chechnya. The struggle was often bitter and bloodthirsty. Under tsarist Russia, the Chechens were humiliated, betrayed, killed, tortured, deported and kidnapped. Under communism, the government tried russification and sovietization as a means to control the Chechens. All efforts to subdue Chechnya did not weaken the Chechen people. Chechens continuously united and fought back with more determination not to surrender. Contrary to the expectations of the Russians, what started as a revolution against occupation turned into a jihad against the Russians organized by the Chechens. One can say that racism was a major factor that contributed to the harsh punishments administered by the Russians.

Chechnya is situated in the northern part of the Caucasus region which is made up of about forty ethnic groups of Christian and Muslims.[1] Geographically, Chechnya has a large plain in the north with hills in the south bordering the Caucasus Mountains. When the Russians first encountered the Chechens, in the beginning of the eighteenth century, they viewed their local traditions as being very primitive. Rather than having a central authority, Chechen society was divided into clans with proud warriors who valued their freedom and rejected any authority that came from outside their clan. They respected and obeyed the elders of their families. When attacked, they rebelled as a group not as individuals. They believed in equality, hospitality, and a spirit of sacrifice for the clan and family but also in vindictiveness towards their enemies. Alexander Solzhenitsyn provided a very good description of the Chechens:

> There was one nation which would not give in, would not acquire habits of submission-and not just individual rebels among them, but the whole nation to a man. These were the Chechens . . . The Chechens never sought to please, to ingratiate themselves with the bosses; their attitude was always haughty, and indeed openly hostile. They treated the laws on universal education and the state curriculum with contempt, and to save them from corruption would not send their girls to school, nor indeed all their boys.[2]

The Chechen way of life is well captured by the symbol they chose for their nation: the wolf. The Chechen author Lenna Usmanov explained that:

> The wolf is the only creature that dares to take on someone stronger than himself. The wolf's insufficient strength is compensated for with limitless audacity, courage and adroitness. If however, he has lost the battle, he dies silently, expressing neither fear nor pain. And he always dies facing the enemy.[3]

The first encounter with the people of the Caucasus came during the reign of Peter the Great, who tried to impose Russian rule in the area and expand his territory in the South. Like his predecessors, he wanted an opening to the Black Sea, which at that time, was under the control of the Ottoman Empire. Peter the Great managed to set up a line of defense for the region with Cossack settlements, despite the strong opposition of the Mountaineers (the Chechens). The Russians built fortresses on the land that traditionally belonged to the Mountaineers. In retaliation, the Chechens executed raids inside Russian land, which were followed by Russian punitive actions with the purpose to inflict large number of casualties and material damages. From that time on, there was tension between Chechen and Russian authorities.

Chechnya and Russian Expansion

Catherine the Great who pushed the defense line closer to the Black Sea, continued the Russian policy of expansion to the south. Catherine's aid, Prince Potemkin, explained that expansion would "bar the mountain people of different names from those areas to be exploited by our subjects."[4] Russian officials used force to bring the tribes of the Caucasus into submission because they believed that Chechens were "Asiatics" or primitive tribes who could only understand violence.

The same policy that employed harsh treatment upon those viewed as primitives was continued by Catherine's successor Alexander I. Russia had to prove to the West that it was a colonial power. Alexander appointed General Alexei Yermolov to the post of Proconsul of the Caucasus. General Yemolov was extremely xenophobic against non-Russians. He considered the Chechens to be "the basest of the bandits who attack the Caucasian line" and Chechnya, "May rightly be called the nest of all the bandits."[5] Yermolov's treatment of the Chechens was one of extreme cruelty. He razed entire villages and executed many villagers without trials. In 1819, the village of Dadi Yurt was attacked. After the men were killed, the women took their place or committed suicide rather than surrender to the Russians. Chechen wives and daughters were often raped and humiliated by Russian victors.[6] Land belonging to Chechens was given to the Cossacks and those who collaborated with the Russians. Yemolov's actions provoked a deep and lasting hatred towards Russia. As the British explorer, Lyall, commented that the Russian destruction of villages were considered acts "unjustified in the eyes of God and man."[7]

One might say, without doubt, that Yermolov did not understand the Chechens. He did not abandon his cruel methods because he believed that "Condescension in the eyes of the Asiatics is a sign of weakness, and out of pure humanity, inexorably severe."[8] He is also attributed with the statement "the only good Chechen is a dead Chechen."[9] Aleksei Yermolov was considered a hero. He was the conqueror of the Caucasus. Others who had open contempt for "Asiatics," shared his views. Aleksandr Griboedov was in the Foreign Service and knew General Yermolov and the way he dealt with the people from the Caucasus. Regarding the General's attitude, he commented: "He subdues the disobedient with arms: hangs them, burns their villages, but what is to be done? I cannot justify his arbitrary actions according to the law, but recall that he is in Asia-here even a child reaches for a knife."[10]

Alexei Yermolov failed whenever he used military force against the Chechens. The campaign ended up in humiliating defeat for the Russians, but it set up a pattern that would continue over the following two centuries. The use of punitive expeditions strengthened the determination of the Chechens to unite under a leader, to organize, and to strike back at the regime that tried to eliminate them. Historian Moshe Gammer, the author of *The Lone Wolf and the Bear*, found an explanation of the Russian failure to control Chechens as residing in their contempt for the people of the mountains, viewed as primitive "Muslims," "Asiatics" and "Tartars."[11]

In their struggle against Russian occupation, Chechens turned to religion and religious leaders as a unifying and inspirational focus. In the eighteenth and nineteenth century Sufism attracted followers because it insisted on strict discipline that fit well with the warrior brotherhood that pre-dated the conversion to Islam.

There were two branches of Sufism: Naqshbandya, a more aggressive form of Islam and Qadyria, which preached non-resistance. Initially, Naqshbandya was the more attractive branch and had many followers. According to Moritz Wagner, the author of *Travel in Persia*, the Islamic passion was the direct result of the hatred of the Russian supremacy, which as he stated, "facilitates the cohesion of tribes speaking different idioms, under one head, and impedes the progress of conquest to the numerous Russian hosts."[12] People rallied around spiritual leaders who became military leaders as well. One example was Imam Shamil who enforced the laws of the *Koran* and organized frequent raids against the Russians.

The Russians continued to hammer the Chechen villages but, despite overwhelming forces, achieved no results. During the reign of Tsar Nicholas I in 1844 the situation seemed out of control. The Tsar sent more troops to Chechnya under a new commander. Again, the Russian army was trapped and nearly annihilated. While the Chechens scored victories against their enemy, they paid a heavy price with thousands killed. The Russian expeditions became more forceful and frequent. Their goal was to destroy the village life of the Chechens and to force them to abandon their homes, and migrate to Russian dominated territories. Some governors tried to do "ethnic cleansing" by persuading the insubordinate elements of the Chechen society to settle in Turkey. The Turkish government agreed to allow the migrants to settle in Asia Minor. Between 1864-5, Grand Duke Michael encouraged the "most untamed' to migrate and in the summer of 1865 some 5,000 families left to live in Turkey.[13] The Chechens perceived this exodus as an "ethnic catastrophe that deprived the people of its finest sons."[14] LeoTolstoy wrote that the inhabitants of the villages:

> Were confronted with the choice of remaining there and restoring the frightful effort what had been produced with such labor and yet, so lightly and senseless destroyed, facing every moment the possibility of a repetition of what had happened, or to submit to the Russians- contrary to their religion and despite the repulsion and contempt they felt for them.[15]

The Crimean War (1854-1856) raised the hopes of the Mountaineers for independence. The Chechens believed that the Ottoman Empire, supported by Britain and France, might defeat Russia. It was a great disappointment to learn that Russia won. Some Chechens gave up fighting thinking that if three great powers of the world could not defeat Russia that the chances for a small group of people to resist such a giant were very slim. Those who accepted Russian rule were allowed to live. Others remained in the deep forests and continued to fight from there.

By the 1860s, Russian authorities managed to take control of most of Chechnya. They used military actions with tactics such as divide and rule, deportation, and rewarding those who supported their authority. Contributing to the Chechens' submission was the adoption of Qadiryya, the other branch of Sufism. The man who introduced Qadiryya was Sheikh Kunta. He preached individual salvation and advocated that the retreat from worldly affairs did not equate to being a less faithful Muslim. The Russian officials welcomed Sheikh Kunta in the beginning, but later on he was arrested on charges of being a fanatic religious leader. His arrest was followed by more violence, killings, and imprisonment of Chechens. True to their traditions and customs the Chechens continued with sporadic uprisings to the twentieth century. Most of the fights took place in the forests in the form of ambushes. The conflict between the Russians and the Chechens never completely died out and continued with heavy losses on both sides.

Russian Views of Chechens

One might wonder why Russia fought for this piece of rugged land. The author Anatol Lieven identified a couple of reasons to explain Russian behavior. One reason was the desire to spread their sphere of influence in that area. Russia had many conflicts with Turkey. If a war ever broke out between the two powers, the Russians were convinced that the Chechens would join the Turkish troops.[16] The second reason was to stamp out "banditry." Among the Chechens, it was a tradition for young men to fight. It was a social obligation and a form of resistance to Russian occupation. Chechens did not recognize Russian authority; therefore, there was nothing to stop the young men from organizing raids against the Russians. When the Russians started the war against Chechnya, these bandits became popular heroes, protected by the people. They attacked Russian convoys and forts. These "bandits" would continue to do so into the next century.

Russians viewed Chechens as very primitive and their attitude towards other cultures was not too different from that of other imperialist powers. The Russian government considered it their duty to try to civilize them, using that as justification in trying to occupy the North Caucasus. This attitude was clearly outlined by Alexander Gorchakov, Russian Foreign Minister, in 1864, in a letter to the tsar:

> The position of Russia in Central Asia is that of all civilized states which are brought into contact with half-savage, nomad population possessing no fixed social organization. In such cases, it always happens that the more civilized State is forced, in the interests of the security of its frontier and its commercial relations, to exercise a certain ascendancy over those whom their turbulent and unsettled character make most undesirable neighbors. First, there are raids and acts of pillage to put down. To put a stop to them, the tribes of the frontier must be reduced to a state of more or less perfect submission . . . It is a peculiarity of Asiatics to respect nothing but visible and palpable force.[17]

Not everybody agreed with this point of view. The famous Russian writer, Leo Tolstoy wrote:

> Under the pretext of self-defense (even though attacks are always provoked by the powerful neighbor) or the pretext of civilizing the ways of a savage people (even though that savage people is living a life incomparable better and more peaceable than the 'civilizers'), or else under other pretext, the servants of large military states commit all sorts of villainy against small peoples, while maintaining that one cannot deal with them otherwise.[18]

The prejudice, betrayals, killings and deportations continued into the twentieth century under the Soviet regime.

The Communists and Chechnya

After the communists took over Russia, many nations within the former Russian Empire declared independence and the Chechens were among them. In

1918, the Chechens and their neighbors, Daghestanis, set up the North Caucasus Republic. In their struggle to gain support, the Bolsheviks appealed to the non-Russians and promised things such as cultural independence, religious freedom, and the right to secede. Many Muslims, like other people in Russia, were lured by these promises and believed in Lenin. In the civil war that followed the Russian Revolution, the Chechens joined the Red Army in war against the White Army led by General Denikin who opposed secession. Once the White Army was eliminated, the Chechens, like other minorities were faced with the process of sovietization nationalism, which became a bourgeoisie concept. The Muslim religion was discouraged and ethnic identity was repressed. Intellectuals and the clergy, who played such an important role in the life of the Chechens, were liquidated through accusations of "counter-revolutionary activity" and "bourgeois nationalism."

The communists intensified the process of russification in dealing with the non-Russians. New schools were opened without any link to religion. The Arabic alphabet was labeled "an alphabet of exploitation"[19] and the Cyrillic alphabet, along with the Russian language, became obligatory. These measures were implemented "at the request of the people" and were meant to mould a new identity—*Homo Sovieticus*. This was a strike at the very soul of the people in the Caucasus Mountains. The Communists eliminated the governments of the independent republics. Russian troops plundered the land, confiscated food supplies, and forced people to join the Russian army. The reaction of the Chechens was quick. Like in the past, they started attacking Russian convoys. This was the second war since the 1917 revolution but this time it was against the communists. The war lasted about one year, 1920-1921, but various forms of resistance did not stop until 1925.[20] Despite food shortages and forced relocation of about 10,000 people, the Chechens waged a guerrilla war against the much larger Soviet force even during Stalin's reign of terror.[21]

Collectivization met resistance everywhere. The Soviet government introduced a new method of economic control- grain requisitioning. It affected all the peasants but the effects were stronger in the region of the northern Caucasus. Grain requisition produced starvation that killed thousands of people. This time it was not the religious leaders or the clan leaders to inspire the people but members of the Chechen Communist Party who felt that they were betrayed by Lenin and his Bolsheviks. Stalin promised an amnesty if they would give up fighting. When the Chechens gave up their hiding places in the mountains and returned to their homes they were arrested, put in show trials, labeled "enemies of the people", and then imprisoned, exiled or shot.[22]

In 1937, Stalin's purges began. Nobody was safe anymore. NKDV, the Soviet secret police, arrested 14,000 men representing 3% of the population. This is how an eyewitness described those events:

> As it would have been impossible to carryout the death sentence pronounced by the troika within the assigned time, a 'special' execution hall was established for the extermination of large groups" . . . That chamber was made up of concrete and "hermetically sealed from the outside world. Revolving firing positions were fixed into the walls and the ceiling from the exterior." The bodies were carried off to a mass grave.[23]

Among those victims were Chechen Communist Party members who supported the Bolsheviks and believed in their communist ideology.

During WWII, the Chechens again attempted to free themselves from the Soviet regime. Some Chechens wanted to join the Germans, hoping that they would get independence. After the defeat of Germany, Stalin decided to get rid of those problem people in the Caucasus once and for all. In 1944, thousands of agents of the Soviet secret police, NKDV, gathered together most of the Chechen and Ingush population, telling them that they would be deported within one hour.[24] About 500,000 people were deported. It has been estimated that about 78,000 died on the way. Those who could not be evacuated because of weather or difficult terrain were killed. Husbands were separated from their wives and children were separated from their parents if, during that fatal hour allowed to prepare for the exile, they were not united. Mosques were burnt and patients in the hospitals were executed.[25] The Chechens and other groups from the Caucasus Mountains were resettled in Kazakh and Kyrgyz SSR as well as Siberia. They were not allowed to leave the premises without permission.

This deportation is considered by the Chechens to be genocide. To understand the extent of that event, one can look at Soviet censuses taken 1926-1939. For that period the population growth was 28%, despite the purges, collectivization, and revolts. Between 1939 and 1959, the growth of the population increased by only 2%.[26] This is what a British journalist said about the deportation:

> Because this was punishment based on race, the deportation has become part of the national identity of the Chechens, Ingush, Karachai, and Balkars. Like Jewish holocaust survivors, it is an event which quietly dominates both the individuals' lives and the nation as a whole. Everyone without exception is a victim. Even for those born after, the tragedy is impossible to put aside, since their parents, relatives, village and entire people suffered.[27]

In Groznyy, the capital of Chechnya, there is a monument that serves as a reminder of this atrocity. It reads: "We will not weep; we will not weaken; we will not forget."[28] It is an important statement that sums up who the Chechens are, what resulted from intensive Russian oppression, and how their consciousness was shaped by past experiences. It was Russian policy, based on racial hatred that united the Chechens and made them organize to put up a strong resistance against an authority that they would not recognize.

By 1956, as part of de-Stalinization program, the new Soviet president, Nikita Khrushchev described the deportation as monstrous and allowed the Chechens to return to their land.[29] Many of the Chechens and Ingush did not get their land and homes back. They were settled in industrial centers to provide labor, on one hand and, on the other, to be easily supervised. In an effort to dilute the ethnic tensions, the borders of the Chechen-Ingush Republic were redefined, to include more pro-Russians people. One way to attract Russian emigrants was to offer them better salaries. By the 1980s, there was an increased industrialization in such areas as refineries, gas, machinery for the oil industry, and medical instruments. However, despite the fact that specialists were needed there was no real effort to engage the young Chechens in these activities. The

Russians filled most of the positions for trained specialists, leaving agriculture for the Chechens. In 1980s the largest petrochemical company in Chechnya hired 50,000 workers and engineers and out of these only a few hundreds were Chechens.[30] This intensified the feeling among the Chechens that they were discriminated against and that many opportunities were denied to them.

During the Khrushchev administration, the process of Sovietization continued through campaigns designed to eradicate "the reactionary past," the traditions and religion. New schools were set up where children were taught in Russian. These measures were introduced under the slogan of "getting together" the people of the Soviet Union. Despite the efforts of the soviet officials to change the Chechens, there was an increase in nationalism and their traditions did not disappear. This is shown in a report of a KGB agent in 1966 in which he describes the "harmful activity " of the elder generation and religious authority who continued to incite hate against the Soviet state and predict its demise.[31] For the next three decades, there were not so many uprisings. People were too busy trying to survive. There was an improvement in the standard of living and this contributed to the relative calm. Although religion was discouraged, Islam continued to play a unifying role in the lives of the Chechens.

The Gorbachev Government and Chechnya

In 1985, Mikhail Gorbachev became Secretary General of the Communist Party. He introduced two concepts perestroika (restructuring) and glasnost (openness). His desire to restructure the political and economic system of the Soviet Union failed and, paradoxically, led to the collapse of the empire. The truth that was denied for decades resurfaced and exposed the real face of communism. In 1988 the Chechens set up the Chechen Ingush Popular Front in Support of Perestroika (CHINFSP). They pushed for moderate demands such as freedom of religion, compensation for the deportees, protection of Chechen and Ingush culture, and commemoration of the deportation.[32] The organization included Chechen members of the intelligentsia, businessmen, and local Russians. For the first time, the head of this organization was a Chechen, Doku Zavgayev. Two years later, in 1990, another organization was set up with more radical composition—the All National Congress of the Chechen People (OKCHN) led by Major–General Jobar Dudayev. A Chechen born before the deportation, Dudayev served in the Soviet Air Force, and earned a highranking position. Meanwhile, in Moscow, tensions mounted between Mikhail Gorbachev, supported by Soviet loyalists and Boris Yeltsin. Yeltsin was backed by a Russian middle class disappointed with Gorbachev's lack of direction and by ethnic groups who hoped for a radical change in their status. The conflict ended in 1991 when Yeltsin became the Russian president.

Jobar Dudayev denounced the putsch in Moscow and staged a mass demonstration in Grozny demanding the resignation of the Supreme Soviet. As commander of the Chechen National Guard, reinforced with criminal elements that had been released from prisons, Dudayev took control of Chechnya and declared independence of his country. Despite his high rank in the Soviet Army, Dudayev was anti-Russian and anti-communist. He used the people's feelings against the Russians to further his political agenda. He was surrounded by criminal elements and used them in any way he could to maintain his control.

Initially, Yeltsin saw an ally in Dudayev against pro-Gorbachev elements. However, with the collapse of the Soviet Union, he realized further territorial disintegration would spell disaster for his presidency. Russian officials tried to negotiate with Dudayev a compromise as long as Chechnya would remain part of Russian Federation. The talks failed mainly because Dudayev alienated the Russians and the Chechens with his lack of political understanding.[33] A Western journalist expressed tThe same idea:

> Dudayev, with his macho fantasies and total disregard for democracy, bore a particular guilt for what was about to happen. When there were chances for negotiations, he baited the Russian bear; when compromise might have kept peace, he threatened war. He began his rule with a threat in November 1992, to blow up a Russian nuclear power, and on the eve of the war, he threaten to kill prisoners, and his former minister repeated the threat about nuclear power.[34]

Chechnya after the Fall of Communism

In 1991, Chechnya declared independence and Dudayev became its first president. The Russian government wanted to invade Chechnya right away but, due to the chaos that followed the collapsed of the former Soviet Union, it was postponed. There were, however, attempts to de-stabilize Dudayev's regime. Chechnya's independence was neither recognized nor denied.

Dudayev faced the same problems in Chechnya that were rampant in the rest of Russia after the fall of communism—a weak economy, corruption, high unemployment, and high criminality. The Russian military feared that Chechnya would turn into a criminalized state. The Chechens were involved in illegal export of oil, forged money and drugs. Many of these were done with the blessing of Dudayev and Russian members of the government in Moscow. Dudayev admitted in 1993 that he had $70 million in different foreign banks.[35] The idea of Chechnya as a criminalized state was further emphasized by the newspapers, which condemned the leniency of the Russian government towards the criminal elements. In 1992, there were many rallies calling for the expulsion of Caucasians. This attitude towards the Caucasians is clearly explained by a police chief from Moscow, Andrei Shchavlev:

> Most of our crimes are committed by the Caucasians. They have dark complexions, large noses so they are easily to spot and detain...They go into bars, beat up men, steal their women, they bring girls into dorms, force them to take drugs...these drive all the best cars- Audi, BMWs, Mercedes- but they have very low culture." He continued saying that "these Caucasians flooded the city and have caused a lot of trouble. There is no doubt, Muscovites want them out."[36]

One cannot deny the presence of a strong criminal element in Chechnya, but looking at the history of the people, one can see the reasons. An old Chechen, Haji Mahomet, explained the killings among the Chechens:

One reason for the killings and the feuds is that the Chechen people always loved arms. Every man who was a man had to carry arms, and know how to use them. A man without arms would be humiliated, challenged to fight...Though as result men did not hit each other, because the other man would immediately go for his weapons, and in general, quarrelsome men are not respected; the man with respect was the man who did not look for fights but would defend himself bravely if attacked.[37]

In their desire to undermine Chechen traditions, the Russians destroyed the authority in the clan. The young generation of Chechens lacks the discipline that their fathers had:

Today, there is not such respect for tradition. Youths hit each other more easily, use their weapons more easily, partly because of the spread of alcohol, a great disgrace, and a crime-thanks to the Soviet rule.[38]

With high unemployment, many were forced to migrate to find jobs or turned to criminal activities. Many Chechens and Ingush people were imprisoned annually. There were conflicts among clans and fights between clans and Russians. Religious leaders who preached hatred and incited fanaticism also fanned the conflicts. All of these factors contributed to the Chechen scornful attitude towards a society that did not welcome them. A number of bus hijackings by the militants, triggered the intervention of the Russian army in 1994. There were other reasons for military intervention, such as the oil pipeline from Azerbaijan to the port Novorossisk passed through Chechnya, making this region an important economic and strategic point.

The Russian Chechen Conflict

The first war lasted two years between 1994 and 1996 and ended up with a victory for the Chechens. When the war started, the reaction of the Russian was mixed. Those Russians living in the south supported the intervention. Among those in central part of Russia only 45% were in favor of a military intervention.[39] In Moscow, only 13% supported the action.[40]

During the war a lot of civilians became victims both of BOYEVIKI, Chechens militants, and of Russian soldiers. Valery Tishkov, the author of Chechnya—Life in a War Torn Society, argued that, contrary to the statements of Dudayev, that Chechens do not attack other Chechens, there was a lot of violence against regular Chechens who did not share too much enthusiasm for war and against Russians, not because of their ethnicity, but because they had expensive possessions.[41] The federal troops persecuted those Chechens suspected of collaborating with the militants.

An old Chechen, who worked in a store, saw first hand how the *Boyeviki* and the federals operated:

At times the Russians and the *Boyeviki* would hold different sides of the same street, with the civilian population between them. They would visit each other amicably and share tobacco and liquor, and they would shoot population from both sides. How can you understand such a war?

Then, they would begin ransacking our stores. The director had bid me stand guard and I buried the keys where they could not be found, thinking, let them beat me all they like. I would not betray that secret. They robbed the store all the same, but how? First the Russians would come-eat, drink and be off. Then the boyeviki would follow, eating drinking and grabbing all they could. When they had taken everything down that wasn't nailed down, they began to saw off the pipes, as if they could eat them up in the mountains.[42]

The *Boyeviki*, however, were only a small part of the population. As one Chechen teacher said they are, "far from representing the Chechen people."[43] They were "idlers, and parasites" who "envied hard working people who tried to make a decent living."[44] Chechens opposed the war but once it started, they fought to defend their families and dignity.

During the war a new character appeared: Shamil Basayev the most ferocious among the Chechen fighters and Russia's most wanted terrorist. He was unconventional, defiant and calculated. He fought in support of Yeltsin because, as he mentioned, he knew that, "if the Communists won, it would be the death of independence for Chechnya."[45] He came from a family of fighters and he wanted to set up an imamate in his country. In 1995, during a Russian bombardment, a bomb fell on Basayev's uncle's house, killing eleven members of his family. Among them were Basayev's wife, children, and sister. Basayev decided to take the war to Russia. Accompanied by 142 fighters, Basayev attacked the police headquarters and the hospital in the town of Budennovsk. They killed all the police troops in sight and in the hospital. The siege left 143 dead and more than 400 wounded. Any offer from the Russians to stop the attack was dismissed. He was ready to use pregnant women as shields if the Russian government would not agree to a ceasefire of the war.[46]

In an interview with Anatol Lieven, when asked about morality of his action, Basayev answered: "Who cares about our moral position? Who, from abroad helped us, while Russia has brutally ignored every moral rule?"[47] His mission was successful and in Chechnya he got a hero's welcome because he challenged the Russians on their own territory. In an interview with Svoboda Radio, Movladi Udugov, Chechen propagandist, and Dudayev's press secretary, declared: "We consider this an act of heroism; it was a valuable prize and we admire and have deep respect for those who died to save our people."[48]

The Russians agreed to sign a peace agreement in 1996. The war was devastating. It was estimated that between 40,000 and 100,000 died and 300,000-400,000 left the country.[49] These were primarily Chechen professionals who were the only ones capable of bringing law and order in Chechnya. Many of those who remained in Grozny died from shock and ill health. Among the Russians, according to a report of the Defense Ministry about 25,000 perished, were wounded, or were missing in action.[50] The conflict did not end despite peace agreements. As a result of warlords, and Islamic radicals, anarchy dominated the country. Unemployment was 33% while education was practically non-existent. Some people resorted to counterfeiting result in approximately 4 billion bills forged in Chechnya. Stealing oil directly from the pipeline was very profitable. Even before the war, profits from the oil refineries were huge. In 1993, the Chechen Council of Ministers reported that 47,000 tons of oil products worth approximately 4 billon dollars went missing in the first three months of the year.[51] That was estimated to be $100-$900 million profit for Dudayev and his accomplice in Chechnya and in Russia.[52] Many saw the first war as a mafia war:

> This is not a conflict between the Chechen and Russian people. It is a personal conflict between Dudayev and various clans, lining their pockets on oil deals, the arms trade and drug trafficking.[53]

In 1994, it was estimated that 4,300 gangs were in Russia and 600 out of these were ethnic groups.[54] Dudayev's regime and the actions of people like Shamil Basayev turned people against them, both inside and outside the country. This played into Russian prejudices about the Chechens. Many Chechen intellectuals opposed the use of terrorist methods and resented the fact that their country is considered by many to be a nation of criminals. This is what one of them said:

> Around the world, we are portrayed as a wild and mafia–ridden tribe. But in real life, the Chechens are a different nation. We have high culture. Somebody came, imposed this regime on us, and it has changed us. This regime brought the most undignified instincts out of us.[55]

After the first war, Moscow almost recognized the independence of Chechnya but negotiations that were supposed to be concluded in the following five years were never completed. In 1997, Aslan (Khalid) Maskhadov won the presidential election. The new president was faced with a disastrous situation. The country was in ruin. Although Moscow promised help to the Chechens, it never materialized. Many who fought in the war returned to no jobs and no houses. Some attached themselves to the warlords and turned to crime.

One major problem was that hostage taking developed into "a branch of Chechnya's economy,"[56] and brought millions of dollars. These kidnappings were done for ransom and if ransom was not paid the hostages met a gruesome death. By 1999 there were 851 people missing and the sale of the captives put about 200 million in the pockets of the criminals. Anybody could become a target: foreigners, Russians, children, and women who were forced to perform services for the armed groups.[57] President Maskhadov recognized the gravity of the situation but was unable to stop it. There were several attempts on his life too. The response of the Russian authorities to the situation was weak. Moscow was disappointed with Mashkadov for failing to establish order in Chechnya.

Another problem for the new president was that warlords had taken control over certain areas and refused to relinquish their power. One of them was Shamil Basayev who wanted to "decolonize" the Caucasus and set up a shura (Council) that defied Maskhadov's authority. In 1999, Basayev and Emir Khattab, born in Saudi Arabia, invaded Dagestan to help their allies there. Basayev and Khattab wanted an Islamic state with strict Islamic laws. Islamization was a great concern for Moscow. Some Wahhabis, like Khattab, went to Chechnya as volunteers from different Arab countries. Moscow reacted swiftly and sent troops to put down the rebels and that marked the second war with Chechnya.

During the same year, there were approximately 300 explosions in residential areas around Moscow. The Russian people were shocked and concern for safety became the number one priority. Vladimir Putin promised to take a strong position against these acts of terrorism. According to Lilia Shevtsova, the author of *Putin's Russia*, police in Moscow rounded up all the Chechens and all those who looked Chechen. However, there was no evidence that the Chechens were involved in those acts and many suspected the participation of the Russian secret services in the explosion. Putin received great support in his "anti-terrorism" actions.[58]

With violence escalating on both sides, Russian troops conducted pogroms against civilians, leaving behind the bodies of those who did not or could not cooperate with the federal troops. Whole villages were destroyed and many mosques were burnt. Soldiers defecated in the mosques. Women who cleaned up the human waste from the mosques exclaimed "And they call themselves civilized people! And say we are from the Middle Ages or something! Damn those Russians! We'll never forget this! What mothers gave birth to these monsters?"[59] The militants killed those suspected of cooperating with Federal troops or those who did not show enthusiasm for the fight against the Russians.

The media did not help in the conflict. Western journalists were prevented from going to Chechnya on account of the kidnapping. Russian journalists, like the author Anna Politkovskaia, who dared to criticize their own government were removed or killed. Many in the Russian and Chechen media fanned the hatred between the people. The Chechens defined their enemy as the "federals," the infidels, or the Russians. In the Russian media, the Chechens are "terrorists," "bandits" or "not like us" (the Russians).

The Western media and human rights organization were rather weak in their reaction to what was happening in Chechnya. It was only when the western hostages were taken that they asked for investigations. Organizations like Human Rights Watch blamed the Russian troops and the forces of the Chechen security forces for the increased number of missing person cases. Akhmed Kadyrov, the new pro-Russian president elected in 2000 pointed to the federal troops for the abductions.[60] The Russian commander of the Regional Operation Headquarters in Chechnya came to the conclusion that there were criminals among the Chechens and among the federal forces, "unfortunately, besides the bandits, representatives of the federal forces and law enforcement agencies also take part in the abductions of the residents of the republic."[61]

It has been determined that the investigations of these disappearances ended for lack of evidence regarding the identity of the perpetrators. In 2004out of 1,783 cases of abductions in Chechnya 1,469 were dismissed.[62] The use of torture in investigations drew the attention of the UN Committee Against Torture. The committee sent a letter to Moscow, to stop and prevent these acts.[63] The second war was over by the year 2000 with the Russians claiming victory. Chechnya had increased autonomy within the Russian borders. The question of independence was not a negotiation point.

Chechnya after the Conflict

Despite President Putin's assurance that the situation in Chechnya was normal, the violence continued. The following years were marked by terrorist attacks on Russian soil. In 2002, the rebels took 763 hostages in a Moscow theatre. Special Forces released a gas into the theatre that killed the rebels and 100 of the hostages. In 2003, there were eleven bomb attacks in Russia. In 2004, the rebels executed a horrific attack on a school in Beslan that resulted in 335 people dead out of which 156 were children.[64] The first war on Chechnya was very unpopular with the Russians. In a poll, only 54% of the population wanted the troops to withdraw. With the second war, 60% to 70% were in favor of military operation in Chechnya.[65] However, the casualties of the war among the Russians made them rethink the situation.

The conflict in Chechnya brought significant changes for both the Russians and the Chechens. Over 200 years of violence proved that military actions were not working. In Chechnya there was a radicalization of the younger generation after seeing the devastation and cruelty to which their families were subjected. Their participation in the war was the result of anger rather than political considerations. A Chechen mother tried to make sense of the situation that she found herself in:

> Russia has turned us into cattle. It is driving our youth into the arms of whoever comes along first and says "Go with us." I even thing like this now: I'd rather the bearded ones, the Wahhabis, beat us with sticks for vodka. A stick is still better than an exploding bullet. Sticks and stones won't break your bones. Most of all now, we want to know the rules of the game. We want to understand which of us you don't understand. And why? What should be tortured for? What are the reasons we've been commended to kill? To kidnap? Right now we don't understand anything and everyone is being destroyed in turn-those who were with Wahhabis and those who were against them. Most of all, those in the middle who weren't with anyone. Like our Imam.[66]

Another result was that an increased number of people turned to religion, but Chechens faced a different kind of Islam: Wahhabism - an extreme Islamic faith. The Wahhabists have weapons and will use violence against those who seemed to be relaxed in their religion. They are feared as much as the federals.

Russian perceptions of Chechens and their way of dealing with them have not changed since the beginning of the nineteenth century. The fact that Chechens committed crimes in Russia did not help their cause. On the contrary, many westerners who watched the events that took place in Beslan and the Moscow theatre were appalled. Although the militants do not represent all Chechens they are active and their methods are fueling the hate and mistrust of the Russians.

Russian society today is marked by an alarming increase in hate crimes against minorities. It is the neo-Nazi groups, about fifty of them, who are operating in the country under the slogan, "Russia for Russians." These gangs are organized in cells, like Al Qaeda; they attack and then they disperse. Alexei, a member of one of these groups stated, "We are a white man's Al-Qaeda. We don't care how many ethnic minorities end up dead; the more the better. The time of our jihad has come."[67] He also stated that he did not consider himself Russian, "We belong to the white race."[68] This same individual had only contempt for Alexander Pushkin, a genius of Russian literature, for being the descendent of an Abyssinian slave.[69] His hero was Timothy McVeigh, executed in 2001, for killing 168 people in the Oklahoma bombing.[70]

Vyacheslav Sukhachev, a professor of sociology in St. Petersburg, said that racism is seeping into mainstream society.[71] A poll taken in July 2008 by the All Russian Center for the Public Opinion Studies showed that 61% of those polled supported the slogan "Russia for Russians." In another study by the Ekspertiza Foundation, a think tank, shows that 60% of those polled wanted to limit the presence of the people of Caucasus in the country.[72] Many Russians, worn out by the war with Chechnya, blamed everything on the people of Caucasus and encouraged this propaganda. Race crimes increased six times in the first half of 2008. Extremist groups are targeting people of non-Slavic appearance.

Racism was also a part of some political parties such as The Liberal Democratic Party led by Vladimir Zhirinovski, Motherland Party, and even the Communist Party. It was Zhirinovski who said that the people of Caucasus "must separate from us completely and never come over here!"[73] Yuri Belyayev, leader of the Freedom Party, a neo-Nazi organization, complained that Vladimir Putin was not tough enough with the nonwhite immigrants who are invading the country. He justified the actions of the neo-Nazi groups as self-defense.[74]

A new party, named The Nationalist Socialist Society, wanted to build a unitary Russian state. Alex, one of its members, believed that the use of genetics would lead to racial purity. A graduate of a Moscow university, he and his colleagues intended to get positions in business and politics in order to make people accept this ideology because, as he put it "it will get us further than just drawing blood in the streets."[75] Alex, like other Russians, has an "us" against the "others" mentality. In 2007, Christof Puzel, a journalist who works for Current TV, founded by Vice President Al Gore, investigated some of these Russian gangs. These skinheads executed over 300 assaults and out of these, forty-seven ended up in death. According to Puzel, there are about 50,000-70,000 skinheads in Russia, which constitutes more than half of the total number of skinheads in the world.[76]

Many ethnic groups complain that hate crimes are dealt with like simple acts of hooliganism and that the justice department does not take them seriously.[77] According to Itar-Press news agency, people of color including immigrants from Asia and Africa, are threatened by skinheads.[78] Izvestia newspaper revealed that many companies have an unofficial policy not to hire people of color because they cannot guarantee their safety.[79] These are educated people affected by ultra nationalism and xenophobia. Some blamed the rise in hate crimes on suppressed political conditions that create a need to find an enemy to explain the misfortunes of the people. Others say that Putin did not support racism but that he had no strategy to stop it. However, the former president emphasized the connection between the Chechen militants to Al Qaeda in order to get support for his intervention in Chechnya. In 2003, the United States declared two organizations based in Chechnya as terrorist groups. Ariel Cohen, a Research Fellow from the Heritage Foundation, argued that instability in the Caucasus might increase the threat of WMD. He also suggested that the USA should assist Russia in isolating Islamic militants in Chechnya and also to help with the rebuilding of Chechnya.

Conclusion

The conflict between Chechnya and Russia has lasted more than 200 years. The Russians wanted to keep Chechnya within the Russian Federation although they had only contempt for the Chechen people. The Chechens were lied to, were discriminated against, exiled, and killed. Many Chechens who saw their families destroyed became radicalized. These militants used terrorist methods against the Russians and even against those Chechens who did not share their beliefs. However, these criminals would appear to some Chechens as heroes because they had the courage to oppose a mighty country like Russia.

After the fall of communism, extreme nationalism showed its ugly face. Russian society seemed to be divided between the Slavs (superior groups) and the non-Slavs (inferior groups). The terrorist methods used by the militants such as kidnapping and beheadings made many Russians perceive Chechnya as a criminal state. These Nazi gangs felt threatened by the immigrants because of the high cost of living and low birth rate. They perceive the non-Slavs working in Russia as a threat to the very core of the white race. Some Chechens, caught between the federal troops and the militants, decided to settle somewhere else, to protect their families. However, in their new places of settlement, they face job discrimination and even violence.

On both sides of the conflict, there are people fighting against racism. There are people in Russia who demonstrate against extreme nationalism. There are also educated moderates in Chechnya who oppose the methods of the militants and their use of violence. In recent years, the Russian government has helped with the rebuilding of Chechnya and violence has reduced. In a multi-ethnic country such as the Russian Federation, the safeguard of human rights, and equality for all groups is a necessary condition for maintaining territorial integrity.

Notes

1. Robert Seeley, *Russo-Chechen Conflict: A Deadly Embrace* (Portland: Frank Cass Publications, 2001), 5.
2. Anatol Lieven, *Chechnya: Tombstone of Russian Power* (New Haven: Yale University Press, 1998), 347.
3. Moshe Gammer, *The Loan Wolf and the Bear: Three Centuries of Chechen Defiance of Russian Power* (Pittsburg: University of Pittsburg Press, 2005), 5.
4. Gammer, 13.
5. Ibid., 33.

6. Ibid., 35.
7. Seely, 35.
8. Gammer, 37.
9. Lieven, 306.
10. Angela Brintlinger, "The Persian Frontier: Griboedov as Orientalist and Literary Hero," *Canadian Slavonic Papers* (2003), 396.
11. Seely, 36.
12. Ibid., 37.
13. Gammer, 80.
14. Ibid.
15. Ibid., 62.
16. Lieven, 312.
17. Ibid., 313.
18. Ibid.
19. Gammer, 146.
20. Seely, 76.
21. Ibid.
22. Ibid., 78.
23. Gammer, 154.
24. Lieven, 319.
25. Ibid.
26. Gammer, 174.
27. Ibid.
28. Lieven, 320.
29. Seely, 87.
30. Valery Tishkov, *Chechnya: Life in a War-Torn Society* (Berkeley: University of California Press, 2004), 41.
31. Gammer, 193.
32. Ibid., 200.
33. Ibid., 207.
34. Ibid.
35. Seely, 184.
36. Ibid., 187.
37. Lieven, 29.
38. Ibid.
39. Seely, 235.
40. Ibid.
41. Tishkov, 91.
42. Ibid., 105.
43. Ibid., 101.
44. Ibid., 103.
45. Paul J. Murphy, *The Wolves of Islam: Russia and the Fear of Chechen Terror* (Washington, D.C.: Brassey's Inc., 2004), 9.
46. Ibid., 22.
47. Lieven, 33.
48. Murphy, 23.
49. Gammer, 210.
50. Ibid.
51. Seely, 198.
52. Ibid., 199.
53. Ibid., 199.
54. Ibid., 182.

55. Ibid., 293.
56. Tishkov, 107.
57. Ibid., 117.
58. Lilia Shevtsova, *Putin's Russia* (Washington, D.C.: Carnegie Endowment for International Peace, 2003), 38.
59. Anna Politkovskaya, *A Small Corner of Hell: Dispatches from Chechnya* (Chicago: The University of Chicago Press, 2003), 93.
60. See *Human Rights Watch* "Worse than a War: Disappearances in Chechnya-A Crime Against Humanity."
61. Ibid.
62. Ibid.
63. See *EU Letter to Foreign Minister Rupel in Advance of EU-Russia Troika Meeting.*
64. David Johnson and B. Brunner, *Timeline of Key Events in Chechnya, 1830-2006,* at http://www.infoplease.com/spot/Chechnyatimel.htm.
65. Shevtsova, 39.
66. Politkovskaya, 117.
67. Yuri Zarakhovich, "From Russia with Hate (Russian Neo-Nazi)," *Time* August, 2004, 2-3.
68. Ibid.
69. Ibid.
70. Ibid.
71. Ibid.
72. Ibid.
73. Ibid.
74. Ibid.
75. Ibid., 4.
76. See Harris.
77. See "Hate Killings Shake Moscow's Ethnic Communities" in *The Other Russia* at http://www.theotherrussia.org/2008/02/22/hate-killings-shake-moscow
78. Ibid.
79. Ibid.

References

Brintlinger, Angela. "The Persian Frontier: Griboedov as Orientalist and Literary Hero." *Canadian Slavonic Papers.* (September 2003): 271-293.
"Disappearances in Chechnya as a Crime Against Humanity." *Human Rights Watch.* August 6, 2008. http://hrw.org/backgrounder/eca/chechnya0305/3.html
Gammer, Moshe. *The Lone Wolf and the Bear: Three Centuries of Chechen Defiance of Russian Power.* Pittsburg: University of Pittsburg Press, 2005.
"EU: Letter to Foreign Minister Rupel in Advance of EU-Russia Troika Meeting." *Human Rights Watch.* http://hrw.org/english/docs/2008/01/31/russia18985.htm December 7, 2008.
Johnson, David. "Timeline of Key Events in Chechnya, 1830-2006." *Chechnya Timeline.* http://www.infoplease.com/spot/chechnyatime1.htm August 17, 2008.
"Killings Shake Moscow's Ethnic Communities." *The Other Russia.* August 6, 2008. http://www.theotherrussia.org/2008/02/22/hate-killings-shake-mosco
Lieven, Anatol. *Chechnya Tombstone of Russian Power.* New Haven: Yale University Press, 1998.

Maximishin, S. "From Russia With Hate." *Time.* December 5, 2008. http://www.time.com/time/magazine/article/0,9171,674718-2,00.html

Murphy, Paul J. *The Wolves of Islam: Russia and the Faces of Chechen Terror.* Washington, D.C.: Brassey's Inc., 2004.

Politkovskaya, Anna. *A Small Corner of Hell: Dispatches from Chechnya.* Chicago: The University of Chicago Press, 2003.

Seely, Robert. *Russo-Chechen Conflict, 1800-2000: A Deadly Embrace.* Portland: Frank Cass Publishers, 2001.

Shevtsova, Lilia. *Putin's Russia.* Washington, D.C.: Carnegie Endowment for International Peace, 2003.

Tishkov, Valery. *Chechnya Life in a War-Torn Society.* Berkeley: University of California Press, 2004.

Zarakovich, Yuri. "From Russia with Hate (Russian Neo-Nazis)." *Time.* August, 2004. 2-3.

Contributors

Julius O. Adekunle holds a Ph.D. in African History from Dalhousie University, Halifax, Canada. He is Professor of African History in the Department of History and Anthropology at Monmouth University, West Long Branch, New Jersey. He taught in Nigeria and Canada (at Dalhousie University and St. Mary's University, both in Halifax). He also taught at Tennessee State University, Nashville. His research interests include ethnicity, religion and politics, and political leadership in Africa. He is the author of *Politics and Society in Nigeria's Middle Belt: Borgu and the Emergence of a Political Identity* (2004) and *Culture and Customs of Rwanda* (2007). Julius has contributed numerous articles and essays to edited volumes and texts on the subject of African history. He is currently working on an edited volume on religion and politics in Nigeria.

David L. Brunsma received his Ph.D. in sociology from Notre Dame in 1998 and specializes in critical race theory, social psychology, sociology of education, and the sociology of culture. His research includes the strategies and negotiated manifestations of racial identity in the post civil rights era as illuminated by the interplay of social, structural, cultural/symbolic, interactional, and biographical narrative life structures with an emphasis on biracial people in the United States. He is also one of the premiere scholars in the country on the impact of school uniform policies in public schools. The results of his research on biracials in the U.S. have appeared in numerous journals, edited volumes, as well as a book with Kerry Ann Rockquemore titled *Beyond Black: Biracial Identity in America* (Sage Publications, 2001). He is currently working on a book tentatively titled *Race(ing) and E(race)ing the Child: Parental Strategies of Socializing the Multiracial Child* (with Kerry Ann Rockquemore). His work on the uniform school movement has been published in a book titled *A Symbolic Crusade: The School Uniform Movement and What It Tells Us About American Education* (Rowman & Littlefield Education, 2004). He is currently an Associate professor in the Department of Sociology at the University of Missouri, Columbia.

G. Reginald Daniel Ph.D., Professor, Department of Sociology, University of California, Santa Barbara; Affiliated Faculty, Department of Black Studies, Latin American and Iberian Studies, History, Asian American Studies, and Chicana and Chicano Studies. Since 1989, he has taught "Betwixt and Between," which is one of the first and longest-standing university courses to deal specifically with the question of multiracial identity comparing the U.S. with various parts of the world. He has published numerous articles and chapters that cover this topic. His books entitled *More Than Black? Multiracial Identity and the New Racial Order* (2002) and *Race and Multiraciality in Brazil and the United States: Converging Paths?* (2006) are a culmination of much of his thinking on the relationship between social structure and racial formation—especially multiracial identities. In addition, Daniel has received a great deal of media attention and participated as a panelist at various conferences on the topic of multiracial identity. Also, he is a member of the Advisory Board of AMEA (Association of MultiEthnic Americans) and the Advisory Council of the Mixed Heritage Center of MAVIN Foundation, and a former Advisory Board member of Project RACE (Reclassify All Children Equally). These are among the most prominent organizations involved in bring about changes in the collection of official racial and ethnic data, as in the decennial census, which makes it possible for multiracial-identified individuals to acknowledge their various backgrounds.

Marsha J. Darling Ph.D. is a Professor of history and interdisciplinary studies at Adelphi University located in Garden City, New York where she has taught courses on African American history, ethnicity in America, and Black culture. Her research interests include studies on gender, race, poverty and the new genetics in the "Gene Age." She is the editor of the multivolume work *Race, Voting, Redistricting and the Constitution: Sources and Explorations on the Fifteenth Amendment* (2001) and the text *Political Environments: A Publication of the Committee on Women, Population, and the Environment* (2007).

Johanna E. Foster specializes in the sociology of gender and the intersections of social inequalities. She holds a Bachelor's degree in Interdisciplinary Studies from The American University, a Master's degree in Applied Sociology with a concentration in Gender and Social Policy also from The American University, and a Doctorate in Sociology/Gender Program from Rutgers, The State University of New Jersey. She has published in the areas of gender and feminist theory, the sociology of women's health, social movements, and the sociology of race. Her work has appeared in *Gender & Society, Sociological Forum, Research in Political Sociology*, and as a chapter in the upcoming book edited by David Brunsma, *Mixed Messages: Multiracialism and Movements for Social Justice*. In 2001, Dr. Foster co-founded *College Connections: Higher Education for Women in Prison*, a not-for-profit association that works to bring credit-bearing, college-level courses to women incarcerated at Taconic Correctional Facility, a medium security prison in Westchester County, New York. She currently serves as a co-coordinator for *College Connections* as well as a volunteer professor. Along with her work with incarcerated women in New York, Dr. Foster also works with colleagues in New Jersey to expand educational and training programs for women incarcerated at Edna Mahan Correctional facility.

Dru C. Gladney is currently a special- researcher for China and Central Asia at the Asia-Pacific Center for Security Studies in. Honolulu, He is currently on leave from Professor of Asian Studies and Anthropology at the University of Hawaii at Manoa in the School of Hawaiian, Asian, and Pacific Studies. In addition to a Ph.D. in Social Anthropology from the University of Washington, Seattle, in 1987, Dr, Gladney has three M.A. degrees. He has been a Fulbright Research Scholar in Turkey and China~ and has held faculty positions and post-doctoral fellowships at Harvard University, the University of Southern California, and the Institute for Advanced Study, Princeton. Dr. Gladney conducted field research in China for more than three years as well as more recent projects in Kazakhstan, Kyrgyzstan, and Turkey He is author of the award-winning book, ' *Muslim Chinese: Ethnic Nationalism in the People's Republic* (Harvard University Press, 1996, 1st edition 199 1) as well as three new books—*Ethnic Identity in China: The Making of a Muslim Minority Nationality* (Harcourt Brace, 1998); *Making Majorities: Constituting the Nation in Japan China Korea Mak7ysia TV4 Turkey and the US.* (Editor, Stanford University Press, 1998); and *Dislocating China: Muslims, Minorities, and Other Sub-Altern Subjects* (London, C. Hurst, forthcoming). He has published over 50 academic articles and his research has been regularly featured in interviews on CNN and in *Newsweek, Time Magazine, International Herald Tribune, Los Angeles Times, and the New York Times*.

Gary L. Haddow received his B.A. in sociology from the University of California, Santa Barbara. He has taken many courses focusing on multiracial identity and racial theory, as well as performed extensive research on multiraciality in Brazil, South Africa, and the United States. In 2007, Gary spent three months researching first-hand the multiracial phenomenon and racial order of South Africa. Committed to understanding the experience and identity formation of multiracial individuals, Gary conducted an Honor's Senior Thesis during the final year of his undergraduate career. Entitled "In Between Spaces: Understanding Multiracial Students at UCSB," this thesis is based on interviews of multiracial undergraduates at the University of California, Santa Barbara in the hopes of gaining insight into how they formulate their racial identity. A citizen of the United Kingdom, Gary will be continuing his education in graduate school either in the United States or in the United Kingdom.

Reza Hasmath is a Sociologist based at the University of Cambridge. His research examines the management of ethnic differences in North America and East Asia. He has recently completed *China in an Era of Transition: Understanding Contemporary State and Society Actors* (Palgrave) and *Multiculturalism: The Great Marketing Strategy? An International Perspective* (UBC Press).

Philomina Okeke-Ihejirika is professor of Gender, Development and Transnational Studies in the Women's Studies Program of the University of Alberta, Edmonton, Canada. She is also an adjunct professor in the Social Science Faculty of Nnamdi Azikiwe University, Nigeria. Her research and teaching focus on Gender and Development in Africa as well as on Gender Issues in Migration and Settlement in Canada. Her publications in journals and books reflect a continuing contribution to the debates in these fields, including her highly acclaimed volume—Negotiating Power and Privilege: Igbo Career Women in Contemporary Nigeria (Ohio University Press, 2004). Dr Okeke-Ihejirika is actively involved in building cross-Atlantic linkages with scholars, academic institutions, and local communities with the aim of improving the conditions of women's life Africa. She also works with international organizations such as the Rotary International Foundation as well as various immigrant serving organizations and social agencies in Canada.

Indira Jalli is a scholar based in India. She has a graduate degree in philosophy and a doctoral degree in political science. The topic of her MA in philosophy was "Sexual Violence against Dalit Women: A Case of Rape" in which she deconstructed mainstream feminist theory through a discussion of Indian law and case studies. Her dissertation is entitled "Contemporary Post-Colonial Theory: A Dalit Feminist Critique" in which she explained the loopholes in post-colonial theory as associated with studies of dalit women. She is also a social activist and poet writing in both Telugu and English.

Andrew Jolivette is an associate professor in American Indian Studies, Educational Leadership, and Critical Race and Resistance Studies at San Francisco State University. He is a mixed-race studies specialist with a particular interest in Comparative Race Relations, the Urban Indian Experience, People of Color and Popular Culture, Critical Mixed Race Studies and Social Justice, Creole studies, Black-Indians, and mixed-race health disparities. He has been an Adjunct Professor in the Department of Sociology at the University of San Francisco and a Researcher with the University of California, San Francisco on issues of racial violence among African American and Latino/a youth in the Bay Area. He is the author of two books, *Cultural Representation in Native America* (AltaMira Press), which is a part of the Contemporary Native American Communities Series and *Louisiana Creoles: Cultural Recovery and Mixed Race Native American Identity* (Lexington Books, January, 2007). He is currently working on a third book, *Mixed Race Gay Men and HIV: A Community History* where he will explore how race and sexuality intersect to create social and sexual risk.

DeMond S. Miller is a professor of sociology and research scientist/director of the Liberal Arts and Sciences Institute for Research and Community Service at Rowan University (Glassboro, New Jersey). He has worked as an evaluator for alcohol and tobacco social norms projects and as principal investigator to facilitate research projects involving: environmental issues and community satisfaction. His primary area of specialization is environmental sociology, disaster studies (disaster mitigation and preparedness, and response), the study of the social construction of place, community development, and social impact assessment. His work has appeared in numerous journals and edited volumes including *Through the Eye of the Katrina: Social Justice in the United States.* He is the author, along with J. Rivera, of *Hurricane Katrina and the Redefinition of Landscape.*

Hilde Neus is a writer, independent scholar, and associate of the Suriname Museum Foundation. She has delivered several papers at various international conferences on the topic of women in Caribbean literature and society. Her research interests include women, gender studies, and literature.

Jason D. Rivera earned a graduate degree in public administration from Rutgers University-Camden and is currently a research associate at the Richard Stockton College of New Jersey. His research interests have focused on public policy and disaster mitigation, relief, and social justice. He has published articles in several scholarly outlets including *The Journal of Public Management and Social Policy* and *The International Journal of the Humanities.* He is the co-author of a text on hurricane Katrina with DeMond Miller.

Kerry Ann Rockquemore is an associate professor of sociology and African American Studies at the University of Illinois, Chicago. Her research interests include racial identity development, racial socialization, interracial families, gender, children and youth. She is the author of *Beyond Black: Biracial Identity in America (2001)* and *Raising Biracial Children (2005).* She is the author of multiple articles and books chapters and her work has been featured in the *New York Times* and ABC's 20/20.

Rainier Spencer is professor and director of Afro-American Studies in the Department of Anthropology & Ethnic Studies at the University of Nevada, Las Vegas. He is the author of *Spurious Issues: Race and Multiracial Identity Politics in the United States* (Westview, 1999) and *Challenging Multiracial Identity* (Lynne Rienner, 2006). His work focuses on the ways biological race is deployed by lay and scholarly advocates of multiracial identity and by the popular media.

Magid Shihade received his Ph.D. in interdisciplinary and Near East/Middle East Studies from the University of Washington. He has served as an adjunct and visiting faculty member at various institutions including the University of Pittsburg where he has taught courses on the Middle East. His research interests include sectarian violence, nationalism, colonialism and modernity. He has contributed essays to journals, edited volumes, and attended conferences on the subject of resistance studies. He is currently a research associate in Middle East/South Asian Studies at the University of California, Davis.

Mariana Tepfenhart is currently an instructor of history at Monmouth University located in West Long Branch, New Jersey where she teaches Western Civilization in

World Perspective and Russian history. Her research interests include the history of modern Russia, global affairs, and ethnic conflicts.

James M. Thomas is a PhD student in Sociology at the University of Missouri. His substantive interests are in sociological theory, culture, and social justice. His previous publications and conference presentations have focused on Jewish identities, racial formation, and reparations within a human rights model. His current project looks at the ways in which stand-up comedy both operates within and challenges lay knowledge on race, class, gender, and sexuality.

Kwyku Osei Tutu is an instructor of history at Essex County Community College located in Newark, New Jersey where he has taught courses on World Civilization and African history. His research interests include the history of Africa and African Americans.

Francis Wardle earned his Ph.D. in Education from the University of Kansas. He is the founder and Director of the Center for the Study of Biracial Children and the author of books, articles, and essays on the subject of mixed race children including *Meeting the Needs of Multiethnic and Multiracial Children in Schools* (2003) and *Introduction to Early Childhood Education: A Multidimensional Approach to Child-Centered Care and Learning* (2002). He has also taught courses on education and psychology for the University of Phoenix in Colorado and Red Rock Community College.

Hettie V. Williams completed her graduate work in history at Monmouth University in 2000. Her research interests include race, identity, and the cultural history of African Americans; recent American history; studies in the African Diaspora; and gender. She has taught survey courses in U.S. history, world history, and Western Civilization and upper division courses on the history of African Americans. She has published various entries and essays for several volumes and recently completed a text on the American civil rights movement entitled *We Shall Overcome to We Shall Overrun: The Collapse of the Civil Rights Movement and the Black Power Revolt (1962-1968)*. Currently, she teaches as a lecturer of African American history in the Department of History and Anthropology at Monmouth University.

Index